Understanding Economics

A Contemporary Perspective

Understanding Economics

A Contemporary Perspective

Mark Lovewell, B.A., M.A.

Ryerson Polytechnic University
Toronto, Ontario

McGraw-Hill Ryerson

Toronto New York Burr Ridge Bangkok Auckland Bogotá
Caracas Lisbon London Madrid Mexico City Milan
New Delhi Seoul Singapore Taipei

McGraw-Hill
Ryerson Limited

A Subsidiary of The **McGraw-Hill** Companies

Understanding Economics: A Contemporary Perspective
Lovewell

ISBN: 0-07-552901-7

2 3 4 5 6 7 8 9 10 BBM 7 6 5 4 3 2 1 0

Printed and bound in Canada

Sponsoring Editor: Joan Langevin
Production Editor: Rachel Mansfield
Associate Editor: Jenna Wallace
Developmental Editor: Daphne Scriabin
Production Co-ordinator: Nicla Dattolico
Cover and Interior Design: Dianna Little
Cover Illustration: "Déjà Vu," by Larry Limnidis
Electronic Page Composition: Lynda Powell
Printer: Transcontinental Printing Inc.

Canadian Cataloguing in Publication Data

Lovewell, Mark A.
Understanding economics: a contemporary perspective

Includes bibliographical references and index.
ISBN 0-07-552901-7

1. Economics. 2. Canada – Economic conditions. I. Title.

HB171.5.L76 1998 330 C97-932368-1

This book is dedicated to

Marina

CONTENTS

Acknowledgments x
Introduction xi
Skills Resource xiii

Part 1 Working With Economics 1

Chapter 1 The Economic Problem **2**
What Economists Do 3
Economic Choice 7
The Production Possibilities Model 8
Economic Systems 11

Chapter 2 Demand and Supply **30**
The Role of Demand 31
The Role of Supply 37
How Competitive Markets Operate 41

Chapter 3 Competitive Dynamics **53**
Price Elasticity of Demand 54
Supply Elasticity 60
Price Controls 63

Part 2 Efficiency and Equity 79

Chapter 4 Costs of Production **80**
Business Organization 81
Production, Costs, and Profit 82
Production in the Short Run 85
Costs in the Short Run 90
Production in the Long Run 94

Chapter 5: The Nature of Markets **109**
Market Structures 110
Demand Differences 115
Nonprice Competition 119
Industrial Concentration 121

Chapter 6: The Role of Profit **133**
Perfect Competition 134
Monopolistic Competition 144
Oligopoly 146
Monopoly 149

Chapter 7: Resource Markets **164**
How Resource Markets Operate 165
Product and Resource Price-Taker 166
Product Price-Maker/Resource Price-Taker 171
Changes in Resource Demand 173
Price Elasticity of Resource Demand 174

Chapter 8 Wages, Rent, Profit, and Interest **187**
Wages and Their Determinants 188
Rent 196
Profit 198
Interest 199

Chapter 9 The Role of Government **213**
The Distribution of Income 214
Poverty 218
The Canadian Welfare Society 221
Taxation 226
Spillover Effects 231

Part 3 Economic Stability 245

Chapter 10 Measures of Economic Activity **246**
Gross Domestic Product 247
The Income Approach 249
The Expenditure Approach 250
GDP and Living Standards 257
Other Economic Measures 260

Chapter 11 Inflation and Unemployment **271**
Inflation 272
Unemployment 280

Chapter 12 Economic Fluctuations **298**
Aggregate Demand 299
Changes in Aggregate Demand 301
Aggregate Supply 307
Changes in Aggregate Supply 308
Equilibrium 312
Business Cycles 317

Chapter 13 Fiscal Policy **331**
Fiscal Policy 332
The Spending Multiplier 336
Impact of Fiscal Policy 344

Chapter 14 Money **360**
Money and Its Uses 361
The Money Market 369
Money Creation 373

Chapter 15 Monetary Policy **387**
The Bank of Canada 388
Monetary Policy 390
Tools of Monetary Policy 393
Inflation and Unemployment 398

Part 4 Canada in the Global Economy 411

Chapter 16 The Foreign Sector **412**
The Balance of Payments 413
Exchange Rates 420
Exchange Rate Systems 427

Chapter 17 Foreign Trade **443**
Canada's Foreign Trade 444
The Case for Trade 448
The Impact of Trade Protection 453
The Case for Trade Protection 456
Trade Policies 460

Chapter 18 Economic Growth **475**
Economic Growth 476
Economic Development 486

Glossary 503
Index 515

ACKNOWLEDGMENTS

I owe a great debt to this book's sponsoring editor, Joan Langevin, as well as to Rachel Mansfield, Daphne Scriabin, Karen Taylor, and Jenna Wallace for their innumerable contributions in casting this book in its final form. There are others who have played a significant editorial role: Andrea Crozier, Laura Edlund, Brenda Hutchinson, and Claudia Kutchukian. I am also grateful to the reviewers of the book for their perceptive comments and criticisms. They include Douglas Beatty, Lambton College; Gary Berman, Humber College; John Brander, University of New Brunswick; Peter Fortura, Algonquin College; Robert Jeacock, Malaspina University College; Marion Jones, University of Regina; Ivo Kvarda, Confederation College; Cal Shaw, George Brown College; William Sinkevitch, St. Clair College; Ian Wilson, St. Lawrence College.

Encouragement has come from past and present colleagues in Ryerson's Economics Department — Tom Barbiero, Ingrid Bryan, Harry Pope, Dagmar Rajagopal, Eric Wright, and Gus Zaks in particular — and from my associates at CJRT-Open College. On a personal note, Marco Blefari, Deborah Brown, and Nicolas Van Praet deserve thanks for welcome diversons while this book was being written. Finally, I would like to acknowledge a special debt to my friend Marina Vitkin, without whose support and good-humoured endurance writing this book would not have been possible.

INTRODUCTION

Present day economics is not just a body of ideas, but a way of thinking. *Understanding Economics: A Contemporary Perspective* reflects this approach by combining economic theory and application in an up-to-date, accessible, and appealing way. The result is a learning tool that explores current issues, emphasizes skills, and facilitates both learning and teaching.

Current Issues

Economics is part of daily life—in the choices we make, in the decisions of communities, governments, and businesses, and in the media. While developing the theoretical framework of economics, *Understanding Economics* offers real-world examples and explores current economic issues. Articles, essays, and interviews stimulate critical thinking, research, application, and more. By providing a balanced and wide range of perspectives, these elements encourage students to evaluate and debate economic issues for themselves. **Sidelines** deals with a wide range of economic issues—for example, growing wage differences in the Canadian economy, the debate over the Bank of Canada's zero-inflation policy, and the increasing significance of cross-border financial flows. Within each chapter, **Advancing Economic Thought** details the ideas of an influential thinker of either the past or the present and allows the student to judge their contemporary relevance. So, for example, Adam Smith's defence of private markets, Karl Marx's theory of capitalist exploitation, and Thomas Malthus's treatment of population growth are featured, as well as Nuala Beck's analysis of the "new economy," Hazel Henderson's environmental and economic ideals, and Muhammad Yunus' grassroots banking scheme practised in Bangladesh. In addition, each chapter includes several points for discussion called **Thinking About Economics**, which help students to interpret and apply the concepts they are learning through a question-and-answer format.

Emphasis on Skills

Application is the key to effective learning. So that students have ample opportunity to apply the knowledge they acquire, this text emphasizes skills throughout. As an initial review and a resource to return to for direction and hints, the **Skills Resource** focuses on the basics of critical thinking, the use of economic language and visual materials, research, and ways of presenting findings. For example, this resource guides students in evaluating their own work or that of others to see that it is precise, logical, and considered; it reviews interpreting and creating tables and graphs; it illustrates economic forecasting; it lists possible resources; it discusses the use of the Internet as a research tool; and it supports essay-writing and debating.

In the body of each chapter, issues relating to the use of **Economics as a Second Language** are highlighted by the icon shown in the margin. Questions appear at the end of each chapter, as well as at the end of all supplementary articles. Selected **online questions** (highlighted by the icon shown in the margin) provide practice in using economics-related resources on the Internet.

Study Aids

So that *Understanding Economics* invites and engages students, care has been taken to write in a clear and readable style, and to use an appealing design. At the same time, a variety of features make this text user-friendly. Every chapter begins with a **Chapter Focus**, which introduces the content students are to learn. Then, each **Brief Review** summarizes key ideas, while margin notes define key terms highlighted in the text. These terms are listed at the end of each chapter under the heading **Key Concepts** for review and are defined again in a central **Glossary** at the end of the book for easy reference. Because interpreting graphs is a challenge for many students, virtually all graphs are paired with tables so that it is possible to see at a glance how they are plotted. This technique not only makes graphs easier to interpret, it also helps students appreciate the usefulness of visual aids in presenting economic information. Lastly, an **Index** helps students access the text in a variety of ways.

Ancillaries

In addition to these in-text features, a **Study Guide** (in book form), and an **Interactive Study Guide** (for computers running MS-Windows) are also available. These guides, each written separately in conjunction with the text, give students the opportunity to test their knowledge of text material.

A range of teaching and testing aids have been developed for use with the text. An **Instructor's Resource Manual** provides instructional strategies and complete solutions to all in-text questions. A **Computerized Test Bank** (provided in MS-DOS and Macintosh versions) gives over 1200 questions and answers in various formats. **Powerpoint Slides** provide highlights of each chapter with the aid of presentation graphics software that comes in both Windows and Macintosh versions. Finally, an **Internet Resource** provides information on using online sources to facilitate the study of current economic issues.

SKILLS RESOURCE

Understanding Economics requires that you interpret, analyze, and apply information. Use this general resource first to review the skills you will need, and then—as you venture further into *Understanding Economics*—for direction and helpful hints.

The Basics of Critical Thinking

Information, ideas, and opinions abound. Whether you are interpreting and analyzing the work of others or developing your own observations, opinions, and arguments, you must use critical thinking skills. Critical thinking involves precise meaning, logic, and consideration of values and perspectives. Evaluate your work and that of others against these basics.

Precise

The rule "Say what you mean and mean what you say" can be applied to all subjects and topics. Keep in mind these questions: What don't I understand? Can I paraphrase this? What really is the point? What might confuse the audience? Where is the meaning clear? Where is it murky?

See that a writer is using terminology precisely or defines terms in the writing. In your own work, use the standard definition that is appropriate to the subject or discipline. If the meaning might be unclear, clarify it.

Statistics can be a particular trouble-spot. With every statistic you use or come across, ask yourself the following: What information is this giving? What definitions are used? What is the basis of this information (for example, a broad study, or a small sample)? How is this relevant to the discussion? How have the numbers been treated? What other factors should be taken into account? What relationships can I see?

See that a statistic means what you think it does, and use it precisely. For example:

- A **measure** differs from an **indicator**. For example, the *measure* of Gross Domestic Product *indicates* living standards. The *measure* of body temperature *indicates* physical health.
- **Average** differs from **median**. An average is the sum of all the values divided by the number of values. The median is the middle value in any group of values. For three hourly wages (of $5, $10, and $30), the average wage is $15, but the median wage is $10.
- **Nominal** figures differ from **real** figures. Nominal dollar values make no adjustments for changes in prices over the years. However, real figures are adjusted using a **base year**, which gives a point of comparison. For example if your nominal income has doubled since the base year at the same time as prices have doubled, your real income has remained the same.
- Percentages sometimes cause confusion. If you are to calculate the percentage difference between two numbers, determine what is the base

from which the percentage is calculated, then divide the difference between the two numbers by the base number and multiply by 100 percent. For example, if a price increases from $1 to $3, it has risen by 200 percent [(($3 – $1) ÷ $1) × 100%]. In this case, $1 is the base number. If, on the other hand, a price decreases from $3 to $1, the base number is now $3. The percentage fall in price is therefore 67 percent [(($1 – $3) ÷ $3) × 100%].

- Many statistics are **rounded**—for example, to the nearest whole number or nearest thousand.

Logical

Logical arguments move from one point to the next in a reasonable and orderly way. Reasons should support each point, and the points should follow some order, often a cause-and-effect order. The **scientific method**, which we outline in Chapter 1, gives one model for a logical approach. In the case of a written or spoken argument, we should be able to answer the following questions: What points does the author make? How does the author support each point? How do the points connect and are the connections valid? What is the main point or conclusion?

Read your own work and that of others carefully for the following problems:

- **Personal arguments**. A personal argument attacks an opponent rather than the opponent's reasoning. Personal arguments often appear when economic issues are debated in the political arena. For example, a government's expansionary fiscal policy might be disparaged as being the work of "doctrinaire socialists" rather than being criticized on its own merits.
- **False analogy**. Arguments can often be supported with analogies, or comparisons between two different things. For example, the flow of incomes and spending in an economy is sometimes likened to a circular flow of water. However, one extension of this analogy—that the flow of incomes and spending in an economy would stop unless propelled by some outside force—is false. Each analogy must be checked against the facts.
- **False causation**. Simply because two trends take place at the same time does not mean one trend is causing the other. For example, a trend toward more students staying in school and a trend toward more part-time jobs does not mean that the first necessarily causes the second, or vice versa. In each case, examine the situation to see how the factors are related, if at all.
- **Fallacy of composition**. What is true for one component of a group—say, an individual—is not necessarily true for the group as a whole. For example, just because higher savings benefit an individual household does not mean that they necessarily help the entire economy, since a rise in saving can cause spending and production in an economy to fall. Examine each generalization carefully.

Considered

Our experiences and background have implications for how we see the world; they inform our perspectives. Because many of the issues explored in *Understanding Economics* deal with how we think things "ought" to be, they bring up questions of values—for example, how you value extra leisure time against more possessions. The key to critical thinking is recognizing and examining our perspectives (including our assumptions) and considering the perspectives of others. A blinkered view of the world—one that doesn't consider the perspectives of others—makes for a poor, unbalanced argument.

Examine your own work and that of others carefully for the following:

- **Opinions**. Are any opinions stated clearly, explained, and supported? Are any not stated but apparent? Remember that opinions are not the sign of dubious critical thinking. In fact, explicit opinions are preferable to unexamined perspectives in most cases.
- **Statement of specific assumptions**. If assumptions are not clearly identified, can they be inferred? Are the stated assumptions overly simplistic or irrelevant? For example, in an argument about product demand it is too simplistic to assume that the number of units bought stays constant, while detailed assumptions concerning how a product is supplied are irrelevant.
- **Emotional language**. While emotional language may suit some persuasive arguments (for example, political speeches, letters to the editor, advertising), it can mask lack of evidence, or may suggest a biased view. Emotional language—which usually lays blame—is especially common in the popular media. If you are faced with emotional language, try to decide whether an argument would be equally effective without it. Also keep in mind that emotional language does not always signify that an argument is unreasonable, and that arguments expressed in reasonable language can also be flawed.
- **Distortions of fact, or faulty logic**. Double-check for misrepresentations and errors in logic in your reading.

Finally, ask yourself whether alternative perspectives have been considered and addressed. If not, why not? Keep in mind that arguments supporting the current state of things are not necessarily more objective than those that do not.

To summarize the basics of critical thinking, consider the task of **forecasting**. Suppose you are asked to use a current economic statistic that is in the news to try to forecast future values. To make a prediction concerning the prime interest rate, for example, you must define precisely the problem and terminology, decide which factors affecting interest rates will be most crucial in the near future, and try to weigh the importance of each of these factors in affecting the statistic's current value. Look to economic theory and economists for help; consult newspapers and magazines to see how closely your own hypothesis corresponds to the opinions of professional economic forecasters. Develop an argument, which you will support and check carefully for errors in logic—for example, what factors cause what. Then, present your forecast and evidence precisely, logically, and having considered a range of perspectives. Later, you will likely want to evaluate your forecast against what actually happened. Because forecasting is an extremely difficult task, consider yourself successful if you predicted the same direction of change.

Economics as a Second Language

Because economics involves an extensive vocabulary of specialized terms, it is closely linked to the way we use language. In each chapter, you will find passages highlighted by the icon shown in the margin. These passages help you learn the proper use of economics as a "second language" by exploring the following issues:

- **Precise Definitions** With few exceptions, economic terms—such as "rent" and "aggregate demand"—have precise definitions. But some terms—such as "income equity" and "full employment"—have more than one possible interpretation. When using such potentially ambiguous terms, specify how you are using them.
- **Special Meanings** Terms may have a different meaning in economics than they do in everyday language. For example, in economics "investment" typically refers to business purchases of materials, equipment, and buildings rather than to purchases of financial assets such as stocks and bonds.
- **Descriptive Images** Sometimes economic terms provide a way of describing abstract concepts in a concrete way. Such descriptive images can clarify an argument's underlying logic. For example, the view that education is acquired by individuals to raise their income-earning potential is neatly summarized by the term "human capital."
- **Loaded Language** Descriptive images are not the only way to give language suggestive power. Loaded language, which appears straightforward but subtly colours economic arguments, is common in economics. For example, supporters of a market economy often call it a "free market system," to emphasize the freedom of choice that comes with private markets. Critics of a market economy usually refer to it instead as "capitalism," since this suggests the power of owners of capital in this economic system. Loaded language helps reveal a writer's implicit assumptions. Though loaded language can be misused, arguments that contain this language are not necessarily wrong.

Visual Materials

Because visual materials can present complex information at a glance, they are often used in economics. Whether you are interpreting or creating visual materials, keep the following advice in mind.

Tables

Tables present *related* information in **columns** (groups of information presented vertically) and **rows** (horizontal lines of information). A **heading** usually appears at the top of each column to describe the information presented; check the column heading to ensure you understand what information is being presented. Tables are "read" left to right—giving the **independent variable** first, at the left. When reading or creating complex tables, use a grid to help you line up information. Double-check at each stage any calculations you must make. Label your table for easy reference and to summarize the relationship it presents. Note that some tables are called **schedules** when they present, for example, the demand and/or supply information for a product.

Often you will need to examine tables for relationships and trends. Consider the following table. In the left column, the numbers are increasing; in the right column, the numbers are decreasing. Based on the hypothetical information in the table, we can say that as the price of compact discs goes up, the quantity sold goes down.

Sales of Compact Discs

Price per CD ($)	CDs Sold (no. of CDs)
4	16
8	12
12	8
16	4

Now consider this table, which shows hypothetical data for a particular country. It shows that, between years 1 and 2 sales of compact discs and cassettes have increased, while sales of long-playing records have decreased.

Sales Per Year (millions of units)

Year	Cassettes	Long-Playing Records	Compact Discs
1	14	11	2
2	17	6	23

Especially when interpreting and analyzing tables that have many columns and rows, you might find it easiest to look at the trend in each column, then start examining the possible relationships among columns and the trends they demonstrate.

Graphs

Related information also can be presented on a graph. Note on the following example how the horizontal line—called the **x-axis**—and the vertical line—called the **y-axis**—form an L-shape to meet at a **point of origin**. The range of values for one variable is indicated on each axis, and each axis is labelled, including the **units**. To graph correctly, the **scale** must be consistent—for example, if the height of the first square on the grid equals $2, the height of each subsequent square must also equal $2. In economics, the **independent variable** is usually plotted on the y-axis. In our example, using the price to give the **y co-ordinate** and CDs sold to give the **x co-ordinate**, we can plot the points shown. Joining the points together gives a **curve**. The term "curve" is used even for a straight line.

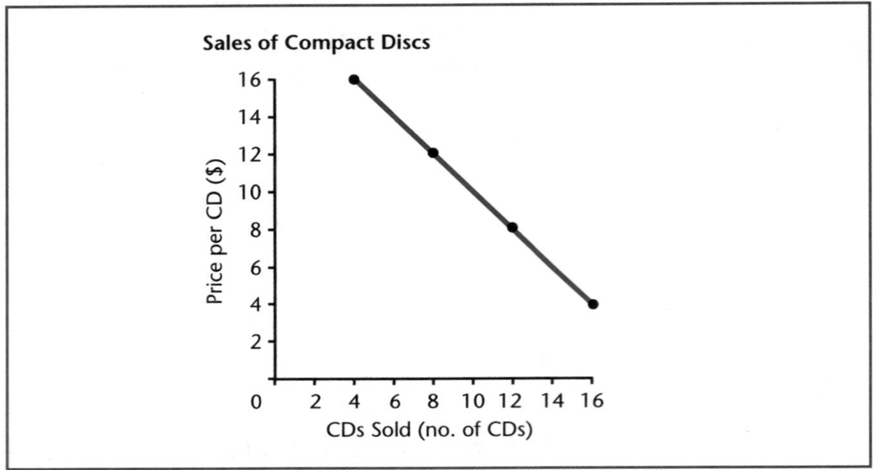

The resulting curve shows the relationship of the two variables. Note that a graph can relate more than two factors. For example, a third factor—the costs to the CD manufacturer—could be added if the graph's y-axis were changed to represent general dollar amounts.

Curves can depict a variety of relationships and are described in *Understanding Economics* in particular ways. For example, the curve that illustrates prices and CDs sold shows that as price decreases, the quantity sold increases. In the text, we describe this as having a **negative (downward) slope** ("downward" because graphs, like tables, are "read" left to right and the curve slopes downward to the right). If, in contrast, quantity sold increases as price increases, the slope would be described as having a **positive (upward) slope**.

The **slope of a curve** demonstrates another aspect of the relationship—for example, whether the decline in CD sales is the same as the increase in price. In this case it is, and our graph demonstrates this by showing a curve at a 45-degree angle. Other relationships will be represented by curves that we describe as **horizontal**, **flattened**, **steep**, and **vertical**.

Whenever possible, the terms "steep" and "flattened" should be precisely defined. This is because the slope of a curve depends on the scale used on the x- and y-axes. Take the CD example again. If the scale of the y-axis is reduced or increased, the slope appears to change. This problem is overcome by calculating the numerical value of the slope, which is the change in the variable on the y-axis divided by the related change in the variable on the x-axis. In this example, where the decline in CD sales is exactly equal to the increase in price, the slope has a value of –1. Any line whose slope has an absolute value greater than 1 (such as 2 or 3) is described as steep, while lines whose slopes have an absolute value less than 1 (such as 0.5 or 0.25) are said to be flattened.

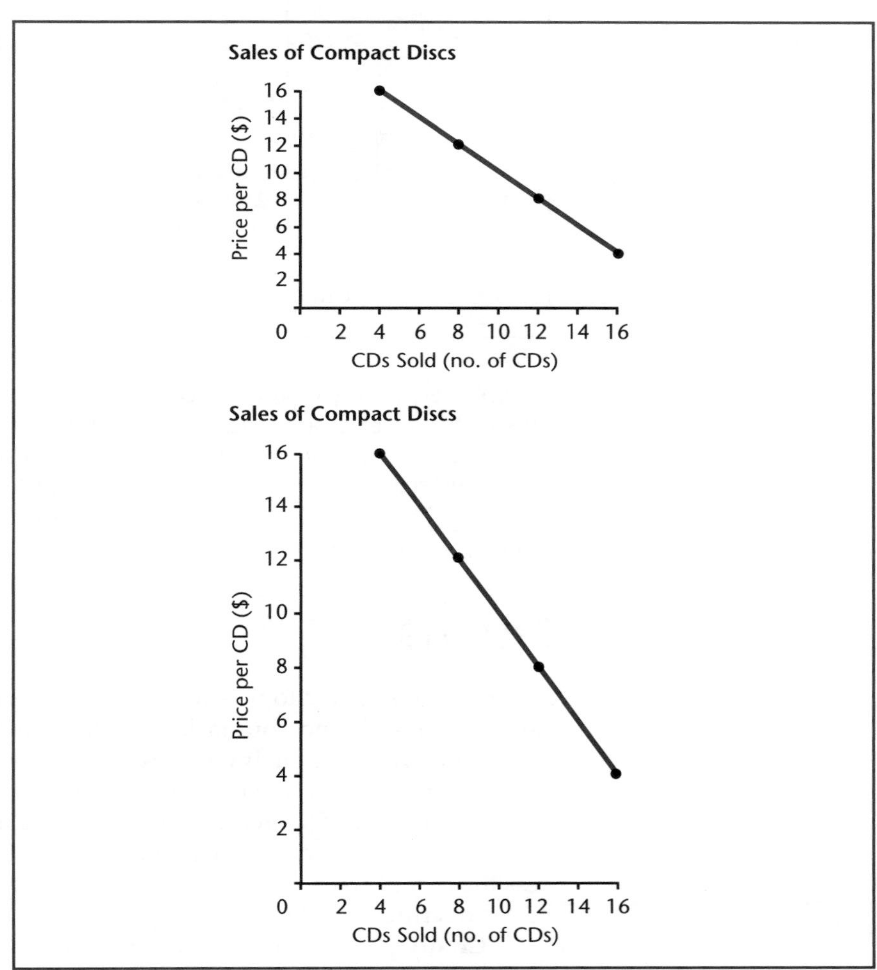

When asked to *draw* or *create* a graph, develop and label the graph precisely based on the information given. If instead you are asked to sketch a graph, develop a graph with labelled axes and a curve demonstrating the relationship of the variables. When "reading" or developing graphs, use a grid for precision. Label the x- and y-axes carefully, remembering to note units of measurement. Title your graphs for easy reference and to summarize the relationship shown.

Note that, depending on the information, graphs can take a variety of forms. For example, the information about sales of cassettes, long-playing records, and compact discs could be presented in a **bar graph**. The same basic principles of graphing apply. When various types of information are shown, as in the graph below, a legend must be included to identify the different types of bars.

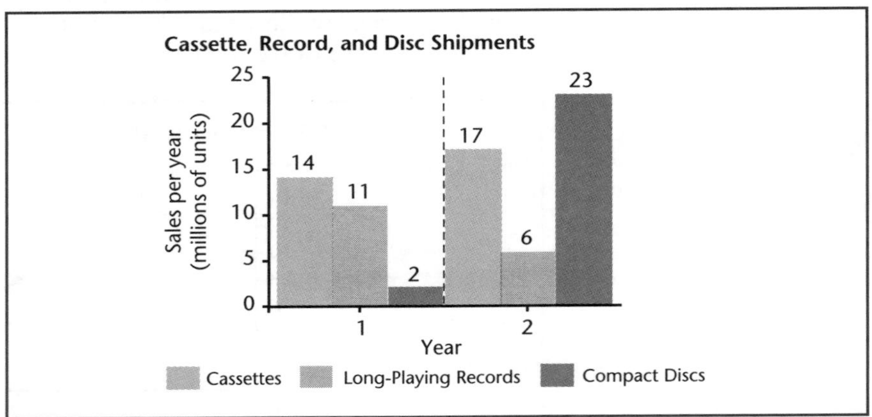

When interpreting any graph, consider these questions: What are the variables? What trends are evident? What relationships are suggested? Why? Particularly in macroeconomics, you might also ask: What additional factors could have caused this result (for example, a sudden downturn in the economy)? What is the context for this information (for example, expansionary years)? Why?

Research

When you research a topic—for example, to write a research paper—first define your topic and your task carefully so that you do not waste time as you gather information. If your research takes you in a different direction from what you had planned, check with your teacher.

Use a range of sources. By doing so, you are more likely to be able to see your topic from different angles, address the relevant factors, and access the best sources. Evaluate your sources against one another using the basics of critical thinking.

Credit all your sources, both to recognize the debt you owe to others and to allow readers to refer to the sources themselves. As you collect information, note what is a direct quotation, what is a paraphrase, and what is a summary, and note the exact source. For example:

- for articles—author's name, article title, newspaper or magazine title, date of issue, and page number(s)

- for books—author's name, book title, place of publication, publishing company, year of publication, and page number(s)
- for television sources—television station, program name, date, and time of airing
- for CD-ROM (Compact Disc–Read Only Memory) material—author's name, title of article/text portion, date, newspaper/magazine/encyclopedia title, edition, and CD-ROM title

Depending on your topic, you might do primary research, secondary research, or a combination of both. **Primary research**, in such forms as interviews and surveys, involves you in gathering "raw" information. **Secondary research**, which is based on the work of others, allows you to acquaint yourself with a range of opinions and to use data that would be difficult or impossible to collect on your own.

Valuable Sources

The research sources immediately available to you are probably newspapers (specifically their business sections), news magazines (such as *Maclean's*), business newspapers (such as *The Financial Post*), business magazines (such as *The Globe and Mail Report on Business Magazine, Forbes, The Economist*), and any collections of news clippings at your library. Some sources, such as *Maclean's*, may be available to you on CD-ROM, while others may be indexed on CD-ROM (for example, within the Canadian Business and Current Affairs Index and the Canadian Index). Alternatively, most libraries have indices in book form.

In addition, consider the following sources:

- *The Canadian Encyclopedia* and the annual *Canadian Global Almanac* for details on economic institutions in Canada
- E-Stat for Statistics Canada data on the Canadian economy, society, and population in CD-ROM format, as well as Statistics Canada publications, such as the biennial *Canada Year Book*, the monthly *Canadian Economic Observer* and its annual historical supplement, the quarterly *Perspectives on Labour and Income*, plus other more detailed publications on particular topics listed in Statistics Canada's catalogue
- Canadian BusinessDisc and Canadian NewsDisc on CD-ROM
- the Bank of Canada's quarterly *Bank of Canada Review* and the Department of Finance's annual *Economic and Fiscal Reference Tables* for recent economic statistics, especially on monetary and financial matters
- the World Bank's annual *World Development Report* and the monthly *OECD Main Economic Indicators* for international statistics
- federal and provincial government bookstores for annual budget papers

Using the Internet

By making millions of documents available with just a few strokes at a computer keyboard, the Internet offers important benefits as a research tool. As more documents become available, the range of this online information will continue to expand rapidly.

Internet documents have their own distinctive features. One is "live" links to other online sources. These links are not as structured as more traditional search techniques, but they often lead to unexpected information. Online sources can also be easily updated or tailored to the demands of users through interactive programs. This may create headaches for the Internet researcher, since information found once may be difficult to retrieve again. But it makes the Internet the perfect vehicle for statistical data and news — topics richly covered in online documents. Shrinking library budgets and rising publication costs mean that many government documents are now most easily available in online form. Important examples are Statistics Canada's daily reports of newly released information (at http://www.statcan.ca) and summaries of the Bank of Canada's reports on current monetary policy (at http://www.bank-banque-canada.ca). But traditional research methods still have advantages when you are looking for more timeless information. Therefore, keep in mind that online resources are most effective when employed alongside other research methods.

Always credit Internet documents used in your work. To refer to an online source, include the author's name, article title, title of periodical or journal (where appropriate), date of publication or last update, publication medium (online), computer network (e.g., World Wide Web), the document's electronic address, and the relevant page number (including the document's total number of pages, since this differs depending on the browser used).

Throughout the text, you can practise using the Internet by answering the online questions, which are highlighted with the icon shown in the margin. For further information on the Internet, consult the online guide that accompanies *Understanding Economics*. This guide outlines Internet sources relevant to an introductory economics course. It also provides "live" links to instructors and students using *Understanding Economics* (Instructors can apply for a class licence at the following Web address: http://www.mghr.com/college/)

Presentation

Based on your research, you should be able to present the results in an essay, an oral presentation, or a debate. Once again, evaluate your work against the basics of critical thinking. Whatever the form of your presentation, you should be able to state the thesis or main argument, give support, and address your points in a logical and orderly way. Prepare an outline to ensure that your presentation is well-structured and organized.

Essay

An essay should be written in a concise and easy-to-follow style. Remember that your general purpose is to inform and persuade, rather than to overwhelm your reader with complicated concepts and terminology. Keep in mind your specific task and the expectations of readers. Double-check to see that, in fact, your essay does what it was supposed to—for example, "explain," "support or refute," "compare," or "analyze." State your thesis clearly in your introduction, provide any background information your readers will need, support for your thesis, and a conclusion, which restates your thesis. Repeatedly revise and edit your writing before handing in the final version.

Class Presentation

Though less formal than an essay, a class presentation requires the same steps of research and preparation. Again, you should structure your discussion using an outline, and credit any sources during your presentation.

Debate

Usually when you debate, the thesis is provided for you. In a formal debate, two sides debate a statement or **proposition**. The side arguing for the proposition, called the **affirmative**, and the side arguing against the proposition, called the **negative**, each have a set period of time to make their original arguments, after which each side is allowed time for a **rebuttal** of the other's arguments. Informal debates often include a statement of the argument and support by either side, then discussion and resolution. In both types of debates, research and preparation are key. Consider all sides of the argument. It is also important to remember that the purpose of a debate is to persuade, not to create conflict. Effective debating therefore combines logic and tact.

Sources

M. Neil Brown and Stuart Keeley, *Asking the Right Questions* (Englewood Cliffs, NJ: Prentice-Hall, 1990).

Stanley L. Brue and Donald R. Wentworth, *Economic Scenes*, 5th ed. (Englewood Cliffs, NJ: Prentice-Hall, 1992).

Robert Case, *Reading Critically* (Toronto: OISE Press, 1981).

Catherine Harris, "A Guide to Using Statistics," *Canadian Economic Observer* (Ottawa: Statistics Canada, February 1990), pp. 19–33.

Darrel Hugg, *How to Lie with Statistics* (New York: W.W. Norton, 1954).

David P. Kreutzer, *Systems Thinking and Dynamic Modeling* (Cambridge, MA: Gould-Kreutzer Associates, 1994).

Donald McCloskey, *If You're So Smart* (Chicago: University of Chicago Press, 1990).

W. Edgar Moore, H. McCann, and J. McCann, *Creative and Critical Thinking*, 2nd ed. (Boston: Houghton Mifflin, 1985).

ANALYSIS AND APPLICATION

1. Calculate each of the following, rounding your answers to one place after the decimal point. In each case, explain your reasoning:
   a. the percentage change when a person's annual income falls from $28 225 to $23 158
   b. the percentage change when a country's exports rise from $20.3 billion to $32.7 billion
   c. a business's profit after a 21.2 percent increase from $402.3 million
   d. an economy's employment level after a 8.2 percent decrease from 12.7 million workers

2. Each statement below contains a logical problem—either a personal argument, false analogy, false causation, or fallacy of composition. In each case, identify the problem and briefly explain your answer.
   a. "When a person loses his or her job, total employment in the economy falls."
   b. "Canada's exports to foreign countries have risen because of the accompanying increase in Canadian interest rates."
   c. "Buying shares on the stockmarket is very much like purchasing a lottery ticket—you are making a gamble with a very low chance of success."
   d. "The argument that governments should stay out of the economy is illogical because it is supported only by extreme conservatives."

3. The table below shows how annual CD purchases in a given region are related to the average yearly income of the region's consumers.

CD Purchases

Income ($ thousands)	CDs Purchased (thousands of CDs)
40	18
30	14
20	10
10	6

   a. CD purchases can also be affected by variables other than income. For example, if there is a rise in the price of CDs how will the numbers in the table change? What assumption needs to be made about the price of CDs to analyze the relationship in the table?
   b. Draw a graph that shows the curve associated with the numbers in the table.
   c. Calculate the slope of the curve you have drawn between the income levels of $30 000 and $40 000. Is this slope positive or negative? Is it constant at all other given values of income and CDs purchased? Explain.

4. The following graph shows the relationship between the hourly wage in the construction industry and the number of construction workers employed.

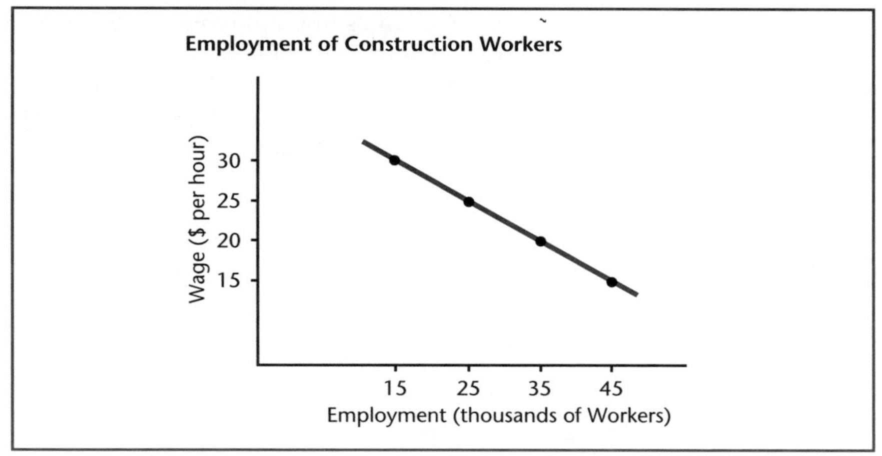

   a. Prepare a table that presents the information shown by the four highlighted points on the graph. Make sure to label your table.
   b. Estimate how many construction workers will be employed if the hourly wage falls to $10. Use the table to explain your answer.
   c. Your answer in part b. is based on an assumption concerning the relationship you are analyzing. What is this assumption?

5. The table below shows the lost time (measured in thousands of person-days) due to work stoppages in Canada in various years between 1980 and 1995.

Time Lost in Work Stoppages (thousands of person-days per year)

Year	Manufacturing	Construction	Transportation
1980	3 137	1 107	729
1985	1 578	11	479
1990	2 474	1 150	400
1995	722	202	277

Source: Statistics Canada, *Historical Statistical Supplement, 1995/6,* (July 1996) cat. no. 11-210, vol. 8, p. 38.

   a. Convert the data shown in the table into a bar graph.
   b. Which of the three industry groups has experienced the biggest percentage change in time lost to work stoppages between 1980 and 1995? the smallest percentage change?

6. Access Statistics Canada's website (at http://www.statcan.ca). Then use the links to "Canadian Dimensions" to find the two most recent annual values for the following variables:
   a. Canada's total population
   b. Canada's unemployment rate, measured as a percentage
   c. total imports of goods into Canada, valued in Canadian dollars
   d. total exports of goods from Canada, valued in Canadian dollars
   e. the exchange rate, measured in terms of U.S. dollars per Canadian dollar

Part One

Working With Economics

The Age of Chivalry is gone—that of sophisters, economists, and calculators has succeeded.

— Edmund Burke, British political writer

Chapter One
The Economic Problem

Economy is the art of making the most out of life.
—George Bernard Shaw, Irish playwright

Just as variety adds spice to life, so choice enlivens our everyday existence. Some choices are minor—which pair of shoes to buy, or whether to have a pizza or a hamburger for lunch. Others are more important—where to live, and what career to pursue. Because our resources are limited, every one of our choices has a price. This is a basic fact of human existence that applies equally to individuals and societies. Individuals must decide how to use their limited time and budgets. Societies, meanwhile, must decide how to employ a fixed supply of resources. Thus, both individuals and societies can use economics to analyze their choices and make the best possible decisions.

CHAPTER FOCUS

This chapter focuses on the following:

- the economic problem—the problem of having needs and unlimited wants, but limited resources—that underlies the definition of economics
- the types of reasoning that economists use
- the production choices an entire economy faces, as demonstrated by the production possibilities model
- the three basic economic questions and how various economic systems answer them
- the main economic goals of the Canadian economy and the ways in which they are related

WHAT ECONOMISTS DO

The Economic Problem

economic problem: the problem of having unlimited wants, but limited resources with which to satisfy them

Every day, we make choices to meet our wants. Wants vary widely from person to person; we may have a special preference for ice-cream sundaes or chocolate cakes, rock concerts or classical recitals, video games or comic books. Because we face so many choices, the sum total of wants is virtually unlimited. Our resources, however, are not. Thus we have the **economic problem**.

Thinking About Economics

The famous Indian statesman, M.K. (Mahatma) Gandhi, once said, "There is enough for the needy, but not for the greedy." What are the implications of this belief for the economic problem?

Gandhi's statement reveals a way the economic problem can be solved without the help of economics—by curbing our selfish wants. Is such a scenario feasible? In some cultures, and for idealistic individuals or small groups, it can be. However, attempts to control the wants of large groups of people have tended to be spectacular failures.

economic resources: basic items that are used in all types of production, including natural, capital, and human resources

The limited nature of resources—or scarcity—requires that we make choices based on both noneconomic factors, such as the need for security, *and* economic factors. For many individuals, time and money are most scarce. For societies as a whole, it is the basic items used in all types of production, known as **economic resources**, that are scarce. These resources come not only from nature, but also from human effort and ingenuity. Economic resources are often categorized as natural resources, capital resources, and human resources.

natural resources: the resources from nature that are used in production, including land, raw materials, and natural processes

Natural Resources

Natural resources represent nature's contribution to production. These resources include not only land—used for farms, roads, and buildings—but also raw materials such as minerals and forests. As well, natural resources include useful natural processes such as sunlight and water power.

capital resources: the processed materials, equipment, and buildings used in production; also known as capital

Capital Resources

In economics, **capital resources**, or capital, refers to the real assets of an economy—the processed materials, equipment, and buildings that are used in production. An example is a newspaper printing plant and its printing presses, as well as the processed inputs—paper and ink—used

to make newspapers. The term "capital" has a special meaning in economics. As economic resources, capital resources do *not* include financial capital such as stocks and bonds. A person's shares in Canadian Pacific, for example, do not add to the economy's stock of real capital. Similarly, the bonds issued by a company such as Bell Canada are viewed as financial capital by their holders, but not as real capital by economists.

Human Resources

labour: human effort employed directly in production

entrepreneurship: initiative, risk-taking, and innovation necessary for production

There are two main types of human resources used in production. **Labour** represents human effort employed directly in production, such as the work of a computer programmer, store clerk, factory supervisor, or brain surgeon. On the other hand, **entrepreneurship** is the initiative, risk-taking, and innovation necessary for production. It includes the efforts of the inventor who brings a new product to the market, the head of a multimillion-dollar corporation, the owner of a small variety store, and the student who starts a summer house-painting business. Entrepreneurship is often difficult to pinpoint, but it is this that brings together the natural resources, capital resources, and labour in order to produce a good or service.

Resource Incomes

Economic resources have corresponding incomes, which reflect their contributions to production. When a natural resource is employed, its owner receives a rent, which is the payment for supplying the resource. Similarly, providers of capital resources (as well as providers of financial capital such as bonds) receive an income in the form of interest. Finally, people are paid wages for their labour and profit for their entrepreneurship.

Economics Defined

economics: the study of how to distribute scarce resources among alternative ends

Arising from unlimited wants and scarce resources, **economics** is the study of how to distribute limited resources among alternative ends. Economics is divided into two branches, which are studied separately: microeconomics and macroeconomics.

Microeconomics

microeconomics: the branch of economics that focuses on the behaviour of individual participants in various markets

Microeconomics focuses on the behaviour of individual participants in various markets. How do people decide on the quantities of a particular resource they will consume? How do businesses decide on the quantities of a particular product they will produce? How are prices set within markets? What determines how incomes are distributed to the various participants in an economy? These are the sorts of questions studied in microeconomics.

Macroeconomics

macroeconomics: the branch of economics that takes a wide-ranging view of the economy, studying the behaviour of economic sectors

In contrast, **macroeconomics** takes a more wide-ranging view of the economy. It is concerned with entire economic sectors, which are treated as separate entities. The four important sectors in the economy are households, businesses, government, and foreign markets. How these sectors interact determines a country's unemployment rate, general level of prices, and total economic output. Explaining these larger economic forces is the central task of macroeconomics.

Economic Models

economic models: generalizations about or simplifications of economic reality; also known as laws, principles, or theories

Economists use models to help them understand economic behaviour. **Economic models**—also known as laws, principles, or theories—are generalizations or simplifications of economic reality. As an example, think about the Canadian economy, in which literally millions of separate transactions—sales and purchases—are made each day. Trying to keep track of every sale and purchase for the purpose of understanding economic activity would be impossible. Instead, economists build useful abstractions of reality that allow them to see the basic workings of the economy. In other words, a good economic model allows economists to see the forest instead of the trees.

Without even realizing it, we regularly use models. When driving in unfamiliar territory, for example, we often depend on maps. Although an aerial photograph of our route would be the most realistic representation, it is virtually useless as a driving guide. A road map, however, gives exactly the detail needed to find the way. Similarly, a good economic model can help us understand some facet of economic behaviour without overwhelming us with details.

Cause and Effect

variables: factors that have measurable values

independent variable: the variable in a causal relationship that causes change in another variable

dependent variable: the variable in a causal relationship that is affected by another variable

How, can economic models help explain economic trends and behaviour? Usually by including two or more **variables**, or factors that have measurable values. For example, the price of an item and the quantity that is purchased of that item are two variables. In a model, variables are connected by a causal relationship, meaning that one variable is assumed to affect another. Suppose a model states that a rise in the price of cellular phones reduces the number of cellular phones purchased. In this case, the variable that is causing the other to change—known as the **independent variable**—is the price of cellular phones. The variable that is being affected—called the **dependent variable**—is the number of cellular phones purchased.

Inverse and Direct Relationships

inverse relationship: a relationship in which a change in the independent variable causes a change in the opposite direction of the dependent variable

direct relationship: a relationship in which a change in the independent variable causes a change in the same direction of the dependent variable

A model proposes what effect one variable will have on another. If the value of one variable is expected to increase as the value of another variable decreases, the variables have an **inverse relationship**. An increase in cellular phone prices that reduces the number of phones sold is an example of an inverse relationship. Two variables can have a **direct relationship**, meaning that, when the independent variable rises or falls, the dependent variable moves in the same direction. A rise in the hourly wage of bank tellers that causes a corresponding rise in the number of people who wish to work in this occupation is an example of a direct relationship.

The Need for Assumptions

In order to focus on the relationship between two variables, economists must make assumptions to temporarily simplify the real world. Let's return to the relationship that states that the quantity of cellular phones purchased is inversely related to their price. Economists must assume that another factor—such as consumer incomes—is not affecting purchases of cellular phones. Assuming that all other factors affecting a dependent variable remain constant is common in economics. This assumption is known as ***ceteris paribus*** (pronounced kay'-teh-rees pah'-ri-bus), which is the Latin expression for "all other things remaining the same." The ceteris paribus assumption, as well as any other assumptions that are made, should be outlined explicitly in an economic model.

ceteris paribus: the assumption that all other things remain the same

Positive and Normative Economics

In using economic models we need to distinguish between two types of economic enquiry: positive and normative economics.

positive economics: the study of economic facts and how the economy operates as it does

Positive economics (sometimes called *descriptive economics*) is the study of economic reality and why the economy operates as it does. It is based purely on economic facts rather than on opinions. This type of economics is made up of positive statements, which can be accepted or rejected through applying the scientific method. "Canadians bought 5 million CDs last year" is a positive statement—a simple declaration of fact. A positive statement can also take the form of a condition that asserts that if one thing happens, then so will another: "If rent controls are eliminated, then the number of available rental units will increase." Both declarations of fact and conditional statements can be verified or disproved using economic data.

normative economics: the study of how the economy ought to operate

In contrast, **normative economics** (also called *policy economics*) deals with how the world ought to be. In this type of economics, opinions or value judgements—known as normative statements—are common. "We should reduce taxes" is an example of a normative statement. So is "A 1 percent rise in unemployment is worse than a 1 percent rise in inflation." Even people who agree on the facts can have different opinions regarding a normative statement, since the statement relates to questions of ethical values.

BRIEF REVIEW

1. The basic economic problem faced by both individuals and societies is that while human wants are virtually unlimited, the resources to fulfil them are limited, or scarce.
2. Economic resources can be categorized as natural resources, capital resources, and human resources. Each resource has a corresponding income.
3. Whereas microeconomics concentrates on the ways consumers and businesses interact in various markets, macroeconomics takes a broader look at the economy as a whole, and highlights such variables as unemployment, inflation, and total output.
4. Economic models contain causal relationships between variables and are based on simplifying assumptions.

ECONOMIC CHOICE

How do people make economic choices? They do so by using effectively the scarce resources they have. Two main factors are involved in this decision-making process: utility and cost.

Utility Maximization

utility: the satisfaction gained from any action

self-interest motive: the assumption that people act to maximize their own welfare

Economists assume that, whenever you make an economic choice, you are trying to maximize your own utility. **Utility** can be defined as the satisfaction or pleasure you derive from any action. Let's examine utility maximization with the illustration of you and your lunch. Economists assume first the **self-interest motive**, that is, that you are primarily concerned with your own welfare. So, when deciding among lunch options that cost the same amount of money, you pick the one that gives the most utility. For example, suppose someone has $2 to spend at a fast-food restaurant. Two options are available: a pizza slice or a low-calorie veggieburger, each with a price of $2. How does this person make a choice? According to economists, the person decides by comparing the utility gained from either product. If the satisfaction from a pizza slice outweighs the pleasures of a veggieburger, they'll buy the pizza. If the opposite applies, the veggieburger will win out.

Opportunity Cost

opportunity cost: the utility that could have been gained by choosing an action's best alternative

Maximizing utility is only one part of making economic decisions. Acquiring anything prevents someone from pursuing an alternative. Instead of measuring cost in terms of money, economists use a concept that accounts for the tradeoffs resulting from any economic choice: **opportunity cost**. The opportunity cost of any action is the utility that could have been gained by choosing the best possible alternative.

The notion of opportunity cost involves more than money. To illustrate, the person who spends $2 to buy a pizza slice at the fast-food restaurant faces an opportunity cost equal to the utility that could have been gained by eating a low-calorie burger instead. If the person chooses the veggieburger, the opportunity cost is the sacrificed pleasure of eating a pizza slice. For a weight-conscious consumer, for example, the utility gained from eating the burger probably outweighs the pleasure from eating the pizza slice. This means that the burger's opportunity cost is lower than the opportunity cost of the pizza slice (even though both have the same monetary price), making the burger the preferred choice for this individual.

The concept of opportunity cost also relates to how we spend time, since time passed in one activity means less devoted to another. Suppose a student is deciding whether to spend a free hour watching a TV program or reading a paperback mystery. The opportunity cost of watching the TV program is the pleasure that could have been gained from reading the mystery. Likewise, the opportunity cost of reading the mystery is the benefit sacrificed by not watching the program.

THE PRODUCTION POSSIBILITIES MODEL

The production possibilities model illustrates the tradeoffs that society faces in using its scarce resources. Like all models, it is an abstraction of the real world based on various simplifications. In this case, the following assumptions are made: only two items are produced, resources and technology are fixed, and all economic resources are employed to their full potential.

Two Products

An immense range of goods and services are produced in the Canadian economy. The production possibilities model, however, narrows the list to only two; for example, VCRs and videotapes.

Fixed Resources and Technology

For the model, it is assumed that there is a set amount of available economic resources and that technology remains constant. However, resources can be moved from the production of one good to the other. Workers who make videotapes, for example, can be shifted to the assembly of VCRs.

Full Production

In the production possibilities model, all economic resources are employed; that is, there is no excess. Also, resources are used to their greatest capacity no matter which good they are producing—in this case, VCRs and videotapes.

The Production Possibilities Curve

production possibilities schedule: a table that shows the possible output combinations for an economy

production possibilities curve: a graph that illustrates the possible output combinations for an economy

In order to maximize the welfare of its citizens, a society must make economic choices. How much of each good should be produced in a certain year given the resources at the society's disposal? A choice is necessary because producing more of one item means making do with less of the other. This choice is illustrated in Figure 1.1. On the left is the economy's **production possibilities schedule**—a table outlining, in this case, the possible combinations of VCRs and videotapes. Expressing the schedule in a graph gives us the economy's **production possibilities curve**. Because making more of one good means making less of the other, there is an inverse relationship between the quantities of VCRs and videotapes produced. Therefore the curve has a negative slope—from left to right, the curve falls.

As Figure 1.1 demonstrates, it might be possible for the economy to make 900 videotapes and assemble 1 VCR in a given year (point *b*). If the output of videotapes is reduced to 600, it might also be feasible for the economy to produce 2 VCRs (point *c*). The extreme cases serve as useful reference points: when all of the economy's resources are devoted to the making of videotapes, a total of 1000 can be produced annually (point *a*), but when the economy devotes all of its resources to making only VCRs, 3 can be made (point *d*).

FIGURE 1.1
The Production Possibilities Model

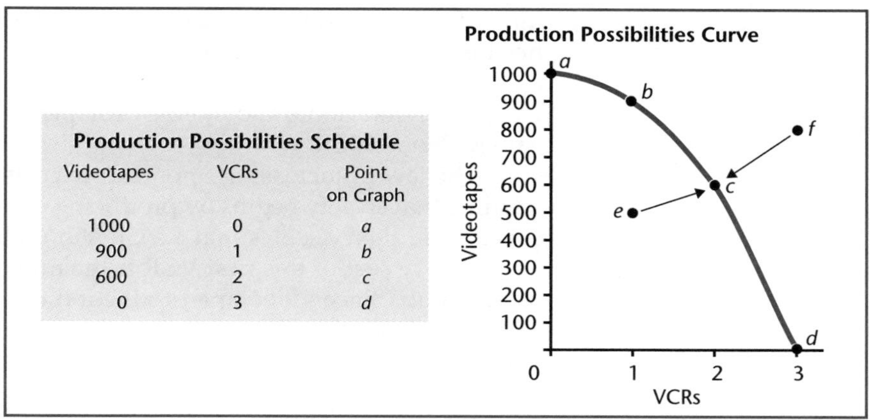

Production Possibilities Schedule

Videotapes	VCRs	Point on Graph
1000	0	*a*
900	1	*b*
600	2	*c*
0	3	*d*

A society must choose among possible combinations of two goods. These combinations are shown in the production possibilities schedule and represented by points on the production possibilities curve. Both the schedule and the curve show that more VCRs can be assembled only if fewer videotapes are produced. Any points within the curve, as illustrated by *e*, are feasible. Those outside the curve, like *f*, are not.

The Role of Scarcity

As well as depicting the economic choices a society faces, the production possibilities curve highlights the scarcity of economic resources. The curve is a boundary between all those output combinations that are within reach of an economy, and all those combinations that are unattainable. Anywhere inside the curve, such as point *e* in Figure 1.1, represents a feasible combination of the two products. At point *e*, for example, 500 videotapes and 1 VCR can be produced. The production of both videotapes and VCRs could be increased by moving toward point *c* on the curve. At any point such as *e*, some of an economy's resources are not being fully employed or used to their greatest capacity. Hence, all points inside the curve represent a situation where resources are not being used effectively.

In contrast, point *f* in Figure 1.1 is outside the curve. In this case, the economy would be producing 800 videotapes and 3 VCRs annually. As long as the economy's resources remain constant, this point cannot be reached. More of *both* videotapes and VCRs could be made if point *f* were attainable, but the economy's resources are already being fully utilized at point *c*.

Increasing Opportunity Costs

law of increasing opportunity costs: the concept that as more of one item is produced by an economy, the opportunity cost of additional units of that product rises

The notion of opportunity cost is best seen when moving from one point to another on the production possibilities curve. Notice that the curve in Figure 1.1 bows out to the right. This shape reflects what is called the **law of increasing opportunity costs**, which states that, as more of one product is produced, its opportunity cost in terms of the other product increases. This law arises from the fact that economic resources do not shift perfectly from one use to another. For example, because of training and experience, some workers are better at making videotapes than assembling VCRs. When the first VCR is assembled, it is made using resources suited to VCR assembly rather than to making videotapes. Hence, the number of videotapes sacrificed is relatively small. But if further VCRs are assembled, resources that are not as well suited to this new task must be shifted from making videotapes. Therefore, more and more videotapes have to be given up in order to gain each new VCR.

The law of increasing opportunity costs is illustrated in Figure 1.2. Assume that society begins by producing only videotapes (point *a* on the curve), and then decides that 1 VCR should be assembled (point *b*). The opportunity cost of this first VCR is the number of videotapes that must be given up. Since videotape production falls from 1000 to 900, the new VCR costs 100 videotapes. This is shown on the schedule and, on the curve, appears as the height of the triangle connecting points *a* and *b*. The same reasoning can be applied in moving from points *b* to *c*—as a second VCR is added, videotape production drops from 900 to 600. The opportunity cost of this extra VCR is therefore 300 videotapes. Finally, in moving from points *c* to *d*, videotape production drops another 600 to zero, meaning that the opportunity cost of the third VCR is 600 videotapes. The opportunity cost of each new VCR, in terms of videotapes, therefore rises from 100, to 300, and then to 600.

FIGURE 1.2
The Law of Increasing Opportunity Costs

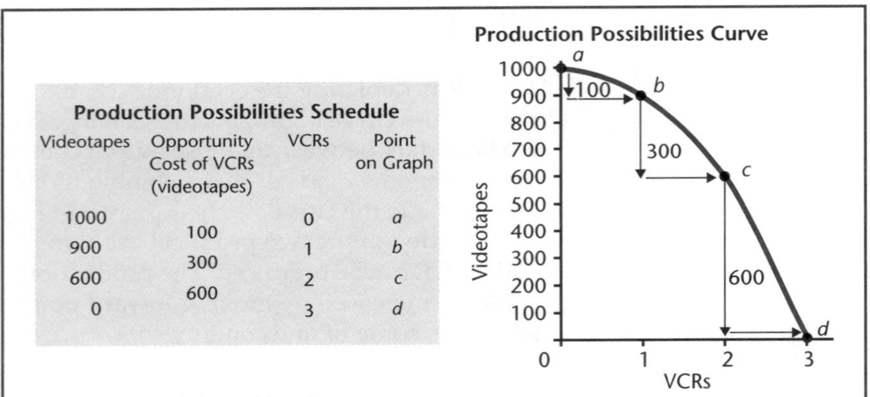

Production Possibilities Schedule

Videotapes	Opportunity Cost of VCRs (videotapes)	VCRs	Point on Graph
1000		0	*a*
	100		
900		1	*b*
	300		
600		2	*c*
	600		
0		3	*d*

As the production of VCRs rises from 0 to 1 unit (from points *a* to *b*), the opportunity cost of the first VCR is 100 videotapes. Further expansion in the output of VCRs comes at higher opportunity costs: 300 videotapes for the second VCR (from points *b* to *c*), and 600 videotapes for the third VCR (from points *c* to *d*).

Thinking About Economics

What happens to the production possibilities curve when the economy's stock of resources increases? Also, what happens if technology improves, allowing the same resources to produce more of both videotapes and VCRs?

In each of these cases, the production possibilities curve shifts to the right, meaning that the area of feasible output combinations expands. As a result, the society can choose output combinations that were previously unattainable—more of both items can now be produced. The economy therefore experiences a growth in total output.

BRIEF REVIEW

1. Economists assume that individuals make economic choices among scarce items by maximizing their own utility while minimizing opportunity cost.
2. The production possibilities curve shows the range of choices faced by an economy. It assumes only two products, fixed resources and technology, and full production.
3. Points inside the production possibilities curve are feasible but indicate that not all resources are being used effectively. Conversely, points outside the curve cannot be reached unless resources increase or technology improves.
4. The fact that economic resources are specialized leads to the law of increasing costs. As the economy's production of any item is expanded, that item's opportunity cost rises.

ECONOMIC SYSTEMS

Basic Economic Questions

Because of the basic economic problem of scarcity, every country, no matter how it chooses to conduct its economic affairs, must answer three basic economic questions: what to produce, how to produce, and for whom to produce.

What to Produce

Countries face economic choices when trying to decide what items to produce, as depicted by the production possibilities curve. For example, making more videotapes means assembling fewer VCRs. Somehow, a country must decide how much of each possible good and service is to be supplied. Should these decisions be based on past practice, the individual choices of consumers, or government decisions?

How to Produce

Once the question of what to produce has been answered, a country must decide how these items should be produced. Which resources should be employed and in what combinations? For example, should farmers use horse-drawn plows and large amounts of labour to produce wheat? Or should they use sophisticated farm machinery and very little labour? And how should these decisions be made? Should the farmers follow tradition, each choose among their many options, or have their production methods specified by government planners?

For Whom to Produce

Each country must also determine how its total output of goods and services will be distributed. How output is divided might be based on custom. Alternatively, each person's ownership of economic resources may be the key factor. Or, the government might distribute output in some other fashion.

economic system: the organization of an economy, which represents a country's distinct set of social customs, political institutions, and economic practices

To answer these three basic economic questions, a country organizes its economy. The result is an **economic system**, which represents the country's distinct set of social customs, political institutions, and economic practices. In the following sections, we will look at three main economic systems: traditional economy, market economy, and command economy. Each of these is a pure or theoretical system, so few economies come close to them. Most economies today are mixed; that is, they combine aspects of the main economic systems. These systems are all founded on different views of what a society's primary aims should be.

Traditional Economy

traditional economy: an economic system in which economic decisions are made on the basis of custom

A **traditional economy** is one in which economic decisions depend on custom, such as a traditional division of work between women and men. The mix of outputs, the organization of production, and the way in which outputs are distributed tend to be passed on relatively unchanged from generation to generation. Religion and culture tend to be considered to be at least as important as material welfare. As recently as a century ago, most people lived in traditional economies, but these economies exist today only in isolated pockets. For example, many farmers in the remote country of Nepal still use traditional methods that have existed for generations. Since they are based on tight social constraints, traditional economies are often resistant to change. Still, the long-term outlook for these economies seems clear: increasingly, they are being broken down by expanding consumer wants and the inability of traditional production methods to meet these wants.

Supporters of traditional economies suggest that they offer the advantage of stability. These economies can also be viewed as beneficial because they emphasize the spiritual and cultural aspects of life. However, critics argue that traditional economies' widespread poverty and social restrictions restrain human potential; people must follow the dictates of custom rather than having the freedom to make their own economic choices.

Market Economy

market economy: an economic system based on private ownership and the use of markets in economic decision-making

In a **market economy** individuals are free to pursue their own self-interest. This type of economy is based on the private ownership of economic resources and the use of markets in making economic decisions. In this system—often referred to as capitalism—households use incomes earned from their economic resources by saving some and spending the rest on consumer products. Businesses, conversely, buy resources from households and employ these resources to provide the consumer products demanded by households. Government performs only the political functions of upholding the legal system and maintaining public security.

The transactions between households and businesses in a market economy are illustrated by the circular flow diagram in Figure 1.3. This diagram includes not only households and businesses, but also two markets.

FIGURE 1.3
The Circular Flow Diagram

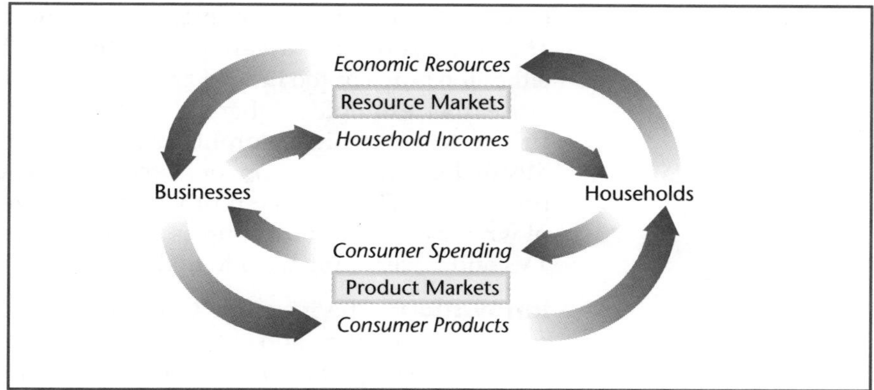

Households and businesses are involved in two main markets, one involving consumer products and the other involving economic resources. While the inner loop represents the clockwise flow of incomes and consumer spending, the outer loop indicates the counterclockwise circulation of resources and products.

market: a set of arrangements between buyers and sellers of a certain item

product markets: markets in which consumer products are traded

resource markets: markets in which economic resources are traded

A **market** is a set of arrangements between buyers and sellers that allows them to trade items for set prices. **Product markets** are those in which consumer products are traded. **Resource markets** are those in which economic resources—natural resources, capital resources, and human resources—are traded.

Households and businesses face each other in both sets of markets. In product markets, households are the buyers of consumer products while businesses are the sellers. In resource markets, the roles are reversed: households sell resources that businesses purchase so they can produce goods and services. Households and businesses are connected by two circular flows. The inner loop in the diagram shows the circulation of payments—both household incomes and consumer spending. The outer loop shows the circulation of consumer products and economic resources in the opposite direction.

Benefits of a Market Economy

Placing markets at the centre of economic activity can have benefits. The main benefits are associated with consumer sovereignty, prices, and innovation.

consumer sovereignty: the effect of consumer needs and wants on production decisions

Consumer Sovereignty Market economies are characterized by **consumer sovereignty**, meaning that the decision of what to produce is ultimately guided by the needs and wants of households in their role as consumers. In other words, consumers use their dollars to "vote" on what types of goods and services should be produced. For example, if households wish to switch some of their consumption dollars from the purchase of stereos to TVs, a chain reaction will occur in the product and resource markets. In product markets, the extra demand for TVs pushes up TV prices, while the lower demand for stereos pushes down stereo prices.

Prices Prices act as an important signalling device in a market economy. They do this by co-ordinating the activities of buyers and sellers to stop either too much or too little of an item from being produced. In the case of our earlier example, higher TV prices provide businesses, lured by the chance to make higher profits, with an incentive to supply more TVs. Meanwhile, the price drop for stereos causes businesses to cut their stereo production. These shifts in production also result in changes in the employment of economic resources, with more resources being used to make TVs and fewer being used to make stereos.

Innovation The incentive to make a profit in a market economy encourages innovation and entrepreneurship, which help to foster advances in technology. Consumers benefit through improvements to existing products and the introduction of completely new products.

Drawbacks of a Market Economy

The main drawbacks of a market economy are associated with income distribution, possible market problems, and potential instability of total output.

Income Distribution Without intervention by governments, the distribution of income in a market economy can create significant inequities. If households' incomes are based solely on the ability to supply economic resources, then some individuals in the economy might not earn enough to provide even for their basic needs.

Market Problems Other deficiencies of market economies arise because private markets do not always operate in a way that benefits society as a whole. Negative external effects of economic activity—for example, pollution—may require intervention by governments to prevent harm to the society. Negative internal effects may also cause governments to step in; for example, when one or a few companies control a certain product market, thus depriving consumers of the advantages of competition.

Instability Finally, market economies can display considerable instability in the total output produced from year to year. Such fluctuations can harm the economy's participants through substantial variations in prices or employment levels.

As a result of these deficiencies, there are very few real-world examples of pure capitalism. The closest approximations have occurred in the past; in particular, during the first half of the nineteenth century in Great Britain.

Command Economy

command economy: an economic system based on public ownership and central planning

Opposite to a market economy is a **command economy**, in which all productive property—natural resources and capital—is in the hands of government, and markets are largely replaced by central planning. Rather than being based on consumer sovereignty and individual decision-making, command economies rely on planners to decide what should be produced, how production should be carried out, and how the output should be distributed. For example, in a market economy, decisions made by households about how much to consume and how much to save determine the split between consumer and capital products. In a command economy, however, central planners determine the split, based on their judgement of the future needs of the entire economy.

Benefits of a Command Economy

The reliance on planning rather than markets gives command economies some possible benefits related to income distribution and economic growth.

Income Distribution A country that adopts a command system can choose to distribute income among its citizens based on considerations other than purely economic ones. In these economies, an attempt is usually made to distribute income more equally than would be the case with market economies.

Economic Growth Central planners can focus on promoting the rate of economic growth by devoting more resources to capital goods than would be the case in a market economy. This strategy can be particularly effective when an economy is first building a manufacturing sector. During this stage of development, economic growth is closely tied to the quantity of capital goods, such as machines and factories, that an economy possesses.

Drawbacks of a Command Economy

Command economies also have serious drawbacks related to planning, efficiency, and individual freedom. Because of these deficiencies, pure command economies are almost as rare as pure market economies; the closest approximation in contemporary times is North Korea.

Planning Difficulties Trying to plan an entire economy is a difficult task requiring a tremendous amount of information that is unlikely to be at the planners' disposal. Incorrect estimates of future conditions are all too easy to make, leading to overproduction of some items and underproduction of others.

Inefficiencies Government ownership of productive property can lead to waste and inefficiency, since command economies cannot depend on the lure of profit to promote the efficient use of resources. Without markets to control individual self-interest, corruption of government officials is also a frequent problem. As well, because planners emphasize quantity by setting production quotas, the quality of goods and services can suffer.

Lack of Freedom Opponents of command economies also suggest that putting so much power into the hands of government stifles individual freedom. Because central planners are responsible for so many economic decisions, people living in command economies have limited economic choices. All too often, critics contend, command economies are associated with a lack of political freedom as well.

Mixed Economy

modern mixed economy: an economic system that combines aspects of a market economy and a command economy; production decisions are made both in private markets and by government

Most countries fall between the extremes of traditional, market, and command economies. A **modern mixed economy** is one that combines both the use of markets and a significant government presence in economic decision making. Modern mixed economies have proven very popular and take a variety of forms, depending on the relative importance given to private markets and to the economic functions of government. In some countries, such as Canada and the United States, markets play the dominant economic role. In other countries, such as Sweden, the government's economic role is more important. All three examples are illustrated in Figure 1.4, which depicts the range of possible modern mixed economies (along the top edge of the triangle) that exist between the two poles of pure market and command economies.

While modern mixed economies vary widely, they have some common attributes. Each one includes a private sector, in which economic activity is dominated by markets and there is private ownership of productive resources. Each of these economies also includes a public sector, in which governments conduct economic activity—often without the use of markets—and own productive resources.

In most modern mixed economies, the distinction between the private and public sectors is not clear-cut. Governments can intervene in the private sector by levying taxes or providing subsidies to some industries. In Canada, for example, the federal government plays a part in the private sector through personal and corporate taxes and the subsidies it provides to business. Government also intervenes in the private sector by imposing regulations, such as environmental laws, on businesses. In addition, the government owns some companies, such as Canada Post.

Countries with entirely traditional economies are rare. However, some countries still possess a significant traditional sector, in which

FIGURE 1.4
The Range of Economic Systems

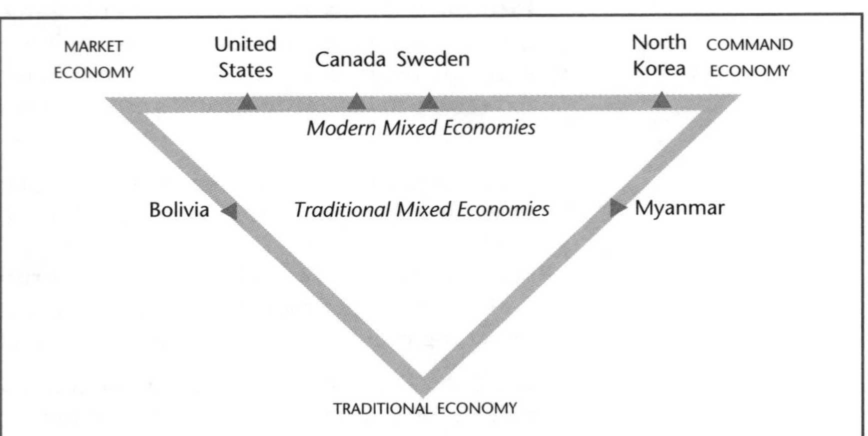

Real-world economies can be positioned on or within a triangle whose points make up the three basic types of economic systems: traditional, market, and command. Countries with surviving traditional sectors combine them with either an emerging market economy (as in Bolivia) or a command economy (as in Myanmar).

economic activity is based on custom and traditional production methods. Economies that possess a traditional sector alongside more modern sectors are known as **traditional mixed economies**. An example is Bolivia, where market-driven industries such as mining co-exist with a traditional sector of peasant farmers. These economies can also involve traditional and command economies, as in the case of Myanmar (formerly Burma). Both of these examples appear in Figure 1.4, in which traditional mixed economies appear on the two sides of the triangle.

traditional mixed economies: economic systems in which a traditional sector co-exists with modern sectors

Conflicts

Mixed economies must deal with the inevitable conflicts among their component sectors. Each sector emphasizes a distinct view of society's underlying aims—the focus on self-interest in a private sector, wider national objectives in a public sector, and continuity in a traditional sector. As the sectors interact, differences in these views are sure to cause friction.

As an example, consider one of Canada's few remaining traditional industries—the Atlantic inshore fishery, which is based on the tradition of small, family-owned business. Canadians view government subsidies to those working in this industry in different ways. Some Canadians resent their taxes being used to prop up an uncompetitive industry. Others see these subsidies as a necessary form of regional aid. Still others view the issue not as an economic one, but as a cultural one, since fishing has traditionally been an important part of Atlantic Canada's economy.

Economic Goals

Choosing economic goals is an issue of normative economics. In other words, it requires making value judgements. The economic goals that various countries strive for are often similar. In 1964, the Economic Council of Canada—which, until recently disbanded, was a federal "think tank" on economic issues—listed what it considered to be the five main goals of the Canadian economy: economic growth, full employment, price stability, income equity, and a viable balance of payments. Many Canadians would add to the list economic efficiency and environmental sustainability.

These seven goals are the focus of later parts of this text. Part 2 of the text centres on how an economy can best achieve the goals of economic efficiency and income equity. Part 3 concentrates on how to attain both price stability and full employment. Finally, Part 4 focuses on issues related to ensuring a viable balance of payments and economic growth. The goal of environmental sustainability is addressed throughout the text. For now, the significance of each of these goals will be briefly summarized.

Economic Efficiency

economic efficiency: employing scarce resources in such a way as to derive the highest benefit

In general, **economic efficiency** means getting the highest benefit from an economy's scarce resources. In other words, efficiency requires that scarce economic resources be employed in a way that maximizes utility.

Income Equity

Income equity is achieved when a country's total output is distributed fairly. This begs the question, "What is fair?" Is it fair that the salary of a bank executive is many times higher than the year's wages of a part-time gardener? Because value judgements come into play, defining and satisfying the goal of income equity is controversial.

Price Stability

inflation: a rise in the general level of prices

To achieve price stability, Canadian governments try to minimize the country's rate of inflation. **Inflation** is a rise in the general level of prices. As the average price level in the economy increases, households must pay more to buy the same items as before. In other words, the purchasing power of a single dollar falls. Meanwhile, people's money incomes do not necessarily increase along with these higher prices. Those households whose incomes stay the same or grow only slightly are hurt by inflation because they can buy fewer goods and services than they could before.

Full Employment

unemployment rate: the percentage of a labour force that is involuntarily unemployed

The Canadian government endeavours to minimize involuntary unemployment in the labour force. The labour force can be defined as those people who are working, plus those who are involuntarily unemployed and actively seeking employment. The **unemployment rate** is the percentage of the country's labour force that is involuntarily unemployed.

The costs of involuntary unemployment are significant both to jobless people and to the entire economy. Being without work represents a waste of personal potential and can bring economic hardship to the unemployed and their families. For the Canadian economy, a high unemployment rate means a lower total output than could otherwise be produced. In terms of the country's production possibilities curve, economic activity takes place within the curve, where resources are not used to their full potential.

Viable Balance of Payments

balance-of-payments accounts: a summary of all transactions between Canadians and foreigners that involve exchanging Canadian dollars for other currencies

Canadians, like people of other nations, engage in a constant flow of imports, exports, and financial dealings with other countries. These international flows—including importing, exporting, borrowing, and lending—are of great significance to the Canadian economy, since the annual value of trade per person in Canada is higher than that for citizens of any other country in the world. The **balance-of-payments accounts** summarize all transactions between Canadians and foreigners that involve exchanging Canadian dollars for other currencies, such as American dollars or British pounds. Because of Canada's dependence on foreign markets, it is important that Canadian imports and exports should roughly balance one another. Similarly, financial flows in and out of the country need to be more or less evenly matched. As long as these conditions are met, then Canada exhibits a viable balance of payments.

Economic Growth

economic growth: an increase in an economy's total output of goods and services

Economic growth, or an increase in the total output of goods and services, is depicted by an outward shift in the production possibilities curve. A rise in the amount of available resources or an improvement in technology can lead to this outward shift. Economic growth is an important national goal because it helps to raise the average standard of living for Canadians. Thus, over recent decades the entire Canadian economy has expanded considerably and individual Canadians are better off than they were in previous decades. For example, an average Canadian worker in the early 1990s could buy over three and a half times as much with his or her income than could an average worker in the early 1920s. Maintaining a healthy rate of growth in the Canadian economy will ensure that future generations will achieve even higher living standards.

Environmental Sustainability

Economic activity must be carried out so that the quality of our physical environment can be sustained without significant harm. Already, the world's air, water, and land resources have seriously deteriorated, so much so that there are signs that irreversible damage has occurred. To eliminate, or at least minimize, these problems in the future requires adjustments in the way economic activity is now conducted, especially in industrialized countries such as Canada.

Complementary Goals

In some cases, success in reaching one economic goal makes another goal easier to achieve. Goals that are related in this way simplify the task of those in charge of government economic policy, and are said to be complementary. Full employment and economic growth, for example, are considered complementary goals, since government policies that help to push up employment levels in an economy also lead to expanded national output.

Conflicting Goals

Some economic goals, however, are bound to conflict, so that attaining one goal makes another goal more difficult to achieve. For example, price stability and full employment frequently clash, because government measures that bring down the rate of inflation often restrain the level of production in an economy, thus raising the unemployment rate. Similarly, income equity and economic efficiency often clash, since efforts to make the distribution of income more fair can reduce incentives for households to supply their resources. This can mean that an economy's resources are used less efficiently than before. Conflicts like these mean that government policy-makers must set priorities, and this can mean that one goal is achieved at the cost of another.

BRIEF REVIEW

1. Three basic economic questions must be answered by every country: what to produce, how to produce, and for whom to produce.
2. Traditional economies stress the role of custom and tradition. Market economies rely on private property and the operation of markets. Command economies depend on publicly owned property and central planning.
3. Modern mixed economies combine features of both market and command economies in different degrees. Traditional mixed economies include both traditional and modern sectors.
4. The main goals of the Canadian economy are economic efficiency, income equity, price stability, full employment, a viable balance of payments, economic growth, and environmental sustainability. Some of these goals are complementary while others are conflicting.

KEY CONCEPTS

economic problem
economic resources
natural resources
capital resources
labour
entrepreneurship
economics
microeconomics
macroeconomics
economic models
variables
independent variable
dependent variable
inverse relationship
direct relationship
ceteris paribus
positive economics
normative economics
utility
self-interest motive
opportunity cost
production possibilities schedule
production possibilities curve
law of increasing opportunity costs
economic system
traditional economy
market economy
market
product markets
resource markets
consumer sovereignty
command economy
modern mixed economy
traditional mixed economies
economic efficiency
inflation
unemployment rate
balance-of-payments accounts
economic growth

ANALYSIS AND APPLICATION

1. Specify whether the following relationships are direct or inverse.
   a. The drop in the price of compact discs reduces the quantity purchased of cassette tapes.
   b. The rise in the average salary of computer programmers increases the number of people seeking a career in computer programming.
   c. The fall in the price of wheat fertilizer increases the amount of wheat planted by farmers.
   d. An increase in the income tax rate paid by households reduces the amount of consumption spending in the economy.

2. Identify the following statements as positive or normative. In each case, explain your answer.
   a. In order to stimulate economic growth, more capital goods and fewer consumer goods should be produced in the Canadian economy.
   b. Inflation in Canada is currently lower than in most other countries.
   c. If a country experiences lower levels of economic efficiency, citizens of the country will experience a decrease in living standards.
   d. The Canadian government should be more concerned with ensuring environmental sustainability and less concerned with achieving low inflation.

3. A consumer would gain more utility from purchasing a TV than from purchasing a stereo, even though both products have the same price of $600. How can the consumer's decision to purchase the TV be explained using the concept of opportunity cost?

4. Below is a production possibilities schedule for a hypothetical economy that produces only two goods—skateboards and bicycles.

Production Possibilities Schedule

Production Scenario	**Skateboards**	**Bicycles**
A	40	0
B	38	1
C	32	2
D	20	3
E	0	4

   a. Graph this production possibilities schedule, putting skateboard output on the vertical axis and bicycle output on the horizontal axis. (Make sure the numerical scales you choose for each axis are sufficient to plot the points on the curve.) Describe the shape of the curve you have drawn and explain the reason for this shape.
   b. Calculate the opportunity cost of bicycles in terms of skateboards when the economy moves from points B to C. What is the new opportunity cost for bicycles when the economy moves from point C to D? Do your answers illustrate the law of increasing opportunity costs? How?
   c. Can the economy produce 38 skateboards and 2 bicycles? Why or why not?
   d. If 32 skateboards and 1 bicycle are produced, how would you describe production in this economy?

5. The table below shows the size of the private, public, and traditional sectors in three hypothetical countries.

Sector Sizes in Three Countries (% of country's total economy)

	Private Sector	Public Sector	Traditional Sector
Country A	60%	40%	0%
Country B	30%	0%	70%
Country C	0%	80%	20%

a. Drawing a diagram based on Figure 1.4, show the approximate position of each of these three countries in the diagram.
b. Which of these countries likely has the most stable culture? the most equal distribution of income? the greatest economic freedom? Explain.
c. Traditional sectors in most countries are continually shrinking. On your diagram, portray the movement caused by an increase in the private sector in Country B and an increase in the public sector in Country C.

6. Identify a pair of complementary economic goals and a pair of conflicting economic goals (other than those cited in the chapter). In each case, explain why these goals are related in the way you suggest.

7. (Advanced Question)

Annual Inflation and Unemployment Rates in Canada, 1980–1995

	Inflation (%)	Unemployment (%)		Inflation (%)	Unemployment (%)
1980	10.2	7.5	1988	4.0	7.8
1981	12.4	7.6	1989	5.0	7.5
1982	10.9	11.0	1990	4.8	8.1
1983	5.7	11.9	1991	5.6	10.4
1984	4.4	11.3	1992	1.5	11.3
1985	3.9	10.5	1993	1.8	11.2
1986	4.2	9.6	1994	0.2	10.4
1987	4.4	8.9	1995	2.1	9.5

Source: Statistics Canada, *Historical Statistical Supplement, 1995/6,* (Ottawa, 1996), pp. 30, 43.

a. For the years shown in the table above, calculate Canada's misery index, which is the sum of a country's inflation and unemployment rates, expressed as percentages. Construct a table showing your results.
b. What was the average value of the misery index during the years 1980–95? In which years was the index greater than the average value? In which years was it less?

c. What does the misery index indicate? How are the inflation rate and the unemployment rate weighted in this index? Would everyone agree with this weighting? Explain.

8. Access the Penn World Tables (at http://cansim.epas.utoronto.ca:5680/pwt/pwt.html). Using the most recent year's statistics available, rank the following economies—Canada, United Kingdom, Finland, Hong Kong—by the size of government in each economy. What does your ranking suggest about the systems chosen by each economy?

Advancing Economic Thought

THE FOUNDER OF MODERN ECONOMICS

Adam Smith and the Invisible Hand

Smith and His Influence

Adam Smith (1723–1790) is known as the father of present-day economics. While he deserves his reputation as a trailblazer, his greatest talent was in combining innovative ideas—many conceived by others—into a theory that had a profound influence on economic thinking, not only in his own time but ever since.

The son of a middle-class Scottish family, he was an avid student, attending universities in both England and Scotland. At the University of Glasgow, he gained a reputation as the classic absent-minded professor who, when distracted by some difficult theoretical problem, would walk for hours, oblivious to his surroundings.

Smith first made a name for himself through his writings in philosophy. He then turned his attention to economic issues. In 1776, after years of research, he published his classic work, *An Inquiry Into the Nature and Causes of the Wealth of Nations,* which brought him both fame and a modest fortune. For generations the book was a standard in economics, and it can still be read profitably today.

Adam Smith
Source: The Bettman Archive

The Industrial Revolution

Smith lived at the beginning of the Industrial Revolution. In the latter half of the 1700s and early 1800s, agriculture lost its central role in the British economy. Through a host of technological innovations, a powerful new manufacturing sector based on labour-saving machinery and steam power took its place. By transforming the lives of common people, this revolution had a profound social and economic impact in many countries, but first in Britain:

> The Industrial Revolution marks the most fundamental transformation of human life in the history of the world recorded in written documents. For a brief period it coincided with the history of a single country, Great Britain. An entire world economy was thus built on, or rather around, Britain, and this country therefore temporarily rose to a position of global influence and power unparalleled by any state of its relative size before or since, and unlikely to be paralleled by any state in the foreseeable future.[1]

The Division of Labour

When Adam Smith was writing *The Wealth of Nations,* these great changes in the British economy were just beginning. As the title of his book suggests, he wished to explain why some countries become more wealthy than others. Smith viewed the division of labour—the degree to which the job of each worker is a specialized task—as the most significant single cause of economic progress. To support this claim, he provided his famous illustration from the trade of pinmaking:

> The greatest improvement in the productive powers of labour, and the greater part of the skill, dexterity, and judgement with which it is anywhere directed, or applied, seem to have been the effects of the division of labour….
>
> To take an example,...the trade of the pin-maker; a workman not educated to this business,...nor acquainted with the use of the machinery employed in it,...could scarce, perhaps, with his utmost industry, make one pin in a day, and certainly could not make twenty. But in the way in which this business is now carried on, not only the whole work is a peculiar [i.e., particular] trade, but it is divided into a number of branches, of which the greater part are likewise peculiar trades. One man draws out the wire, another straight[en]s it, a third cuts it, a fourth points it, a fifth grinds it at the top for receiving the head; to make the head requires three distinct operations; to put it on is a peculiar business, to whiten the pins is another; it is even a trade by itself to put them into the paper; and the important business of making a pin is, in this manner, divided into about eighteen distinct operations, which, in some manufactories, are all performed by distinct hands, though in others the same man will sometimes perform two or three of them.[2]

Smith mentioned that he visited a small factory where, through the division of labour, 10 employees produced a total of 48 000 pins a day—4800 times the estimated product of 1 pin per worker when the division of labour was not used!

The Invisible Hand

The benefits associated with the division of labour are not the only reason why some nations are better off than others, according to Smith. Economic progress is also spurred by the self-interest motive, or the desire individuals have to increase their own happiness. "It is not from the benevolence of the butcher, the brewer, or the baker that we expect our dinner," Smith stated, "but from their regard to their own interest. We address ourselves, not to their humanity but to their self-love, and never talk to them of our own necessities but of their advantages."[3] In other words, if people are free to pursue their own private interests, they act in a way that aids the economy as a whole. What causes this is competition. As long as there are many businesses selling a product, the product's price will be driven down to a point where it covers only the businesses' costs, including a reasonable profit for the owners. If the price of the product were any higher, others would enter the industry in order to gain excess profits.

Because consumers can buy the product at the lowest possible price, they reap the ultimate rewards of competition.

In more general terms, the forces of individual self-interest and competition ensure that resources are used in ways that promote economic growth and national prosperity. To explain his theory, Smith used a term that has become part of everyday language. He said that the forces of market competition act like an "invisible hand," so that self-interested behaviour can work to the benefit of all society.

The Principle of *Laissez Faire*

Although Adam Smith pointed out the potential benefits of people's selfish actions, he was not merely acting as a mouthpiece for the business class. As he was quick to point out, individual self-interest ceases to benefit society when competition is lacking. In the case of a monopoly, where a single producer controls an entire market, the business class's selfish motives cause price to be driven to the highest value that the market will bear, meaning that consumers suffer.

Often it is governments that cause monopolies to flourish, said Smith, by offering privileges to a chosen firm. In fact, governments themselves can be considered a type of monopoly. All too frequently, Smith argued, public officials engage in political favouritism or misuse their power for private ends. In doing so, they illustrate how selfish behaviour, when unimpeded by private competition, harms rather than helps society.

Given his sceptical view of government actions, Smith asserted the principle of *laissez faire,* the French term for "let things be"—meaning that, in general, governments should interfere as little as possible in the day-to-day operations of private markets.

Relevance for Today

While modern economists, as a rule, express admiration for Smith's achievements, some of them question the suitability of his theories in contemporary times. They suggest that Smith's "invisible hand" only operates when an economy is made up of many small businesses. However, most modern markets do not meet these requirements. A contemporary American economist named Robert Heilbroner upholds this view:

> Today's market mechanism is characterized by the huge size of its participants: giant corporations and equally giant labor unions obviously do not behave as if they were individual proprietors and workers. Their very bulk enables them to stand out against the pressures of competition, to disregard price signals, and to consider what their self-interest shall be in the long run rather than in the immediate press of each day's buying and selling.[4]

Other economists claim that Smith's conclusions are just as relevant today as they were 200 years ago. Although huge corporations are an important factor in contemporary economies, so are small businesses. And, as various nations become integrated into a single global economy, international competition among companies—both large and small—is playing a greater role than ever before.

Supporters of Smith's relevance also point to the recent growth of private markets in formerly communist and socialist states. They argue that now, even more than before, private competition is preferred over government intervention.

Notes

[1] From *Industry and Empire: From 1750 to the Present Day* by E.J. Hobsbawm (Harmondsworth: Penguin, 1969), p. 13, copyright © E.J. Hobsbawm, 1968, 1969. Reprinted by permission of Simon & Schuster, Inc.

[2] Adam Smith, *The Wealth of Nations* (Harmondsworth: Penguin, 1983), pp. 109–10.

[3] Ibid, p. 119.

[4] *The Worldly Philosophers*, 6th ed. (New York: Simon and Schuster, 1986), p. 59. Copyright © 1953, 1961, 1967, 1972, 1980, 1986, 1992 by Robert L. Heilbroner. Copyright renewed © 1981, 1989 by Robert L. Heilbroner. Reprinted by permission of Simon & Schuster, Inc.

1. The reasons for the output-enhancing effect of the division of labour can be inferred from Adam Smith's illustration of a pin-making factory.
   a. Explain in your own words why the division of labour can lead to increased output in a production process such as pin-making.
   b. Do you think the use of more specialized machinery in pin-making would also lead to increased output? Why or why not?

2. In each of the following cases, use Adam Smith's concept of the invisible hand to explain the events that occur if the relevant markets are competitive and operate without government intervention. In your answers, identify the self-interested behaviour that causes beneficial results.
   a. Because of Good W's sudden popularity, suppliers of this good presently make exorbitant profits.
   b. A new innovation reduces the cost of producing Good X.
   c. Two neighbouring countries, A and B, agree for the first time to allow goods to flow freely between them.

3. Explain why the absence of the invisible hand of competition in the following situations can lead to harmful results for the consumer.
   a. A catering company wins the exclusive right to sell food in a stadium.
   b. By keeping out potential rivals, a few large corporations control sales of Good Y.
   c. A labour union, which by law includes all workers involved in the production of Good Z, manages on the basis of a strike threat to gain a significant wage increase from employers.

SIDELINE

ECONOMICS AS AN ART

The Craft of Economic Thinking

The Role of Assumptions

One of the most common criticisms of economics is summarized by a well-known joke:

> Three hungry castaways—a physicist, a geologist, and an economist—are stranded on a desert island with a single can of beans to eat, and no can opener.
>
> "I've got the answer," announces the physicist, after thinking about how to extract the beans. "We'll focus sunlight through my eyeglasses to burn a hole in the can."
>
> "Are you crazy?" replies the geologist. "You'll burst it and spill out the beans. Let's punch a hole with a sharp rock."
>
> The economist smiles and shakes his head at their thick-headedness. "No, it's much easier than either of you think. Let's just assume we have a can opener."

As the joke implies, economists depend extensively on assumptions, some of them rather creative. Scientists such as physicists and chemists also make assumptions, but theirs are more often assumptions that can be tested in controlled laboratory experiments. They can duplicate circumstances and isolate the variables they are studying from external factors. Economists rarely have this luxury. When people's economic behaviour is studied in artificial laboratory settings, it does not necessarily match real life. To isolate a relationship between two or more variables requires abstracting from the complexity of the real world, then verifying these economic models by studying transactions in actual markets.

Economics as an Art

Many economists prefer to think of their subject simply as a discipline, rather than as a science like physics or chemistry. They argue that creating models of economic reality requires the talent of being able to represent reality in the most "economical" way possible. A good economic model is therefore a little like a sketch by an expert artist such as Leonardo da Vinci; just a few well-chosen lines capture the appearance of the subject, as does da Vinci's sketch below.[1]

*A good economic model is like an artist's sketch. (*Portrait of a Young Woman *by Leonardo da Vinci.)*

Source: The Royal Collection © 1994. Her Majesty The Queen.

The art of model-building in economics is complicated by the fact that economics is a discipline that analyzes human behaviour. The way we behave depends partly on our social surroundings: the political, cultural, and economic aspects of the society we live in. Changes in these social surroundings can affect human behaviour; when this happens, economic models may have to be altered as well. This leads to a complex interaction between economics and the reality it tries to explain:

> Economics is an ever-changing discipline. Partly a product of the great ideological debates about the way human society ought to be organized, it also influences the outcome of those debates.

> Partly based on a theoretical search for abstract truths, it is also rooted in the realities of public policy and the climate of opinion. Partly an explanation of how and why an economic system functions, it is affected by the ways in which economic systems change.[2]

Just as a piece of art is a product of the time and place in which the artist lived, so an economic model reflects the society in which it was developed.

Interestingly, the twentieth century's most illustrious economist, John Maynard Keynes, viewed his subject as science and art. According to Keynes, an economist "must be purposeful and disinterested in a simultaneous mood; as aloof and incorruptible as an artist, yet sometimes as near the earth as a politician."[3] Given such tough requirements, a first-rate economist is a rare creature indeed. As we'll see in later chapters, Keynes himself was someone who possessed the talents necessary to build a simple yet powerful model of the economy. In fact, his theories form the basis of macroeconomics as we know it today.

Notes

[1] This comparison is made by Maurice Levi in *Economics Deciphered: A Layman's Survival Guide* (New York: Basic Books, 1981), p. 10.

[2] From *The Age of the Economist*, 6th ed., by Daniel R. Fusfeld, copyright © 1990 Scott, Foresman and Company. Reprinted by permission of HarperCollins College Publishers.

[3] John Maynard Keynes, *Essays in Biography* (London: Macmillan, 1972) p. 174

1. For each case below, identify one variable that must be assumed constant to analyze this relationship.
   a. The price of tomatoes affects the amount of tomatoes offered for sale in a farmers' market.
   b. The wage rate paid to gold-miners affects the number of gold-miners that companies choose to employ.
   c. The price of a certain type of machine affects the number of these machines purchased by businesses.

2. Explain whether each of the economic concepts below is equally relevant in all societies. If not, give an example where the concept might not apply.
   a. opportunity cost
   b. self-interest motive
   c. capital resources

Chapter Two
Demand and Supply

Teach a parrot to say demand and supply, and you've created an economist.
— An old joke

Each day, we buy an assortment of goods and services—a meal, a snack, maybe a magazine. What determines the price of the french fries we buy at lunchtime? The selection of chocolate bars we find at our local variety store? The types of articles we find in the magazines we read? The answer to all of these questions is demand and supply. In this chapter, we will study the impact of these two forces on our daily lives by analyzing how they operate in individual markets. We'll also see how the "invisible hand" of competition coordinates the plans of buyers and sellers through the interaction of demand and supply.

CHAPTER FOCUS

This chapter focuses on the following:

- the interaction between demand and supply within product markets
- the nature of demand, changes in quantity demanded, changes in demand, and the factors that affect demand
- the nature of supply, changes in quantity supplied, changes in supply, and the factors that affect supply
- how markets reach equilibrium—the point at which demand and supply meet
- the effects of changes in demand and supply on market equilibrium

THE ROLE OF DEMAND

A product market exists wherever households and businesses buy and sell consumer products—either face-to-face, or indirectly by mail, telephone, or computer. Some markets, such as the market for crude oil, are global in scope. Others, such as the market for hot dogs at a local baseball game, are tiny by comparison.

What Is Demand?

demand: the relationship between the various possible prices of a product and the quantities of that product consumers are willing to purchase

quantity demanded: the amount of a product consumers are willing to purchase at each price

Because households are buyers in product markets, their behaviour can be analyzed using the concept of **demand**, which is the relationship between the various possible prices of a product and the quantities consumers will purchase at each price. In this relationship, price is the independent variable. **Quantity demanded**—the amount of the product that consumers are willing to purchase at each price—is the dependent variable. To isolate the relationship between these two variables, all other factors affecting price and quantity demanded are assumed to remain constant. Recall that this is the assumption of *ceteris paribus*—"all other things remaining the same."

The Law of Demand

Is the relationship between price and quantity demanded direct or inverse? To answer this question, consider the example of strawberries you might eat during a month. As shown in the table in Figure 2.1, you might buy two kilograms per month when each kilogram is priced at $2.00. If the price rises to $2.50, you will likely purchase less strawberries, perhaps

FIGURE 2.1
An Individual's Demand Schedule and Curve

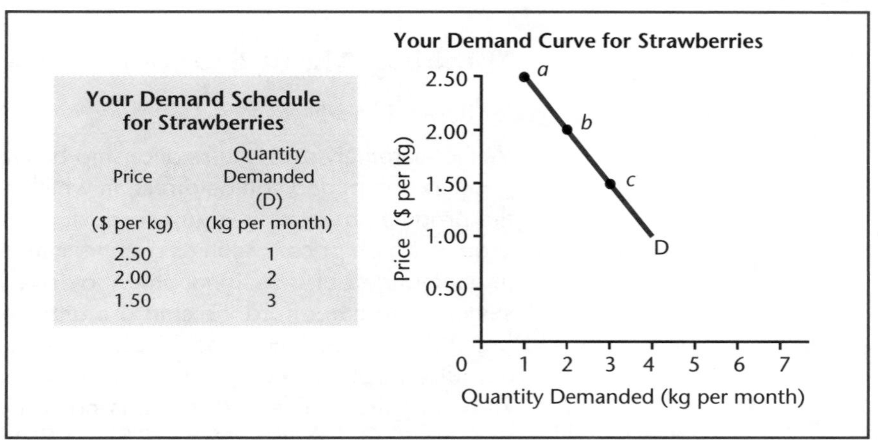

Your Demand Schedule for Strawberries

Price ($ per kg)	Quantity Demanded (D) (kg per month)
2.50	1
2.00	2
1.50	3

The demand schedule shows that as the price of strawberries falls, you are willing to purchase more strawberries. The demand curve D depicts this same inverse relationship between price and quantity demanded. For example, a fall in price from $2 to $1.50 causes quantity demanded to rise from 2 kg (point *b*) to 3 kg (point *c*).

one kilogram per month at this new price. Conversely, if the price falls to $1.50, you will probably buy more strawberries per month. At this lower price strawberries become a better deal in terms of the satisfaction you get from each dollar spent. Thus you may decide to increase your purchases to three kilograms per month. This inverse relationship between price and quantity demanded, when all other factors are kept constant, is known as the **law of demand**.

law of demand: states that there is an inverse relationship between a product's quantity demanded and its price

The Demand Curve

The quantities demanded of a product at various prices can be expressed in a **demand schedule** like the one in Figure 2.1. Expressing the schedule in a graph, as shown on the right in Figure 2.1, gives us the consumer's demand curve, D, for strawberries. The **demand curve** is drawn by placing the price of strawberries on the vertical axis and the quantity demanded on the horizontal axis. Note that the independent variable (price) is on the vertical axis, while the dependent variable (quantity demanded) is on the horizontal axis. This is a choice economists have made that differs from the convention in mathematics, in which the independent variable (x) is on the horizontal axis and the dependent variable (y) is on the vertical axis.

demand schedule: a table that shows possible combinations of prices and quantities demanded of a product

demand curve: a graph that expresses possible combinations of prices and quantities demanded of a product

The demand curve's negative (downward) slope reflects the law of demand: an increase in the product's price decreases the quantity demanded, and vice versa. Changes such as these are examples of a **change in quantity demanded**, and produce a movement *along* the demand curve. For example, an increase in the price of strawberries from $1.50 to $2 decreases the quantity demanded per kilogram from three kilograms (point *c* on the demand curve) to two kilograms (point *b*).

change in quantity demanded: the effect of a price change on quantity demanded

Thinking About Economics

Is the law of demand ever broken?

While extremely rare, the relationship between a product's price and quantity demanded can be direct, in which case the demand curve for the product has a positive (upward) slope. This may happen when a product's high price is seen as a status symbol. For example, the quantity demanded of a designer shirt may rise when its price rises. Consumers who can afford the shirt are attracted to the item because its high price makes it more fashionable than before. This situation, which can also apply to such products as luxury perfumes and watches, is known as the "Veblen effect." It is named after a famous American economist, Thorstein Veblen (1857–1929), who criticized such purchases and coined the memorable term conspicuous consumption to describe them.

Market Demand

market demand: the sum of all consumers' quantity demanded for a product at each price

Market demand, which can again be shown as a schedule or a curve, is the sum of all consumers' purchases, or quantity demanded, at each price. This is illustrated in Figure 2.2 in the unlikely case that there are just two consumers in the strawberry market—you and a friend—with individual demand curves D_0 (yours) and D_1 (your friend's). While you purchase two kilograms at a $2 price, your strawberry-loving friend purchases three kilograms at this same price. The total quantity demanded in the market is therefore five kilograms. Repeating this procedure at every possible price gives the market demand curve, D_m, on the lower right in Figure 2.2.

Changes in Demand

Earlier, we stated that to study the relationship between price and quantity demanded that all other factors affecting these variables must be assumed constant. Now, let us examine these other factors, which are

FIGURE 2.2
The Market Demand Schedule and Curve

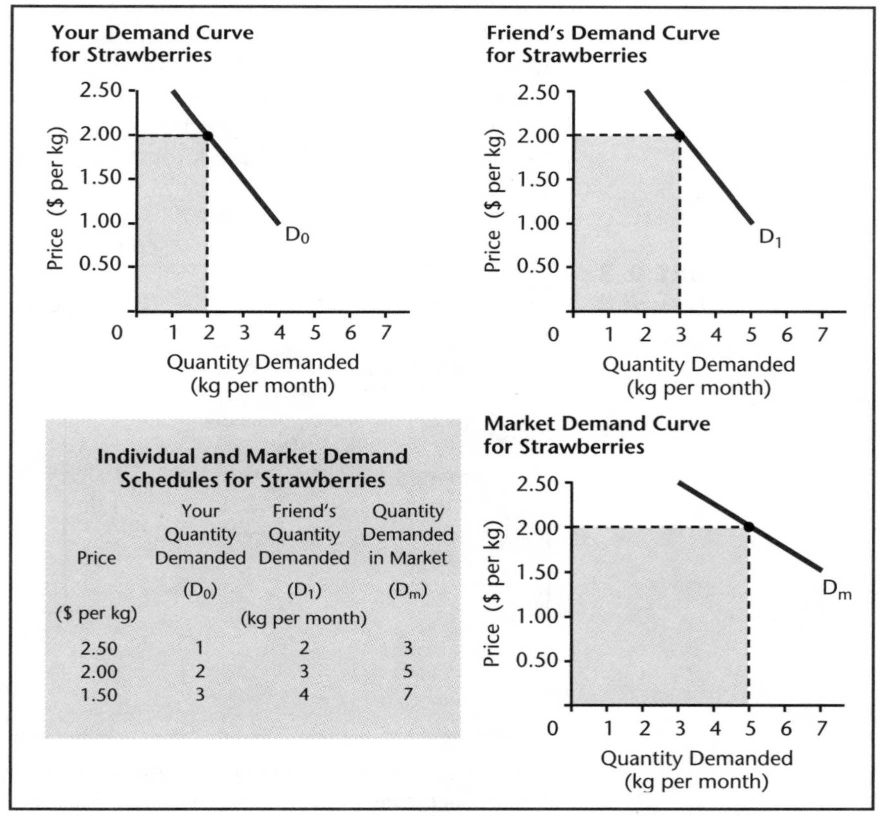

Individual and Market Demand Schedules for Strawberries

Price ($ per kg)	Your Quantity Demanded (D_0)	Friend's Quantity Demanded (D_1)	Quantity Demanded in Market (D_m)
	(kg per month)		
2.50	1	2	3
2.00	2	3	5
1.50	3	4	7

There are only two consumers in the strawberry market: you and a friend, with demand curves D_0 and D_1. The market demand curve, D_m, is found by adding the number of kg purchased by both consumers at each possible price. For example, at a price of $2, you buy 2 kg and your friend buys 3, giving a quantity demanded in the market of 5 kg at this price.

demand determinants: factors that can cause an increase or a decrease in a product's demand

known as **demand determinants**. Demand determinants are factors that can cause the entire market demand curve to shift. The five main demand determinants are the number of buyers in a market, their average income, the prices of other products, consumer preferences, and consumer expectations about future prices and incomes. With each determinant, it must be assumed that all other factors remain constant.

Number of Buyers

increase in demand: an increase in the quantity demanded of a product at all prices

decrease in demand: a decrease in the quantity demanded of a product at all prices

When the number of buyers for a certain product increases, more purchases are made. Thus the product's quantity demanded increases, whatever its price. The result is called an increase in demand. In a graph, an **increase in demand** is shown as a shift of the *entire* demand curve to the right. When the number of buyers in a market decreases, quantity demanded also decreases at every price, thus causing the entire demand curve to shift to the left. This result is called a **decrease in demand**.

Both cases are illustrated in Figure 2.3 using a hypothetical market for strawberries. The initial quantities demanded in the market are shown in the demand schedule, under D_0. When demand increases, quantity demanded increases at every possible price. For example, at a price of $2, quantity demanded increases from 9 to 11 million kilograms. Thus, on the graph, the original demand curve (D_0) shifts to the right, giving a new demand curve (D_1). When demand decreases, quantity demanded decreases at every price. For example, at a price of $2, quantity demanded decreases from 9 to 7 million kilograms. Thus, the demand curve shifts to the left, from D_0 to D_2.

FIGURE 2.3
Changes in Demand

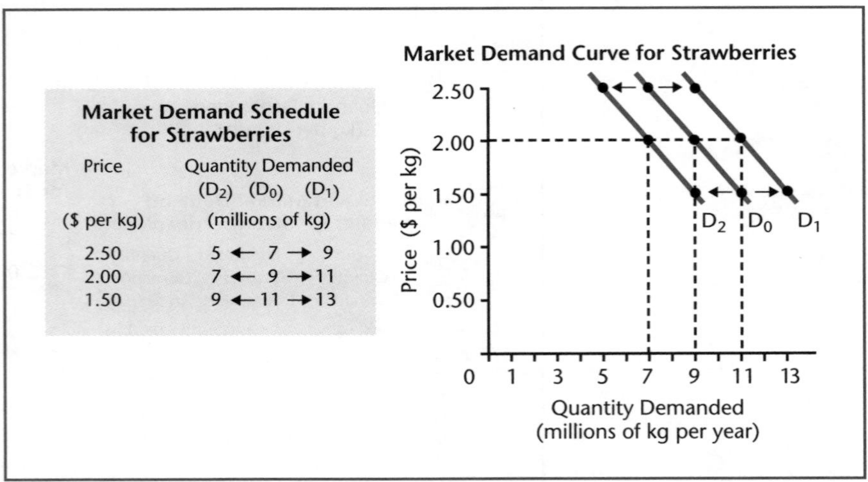

Market Demand Schedule for Strawberries

Price ($ per kg)	Quantity Demanded (millions of kg) (D_2)	(D_0)	(D_1)
2.50	5 ←	7	→ 9
2.00	7 ←	9	→ 11
1.50	9 ←	11	→ 13

When the number of buyers in a market increases, the quantity demanded of strawberries increases at every possible price. Each point on the demand curve therefore shifts to the right from D_0 to D_1, as from 9 to 11 million kg at a price of $2 per kg. Similarly, a decrease in the number of buyers pushes down the quantity demanded at every price, shifting the demand curve to the left from D_0 to D_2, as from 9 to 7 million kg at a $2 price.

Income

When consumers' incomes increase, they purchase more luxury products such as expensive jewellery and caviar. Purchases of more basic items, such as milk and shoes, also rise, but by a smaller proportion. Whether for luxury products or for necessities, demand increases, thus shifting the entire demand curve to the right. Products whose demand changes directly with income are known as **normal goods**. There are a few products, known as **inferior goods**, for which incomes have the opposite effect. Turnips and second-hand suits are examples. As incomes rise, consumption of these products falls as buyers switch from turnips to more expensive vegetables, and from second-hand to new suits. The result is a decrease in demand for these products, reflected in a shift to the left of the entire demand curve.

normal goods: products whose demand changes directly with income

inferior goods: products whose demand changes inversely with income

Prices of Other Products

Substitute goods are products that can be consumed in place of one another. When the price of a product rises, consumers choose to purchase more of any reasonable substitute available, thus shifting the substitute product's demand curve to the right. For example, a higher price for butter causes some consumers to switch to margarine, increasing the demand for margarine. If the price of butter falls, however, there will be a decrease in the demand for margarine.

substitute goods: products that can be consumed in place of one another

Complementary goods are products that are consumed together, such as cars and gasoline, or compact discs and compact disc players. In the case of complementary goods, an increase in the price of one product causes a decrease in demand for its complement. For example, if the price of cars rises, the demand for gasoline falls. The reverse is also true: a fall in the price of compact discs leads to a rise in demand for compact disc players.

complementary goods: products that are consumed together

Consumer Preferences

People's preferences also affect buying patterns. A significant shift in consumer concerns over nutrition, for example, causes an increase in the demand for nutritious foods. Consumer preferences are also influenced by current fashion or advertising, as in the case of clothing. This is illustrated by a sudden fad for Doc Martens shoes, which increases their demand and shifts this product's demand curve to the right.

Consumer Expectations

The expectations that consumers have about future changes in prices and their own incomes affect their current purchases. For example, if a majority of consumers expect the price of laptop computers to fall, the current demand for laptops decreases. This is because consumers will delay their purchases of laptops until the expected drop in price occurs. Alternatively, if consumers expect their incomes to grow and the prices of products they buy to remain constant—in other words, if they expect their standard of living to rise—their current demand for normal goods will increase and their current demand for inferior goods will decrease.

Change in Quantity Demanded Versus Change in Demand

The terms *change in quantity demanded* and *change in demand*, have special meanings in economics. Both types of change are shown in Figure 2.4. As we have seen, a change in quantity demanded results from a change in the product's own price. For example, the number of skis purchased will increase when the price of skis decreases, as shown in the graph on the left in Figure 2.4. Here a movement (from point *a* to point *b*) occurs along demand curve D_0, since varying the product's own price does not alter the position of the curve. An increase or decrease in demand, however, results from a change in a demand determinant. The graph on the right shows how an increase in incomes increases the demand for skis, which are a normal good, causing a shift of the entire demand curve for skis from D_0 to D_1.

FIGURE 2.4
Change in Quantity Demanded and Change in Demand

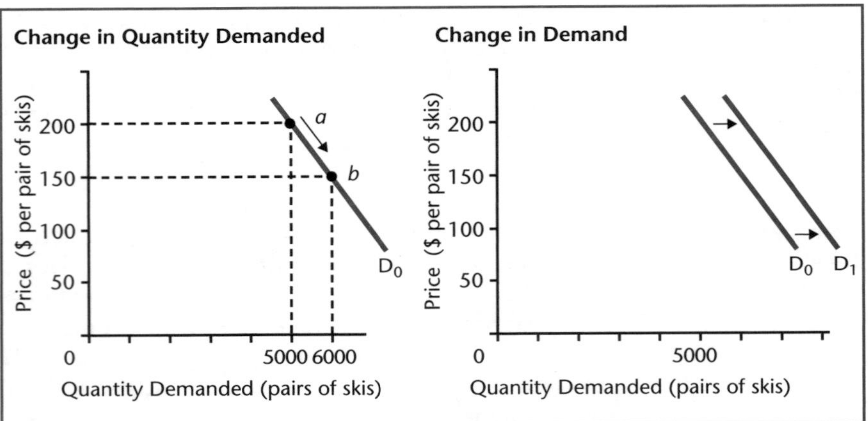

A change in quantity demanded is shown in the left graph as a movement along a single demand curve, D_0, that results from a change in the product's own price. There is a rise in quantity demanded from 5000 to 6000 pairs of skis when the price of skis drops from \$200 to \$150 a pair, causing a movement from point *a* to point *b*. A change in demand is shown in the right graph as a shift in the entire demand curve to the right, from D_0 to D_1. This shift results from a change in a demand determinant, such as consumer incomes.

BRIEF REVIEW

1. In product markets, demand represents the decisions of households purchasing consumer items.
2. The demand curve for a particular product shows the relationship between its price and the quantity demanded, either by an individual consumer or in the market as a whole. According to the law of demand, price and quantity demanded are inversely related.
3. A change in quantity demanded is shown by a movement along a product's demand curve and is caused by a change in the product's own price.
4. A change in demand is shown by a shift of the entire demand curve and is caused by a change in a demand determinant: the number of buyers, their average income, the prices of other products, consumer preferences, or consumer expectations about future prices and incomes.

THE ROLE OF SUPPLY

What Is Supply?

supply: the relationship between the various possible prices of a product and the quantities of the product that businesses are willing to supply

quantity supplied: the amount of a product businesses are willing to supply at each price

market supply: the sum of all producers' quantity supplied at each price

In product markets, supply is related to the selling activity of businesses. The role of supply is most easily analyzed in competitive markets where the "invisible hand" of competition, identified by Adam Smith, operates. Because the actions of sellers are independent from those of buyers in these markets, the role of supply can be studied separately. In any competitive market, **supply** is the relationship between the various possible prices of a product and the quantities of the product that businesses are willing to put on the market. While the independent variable is again price, the dependent variable is now **quantity supplied**—the amount of the product that businesses are willing to supply at each price. Once again, we can consider both individuals (in this case, individual businesses) and groups (in this case, all businesses producing the same product). **Market supply** is the sum of all producers' quantities supplied at each price. As before, all other factors that affect supply are assumed to be constant.

The Law of Supply

law of supply: states that there is a direct relationship between a product's quantity supplied and its price

When price changes, quantity supplied changes in the same direction. If the price of strawberries rises, for example, farmers find it desirable to increase the quantity of strawberries they supply, because the higher price provides the lure of increased revenue for every unit produced. This direct relationship between price and quantity supplied, when all other factors are kept constant, is called the **law of supply**.

The Supply Curve

supply schedule: a table that shows possible combinations of prices and quantities supplied of a product

supply curve: a graph that expresses possible combinations of prices and quantities supplied of a product

change in quantity supplied: the effect of a price change on quantity supplied

The law of supply can be illustrated in a **supply schedule**, such as that for the strawberry market in Figure 2.5. Expressing the schedule in a graph gives us the **supply curve** for the strawberry market. As with the demand curve, a change in a product's price causes a movement *along* the supply curve, thus a **change in quantity supplied**. This is illustrated in Figure 2.5 by the movement from point *f* to point *e* on the supply curve. Because of a drop in the price of strawberries from $2.50 to $2.00 per kilogram, the quantity supplied by farmers drops from 13 to 9 million kilograms. The positive (upward) slope of the supply curve illustrates the direct relationship between price and quantity supplied.

Changes in Supply

supply determinants: factors that can cause an increase or a decrease in a product's supply

While price changes will cause changes in quantity supplied, other factors cause supply to change. These factors, which cause the entire supply curve to shift, are known as **supply determinants**. The five main supply

FIGURE 2.5
The Market Supply Schedule and Curve

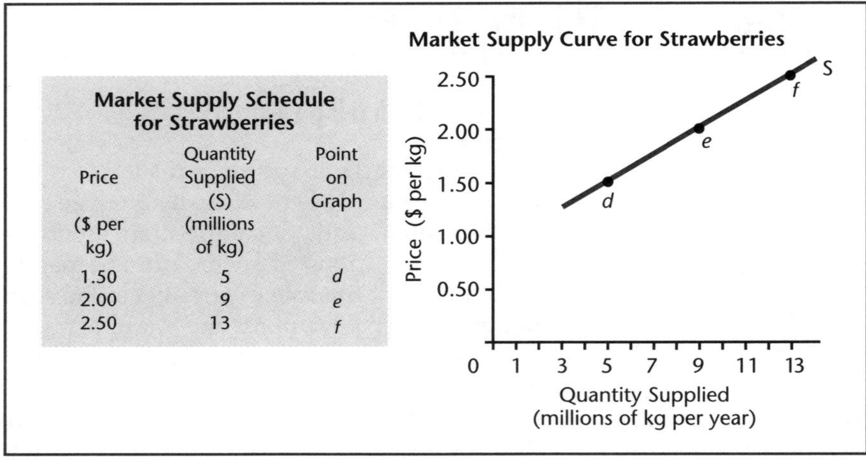

Market Supply Schedule for Strawberries

Price ($ per kg)	Quantity Supplied (S) (millions of kg)	Point on Graph
1.50	5	*d*
2.00	9	*e*
2.50	13	*f*

The supply schedule shows that when the price of strawberries falls, as from $2.00 to $1.50 per kg, then quantity supplied also falls, from 9 million (point *e*) to 5 million kg (point *d*), as farmers find it profitable to produce fewer units. The positively sloped supply curve S indicates a direct relationship between price and quantity supplied.

determinants are the number of producers, resource prices, the state of technology, changes in nature, and the prices of related products. Once again, with each determinant, we must assume that all other factors remain constant.

Number of Producers

increase in supply: an increase in the quantity supplied of a product at all prices

decrease in supply: a decrease in the quantity supplied of a product at all prices

An increase in the number of businesses in an industry causes an **increase in supply**, thus giving a higher quantity supplied at each price, and shifting the supply curve to the right. In contrast, a decrease in the number of businesses in the industry creates a **decrease in supply**, and a corresponding shift of the supply curve to the left. Both cases are illustrated in Figure 2.6 for the strawberry market. The column marked S_0 in the supply schedule gives the quantity supplied by the original number of producers. When the number of producers increases, so does the quantity supplied (indicated by column S_1) at every possible price—for example, from 9 to 11 million kilograms at a price of $2. Thus the supply curve shifts to the right, from S_0 to S_1. Conversely, a decrease in the supply of the product causes the quantities supplied (indicated by column S_2) to decrease at each possible price, from 9 to 7 million kilograms at a price of $2. The supply curve therefore shifts to the left, from S_0 to S_2.

Resource Prices

As discussed in the previous chapter, businesses buy various resources, such as capital resources and natural resources, to produce goods. If there is a price increase for a resource used in a particular industry, costs for businesses in that industry increase. As a result, fewer units of the

FIGURE 2.6
Changes in Supply

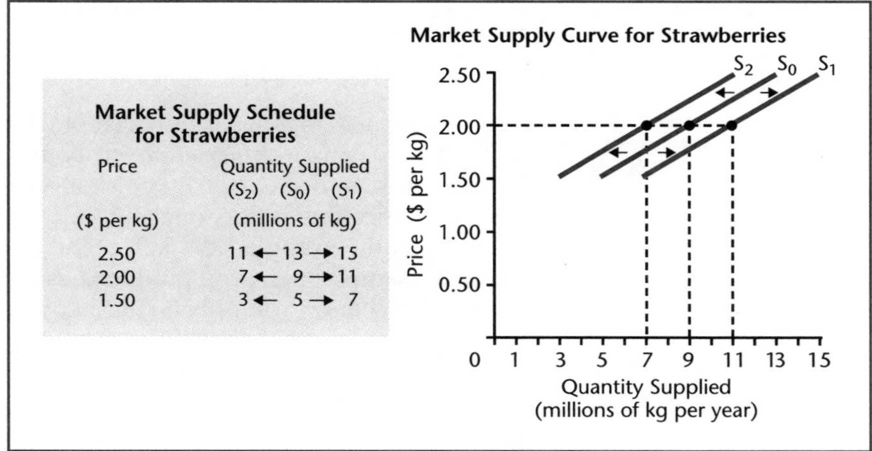

Market Supply Schedule for Strawberries

Price ($ per kg)	Quantity Supplied (millions of kg) (S_2)	(S_0)	(S_1)
2.50	11 ←	13	→ 15
2.00	7 ←	9	→ 11
1.50	3 ←	5	→ 7

When the number of strawberry producers increases in a market, the quantity supplied of strawberries increases at every possible price. Each point on the supply curve shifts to the right from S_0 to S_1, as from 9 to 11 million kg at a price of $2 per kg. In contrast, a decrease in the number of producers decreases the quantity supplied of stawberries at every price, shifting the supply curve to the left from S_0 to S_2, as from 9 to 7 million kg at a $2 price.

product can be produced for the same expenditure. Thus businesses will tend to cut back on production, causing the supply curve to shift to the left. For example, an increase in the wages of workers in the apple industry causes a decrease in the supply of apples.

State of Technology

Technological progress affects the supply curve by allowing businesses to use more efficient production methods. With increased efficiency, more units can be produced at every price, so supply will increase. Use of a better grain fertilizer, for instance, causes the supply of barley to increase, shifting the supply curve to the right.

Changes in Nature

Changes in nature—for example, an early frost, record high temperatures, a flood, or an earthquake—can affect the supply of many products, especially agricultural products. A cold, rainy summer in Canada's prairies, for example, will decrease the supply of grains such as wheat. The market supply curve for wheat will therefore shift to the left.

Prices of Related Products

A product's supply can be influenced by changes in the prices of other products. For example, declines in the price of tobacco during the early 1990s caused some Ontario farmers to switch to ginseng, a medicinal root that is popular in East Asia. As a result, the supply for ginseng increased, resulting in a shift to the right of the supply curve.

Change in Quantity Supplied Versus Change in Supply

As in the case of demand, it is important to distinguish between *a change in quantity supplied* and a *change in supply*, both of which are shown in Figure 2.7. An increase or decrease in quantity supplied is the effect of a change in a product's price, and is illustrated by a movement along the supply curve. As shown in the graph on the left, a rise in the price of ginseng, which raises the quantity of ginseng produced, is a change in quantity supplied. In contrast, a change in supply is caused by a change in a supply determinant. A change in supply shifts the *entire* supply curve. As shown in the graph on the right, a decrease in the price of tobacco increases the supply of ginseng, causing a shift in the entire supply curve to the right.

FIGURE 2.7
Change in Quantity Supplied and Change in Supply

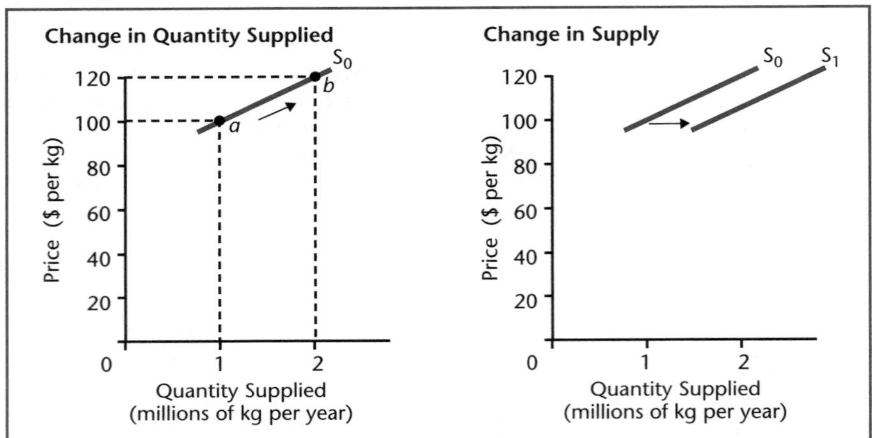

A change in quantity supplied is shown in the left graph as a movement along a single supply curve, S_0, that results from a change in the product's own price. There is a rise in quantity supplied from 1 to 2 million kg of ginseng when the price of ginseng rises from $100 to $120 a kg, causing a movement from point *a* to point *b*. A change in supply is shown in the right graph as a shift in the entire supply curve to the right, from S_0 to S_1. This shift results from a change in a supply determinant—for example, a drop in the price of a related product such as tobacco.

BRIEF REVIEW

1. In product markets supply is the relationship between the various possible prices of a consumer item and the quantities of the item that businesses are willing to put on the market.
2. The law of supply states that there is a direct relationship between the two variables of price and quantity supplied.
3. A change in quantity supplied is caused by a change in price, and is shown as a movement *along* the supply curve.
4. A change in supply is caused by a change in a supply determinant, and is shown as a shift of the *entire* supply curve. The five supply determinants are the number of producers in a market, resource prices, the state of technology, changes in nature, and the prices of related products.

HOW COMPETITIVE MARKETS OPERATE

Market Equilibrium

market equilibrium: the stable point at which demand and supply curves intersect

In competitive markets, demand and supply play a key role in coordinating the decisions of consumers and producers. Changes in price drive demand and supply to a point of stability, known as **market equilibrium**, where the demand and supply curves intersect. Whenever the market is out of equilibrium—supply can't keep up with demand, for example—the market tries to right itself and achieve equilibrium. To see how equilibrium is achieved, consider the example of the strawberry market that appears in Figure 2.8.

Effects of a Surplus

surplus: an excess of quantity supplied over quantity demanded

At a price of $2.50 per kilogram, the quantities demanded and supplied of strawberries are 7 and 11 million kilograms, respectively. The quantity supplied exceeds the quantity demanded, so there are 4 million more kilograms of strawberries for sale than consumers wish to purchase. This excess is called a **surplus**. As a result of this surplus, producers are holding unwanted inventories.

The pressures produced by a surplus in a competitive market cause the price to fall. As the price falls, two adjustments take place. First, consumers buy more at the lower price, so that the quantity demanded rises. This increase in quantity demanded is shown as a move down the demand curve in Figure 2.8. Second, producers offer less for sale, so that the quantity supplied drops. This decrease in quantity supplied is shown as a

FIGURE 2.8
Movement of Price Toward Equilibrium

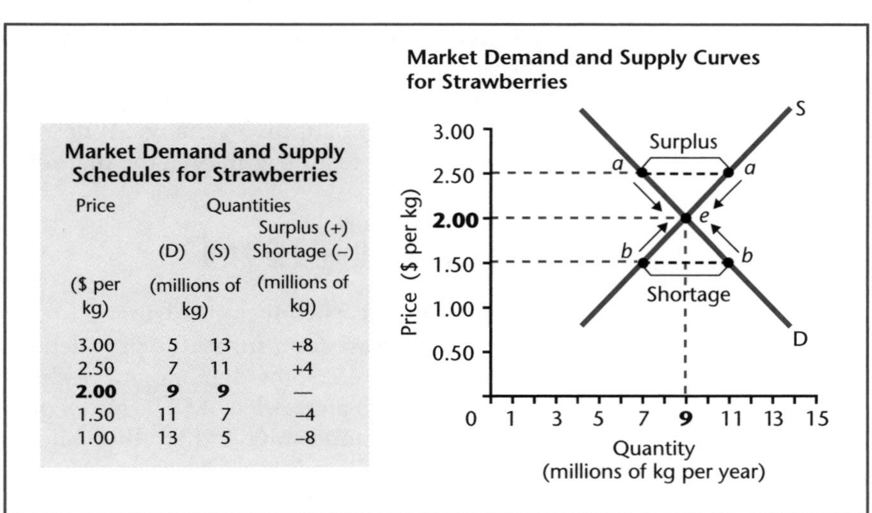

Market Demand and Supply Schedules for Strawberries

Price ($ per kg)	Quantities (D) (millions of kg)	(S) (millions of kg)	Surplus (+) Shortage (–) (millions of kg)
3.00	5	13	+8
2.50	7	11	+4
2.00	**9**	**9**	—
1.50	11	7	–4
1.00	13	5	–8

As shown in both the schedule and the graph, when price (at points *a*) is above its equilibrium level of $2, the quantity of strawberries supplied exceeds the quantity demanded, creating a surplus. This causes price to fall until both quantities demanded and supplied equal 9 million kg at the equilibrium point (point *e*). If price (at points *b*) is below equilibrium, a shortage results. Price is forced higher until its $2 equilibrium level (point *e*) is again reached.

move down the supply curve in Figure 2.8. Both responses reduce the surplus until price comes to rest where quantity supplied matches quantity demanded. Once this happens, the market has reached a stable equilibrium point—at a price of $2 in the case of the strawberry market. At this point, the amount of the product exchanged (9 million kilograms) is simply called "quantity," and can refer to either quantity demanded or quantity supplied.

Effects of a Shortage

shortage: an excess of quantity demanded over quantity supplied

When price is below equilibrium, the quantity of strawberries that consumers wish to purchase exceeds the quantity supplied. This excess of quantity demanded over quantity supplied is called a **shortage**. Because of this shortage, some consumers are unable to purchase strawberries. For example, at a price of $1.50, the quantities demanded and supplied in the strawberry market are 11 and 7 million kilograms, respectively, giving a shortage of 4 million kilograms.

A shortage in a competitive market pushes price higher. Both consumers and producers respond to the price increase. Consumers purchase less, decreasing quantity demanded. At the same time, producers provide more for sale, raising quantity supplied. As a result of these movements up the demand and supply curves in Figure 2.8, the shortage shrinks until the quantities demanded and supplied are again equal at the equilibrium point.

The Role of Price

Notice that, if there is either a shortage or a surplus, the price in a competitive market changes until equilibrium is attained. Only at this point is the pressure for further adjustments eliminated. The market then remains at equilibrium until changes in some demand or supply determinant cause demand or supply to change. Whenever this happens, the shortage or surplus that results will force the market to a new equilibrium point.

Changes in Demand

Consider the case in which the demand for strawberries increases because of a price increase for a substitute product, such as cherries. As a result, as shown in Figure 2.9, the demand curve shifts to the right, from D_0 to D_1. From an equilibrium price of $2.00 and a quantity of 9 million kilograms, quantity demanded shifts to 13 million kilograms. Quantity supplied lags behind, at 9 million kilograms, thus creating a shortage of 4 million kilograms in the market (13 million – 9 million). For the market to right itself, price and quantity supplied both push up to a new equilibrium price of $2.50 and quantity of 11 million kilograms. So, with an increase in demand, the equilibrium values of both price and quantity rise. A decrease in demand would have the opposite effect, causing the equilibrium values of both price and quantity to fall.

FIGURE 2.9
Effects of Changes in Demand on Equilibrium

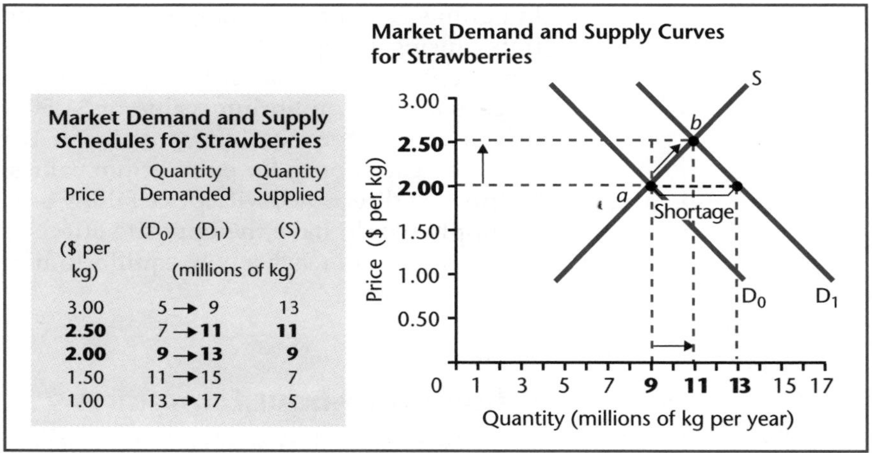

Market Demand and Supply Schedules for Strawberries

Price ($ per kg)	Quantity Demanded (D_0) → (D_1) (millions of kg)	Quantity Supplied (S) (millions of kg)
3.00	5 → 9	13
2.50	7 → **11**	**11**
2.00	**9** → **13**	**9**
1.50	11 → 15	7
1.00	13 → 17	5

When the demand curve shifts to the right, from D_0 to D_1, there is a shortage of 4 million kg at the original equilibrium price of $2.00 (point *a*). As a result, price rises until a new equilibrium point of demand and supply is reached, at point *b*, with a price of $2.50 and a quantity of 11 million kg. Both equilibrium price and equilibrium quantity rise from their original values of $2.00 and 9 million kg.

Changes in Supply

The effects of a change in supply can be outlined in a similar fashion. For example, the supply of strawberries may increase because new producers enter the industry. As a result, as shown in Figure 2.10, the supply curve shifts to the right, from S_0 to S_1. From an equilibrium price of $2.00 and quantity of 9 million kilograms, quantity supplied shifts to 13 million

FIGURE 2.10
Effects of Changes in Supply on Equilibrium

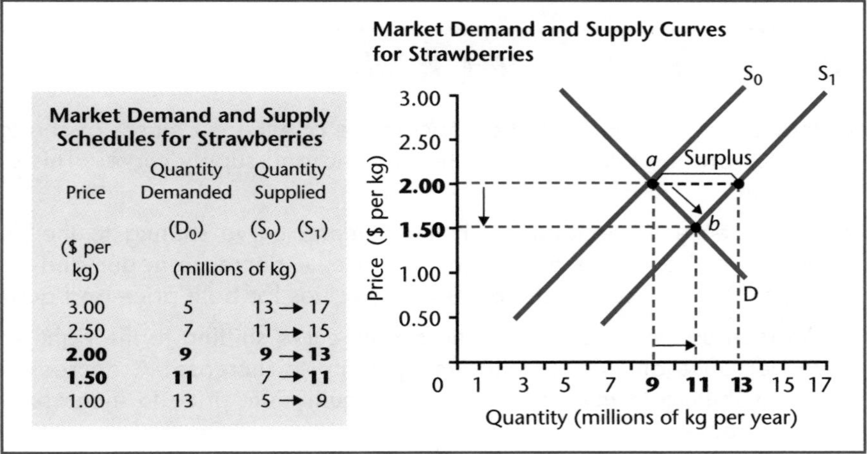

Market Demand and Supply Schedules for Strawberries

Price ($ per kg)	Quantity Demanded (D_0) (millions of kg)	Quantity Supplied (S_0) → (S_1) (millions of kg)
3.00	5	13 → 17
2.50	7	11 → 15
2.00	**9**	**9** → **13**
1.50	**11**	7 → **11**
1.00	13	5 → 9

When the supply curve shifts to the right, from S_0 to S_1, there is a surplus of 4 million kg at the original equilibrium price of $2.00 (point *a*). As a result, price falls until a new equilibrium point of demand and supply is reached at point *b*, with a price of $1.50 and a quantity of 11 million kg. In this case, the equilibrium values for price and quantity move in opposite directions, with price falling from $2.00 to $1.50, and quantity rising from 9 million to 11 million kg.

kilograms. Quantity demanded lags behind at 9 million kilograms, thus causing a surplus of 4 million kilograms in the market (13 million – 9 million). For the market to right itself, price is driven down until it reaches a new equilibrium value of $1.50, and quantity demanded is driven up to a new equilibrium value of 11 million kilograms. So, with an increase in supply, the equilibrium values of price and quantity move in opposite directions, with price falling and quantity rising. A decrease in supply would have the opposite effects: price would rise and quantity would fall to reach a new equilibrium point.

Thinking About Economics

Does a change in demand affect quantity supplied, or does a change in supply affect quantity demanded?

Both situations apply. A shift in the demand curve has a significant impact on quantity supplied. Notice in Figure 2.9, for example, that an increase in demand causes a movement upward along the supply curve, meaning that quantity supplied rises as well. Thus, a change in demand pushes quantity supplied in the same direction. With an increase in supply, as depicted in Figure 2.10, there is a movement downward along the demand curve, which causes an increase in quantity demanded. A change in supply therefore drives quantity demanded in the same direction.

BRIEF REVIEW

1. In a competitive market, the appearance of either surpluses or shortages forces price and quantity toward the intersection of the demand and supply curves. This point represents market equilibrium.
2. An increase in demand—with the demand curve shifting to the right—causes the equilibrium values for both price and quantity to rise. A decrease in demand—with the demand curve shifting to the left—causes the equilibrium values for both price and quantity to fall.
3. An increase in supply—with the supply curve shifting to the right—causes the equilibrium price to decrease and the equilibrium quantity to increase. A decrease in supply—with the supply curve shifting to the left—causes the equilibrium price to increase and the equilibrium quantity to decrease.

KEY CONCEPTS

demand
quantity demanded
law of demand
demand schedule
demand curve
change in quantity demanded
market demand
demand determinants
increase in demand
decrease in demand
normal goods
inferior goods
substitute goods
complementary goods
supply
quantity supplied
market supply
law of supply
supply schedule
supply curve
change in quantity supplied
supply determinants
increase in supply
decrease in supply
market equilibrium
surplus
shortage

ANALYSIS AND APPLICATION

1. During a given week, Student 1 demands 5 milkshakes at a price per milkshake of $2, 7 at $1.80, 9 at $1.60, and 11 at $1.40. Student 2 demands 4 milkshakes at a price of $2, 5 at $1.80, 6 at $1.60, and 7 at $1.40.
   a. In side-by-side diagrams, graph the demand curves D_1 and D_2 for each student, putting the price of a milkshake on both the vertical axes and the number of milkshakes demanded by one of the students on each horizontal axis. (Make sure that the scales you choose for each axis are sufficient to plot all points on the curves.)
   b. In your own words, explain why the amount of milkshakes demanded by each student rises as the price of milkshakes falls.
   c. Assuming that the two students are the only consumers in the market, construct a table showing the market demand schedule. Draw the market demand curve D_m and explain how it can be derived from the individual student's demand curves.

2. In a certain apple market, 80 000 kilograms are offered for sale each week at a price per kilogram of $2, 160 000 at $3, and 240 000 at $4.
   a. Construct a table showing the market supply schedule for apples, then graph the market supply curve for apples (S_0).
   b. In your own words, explain why the amount of apples offered for sale rises as the price of apples increases.
   c. Using both your table and graph, outline what happens if the amount of apples offered for sale each week increases by 40 000 kilograms at each possible price.

3. For each product highlighted in italics, sketch a graph (without numbers on the axes) showing the change in either demand or supply. Explain your answers.
   a. Medical researchers discover that consumption of *blueberries* reduces the risk of cancer.
   b. New automated equipment is introduced in the production of *silicon chips*.

c. A significant rise in the price of ice cream affects the market for *ice-cream cones*.
d. Higher airplane prices have an impact on *air travel*.
e. An influx of new residents into a small town influences *housing* purchases.
f. A fall in average consumer incomes affects purchases of *bologna*.
g. A drop in the price of laptop computers influences the consumption of *desktop computers*.
h. Unusually cold weather in Central America harms the *coffee* harvest.
i. A rise in the price of wheat affects the production of *barley*.
j. A widespread expectation of higher future incomes affects sales of *automobiles*.

4. Identify one possible cause for each event below.
   a. The demand for electric-powered cars decreases.
   b. The quantity supplied of milk decreases.
   c. The supply of Atlantic cod increases.
   d. The quantity demanded of CDs increases.

Market Demand and Supply Schedules for Baseball Caps

Price ($ per cap)	Quantity Demanded (caps per week)	Quantity Supplied (caps per week)	Surplus (+) or Shortage (–)	Effect on Price (up or down)
$20.00	9 000	15 000	______	______
17.50	10 000	13 000	______	______
15.00	11 000	11 000	______	______
12.50	12 000	9 000	______	______
10.00	13 000	7 000	______	______

5. a. Copy out the table above, which shows demand and supply schedules in a hypothetical competitive market for baseball caps. Fill in the appropriate numerical values for the surplus or shortage of caps in the fourth column and the effect on price in the fifth column.
   b. Identify the equilibrium quantity and price. Explain why no other price could represent the equilibrium value.
   c. Suppose the demand schedule in this market changes so that 12 000 caps are demanded at a price of $20, 13 000 are demanded at $17.50, 14 000 at $15, 15 000 at $12.50 and 16 000 at $10. Is this an increase or decrease in demand? Explain.
   d. Create a new table like the one you copied out in part a. to show the demand and supply schedules in this market after the change in demand. Identify the new equilibrium price and quantity. Why is the equilibrium price found in part b. no longer applicable?
   e. Describe the process that causes the market to move from its initial to its new equilibrium.

Market Demand and Supply Schedules for Inline Skates

Price ($ per pair)	Quantity Demanded (thousands of pairs per week)			Quantity Supplied (thousands of pairs per week)		
	D_0		D_1	S_0		S_1
$200	45	→	20	95	→	70
175	55	→	30	80	→	55
150	65	→	40	65	→	40
125	75	→	50	50	→	25
100	85	→	60	35	→	10

6. a. For the schedules above, draw a graph showing the initial demand and supply curves (D_0 and S_0) for inline skates. Identify the original equilibrium price and quantity.
   b. Because of heightened concerns over injuries, the demand for inline skates changes from D_0 to D_1. On the same graph used in part a., draw the new demand curve and indicate the new equilibrium price and quantity associated with D_1 and S_0. How do these equilibrium values compare with those in part a.?
   c. Now, due to a rise in wages, the supply of inline skates changes from S_0 to S_1. On the same graph used in parts a. and b., draw the new supply curve and indicate the new equilibrium price and quantity associated with D_1 and S_1. How do these equilibrium values compare with those found in part b.?

7. How will the following events affect equilibrium price and quantity in a competitive market? In each case, sketch a graph to help explain your answer.
   a. A drop in consumer incomes influences the demand for drycleaning.
   b. Declining numbers of law school graduates affect the supply of legal services.
   c. An expanding proportion of elderly people in the population has an impact on the demand for chiropractors.
   d. A cost-saving technological innovation influences the supply of computer modems.

8. (Advanced Question)
   Each of the following events affects the demand or supply of the product highlighted in italics. Does the relevant curve shift right, left, or possibly in either direction?
   a. Computer prices fall and at the same time consumer incomes rise, affecting the demand for *software programs*.
   b. The price of coal-mining equipment rises at the same time as the wages paid to coal-miners fall, affecting the supply of *coal*.
   c. The price of frozen dinners drops at the same time as consumer incomes fall, affecting the demand for *instant macaroni-and-cheese dinners*.
   d. Prices of building materials fall at the same time as the prices of residential housing rise, affecting the supply of *commercial buildings*.

Advancing Economic Thought

SPOILT FOR CHOICE

William Stanley Jevons and Utility Maximization

Jevons and His Influence

Demand can be related to human psychology if you think of people making purchases to maximize their utility based on their limited budgets. Remember that utility is the satisfaction each individual gains from consuming a variety of goods and services.

William Stanley Jevons (1835–1882), a nineteenth-century English economist, is best known for applying the concept of utility to economics and developing a model of consumption. Jevons found his life turned upside down when, in his teens, his rich family went bankrupt. He was forced to break off his studies to find a job. After working for five years in Australia—during which Jevons taught himself economics—he had earned enough to return to England and complete his formal education. He went on to become a university professor, a shy man who established his reputation primarily through his writings.

William Stanley Jevons
Source: Stock Montage

The Law of Diminishing Marginal Utility

Jevons based his model of consumption on the assumption that utility can be measured in units, which he called "utils." According to Jevons, a consumer's total utility—or overall satisfaction gained from consuming a particular product—depends on the number of units he or she purchases. Consider the example of a student drinking cups of cappuccino at a sidewalk café on a summer afternoon. As shown in Figure A, the student's total utility increases with every additional cup he drinks, but each new cup gives him less *extra* pleasure than the one before. This is illustrated in the top graph by the increases in total utility between *ab* and *bc*, and then *cd* and *de*: the shaded areas get steadily smaller. These shrinking areas are highlighted on the marginal utility graph. For each extra cup he drinks, the student's marginal—or extra—satisfaction is less.

The fall in marginal utility at higher consumption levels led Jevons to state what has become a general rule in economics. The *law of diminishing marginal utility* states that, as a consumer purchases more units of a particular product in a given time period, that consumer's extra satisfaction from each additional unit falls. According to Jevons, common sense suggests that this law applies to the consumption of virtually all products. Other economists developed their own versions of the law of diminishing marginal utility, but Jevons' version has remained the most influential.

FIGURE A Total and Marginal Utility

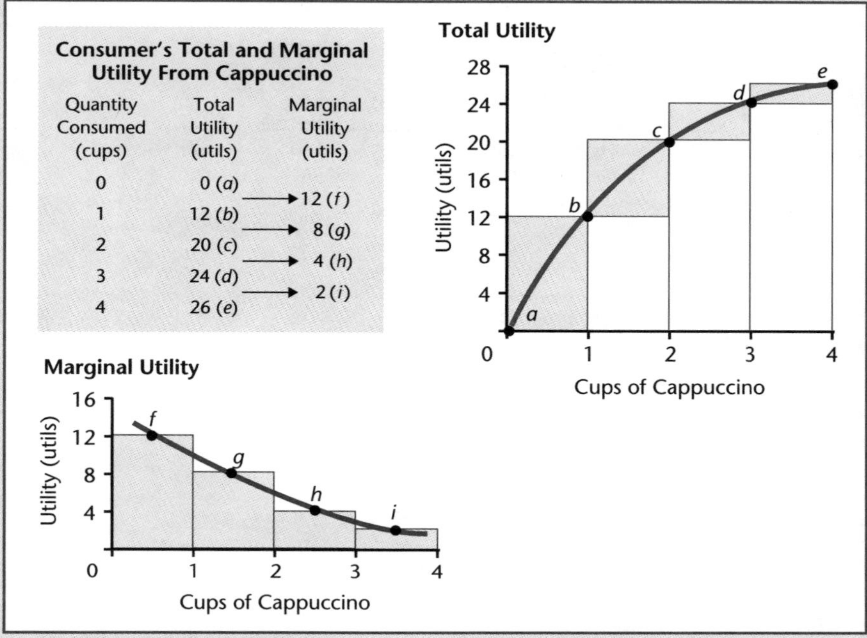

Consumer's Total and Marginal Utility From Cappuccino

Quantity Consumed (cups)	Total Utility (utils)	Marginal Utility (utils)
0	0 (*a*)	
		12 (*f*)
1	12 (*b*)	
		8 (*g*)
2	20 (*c*)	
		4 (*h*)
3	24 (*d*)	
		2 (*i*)
4	26 (*e*)	

As illustrated on the top graph, as the student drinks more cups of cappuccino, his total utility continues to rise, but at a decreasing rate. Each new cup provides less added satisfaction than the one before. That each additional cup provides less marginal utility is also illustrated in the lower graph.

Choosing One Product Over Another

One of the most important uses of the law of diminishing marginal utility is in helping to understand how much consumers choose to spend on various products. Consider again the student visiting a sidewalk café one afternoon. He arrives with $4 in his pocket and plans to spend it all on $1 cappuccinos and $2 Danish pastries. To get the most out of his $4, the student should use it in a way that gives him the greatest added satisfaction from each new dollar. In other words, he should make each purchase based on which item gives him the highest marginal utility per dollar. These figures can be found by dividing the student's marginal utilities for cappuccinos and pastries by their prices.

When making his first purchase, the student can choose either 12 utils in extra satisfaction from a cappuccino or 16 utils from a pastry, as shown in columns 2 and 5 of the schedule in Figure B. His marginal utilities per dollar are shown in columns 3 and 6, and on the graphs. Because the 12 utils (12 ÷ $1) per dollar spent on cappuccinos exceeds the 8 utils (16 ÷ $2) per dollar spent on pastries, the student buys a cappuccino. For his second purchase, the student compares the 8 utils (8 ÷ $1) per dollar he could spend on the second cappuccino with the 8 utils per dollar he

FIGURE B The Utility Maximizing Rule

Cups of Cappuccino (price = \$1)			Danish Pastries (price = \$2)		
(1) Quantity	(2) Marginal Utility (MU) (utils)	(3) Marginal Utility per \$ ($MU/P_1 = MU/\$1$) (utils)	(4) Quantity	(5) Marginal Utility (MU) (utils)	(6) Marginal Utility per \$ ($MU/P_2 = MU/\$2$) (utils)
0			0		
1	12	12	**1**	16	**8**
2	8	**8**	2	12	6
3	4	4	3	8	4
4	2	2	4	4	2

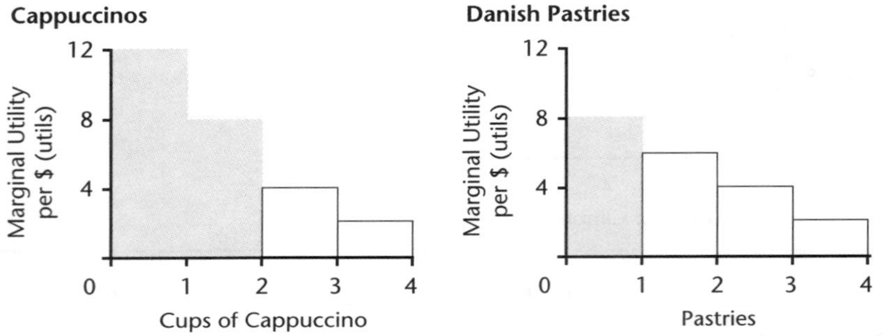

This student buys cappuccinos and pastries until his marginal utility per dollar (MU ÷ P) is the same for both items. Given his \$4 budget, he buys 2 cappuccinos and 1 pastry (the highlighted figures in the table and shaded bars in the two graphs). With these purchases, the student's marginal utility per dollar for each product equals 8 utils. The utility-maximizing rule ($MU \div P_1 = MU \div P_2$) is therefore satisfied.

could spend on his first pastry. Since these marginal utilities per dollar are equal, he buys both items, exhausting his \$4.

The Utility-Maximizing Rule

According to the utility-maximizing rule, the student keeps buying both products until the marginal utility per dollar from both cappuccinos and pastries is the same ($MU \div P_1 = MU \div P_2$). This economic law, which Jevons developed, applies no matter how many items are being bought. By following the rule, consumers maximize their overall satisfaction, or total utility, from a whole range of products.

Relevance for Today

Jevons' model rests on the assumption that utility is measurable in set units. While his critics suggested that this assumption is unrealistic, others argued that it is a legitimate way to simplify reality. By assuming that utility could be measured, Jevons made a verifiable conclusion concerning the relationship between two observable variables—the quantity of a product individuals wish to consume and the price they pay—and the result is unaffected by how this satisfaction is measured. More recently, economists have used utility theory without assuming measurable units of satisfaction. As long as consumers can say they prefer one set of products to another (without having to state exactly how much more they prefer it), conclusions like those drawn from the law of diminishing marginal utility and the utility-maximizing rule can still be reached.

Consumer X's Utility Maximization Table

Consumption of A (price = $2)			**Consumption of B (price = $4)**		
Units of A	**Total Utility (utils)**	**Marginal Utility (utils)**	**Units of B**	**Total Utility (utils)**	**Marginal Utility (utils)**
0	0		0	0	
1	11	___	1	10	___
2	20	___	2	18	___
3	27	___	3	24	___
4	32	___	4	28	___
5	35	___	5	30	___

1 a. **Copy and complete the table showing the utility Consumer X gains from products A and B.**

b. **Find the combination of A and B that maximizes Consumer X's utility if her total expenditure on these two products is $22. Explain your answer using the utility-maximizing rule.**

c. **If Consumer X's total expenditure on products A and B falls to $12 while the prices of A and B remain unchanged, what is her new utility-maximizing combination of A and B? Again explain your answer.**

2. **As a guest at a party, you perceive the price of rootbeer provided by your host as being very close to zero. How will your consumption of rootbeer differ at the party than if you were at home consuming rootbeer you bought yourself? Use the utility-maximizing rule and the law of diminishing utility to explain your answer.**

SIDELINE

UPSIDE-DOWN ECONOMICS

Economic Secrets of the Software Industry

Everything produced has a price — or does it? Why is it that some valuable forms of software are freely available to consumers? As the following article explains, it is because of the unconventional ways that software businesses try to influence demand for the products they sell.

Id Software of Mesquite, Texas, created Doom, one of the all-time megahit computer games. Id hopes to do it again. They spend one or two million dollars developing a game, then give it away. To be more precise, they distribute an abbreviated but fully functioning version of the game free of charge over the Internet. The net result is that this puny company has put its games on millions of hard drives around the world — and made $16 million in 1995.

Id has mastered the peculiar economics of the software industry. That the software industry operates under economics of any kind may come as a surprise. But successful companies like id understand software economics as if it were — as a Doom instruction might put it — smashed into their heads with a club.

The beauty of the software business — or its curse, depending on who's talking — is that once a company gets a firm foothold in a market, that foothold can morph into a fortress. In other words, winners win big, losers lose big.

The value of software increases if the company that makes it can persuade other parties to create additional products that work with it. Microsoft's strategy is: "People don't buy Windows just to use Windows," says Microsoft group vice president Nathan Myhrvold, "but to take advantage of the different hardware and various software applications. If you're clever, you can create a volunteer army of companies building around your product, and create a buzz that helps people choose your product."

Once people learn a program, there are powerful incentives to stick with it. The cost of switching to a new product may well outweigh the benefit — even if the new product is in some ways superior to the old. The term for creating a customer base that is essentially captive is "lock-in."

These new rules of the economics of software are now being adapted to the industry's new world: software that works with the Internet. By giving away a terrific product — the Navigator Web browser — Netscape made it clear that computer users are ready to embrace the Web. That, in turn, lured thousands of software developers, who now write add-on products designed to work with Navigator.

Another economically savvy competitor is Sun Microsystems. By making its programming language, Java, work on any operating system, Sun hopes to reduce the switching costs of people currently locked into Windows. Of course, you can't make money by just giving away hot technology. Application developers and end users get Java for free. But developers who want to embed it in their products have to buy a licence.

Until the mid-eighties, Netscape's Jim Clark was one of the sceptics. "I thought it was a flawed economic proposition, that there's no way you're going to make money on something that people can just copy," he says. "It's amazing what watching Bill Gates get wealthy did for my perspective."

Source
James Aley, "Give It Away and Get Rich!" in *Fortune*, 10 June 1996, Time Inc.

1. When end users of software can use it for free, who is paying the opportunity cost? Explain, giving examples from the article.
2. How does freely providing a piece of software affect the position of the producer's demand curve in the future? Can you think of other industries where the same relationship can be found?

Chapter Three
Competitive Dynamics

Everything is worth what its purchaser will pay for it.

— Publilius Syrus, ancient Roman writer

Most markets work so well that we take them for granted. Usually, when we wish to acquire goods and services—a fresh loaf of bread, a pair of shoes in the right size and style, a last-minute holiday package to a Caribbean island—they can be bought quickly and conveniently. If you take a minute to think about it, you will realize what a significant achievement this is. In this chapter, we will examine in more detail the ways that competitive markets accomplish this task through the interplay of demand and supply. We'll also see how governments can intervene in this process.

CHAPTER FOCUS

This chapter focuses on the following:

- price elasticity of demand and its impact on sellers' revenue
- price elasticity of supply and the links between production periods and supply
- price controls that governments use to override the "invisible hand" of competition, and their effects

PRICE ELASTICITY OF DEMAND

price elasticity of demand: the responsiveness of a product's quantity demanded to a change in its price

From Chapter 2 we know that if the price of a video game falls, then the number of games purchased rises. But by how much? If price is reduced by half, will quantity demanded double or triple, or will it rise by a smaller proportion, such as 10 percent or 20 percent? To answer these questions, we need to understand the **price elasticity of demand** (also called demand elasticity). Price elasticity of demand is the extent to which consumers (and the quantity they demand) respond to a change in price.

Elastic and Inelastic Demand

elastic demand: demand for which a percentage change in a product's price causes a larger percentage change in quantity demanded

inelastic demand: demand for which a percentage change in a product's price causes a smaller percentage change in quantity demanded

Consumers can be very responsive or very unresponsive to price changes. Consider Figure 3.1, which shows the demand curves for a sidewalk vendor selling ice-cream cones in two seasons. During the winter, the vendor raises her price by 20 percent, from $2.00 to $2.40. The result is that monthly quantity demanded decreases by 50 percent, from 1000 to 500 cones. If a given percentage change in price causes a *larger* percentage change in a product's quantity demanded, the product has **elastic demand**. Thus, the vendor faces elastic demand in the winter, as shown in the graph on the left. When the vendor increases her price in the summer by 20 percent, from $2.00 to $2.40, monthly quantity demanded decreases only from 2000 to 1800 cones, or 10 percent. If a given percentage change in price causes a *smaller* percentage change in quantity demanded, the product has **inelastic demand**. Inelastic demand for ice-cream cones is shown in the graph on the right.

FIGURE 3.1 Elastic and Inelastic Demand Curves

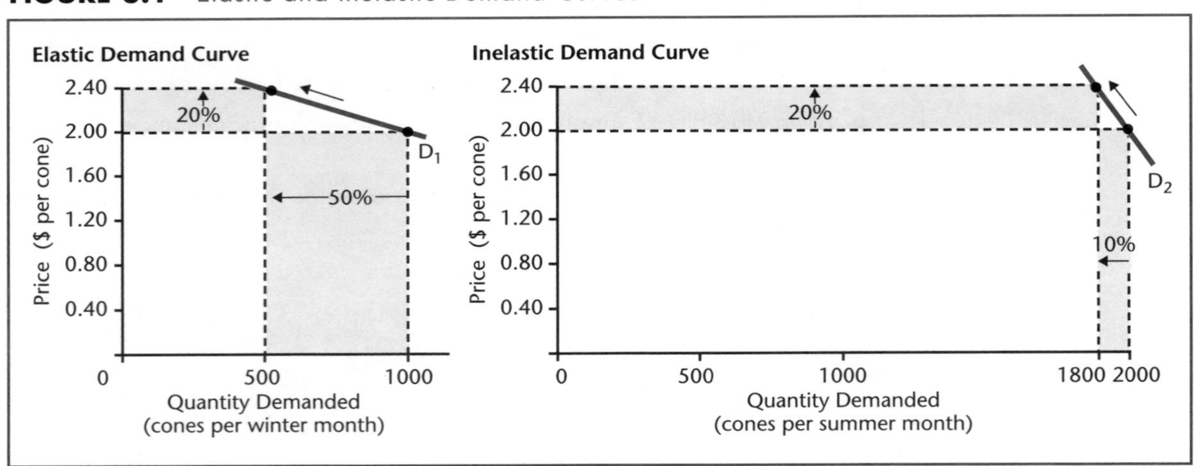

A sidewalk vendor faces an elastic demand curve for ice-cream cones, D_1, shown on the left graph. Here, a 20 percent increase in price from $2.00 to $2.40 leads to a greater 50 percent decrease in quantity demanded, from 1000 to 500 cones. The graph on the right shows an inelastic demand curve, D_2, for the vendor's cones. The same 20 percent increase in price now leads to a smaller 10 percent decrease in quantity demanded, from 2000 to 1800 cones.

Perfectly Elastic and Perfectly Inelastic Demand

perfectly elastic demand: demand for which a product's price remains constant regardless of quantity demanded

perfectly inelastic demand: demand for which a product's quantity demanded remains constant regardless of price

There are two extreme cases of demand elasticity. When a product has **perfectly elastic demand**, its price remains constant whatever quantities are demanded. Because price never varies, the demand curve is horizontal, as shown in Figure 3.2, on the left. Consider the example of an individual producer, a soybean farmer, who is a *price-taker*. This means that the farmer has no influence over the market price of soybeans, since the farmer's operations are too insignificant to affect the market. This farmer would face demand as illustrated by the demand curve D_3. Because the same $100 price per tonne of soybeans applies at all possible amounts demanded, the farmer faces a perfectly elastic demand curve. In contrast, when a product has **perfectly inelastic demand**, quantity demanded is completely unaffected by price. This situation creates a vertical demand curve, as shown in Figure 3.2, on the right. An example is the demand for insulin: since this product is essential to people who have diabetes, they are willing to pay any price for a certain quantity of insulin. This means that the market demand curve for insulin, D_4, is vertical at a given quantity demanded, such as 1000 L.

Price Elasticity of Demand and Total Revenue

total revenue: the total income earned from a product, calculated by multiplying the product's price by its quantity demanded

Demand elasticity plays a role in determining what effect a price change has on **total revenue** (TR). Total revenue is defined, either for an individual business or for all businesses producing the same product, as the price of a product multiplied by its quantity demanded:

$$TR = P \times Q_d$$

FIGURE 3.2 Perfectly Elastic and Perfectly Inelastic Demand

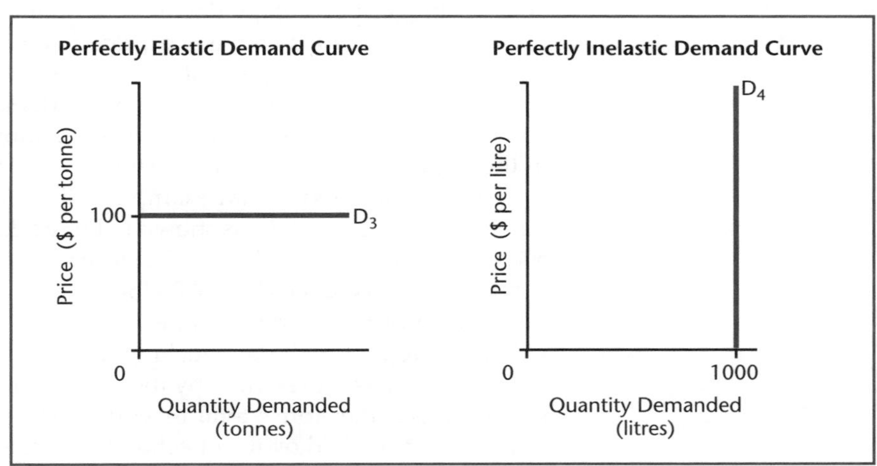

A single farmer of soybeans might face a perfectly elastic demand curve, as shown on the left graph, with a constant price of $100 per tonne. In contrast, a producer of insulin might face a vertical or perfectly inelastic demand curve, as shown on the right graph, with the quantity demanded constant at 1000 L.

Thinking About Economics

Is the slope of the demand curve related to the price elasticity of demand?

Except in cases of perfectly elastic and perfectly inelastic demand, there is no automatic connection between the slope of the demand curve and a product's price elasticity of demand. This is because the slope of the demand curve reflects the change in price divided by the change in quantity demanded, while elasticity is expressed in terms of *percentage* changes in price and quantity demanded. There is a loose connection between the two concepts, however, as shown in Figure 3.1. When two demand curves—one fairly flat and one more steep—are drawn on the same set of axes, the flatter curve (D_1) is more elastic than the steeper curve (D_2) over a given price range. This is because the flatter curve (D_1) is associated with a greater adjustment in quantity demanded, and hence a more elastic demand.

For example, if the price of a certain product is $4 and 1000 units are purchased, then the total revenue generated is $4000 ($4 × 1000).

Consider how a rise in a product's price affects total revenue for businesses selling the product. The higher price, by itself, increases the revenue pocketed by the sellers, but the accompanying decrease in quantity demanded has the opposite effect. It is the price elasticity of demand that determines which of these two effects—the increase in price or the decrease in quantity demanded—has the greater influence on sellers' total revenue.

Elastic Demand

If demand for a product is elastic, price changes cause large variations in quantity demanded. Since a price increase of a certain percentage causes an even bigger percentage decrease in quantity demanded, sellers' total revenue is reduced. Likewise, a price decrease of a certain percentage causes an even bigger percentage increase in quantity demanded, thus raising total revenue for sellers. So, when demand is elastic, total revenue and the change in price have an inverse relationship—total revenue shifts in the opposite direction to the change in price.

Let's take a look at an example. All-U-Want Videos faces an elastic demand for video rentals, as shown in Figure 3.3. At a price of $5 per video, 500 videos are rented each day. The store's total revenue at this point on the demand curve is $2500 ($5 × 500 videos). This total revenue is represented by the area of the shaded rectangle AB. At a price of $3 per video, 1500 videos are rented each day, pushing up total revenue to $4500 ($3 × 1500 videos), which is represented by the shaded area BC. Therefore, a decrease in price raises the store's total revenue, because the effect of the price decrease is outweighed by the effect of the increased quantity demanded.

Inelastic Demand

When the demand for a product is inelastic, changes in price have little effect on quantity demanded. Since an increase in price leads to a smaller

FIGURE 3.3
Revenue Changes With Elastic Demand

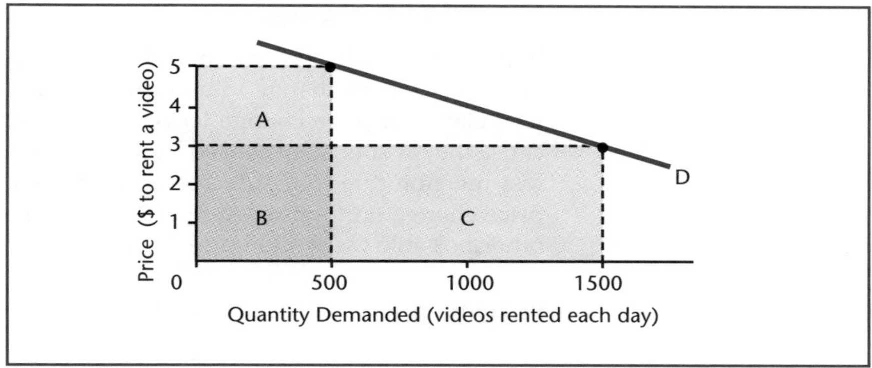

With elastic demand, a decrease in the rental price from $5 to $3 (a 40 percent fall) causes an increase in daily rentals from 500 to 1500 (a 200 percent rise). Total revenue for the business increases from the area AB ($2500 = $5 × 500) to the area of BC ($4500 = $3 × 1500). Thus, the changes in price and total revenue are in opposite directions.

percentage decrease in quantity demanded, the sellers' total revenue increases. Similarly, a decrease in price causes a smaller percentage increase in quantity demanded, thus causing total revenue to fall. Therefore, when demand is inelastic, price and total revenue have a direct relationship—total revenue shifts in the same direction as the change in price. Take, for example, a ride at an amusement park that has inelastic demand, as shown in Figure 3.4. With a price of $2, there are 10 000 riders a day. Total revenue for the ride's operator is therefore $20 000, as shown by the shaded area FG. If price increases to $3, there are 8000 riders a day and a total revenue of $24 000, as shown by the shaded area EF. Therefore, an increase in price adds to the total revenue, because the price increase more than compensates for the reduced quantity demanded.

FIGURE 3.4
Revenue Changes With Inelastic Demand

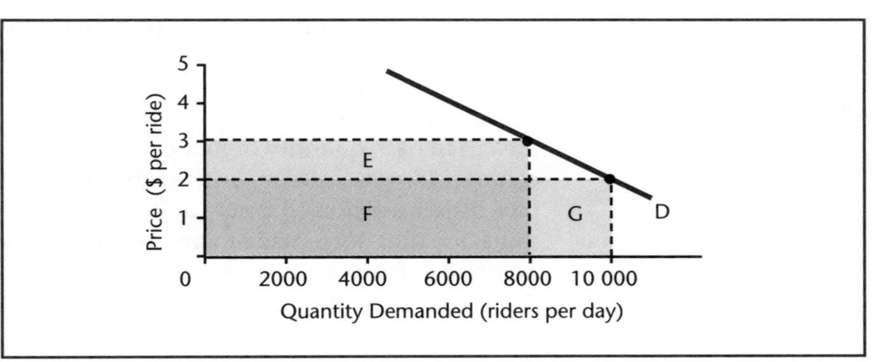

Because demand is inelastic, a rise in the price of the ride $2 to $3 (a 50 percent increase) causes a smaller percentage drop in daily ridership from 10 000 to 8 000 (a 20 percent decrease). As a result, total revenue for the ride's operator grows from FG ($20 000 = $2 × 10 000) to EF ($24 000 = $3 × 8 000). The changes in price and total revenue are therefore in the same direction.

Unit-Elastic Demand

unit-elastic demand: demand for which a percentage change in price causes an equal change in quantity demanded

In the case of **unit-elastic demand**, a percentage change in price causes an *equal* percentage change in quantity demanded. Thus, when demand is unit-elastic, a price change leaves total revenue unchanged. This is because the revenue gain caused by a price increase is precisely offset by the lost revenue due to the decrease in quantity demanded. The effect of a price change on total revenue in this case is summarized, along with all other possible cases, in Figure 3.5.

FIGURE 3.5 Demand Elasticity and Changes in Total Revenue

	Price Change	Change in Total Revenue
Elastic Demand	up	down
	down	up
Inelastic Demand	up	up
	down	down
Unit-Elastic Demand	up	unchanged
	down	unchanged

Factors That Affect Price Elasticity of Demand

Four factors affect a product's price elasticity of demand: the portion of consumer incomes devoted to buying the product, consumer access to substitutes, whether the product is a necessity or a luxury, and the time consumers have to adjust to price changes.

Portion of Consumer Incomes

If the price of a product represents a hefty portion of consumer incomes, consumers will be more responsive to price changes. For those consumers who are deciding whether or not to buy a stereo, for example, a price change can determine whether they make the purchase. If stereo prices are cut in half, quantity demanded will rise by a considerably higher percentage. In contrast, consumers who are deciding how much sugar to buy pay little attention to price; a 50 percent drop in the price will cause a much smaller percentage increase in the amount of sugar purchased. The demand for big purchases, therefore, tends to be more elastic than the demand for smaller purchases.

Access to Substitutes

If there are many close substitutes for a product, consumers will be more responsive to changes in the product's price, because they have more options and can easily change their buying patterns. The demand for a particular brand of athletic shoes, for example, will be more elastic than the demand for athletic shoes in general. If only one brand becomes more expensive, its quantity demanded will plummet as consumers substitute cheaper brands. A rise in the price of all athletic shoes, however, will not radically affect quantities purchased. As this example illustrates, the more narrowly a product is defined, the more elastic its demand will be.

Necessities Versus Luxuries

Recall that necessities are essential items—such as bread and milk—that satisfy basic needs rather than wants. Consumers tend to buy similar amounts of necessities regardless of their price; thus necessities tend to have inelastic demand. In contrast, products such as tourist travel, expensive sports cars, and yachts are luxuries that buyers can easily live without. Because these items are expendable, their demand tends to be elastic.

Time

Demand tends to become elastic over time. In the short run, consumers don't generally respond greatly to price. For example, immediately after a price increase, eaters of nachos will not modify their buying habits significantly, and users of furnace oil will continue to purchase furnace oil, regardless of price. Over time, however, consumers change their habits and needs: nacho-eaters might reduce their consumption, and homeowners might change their furnaces so as to use less fuel.

BRIEF REVIEW

1. Price elasticity of demand is the responsiveness of a product's quantity demanded to changes in the product's price.
2. When demand is elastic, a given percentage change in price causes a larger percentage change in quantity demanded. When demand is inelastic, a given percentage change in price causes a smaller percentage change in quantity demanded.
3. Demand is perfectly elastic when the price of a product is constant at all quantities demanded. Demand is perfectly inelastic when the quantity demanded of a product is constant at all prices. Demand is unit-elastic when a percentage change in price causes an equal percentage change in quantity demanded.
4. Price and total revenue have an inverse relationship when demand is elastic, but a direct relationship when demand is inelastic. When demand is unit-elastic, total revenue is constant regardless of price.
5. Four factors affect the price elasticity of demand of a product: the portion of consumer incomes the product accounts for, access to substitute products, whether the product is a luxury or a necessity, and the amount of time that elapses after a price change.

SUPPLY ELASTICITY

price elasticity of supply: the responsiveness of a product's quantity supplied to a change in price

As discussed earlier, price elasticity of demand measures the responsiveness of consumers to a change in a product's price. Similarly, **price elasticity of supply** (also called supply elasticity) measures the responsiveness of producers (and the quantity they supply) to changes in the product's own price.

Elastic and Inelastic Supply

elastic supply: supply for which a percentage change in a product's price causes a larger percentage change in quantity supplied

inelastic supply: supply for which the percentage change in a product's price causes a smaller percentage change in quantity supplied

In the case of **elastic supply**, a certain percentage change in the product's price leads to a larger percentage change in its quantity supplied. In other words, the quantity that producers are willing to offer for sale is very responsive to price changes. Consider the example of a tomato producer, as in Figure 3.6. As shown in the graph on the left, if the price of tomatoes increases by 50 percent, from \$2 to \$3 per kilogram, the quantity of tomatoes supplied annually increases from 100 000 to 200 000 kg—a 100 percent increase. If, as shown in the graph on the right, the identical 50 percent price increase for tomatoes causes a much smaller 20 percent increase in quantity supplied—from 100 000 to 120 000 kg—then we have **inelastic supply**. In other words, if a product has inelastic supply, a given percentage change in price results in a smaller percentage change in quantity supplied.

As in the case of demand elasticity, the price elasticity of supply is not the same as the slope of the supply curve. However, when two supply curves are drawn on the same set of axes, as in Figure 3.6, then—over a certain price range—the flatter curve (S_1) is more likely to be elastic than the steeper curve (S_2).

FIGURE 3.6
Elastic and Inelastic Supply

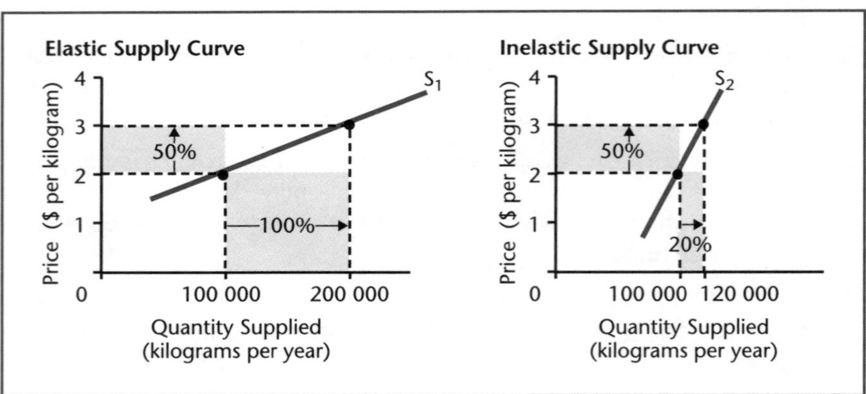

An elastic supply curve for tomatoes, S_1, is shown on the left. A 50 percent increase in price from \$2 to \$3 per kilogram leads to a greater 100 percent increase in quantity supplied, from 100 000 to 200 000 kg. The graph on the right shows an inelastic demand curve, S_2, for tomatoes. The same 50 percent increase in price now leads to a smaller 20 percent increase in quantity supplied, from 100 000 to 120 000 kg.

Factors That Affect Supply Elasticity

The main factor that affects the price elasticity of supply is the passage of time. In competitive markets, three production periods can be distinguished: the immediate run, the short run, and the long run. The price elasticity of supply differs in each period. In Figure 3.7, we illustrate elasticity for each of the three production periods in the market for strawberries.

immediate run: the production period during which none of the resources required to make a product can be varied

perfectly inelastic supply: supply for which a product's quantity supplied remains constant regardless of price

short run: the production period during which at least one of the resources required to make a product cannot be varied

The Immediate Run

The **immediate run** is the period during which businesses in a certain industry can make no changes in the quantities of resources they use. In the case of strawberry farming, the immediate run may be for a month. For example, if the price of strawberries suddenly jumps as a result of an increase in demand, then, during the immediate run, farmers are unable to increase their production. Because quantity supplied is constant, the supply curve (S_1), shown on the left, is vertical at a quantity such as 750 000 kg, Thus, for the immediate run, the supply is said to be **perfectly inelastic**.

The Short Run

The **short run** is the period during which the quantity of at least one of the resources used by businesses in an industry cannot be varied. In the case of strawberry farming, the short run is less than a year. If there is a rise in the price of strawberries from $2.00 to $2.50, then during the short run, farmers can increase their production by, for example, using more labour and maximizing the crop with mulch or fertilizers, but they cannot bring more land into production until the next growing season. In this case, illustrated in the middle graph, the price rise causes an increase in quantity supplied from 9 to 11 million kilograms. The supply curve (S_2)

FIGURE 3.7 Time and Price Elasticity of Supply

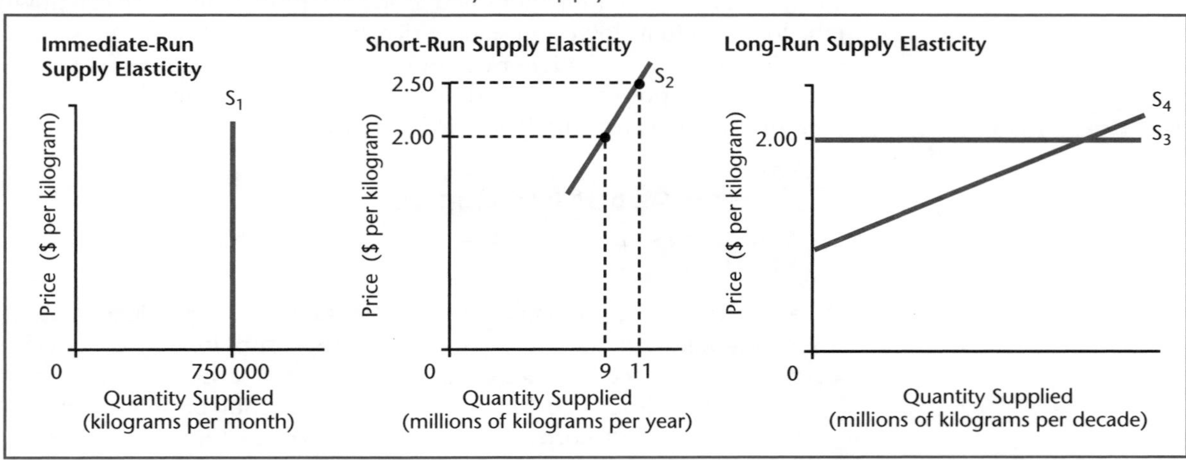

The immediate-run supply curve S_1 for strawberries is perfectly inelastic at 750 000 kg, since a price change does not affect quantity supplied. The short-run supply curve S_2 is either elastic or inelastic, with quantity supplied varying in the same direction as price. The long-run supply curve S_3 shows the case of a constant-cost industry, where supply is perfectly elastic since price is constant at $2 per kilogram for every possible quantity supplied. The long-run supply curve S_4 shows the case of an increasing-cost industry, where price rises as quantity supplied rises.

for the short run may be either elastic or inelastic. This depends on whether a given percentage change in price causes a bigger or smaller percentage variation in quantity supplied.

The Long Run

long run: the production period during which all resources required to make a product can be varied, and businesses may either enter or leave the industry

In the **long run**, the quantities of all resources used in an industry can be varied. Also, businesses may enter or leave the industry. In the case of strawberry farming, the long run is a period longer than a single growing season—perhaps as long as a decade. Over this period, a rise in the price of strawberries will cause a temporary increase in total revenues beyond what they have been in the past. The lure of these larger revenues leads to more resources being devoted to strawberry production. Not only will existing farmers expand their operations, but new farmers will enter the market. Both of these changes increase the quantity supplied of strawberries. Two results are then possible, depending on whether the industry exhibits constant costs or increasing costs at the new, higher production levels.

constant-cost industry: an industry that is not a major user of any single resource

perfectly elastic supply: supply for which a product's price remains constant regardless of quantity supplied

If strawberry farming is a **constant-cost industry**, the increase in quantity supplied following a short-run rise in the price of strawberries has no effect on resource prices, since strawberry farmers are not major users of any single resource. The lure of extra revenues keeps production expanding in the long run until the price of strawberries is driven back to its original level. Thus, the price of strawberries does not vary in the long run, regardless of quantity supplied. This means that a constant-cost industry, as shown on the right in Figure 3.7, exhibits a horizontal long-run supply curve (S_3). For the long run, then, supply is said to be **perfectly elastic**.

increasing-cost industry: an industry that is a major user of at least one resource

If strawberry farming is an **increasing-cost industry**, an increase in quantity supplied leads to an increase in the price of a single resource, such as land or farm machinery. This increase results because the industry is a major user of this resource. Again, a short-run rise in the price of strawberries causes production to grow as farmers take advantage of extra revenues. At higher levels of quantity supplied, however, price is again driven down in the long run to its lowest possible price, but price is now above its initial level, since farmers face higher per-unit costs. Hence, the long-run supply curve (S_4) has a positive (upward) slope but is very elastic, showing how quantities supplied are highly sensitive to price changes.

Thinking About Economics

Are the time spans for the three production periods—immediate run, short run, and long run—similar in all industries?

The time spans are not similar in all industries, because production periods depend on the duration, complexity, and inputs for each product's production. In agriculture, the growing season and the life cycle of a specific crop determine the three production periods. In craft industries—such as carpentry or pottery made by hand—where resource quantities can be changed relatively quickly, all three production periods can be much shorter than in agriculture. In contrast, for a complicated manufacturing process, such as airplane production, resource quantities can only be adjusted slowly, thus making the three production periods longer even than in agriculture.

BRIEF REVIEW

1. Price elasticity of supply is the responsiveness of a product's quantity supplied to changes in the product's price.
2. When supply is elastic, a given percentage change in price causes a larger percentage change in quantity supplied. When supply is inelastic, a given percentage change in price causes a smaller percentage change in quantity supplied.
3. Price elasticity of supply is dependent mainly on the production period. In the immediate run, supply is perfectly inelastic, meaning that a change in price has no effect on quantity supplied. In the short run, supply may be elastic or inelastic.
4. In the long run, price elasticity of supply depends on the industry's use of resources. In a constant-cost industry (not a major user of any one resource), supply in the long run is perfectly elastic, with a constant price at all possible quantities supplied. In an increasing-cost industry (a major user of at least one resource), the long-run supply is very elastic, with price rising gradually at higher quantities supplied.

PRICE CONTROLS

price floor: a minimum price set above equilibrium

price ceiling: a maximum price set below equilibrium

Sometimes governments see fit to control prices, thus overriding the forces of demand and supply and the "invisible hand" of competition. There are two types of price controls. A **price floor** is a minimum price set *above* the level that would exist in equilibrium. An example is agricultural price supports. A **price ceiling** is a maximum price set *below* the equilibrium level. An example is rent controls. Notice that "floor" and "ceiling" have special meanings in economics. A price floor must be higher than equilibrium. Otherwise the floor would have no effect on the price prevailing in the market. Similarly, a price ceiling must be lower than equilibrium. Otherwise it would be irrelevant.

Demand and supply can be used to analyze the effects of government programs to control prices. Because analyzing price controls also involves weighing one goal against another, the analysis depends on value judgements and so is part of normative economics.

Agricultural Price Supports

Agricultural markets, with their many independent buyers and sellers, are among the most competitive in the Canadian economy. These markets therefore provide a useful example of the potential difficulties encountered by competitive producers.

Given the nature of demand and supply for most agricultural products, farmers face product prices that can fluctuate widely. Products such as milk and wheat are viewed as necessities by consumers, so demand curves for these items are inelastic, especially in the short run. Similarly, the short-run supply curves for most agricultural products are inelastic, because farmers find it difficult to vary quantity supplied over brief time periods.

Inelastic demand and supply in agricultural markets mean that changes in either demand or supply lead to relatively large price changes. This is illustrated in Figure 3.8, using a hypothetical market for wheat. A decrease in the supply of wheat, due to unfavourable weather, leads to a fairly small decrease in the equilibrium quantity, but a considerable rise in price.

FIGURE 3.8
Price Fluctuations in Agriculture

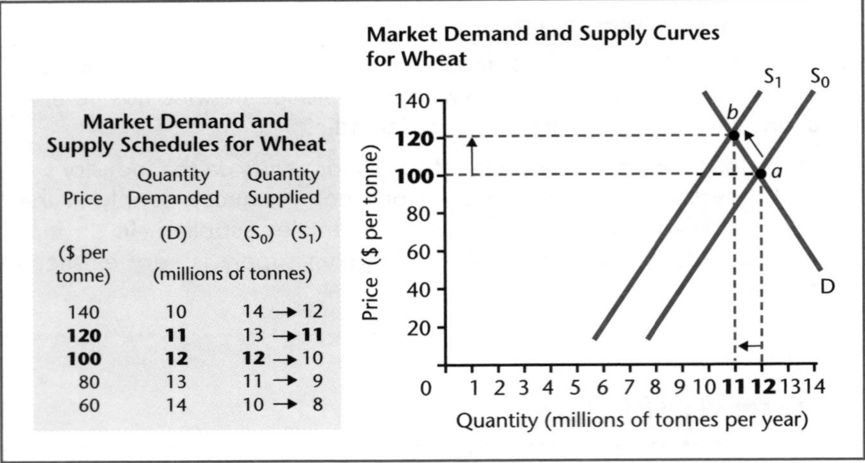

Market Demand and Supply Schedules for Wheat

Price	Quantity Demanded	Quantity Supplied
	(D)	(S_0) (S_1)
($ per tonne)	(millions of tonnes)	
140	10	14 → 12
120	**11**	13 → **11**
100	**12**	**12** → 10
80	13	11 → 9
60	14	10 → 8

Because both the demand and the supply for wheat are inelastic in the short run, a decrease in supply caused by a factor such as unfavourable weather has a relatively large effect on price, with its equilibrium value rising 20 percent from $100 (point *a*) to $120 (point *b*) per tonne. At the same time, equilibrium quantity adjusts by a smaller percentage, from 12 to 11 million tonnes.

Unstable prices, therefore, can cause large fluctuations in farmers' incomes. In years when prices are high, farmers can make substantial revenues, but low prices cause revenues to plummet. Over the long term, farmers also face pressures from the introduction of more sophisticated and expensive production techniques, which make small producers less able to compete with large agribusinesses. Consequently, many Canadian farmers have decided that the returns from agriculture are no longer worth the effort. Canada's farm population is undergoing a gradual but persistent decline, as shown in Figure 3.9.

To counter these difficulties, farmers often request that governments intervene in markets to stabilize prices at favourable levels. In the past, federal and provincial governments have usually responded positively to these demands, not only out of a desire to stabilize prices and farm incomes, but also because the family farm represents a traditional institution that many Canadians wish to see maintained through government intervention.

One type of government program is price supports, illustrated by a hypothetical market for milk in Figure 3.10. Without government intervention, this market would reach an equilibrium price of $1.10 per litre and an associated quantity of 60 million litres sold per year. A government agency pays a minimum or floor price such as $1.30, which is above the equilibrium level. The floor price has two effects: quantity demanded

FIGURE 3.9 Canadian Farm Population (thousands)

	Canada	Nfld	PEI	NS	NB	Que	Ont	Man	Sask	Alta	BC
1931	3289.2	n.a.	55.5	177.7	180.2	777.0	801.0	256.3	564.0	375.1	102.4
1941	3152.5	n.a.	51.1	143.7	163.7	838.9	704.4	249.6	514.7	384.0	102.4
1951	2912.0	20.0	46.9	115.4	149.9	792.8	702.8	219.2	399.5	345.2	120.3
1956	2746.8	13.1	43.3	98.9	129.0	765.5	683.1	206.7	362.2	332.2	112.7
1961	2128.4	11.1	34.8	58.0	63.3	585.5	524.5	172.9	305.7	287.8	84.7
1966	1960.4	9.2	31.0	46.3	52.0	507.9	498.0	161.7	281.1	286.1	91.4
1971	1489.6	5.2	21.3	27.0	27.5	334.6	391.7	131.2	233.8	237.9	79.4
1976	1056.6	1.5	12.3	12.5	12.2	198.2	286.4	101.9	193.1	190.8	47.8
1981	1039.9	1.9	12.0	17.7	15.0	186.4	279.8	96.4	180.3	190.8	59.7
1986	890.5	1.7	10.3	14.2	12.1	143.4	232.8	84.7	161.5	178.1	51.8
1991	867.3	2.0	8.7	12.8	11.0	128.4	226.8	79.6	159.7	177.2	61.1

Canada's total farm population (which includes all those, including dependents, who depend on farming as their primary source of income) has fallen consistently since 1931. This trend is also reflected in each of the provinces, although there have been several periods during which farm population in some provinces has stayed constant or even increased.

Sources: *The Canadian Global Almanac* 1992, p. 642; (Toronto: Global Press, 1992) adapted from Statistics Canada, *Trends and Highlights of Canadian Agriculture and Its People* (December 1992), cat. no. 96-303E, p. 29. Reproduced by authority of the Minister of Industry, 1997.

decreases from 60 to 59 million litres, and quantity supplied increases from 60 to 62 million litres. Both effects lead to a surplus of the commodity of 3 million litres per year (62 million – 59 million), which the government agency purchases.

Winners and Losers

Farmers are the obvious winners from price supports. The program causes both price and quantity supplied to increase and also raises farmers'

FIGURE 3.10
Effects of Price Supports

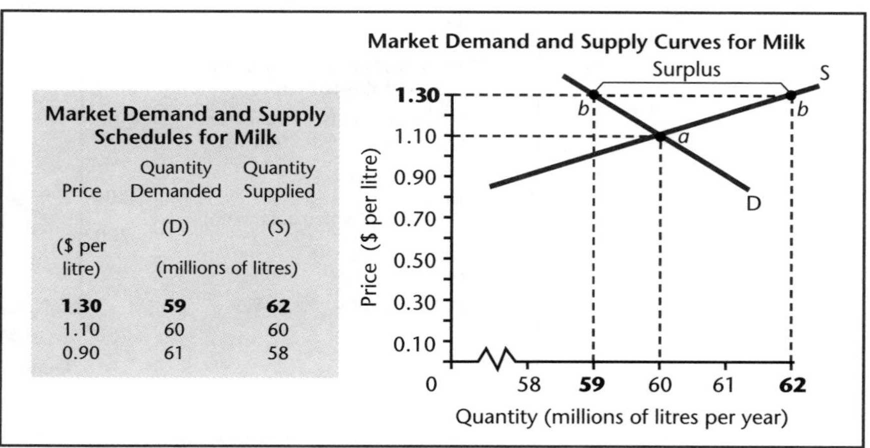

Market Demand and Supply Schedules for Milk

Price ($ per litre)	Quantity Demanded (D) (millions of litres)	Quantity Supplied (S) (millions of litres)
1.30	**59**	**62**
1.10	60	60
0.90	61	58

Because the equilibrium price for milk (point *a*) is considered too low, the government agency imposes a price floor of $1.30. This creates a milk surplus of 3 million litres, at points *b*. As long as the demand and supply curves remain the same, this surplus will recur each year, and the government agency's stock of milk will increase.

revenues. Consumers lose because of the higher prices they pay, while taxpayers lose because they must foot the bill for the government agency's purchases of surplus products. Finally, by causing economic resources to be devoted to the production of unneeded agricultural surpluses, this program also works to the disadvantage of society as a whole. Are the benefits to farmers worth the costs to consumers, taxpayers, and the rest of society? The answer to this question depends on how important you consider the stability and health of the farming sector to be in relation to the costs of supporting the agricultural sector.

Rent Controls

Another way that governments override the "invisible hand" of competition is with price ceilings, which are upper limits to a price such as rent. For example, a rent-control program was imposed on rental housing in Ontario in the 1970s due to pressure from tenant lobby groups. The effect of rent controls in a hypothetical large community with a competitive rental market is shown in Figure 3.11, assuming that all rental units in this market are identical. Without a rent-control program, equilibrium in the market would occur at a monthly rent per unit of $500 and a total of 2000 units rented per month. Controls push rents below the equilibrium level, to a value of $300. Consequently, quantity demanded increases from 2000 to 2300 units as more consumers enter the market. At the same time, quantity supplied falls from 2000 to 1500 units as landlords find it profitable to provide fewer units than before. The result of this artificially low rent is a shortage of 800 (2300 – 1500) rental units. This shortage makes itself felt through a low vacancy rate for units, meaning that an unusually small percentage of units are available for

FIGURE 3.11
Effects of Rent Controls

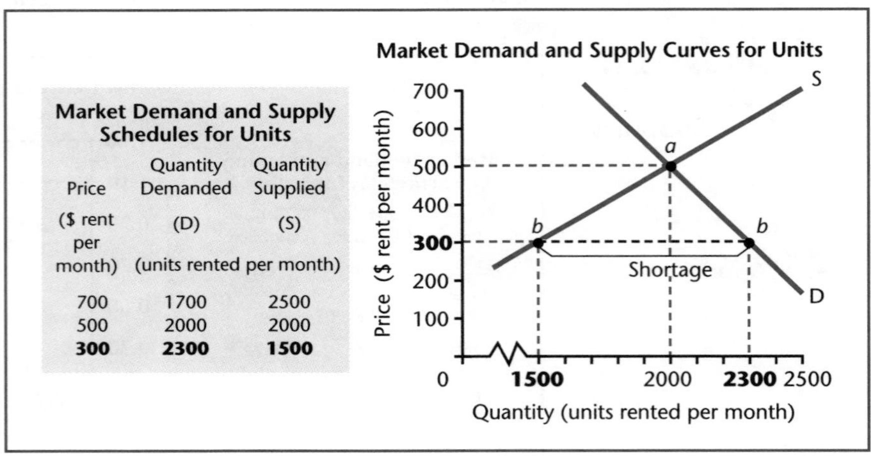

Market Demand and Supply Schedules for Units

Price ($ rent per month)	Quantity Demanded (D) (units rented per month)	Quantity Supplied (S) (units rented per month)
700	1700	2500
500	2000	2000
300	**2300**	**1500**

Rent controls force price below the equilibrium level, from $500 (point *a*) to $300 (points *b*). Quantity demanded, originally at 2000, rises to 2300 units at the new price, while quantity supplied falls to 1500 units. The price ceiling thus causes a shortage of 800 units (2300 – 1500).

rent at any given time. Quantity supplied is reduced in two ways: new rental construction is cut back, and some existing buildings are demolished or converted to other uses. In the 1980s, for example, many residential buildings in Ontario were turned into co-operatively-owned condominiums.

Winners and Losers

According to many critics, rent controls harm society as a whole by driving economic resources away from an important housing market and creating a shortage. Because of the restraints placed on landlords in setting their own price, they are particularly hurt by such controls. Some tenants gain from controls, especially middle-class tenants who have the connections and credentials to acquire the most desirable units. However, the shortage caused by controls pushes many poorer tenants into unregulated units, such as basement flats and rooming houses, with rents that are often higher than for units in the controlled market. Therefore, not only do rent controls lower the stock of rental housing, but they can affect different income groups unfairly.

Thinking About Economics

How do rental market participants cope with shortages caused by controls?

As a rule, shortages foster underground markets. In the case of rental housing, some landlords and tenants who are subletting their apartments to other tenants charge a fee to choose among people on waiting lists. These fees, or bribes, are known as "key money" and are illegal. To get around the law, key money often takes imaginative forms, such as forced purchases of furnishings at exorbitant prices.

BRIEF REVIEW

1. For various reasons, governments sometimes choose to intervene in markets to override the "invisible hand" of competition. Price controls are one form of intervention, and take the form of price floors and price ceilings.
2. Setting a price floor, or a minimum allowable price, in a competitive market tends to cause surpluses.
3. Setting a price ceiling, or a maximum allowable price, in a competitive market tends to cause shortages.

KEY CONCEPTS

price elasticity of demand
elastic demand
inelastic demand
perfectly elastic demand
perfectly inelastic demand
total revenue
unit-elastic demand

price elasticity of supply
elastic supply
inelastic supply
immediate run
perfectly inelastic supply
short run

long run
constant-cost industry
perfectly elastic supply
increasing-cost industry
price floor
price ceiling

ANALYSIS AND APPLICATION

1. Explain whether demand for each of the following is likely to be inelastic, elastic or unit-elastic. Given your answers, outline whether sellers' total revenue will increase, decrease, or stay constant if each item's price increases.
   a. milk
   b. a particular computer model
   c. yachts

2. In each case below, determine the effect on sellers' total revenue and identify whether the demand curve is elastic, inelastic, or unit-elastic:
   a. price falls from $2 to $1.50 along the market demand curve for strawberries (D_m) shown in Figure 2.2 in Chapter 2
   b. price rises from $150 to $200 along the original demand for skis (D_0) shown in Figure 2.4 in Chapter 2
   c. price drops from $12 to $8 along the demand curve for CDs shown on p. xvi of the Skills Resource

Market Demand and Supply Schedules for Leather Jackets

Price ($ per jacket)	Quantity Demanded (jackets per year)	Quantity Supplied (jackets per year)
$10	69 000	108 000
8	77 000	77 000
6	86 000	53 000
4	94 000	31 000
2	103 000	19 000

3. a. Use the table above to draw a graph showing the market demand curve and supply curves (D_0 and S_0) for a hypothetical market for leather jackets. On your graph, indicate the equilibrium price and quantity.
   b. Due to an increase in the number of producers in this market, the annual quantity supplied in this market increases by 33 000 jackets at every price. On the same graph you have drawn in

part a., show the new market supply curve (S_1), and indicate the new equilibrium price and quantity.

c. Calculate the change in total revenue for producers in this market due to the shift from S_0 to S_1. Is the demand for leather jackets between the old and new equilibrium points inelastic or elastic? Explain.

4. In the silver market, 1 million ounces are offered for sale each month by producers at the initial price of $6 per ounce. The price then rises to $8.
   a. What happens to the quantity supplied of silver in the immediate run at the new $8 price? Sketch the immediate-run supply curve to explain your answer.
   b. In what direction will the quantity supplied of silver change in the short run at the new $8 price? Sketch the short-run supply curve to explain your answer.
   c. How will the price of silver change in the long run if this is a constant-cost industry? an increasing-cost industry? Sketch long-run supply curves to explain your answers.

Market Demand and Supply Schedules for Cream Cheese

Price ($ per kilogram)	Quantity Demanded (thousands of kilograms per year)	Quantity Supplied (thousands of kilograms per year)		
	D_0	S_0		S_1
$4.50	560	1350	→	1890
4.00	590	1130	→	1420
3.50	630	890	→	960
3.00	670	670	→	670
2.50	700	440	→	380

5. a. Using the table above, draw a graph showing the demand curve (D_0) and the short-run supply curve (S_0) for cream cheese. Identify the equilibrium price and quantity in the absence of government intervention, and calculate consumers' total expenditure and the total revenue received by producers.
   b. After lobbying by the dairy industry, the government imposes a price support for cream cheese of $4 per kilogram, and agrees to purchase any unsold portion of the product at the $4 price. Outline the short-run effect of this program on consumers and producers.
   c. In the long run, the annual supply curve for cream cheese becomes S_1. How do the long-run effects of the $4 price support differ from the short-run effects on consumers and producers?
   d. Is the price-support program more costly to taxpayers in the short run or in the long run? Explain.

Market Demand and Supply Schedules for Apartments

Price ($ per month)	Quantity Demanded (thousands of units rented per month)			Quantity Supplied (thousands of units rented per month)
	D_0		D_1	S_0
$800	14.5	→	18.4	18.4
700	17.3	→	21.2	17.3
600	19.5	→	23.4	16.4
500	22.0	→	25.9	15.6
400	23.7	→	27.6	14.2

6. For the schedules above, draw a graph showing the original demand curve (D_0) and supply curve (S_0) for apartments in a particular community.
   a. Identify the equilibrium price and quantity in the absence of government intervention.
   b. Using your graph, outline how a $500 price ceiling imposed by the government affects this market. In your answer, make sure to distinguish between tenants who are able to rent apartments at the ceiling price and those who are unable to do so.
   c. An increase in the price of single-family dwellings in the community causes the demand for apartments to shift from D_0 to D_1. Draw this demand curve on your graph, and explain how it influences the impact of the $500 ceiling price on tenants.

7. (Advanced Question)
   The total annual revenue for producers of a given product, called widgets, is always $10 million regardless of the price of widgets.
   a. On the basis of this information, plot the market demand curve for widgets.
   b. How would you describe the elasticity of this demand curve? Explain.

8. Access Statistics Canada's website (at http://www.statcan.ca).
   a. Use the links within "Canadian Dimensions" to find the two most recent annual values for (i) average weekly earnings in residential building and development industries, (ii) the index of new housing prices throughout Canada, and (iii) housing starts in Canada.
   b. Calculate the percentage changes in the three variables between the two years.
   c. Based on the model of demand and supply, predict how the change in average weekly earnings in the residential construction industry between the two years should have affected the price of housing and the quantity of new houses in Canada.
   d. Is your prediction in part c. supported by the results in part b.? If not, what could explain the apparent inconsistency?

GETTING MORE THAN YOU BARGAINED FOR

Alfred Marshall and Consumer Surplus

Advancing Economic Thought

Marshall and His Influence

The Englishman Alfred Marshall (1842–1924) contributed more to the study of microeconomics and the way it is taught today than any other economist. He was the first to establish the use of demand and supply graphs, for example, and the way we conceive of such tricky notions as equilibrium and elasticity owes much to his clear-headed, logical approach.

Marshall was a student at Cambridge University, and went on to spend most of his life there as a professor. Trained as a mathematician, he then switched to economics. Marshall became a model for twentieth-century economists and taught some of the most famous ones.

Consumer Surplus

One of Marshall's most useful contributions related to the interpretation of demand curves. He realized that an individual's demand for a certain item can be seen in two ways. Figure A shows the demand for pizza by an individual pizza lover. Recall that an individual's demand curve tells us how much a person is willing to spend on each unit of the product—in other words, what her quantity demanded is at each price. The curve shows that this consumer will buy one pizza at a price of $12, two pizzas at a price of $9 each, and three pizzas at a price of $6 each. According to Marshall, the demand curve can also be viewed in the opposite way. The height of the demand curve at each quantity is the maximum price the consumer is willing to pay for that unit. Therefore, in this example, the consumer is willing to pay up to $12 for her first pizza of the week, $9 for her second, and $6 for her third.

Alfred Marshall
Source: By permission of the Master and Fellows of St. John's College, Cambridge

Marginal Benefit

The maximum price a consumer will pay for a certain unit of a product indicates the extra satisfaction, expressed in dollar terms, that he or she receives from consuming that unit. This marginal benefit is closely associated with marginal utility—Jevons' notion of extra satisfaction gained—but is measured in dollars instead of imaginary "utils." While our pizza consumer gains $12 worth of marginal benefit from her first pizza of the week, the second pizza gives her $9 in marginal benefit, and the third only $6, regardless of the actual price.

Total Benefit

Since any total value is simply the sum of all possible marginal values, it is possible to use marginal benefits to find the consumer's total benefit—in this case, the total amount of satisfaction derived from eating pizzas during the entire week. Our consumer receives marginal benefits of $12, $9, and $6 for the first three pizzas she eats each week. The sum of these three numbers—$27—gives the total benefit gained weekly from pizza consumption. This total benefit is shown as area AB under the demand curve, between zero and three pizzas.

Consumer Expenditure

A consumer's expenditure on a product is simply the market price multiplied by the number of units purchased. With a price of $6 and her consumption of three pizzas per week, our consumer faces a weekly bill of $18. This dollar amount, which represents revenue to the seller, is shown as area B on the graph.

FIGURE A Consumer Surplus for an Individual

Consumer's Demand Schedule for Pizzas

Price ($ per pizza)	Quantity Demanded (D) (pizzas)	Total Benefit ($)
12	1	12
9	2	21 (12 + 9)
6	3	27 (12 + 9 + 6)

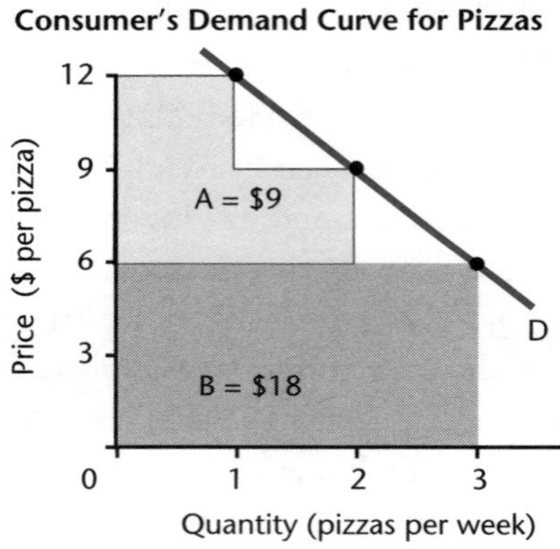

The consumer pays $6 for each of the 3 pizzas, but gets more marginal benefit from the first 2 pizzas. At 2 pizzas, for example, the $9 marginal benefit can be split into the $6 market price and the $3 surplus for that pizza. The consumer's total benefit from eating pizzas is area AB ($12 + $9 + $6 = $27) and the total expenditure is area B ($3 x 6 = $18). So consumer surplus is area A ($27 – $18 = $9).

Consumer Surplus

Marshall realized that individuals usually receive more satisfaction from consuming a product than they actually pay for it. This consumer surplus is defined as the net benefit to the consumer from buying a product at its market price, and is found by subtracting the consumer's expenditure from the total received benefit. In the case of our pizza lover, her consumer surplus from pizzas is $9 ($27 – $18). On the graph, consumer surplus is the difference between total benefit (area AB) and expenditure (area B), giving area A.

With the help of the market demand curve, the notion of consumer surplus can be extended to an entire market, as illustrated for the pizza market in Figure B. The market demand curve shows that, at a price of $6, consumers buy 100 000 pizzas per week. By adding together the marginal benefits for each consumer, total benefit appears as the entire area AB beneath the demand curve, up to a quantity demanded of 100 000 pizzas. In contrast, the total expenditure equals the rectangular area B. Because 100 000 pizzas are purchased at $6, this area equals $600 000 ($6 × 100 000). The consumer surplus for the entire market is the difference between total benefit (area AB) and total expenditure (area B), or the triangular area A. Because this triangle has a height of $10 ($16 – $6) and a width of 100 000, its area equals $500 000 [($10 × 100 000) ÷ 2].

FIGURE B Consumer Surplus for a Market

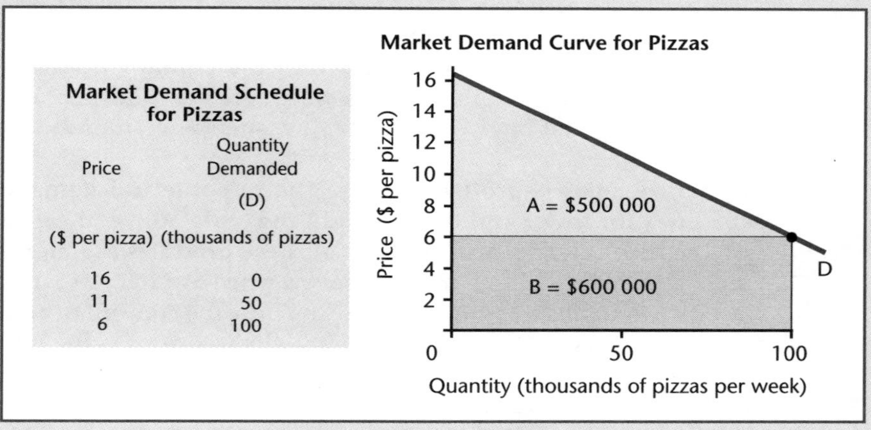

Market Demand Schedule for Pizzas

Price ($ per pizza)	Quantity Demanded (D) (thousands of pizzas)
16	0
11	50
6	100

When consumers in the pizza market are charged a price of $6, they consume 100 000 pizzas. Adding up consumers' marginal benefits for all 100 000 pizzas gives a total benefit in the market equal to area AB. At the same time, consumers' total expenditure on pizzas is area B ($600 000). The total consumer surplus in the market is found by subtracting area B from area A, so it is equal to area A ($500 000).

Relevance for Today

Marshall's concept of consumer surplus for an entire market has a wide range of applications. In evaluating a government policy such as rent controls or price supports, economists often try to calculate the policy's effect on consumer surplus in the affected market. If the consumer surplus is larger with the policy than without it, then the policy is worthwhile, since it increases the net benefit to consumers. Using the notion of consumer surplus in this way assumes that people's satisfaction can be added together in dollar terms, a simplification that is not always appropriate. However, as a rough guide to how different policies affect consumer welfare, the concept is extremely useful.

Market Demand Schedule for Water		Market Demand Schedule for Diamonds	
Price ($ per litre)	Quantity Demanded (millions of litres per year)	Price ($ per carat)	Quantity Demanded (thousands of carats per year)
1000	0	500	0
800	0.2	400	50
600	0.4	300	100
400	0.6	200	150
200	0.8	100	200
0	1.0	0	250

1. **Early economists, including Adam Smith, argued that utility could not be the main determinant of a product's price. To prove this point, they cited a puzzling fact known as the paradox of value. Some of the most useful items, such as water, are very inexpensive, while other items that have little real value, such as diamonds, are very expensive.**
   a. **Define consumer surplus, and use the hypothetical demand schedules for water and diamonds in the table above to calculate the consumer surplus for each of these products if water is freely available while diamonds have a price of $100 per carat.**
   b. **Based on your answer to part a., outline how the concept of consumer surplus can be used to explain the paradox of value.**

2. **A market for economics textbooks in a certain country exhibits a linear demand curve, with an annual quantity demanded of 80 000 books at a price of $40, 40 000 at a price of $60, and zero at $80.**
   a. **Graph the demand curve, and calculate the consumer surplus in the market if price is $40.**
   b. **The government now imposes a tax of $20 per economics textbook sold in the country, which increases price to $60. What happens to the consumer surplus?**
   c. **The revenues from this tax are used to reduce the price of economics textbooks sold in a distant low-income country. As a result, the consumer surplus for economics students in the foreign country rises by $1 million. Is the loss to domestic students outweighed by the gain for foreign students? Explain.**
   d. **What assumption is this analysis based on?**

A CALCULATING QUESTION

How to Calculate Elasticities

Price Elasticity of Demand

Businesses that can adjust the prices they charge frequently attempt to estimate the effect any price change would have on total revenue. By calculating the impact of their product's price elasticity to see whether or not a change in price would be to their advantage, businesses quantify elasticity—that is, they give it a numerical value.

As we will find in the following example, the larger this numerical value, the greater the price sensitivity—or price elasticity—of the product's demand. If the value is greater than 1, then quantity demanded is sensitive to price changes, and demand is elastic. If the value is less than 1, the quantity demanded is unresponsive to price changes, and demand is inelastic. If the value is 1, then the product is unit-elastic.

Recall the case of All-U-Want Videos (Figure 3.3), which rents 500 videos a day at a price of \$5 each, and 1500 videos when the price drops to \$3. All-U-Want Videos can use the following formula to calculate the price elasticity of demand. In the formula, Qd stands for quantity demanded, and Δ stands for change. (The symbol Δ is the Greek capital letter "delta," which signifies a change in some variable.)

$$\text{Price elasticity of demand} = \frac{\Delta Q_d \div \text{average } Q_d}{\Delta \text{ price} \div \text{average price}}$$

$$= \frac{(1500 - 500) \div [(1500 + 500) \div 2]}{(\$3 - \$5) \div [(\$3 + \$5) \div 2]}$$

$$= \frac{1000 \div 1000}{-\$2 \div \$4}$$

$$= \frac{1}{-^1/_2}$$

$$= (-)2$$

In the numerator and denominator of this formula, the changes in quantity demanded and price, respectively, are divided by each variable's average value. The average quantity demanded is found by adding together the new and old quantities demanded, and then dividing by 2. The same method is used to derive the average price, which is the sum of the new and the old prices divided by 2. Therefore, in the example of All-U-Want Videos, the price elasticity is 2, which means that a certain percentage change in price (calculated using average price) causes twice that percentage change in quantity demanded (calculated using average quantity demanded). Note that the answer is a pure number with no units attached. Its negative sign is also ignored, so that the number is always considered to be positive. A step-by-step approach to calculating the price elasticity of demand is outlined in Figure A.

FIGURE A Calculating the Price Elasticity of Demand

The value of the price elasticity of demand can be calculated by completing the following steps, which are illustrated using the demand faced by All-U-Want Videos.

1. Find the new and old quantities demanded (1500 and 500 videos) and the new and old prices (\$3 and \$5).
2. Calculate the changes in quantity demanded (1500 – 500 = 1000) and price (\$3 – \$5 = –\$2).
3. Calculate the average quantity demanded [(1500 + 500) ÷ 2 = 1000] and the average price [(\$3 + \$5) ÷ 2 = \$4].
4. Insert the values found in steps 2 and 3 into the elasticity formula:
   $(\Delta Q_d \div \text{average } Q_d) \div (\Delta \text{ price} \div \text{average price}) = (1000 \div 1000) \div (-\$2 \div \$4) = -2$.

SIDELINE

Price Elasticity of Supply

Supply elasticity is calculated in a similar way to demand elasticity. When the price elasticity of supply has a value greater than 1, quantity supplied is sensitive to price changes, and supply is elastic. If the value is less than 1, quantity supplied is unresponsive to price changes, and supply is inelastic.

Consider the case of the tomato industry with an elastic supply curve (Figure 3.6). When the price of tomatoes rises from \$2 to \$3 a kilogram, the quantity supplied by farmers increases from 100 000 to 200 000 kg. The value of the price elasticity of supply for this industry can be found using the following formula, in which Q_s stands for quantity supplied.

Therefore, the tomato suppliers face a price elasticity of supply of 1.67, which means that a certain percentage change in price causes a percentage change in quantity supplied that is 1.67 times as large (when both percentage changes are calculated using average values). Because there is a direct relationship between price and quantity supplied, the changes in these two variables are always in the same direction. Thus, the numerator and the denominator of the supply elasticity formula are either both positive or both negative, giving a final answer that is always positive. Like the numerical value of demand elasticity, this is a pure number with no units attached. A step-by-step approach to calculating the price elasticity of supply is outlined in Figure B.

$$\text{Price elasticity of supply} = \frac{\Delta Q_s \div \text{average } Q_s}{\Delta \text{ price} \div \text{average price}}$$

$$= \frac{(200\,000 - 100\,000) \div [(200\,000 + 100\,000) \div 2]}{(\$3 - \$2) \div [(\$3 + \$2) \div 2]}$$

$$= \frac{100\,000 \div 150\,000}{\$1 \div \$2.50}$$

$$= \frac{0.667}{0.4}$$

$$= 1.67$$

FIGURE B Calculating the Price Elasticity of Supply

The value of the price elasticity of supply can be calculated in a similar series of steps. Here, the market supply of tomatoes is used as an example.

1. Find the new and old quantities supplied (200 000 and 100 000kg) and the new and old prices (\$3 and \$2).
2. Calculate the changes in quantity supplied (200 000 – 100 000 = 100 000) and price (\$3 – \$2 = \$1).
3. Calculate the average quantity supplied [(200 000 + 100 000) ÷ 2 = 150 000] and the average price [(\$3 + \$2) ÷ 2 = \$2.50].
4. Insert the values found in steps 2 and 3 into the elasticity formula: (ΔQ_S ÷ average Q_S) ÷ (Δ price ÷ average price) = (100 000 ÷ 150 000) ÷ (\$1.00 ÷ \$2.50) = 1.67.

Market Demand Schedule for Canoes

Price ($ per canoe)	Quantity Demanded (canoes per month)
$800	400
600	800
400	1200
200	1600

1. a. Use the market demand schedule for canoes shown above to find total revenue at each given price.
   b. Based on your answer to part a., state whether the market demand for canoes is elastic, inelastic, or unit elastic in the three price ranges $800 to $600, $600 to $400, and $400 to $200.
   c. Compute the numerical values of demand elasticity in the three relevant price ranges.
   d. Are your answers to parts b. and c. consistent? Explain.
   e. Graph the market demand curve for canoes (D) and calculate the numerical value of its slope. Does a demand curve with a constant slope have a constant numerical elasticity? Explain.

2. a. Compute the numerical values of supply elasticity for the market supply curve for strawberries (S) shown in Figure 2.5 in the two price ranges $1.50 to $2.00, and $2.00 to $2.50.
   b. Is supply elastic, inelastic, or unit-elastic between prices $1.50 to $2.50?
   c. Does a supply curve with a constant slope have a constant numerical elasticity? Explain.

Part Two

Efficiency and Equity

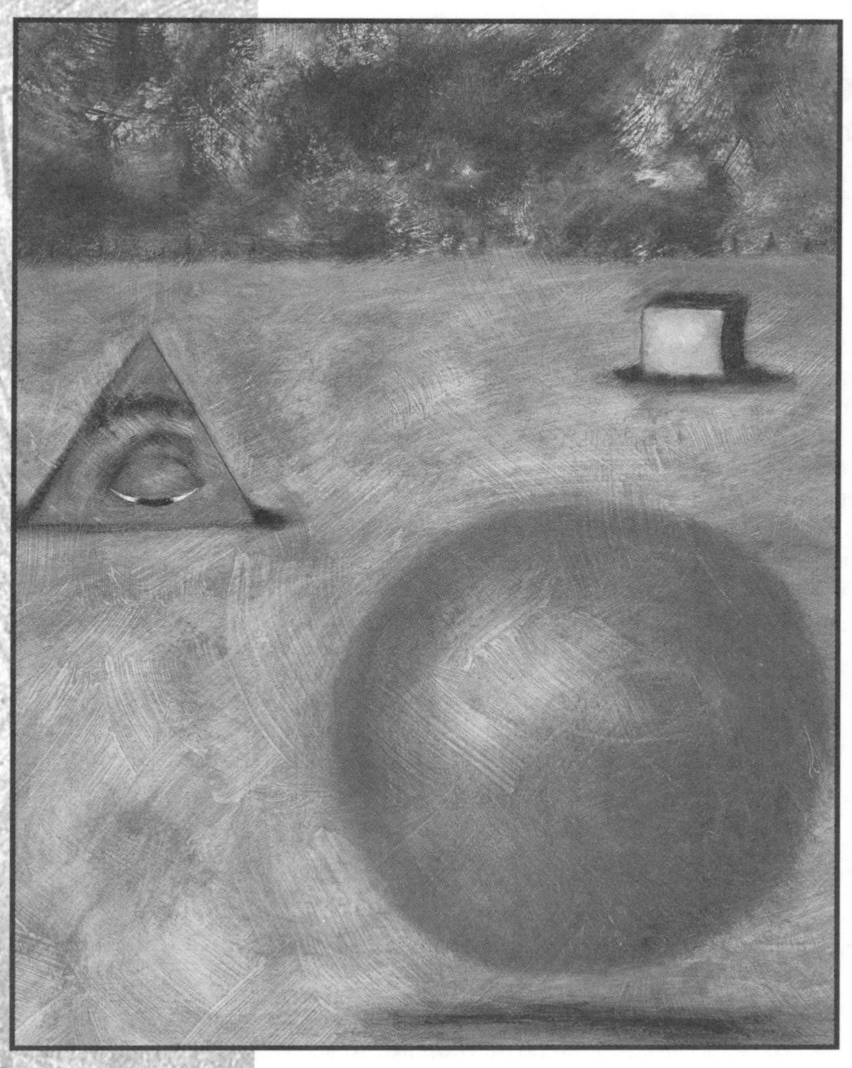

That action is best which procures the greatest happiness for the greatest numbers.

— Francis Hutchinson, British philosopher

Chapter Four
Costs of Production

Knowledge is the only instrument of production that is not subject to diminishing returns.
—J.M. Clark, American economist

There is an old saying: "There's no such thing as a free lunch." In other words, everything has a cost. This chapter highlights one of the most important types of cost—how production creates expenses for businesses. In the future, if not already, most of us will have a close connection with a business as an employee or owner. All of us have a connection to businesses by virtue of being consumers. For now, we will ignore the selling side of business to look at how businesses are organized, how they make decisions about production processes, and how they deal with production costs. In later chapters, we will look again at sales revenues to see the crucial role production costs play in determining the profits companies earn.

CHAPTER FOCUS

This chapter focuses on the following:

- major organizational forms of business—sole proprietorships, partnerships, and corporations
- economic costs (explicit and implicit) of production, and economic profit
- short-run (total, average, and marginal) products and costs, and the law of diminishing marginal returns
- long-run results of production (increasing returns to scale, constant returns to scale, and decreasing returns to scale), and long-run costs

BUSINESS ORGANIZATION

business: an enterprise that brings individuals, financial resources, and economic resources together to produce a good or service for economic gain

A **business** is an enterprise that brings individuals, financial resources, and economic resources together to produce a good or service for economic gain. There are about one million businesses in Canada. Of that number, many are small; more than three-quarters of Canadian businesses have annual sales revenues of less than $5 million. However, 5000 businesses together account for almost half the total revenue received by Canadian business as a whole.

The vast majority of businesses take one of the following forms: sole proprietorship, partnership, or corporation. A co-operative, which is a business owned and run jointly by its members, is significant in certain sectors and regions but is overall a less popular option.

Sole Proprietorships and Partnerships

sole proprietorship: an unincorporated business that is owned by a single person

partnership: an unincorporated business that is owned by two or more people

A business that is owned by a single person is a **sole proprietorship**. A business that is owned by two or more people is a **partnership**. There are few legal restrictions on establishing these forms of business, and their simple structure gives them the flexibility to adapt to new market situations. However, they are a viable option only for small enterprises. This is because of the principle of unlimited liability, which means that owners of sole proprietorships and partnerships are responsible for their company's obligations. In other words, the personal belongings and private savings of the owners may be seized to pay off lenders and suppliers if a business cannot pay its outstanding debts.

Corporations

corporation: a company that has a legal status independent of its owners

A **corporation** is a company that has a legal status independent of its owners. In the eyes of the law, a corporation is a legal entity, like a person, and has the obligations of any person doing business. Ownership in a corporation is gained by buying shares. The shares of many corporations are bought or sold among a wide range of individuals, making the connection between the corporation and its owners looser than for sole proprietorships or partnerships. Many shareholders have nothing to do with the day-to-day operations of the business, but the money they invest allows the corporation to be formed and to expand.

The process of establishing a corporation, which involves government fees and lawyers' bills, is sometimes too expensive for small businesses. But most large businesses find the convenience of operating as a corporation worth the expense. Corporate shareholders enjoy the advantage of limited liability, meaning they can lose only what they put into the business. Given this protection to owners, a large corporation can raise funds by selling shares to many interested buyers. In manufacturing, corporations are the prevalent form of business organization. Figure 4.1 shows the significance of corporations in Canadian manufacturing, both in terms of the percentage of all enterprises and their share of sales.

FIGURE 4.1 Types of Businesses in Canadian Manufacturing (1993)

	Percentage of Total Businesses	Percentage of Total Sales Revenue
Sole Proprietorships	<2%	<1%
Partnerships	<1%	1%
Corporations	98%	98%
Co-operatives	<1%	<1%
	100%	100%

In 1993, about 98 percent of all Canadian manufacturers were corporations, and these corporations also accounted for 98 percent of manufacturers' total sales revenue.

Source: Adapted from Statistics Canada, *Manufacturing Industries of Canada, 1993* (December 1995), cat. no. 31-203, pp. 196–97. Reproduced by authority of the Minister of Industry, 1997.

PRODUCTION, COSTS, AND PROFIT

production: the process of transforming a set of resources into a good or service that has economic value

inputs: the resources used in production

output: the quantity of a good or service that results from production

Production is the process of transforming a set of resources into a good or service that has economic value. The resources used in production are known as **inputs**. Recall that natural resources, capital resources, and human resources are the three economic resources used in production. Inputs for most businesses include all three of these *factors of production*. **Output** is the result of this production, the quantity of a good or service that is produced.

Businesses and the industries in which they operate fall into one of three sectors depending on the type of production: primary, secondary, or service (also known as "tertiary"). The primary sector includes industries that extract or cultivate natural resources, such as mining, forestry, fishing, and agriculture. The secondary sector involves fabricating or processing goods and includes, among other industries, manufacturing and construction. Finally, the service sector includes trade industries (both retail and wholesale) such as banking and insurance, and the new information industries. Despite the differences among these three sectors, they all follow the same production principles.

Productive Efficiency

labour-intensive process: a production process that employs more labour and less capital

capital-intensive process: a production process that employs more capital and less labour

In producing a certain good or service, businesses can typically choose from several processes, each using a different combination of inputs. A **labour-intensive process** is one that employs more labour and less capital to produce a certain quantity of output. Conversely, a **capital-intensive process** uses more capital and less labour to produce the same quantity of output.

Suppose you have started a small clothing company, Pure 'n' Simple T-Shirts with a $100 000 inheritance. You rent a building to use as a factory, and buy a supply of materials. Before hiring workers or buying sewing machines, you discover that you can make 250 T-shirts a day by using one of two possible production processes, each involving a different combination of workers and machines. The combinations of labour and capital employed in each process are shown in Figure 4.2. Process A is labour-intensive, since it requires more workers and fewer machines to produce 250 T-shirts per day. Process B is capital-intensive, since it requires more machines and fewer workers.

FIGURE 4.2: Choosing a Production Process

	Workers (labour)	Sewing Machines (capital)
Process A	4	2
Process B	3	3

Pure 'n' Simple T-Shirts can produce a daily output of 250 T-shirts with one of two possible combinations of workers and sewing machines. Process A is a more labour-intensive process, while Process B is a more capital-intensive process.

productive efficiency: making a given quantity of output at the lowest cost

How does a business decide which production process to use? Owners who want to earn as much profit as possible should try to maximize the business's **productive efficiency**, which means making a given quantity of output with the least costly mix of inputs. Selecting the most efficient process therefore depends both on the quantity of each input used and on the prices of these inputs. Let's look again at the example of Pure 'n' Simple T-Shirts. As the owner, you can maximize your business's productive efficiency by using the lowest-priced combination of workers and sewing machines needed to turn out the daily output of 250 T-shirts. You find that the daily cost of a worker (an hourly wage, plus employee benefits) is $100, while the daily cost of a sewing machine (including wear and tear on the machine, use of electricity, and maintenance) is $25. All other costs for the business (for example, rent of the building) remain constant no matter which process is used, so they can be ignored in making this decision. With Process A, the daily costs of employing four workers and two machines come to $450 [($100 × 4 workers) + ($25 × 2 machines)]. In contrast, the daily costs of employing three workers and three machines with Process B are $375 [($100 × 3 workers) + ($25 × 3 machines)]. In this case, productive efficiency is maximized by using the capital-intensive Process B.

Economic Costs

explicit costs: payments made by a business to businesses or people outside of it

Businesses face two types of costs: explicit costs and implicit costs. Explicit costs are payments made by a business to businesses or people outside of it. **Explicit costs** are also referred to as "accounting costs" because they include all the costs that appear in the business accounting records. These costs include such items as payments made for workers, buildings, machinery, and materials. For Pure 'n' Simple T-Shirts, for example, the explicit costs of producing 250 T-shirts a day using Process B include $375 for labour and machinery. In addition, the business may face a whole range of other accounting costs that add up to $675 per day. The daily explicit costs for the business are therefore $1050 ($375 + $675).

implicit costs: the owner's opportunity costs of being involved with a business

normal profit: the minimum return necessary for owners to keep funds and their entrepreneurial skills in their business

In contrast, **implicit costs** are estimates of what owners give up by being involved with a business—the opportunity cost, in other words, of pursuing this course of action over another. Implicit costs relate to the resources provided by the owners. One implicit cost is **normal profit**, or the minimum return that owners must receive to keep their funds and their entrepreneurial skills tied up in their business. To calculate normal profit, owners must determine the highest possible return they could have received by using their funds and entrepreneurial skills in another way. Consider again the T-shirt company. You might estimate that, rather than making T-shirts, you could use your $100 000 to purchase a partnership in your friend's catering business, which would provide you with a return of $50 a day. Another implicit cost is the wages that owners sacrifice by providing labour to the business. If, for example, you devote labour by working as the manager of Pure 'n' Simple T-Shirts, you might estimate the value of your work as $150 a day, which is what you could earn by working for someone else. The sum of these two costs means that the implicit costs for Pure 'n' Simple T-Shirts are $200 ($50 + $150) per day.

economic costs: a business's total explicit and implicit costs

Recall that economists define "cost" as opportunity cost, which includes any sacrificed opportunity that results from some course of action, even if no outright monetary payment is made. Thus, the **economic costs** encountered by a business are all the opportunity costs involved in production, and include both explicit and implicit costs. So, for Pure 'n' Simple T-Shirts, the explicit costs of producing 250 T-shirts per day are $1050, and the implicit costs are $200. The total economic costs faced by the business are therefore $1250:

$$\begin{aligned}\text{Economic costs} &= \text{explicit costs} + \text{implicit costs}\\ \$1250 &= \$1050 + \$200\end{aligned}$$

Economic Profit

economic profit: the excess of a business's total revenue over its economic costs

When economic costs are subtracted from total revenue, the excess is known as **economic profit**. If this gives a negative figure, the business faces a negative economic profit, or a loss. The daily economic profit of Pure 'n' Simple T-Shirts can be found by calculating total revenue and subtracting economic costs. If 250 T-shirts are sold at a price of $6 each, then the total revenue gained by producing 250 T-shirts is $1500 ($6 × 250 shirts). When the economic costs of $1250 are deducted, we get an economic profit of $250 ($1500 – $1250):

$$\begin{aligned}\text{Economic profit} &= \text{total revenue} - \text{economic costs}\\ \$250 &= \$1500 - \$1250\end{aligned}$$

BRIEF REVIEW

1. The major forms of business organization are sole proprietorship, partnership, and corporation. Sole proprietorships and partnerships are common choices for small businesses, while larger businesses tend to be corporations.
2. Production processes may be labour-intensive or capital-intensive. To achieve productive efficiency, a business must choose the production process that is the cheapest way to produce a certain quantity of output.
3. Economic costs, as opposed to accounting costs, include both explicit costs (payments to those outside the business) and implicit costs (opportunity costs owners sustain by running the business).
4. Economists measure profitability using economic profit, which is found by deducting both explicit and implicit costs from a business's sales revenue.

PRODUCTION IN THE SHORT RUN

Recall from Chapter 3 that the short run is the period during which quantities of one or more of a business's inputs cannot be varied. In manufacturing, companies usually cannot adjust the quantity of machinery they use or the size of their factories on short notice. In agriculture, there is typically an additional quantity that cannot be varied—the land available for cultivation. Inputs that cannot be adjusted in the short run are known as **fixed inputs**. Inputs that can be adjusted are known as **variable inputs**. Typically, variable inputs in the short run include the labour and materials a business uses in production. For example, as owner of Pure 'n' Simple T-Shirts, you are considering adjusting your current production of 250 shirts a day. You have already bought three sewing machines and cannot acquire more without a considerable delay. Hence, the three machines represent a fixed input for your business in the short run. But you can change the number of workers you employ, so labour represents a variable input in the short run.

fixed inputs: inputs whose quantities cannot be adjusted in the short run

variable inputs: inputs whose quantities can be adjusted in the short run

Total, Average, and Marginal Product

To increase production of a certain good or service, a business must employ more of all variable inputs, including workers. The result is a rise in **total product**, which is the overall quantity (q) of output associated with a given workforce. The employment of labour is a convenient measure of a company's scale of production, since labour is a variable input in making virtually all products. But businesses also use other variable inputs, such as natural resources or semi-processed goods.

total product: the overall quantity of output produced with a given workforce

Once again, let's look at Pure 'n' Simple T-Shirts. Say you conduct a few experiments to see what happens to total product for your business when the number of workers employed is changed but the number of sewing machines—three—remains constant. As shown in columns 1 and 2 of Figure 4.3, an increase in workers from three to four causes an increase in total production from 250 to 270 shirts per day.

FIGURE 4.3: Production in the Short Run

(1) Labour (L) workers per day	(2) Total Product (q) (T-shirts per day)	(3) Marginal Product ($\Delta q/\Delta L$) (T-shirts per day)	(4) Average Product (q/L) (T-shirts per day)
0	0		—
		80	
1	80		80
		120	
2	200		100
		50	
3	250		83.3
		20	
4	270		67.5
		10	
5	280		56
		–10	
6	270		45

As the number of workers increases, total product increases until the fifth worker is hired. Marginal product peaks when the second worker is hired and becomes negative at the same point that total product begins to drop. Meanwhile, average product peaks at 2 workers.

average product: the quantity of output produced per worker

marginal product: the extra output produced by an additional worker

In addition to total product, two other concepts are important when analyzing production in the short run. **Average product** is the quantity of output produced per worker, and is found by dividing total product (q) by the quantity of labour (L) employed. **Marginal product**, in contrast, is the extra output produced when an additional worker is hired. Marginal product is calculated by dividing the change in total product (Δq) by the change in the amount of labour employed (ΔL). (The symbol Δ is the Greek capital letter "delta," which signifies a change in some variable.)

Columns 3 and 4 of Figure 4.3 list the marginal and average products for Pure 'n' Simple T-Shirts. When employing three workers, the workforce's average product is 83.3 shirts per day (250 shirts ÷ 3 workers). If a fourth worker is added, the marginal product of this worker is 20 shirts, which comes from subtracting the old total product (250 shirts) from the new total product (270 shirts), and dividing the difference by the change in the workforce from three to four:

$$\text{Average product} = \frac{\text{total product (q)}}{\text{number of workers (L)}}$$

$$83.3 \text{ shirts} = \frac{250}{3}$$

$$\text{Marginal product} = \frac{\text{change in total product } (\Delta q)}{\text{change in workforce } (\Delta L)}$$

$$20 \text{ shirts} = \frac{(270 - 250)}{(4 - 3)}$$

Thinking About Economics

Since marginal product is the "extra" product created by a change in an input, it relates to two levels of inputs. How can this be shown in a table or on a graph?

In a table, such as Figure 4.3, marginal product is shown halfway between the values for total and average product. This is because marginal product is defined as a change from one employment level to another. So, for example, in column 3 the marginal product of 20 shirts for the fourth worker is shown between the rows for 3 and 4 workers. The same principle also applies to expressing the marginal product on a graph; the marginal product of 20 shirts for the fourth worker will be plotted halfway between the horizontal co-ordinates for 3 and 4 workers.

Diminishing Marginal Returns

law of diminishing marginal returns: at some point, as more units of a variable input are added to a fixed input, the marginal product will start to decrease

The marginal product values in Figure 4.3 reflect a law that applies to production in the short run. According to the **law of diminishing marginal returns**, at some point—as more units of a variable input are added to a fixed input—the marginal product will start to decrease, since the new units of the variable input (for example, workers) are being added to an increasingly scarce fixed input (for example, land).It is possible to prove the law of diminishing returns through a type of argument known by the Latin term *reductio ad absurdum* (pronounced *re-dook´-shio ad absurd´-um*). This type of argument verifies a statement by showing that its opposite leads to absurdity. For the law of diminishing marginal returns, consider what would happen if you used a flower pot to grow food. If the law of diminishing marginal returns were false, then, as you used more labour, the total product of food grown in the flower pot would rise at a faster and faster rate, until the world's entire food supply could be provided from this single pot. Since this conclusion is obviously absurd, the law of diminishing marginal returns must be true.

Three Stages of Production

Pure 'n' Simple T-Shirts' total product is shown in the top graph of Figure 4.4, and its marginal product and average product are shown in the bottom graph. Both graphs can be divided into three ranges. In the bottom graph's first range, marginal product rises as more workers are added. In the top graph's first range, total product rises at a higher and higher rate, giving the curve a positive slope that gets steeper. During the second range marginal product begins to fall, but is still positive. Total product in this second range continues to rise but at a lower rate, so that the curve becomes flatter. In the final range marginal product falls below zero and total product decreases. Points in this last range will never be chosen by the business.

Average Versus Marginal Product

The shape of the average product curve reflects an important series of rules governing the relationship between average and marginal values. The average rises if the marginal value is above the average value. The average value stays constant if it equals the corresponding marginal value. Finally, the average value falls if the marginal value is below the average value.

These rules are borne out by the bottom graph in Figure 4.4. At first, marginal product is above average product, so that average product must

FIGURE 4.4
Total, Marginal, and Average Product

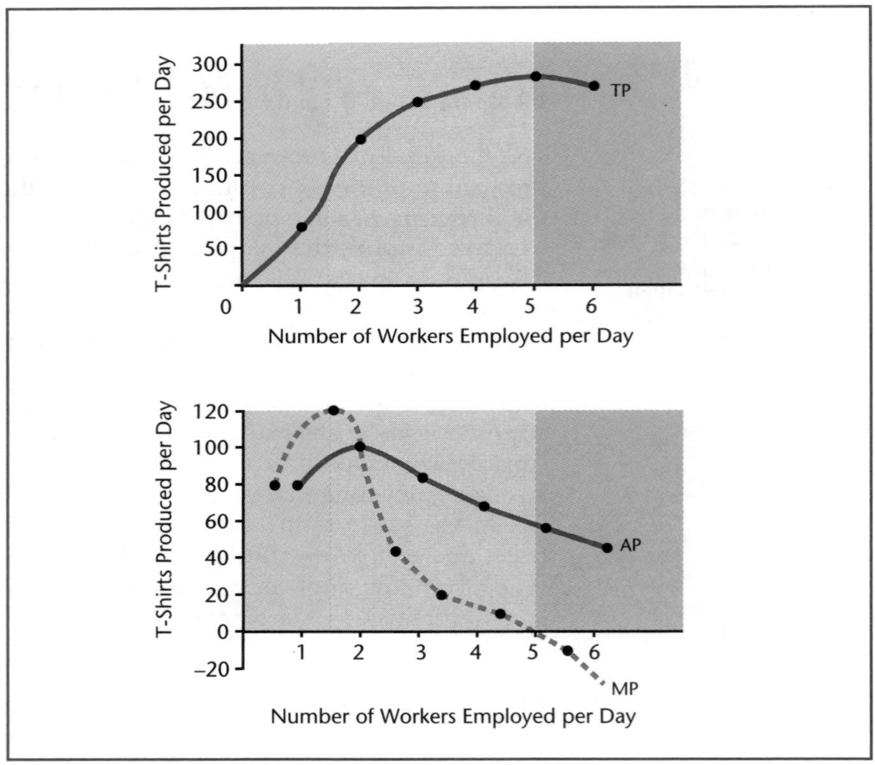

Pure 'n' Simple T-Shirts' total product curve is hill-shaped, with its peak at 5 workers and its slope dependent on the behaviour of marginal product. The first range, where marginal product rises, applies during the hiring of the first 2 workers. In the second range, during the hiring of the third, fourth, and fifth workers, marginal product falls and is positive. In the last range, from the sixth worker onward, marginal product falls and is negative. The shape of the average product curve can be linked to marginal product, since average product reaches a maximum where it crosses the marginal product curve at 2 workers.

be rising. At two workers, average product crosses the marginal product curve, so that values for both must be equal. Here average product is constant, meaning it has a zero slope. Beyond this point, marginal product is below average product, causing average product to fall.

The rules that connect marginal and average values apply in a variety of situations. To help explain these rules, we'll use an illustration every student is familiar with—marks. Suppose there are two tests in a course, each worth 50 marks, with a student's final grade calculated as the sum of the two marks. A student's *marginal mark* is the mark on each test, while her *average mark* is the total earned so far divided by the number of completed tests. For example, say the student has received a marginal mark of 36 out of 50 on the first test. Her initial average is also 36, which comes from dividing 36 by 1, as shown in Figure 4.5. If the student receives a marginal mark of 34 out of 50 on the second test, her average on the two tests falls to 35 [(36 + 34) ÷ 2]. The student's average mark has declined, because her new marginal mark of 34 is below her previous average of 36. On the other hand, she may get another mark of 36 on the second test. Because her new marginal mark is the same as her previous average, this student's average stays the same at 36 [(36 + 36) ÷ 2]. Finally, if the student receives a mark of 38 on the second test, her average rises to 37 [(36 + 38) ÷ 2]. In this case, her average rises because her new marginal mark is greater than her previous average. All three of these cases are shown in Figure 4.5.

FIGURE 4.5: A Student's Marginal and Average Marks

		Marginal Mark	Average Mark
Test 1		$\frac{36}{50}$	$\frac{36}{1} = 36$
Test 2	(Case A)	$\frac{34}{50}$	$\frac{(36 + 34)}{2} = 35$
	(Case B)	$\frac{36}{50}$	$\frac{(36 + 36)}{2} = 36$
	(Case C)	$\frac{38}{50}$	$\frac{(36 + 38)}{2} = 37$

On the first test, the student receives a mark of 36, which represents both her marginal and average marks. In Case A, the marginal mark of 34 on the second test is below the previous average, so the average mark falls to 35. In Case B, the marginal mark on the second test equals the previous average, so the average stays the same at 36. In Case C, the marginal mark of 38 on the second test is above the previous average, so the average mark rises to 37.

COSTS IN THE SHORT RUN

fixed costs: economic costs for inputs that remain fixed at all quantities of output

variable costs: economic costs for inputs that vary at each quantity of output

total cost: the sum of all fixed and variable costs at each quantity of output

In the short run, just as businesses use fixed and variable inputs, they face corresponding fixed and variable costs. **Fixed costs** (FC) do not change when a business changes its quantity of output, since these costs relate to fixed inputs such as machinery and land. **Variable costs** (VC), in contrast, relate to variable inputs, which change when a business adjusts the quantity produced. The most important variable costs are wages and payments for materials used in production. **Total cost** (TC) is the sum of all inputs, both fixed and variable, and is found by adding fixed and variable costs at each quantity of output.

The short-run costs for Pure 'n' Simple T-Shirts are shown in Figure 4.6. The company's fixed costs (column 3) reflect its expenditures on such inputs as factory rent and machinery, and are a constant $825, regardless of how many shirts are produced. In contrast, variable costs (column 4) rise along with output. Therefore, at the level of three workers, total cost (column 5) is $1250 ($825 + $425):

Total cost (TC) = fixed cost (FC) + variable cost (VC)
$1250 = $ 825 + $425

FIGURE 4.6: Short-Run Costs for Pure 'n' Simple T-Shirts

(1) Labour (L)	(2) Total Product (q)		(3) Fixed Costs (FC)	(4) Variable Costs (VC)	(5) Total Cost (TC) (FC + VC)		(6) Marginal Cost (MC) (ΔTC/Δq)	(7) Average Fixed Costs (AFC) (FC/q)	(8) Average Variable Costs (AVC) (VC/q)	(9) Average Cost (AC) (AFC + AVC)
0	0		825	0	825					
		→ 80				→ 140	1.75			
1	80		825	140	965			10.31	1.75	12.06
		→ 120				→ 160	1.33			
2	200		825	300	1125			4.13	1.50	5.63
		→ 50				→ 125	2.50			
3	250		825	425	1250			3.30	1.70	5.00
		→ 20				→ 110	5.50			
4	270		825	535	1360			3.06	1.98	5.04
		→ 10				→ 105	10.50			
5	280		825	640	1465			2.95	2.29	5.24

Columns 1 and 2 are from Figure 4.3, while columns 3 and 4 represent possible fixed and variable costs for the business. The remaining columns are based on calculations shown in the table. Total cost in column 5 is the sum of the fixed and variable costs. Marginal cost in column 6 is found by dividing the *changes* in total cost by the *changes* in total product. Columns 7 and 8 are derived by dividing fixed and variable costs by total product. Average cost in column 9 is the sum of the average fixed and average variable costs.

Marginal Cost

"Marginal" has a different interpretation when referring to cost rather than product. While marginal product is defined in terms of each new unit of labour, with cost the focus switches to new units of output instead.

marginal cost: the extra cost of producing an additional unit of output

Marginal cost (MC), or the extra cost of producing an additional unit of output, is one of the most important cost concepts in economics. Marginal cost is found by calculating the change in total cost (ΔTC) that results whenever a new worker is hired, and then dividing this change by the change in total product (Δq) that results from employing another worker. So, for example, the marginal costs for Pure 'n' Simple T-Shirts at each output level are shown in column 6 of Figure 4.6. When the fourth worker is hired, total cost in column 5 rises by \$110 (\$1360 – \$1250), and total product, in column 2, increases by 20 shirts (270 – 250). Therefore, the marginal cost of each of these additional 20 shirts is \$5.50 (\$110.00 ÷ 20 shirts).

$$\text{Marginal cost (MC)} = \frac{\text{change in total cost } (\Delta TC)}{\text{change in total product } (\Delta q)}$$

$$\$5.50 = \frac{\$110.00}{20 \text{ shirts}}$$

Figure 4.7 shows that the marginal cost curve is shaped like the letter ("J" or the Nike "swoosh"). Early in the process of adding labour, the addition of each new worker produces a proportionally greater increase in output than in the existing labour. So, the marginal cost connected with

FIGURE 4.7
The Marginal Cost Curve

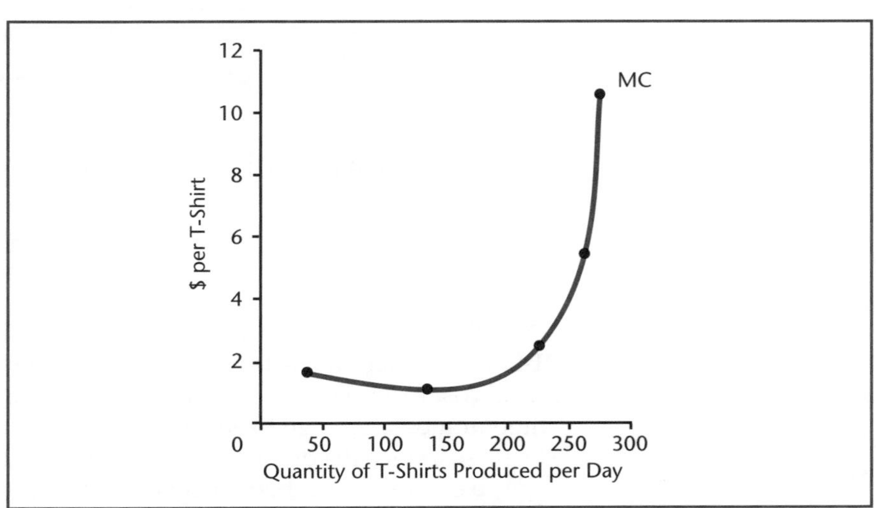

As illustrated by the case of Pure 'n' Simple T-Shirts, the marginal cost curve (MC) is shaped like the letter "J." At low output levels, the extra cost of each unit produced falls. However, the marginal cost of each new unit starts to rise when marginal product begins to fall.

each new worker falls for each extra unit of output as long as marginal product keeps increasing. But at some point marginal product starts to decline. From this point, each new worker produces fewer extra units of output than the previous worker, and the marginal cost connected with adding a new worker is greater for each extra unit of output. Marginal cost therefore rises as long as marginal product continues to fall.

Per-Unit Costs

While marginal cost is based on changes in a business's total product, per-unit costs are expressed in terms of a single level of output. These costs are related to a business's fixed costs, variable costs, and total costs. Hence, there are three separate types of per-unit costs: average fixed cost, average variable cost, and average cost.

Average Fixed and Average Variable Cost

average fixed cost: the fixed cost per unit of output

average variable cost: the variable cost per unit of output

Average fixed cost (AFC) is the fixed cost per unit of output, and is calculated by dividing the business's fixed costs (FC) by its total product (q). Similarly, **average variable cost** (AVC) is the variable cost per unit of output, and is calculated by dividing the business's variable costs (VC) by total product (q). For example, for Pure 'n' Simple T-Shirts, the average fixed and average variable costs are found in columns 7 and 8 of Figure 4.6. When three workers are employed, the business's fixed costs of $825.00 are divided by the total product of 250 shirts, giving an average fixed cost of $3.30. Similarly, the $425.00 variable costs at this employment level are divided by 250 shirts, resulting in an average variable cost of $1.70.

$$\text{Average fixed cost (AFC)} = \frac{\text{fixed costs (FC)}}{\text{total product (q)}}$$

$$\$3.30 \text{ per shirt} = \frac{\$825.00}{250 \text{ shirts}}$$

$$\text{Average variable cost (AVC)} = \frac{\text{variable costs (VC)}}{\text{total product (q)}}$$

$$\$1.70 \text{ per shirt} = \frac{\$425.00}{250 \text{ shirts}}$$

Figure 4.8 shows in a graph the average fixed cost for Pure 'n' Simple T-Shirts. When no shirts are produced, the denominator of the average fixed cost formula is zero, meaning that average fixed cost is an infinitely high number. Average fixed cost then falls as the business's total product increases, since the denominator in the formula rises. Therefore, the average fixed cost curve has a negative (downward) slope, which becomes flatter as output rises.

In contrast, the average variable cost curve shown in Figure 4.8 is saucer-shaped, reflecting its connection with the associated marginal cost curve. At the initial quantities of output, marginal cost is below average variable cost, causing average variable cost to decline. (In terms of our

FIGURE 4.8
The Family of Short-Run Cost Curves

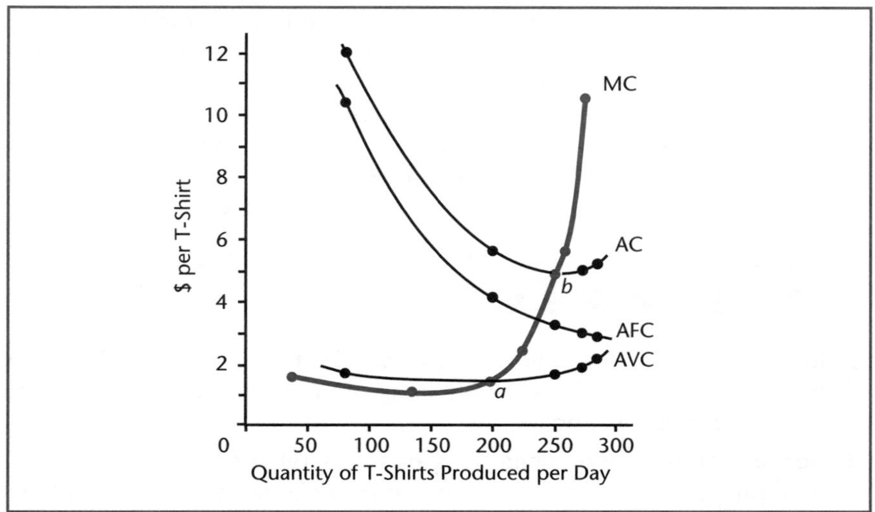

Pure 'n' Simple T-Shirts illustrates the family of short-run cost curves. When a business's output of a certain product rises, the average fixed cost curve (AFC) falls. The average variable cost curve (AVC) declines until it reaches point *a*, where it meets the marginal cost curve (MC), after which the AVC curve rises. The average cost curve (AC) also falls, and then rises. It reaches a minimum at point *b*, where it meets the MC curve.

previous example, this is the case where a student's marginal mark is below her initial average, causing her average mark to fall.) Once the two curves meet (at point *a*)—where the marginal and average values are equal—the average variable cost curve has a zero slope and reaches its minimum. At higher output levels, marginal cost is above average variable cost, causing average variable cost to rise (just as a student's marginal mark that is higher than her initial average leads to a rise in her average mark).

Average Cost

average cost: the sum of average fixed cost and average variable cost at each quantity of output

Average total cost, or simply **average cost** (AC), is the business's total cost per unit of output. Average cost is the sum of average fixed cost and average variable cost at each quantity of output. So, for example, in column 9 of Figure 4.6, when Pure 'n' Simple T-Shirts produces 250 shirts, average fixed cost is $3.30 and average variable cost is $1.70, giving an average cost of $5.00 ($3.30 + $1.70)

Average cost (AC) = average fixed cost (AFC) + average variable cost (AVC)
$5.00 per shirt = $3.30 + $1.70

Like the average variable cost curve, the average cost curve in Figure 4.8 is saucer-shaped. It represents the sum of the values plotted for the average fixed cost curve and the average variable cost curve. At an output level of 250 shirts, for example, the $5.00 average cost is the sum of the heights of the average fixed cost curve ($3.30) and the average variable cost curve ($1.70). At lower output levels, average cost is high because of average fixed cost. Once average cost has passed its lowest point, its rise is due to the impact of expanding average variable cost. The average cost curve reaches its minimum at point *b*, where it intersects the marginal cost curve. This relationship parallels the relationship between the average variable cost and marginal cost. Therefore, marginal cost provides the minimum values for both the average variable cost curve and the average cost curve. In each case, an average value remains constant when it equals its associated marginal value.

BRIEF REVIEW

1. In the short run, production is governed by the law of diminishing marginal returns which states that, as more units of a variable input are added to a fixed input, the marginal product will start to decrease at some point.
2. Because of the law of diminishing marginal returns, the marginal product curve is hill-shaped. The total and average product curves are also hill-shaped, because of their connections with changes in marginal product.
3. Marginal cost, or the extra cost of producing another unit of output, is inversely related to marginal product. The marginal cost curve is shaped like the letter "J."
4. Average fixed cost represents fixed costs per unit of output. Its curve has a negative slope and is flatter at higher output levels. Average variable cost, or variable costs per unit of output, has a saucer-shaped curve that reaches its minimum where it crosses the marginal cost curve.
5. Average cost, or total cost per unit of output, is the sum of average fixed and average variable costs at given output levels. The curve for average cost is saucer-shaped, and reaches a minimum where it intersects the marginal cost curve.

PRODUCTION IN THE LONG RUN

As we discussed in Chapter 3, the long run is the period in which quantities of all resources used in an industry can be adjusted. So, even those inputs that had been fixed in the short run—such as machinery, buildings, and cultivated land—can be adjusted in the long run. Because all inputs can vary in the long run, the law of diminishing marginal returns no longer has the same importance as in the short run. Instead, new questions arise. If a business expands all inputs used to produce a certain product, how will the output of the product vary, and what effect will these changes have on costs? There are three possible results: increasing, constant, and decreasing returns to scale.

Increasing Returns to Scale

increasing returns to scale: a situation in which a percentage increase in all inputs causes a larger percentage increase in output

Increasing returns to scale (also known as economies of scale) occur when a business expands all inputs for a certain product by a given percentage and the output rises by an even higher percentage. For example, if a car manufacturer doubles all inputs used to make a certain car model (that is, expands all inputs by 100 percent), and total output of the car more than doubles (rising by, for example, 150 percent), the manufacturer enjoys increasing returns to scale. Virtually all businesses experience increasing returns to scale over the initial range of output. There are three basic causes: division of labour, specialized capital, and specialized management.

Division of Labour

As Adam Smith illustrated with the pinmaking factory over two centuries ago, increases in the scale of production and worker specialization can go hand in hand. Performing fewer tasks allows workers to become more efficient at their jobs. As a result, Smith concluded, quantities of output tend to rise more quickly than the number of workers producing them. The impact of the division of labour is just as prevalent today in labour-intensive production. For example, if a very small restaurant where workers do everything expands, then workers can begin to specialize in either food preparation or service, thus making both sets of workers more efficient in the tasks they do.

Specialized Capital

In most manufacturing industries, a greater scale of production is associated with the use of specialized machinery. If a car manufacturer raises the quantity of all its inputs, for example, capital equipment can have more specialized functions, so that it performs fewer tasks more efficiently than before.

Specialized Management

The same principle that underlies the division of labour applies to management. When the scale of production is small, there are few managers. Each is forced to deal with a wide range of duties, some of which they are better at performing than others. An accounting expert may need to devise a marketing strategy, or a production manager may have to deal with personnel problems. Along with an enlarged scale of production, more managers are hired, with each assigned to the area in which he or she has the most expertise.

Constant Returns to Scale

constant returns to scale: a situation in which a percentage increase in all inputs results in an equal percentage increase in output

In contrast to increasing returns to scale, in the case of **constant returns to scale**, a business that expands inputs a given percentage will see output rise by the same percentage. This may be the case for the artisan making pottery; doubling her input also doubles her output. Constant returns to scale usually result when making more of an item requires repeating exactly the same tasks used to produce previous units of output.

Decreasing Returns to Scale

decreasing returns to scale: a situation in which a percentage increase in all inputs causes a smaller percentage increase in output

The last possible case is **decreasing returns to scale**, or diseconomies of scale, in which a business that expands inputs to a product's production by a certain percentage sees output rise by a smaller percentage. For example, a 100 percent expansion in all inputs used by a copy shop may lead to its output rising by only 75 percent. There are two major reasons for decreasing returns to scale: management difficulties and limited natural resources.

Management Difficulties

Continual expansion in the scale of production will eventually make a business so cumbersome to administer that managers face problems in co-ordinating operations to ensure efficient production. Virtually all businesses reach an output level above which management difficulties cause decreasing returns to scale to become dominant.

Limited Natural Resources

In primary industries, such as fishing or forestry, a business may be able to acquire only a limited supply of easily available natural resources, even in the long run. In this case, an output level is reached above which further increases in all inputs lead to a smaller rise in output, resulting in decreasing returns to scale.

Costs in the Long Run

The concept of returns to scale is useful in analyzing the effect on a business's costs when inputs that are fixed in the short run become variable. Figure 4.9 shows the case of a magazine publishing company that expands its printing plant three times, and faces a different short-run average cost curve for each plant size. With each expansion of the plant, the curve shifts to the right, demonstrating the effects of the increased output.

When the plant is first expanded, the short-run average cost curve falls from AC_1 to AC_2. This shift results from increasing returns to scale. Recall that average cost is found by dividing total cost by the quantity of output. With increasing returns to scale, output rises more rapidly than the total cost of inputs, so that average cost falls as the scale of production expands.

With the second plant expansion, the shift of the short-run average cost curve (from AC_2 to AC_3) reflects constant returns to scale. Output and the total costs of inputs rise at the same rate when the plant is expanded this second time, so the average cost curve moves horizontally as the output of magazines rises.

With the final plant expansion, the company's short-run average cost curve not only shifts to the right but also rises (from AC_3 to AC_4). This shift reflects decreasing returns to scale. Since the printing plant's output is rising less rapidly than the total cost of input costs, the average cost curve rises as the production of magazines continues to increase.

Long-Run Average Cost

long-run average cost: the minimum short-run average cost at each possible level of output

A business's **long-run average cost** in producing a certain product is the lowest value of short-run average cost at each possible level of output. Figure 4.9 shows that the long-run average cost curve is made up of the lowest possible points from the short-run average cost curves. Given a wide range of possible plant sizes, the long-run AC curve is smooth and

FIGURE 4.9
Long-Run Average Costs

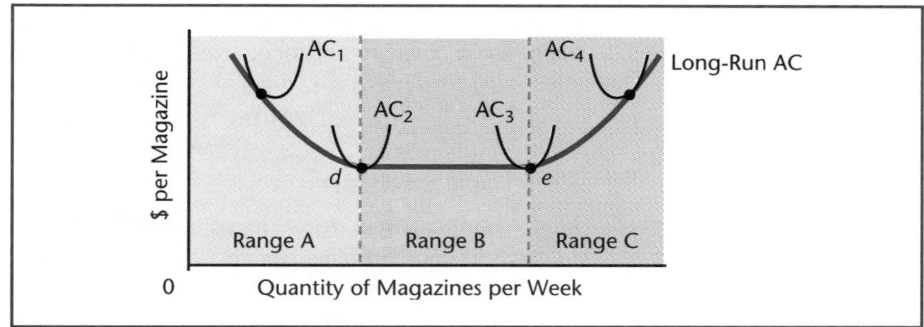

With many possible plant sizes, the long-run average cost curve for producing a product such as magazines is found by adding the lowest possible short-run average costs at every quantity, which results in a single point being included from each short-run curve. The long-run AC curve has three ranges. Range A has a negative slope, reflecting increasing returns to scale between the average cost curves AC_1 and AC_2. Range B is horizontal, indicating the constant returns to scale between AC_2 and AC_3. Range C has a positive slope, showing decreasing returns to scale beyond the AC_3 curve.

saucer-shaped, with only one point represented from each short-run curve. As depicted in Figure 4.9, long-run average cost falls in the initial output Range A because of increasing returns to scale, remains the same in Range B due to constant returns to scale, and rises in Range C because of decreasing returns to scale.

Industry Differences

While virtually all businesses face a saucer-shaped long-run average cost curve, these curves are not necessarily symmetrical for all industries. Often in an industry, one range (or portion of the curve) will dominate the long-run average cost. Figure 4.10 illustrates long-run average cost curves characteristic of manufacturing industries, craft industries, and primary industries.

Manufacturing Industries

Manufacturing industries tend to exhibit an extended range of increasing returns to scale due to the degree to which specialization is possible in the use of both labour and capital. This is particularly true of companies in which assembly-line techniques are used. It is not until output is very large that the conditions leading to constant returns to scale and decreasing returns to scale become relevant. The long-run average cost curve faced by businesses in most manufacturing industries is shown in Figure 4.10, on the left. In this case, the curve falls over a wide range of input levels before briefly levelling out, and then rising.

Craft Industries

In contrast, craft industries are dominated by constant returns to scale. Because raising output levels of crafts tends to depend on repeating exactly the method of production, an increase in input usually results in an equal increase in output. Hence, except at very low or very high levels of output, the long-run average cost curves for producers of items such as handmade pottery are horizontal, as in the middle graph of Figure 4.10.

Primary Industries

Decreasing returns to scale, meanwhile, are most prevalent for businesses in primary industries, as in some types of fishing, where the limits of resource supplies are particularly acute. In this case, the slope of the long-run average cost curve becomes positive at a relatively low level of output, as shown in Figure 4.10, on the right.

FIGURE 4.10
Possible Long-Run Average Cost Curves

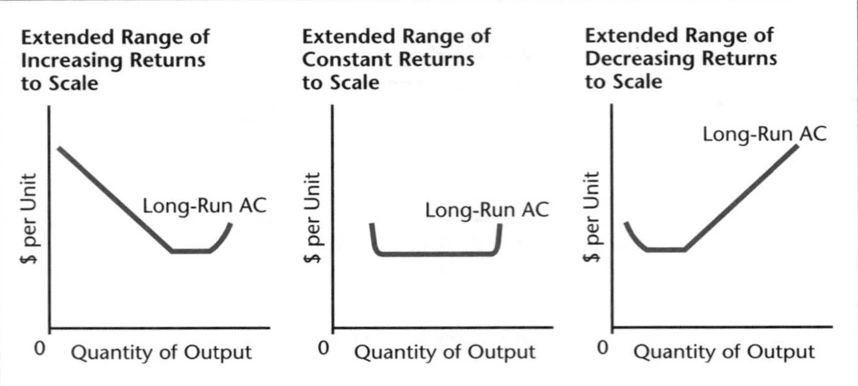

In the left graph, the long-run AC curve's negative slope dominates, illustrating a wide range of increasing returns to scale, as usually occurs in assembly-line manufacturing. The middle graph shows the long-run AC curve when the horizontal range of constant returns to scale dominates, which is characteristic of craft industries. In the right graph, the positive slope dominates, illustrating the range of decreasing returns to scale, as is common in primary industries.

Thinking About Economics

How do returns to scale influence the size of businesses in a certain industry?

The predominance of increasing returns to scale in an industry raises the chances that businesses in the industry are large. Because of their lower long-run average costs, big companies have a competitive advantage over smaller rivals. It is increasing returns to scale, for example, that explain the gigantic size of most companies in the automobile industry. In contrast, smaller companies tend to prevail in industries characterized by constant or decreasing returns to scale, because there is no cost disadvantage associated with low output levels.

BRIEF REVIEW

1. When, in the long run, all inputs can be varied, there are three possible results for a business: increasing, constant, and decreasing returns to scale.
2. Increasing returns to scale exist when a given percentage change in inputs causes an even greater percentage change in output. Division of labour, specialized capital, and specialized management are the major causes.
3. Constant returns to scale exist when a given percentage change in inputs causes an equal percentage change in output. When production of any additional product depends on repeating exactly the tasks used to produce the previous product, constant returns prevail.
4. Decreasing returns to scale exist when a given percentage change in inputs causes a lower percentage change in output. Management difficulties and limited natural resources are the major causes.
5. The long-run average cost curve is saucer-shaped, reflecting ranges first of increasing, then constant, and finally decreasing returns to scale.
6. In general, increasing returns to scale dominate in manufacturing industries, constant returns to scale dominate in craft industries, and decreasing returns to scale dominate in primary industries.

KEY CONCEPTS

business
sole proprietorship
partnership
corporation
production
inputs
output
labour-intensive process
capital-intensive process
productive efficiency
explicit costs
implicit costs
normal profit
economic costs
economic profit
fixed inputs
variable inputs
total product
average product
marginal product
law of diminishing marginal returns
fixed costs
variable costs
total cost
marginal cost
average fixed cost
average variable cost
average cost
increasing returns to scale
constant returns to scale
decreasing returns to scale
long-run average cost

ANALYSIS AND APPLICATION

1. Give an example of a business for which the most appropriate form of organization is:
   a. either a sole proprietorship or partnership
   b. a corporation

2. Which production process shown in Figure 4.2 maximizes productive efficiency for Pure 'n' Simple T-shirts in the following cases? If your answers differ from the case in the text, explain why.
   a. the daily cost of a worker is $20 and the daily cost of a sewing machine is $25
   b. the daily cost of a worker is $100 and the daily cost of a sewing machine is $150

3. Rodriguez operates a variety store that provides an annual revenue of $480 000. Each year he pays $25 000 in rent for the store, $15 000 in business taxes, and $350 000 on products to sell. He estimates he could put the $80 000 he has invested in the store into his friend's restaurant business instead and earn an annual 20 percent profit on his funds. He also estimates that he and his family could earn a total annual wage of $90 000 if they worked somewhere other than the store.
   a. Calculate the total explicit costs and total implicit costs of running the variety store.
   b. What is the accounting profit of the variety store?
   c. What is the economic profit?
   d. In what way is economic profit superior to accounting profit as an indicator of the overall performance of this business? Given the advantages of economic profit as a performance indicator, explain why the concept of economic profit is not often used in accounting.
   e. Should Rodriguez consider closing down this business? Why?

4. Identify each of the following short-run costs as either variable or fixed:
   a. depreciation charges for a construction firm
   b. employee health benefits for an automobile-parts manufacturer
   c. lumber costs for a pulp-and-paper producer
   d. property insurance for a restaurant
   e. gasoline bills for a taxi company

5. Daily production for Pot-Works, a flowerpot maker, varies with the number of workers employed, as shown in the table below.

Short-Run Production for Pot-Works

(1) Labour	(2) Total Product (pots per day)	(3) Marginal Product (pots per day)	(4) Average Product (pots per day)
0	0		
1	100	___	___
2	280	___	___
3	510	___	___
4	560	___	___
5	540	___	___

a. Copy out and complete the table.
b. On one graph, draw the total product curve. On another graph, draw the marginal product and average product curves. Explain the relationships between these curves.
c. On your graphs, identify the ranges where marginal product rises, where marginal product falls and is positive, and where marginal product is negative.

6. The short-run costs for a parking lot are shown in the table below.

Short-Run Costs for a Parking Lot

(1) Labour (workers employed)	(2) Total Product (cars parked per day)	(3) Marginal Product (cars parked per day)	(4) Fixed Costs	(5) Variable Costs	(6) Total Cost	(7) Marginal Cost	(8) Average Fixed Cost	(9) Average Variable Cost	(10) Average Cost
0	0		60	0	___				
1	120	___	60	180	___	___	___	___	___
2	280	___	60	360	___	___	___	___	___
3	410	___	60	540	___	___	___	___	___
4	520	___	60	720	___	___	___	___	___
5	580	___	60	900	___	___	___	___	___

a. Copy out and complete the table.
b. At which employment level does marginal product begin to fall? How is this point related to the behaviour of marginal cost in column (7)?

c. On one graph, draw the marginal product curve for this business. On another graph, draw the curves for marginal cost, average variable cost, and average cost.
d. Using your graph of the business's cost curves, identify the output at which average variable cost and marginal cost have the same value. At what output do average cost and marginal cost have the same value?

7. For the following industries, state whether the long-run average cost curve has an extended range with a negative slope, a positive slope, or a zero slope. In each case, explain how your answer relates to returns to scale.
   a. handcrafted pottery
   b. consumer electronics
   c. wine-making

8. (Advanced Question)
   Pot-Works, the flowerpot maker in question 5, has $500 in daily fixed costs and a single variable input (labour), with each worker paid a daily wage of $120.

Short-Run Costs for Pot-Works

(1) Labour (workers employed)	(2) Total Product (flowerpots per day)	(3) Fixed Costs	(4) Variable Costs	(5) Total Cost	(6) Marginal Cost
0	0	___	___	___	
					___
1	100	___	___	___	
					___
2	280	___	___	___	
					___
3	510	___	___	___	
					___
4	560	___	___	___	

a. Copy out and complete the above table.
b. In one graph, draw the fixed cost, variable cost, and total cost curves for this business. In another graph, draw this business's marginal cost curve.
c. Outline the relationship between variable cost, total cost, and marginal cost as this business's output increases.
d. Referring to the graph accompanying your answer to Question 5 above, explain how variable cost and total cost for this business illustrate the law of diminishing marginal returns.

9 a. Access Statistics Canada's website (at http://www.statcan.ca). Then use the links to "Canadian Dimensions" to find the percentage of Canada's workforce (excluding those in unincorporated businesses and farming) employed in the service sector. Your calculations should be based on the most recent annual statistics available.

b. Use the same source of online information to find the percentage of each province's and territory's workforce (with the same exclusions as above) employed in the service sector. Which provinces and territories have the lowest and highest percentages?

Advancing Economic Thought

CRITIC OF THE MODERN CORPORATION

John Kenneth Galbraith and the Role of Management

Galbraith and His Influence

John Kenneth Galbraith has been one of Canada's most notable intellectual exports. Born in 1908 near Port Talbot, Ontario, he studied agricultural economics at what is now the University of Guelph. He then emigrated to the United States, where, as a professor at Harvard University, he became one of the most widely known economists of the past few decades.

A prolific writer, Galbraith caused considerable debate in the 1960s and 1970s about the role of the modern corporation. He popularized the view that corporate managers possess the real decision-making power in modern capitalist economies. These managers, according to Galbraith, are more interested in their own prestige and income than they are in making profit.

John Kenneth Galbraith
Source: UPI/Bettmann

Financing Corporate Activity

To follow Galbraith's argument, we must first consider how corporations finance their operations. Unlike other types of businesses, corporations can acquire funds by issuing stocks and bonds.

Stocks Corporations sell stocks (also known as shares) through the stock market to buyers, who are known as shareholders. Stockbrokers act as go-betweens in this market, buying and selling stocks on behalf of their customers. People who purchase stocks of a certain corporation do so because they expect to receive dividends, which are periodic payments by the corporation to its shareholders. Shareholders may also expect the price, or resale value, of a company's stock to increase as its profit outlook improves. However, there are no guarantees to shareholders—the company may not perform as expected and dividends may not be declared (corporations are not required to pay dividends). Also, changing conditions in the stock market can cause price fluctuations for a wide range of stocks.

Bonds Corporations can also raise funds by selling bonds. A bond is a type of loan that is governed by a formal contract, which sets out when the borrower will provide interest payments, and also when the original amount of the loan (known as the principal) will be paid back to the bondholder. Bonds differ from other loan contracts in that they can be bought and sold. If the bondholder wishes to convert a bond into cash, he or she does not return the bond to the borrower, but sells it to an interested buyer. Unlike shareholders, bondholders are considered to be lenders to the corporation, rather than its owners. Unless a corporation becomes insolvent, bondholders have no say in the company's operations.

Separation of Ownership and Control

According to Galbraith, the ways that corporations raise funds can cause a separation of ownership and control. Most large corporations have no single shareholder owning a significant portion of the shares, but are owned and managed by different groups. On the one hand, the owners are the corporation's shareholders, who receive income through dividends and higher stock prices. On the other hand, the corporation's managers are, strictly-speaking, employees. The interests of these two groups, according to Galbraith, do not coincide. A corporation's managers may be more interested in maximizing the company's sales revenue rather than its profit, since, as the corporation expands, so will the managers' salaries and power in the organization. Managers may also siphon off profit by providing themselves with generous perks and rewards. While such actions go against shareholder interests, managers do not have to fear reprisals as long as the stake of each shareholder in the company is small enough to rule out a costly examination of management actions.

Relevance for Today

Galbraith's outlook has been influential with the general public and with some economists, although others downplay its relevance. His critics suggest that recent developments in stock markets have tended to increase the power of shareholders over management. During the 1980s, much attention was focused on the frequency of corporate takeovers, in which one company buys a sufficiently large portion of another company's shares to control its operations. Corporate takeovers can either be friendly or hostile, depending on how those taking over a company view its current managers. When a takeover is hostile, managers are often turfed out, especially if they have been looking after their own interests rather than maximizing the company's profit. According to Galbraith's critics, the ever-present threat of a hostile takeover helps to ensure that managers act in the shareholders' interests. Critics also cite the growing clout of investment funds, whose administrators often own significant portions of even a large corporation's shares, giving them control over the behaviour of the corporation's managers. In the United States, for example, pension funds and other large institutions own over half the shares of big companies, a rise from just 16 percent in 1965.

1. **Outline the advantages and disadvantages of (a) stocks, and (b) bonds, both to corporations and to individual wealthholders.**
2. **What attributes make a corporation a likely object for a hostile takeover bid? Explain what makes these attributes significant.**

SIDELINE

THE PROFIT GAME

Measuring Business Performance

Economists and accountants differ in how they look at costs and profits. Although economists consider the broader picture of opportunity costs, they must still understand the concepts accountants use to measure a business's performance. Business performance is measured using two basic accounting records: *balance sheets* and *income statements.*

The Balance Sheet

A balance sheet shows a business's financial position at a particular point in time; thus, it gives a "snapshot" of the business's financial status at that time.

One side of the balance sheet lists the business *assets,* or items of value that the business owns. The other side of the balance sheet lists the claims against the business assets. These claims are either *liabilities,* which are the company's obligations to make payments to others, or *owner's equity,* which represents the owner's stake in the business (there may also be more than one owner). Owner's equity is found by adding the value of all assets, and then subtracting the value of all liabilities.

A balance sheet can be used for several purposes, one of which is to help determine a business's *solvency,* or its ability to meet its debts. To measure solvency, accountants calculate the business's debt/equity ratio, which is the total value of the liabilities divided by the owner's equity. A low value for this ratio is a sign of financial health, since the company can likely pay off any upcoming obligations it has to lenders.

Take, for example, Jumbo-Dogs, a sidewalk cart owned by your friend, who used some savings and a loan from his parents to start the business after graduating. As shown in Figure A, the business has three assets: a bank deposit, food inventory, and a hot-dog cart. The business has one liability, its outstanding $2000 loan, along with owner's equity of $5000. The debt/equity ratio for the business is therefore 0.4, which is found by dividing the value of liabilities by the value of owner's equity:

$$\text{Debt/equity ratio} = \frac{\text{total liabilities}}{\text{owner's equity}}$$

$$0.4 = \frac{\$2000}{\$5000}$$

Compared to most businesses, Jumbo-Dogs has a low debt/equity ratio, meaning that there is little chance that it will soon become insolvent. At present, the business's cash holdings of $1900 are almost equal to its outstanding debt of $2000. Even if the entire loan came due in the very near future, the $100 inventory could soon be turned into cash as well. Assets that can be quickly transformed into money are known as *liquid assets.*

The Income Statement

An *income statement* measures a business's activities over a given period of time. The income statement lists both the business's total sales (or revenue earned) and total expenses (the explicit costs incurred over the period of time). The difference between sales and expenses is the business's profit. The income statement for Jumbo-Dogs is shown in Figure B.

FIGURE A Balance Sheet for Jumbo-Dogs

Balance Sheet
December 31, 1998

Assets		**Liabilities**	
Cash	$1900	Loan from parents	$2000
Food inventory	100		
Hot-dog cart	5000	**Owner's equity**	5000
	$7000		$7000

The assets of the business include cash of $1900, unsold food inventory of $100, and the hot-dog cart, which has an estimated value of $5000. The claims on company assets include the $2000 remaining on the loan from the owner's parents as well as $5000 in owner's equity.

Depreciation

One explicit cost that deserves special note is *depreciation,* or the reduction in the value of a company's long-lived tangible, or durable, assets.

(Land is a special durable asset that does not depreciate — except when improper use degrades its value — because it lasts indefinitely.) Depreciation is the result of age and wear and tear on an asset. As an asset depreciates, its value on the business's balance sheet falls. Every year, a depreciation charge is subtracted from the income statement. Each of these depreciation charges reflects a portion of the original payment made to purchase the asset.

Let's consider Jumbo-Dogs again. At the beginning of the year, the owner bought a hot-dog cart for $6000. Because the cart has an expected life span of six years, the value is depreciated over the six-year life, giving a yearly depreciation of $1000 ($6000 ÷ 6 years). Therefore, at the end of the first year, the hot-dog cart has a value of $5000, and the income statement in Figure B shows a depreciation charge of $1000.

Durable assets have different life spans, so they depreciate at different rates. For example, because a building is a longer-lasting asset than most machinery, the annual depreciation charge for a building is usually proportionately less than that for machinery. Of all the explicit costs, depreciation is the only item that does not entail a payment of cash by the business in the same year it appears on the income statement. In the example of Jumbo-Dogs, the $1000 depreciation charge is not withdrawn from the deposits of the company. Therefore, to reflect the cash position of the company for the year, the depreciation charge would be added to the accounting profit.

Accounting Versus Economic Profit

The main purpose of an income statement is to show the business's accounting profit, which appears at the bottom of the statement, and is found by deducting total expenses from total sales. So, Jumbo-Dogs has an accounting profit, or "bottom line," of $30 000, as shown in Figure B and below.

Accounting profit = total revenue – explicit costs
$30 000 = $50 000 – $20 000

FIGURE B Income Statement for Jumbo-Dogs

Income Statement
For the year 1998

Total Sales		$50 000
Expenses		
Food	$15 000	
Fuel	3 500	
Depreciation	1 000	
Interest on loan	500	
Total expenses		$20 000
Total profit		$30 000

The business's accounting profit of $30 000 is found by deducting total explicit costs of $20 000 from its total revenue of $50 000. The explicit costs include payments for food and fuel (for a propane tank), $500 interest on the business's loan, and wear and tear on the hot-dog cart—depreciation—estimated at $1000.

It is important to keep the various definitions of profit distinct. Because accountants consider only a business's explicit costs in their measure of profit—whereas economists consider both explicit and implicit costs — accounting profit always exceeds economic profit by the amount of implicit costs, which include an estimate of the normal profit that owners must receive to keep their funds and entrepreneurial skills in a business. Therefore, calculating the economic profit of Jumbo-Dogs would involve measuring not only total sales and total expenses, but also the business's implicit costs, as shown in Figure C. Imagine the owner estimates that, by working for the company, he sacrifices $25 000 a year in wages. In addition, he estimates that he could have earned $3000 a year by devoting his funds and entrepreneurial skills to another business. This $3000 is called a normal profit. Implicit costs therefore equal $28 000. As a result, Jumbo-Dogs' implicit costs of $28 000—as well as its explicit costs of $20 000—are subtracted from the $50 000 in total revenue to give an annual economic profit for the company of $2000 [$50 000 – ($28 000 + $20 000)].

FIGURE C Calculation of Economic Profit for Jumbo-Dogs

Total Revenue		$50 000
Explicit Costs		
Food	$15 000	
Fuel	3 500	
Depreciation	1 000	
Interest on loan	500	
Total explicit costs		$20 000
Implicit Costs		
Owner's wage	$25 000	
Normal profit	3 000	
Total implicit costs		$28 000
Economic profit		$ 2 000

Jumbo-Dogs' economic profit is calculated by subtracting both explicit and implicit costs—$20 000 and $28 000, respectively—from total revenue. The $2000 economic profit is lower than the $30 000 accounting profit, shown in Figure B, by the $28 000 in implicit costs.

1. A computer programmer operates a business, Readyware Solutions, from her own home. On January 1, 1999, she has a bank deposit for her business with a value of $750. She is owed $1750 in the form of an overdue customer's account, which she expects to be paid in full during the next few weeks. Her business owns computer equipment worth $3250 and office furniture worth $1500. She owes $4250 on a bank loan she has borrowed to operate her business and $1525 which she has yet to pay on a bill she owes for purchases of business supplies.
   a. Create a balance sheet for Readyware Solutions.
   b. Calculate this business's debt-equity ratio. Based on this ratio, and the business's holdings of liquid assets, how would you describe its current financial situation?

2. During 1998, total sales for Readyware Solutions were $35 400, wages for an assistant programmer were $20 600, costs for business supplies were $2300, depreciation charges on office furniture and computer supplies were $1100, and payments on the bank loan were $800.
   a. Create an income statement for Readyware Solutions and calculate the business's total accounting profit.
   b. What does the information in its income statement suggest about the profitability of Readyware Solutions? Explain.

Chapter Five
The Nature of Markets

Modern business is a complex, fast-moving thing. The fit and educated survive. The remainder go into politics.
—Herbert Surplis, Canadian journalist

How do the operations of a giant company like Bell Canada differ from those of a small-town restaurant or a single broccoli farmer? From an economist's perspective, the main distinction is the type of market in which each producer does business. In this chapter, we'll examine the four market structures and how much businesses within each can influence the prices and demand for the products they sell. We'll also consider how a company's ability to influence its market position affects the interests of consumers.

CHAPTER FOCUS

This chapter focuses on the following:

- the four market structures—perfect competition, monopolistic competition, oligopoly, and monopoly—and the characteristics of each
- the demand conditions for businesses in each market structure
- nonprice competition through product differentiation and advertising
- industrial concentration—how it is measured, and the arguments for and against it

MARKET STRUCTURES

While product markets come in all shapes and sizes, each has one of four structures: perfect competition, monopolistic competition, oligopoly, or monopoly. The number of businesses involved in the market, whether or not a standard product is being sold, and the ease with which businesses can enter and exit the industry all determine the market structure.

Perfect Competition

perfect competition: a market structure characterized by many buyers and sellers of a standard product and easy entry to and exit from the industry

The ideal form of competition allows for the unobstructed operation of demand and supply forces, as outlined in previous chapters. This market structure, known as **perfect competition**, has three main characteristics: many buyers and sellers, a standard product, and easy entry to and exit from the industry. In a perfectly competitive market, businesses consider the price of the product they sell to be determined by the forces of demand and supply. While common in primary industries such as agriculture and markets for financial assets such as stocks, bonds, and foreign currencies, perfectly competitive markets are not common in most other sectors of the economy.

Many Buyers and Sellers

The most important feature of perfectly competitive industries is that there are large numbers of buyers and sellers. For example, in the Canadian broccoli market there are many consumers and many farmers. As a result, no single participant is large enough to affect the prevailing price in the industry.

Standard Product

In a perfectly competitive market, each business supplies a product that is indistinguishable from that of other businesses. One farmer's crop of broccoli, for example, is not noticeably different from that same variety of broccoli produced by other farmers.

Easy Entry and Exit

Finally, for a market to be perfectly competitive, businesses must be free to enter or exit the industry. Compared with most other industries, for example, it is relatively easy for farmers to transfer resources from the production of other crops to the growing of broccoli, since agricultural land has a wide variety of uses. Similarly, farmers can leave the broccoli market with little difficulty by devoting resources to alternative agricultural uses.

Monopolistic Competition

monopolistic competition: a market structure characterized by many buyers and sellers of slightly different products and easy entry to and exit from the industry

Monopolistic competition is the structure most prevalent in the service sector, and applies, for example, to the restaurant industry. This market structure is characterized by a large number of businesses (though not as many as in a perfectly competitive industry), perceptible differences among the products of competitors, and easy entry and exit of businesses. Product differences can be related to location, quality, or the image consumers have of each product.

Oligopoly

oligopoly: a market structure characterized by only a few businesses offering standard or similar products and restricted entry to the industry

An **oligopoly** is a market in which there are only a few businesses, and entry to the industry is restricted. Oligopolies are extremely common in the Canadian economy, as illustrated by the steel, automobile, and insurance industries. The products sold in oligopolies may or may not vary, depending on the particular market. For example, in the steel industry, a standard product is produced, whereas the automobile and insurance industries offer some variety among their products.

Monopoly

monopoly: a market structure characterized by only one business supplying a product with no close substitutes and restricted entry to the industry

A **monopoly** is an industry in which a single business supplies a product with no close substitutes. This market structure is the exact opposite of perfect competition. Monopolies are relatively common in the Canadian economy. Cable TV companies, for example, often have a monopoly in particular regions of the country, and notable Canadian monopolies include Canada Post and Via Rail. Monopoly companies are not always large; small companies, such as a caterer with exclusive rights to sell food at a certain sports stadium, can be monopolies as well.

Entry Barriers

entry barriers: economic or institutional obstacles to businesses entering an industry

Markets that are oligopolies and monopolies require entry barriers to continue as such. **Entry barriers** are economic or institutional obstacles that stop potential competitors from setting up in an industry where economic profits are being made. There are six main entry barriers: economies of scale, market experience, restricted ownership of resources, legal obstacles, market abuses, and advertising.

Increasing Returns to Scale

natural monopoly: a market in which only one business is economically viable because of increasing returns to scale

In industries where established companies benefit from increasing returns to scale, and therefore decreasing average costs when output increases in the long run, small companies just entering the market will be unable to charge as low a price. In the extreme case, known as a **natural monopoly**, increasing returns to scale mean that it makes sense to have only one supplier of a product, given the size of the market. This applies to public utilities, which provide a product such as water, and services such as public transit. Having more than one company would require a large-scale duplication of inputs, thus leading to high per-unit costs and product prices.

While the concept is applicable to some markets, the term "natural monopoly" can be misleading, since there is nothing "natural" about this concept. For example, the telephone industry was once considered a natural monopoly, until recent technological innovations—such as cellular phones and Internet phone services—made it possible to have competition. Similarly, cable TV companies that were once regional monopolies are gradually losing this status because of new forms of satellite delivery.

Market Experience

Even in cases where increasing returns to scale are not predominant, well-established businesses may have a cost advantage over potential rivals simply because of their experience. A business can learn from experience how to supply a product more efficiently, thus decreasing its per-unit costs at all possible output levels.

Restricted Ownership of Resources

When one or a few businesses control supplies of a resource to make a product, they effectively bar other businesses from entering the industry. One example of such control is the South African company De Beers, which owns or controls over 75 percent of the world's supply of diamonds.

Legal Obstacles

Legislation regarding, for example, patents or licences can act as barriers to entry. A patent gives the exclusive right to produce, use, or sell an invention for a given period (now 20 years in Canada). This exclusive right allows individuals and companies to reap some rewards of their innovations. Companies can become monopolies with patented products, as did the patent-holder for the artificial sweetener aspartame, known as Nutrasweet. Government licensing, too, can create closed or regulated markets. For instance, only Canada Post has the legal right to provide regular mail service, making it a monopoly in this industry. Similarly, only a certain number of Canadian television or radio stations have broadcast rights within different regions of the country, thus making these broadcasting industries oligopolies.

Market Abuses

Established businesses in an industry may use unfair practices to maintain their dominant positions. A business might, for example, temporarily drop the price of its product below average cost to drive a new competitor out of business. This illegal strategy is known as **predatory pricing**. At one time, predatory pricing was used in the international airline industry; some large companies would cut fares only to increase them once upstart competitors had gone into bankruptcy.

predatory pricing: an unfair business practice of temporarily lowering prices to drive out competitors in an industry

Advertising

The use of advertising as an entry barrier is most common in oligopolies, such as the beer and soft-drink industries. Because consumer preference for these products is so dependent on promotion, established companies with large advertising budgets can often stop small competitors from gaining a significant toehold in these markets. For example, Canada's two largest beer companies, Molson Breweries and John Labatt Ltd., use advertising to help them maintain their sales, which represent over 90 percent of total quantity demanded in the Canadian beer market.

Market Power

market power: a business's ability to affect the price of the product it sells

Businesses in perfectly competitive markets—or perfect competitors, as they may be called—are price-takers because they are forced to take the price for their product that is set by the market forces of demand and supply. In contrast, businesses in the remaining three types of markets have some influence over a product's price, so they are price-makers. In other words, these businesses have some measure of **market power**, or the ability to affect the price they charge. A business's market power depends on how easy it is for buyers to find substitutes for the business's output.

As a rule, a business in a monopoly (a monopolist) has the most market power. It deals with no competitors and has the largest possible size in relation to the industry. Because the monopolist sells a product with no close substitutes, the product's demand curve tends to be less elastic than for other products. A company in an oligopoly (an oligopolist) commonly has substantial market power because of the small number of competitors and the company's large size relative to the industry. A business in a monopolistically competitive market (a monopolistic competitor) has less market power because it faces many competitors and is small in relation to its market. Moreover, because it sells a product with close substitutes, its demand curve is relatively elastic. Finally, a perfect competitor has no market power because of its role as a price-taker.

Thinking About Economics

Can businesses use market power to charge different prices to various consumers?

Yes. For example, a municipal bus company may offer a discount to students rather than have them not riding the bus at all, a restaurant owner may lower the price of a meal for a lunch special and keep it high for dinner, or an airline will charge lower fares to tourists than to business travellers. This practice, known as "price discrimination," can be used to increase profits by any business with market power, as long as the business can stop customers who pay different prices from exchanging the products between themselves, and the business can distinguish between buyers willing to pay high and low prices by using a condition such as the consumer's age or the time of day when the product is consumed.

FIGURE 5.1 Attributes of Market Structures

	Perfect Competition	Monopolistic Competition	Oligopoly	Monopoly
Number of Businesses	very many	many	few	one
Standard Product	always	never	sometimes	not applicable
Entry and Exit of New Businesses	very easy	fairly easy	difficult	very difficult
Market Power	none	some	some	great
Example	farming	restaurants	automobile manufacturing	public utilities

BRIEF REVIEW

1. Product markets have one of four structures: perfect competition, monopolistic competition, oligopoly, or monopoly.
2. Market structure, or the degree of competition in a market, is determined by the number of buyers and sellers in the market, whether or not a standard product is being sold, and the ease with which businesses can enter or exit the market.
3. In monopolies and oligopolies, potential competitors face the entry barriers of increasing returns to scale, market experience, restricted ownership of resources, legal obstacles, market abuses, and advertising.
4. A business's market power, or ability to be a price-maker, tends to be greater for monopolists than for oligopolists, and greater for oligopolists than for monopolistic competitors. Perfect competitors possess no market power.

DEMAND DIFFERENCES

As we saw in Chapter 4, producers face the same sorts of costs. However, because of the different market structures in which they operate, producers face significantly different demand conditions.

Perfect Competition

business's demand curve: the demand curve faced by an individual business, as opposed to an entire market

Because a perfect competitor is a price-taker, it must accept the price dictated by the market forces of demand and supply. Thus, the individual **business's demand curve** is different from the market demand curve. Recall that the market demand curve (D_m) has a negative slope, given that price and quantity demanded are inversely related. Because a perfect competitor is one of many businesses in a market, the quantity it chooses to supply has no effect on equilibrium price and quantity in the market. See the graph for the T-shirt market in Figure 5.2. On the left, the intersection of the market demand and supply curves, D_m and S_m, gives the equilibrium price of $6 per T-shirt. No matter how many shirts Pure 'n' Simple T-Shirts supplies, it will sell all it produces at a price of $6 per shirt. Thus, the individual business's demand curve, D_b, is horizontal, or perfectly elastic, at a price of $6 as shown on the right in Figure 5.2.

Monopolistic Competition

Because it has some ability to influence the price it charges, a monopolistic competitor faces a different type of demand curve. Consider the example of the Jaded Palate, a restaurant that serves highly spiced Cajun food. Customers of this restaurant view its food as distinct from that of nearby restaurants, none of which specialize in this cuisine. If the Jaded

FIGURE 5.2
Demand Faced by a Perfect Competitor

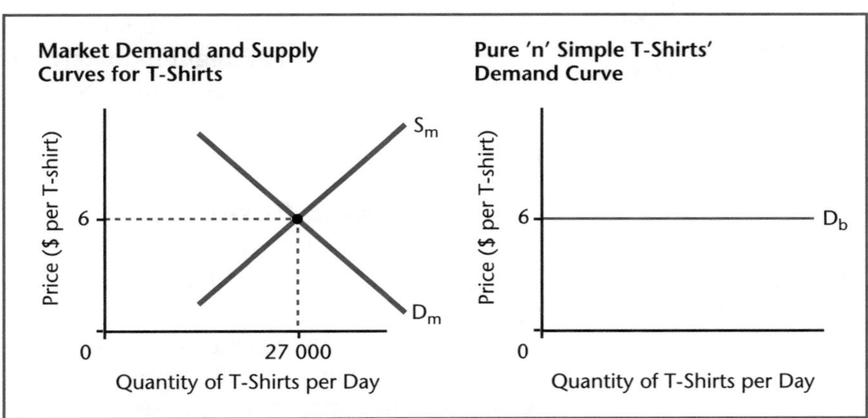

Equilibrium in the T-shirt market occurs where the market demand and supply curves, D_m and S_m, meet as shown in the graph on the left. The equilibrium price ($6) sets the position of the business's demand curve, D_b, in the graph on the right.

Palate raises the average price of its meals from $10 to $11, as shown in Figure 5.3, it will lose some, but not all, of its customers. Quantity demanded will fall from 200 to 100 meals a day. If the restaurant lowers the average price of meals from $10 to $9, there will be an increase in quantity demanded, from 200 to 300. Hence, the restaurant faces the demand curve D. Since customers see other restaurants as possible substitutes, a percentage change in the price of a meal causes an even greater change in quantity demanded. In other words, the monopolistic competitor's demand curve is elastic.

FIGURE 5.3
Demand Faced by a Monopolistic Competitor

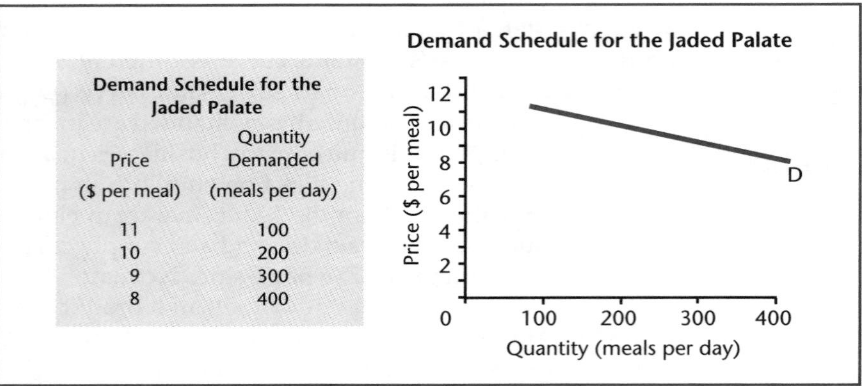

Demand Schedule for the Jaded Palate

Price ($ per meal)	Quantity Demanded (meals per day)
11	100
10	200
9	300
8	400

The restaurant's demand curve, D, has a negative slope, so that a change in price (for example, from $10 to $11) causes an opposite change in quantity demanded (from 200 to 100 meals). Since demand is elastic, the change in quantity demanded is relatively large compared to the initial change in price.

Oligopoly

mutual interdependence: the relationship between oligopolists, in which the actions of each business affect the other businesses

In the case of an oligopoly, the fact that each business makes up a considerable part of the market leads to **mutual interdependence**. This is a situation where businesses in the industry cannot afford to ignore their competitors' actions that might indirectly affect sales. Because of mutual interdependence, businesses in an oligopoly can operate in either of two ways: as rivals, or as fellow players who co-operate to increase combined profits.

Rivalry Among Businesses

market share: a business's proportion of total market sales

Businesses in an oligopoly where rivalry prevails are concerned with maintaining their **market share**, or the proportion of total market sales they control. Because their actions influence rivals, these businesses must take into account the reactions of competitors whenever they consider a price change. They must then predict how the responses of other businesses will influence their own market share.

Let's consider the hypothetical situation of Universal Motors and its luxury car, the Centaur. If Universal Motors increases its price for the Centaur, competitors will likely keep the prices of their luxury cars constant in order to increase their sales. Thus, Universal Motors will lose some of its market share to its competitors. If, in contrast, Universal Motors lowers its price for the Centaur, its competitors will reduce their prices as well, so as not to lose market share. Thus, Universal Motors' market share will remain constant. These actions and reactions among rival companies in an oligopoly are summarized in Figure 5.4.

FIGURE 5.4 Actions and Reactions Among Rivals in an Oligopoly

Action of Company A	Probable Response of Competitors	Effect on Company A's Market Share	Company A's Quantity Demanded
raise price	keep prices constant	product now high-priced, so market share falls	large decrease as market share lost to competitors
lower price	match price drop	since all companies selling at lower price, Company A's market share stays constant	small increase as lower prices for all companies attract new buyers

Now, let's continue the example of Universal Motors in Figure 5.5. If the original price of the Centaur is $30 000, a price increase to $35 000 will cause competitors to keep their prices constant, and the market share for Centaurs will drop from 20 000 to 10 000 cars. The change in quantity demanded (from point *b* to point *a*) causes the demand curve for this price range to be fairly flat. If Universal Motors lowers the price of the Centaur from $30 000 to $20 000, competitors will lower the prices of their cars. Sales

FIGURE 5.5
Demand Faced Among Rivals in an Oligopoly

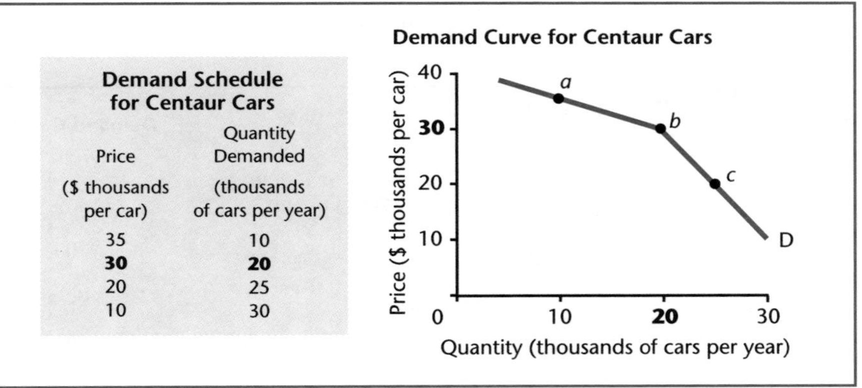

Demand Schedule for Centaur Cars

Price ($ thousands per car)	Quantity Demanded (thousands of cars per year)
35	10
30	**20**
20	25
10	30

The demand curve for Centaur cars is shown as two differently sloped segments. When Universal Motors raises the price above $30 000, competitors keep their prices constant to raise their sales. The results are a substantial drop in the quantity demanded of Centaurs, and a flat demand curve (from point *b* to point *a*). If price moves below $30 000, competitors are forced to drop their prices as well. Thus, quantity demanded for Centaurs increases by only a minor amount, producing a steep demand curve (from point *b* to point *c*).

of Centaurs will increase—from 20 000 to 25 000—but not in equal proportion to the price drop. Thus, the demand curve for this price range (from point *b* to point *c*) is steep. As shown on the graph in Figure 5.5, the result is a **kinked demand curve**—a demand curve with two segments, one fairly flat and one steep, with the kink or bend at the original price of $30 000 (point *b*). This kinked demand curve is typical of oligopolies in which businesses jostle one another for profit and market dominance.

kinked demand curve: a demand curve with two segments, one fairly flat and one steep, that is typical of rival oligopolists

Co-operation Among Businesses

Oligopolists can also co-operate in ways that are against the interests of consumers. In an oligopoly, for example, there may be an unspoken understanding that one company—usually the largest—acts as the price leader. In a case of **price leadership**, other companies will follow any price change initiated by the price leader, and adjust their output accordingly. In the past, price leadership has occurred in the automobile and farm-machinery industries. Oligopolies may take their co-operation even further. When oligopolists band together—either secretly or openly—as if they were a monopoly, they are practising **collusion**. In this case, they act jointly to maximize total profits. To do so, the businesses must first estimate the most profitable output level, and then agree to restrict production in order to keep the total market output down and price high. When this sort of agreement among producers is a formal one, the businesses together are known as a **cartel**. The best-known example of a cartel is OPEC, the Organization of Petroleum Exporting Countries.

price leadership: an understanding among oligopolists that one business will initiate all price changes in the market and the others will follow by adjusting their prices and output accordingly

collusion: oligopolists acting together as if they are a monopoly

cartel: a union of oligopolists who have a formal market-sharing agreement

Monopoly

As sole supplier of a product, a monopolist faces the same demand curve as that for the entire market—a curve with a negative slope. Therefore, the monopolist has considerable ability to influence price. Figure 5.6 gives the example of Megacomp, the only seller of large supercomputers.

FIGURE 5.6
Demand Faced by a Monopolist

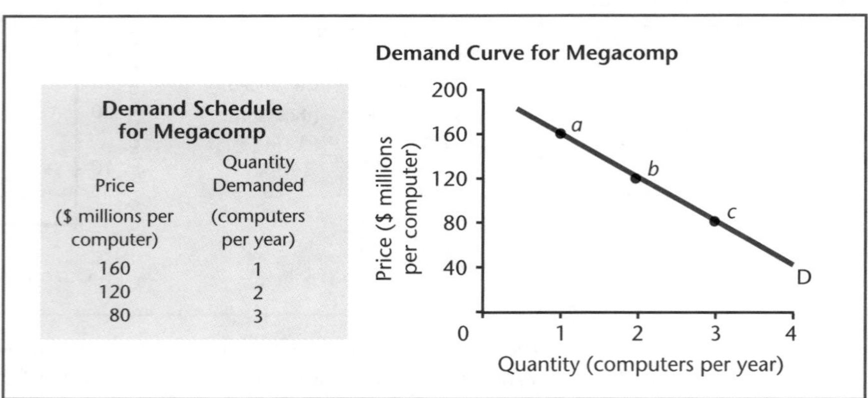

Demand Schedule for Megacomp

Price ($ millions per computer)	Quantity Demanded (computers per year)
160	1
120	2
80	3

The demand curve for the individual business is identical to the market demand curve, D. As D shows, if Megacomp increases the price from $120 million to $160 million, quantity demanded decreases from 2 to 1 computer.

NONPRICE COMPETITION

nonprice competition: efforts to increase demand through product differentiation, advertising, or both

Because of the similarities they share, monopolistic competition and oligopoly are often lumped together in a general category known *as imperfect competition*. In addition to changing product prices, imperfectly competitive firms can compete in another way. **Nonprice competition** refers to the efforts of imperfectly competitive producers to increase demand for their products by swaying consumer preferences. The two strategies used are product differentiation and advertising.

Product Differentiation

product differentiation: efforts to make a product distinct from that of competitors

Product differentiation is a company's attempt to distinguish its product from that of competitors. Designer labels on a clothing manufacturer's jeans, or an "exclusive" set of toppings on a pizza restaurant's product are examples of product differentiation. The changes made to a product may be cosmetic—slick packaging, for example—or they may be substantial, such as providing the product at a more convenient location. Product differentiation has two goals: to increase demand (thus raising the quantity demanded at every price), and to decrease demand elasticity (so that prices can be increased without losing customers to competitors). Meeting both goals increases a business's profit and market power.

Advertising

Advertising can play two roles in imperfectly competitive markets. It can provide the consumer with information, as with newspaper classified ads, and it can promote consumer preferences for a product, as is commonly the case for radio and television ads. Advertising has the same two goals as product differentiation: to increase demand for the product, and to make the demand more inelastic. For example, a producer of athletic shoes, such as Nike, advertises in order to raise the quantity demanded of its shoes at every possible price. The producer also aims to make consumers less likely to switch brands if Nike shoes go up in price. Again, the company's profit and market power are increased if its advertising strategy meets the two goals.

Nonprice Competition and Business

For a single imperfectly competitive business, product differentiation and advertising increase both revenues and costs. Total revenue increases when the demand for the business's product increases and the demand becomes more inelastic. However, the business's total costs increase because of the extra costs of undertaking nonprice competition. If the gain in total revenues outweighs the extra costs of product differentiation and advertising, profits are increased. Whether or not this extra profit can be made depends on how easy it is to influence consumer preferences. Businesses in oligopolies typically find advertising a profitable strategy, especially when large advertising budgets serve as an entry barrier. Not surprisingly, businesses in such markets are Canada's top advertisers, as shown in Figure 5.7.

FIGURE 5.7 Canada's Top Advertisers (1995)

		$ Millions
1.	General Motors of Canada	111.4
2.	Bell Canada Enterprises	94.2
3.	Procter & Gamble	84.2
4.	Hudson's Bay Company	72.3
5.	Vycom Electronics	67.8
6.	Government of Canada	67.6
7.	Sears Canada	67.2
8.	Chrysler Canada	58.2
9.	Viacom Enterprises	57.8
10.	Kraft Canada	57.3

Source: Nielsen Marketing Research.

Nonprice Competition and the Consumer

For the consumer, product differentiation leads to higher prices by raising per-unit costs and enhancing an individual business's market power. However, consumers will likely have more choices because of businesses' efforts to differentiate their products. So, for example, the fact that TVs produced by competing companies are distinctive raises the average price of TVs, but gives consumers a wider selection of possible features than they would otherwise have had.

The impact of advertising on the consumer is also mixed. In some cases, advertising is anti-competitive, leading to more market power for established firms. However, advertising can also increase competition. By giving new companies the chance to familiarize buyers with their products, advertising can offer consumers more choice. In this case, advertising lessens the market power of established businesses and leads to more industry flexibility. An example that portrays both possible effects is the Canadian soft-drink industry. This market is an oligopoly that for decades was dominated by two giant businesses, Coca-Cola and PepsiCo, whose market power was enhanced by their high levels of advertising. However, partly through the effects of advertising, smaller private-label producers (usually connected with supermarket chains) were able to become major players in the early 1990s, with a combined market share of almost 30 percent.

BRIEF REVIEW

1. A perfectly competitive business is a price-taker, and thus faces a horizontal demand curve, with the price being set by the market.
2. A monopolistic competitor faces an elastic demand curve with a negative slope.
3. Oligopolies are characterized by mutual interdependence. Rivalry among oligopolists creates a kinked demand curve because of competitors' responses to price changes. Co-operation among oligopolists may lead to price leadership or collusion. If collusion is formal and explicit, the companies make up a cartel.
4. Monopolists face the demand curve of the entire market—a curve with a negative slope.
5. Product differentiation and advertising are forms of nonprice competition common in imperfectly competitive markets. Their effect on the consumer is mixed.

INDUSTRIAL CONCENTRATION

Concentration ratio: the percentage of total sales revenue earned by the largest businesses in the market

It is usually fairly obvious that an industry is either perfectly competitive or monopolistic. Most industries, however, fall between the two extremes, and therefore represent some form of imperfect competition. It is not always easy to establish whether an imperfectly competitive industry is monopolistically competitive or an oligopoly. The most common indicator is a **concentration ratio**, which is the percentage of total sales revenue in a market earned by the largest business firms.

Concentration ratios are commonly measured for the four largest business firms in any market, in which case they are known as four-firm ratios. An industry might be considered to be a monopolistic competition if its four-firm ratio is below 50 percent. If the four-firm ratio is above 50 percent, the industry is considered to be an oligopoly. So, for example, if a certain market has total annual sales revenues of $100 million, with the four largest companies having sales of $42 million, $27 million, $14 million, and $8 million, the four-firm ratio is 91 percent ($\frac{42 + 27 + 14 + 8}{100} \times 100\%$). In this case, the industry is considered an oligopoly. Concentration ratios for selected Canadian industries are shown in Figure 5.8.

Because of rapidly expanding foreign trade, Canadian manufacturing markets are in a state of flux. Before these changes began in the late 1980s, about half of Canada's manufacturing industries had four-firm ratios of over 50 percent, and could therefore be classified as oligopolies. Many Canadian service industries are concentrated as well. Compared to the United States, Canada has relatively small markets, each of which are more likely to be dominated by just one or a few businesses. It has been estimated that, overall, about three-fifths of Canadian economic activity takes place in concentrated markets that are either monopolies or oligopolies. In the U.S. economy, the corresponding estimate is just over one-fifth.

FIGURE 5.8 Concentration Ratios in Selected Canadian Industries (1988)

	Share of Industry Sales by Four Largest Businesses
Tobacco products	98.9
Petroleum and coal products	74.5
Transportation	68.4
Beverages	59.2
Metal mining	58.9
Paper and allied industries	38.9
Electrical Products	32.1
Printing, publishing, and allied industries	25.7
Food	19.6
Finance	16.4
Machinery	11.3
Retail trade	9.7
Clothing industries	6.6
Construction	2.2

Sales in industries such as tobacco products, beverages, and transportation equipment are dominated by the four top businesses in each industry, indicating high levels of concentration. Meanwhile, in industries such as retail trade, clothing, and construction, the four top businesses in each industry have a much smaller proportion of industry sales, indicating low levels of concentration.

Source: Statistics Canada, *Annual Report of the Minister of Industry, Science and Technology under the Corporations and Labour Unions Return Act, Part 1 — Corporations 1988* (October 1991), cat. no. 61-210, p. 94. Reproduced by authority of the Minister of Industry, 1994.

Concentration ratios are not foolproof indicators of market structure, however. Statistics Canada includes only domestic businesses in its calculations and defines each market as for all of Canada. In markets where there is significant international trade, official concentration ratios underestimate competition by ignoring the role of imports. So, for example, Canada's motor vehicle industry would appear less concentrated if foreign imports were taken into account. In markets that are highly localized, meaning that one or two businesses dominate certain regions, national concentration ratios overestimate the level of competition. For example, while the many radio broadcasters in Canada would result in low official concentration ratios, the fact that most broadcasters operate in highly concentrated regional markets would not be reflected.

The Debate Over Industrial Concentration

industrial concentration: market domination by one or a few large businesses

The effect of market power on the economy can be studied in the context of **industrial concentration**, which refers to the domination of a market by one or a few large companies. Because of their small numbers and great size, these companies possess significant market power. Figure 5.9 gives some indication of how large some individual Canadian companies are in relation to Canadian business as a whole.

FIGURE 5.9 Concentration in the Canadian Economy (1993)

In Nonfinancial Industries, Share of Assets and Share of Revenues for 25 Leading Enterprises

	Assets	Revenues
Foreign	4.4	7.5
Canadian		
Private enterprises	11.2	6.6
Government enterprises	13.1	5.0
	28.7%	19.2%*

*figures may not sum due to rounding

Canada's leading 25 enterprises (ranked by assets) control over a quarter of total assets in nonfinancial industries. Of this, the bulk was controlled by Canadian enterprises—both private and government-owned. In terms of sales revenue in nonfinancial industries, the leading 25 enterprises (ranked by revenues) have a less significant share.

Source: Statistics Canada, *Parliamentary Report of the Minister of Industry, Science and Technology under the Corporations and Labour Unions Return Act, Part 1—Corporations* (April 1995), cat. no. 61-220, p. 48. Reproduced by authority of the Minister of Industry, 1997.

Can industrial concentration work to the advantage of consumers? To answer this question, we must weigh the costs and the benefits of huge companies dominating a given market.

Increasing Returns to Scale Versus Market Power

Defenders of industrial concentration emphasize the role of increasing returns to scale. They say this is especially important in a time when businesses are more likely than ever to compete in huge global markets. In many industries, only large businesses with a substantial market share can produce the quantity of output necessary to take advantage of increasing returns to scale. As a result, these big businesses have lower per-unit costs than would perfectly competitive businesses in the same market. These cost savings may then be passed on to consumers in the form of lower prices. Critics of industrial concentration say that the benefits of economies of scale must be weighed against the market power held by large monopolists and oligopolists. This market power allows big companies to charge a higher price than would occur with more competition in the market.

Technical Innovation

Some people have argued that "big business" is needed to promote innovation and technological advances. However, recent evidence points to the opposite conclusion. Companies in highly concentrated industries—either monopolies or oligopolies—tend not to innovate as rapidly as those in more competitive markets, where the continual jockeying for profit encourages improvements in products and production processes.

BRIEF REVIEW

1. Concentration ratios are measures of the percentage of total sales revenue in a market as earned by the biggest companies within the industry. These ratios suggest the degree of competition in an industry, although they do have some deficiencies.
2. Industrial concentration has its supporters and its critics. The arguments for and against concentration centre around increasing returns to scale, excess market power, and technical innovation.

KEY CONCEPTS

perfect competition
monopolistic competition
oligopoly
monopoly
entry barriers
natural monopoly
predatory pricing
market power
business's demand curve
mutual interdependence
market share
kinked demand curve
price leadership
collusion
cartel
nonprice competition
product differentiation
concentration ratio
industrial concentration

ANALYSIS AND APPLICATION

1. Categorize each seller below based on the type of market it operates in. Explain each of your answers.
   a. a cattle farmer
   b. a company that produces a popular type of word-processing software
   c. a photocopying shop in a large metropolitan area
   d. a seller of Canadian dollars in foreign currency markets
   e. a life insurance company
   f. a liquor store in a remote village
   g. a visual artist
   h. a country that produces a valuable radioactive mineral found in no other part of the world

2. For each case below, state what type of market the business is in and then depict the change using a graph that shows the business's demand curve(s).
   a. a large tobacco company uses advertising to boost its share of the cigarette market in third world countries
   b. a barber shop in a big city benefits from the closing of a nearby barber shop
   c. a lobster fisherman faces a higher lobster price
   d. Canada Post's regular letter delivery is increasingly affected by e-mail and fax machines

3. Find examples in the media of demand changes affecting sellers in each of the four market structures. In each case, outline the impact on the business's demand curve.

4. For each of the following cases of nonprice competition, outline the likely effects on (i) the business undertaking the strategy, (ii) other businesses in the market, and (iii) consumers.
   a. A recording company is the first to produce recordings of a new style of popular music.
   b. A major corporation that makes laundry soap increases the amount it spends on advertising.
   c. A cosmetics firm changes the brand name of one of its perfumes to give it greater appeal to young buyers.
   d. A lawyer starting her practice decides to break with tradition by advertising the prices she charges.

5. An industry is made up of six firms with sales of $50 million, $55 million, $80 million, $30 million, $65 million, and $100 million.
   a. Calculate the industry's four-firm concentration ratio.
   b. How would you categorize this industry?

6. Identify whether official concentration ratios for the following products will tend to overestimate or underestimate the level of competition.
   a. magazines
   b. telephone services

7. (Advanced Question)
   Some cases of price discrimination can be defended as being in the best interests of society while others are indefensible. Give a hypothetical example of each case, and explain the reasoning behind each choice.

8. Canada's chartered banking system, discussed in detail in Chapter 14, is highly concentrated. Use online sources such as the Department of Finance's fact sheet, "The Canadian Financial System" (at http://www.fin.gc.ca/fctsheet/sum95e.html) and the Canadian Bankers Association's "Bank Facts" (at http://www.cba.ca/pub/bankfacts/index.html) to research recent trends in this industry. Based on your research, outline to what extent you believe the high level of concentration in this industry has benefited consumers.

Advancing Economic Thought

PROPHET OF CAPITALISM'S DOOM

The Economic Theories of Karl Marx

Marx and His Influence

Karl Marx (1818–1883) is best known as the founder of the international socialist and communist movements. He was born in the German state of Prussia, studied philosophy, and worked as a journalist before beginning his career as a political activist. Exiled from both Germany and France, he moved to England where, with his close friend Friedrich Engels (1820–1895), he applied his revolutionary views to the fields of philosophy, history, and economics.

Of these three subjects, it was what he called "the confounded ramifications of Political Economy" that gave him the most headaches. In his mammoth three-volume work, *Das Kapital*, Marx developed his theory of economics. He concluded that capitalism, by its very nature, is unjust.

Karl Marx
Source: The Bettmann Archive

Marx's View of Capitalism

Marx's years in England allowed him to witness first-hand the effects of the British Industrial Revolution. By the mid-1800s manufacturing was the mainstay of Britain's economy, and a large portion of the population had moved from rural areas to the burgeoning new cities in hopes of finding jobs in manufacturing. In the long run, the industrial transformation experienced in Britain enhanced the economic well-being of the majority of citizens of industrialized countries. But in Marx's day, the benefits of the Industrial Revolution seemed to be limited to the wealthier members of society. Living conditions were horrendous for the labouring classes in the rapidly expanding urban areas:

> And what cities! It was not merely that smoke hung over them and filth impregnated them, that the elementary public services—water-supply, sanitation, street-cleaning, open spaces, and so on—could not keep pace with the mass migration of men into cities, thus producing, especially after 1830, epidemics of cholera, typhoid and an appalling constant toll [from] air pollution and water pollution... The new city populations...[were] pressed into overcrowded and bleak slums, whose very sight froze the heart of the observer.[1]

Marx's Theory of Capitalism

The Labour Theory of Value Marx blamed these conditions on capitalism itself. His attack was based on his "labour theory of value," in which prices of products depend on how much labour goes into producing them. According to this theory, only company owners (whom Marx called capitalists) have the financial resources to hire workers and sell the resulting output. By paying wages that are less than the value workers contribute to production, company owners are able to skim off a portion of value for themselves. By doing this, they engage in capitalist exploitation of their workforce.

The Theory of Exploitation An example will help explain Marx's theory. It may take a worker four hours to make a shirt and eight hours to make a suit. According to Marx, the price of the shirt should then be half that of the suit; say the prices of the two products are $40 and $80, respectively. If so, workers producing either two shirts or one suit in an eight-hour day create $80 of value. Let's assume that daily wages in the textile trade are $50, and that the cost of materials plus daily wear and tear on the machines each worker uses is $10. The portion of value kept by the capitalist, or each worker's "surplus value," is therefore $20 [$80 – ($50 + $10)] as shown in the table below.

Marx's Theory of Exploitation

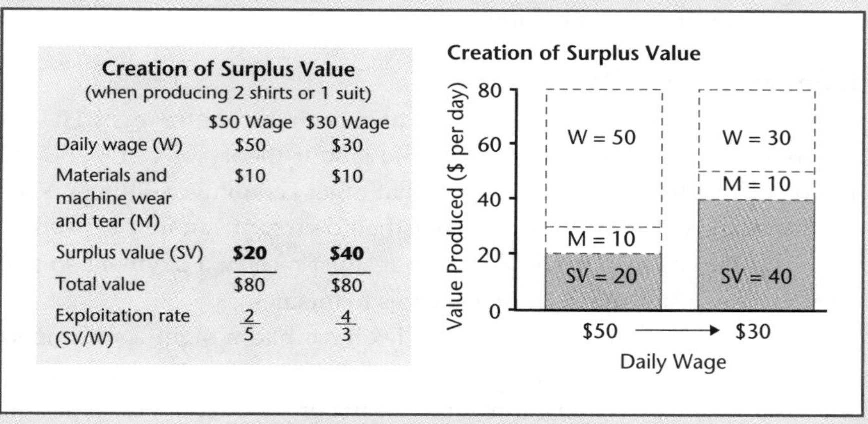

Creation of Surplus Value
(when producing 2 shirts or 1 suit)

	$50 Wage	$30 Wage
Daily wage (W)	$50	$30
Materials and machine wear and tear (M)	$10	$10
Surplus value (SV)	**$20**	**$40**
Total value	$80	$80
Exploitation rate (SV/W)	$\frac{2}{5}$	$\frac{4}{3}$

If daily wages are reduced from $50 to $30, daily surplus value extracted from each worker is increased (the shaded portions in the bar graphs). As a result, surplus value as a proportion of daily wages also increases.

Source: Adapted from Stanley L. Brue, *The Evolution of Economic Thought,* 5th ed. (Fort Worth: The Dryden Press, 1994), p.195.

Dynamics of Capitalism

With time, Marx argued, the rate of exploitation by capitalists would worsen, meaning that surplus value would increase as a proportion of the daily wage. This could happen either through further decreases in wages or a lengthening of the workday.

Decreased Wages Capitalists try to slash wages as much as possible. The daily wage in our example could drop from $50 to $30, while the cost of materials, plus the wear and tear on machines, remains constant at $10.

As a result, surplus value would rise to $40 [$80 – ($30 + $10)]. Surplus value as a proportion of the daily wage would then increase from $20/$50 to $40/$30.

Lengthening of the Workday Capitalists also have an incentive to raise the number of hours workers put in each day. This expands the daily value created by each worker. As long as the daily wage remains the same, surplus value as a proportion of this wage would again rise.

Communist Revolution

Marx believed that capitalist exploitation would worsen the living standards of workers until, finally, workers would violently revolt, first in the nations of Western Europe, which were most industrialized at the time Marx was writing, and later in other parts of the world. The overthrow of capitalism would usher in a socialist age based on common ownership of property. Once socialist ownership had been consolidated, true communism would arrive. Governments would disappear and people would be able to live in complete liberty. Society's guiding principle would then be "from each according to his abilities, and to each according to his needs."[2]

Relevance for Today

Marx's theories have been the source of continuing controversy. His detractors challenge the usefulness of the labour theory of value and the notion of surplus value. They argue that other economic resources, such as capital and entrepreneurship, make their own contributions to production, and that owners of these resources must receive a payment so that they will keep supplying their resources to businesses.

At the same time, Marx's theories have had a significant impact throughout the 20th century. Socialists—who advocate that the community as a whole own and control the means of production, distribution, and exchange—have held power in many parts of the world. Among socialists, communists have accepted the bulk of Marx's theories and applied them in countries subject to communist rule. In most nations, however, Marx's influence has been less direct. Labour movements, for example, owe much to Marx's theories of capitalist exploitation. Through gradual reform, rather than revolution, socialists in countries such as Canada have played a major part in social reform and in creating modern mixed economies in which governments are much more important than they were a century ago.

Notes

[1] Adapted from *Industry and Empire: From 1750 to the Present Day* by E.J. Hobsbawm, (Penguin Books, 1969). Copyright © E.J. Hobsbawm, 1968, 1969. Reprinted by permission.

[2] Karl Marx, *Critique of the Gotha Program*, 1875.

1. **For the textile industry example given previously, imagine that each worker's wages are raised from $50 to $60 per day, while other costs remain the same. Create a bar graph to show the resulting change in surplus value per worker. How does surplus value change as a proportion of the daily wage?**

2. **Imagine that the daily wage of a textile worker remains at $50, but the workday is lengthened to 12 hours, causing each worker to raise production to $120 per day and increasing the other costs (materials and wear on machines) to $15 per worker.**
   a. **Create a bar graph to show the new surplus value per worker.**
   b. **Explain how surplus value changes as a proportion of the daily wage.**
   c. **Explain whether company owners are worse off or better off as a result of the lengthened workday.**

3. **Average living standards for workers in most capitalist countries have risen significantly since the period when Marx was writing. Outline two reasons why Marx's prediction of falling living standards for workers in these countries has proven to be incorrect.**

SIDELINE

PUMPING UP PRICE

The OPEC Cartel

In most countries, collusion is illegal because of its harmful effects on the consumer. Thus cartels that involve private companies operate secretly. However, there is nothing to stop national governments themselves from colluding. No wonder, therefore, that the best-known example of a cartel is an international one. OPEC, the Organization of Petroleum Exporting Countries, is made up of many of the major oil-producing countries, including Algeria, Gabon, Iran, Saudi Arabia, Iraq, Kuwait, Venezuela, Nigeria, Qatar, the United Arab Emirates, Libya, and Indonesia.

OPEC in the 1970s

During the 1970s, OPEC members made spectacular gains. Through market-sharing agreements, these countries limited their production, thus driving the world price of oil from under US$3 per barrel before 1973 to over US$30 by the end of the 1970s. This famous oil shock had major effects on the world economy. There was a huge outflow of "petro-dollars" from oil-importing to oil-exporting countries. While oil producers benefited, bewildered oil consumers suffered.

OPEC's success sprang from two main factors. Because the short-run demand for oil is inelastic, OPEC members could cut quantity supplied by a relatively small amount and still significantly raise the world price and their combined revenues. OPEC's success also hinged on the leadership of Saudi Arabia, by far the largest exporter of oil, whose government preserved the cartel's power and stabilized price by adjusting its national production levels.

OPEC in the 1980s

During the 1980s, OPEC's influence on world oil prices waned because of three trends. First, the high oil prices of the 1970s had gradually forced consumers to find ways to reduce their oil consumption. In the long run, therefore, the demand curve for oil became elastic, with price changes having a much larger effect on quantity demanded than in the short run. Second, the high prices of the 1970s meant that oil sources previously too expensive to be exploited became profitable. As a result, non-OPEC countries—such as Canada, the United States, and Great Britain—tapped these sources, thus raising their production levels and pushing up the total quantity supplied in the oil market. This left OPEC countries with a smaller share of the market. Finally, once oil prices began to fall, some OPEC members responded by secretly selling more oil than they were allowed to supply under the joint agreement.

The temptation to cheat is a potential hazard for all cartels. By producing extra output, a member can raise its own revenues. Sooner or later, however, cheating within a cartel becomes common knowledge. Once this happens, it is likely

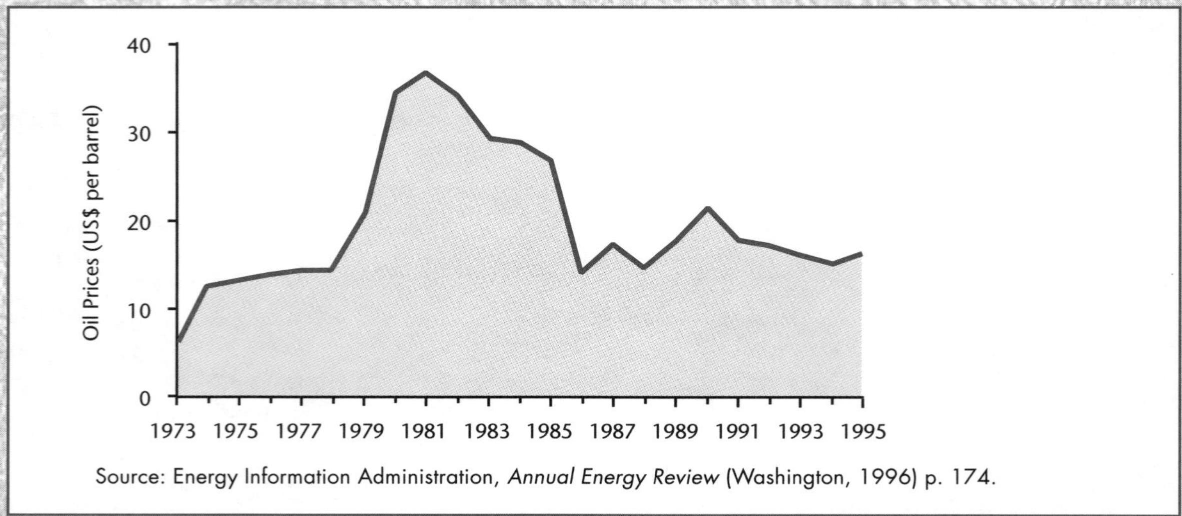

Source: Energy Information Administration, *Annual Energy Review* (Washington, 1996) p. 174.

that the cartel will fall apart as all members disregard the agreement by selling more. Price is then driven back down to its value before the cartel was formed. As OPEC's experience shows, cartels are often only temporarily successful in raising price and profits for the producers involved.

1. Non-OPEC countries supply over half of the international demand for oil, even though they have a much smaller proportion of the world's proven reserves. Explain what effect this imbalance could have on future oil prices.

2 a. Access the Government of Canada's website (at http://canada.gc.ca/) and find the online version of *Canada's Energy Outlook*, published by Natural Resources Canada (NRC). What change in oil prices do NRC analysts forecast between 1992 to 2005?

b. On what prediction concerning OPEC production is this forecast based?

c. Check this forecast against current oil prices by accessing the U.S. Energy Information Administration's *Weekly Petroleum Status Report* (at http://www.eia.doe.gov/).

STOKING THE FIRES OF COMPETITION

Anti-Combines Legislation in Canada

Laws aimed at preventing industrial concentration and abuses of market power are known as anti-combines legislation. Canada's anti-combines laws date back to 1889, but until recently were largely unsuccessful.

That violations were considered criminal offences was one reason for the lack of success. Criminal cases require that guilt be established beyond a reasonable doubt. This requirement does not easily make use of economic analysis—analysis that is so vital to considering anti-competitive behaviour. A second reason is that Canadian governments have traditionally been less opposed to industrial concentration than those in other countries, the United States in particular. Many Canadians have argued that domestic businesses need to be large in order to be internationally competitive, especially in sectors with significant economies of scale. Canada's lawmakers, therefore, have typically given the goal of international competitiveness and efficiency greater weight than domestic competition.

The Competition Act of 1986 was a major reform of Canada's anti-combines legislation. It offered a combination of criminal and civil provisions, strengthened penalties, and built on the almost century-long experience of anti-combines legislation and prosecution. The Act covers business practices that prevent or lessen competition, including the practices described in the following sections. Of these, the first three are still criminal offences, with penalties ranging from fines to possible imprisonment of company executives, while the last two are considered civil matters, which are reviewed by a government-administered panel known as the Competition Tribunal.

Conspiracy

Businesses that conspire or agree to fix prices, allocate markets, or restrict entry to markets can be charged under the Competition Act. In order for a business to be found guilty, its actions must be proven to unduly restrain competition. Violators can face fines of up to $10 million or prison terms of up to five years. One case of conspiracy involved nine real estate boards in five provinces. After complaints from customers and some industry members about commissions, services, and other practices, an investigation began. The Canadian Real Estate Association came forward to settle the matter, which was resolved out of court.

Bid-Rigging

Companies that bid on contracts may arrange among themselves who will win each contract and at what price. By taking turns at winning bids and by inflating prices, all conspirators are winners. Unlike the more general conspiracy charge, bid-rigging is considered an automatic offence; undue restraint does not have to be proven. In a recent case, three heating equipment suppliers were convicted on six counts of sharing out the market, in part by rigging bids; each company was fined $1000 on each count. Penalties are at the courts' discretion, but reflect the seriousness with which the courts view the crime, and so can include, for example, $1 million fines and five-year prison terms.

Predatory Pricing

The policy and practice of temporarily dropping a price for a product below its average cost to drive a new competitor out of business is a criminal offence. In one case, a company provided free supplies of a drug to hospitals. Because the company's goal was to generate long-term sales after eliminating competition, the company was fined $50 000.

Abuse of Dominant Position

Companies that control most of the sales in a market are not allowed to use their dominant position to engage in anti-competitive behaviour. One recent case of abuse involved the Canadian maker of (and former patent-holder for) the artificial sweetener aspartame, known as NutraSweet.[1] According to the findings of the Competition Tribunal, the company had used its power to have several major purchasers of aspartame sign long-term contracts to buy NutraSweet exclusively, rather than the products of the competition. The company was not allowed to enforce these old contracts or to negotiate new ones of the same sort. Typically, the Tribunal requires that the guilty company cease its anti-competitive behaviour. The Tribunal can also use stronger measures to restore competition in the market; for example, by requiring partial break-up of a business into smaller units.

Mergers

A merger is the combining of two companies into one. The Competition Tribunal has the power to prohibit a merger in Canada—no matter what the size or nationality of the companies involved—if the merger could prevent or substantially reduce competition. Exceptions are often made if a merger will increase efficiency and pass on savings to consumers. In practice, it is uncommon for the Tribunal to disallow a merger. Mergers can be of three sorts, depending on the connection between the companies involved.

Horizontal Merger A horizontal merger combines former competitors. One example of a horizontal merger is the 1989 purchase of Wardair by its rival, Canadian Airlines International. Horizontal mergers allow businesses to take advantage of the economies of scale that arise from combining production. Horizontal mergers can also reduce the level of competition in the market, thereby giving the new, combined company more market power and potential profit.

Vertical Merger A vertical merger combines a business and its supplier. A steelmaker that purchases an iron ore mine is one example, as is a fashion design company merging with a clothing wholesaler. Vertical mergers can guarantee a supply of needed inputs or can ensure distribution of the product. For example, McDonald's has taken over many of its food suppliers, and PepsiCo's acquisition of Pizza Hut ensured that PepsiCo soft drinks are sold in these restaurants.

Conglomerate Merger A conglomerate merger combines businesses in unrelated industries. The main reason for such mergers is to help companies smooth out fluctuations in profit that occur during booms and recessions. A company whose profit plummets during a downturn in the economy—a manufacturer of luxury yachts, for example—might decide to purchase a chain of discount hardware stores, which are not affected in the same way.

Sources

Consumer and Corporate Affairs Canada, *Competition Policy in Canada: The First Hundred Years*; Robert S. Nozick and Charlotte Neff, *The Annotated Competition Act* (Toronto: Carswell, 1987), pp. 78, 79, 83.

[1] Fagan and Drew, "Nutrasweet Case to Set Precedent," in *The Globe and Mail*, 10 January 1990, pp. B1, B5.

1. Which of the three sorts of mergers is least likely to lead to a reduction of competition in an industry? Why?

2. Using either media reports or the information included in the Competition Tribunal's website (at http://www.ct-tc.gc.ca/rcteng.htm), summarize a recent case before the Competition Tribunal involving (a) a merger that could lessen competition, and (b) abuse of dominant position.

Chapter Six
The Role of Profit

It is not from the benevolence of the butcher, the brewer, or the baker that we expect our dinner but from their regard to their own interest.
—Adam Smith, Scottish economist

Ask most businesspeople why they are in business and they'll give one answer—to make a profit. In fact, profits are expected, so economists consider "normal profit" an implicit cost of doing business. As the driving force behind business activity, profit is the key to understanding how businesses behave. In this chapter, we'll examine how the quest for profit is carried out by businesses in the four market structures. We'll also look at how profit-making activity leads to significantly different results depending on the extent of competition in a market.

CHAPTER FOCUS

This chapter focuses on the following:

- the profit-maximizing output rule
- how businesses in each market structure maximize profits
- the effects of profit-maximizing behaviour on consumers in each market structure
- the short-run and long-run outcomes of profit-maximizing behaviour
- natural monopolies and how governments regulate them

PERFECT COMPETITION

How do businesses make operating decisions? They do so by comparing a range of potential revenues and costs. All businesses—whether they are perfect competitors, monopolistic competitors, oligopolists, or monopolists, and whatever their product—use the same general methods in pursuing maximum profit. However, each business must apply the methods differently, according to the market structure in which it operates. To examine profit-maximizing decisions and actions, we'll look first at perfect competitors—the "price-takers." As price-takers, perfectly competitive businesses accept one price, and can maximize their profits only by finding the optimum quantity of output.

Revenue Conditions

Given the horizontal demand curve the business faces, the perfect competitor's total revenue (TR), or the overall earnings from selling a product, is calculated by multiplying the product's price by each potential quantity of output (q). For example, if Pure 'n' Simple T-Shirts sells 250 shirts at a price of $6, then its total revenue is $1500 ($6 × 250). In addition to total revenue, the perfect competitor can examine two other revenue concepts to help make operating decisions: average revenue and marginal revenue.

Average Revenue

average revenue: a business's total revenue per unit of output

Average revenue (AR) is the business's total revenue per unit of output (q). When Pure 'n' Simple T-Shirts sells 250 shirts and its total revenue is $1500, its average revenue equals $6 per unit of the product:

$$\text{Average revenue (AR)} = \frac{\text{total revenue (TR)}}{\text{quantity of output (q)}}$$

$$\$6 \text{ per shirt} = \frac{\$1500}{250 \text{ shirts}}$$

Note that average revenue for Pure 'n' Simple T-Shirts equals each shirt's $6 price. For all businesses, regardless of the market structure in which they operate, price will equal average revenue. This is because price can be defined in the same way as average revenue—as the business's total revenue per unit of output. The only exception to this rule occurs when a business practises price discrimination, or charges different prices to different customers for exactly the same product.

Marginal Revenue

marginal revenue: the extra total revenue earned from an additional unit of output

Marginal revenue is the extra total revenue (ΔTR) earned when the business sells another unit of output (Δq). For example, if Pure 'n' Simple T-Shirts has an increase in total revenues from $1500 to $1620 when it increases its output from 250 to 270 shirts, then the marginal revenue of each of these last 20 shirts is $6:

$$\text{Marginal revenue (MR)} = \frac{\Delta TR}{\Delta q}$$

$$\$6 \text{ per shirt} = \frac{\$120}{20 \text{ shirts}}$$

Relationship Between Revenue Conditions and Demand

As the case of Pure 'n' Simple T-Shirts illustrates, average and marginal revenues are always equal for a perfectly competitive business. This follows from the fact that average revenue (or price) is constant at all possible quantities of output. Recall that when an average value such as average revenue is constant, it equals its related marginal value—which in this case is marginal revenue.

Figure 6.1 illustrates the relationships among price, average revenue, and marginal revenue for our example of Pure 'n' Simple T-Shirts. In the table, the values for price (column 1), marginal revenue (column 4), and average revenue (column 5) are identical. The demand curve this perfect competitor faces also represents the business's average revenue and marginal revenue curves. Because the business is a price-taker, this combined

FIGURE 6.1
Revenues for a Perfect Competitor

Revenue Schedules for Pure 'n' Simple T-Shirts

(1) Price (P) ($ per T-shirt)	(2) Quantity (q) (T-shirts per day)	(3) Total Revenue (TR) (P x q)	(4) Marginal Revenue (MR) (ΔTR/Δq)	(5) Average Revenue (AR) (TR/q)
—	0	0		—
6	80	480 →	480/80 = 6	480/80 = 6
6	200	1200 →	720/120 = 6	1200/200 = 6
6	250	1500 →	300/50 = 6	1500/250 = 6
6	270	1620 →	120/20 = 6	1620/270 = 6
6	280	1680 →	60/10 = 6	1680/280 = 6

Revenue Curves for Pure 'n' Simple T-Shirts

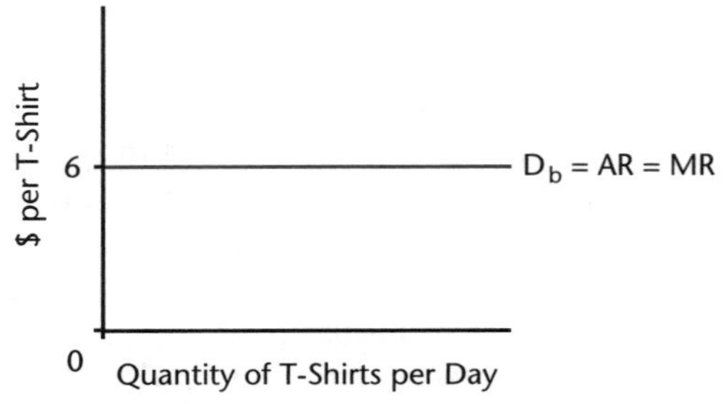

The business's demand schedule is shown in columns 1 and 2 of the table, which also shows that the constant values of price (P), average revenue (AR), and marginal revenue (MR) are identical. In the graph, the business's horizontal demand curve, D_b, also represents its AR and MR curves.

curve shows a constant value at all quantities of output. Thus, for a perfectly competitive business:

Price (P) = Average revenue (AR) = Marginal revenue (MR)

The Short Run

Because the forces that affect perfectly competitive markets in the short run are different from those in the long run, the actions of individual businesses depend on the relevant time period. We'll begin by analyzing how perfect competitors operate in the short run.

Profit Maximization

profit-maximizing output rule: produce at the level of output where marginal revenue and marginal cost intersect

Regardless of the market it operates in, any business can maximize its profit by following a single **profit-maximizing output rule**: produce the quantity of output (q) at which marginal revenue and marginal cost intersect.

Profit-maximizing rule: Marginal revenue (MR) = Marginal cost (MC)

Of course, this may result in an awkward quantity, such as 5.73 units, in which case the producer would choose the closest whole number, such as 6 units.

What happens if the condition MR = MC is not met? If each new unit of output is still providing more extra revenue to the business than it adds in cost, output should be increased in order to maximize profit. So, for example, if a business has a marginal revenue of $3 at its current output level, but the marginal cost of producing this unit is $2, the business is wise to increase its output. Recall that profit is the difference between total revenue and total cost. In this case, each additional unit of output is adding more revenue ($3) than it is costing ($2), so the profit added by this unit is $1. Profit-adding units such as these should be produced no matter how small the contribution to profit. Once output is raised to the level at which marginal revenue and marginal cost are equal, any further increase in output would cause the business's profit to fall. So, for example, if a business produces beyond the output level at which marginal revenue and marginal cost are both $3, the business will soon find the marginal revenue of $3 surpassed by a marginal cost of $4. Hence, each additional unit is subtracting from profit, and output should be returned to the point at which marginal revenue and marginal cost are equal.

So, perfect competitors, like all other businesses, must determine their profit-maximizing output by looking at the business's cost and revenue figures. Pure 'n' Simple T-Shirts, for example, would examine the data in Figure 6.2 and ask: "At what output level does marginal revenue intersect with marginal cost?" If the marginal revenue and marginal cost figures are graphed, as shown, we can see that the profit-maximizing point occurs at point *a*. As the closest associated whole number is 270, Pure 'n' Simple T-Shirts should choose a quantity of 270 T-shirts.

This point can be checked against the table in Figure 6.2. The figures for marginal revenue (column 3) and marginal cost (column 4) would pass through the same values nearest the output of 270 T-shirts (column 1). To verify this result, a business's owners might calculate the total profit they would make at every possible quantity of output. The highest positive (or lowest negative) profit figure in this column corresponds to the profit-maximizing quantity. In the case of Pure 'n' Simple T-Shirts, the owner would subtract total cost (column 8) from total revenue (column 7), to give total profit (column 9). So, scanning column 9, it is clear that the best choice is again at 270 shirts, where total profit reaches its highest value of $260 ($1620 – 1360).

While the profit-maximizing point can be verified with the table, using a graph to find this point has a bonus: the graph immediately shows whether or not the business is earning an economic profit. When price (P) exceeds average cost (AC) at the profit-maximizing output, the business enjoys a short-run economic profit. If price is less than average cost, the business suffers a loss, or negative profit. If the business is at a profit-maximizing output where price and average cost are equal, the business

FIGURE 6.2
Profit Maximization for a Perfect Competitor

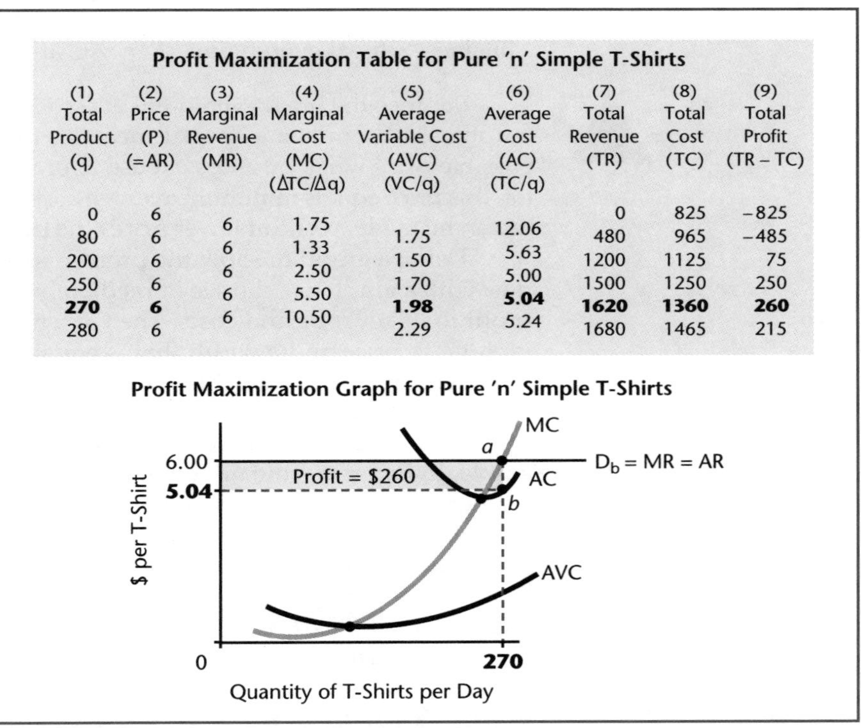

Profit Maximization Table for Pure 'n' Simple T-Shirts

(1) Total Product (q)	(2) Price (P) (=AR)	(3) Marginal Revenue (MR)	(4) Marginal Cost (MC) (ΔTC/Δq)	(5) Average Variable Cost (AVC) (VC/q)	(6) Average Cost (AC) (TC/q)	(7) Total Revenue (TR)	(8) Total Cost (TC)	(9) Total Profit (TR – TC)
0	6					0	825	–825
80	6	6	1.75	1.75	12.06	480	965	–485
200	6	6	1.33	1.50	5.63	1200	1125	75
250	6	6	2.50	1.70	5.00	1500	1250	250
270	**6**	6	5.50	**1.98**	**5.04**	**1620**	**1360**	**260**
280	6	6	10.50	2.29	5.24	1680	1465	215

Profit Maximization Graph for Pure 'n' Simple T-Shirts

The quantity of output at which the business maximizes its short-run profit—or minimizes its short-run loss—is found using either a graph or a table. On the graph, the profit-maximizing output is found where the MR and MC curves intersect at point *a*. Total profit is the area of the shaded rectangle, the width of which is the profit-maximizing output (q) and the height of which is the average revenue (AR) minus average cost (AC) at points *a* and *b*. In the table, this profit-maximizing output occurs where marginal cost (MC) in column 4 passes through the same values as the constant marginal revenue (MR) in column 3. The answer can be verified by calculating total profit at every output level, as in column 9, and then finding the output level at which the highest positive (or lowest negative) profit is possible.

Thinking About Economics

Does the profit-maximizing output rule also apply when a business is making a loss at all possible quantities of output?

Yes. In this case, the profit-maximizing output rule is used to determine the quantity at which the business makes the minimum possible loss. Since a loss is simply a negative profit, this means finding the output level with a negative profit that is closest to zero. For example, if a loss-making business is choosing between two output levels that provide negative profits of –\$100 and –\$300, it can minimize its loss by selecting the first of these output levels.

breakeven point: the profit-maximizing output where price (or average revenue) equals average cost

is making no economic profit, and is said to be at its **breakeven point**. Note, however, that at this point the business is still making a normal profit, so that the owners are paid a sufficient amount to keep their funds and entrepreneurial skills tied up in the business.

Business's breakeven point: P = AC at the profit-maximizing output

Because the breakeven point is associated with a profit-maximizing output, this term has a special meaning in economics. Only at a single possible price will a business choose to break even. For a perfect competitor, this price equals minimum average cost. At higher prices, positive profits can be made, while at lower prices the business can only make a loss.

Using a graph to show the profit-maximizing point has another bonus: with a graph, we can see immediately the relationship of a business's profit to its revenue and costs. The "revenue rectangle" has a height that is equal to price and a width that is equal to the quantity of output. The "cost rectangle" has a height that is equal to average cost and a width that is again equal to the quantity of output. The "profit rectangle" is the area of the revenue rectangle less the area of the cost rectangle. So, for example, in Figure 6.2 the marginal cost curve and marginal revenue curve for Pure 'n' Simple T-Shirts intersect at the profit-maximizing point. As we know from the table also, this point is closest to an output level of 270 shirts and a price of \$6 per shirt. Thus, the company's revenue rectangle has an area of \$1620 (\$6 price × 270 quantity). The cost rectangle has an area of \$1360 (\$5.04 average cost × 270 quantity). The profit rectangle, then, is the shaded area of \$260 profit (\$1620 – \$1360).

When Should a Business Close?

Would Pure 'n' Simple T-Shirts remain in business if it were making a loss? In the short run, the business would likely continue to operate as long as it earned sufficient revenue to pay its variable costs. The remaining fixed costs would have to be paid in the short run whether or not the company stayed in business. As long as a business's total revenue more than covers its variable costs, it is better off remaining in business rather than shutting down and still having to pay its fixed costs. If total revenue were to fall below variable costs, however, the business would not be able to fund even its day-to-day operations, and it would have no choice but to close down.

Recall that total revenue for a business is found by multiplying price by the quantity of output (TR = P × q). Recall also that variable costs are found by subtracting fixed costs from total cost at any given output level (VC = TC – FC), and average variable cost is variable costs divided by quantity (AVC = VC ÷ q). So that we may consider the question of whether or not a business should continue to operate, let's take a look at average variable cost in another way: variable costs equal average variable cost multiplied by quantity (VC = AVC × q). Now, we can establish a relationship between price and average variable cost by looking at the formula for total revenue (TR = P × q), and the formula for variable costs (VC = AVC × q). Recall that as long as variable costs do not exceed total revenue, the company should stay in business; if the variable costs begin to exceed total revenue, the company should shut down. Cancelling the quantity of output (q)—because it is a common element in both these expressions—means that total revenue exceeds variable costs as long as price is greater than average variable cost. Variable costs exceed total revenue when average variable cost exceeds price. At the profit-maximizing output where total revenue and variable costs (or average variable cost and price) are equal, the business reaches its **shutdown point**, which occurs at the point of minimum average variable cost:

shutdown point: the level of output where price (or average revenue) equals minimum average variable cost

Business's shutdown point:

$$TR = VC$$
$$(P \times q) = (AVC \times q)$$
$$P = \text{minimum AVC}$$

Let's consider our example of Pure 'n' Simple T-Shirts in Figure 6.3. When receiving a price of $6.00 per T-shirt (at point *a*), the company is maintaining a positive economic profit. If, for some reason, the price drops to $5.00, the business reaches its breakeven point (point *b*). At the lowest point on the average variable cost curve, at $1.50 (point *c*), average variable cost equals price, thus variable costs equal total revenue.

Pure 'n' Simple T-Shirts' Shutdown Point:

$$TR(\$300) = VC(\$300)$$
$$P \times q\ (\$1.50 \times 200) = AVC \times q\ (\$1.50 \times 200)$$
$$P(\$1.50) = \text{minimum AVC}(\$1.50)$$

Point *c* in Figure 6.3 is Pure 'n' Simple T-Shirts' shutdown point. If the price falls further, to a price such as $1.40 (point *d*), the company closes down its operations, since total revenue which, at 200 units of output, would now be $280 ($1.40 × 200) no longer covers variable costs ($300).

Business's Supply Curve

Figure 6.3 also sheds light on how a change in price influences the operations of a perfectly competitive business. For example, if price falls from $6 to $5, the profit-maximizing output for Pure 'n' Simple T-Shirts changes from 270 to 250 shirts. At the same time, the business's economic profit falls to zero, since point *b* is the breakeven point. Notice that the effect of this price change on the business's quantity supplied is shown as a movement

FIGURE 6.3
Supply Curve for a Perfect Competitor

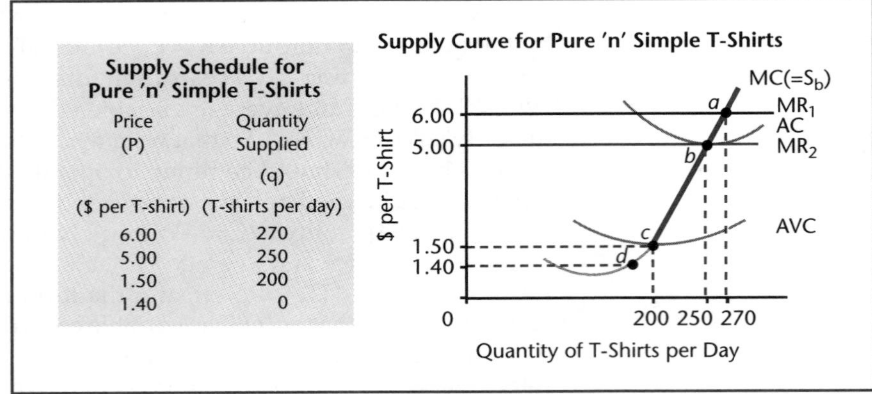

Supply Schedule for Pure 'n' Simple T-Shirts

Price (P) ($ per T-shirt)	Quantity Supplied (q) (T-shirts per day)
6.00	270
5.00	250
1.50	200
1.40	0

At point *a* on the graph, price exceeds average cost (AC) and positive economic profits are made. Point *b* is the breakeven point where price equals AC. At lower prices, the business makes a loss. Point *c* is the business's shutdown point, where price equals average variable costs (AVC). Below the shutdown point—for example, at point *d*—average variable costs would exceed price. The marginal cost curve (MC) above point *c* is the business's supply curve (S), the highlighted part of the curve.

business's supply curve: a curve that shows the quantity of output supplied by a business at every possible price

along the marginal cost curve (MC). Because the various profit-maximizing points for the business are all on the marginal cost curve, at least a portion of it represents the **business's supply curve**, S_b. The business's supply curve shows the quantity of output supplied by the business at every possible price. If price moves below the shutdown point (point *c*), Pure 'n' Simple T-Shirts will no longer be in business and its output will fall to zero. Hence, only that part of the marginal cost curve above this point is the business's supply curve (the highlighted part of the MC curve).

Market Supply Curve

The market supply curve, S_m, for a perfectly competitive industry is created using the supply curves for all businesses in the market. So, for the T-shirt market in which Pure 'n' Simple T-Shirts operates, we have the supply curve S_m as illustrated in Figure 6.4. If there are 100 businesses all identical to Pure 'n' Simple T-Shirts in the industry, then the market supply curve for T-shirts is found by adding the profit-maximizing outputs produced by all 100 businesses at each possible price. Thus, at a price of \$6, the quantity supplied in the market (Q) would be 27 000 shirts (270 shirts × 100 businesses), given that each business's output is 270 shirts.

The Long Run

In the long run, ease of entry into and exit from an industry in a perfectly competitive market becomes a crucial factor. Short-run profits and losses cause perfectly competitive markets to move toward a point of long-run equilibrium. Entrepreneurs enter industries where an economic profit can be expected, and leave those industries where there are losses. Movement

FIGURE 6.4
Supply Curves for a Perfectly Competitive Business and Market

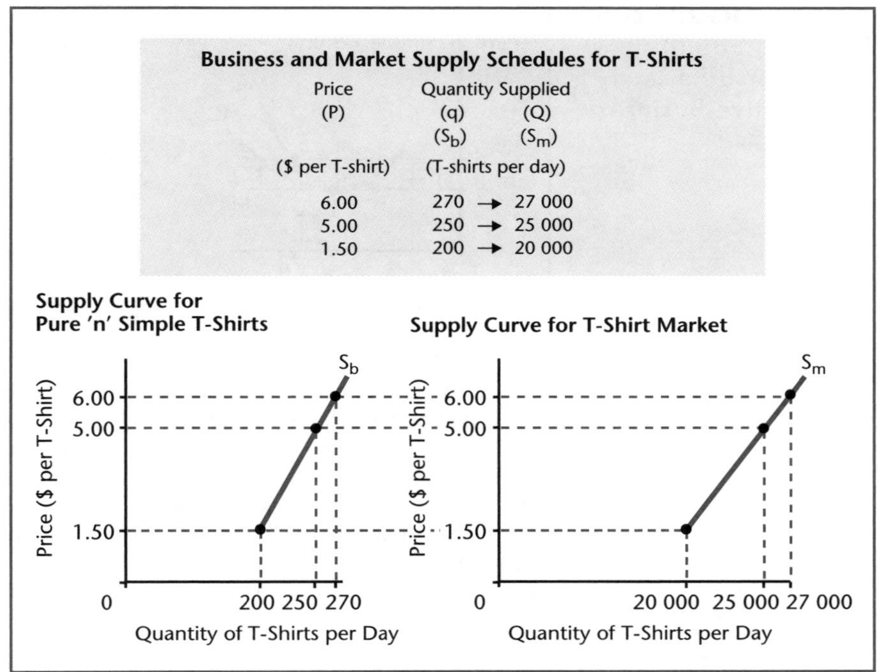

Business and Market Supply Schedules for T-Shirts

Price (P) ($ per T-shirt)	Quantity Supplied (q) (S_b) (T-shirts per day)		Quantity Supplied (Q) (S_m) (T-shirts per day)
6.00	270	→	27 000
5.00	250	→	25 000
1.50	200	→	20 000

If the T-shirt industry is made up of 100 identical businesses, then the market supply curve, S_m, is found by multiplying each output level on Pure 'n' Simple T-Shirts' supply curve, S_b, by 100.

to and from the industry continues until all the businesses in the market reach long-run equilibrium, at which they are just breaking even, with price equalling average cost and a normal profit being made.

The operation of these long-run competitive forces is illustrated in Figure 6.5 for the T-shirt market. We will assume that this is a constant-cost industry in which input prices are fixed regardless of the quantity of T-shirts produced. As a representative business in this industry, Pure 'n' Simple T-Shirts is originally in long-run equilibrium at a price of $5 (point *a* on the left), which is determined by the intersection of the market demand and supply curves, D_0 and S_0, at point *c* on the graph on the right. At this price, Pure 'n' Simple T-Shirts produces 250 shirts per day. Since price equals average cost, it is breaking even, or making zero economic profit. If the market demand for T-shirts increases from D_0 to D_1, the conditions of long-run equilibrium are temporarily broken. The new price in the market is $6, found at the intersection of D_1 and S_0 (point *d*). At this new price, Pure 'n' Simple T-Shirts makes a short-run economic profit, as shown on the graph on the left, since price (point *b*) exceeds average cost. This economic profit acts as a lure to new companies, who enter the industry and cause a shift in the market supply curve to the right, from S_0 to S_1. As a result, price returns to $5. With long-run equilibrium restored (point *e*), businesses in the market are again breaking even with a price equal to average cost, as exemplified by Pure 'n' Simple T-Shirts.

FIGURE 6.5
Long-Run Equilibrium for a Perfectly Competitive Business

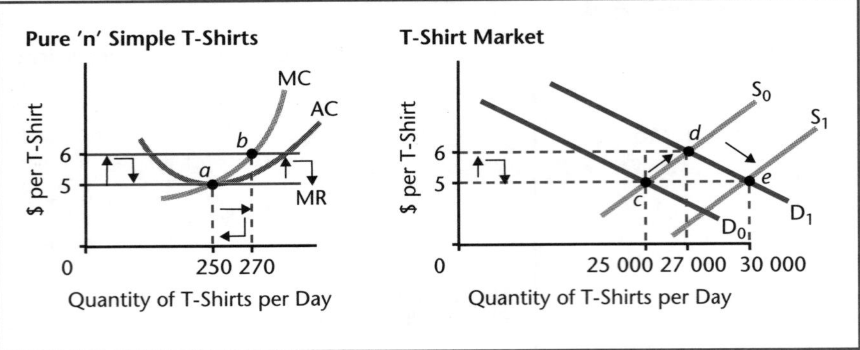

Long-run equilibrium for a perfectly competitive business, such as Pure 'n' Simple T-Shirts, is shown on the left at point *a*, where price equals both marginal cost and minimum average cost. Associated with this point is the equilibrium point *c* for the entire market on the graph on the right. An increase in market demand for T-shirts from D_0 to D_1 shifts equilibrium in the T-shirt market to point *d*, at both a higher price and a higher quantity. At the new profit-maximizing point for the business (point *b* on the left graph), a positive profit is being made, since price now exceeds average cost. The lure of economic profit causes new businesses to enter the market. Assuming that this is a constant-cost industry, the market supply curve shifts to the right, from S_0 to S_1, until price is driven back down to its original level at point *e*. On the left graph, Pure 'n' Simple T-Shirts returns to its long-run equilibrium point *a* because of these competitive forces.

Benefits of Perfect Competition

The long-run equilibrium shown in Figure 6.5 illustrates the advantages of perfectly competitive markets for buyers. It also helps explain Adam Smith's assertion that, through the "invisible hand" of competition, the self-interest of producers ultimately benefits consumers. Because a perfectly competitive market in long-run equilibrium meets two requirements—known as minimum-cost pricing and marginal-cost pricing—consumers will benefit.

Minimum-Cost Pricing

minimum-cost pricing: the practice of setting price where it equals minimum average cost

By operating at the break-even point where price equals minimum average cost, perfectly competitive businesses in long-run equilibrium practise **minimum-cost pricing**. If businesses weren't charging the minimum possible average cost as their price, they would change the scale of production and reduce average costs even further in order to maximize profit. By charging the minimum-cost price of $5 when it is in long-run equilibrium, Pure 'n' Simple T-Shirts, for example, is choosing the least costly combination of inputs. Moreover, it is making zero economic profit, so that all these cost savings are passed on to T-shirt buyers. The purchasing power of consumers' incomes when acquiring T-shirts is therefore maximized.

Marginal-Cost Pricing

marginal-cost pricing: the practice of setting price where it equals marginal cost

In long-run equilibrium, perfectly competitive businesses also practise **marginal-cost pricing**, meaning they produce at an output level where price equals marginal cost. The fact that they do so follows from the equality of marginal revenue and price for perfectly competitive firms. The profit-maximizing output rule means that perfect competitors choose the quantity of output at which marginal revenue and marginal cost intersect. Since marginal revenue and price are identical for individual businesses, the profit-maximizing output rule can be expressed, also, as the condition that price equals marginal cost.

If each business's marginal cost incorporates all possible costs to society, then a perfectly competitive market in long-run equilibrium operates at a price that fully reflects the product's opportunity cost. Furthermore, if all markets in an economy are close to being perfectly competitive, society's scarce resources are distributed among industries in a way that maximizes the overall satisfaction of consumers. This is because the prices of various products accurately reflect the extra costs of producing them. Considering again the example of T-shirts, if they are priced at $6 while the marginal cost of an additional T-shirt is $3, then more of society's resources should be devoted to T-shirt production. Otherwise, consumers who derive less than $6 worth of satisfaction from this product are not purchasing it, even though many of them would be willing to pay more than the product's marginal cost. Production in this market should therefore be increased.

BRIEF REVIEW

1. All businesses—whatever market structures they operate in—can maximize profits by finding the output level at which marginal revenue intersects marginal cost.
2. At the profit-maximizing output a business's economic profit is positive if price is greater than average cost. When price and average cost are equal at the profit-maximizing output, the business is at its breakeven point, with economic profit at zero. If price is lower than average cost, then the business is operating at a loss, or negative economic profit.
3. For a perfect competitor, the breakeven point occurs when price equals minimum average cost. At lower prices, a perfect competitor will continue in business until the shutdown point, where price equals minimum average variable cost. A perfectly competitive business's supply curve is only the portion of its marginal cost curve that is above the shutdown point.
4. In long-run equilibrium, perfectly competitive businesses break even. They also operate at the minimum-cost and marginal-cost prices, thereby benefiting consumers.

MONOPOLISTIC COMPETITION

Because they are price-makers, monopolistic competitors must choose both a level of output and a price when attempting to maximize profits. Thus they apply the profit-maximizing output rule in a different way than do perfectly competitive businesses.

Revenue Conditions

Figure 6.6 shows the relationships among price, marginal revenue, and average revenue for a monopolisitic competitor, the Jaded Palate restaurant. In the table, price (column 1) and average revenue (column 5) are equal, just as they are for perfect competitors. However, marginal revenue and average revenue are no longer necessarily the same. Recall that if an average value such as average revenue declines, then its corresponding marginal value (marginal revenue) is below it. For example, when the Jaded Palate sells its first 100 meals, the restaurant's average and marginal revenues both equal $11. (Remember that marginal values are graphed halfway between the relevant horizontal coordinates.) But once the next 100 meals are added, average revenue falls to $10. For this to

FIGURE 6.6
Revenues for a Monopolistic Competitor

Revenue Schedules for the Jaded Palate

(1) Price (P) ($ per meal)	(2) Quantity (q) (meals per day)	(3) Total Revenue (TR) (P x q)	(4) Marginal Revenue (MR) ($\Delta TR/\Delta q$)	(5) Average Revenue (AR) (TR/q)
—	0	0		
11	100	1100	→ 1100/100 = 11	1100/100 = 11
10	200	2000	→ 900/100 = 9	2000/200 = 10
9	300	2700	→ 700/100 = 7	2700/300 = 9
8	400	3200	→ 500/100 = 5	3200/400 = 8

Revenue Curves for the Jaded Palate

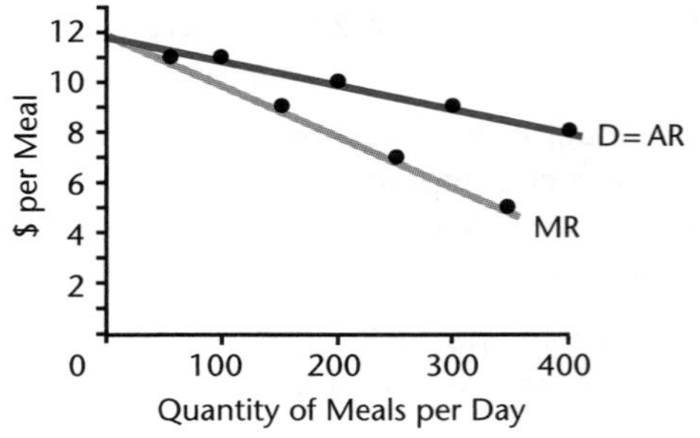

$ per Meal
D = AR
MR
Quantity of Meals per Day

The business's demand schedule is shown in columns 1 and 2. The values for price (P) and average revenue (AR) in columns 1 and 5 are equal, while marginal revenue (MR) in column 4 is the same as P and AR only at their initial values. After this, MR falls more quickly than price, as the graph shows with the demand curve D and its associated MR curve.

happen, the last 100 meals must each have a lower marginal revenue of \$9. Therefore, in the accompanying graph, the demand (D) and average revenue (AR) curves for the Jaded Palate are identical, but the demand and marginal revenue (MR) curves intersect only at their initial points. As the quantity of output for the restaurant rises, marginal revenue drops below price. This follows from the connection between average and marginal values.

The Short Run

Given its ability to choose price, the monopolistic competitor maximizes its short-run profit by first finding the appropriate quantity of output, and then using this quantity level to determine the highest possible price it can charge. These typical profit-making activities are illustrated on the left in Figure 6.7. In addition to the business's demand and marginal revenue curves, the graph shows the relevant curves for marginal cost and average cost. Once again, in order to maximize profit, the business must find the point at which marginal revenue and marginal cost intersect. This is point *a*, which is at the profit-maximizing quantity of 200 meals. Price is then set at \$10 by drawing a vertical line up to the business's demand curve at point *b*, and then across to the price axis.

The Jaded Palate could be making an economic profit or loss in the short run, or it could be breaking even. As in the case of perfect competitors, the answer can be found by comparing price and average cost at the profit-maximizing quantity. Because the price of \$10 is above the \$8 average cost at a quantity of 200 meals (point *c*), the Jaded Palate is making a

FIGURE 6.7
Profit Maximization for a Monopolistic Competitor

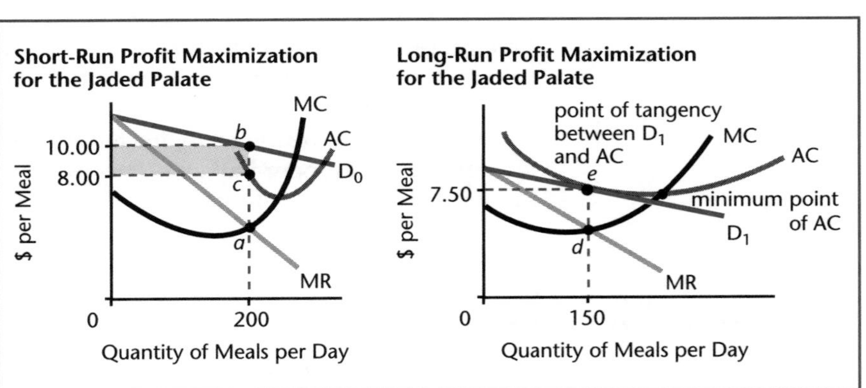

On the left, the business's short-run profit is maximized at point *a*, where the marginal revenue (MR) and marginal cost (MC) curves intersect at a quantity of 200 meals. The \$10.00 price is found by drawing a vertical line up to point *b* on the business's demand curve, D_0, and then across to the price axis. The business's total profit is shown by the shaded rectangle, which has a height equalling the difference between price at point *b* and average cost (AC) at point *c*. The width of the rectangle equals the profit-maximizing output (200 meals). On the right, the long-run profit-maximizing output of 150 meals occurs at the point where MR and MC are equal (point *d*). The price of \$7.50—which equals long-run AC—is point *e* on the business's long-run demand curve (D_1).

positive economic profit. On the graph, the revenue rectangle equals price multiplied by the quantity of output ($10 × 200 meals = $2000), and the cost rectangle equals average cost multiplied by the quantity of output ($8 × 200 meals = $1600). Therefore, the profit rectangle equals $400 ($2000 – $1600) and is shown as the shaded rectangle in the short-run graph.

The Long Run

It is in the long run that the competitive elements of monopolistic competition become evident. Because short-run economic profits are being made in the restaurant industry, new businesses enter the market in the long run. The graph on the right in Figure 6.7 shows how the increase in competition shifts demand (from D_0 to the new D_1 curve) for established restaurants such as the Jaded Palate. The entry of new competitors causes demand for the Jaded Palate to move leftward, because there are now fewer customers at each possible price that the restaurant can charge. The new demand curve, D_1, is also more elastic than D_0, since there are more close substitutes available for the Jaded Palate's product. Once again, the market adjusts: profits go down and, eventually, long-run equilibrium is reached at point *e*. Besides showing the Jaded Palate's demand and marginal revenue curves, the graph on the right shows the marginal cost and average cost curves in the long run. The profit-maximizing point where marginal revenue equals marginal cost now occurs at a quantity of 150 meals (point *d*). The new price is $7.50, which is found at point *e* on the long-run demand curve, D_1.

Note that monopolistic competitors reach neither the minimum-cost nor the marginal-cost pricing conditions in long-run equilibrium. Since average cost and price are equal at point *e* on Figure 6.7, the business is breaking even in the long run. However, this price does *not* equal the minimum point on the average cost curve. This minimum-cost price could only be achieved at a higher output for each business. Figure 6.7 also illustrates that in the long run, for monopolistic competitors, price (point *e*) is greater than marginal cost. This means that too few units of output are produced for price to reflect the product's full opportunity cost.

OLIGOPOLY

We have already seen in Chapter 5 how an oligopoly that is characterized by rivalry among competitors faces a kinked demand curve. Recall that the kinked demand curve is based on the different responses of competitors when the business either raises or reduces its price. In Figure 6.8, when Universal Motors increases the price of its Centaur car, rivals do not increase their prices. Thus, the quantity demanded of Centaurs decreases sharply, giving the flatter segment of the demand curve. Were Universal Motors to decrease its price on the Centaur, rivals would follow suit, so the change in quantity demanded would be small, giving the steeper segment of the demand curve.

FIGURE 6.8
Profit Maximization for an Oligopolist

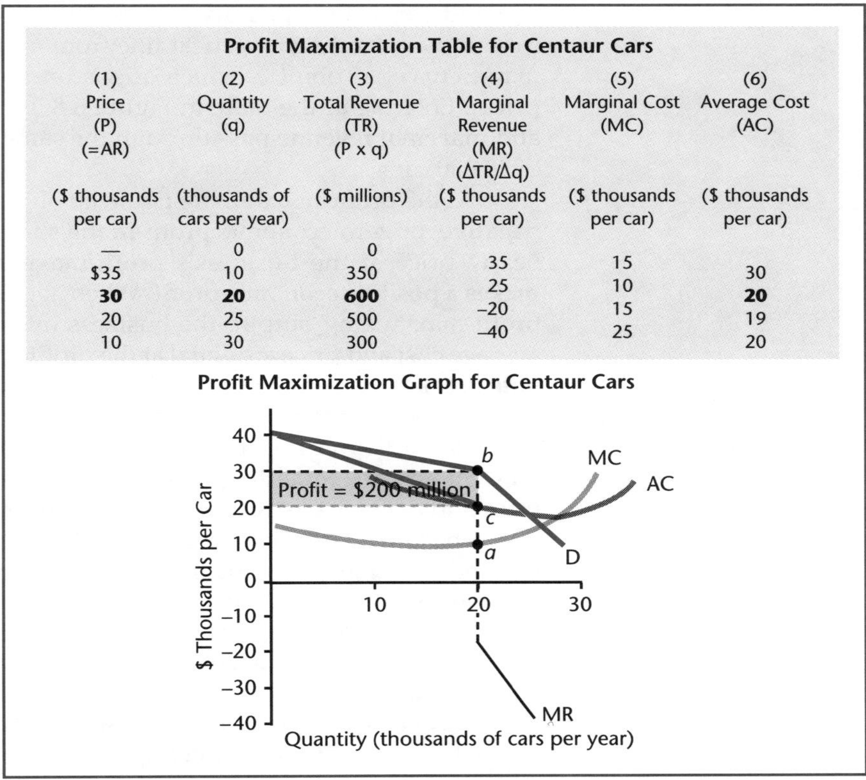

Profit Maximization Table for Centaur Cars

(1) Price (P) (=AR) ($ thousands per car)	(2) Quantity (q) (thousands of cars per year)	(3) Total Revenue (TR) (P x q) ($ millions)	(4) Marginal Revenue (MR) (ΔTR/Δq) ($ thousands per car)	(5) Marginal Cost (MC) ($ thousands per car)	(6) Average Cost (AC) ($ thousands per car)
—	0	0			
			35	15	
$35	10	350			30
			25	10	
30	**20**	**600**			**20**
			–20	15	
20	25	500			19
			–40	25	
10	30	300			20

Profit Maximization Graph for Centaur Cars

In an oligopoly characterized by rivalry, a business faces a kinked demand curve, D, with two segments. The marginal revenue curve also has two segments; however, the segments are separate, so they must be joined with a vertical line. On the graph, the marginal revenue (MR) and marginal cost (MC) curves meet at point *a*, giving a profit-maximizing output level of 20 000 cars. To determine price for these 20 000 cars, we must look to the demand curve; at a quantity demanded of 20 000, the price should be $30 000 (point *b*). According to the table also, the values of marginal revenue (column 4) and marginal cost (column 5) pass through the same values around an output level of 20 000.

Revenue Conditions

The marginal revenue for Centaur cars is shown in the table and on the graph in Figure 6.8. Just as with the demand curve, the marginal revenue curve has two distinct segments. In this case, however, the flatter segment and the steeper segment do not meet, but must be joined by a vertical line at the quantity of 20 000 cars, the quantity associated with the $30 000 price.

Profit Maximization

To maximize profit, the oligopolist, like all businesses, must follow the profit-maximizing output rule. Therefore, Universal Motors should produce at the output level where the marginal revenue and marginal cost curves intersect, at point *a* in Figure 6.8, or 20 000 cars. According to the demand curve, this quantity of cars should be sold at a price of \$30 000 (found by extending a vertical line from a quantity of 20 000 to the demand curve, at point *b*, which aligns on the price axis with a \$30 000 price). Looking at the table in Figure 6.8, we can see that marginal cost and marginal revenue pass through the same values closest to an output of 20 000 cars.

At the profit-maximizing point, an oligopolist may make a positive, negative, or zero economic profit in the short run. When average cost is below price at the business's profit-maximizing output, the business makes a positive economic profit. When average cost is above price at the profit-maximizing output, the business makes an economic loss. When average cost and price are equal at the profit-maximizing output, the business breaks even. In the case of Universal Motors, at the output level of 20 000 cars and the price of \$30 000 (point *b* in Figure 6.8), the average cost is \$20 000 (point *c*). Therefore, the company makes an economic profit on Centaur cars equal to quantity multiplied by the difference between price and average cost, or \$200 million [20 000 × (\$30 000 – \$20 000)]

The kinked demand curve—which applies equally in both the short run and the long run—explains why rival oligopolists tend to keep prices constant even as costs change. In the case of the Centaur illustrated in Figure 6.8, as long as the marginal cost and marginal revenue curves intersect at a quantity of 20 000, Universal Motors will not change its price. Only if marginal cost changed so dramatically that its curve and the marginal revenue curve no longer intersected at 20 000 (the vertical connection between the two segments) would Universal Motors change its price.

As in the case of monopolistic competitors, oligopolists achieve neither the minimum-cost nor the marginal-cost pricing conditions. Because of limited competition created by barriers to entry, an oligopolist that faces rivals can remain indefinitely at one price, such as \$30 000 in Figure 6.8. At this price, the business is making a positive economic profit and fails to reach the output level where average cost is at its lowest value. So, the minimum-cost pricing condition is broken. The condition of marginal-cost pricing is also broken; as Figure 6.8 shows, the price of \$30 000 is greater than marginal cost. The same conclusions apply for colluding oligopolists, as the prices they charge are even higher.

Thinking About Economics

Why are there no supply curves for businesses in imperfectly competitive markets?

A supply curve is relevant only when a business plans how much output to produce at various prices. Perfect competitors do this, but not sellers in other types of markets. Given its demand curve, a monopolistic competitor or oligopolist chooses one output level and then charges the highest possible price the demand allows at that quantity. It is therefore impossible for an imperfectly competitive business to devise a supply curve that is independent of the demand conditions it faces.

BRIEF REVIEW

1. A monopolistic competitor faces a marginal revenue curve that intersects its corresponding demand curve only at their initial (zero) values. From that point, the marginal revenue curve falls faster than does the demand curve.
2. In the short run, a monopolistic competitor can make an economic profit or loss. In the long run, however, competitive forces drive monopolistic competitors to a breakeven point.
3. An oligopolist in a market that is characterized by rivalry faces a marginal revenue curve of two disconnected segments, one steeper than the other. These segments are associated with the two portions of the kinked demand curve.
4. Because of limited competition, oligopolists can make an economic profit even in the long run.
5. Imperfectly competitive businesses satisfy neither the minimum-cost nor the marginal-cost pricing conditions met by perfectly competitive businesses in the long run.

MONOPOLY

Unlike businesses in other market structures, the monopolist does not have to worry about competitors when it chooses its profit-maximizing point. In contrast to the horizontal demand curve the perfect competitor faces, the monopolist faces a negatively sloped demand curve for the entire market.

Revenue Conditions

Figure 6.9 shows the demand and revenue conditions for Megacomp, the sole seller of supercomputers. As for monopolistic competitors and oligopolists, only the initial values for Megacomp's price and marginal revenue (columns 1 and 4 of the table) are equal. As the graph also demonstrates, marginal revenues drop below price when output increases. Notice that the curves look similar to those for the Jaded Palate (Figure 6.7). The difference is that Megacomp's demand curve is less elastic. This is because the monopolist is selling a product with no close substitutes.

Profit Maximization

With its ability to set price, Megacomp applies the profit-maximizing rule in the same way as imperfectly competitive sellers. Both in the short run and the long run, the profit-maximizing output is found where marginal revenue intersects marginal cost. As shown in Figure 6.9, the marginal revenue and marginal cost curves for Megacomp intersect at point *a*, at a quantity of 2 computers. Once again, the price for this output level is determined by the demand curve. At the quantity of 2, the demand curve gives a price (at point *b*) of $120 million. The table shows the same results: marginal revenue (column 4) and marginal cost (column 5) pass through the same values nearest the quantity of 2 computers and price of $120 million.

Like other companies, the monopolist may be making an economic profit or a loss, or it may be breaking even, depending on whether the business's average cost is above, below, or equal to price. Because in our example Megacomp has an average cost of $90 million (at point *c*) that is below the $120 million price (point *b*), it is making a positive economic profit. The business's profit rectangle has a height equal to the distance between points *b* and *c* ($30 million = $120 million – $90 million) and a width of 2 computers, giving a total economic profit of $60 million.

Notice that, like both monopolistic competitors and oligopolists, a monopolist satisfies neither of the conditions for consumer benefit: minimum-cost pricing and marginal-cost pricing. Because the monopolist has no competitors due to barriers to entry, it can keep its price constant in the long run. In the case of Megacomp, this price would be $120 million, as shown in Figure 6.9. Since price does not equal the lowest possible average cost, the minimum-cost pricing condition is not met. Similarly, this price is not equal to the business's marginal cost, meaning that the marginal-cost pricing condition is not met either.

FIGURE 6.9
Profit Maximization for a Monopolist

Profit Maximization Table for Megacomp

(1) Price (P) (AR) ($ millions per computer)	(2) Quantity (q) (computers per year)	(3) Total Revenue (TR) (P x q) ($ millions)	(4) Marginal Revenue (MR) (ΔTR/Δq) ($ millions per computer)	(5) Marginal Cost (MC) ($ millions per computer)	(6) Average Cost (AC) ($ millions per computer)
	0	0			
			160	60	
160	1	160			140
			80	40	
120	**2**	**240**			**90**
			0	70	
80	3	240			83
			–80	150	
40	4	160			100

Profit Maximization Graph for Megacomp

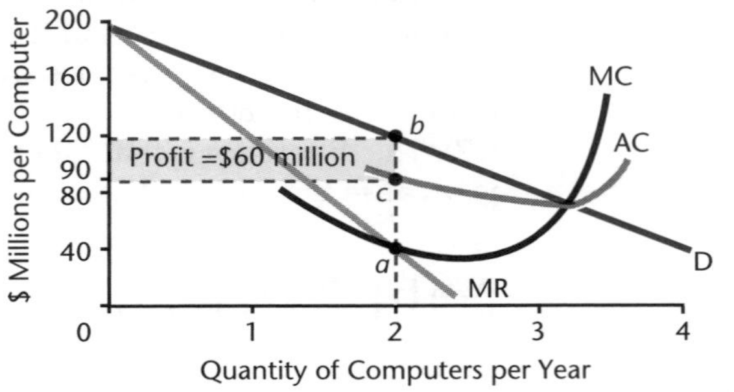

$ Millions per Computer
200
160
120
90
80
40
0
1
2
3
4
Quantity of Computers per Year
Profit =$60 million
MC
AC
MR
D
a
b
c

On the graph, the profit-maximizing output is found at the intersection of the marginal revenue (MR) and marginal cost (MC) curves (at point *a*.) At this output of 2 computers, the demand curve gives a price (at point *b*) of $120 million (determined by drawing a vertical line from the quantity of 2 to the demand curve, then across to the price axis). The table also shows that marginal revenue and marginal cost pass through the same values around an output of 2 computers and a price of $120 million. On the graph, Megacomp's profit ($60 million) is the area of the shaded rectangle, with a height equalling the difference between price (point *b*) and average cost (point *c*), and with a width equalling the quantity of 2.

Thinking About Economics

How easy is it for a monopolist, such as Megacomp, to estimate the profit-maximizing values for price and quantity?

The task requires estimating both demand and costs. Whereas the perfect competitor has an easy time of estimating demand conditions (because market price is the only factor to be determined), monopolists (as well as imperfectly competitive businesses) have a harder task of estimating how much consumers will buy at each possible price. As far as cost estimates are concerned, all businesses must estimate how much explicit and implicit costs would be at each possible output level. When a business sells more than one item, it must also distribute its costs among these various products.

Monopoly Versus Perfect Competition

To see the impact on price and quantity of a monopoly, let's compare them with price and quantity in a perfectly competitive market. To do this, we'll consider what would happen if a perfectly competitive market in long-run equilibrium were transformed into a monopoly.

The market demand and supply curves for the T-shirt industry are shown in Figure 6.10. Equilibrium for a competitive market occurs at the intersection of these curves (point *a*), with a price of $4 and a quantity of 22 000 shirts. If the industry becomes one large company, the market demand curve remains the same despite the change in the market structure. With the transformation to a monopoly, the demand curve for the entire market becomes the business's demand curve. There is a significant change, however. Now that the business is a monopolist, its price (given by the demand curve) and its marginal revenue are no longer equal. Instead, the marginal revenue curve falls below the demand curve, as was the case for Megacomp.

Next let's consider supply. Recall that a perfect competitor's supply curve shows the quantity of output supplied by the business at each possible price, and is represented by a portion of the marginal cost curve. In turn, the market supply curve is the sum of all supply curves of businesses in the market. After the change to a monopoly, production facilities remain the same as before, with inputs originally owned by the perfectly competitive producers now in the hands of one business. When the monopolist combines the cost figures for these various facilities, it finds a marginal cost curve that is merely an extension of the perfectly competitive supply curve, shown in Figure 6.10.

Effects on Price and Quantity

The T-shirt monopoly's profit-maximizing output is 18 000, where the new marginal revenue and marginal cost curves intersect (point *b*). At this output level, the price is $7 (point *c*), as found on the demand curve. Thus, with the transformation from perfect competition to monopoly, T-shirts become more expensive and fewer of them are produced.

FIGURE 6.10
Monopoly Versus Perfect Competition

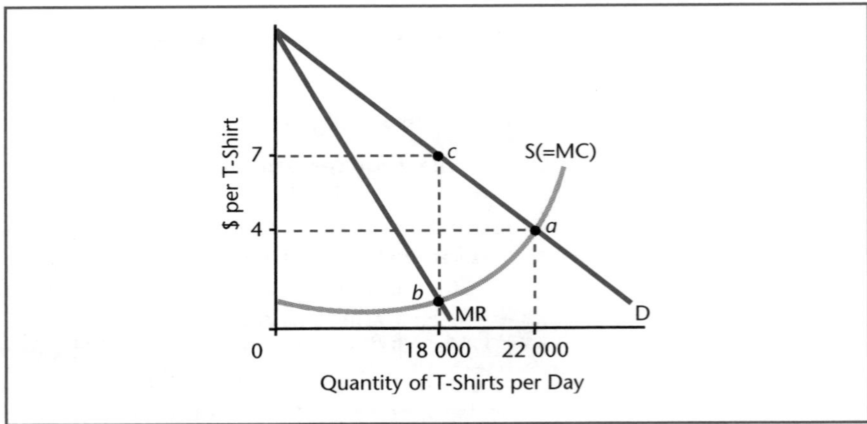

When the T-shirt industry is perfectly competitive, equilibrium occurs at a price of $4 and an output of 22 000, found at the meeting point (*a*) of the market demand and supply curves, D and S. If the industry becomes a monopoly, the profit-maximizing output for the single seller decreases to 18 000, where marginal revenue (MR) and marginal cost (MC) meet (point *b*). The new price of $7 is found on the demand curve (point *c*).

Regulation of Natural Monopolies

When an industry is a natural monopoly, economies of scale mean that the single business can produce a product at a significantly lower per-unit cost than could several companies. To ensure that these cost savings are passed on to the consumer, governments usually intervene in natural monopolies. Either they provide the service through a government-owned corporation (as in the case of Canada Post), or they regulate the single private company in the market (just as the Canadian Radio-television and Telecommunications Commission regulates cable television businesses).

Average-Cost Price

Public agencies that regulate monopolies have a difficult task. Not only must regulators estimate each business's costs, they must also try to choose the "best" possible price for the monopolist to charge. Usually regulators use **average-cost pricing**, so that the monopolist can break even without public funds. As a practical matter, regulators applying the average-cost price do not undertake the cumbersome task of estimating the cost and demand curves of the regulated business. Instead, they control profits directly. A business's **accounting-profit rate**, or rate of return, is its accounting profit divided by owner's equity and expressed as a percentage:

average-cost pricing: the practice of setting price where it equals average cost

accounting-profit rate: a measure of a business's profitability, calculated as its accounting profit divided by owner's equity

$$\text{Accounting-profit rate} = \frac{\text{accounting profit}}{\text{owner's equity}} \times 100\%$$

fair rate of return: the maximum accounting-profit rate allowed for a regulated monopoly

The regulating agency imposes a ceiling, such as 8 percent or 9 percent, on the profit rate the business can earn. This **fair rate of return** is arrived at by estimating how much the business needs to cover both explicit costs (such as wages and outlays on materials) and implicit costs (in particular, the business's normal profits).

While it is often the only viable method of regulation, setting a fair rate of return leads to inefficiencies. Because of profit controls, there is little incentive for the company's managers to control costs. Indeed, the easiest way for the business to raise its price is by inflating costs. Generous perks, bloated payrolls, and plush offices are then paid for by consumers in the form of higher prices. Regulators try to overcome such problems by imposing performance standards on the business, but these standards are difficult to implement.

BRIEF REVIEW

1. The monopolist faces a demand curve that is equal to marginal revenue only at its initial value. Marginal revenue drops more quickly than price as output rises.
2. A monopolist can make a positive economic profit in both the short run and the long run, and meets neither of the minimum-cost and marginal-cost pricing conditions.
3. A monopolist necessarily charges a higher price and produces a lower quantity than would a perfectly competitive industry in the same market.
4. Regulators usually force natural monopolies to charge an average-cost price, where the businesses are just breaking even.

KEY CONCEPTS

average revenue
marginal revenue
profit-maximizing rule
breakeven point
shutdown point
business's supply curve
minimum-cost pricing
marginal-cost pricing
average-cost pricing
accounting-profit rate
fair rate of return

ANALYSIS AND APPLICATION

1. For each of the following cases, (i) create a table showing the business's revenue schedules, (ii) plot the business's demand and marginal revenue curves on a sheet of graph paper, and (iii) explain how the relationship between demand and marginal revenue is affected by the type of market in which this business operates.
   a. A dairy farmer, who sells milk in a perfectly competitive market, faces a price of $2 per litre at possible outputs of 1000, 2000, 3000, or 4000 litres per week.
   b. Biodata Software is the sole seller of a programming language with unique scientific applications. The company finds that each month it can sell 60 copies of the language at a price of $400, and 60 extra copies for each $100 reduction in price.

c. Stan's Coffee Shop operates in a monopolistically competitive market. It sells 100 cups of coffee daily at a price of 95 cents per cup. For each 5-cent reduction in price, it sells 100 extra cups, until a minimum possible price of 80 cents is reached.

d. The Big Hair Company sells shampoo in an oligopoly characterized by rivalry. The business's daily sales are 2000 bottles at a price of \$3, 4000 at \$2.50, 5000 at \$2, and 6000 at \$1.50.

Profit-Maximization Table for a Vegetable Gardener

(1) Price (\$ per kilogram)	(2) Quantity (kilograms per month)	(3) Total Revenue (\$)	(4) Total Cost (\$)	(5) Marginal Revenue (\$ per kilogram)	(6) Marginal Cost (\$ per kilogram)	(7) Average Cost (\$ per kilogram)	(8) Profit (\$)
	0	0	18				___
				___	___		
___	100	48	41			___	___
				___	___		
___	200	96	57			___	___
				___	___		
___	300	144	77			___	___
				___	___		
___	400	192	106			___	___
				___	___		
___	500	240	145			___	___
				___	___		
___	600	288	199			___	___
				___	___		
___	700	336	294			___	___
				___	___		
___	800	384	501			___	___

2. The accompanying table applies to a vegetable gardener who sells carrots at a local farmer's market.
   a. Copy out and complete the table. What type of market does the gardener operate in? Explain.
   b. Identify the gardener's profit-maximizing or loss-minimizing quantity of output (rounded to the nearest 100 kilograms), and explain your answer using the profit-maximizing output rule.
   c. On a sheet of graph paper, plot the gardener's marginal revenue, marginal cost, and average cost curves. On your graph, show the profit-maximizing point identified in part b., as well as the area of profit or loss.
   d. At what price and quantity of output (rounded to the nearest 100 kilograms) would the gardener reach the breakeven point? Show this point on your graph.

3. a. On a sheet of graph paper, plot the total revenue and total cost curves for the vegetable gardener in the previous question.

b. On a separate graph, directly below the one you have drawn in part a., plot the gardener's total profit at the various possible output levels.
c. On your graphs, highlight the profit-maximizing or loss-minimizing quantity of output and discuss how it can be identified.

Profit-Maximization Table for a Fisherman

(1) Price ($ per kilogram)	(2) Quantity (kilograms per day)	(3) Total Revenue ($)	(4) Fixed Costs ($)	(5) Variable Costs ($)	(6) Total Cost ($)	(7) Average Fixed Cost ($ per kilogram)	(8) Average Variable Cost ($ per kilogram)	(9) Average Cost ($ per kilogram)	(10) Marginal Cost ($ per kilogram)
	0	___	400	0	___				
									___
___	90	___	400	55	___	___	___	___	
									___
___	220	___	400	110	___	___	___	___	
									___
___	307	___	400	165	___	___	___	___	
									___
___	360	___	400	220	___	___	___	___	
									___
___	385	___	400	275	___	___	___	___	
									___
___	400	___	400	330	___	___	___	___	

4. A fisherman who sells his mackerel catch in a perfectly competitive market faces revenues and costs shown in the accompanying table.
   a. Copy out and complete the table, assuming that the fisherman sells his catch at a price of 80 cents per kilogram.
   b. On a sheet of graph paper, carefully plot the fisherman's marginal cost, average fixed cost, average variable cost, and average cost curves.
   c. Which of the output levels in the table represents this fisherman's profit-maximizing or loss-minimizing quantity of output? At this quantity, what is the fisherman's profit or loss? Draw the fisherman's marginal revenue curve on your graph and use this curve to identify the profit-maximizing point as well as the area of profit or loss.
   d. On your graph, identify the business's breakeven point, shutdown point, and supply curve. What is the significance of each of these concepts to the fisherman?
   e. If, in the long run, price remains at 80 cents and the total costs shown in the table still apply, what action will this fisherman take? Explain.

5. How do the conditions of minimum-cost and marginal-cost pricing correspond to Adam Smith's notion of the "invisible hand"?

Profit-Maximization Table for Presto Cleaners

(1) Price ($ per shirt)	(2) Quantity (shirts per month)	(3) Total Revenue ($)	(4) Total Cost ($)	(5) Marginal Revenue ($ per shirt)	(6) Marginal Cost ($ per shirt)	(7) Average Cost ($ per shirt)
	0	___	3000			
				___	___	
4.50	1000	___	5000			___
				___	___	
4.00	2000	___	6000			___
				___	___	
3.50	3000	___	7500			___
				___	___	
3.00	4000	___	12000			___
				___	___	
2.50	5000	___	20000			___

6. Presto Cleaners, a small drycleaning shop, operates in a monopolistically competitive market, with revenues and costs as shown in the accompanying table.
   a. Copy out and complete the table, and on a sheet of graph paper plot Presto's demand, marginal revenue, marginal cost, and average cost curves.
   b. Using your graph, identify Presto's profit-maximizing or loss-minimizing quantity of output (rounded to the nearest 1000 shirts) and price, and calculate the area of profit or loss. Explain how these values can be derived using the table.
   c. What will happen to Presto's profit or loss in the long run? Explain.

Profit-Maximization Table for Citrus Delight

(1) Price ($ per carton)	(2) Quantity (thousands of cartons per day)	(3) Total Revenue ($ thousands)	(4) Total Cost ($ thousands)	(5) Marginal Revenue ($ per carton)	(6) Marginal Cost ($ per carton)	(7) Average Cost ($ per carton)
	0	___	50			
				___	___	
2.10	30	___	90			___
				___	___	
2.00	60	___	110			___
				___	___	
1.90	90	___	126			___
				___	___	
1.70	100	___	139			___
				___	___	
1.50	110	___	169			___

7. A producer of fresh orange juice, Citrus Delight, operates in an oligopoly, and has revenues and costs as shown in the accompanying table.
   a. Copy out and complete the table, and on a sheet of graph paper plot Citrus Delight's demand, marginal revenue, marginal cost, and average cost curves. Explain the shapes of the demand and marginal revenue curves.
   b. Using your graph, identify Citrus Delight's profit-maximizing or loss-minimizing quantity of output (rounded to the nearest 30 000 cartons) and price, and calculate the area of profit or loss.
   c. Will Citrus Delight's profit or loss necessarily disappear in the long run? Explain.

Profit-Maximization Table for True North Railways

(1) Price ($ per passenger	(2) Quantity (passengers per day)	(3) Total Revenue ($)	(4) Total Cost ($)	(5) Marginal Revenue ($ per passenger)	(6) Marginal Cost ($ per passenger)	(7) Average Cost ($ per passenger)
	0	___	24750			
				___	___	
350	50	___	26750			___
				___	___	
280	100	___	27750			___
				___	___	
210	150	___	27900			___
				___	___	
140	200	___	28000			___
				___	___	
70	250	___	29000			___
				___	___	
0	300	___	34500			___

8. (Advanced Question)
   True North Railways, which is the sole provider of passenger rail service to a remote community, has revenues and costs shown in the accompanying table.
   a. Copy out and complete the table. On a sheet of graph paper plot True North's demand, marginal revenue, marginal cost, and average cost curves. Would the business ever freely choose to operate in the output range where marginal revenue is negative? Explain.
   b. Using your graph, identify True North's profit-maximizing quantity of output (rounded to the nearest 50 passengers) and price, and calculate the area of profit.
   c. Government officials decide to regulate True North's operations. Use your graph to identify the average-cost price and associated quantity of output (rounded to the nearest 50 passengers) that

regulators could choose. Outline one problem connected with this regulated price.

9. Canada Post has the exclusive right to provide regular mail service in Canada. As a government-owned company that seeks to maximize profits under close public scrutiny, it provides a useful example of a regulated monopoly. Access the 1996 report of the Canada Post Mandate Review (at http://w3.pwgsc.gc.ca/text/cpmr/text/cover_e.html) to research the operations of Canada Post. Based on your research, answer the following questions:
   a. Up until the mid-1990s, has Canada Post made a positive accounting profit? a positive economic profit?
   b. According to the Mandate Review Report, how has Canada Post used its monopoly in regular mail service to gain an advantage in other markets?
   c. Do you think the behaviour outlined in part b. helps or harms Canadian consumers? Explain.

Advancing Economic Thought

CAN CAPITALISM SURVIVE?

Joseph Schumpeter and the Prospects for Capitalism

Joseph Schumpeter (1883–1950) is one of the most famous economists of the twentieth century, and the originality of his ideas and breadth of his learning have been matched by few others. Born to a middle-class business family, he enjoyed an aristocratic upbringing after his father died and his mother married a high-ranking military commander in the Austrian army. Schumpeter studied law and economics at the prestigious University of Vienna. After working as a lawyer, he took up a career as a professor of economics. For a brief period after World War I, he served as the Minister of Finance in the Austrian government. In the 1930s, the political turmoil surrounding the rise of the Nazis in Germany caused him to move to the United States, where he taught for many years at Harvard University.

Schumpeter and His Influence

Schumpeter's work is fascinating because of his ability to combine seemingly contradictory ideas. While a strong supporter of capitalism and private markets, he devised a theory of capitalist development that has interesting parallels with the work of Karl Marx. Like Marx, Schumpeter used not only the tools of economics but also the other social sciences. He was therefore able to highlight the role played by politics and culture in affecting economic conditions.

Joseph Schumpeter
Source: The Bettmann Archive

The crucial player in Schumpeter's theory of capitalism is the entrepreneur. For Schumpeter, entrepreneurs are much more than risk-takers—they are innovators who, through imagination and creativity, supply new products or adopt new types of technology. While not necessarily inventors, they are able to bring fresh ideas to the marketplace. As Schumpeter noted:

> To carry any improvement into effect is a task entirely different from the inventing of it, and a task, moreover, requiring entirely different kinds of aptitudes. Although entrepreneurs of course may be inventors just as they may be capitalists, they are inventors not by nature of their function but by coincidence and vice versa.[1]

Schumpeter saw entrepreneurs as the driving forces of economic progress. He believed that a capitalist system would ensure the fastest possible pace of technological change, because capitalism allows entrepreneurs to keep the profits resulting from their innovations.

According to Schumpeter, the importance of perfectly competitive markets is overrated in economic theory. In real capitalist economies, he said, competition usually takes place between a few rivals in oligopolistic markets. In pursuit of profit and market power, the rivals introduce new products and production methods, which in turn lead to economic growth and revitalize the capitalist system. Schumpeter called this process "creative destruction," since it destroys parts of the economy at the same time as it creates new ones.

Predictions for the Future

Given Schumpeter's opposition to socialism and his strong support for capitalism, we might expect that he would predict the downfall of socialism and final victory of capitalism throughout the world. On the contrary, he believed that in the long run capitalism was doomed, not because of its internal economic contradictions, but because of cultural and political trends flowing from its success. Hence, in answer to the question, "Can capitalism survive?" he gave the straightforward answer, "No. I do not think it can."[2]

According to Schumpeter, because of the advantages they possess, giant companies will gradually take over most industries. In the process, the innovative spirit that once guided them will be crushed, as the imaginative entrepreneur is replaced by the cautious professional manager at the helm of business. Without the entrepreneur, there will no longer be a force in society to support the institution of private property.

At the same time, the growing class of intellectuals—professors, writers, and journalists—that live well off the prosperity provided by the capitalist system, will use their persuasive powers to turn others against capitalism. Therefore, a majority of people will also become opposed to property rights. Why are so many intellectuals hostile to capitalism? Because, stated Schumpeter, most of them are outsiders who are much more competent at criticizing the system than they are at working within it.

Schumpeter predicted that the elimination of the entrepreneur and the new popular hostility toward capitalism would lead to more government involvement in the economy. Attempts would be made by government bureaucrats to smooth out economic fluctuations as well as reduce inequalities in the distribution of incomes. Gradually, the role of private property would shrink, and capitalist societies would turn toward socialism—of either the democratic or the authoritarian variety.

Relevance for Today

It is important to note that Schumpeter developed his theories before and during World War II, before the massive expansion in government activity that took place in developed capitalist countries such as Canada. In the 1960s and 1970s, as criticism of capitalist institutions became common in Canada and other countries, many commentators suggested that

Schumpeter's forecasts contained a good deal of truth. Are his predictions still as applicable in the 1980s and 1990s as they were in previous decades? Some would argue that there has been a resurgence in entrepreneurship and popular support for capitalism that now makes Schumpeter's theories less relevant than they once were.

> During the late 1960s...Schumpeter's predictions seemed to be coming true. Third world nations, newly liberated from Europe, turned to socialism. By the early 1970s, Ph.D.s were driving taxicabs and blasting the establishment. But what did the 1980s bring us? Yuppies, short hair, striped shirts, and a parade of underdeveloped nations trading Das Kapital in for Dress for Success. Even the [former] Soviet Union strives to revise its...economy. Nobody urges centralized planning anymore.... Even if a return to market mechanisms does not magically turn poverty into wealth, at least governments have jettisoned rigid, ideological abhorrence of market economic systems.[3]

But, right or wrong, Schumpeter's work provides a classic example of how economic theorizing can be made to include not only economic factors but also political and social trends.

Notes

[1] Joseph A. Schumpeter, *The Theory of Economic Development* (New York: Oxford University Press, 1961), pp. 88–89.

[2] Joseph A. Schumpeter, *Capitalism, Socialism and Democracy* (New York: Harper & Row, 1976), p. 61, as quoted in *New Ideas From Dead Economists* by Todd G. Buchholz. Copyright © 1989 by Todd G. Buchholz. Used by permission of Dutton Signet, a division of Penguin Books USA Inc.

[3] From *New Ideas From Dead Economists* by Todd G. Buchholz. Copyright © 1989 by Todd G. Buchholz. Used by permission of Dutton Signet, a division of Penguin Books USA Inc.

1. Outline one possible reason why Schumpeter's predictions about capitalism have not been borne out in the 1980s and 1990s.

2. Schumpeter elaborated a theory—first developed by the Russian economist Nikolai Kondratieff—that the world economy fluctuated in "long waves" of 50 to 60 years. To see the ways this theory can be applied, access the website of The Longwave and Social Cycles Resource Centre (at http://web.1-888.com/longwave/lwintro.html).

a. Briefly summarize how long-wave theory can be used to explain cyclical changes in the world economy between the late 1700s and the 1930s.

b. What factor did Schumpeter highlight in explaining these long waves of economic change? What are three other possible arguments to explain the existence of long waves?

c. According to contemporary long-wave theorists, what phase of the long wave is the world economy currently experiencing?

SIDELINE

THE MILK SHAKE MAN COMETH

Ray Kroc and the History of McDonald's

Maximizing profits in real-world businesses often hinges on factors that are difficult to quantify or to include in general economic models. The article below details the importance of some of these intangible factors in determining the success of one of today's best-known corporations.

In 1930, two brothers moved from New Hampshire to California. Their names were Richard and Maurice (Dick and Mac) McDonald and they hoped to break into the movie business. Having little success in the movies, and failing also at running their own movie theater, they decided to enter the newly popular drive-in restaurant business.

Located just east of Pasadena, the McDonald brothers' restaurant opened in 1937. There were three carhops in the parking lot. In short skirts and on roller skates, carhops served their drive-in customers. Dick and Mac made the hot dogs and the shakes and waited on customers who preferred to sit on stools. Their restaurant was clean, it was efficient, and it was a success. They soon had enough money to move to a second, grander location, fifty miles west of Los Angeles in San Bernardino...

Beef and pork sandwiches, ribs, and a barbecue pit laden with specially delivered Arkansas hickory chips were the centerpieces of the San Bernardino McDonald's. The brothers soon realized, though, that the more "we hammered away at the barbecue business, the more hamburgers we sold...[and] my God the carhops were slow. We'd say to ourselves that there had to be a faster way."

There was. Even though they had to close their restaurant for three months, they decided to redesign its entire operation. Paper instead of china, custom-designed grills, and ten hamburgers to the pound would cut costs and optimize efficiency. Dick designed a portable, rotating tray on which two employees could dress hamburgers as it turned. A newly created ketchup squirter would dispense precisely the right amount each time with a single squeeze. Not only would they serve a limited number of items (hamburgers and cheeseburgers; three soft drink flavours, milk, and coffee; chips; and a slice of pie; and the soon to be added fries and a shake), but also those items would be standardized. Every burger would have mustard and ketchup, onions, and two pickles. And they would charge only fifteen cents a burger, half the going rate...

One day in 1954, a curious salesman of milk shake makers appeared on their doorstep...The salesman's name was Ray Kroc and he was amazed at what he saw. Close to opening time, lines of customers formed. When asked, many said they returned daily. Some left with bags full of the fifteen-cent hamburgers.

Immediately Ray Kroc grasped the potential of the McDonald brothers' operation. He asked the brothers if he could have the exclusive right to franchise as a national chain...He was ready to copy everything the brothers did, to improve efficiency where possible and to look for franchises...

Kroc hoped to entice others to purchase the right to start their own McDonald's. In many ways he was selling a dream. To franchisees, McDonald's was supposed to represent the opportunity to earn wealth that had been unreachable...One day, Betty Agate arrived at McDonald's head quarters to sell Bibles. Kroc's secretary is said to have looked at her and immediately asked why she was selling Bibles. She replied, "Making a living."...In many ways the Agates were the type of franchisees Ray Kroc sought. They were hands-on active entrepreneurs. They spent most of their time at the restaurant counting cars, calculating preparation time, and guaranteeing cleanliness and quality. They were the people who would adhere to McDonald's standards because their interests coincided...

To maintain standardization, Kroc was willing to expand gradually...Kroc sold single-store franchises for $950 apiece. Then, if a restaurant owner refused to follow the chain's rules, Kroc would refuse to sell him another franchise. A second way that Kroc committed McDonald's to its restaurants' operations was by basing its franchise income on store performance. McDonald's made its profits from a service fee of 1.9 percent of a store's sales...

In its french fries, its burgers, indeed throughout its menu, uniformity is McDonald's basic goal. One source of uniformity is McDonald's training center, Hamburger University. Located in Oak Brook, Illinois, with three other campuses in Japan, Germany, and England, the school is headed by a "dean," can be attended by 232 students at one time, and, by 1995, had awarded its Bachelor of Hamburgerology degree to 50,000 graduates. Having already learned what they need to know about preparing food, managers attend Hamburger U. for such courses as "Effective People Practices," and team building. They take tests, hear lectures, earn a diploma, and receive academic honors for excellence...

By 1962, McDonald's franchises exceeded 400. In 1974, the chain had 3,000 stores. By 1980 there were 6,200 units. Today the company, through the restaurants it owns, through joint ventures, and through its franchisees, operates more than 14,000 restaurants in seventy-three countries. In 1994, its sales totalled $26 billion.

Source

Abridged from *Econ 101½* by Elaine L. Schwartz. Copyright © 1995 by Elaine L. Schwartz. By permission of Avon Books, pp. 190-196.

1. In what ways were the innovations of the McDonald brothers and Ray Kroc crucial in the development of McDonald's as a successful company?

2. Can the McDonald brothers and Ray Kroc be classified as entrepreneurs, as defined by Schumpeter? Explain.

Chapter Seven
Resource Markets

Nothing like a splendid new resource to start the battles.

—Jean Howarth, Canadian short story writer

Two activities unite all businesses: they sell products and they hire resources. So far, we have concentrated on the selling. Now, we'll start to explore how businesses use economic resources. How many workers should a particular company hire? Is it worthwhile for the business to purchase and use another machine? Should a farmer use more land to grow a crop? In this chapter, we'll focus on how businesses make choices about the economic resources they employ; later, we'll turn our attention to the roles households and governments play in these decisions.

CHAPTER FOCUS

This chapter focuses on the following:

- how businesses maximize profits by choosing how much of each economic resource to use
- the demand for resources by businesses that are price-takers and price-makers in the markets in which they sell their products
- the supply of labour, how wage rates are determined, and labour market equilibrium
- factors that change resource demand
- price elasticity of resource demand and the factors that determine it

HOW RESOURCE MARKETS OPERATE

In past chapters, we have concentrated on product markets—the markets in which consumer goods and services are traded. Now, we'll take a look at the other half of the picture—resource markets, in which economic resources are traded. Recall that in resource markets households sell economic resources to businesses, and households receive incomes in return. So, for their contribution of natural resources (including land), capital resources, and human resources (in particular labour and entrepreneurship), households receive incomes in the form of rent, interest, wages, and profit.

wage: the amount earned by a worker for providing labour for a certain period of time

When analyzing resource markets, economists are especially interested in the way that resource prices are set, since these prices play a crucial role in determining people's incomes. For example, the relevant price in a labour market is the **wage**, which is the amount earned by a worker for providing labour for a certain period. While a wage is usually thought of as a worker's income paid on an hourly basis, the term is used more broadly in economics to include workers' incomes (often known as salaries) paid by the day, month, or year. It is important to remember that resource markets are affected by a wide array of factors. While social customs, governments, and labour unions each play a part in determining resource prices, the interaction of demand and supply remains the central feature in these markets. Indeed, demand and supply conditions often influence resource markets *despite* outside intervention. In this chapter, we focus on the forces of demand and supply.

The Demand for Resources

Unlike the demand for consumer items, the demand for resources is determined indirectly. Since resources are used to produce final goods and services, it is the demand for these products that ultimately determines how much of the resources are demanded. For example, the number of printing presses demanded by a newspaper publishing company depends on the demand for the company's product. If the newspaper attracts more readers, the company will respond by increasing production, and therefore buying more printing presses. Similarly, the number of workers hired by a car manufacturer depends on demand in the car market. A drop in the demand for cars will lower the demand for workers, resulting in hiring freezes and, perhaps, even layoffs.

marginal productivity theory: the theory that businesses use resources based on how much extra profit these resources provide

To calculate resource demand, economists use **marginal productivity theory**, which states that businesses use resources based on how much extra profit these resources provide. Therefore, when deciding whether or not it is profitable to buy one more unit of a resource, businesses consider three factors: the resource's marginal cost, its marginal product, and the marginal revenue provided by each new unit of output produced. To illustrate the resource choices a business makes, we'll look at businesses with varying power in product markets.

PRODUCT AND RESOURCE PRICE-TAKER

Let's first consider the example of a strawberry farm. We'll assume that the strawberry market is perfectly competitive, that the farmer hires labour in a perfectly competitive resource market, and that factors other than output and labour remain constant. So, the farmer hires workers in a market with many buyers and sellers, each of them having no effect on the prevailing price of the resource—namely, the hourly wage for farm workers. Therefore, the strawberry farm is a price-taker in both its product and resource markets.

Marginal Revenue Product

According to marginal productivity theory, a business decides how much of a resource to use based on the resource's marginal product and marginal revenue, in addition to the resource's marginal cost to the business.

Marginal Product

The strawberry farmer must first estimate how much output will be added by hiring each new worker while all other factors remain constant. In other words, the farmer must determine each worker's marginal product. Columns 1, 2, and 3 of the table in Figure 7.1 show the results. For the sake of simplicity, we assume that the marginal product of labour starts to decline with the very first worker. At harvest time, the farmer hires more labour and the total quantity of strawberries picked per hour increases, as shown in column 2. However, the marginal product of labour, shown in column 3, declines. For example, when the second worker is hired, the total product of strawberries rises from 10 to 18 kg, giving a marginal product for the second worker of 8 kg (18 – 10). With the third worker, the total product rises from 18 to 24 kg, giving a marginal product for the third worker of only 6 kg (24 – 18).

Marginal Revenue

Once the marginal product of each worker is determined, the farmer must calculate the marginal revenue gained by selling the additional strawberries. Because the farmer is a price-taker in the perfectly competitive strawberry market, the price of strawberries is constant, and the price and marginal revenue for strawberries are equal. Hence, the farmer only needs to know the price of strawberries to find marginal revenue. Figure 7.1 shows the price of strawberries in column 4 as $2 per kilogram.

marginal revenue product: the change in total revenue associated with employing each new unit of a resource

The effects of marginal product and marginal revenue on the business's demand for labour are summarized by the concept of **marginal revenue product** (MRP), which is the change in total revenue associated with employing each new unit of a resource—in this case, each new worker. Because it represents the *extra* revenue provided by the *extra* units of output produced by each new worker, marginal revenue product incorporates both marginal revenue and marginal product. The

FIGURE 7.1
Labour Demand and Supply for a Product and Resource Price-Taker

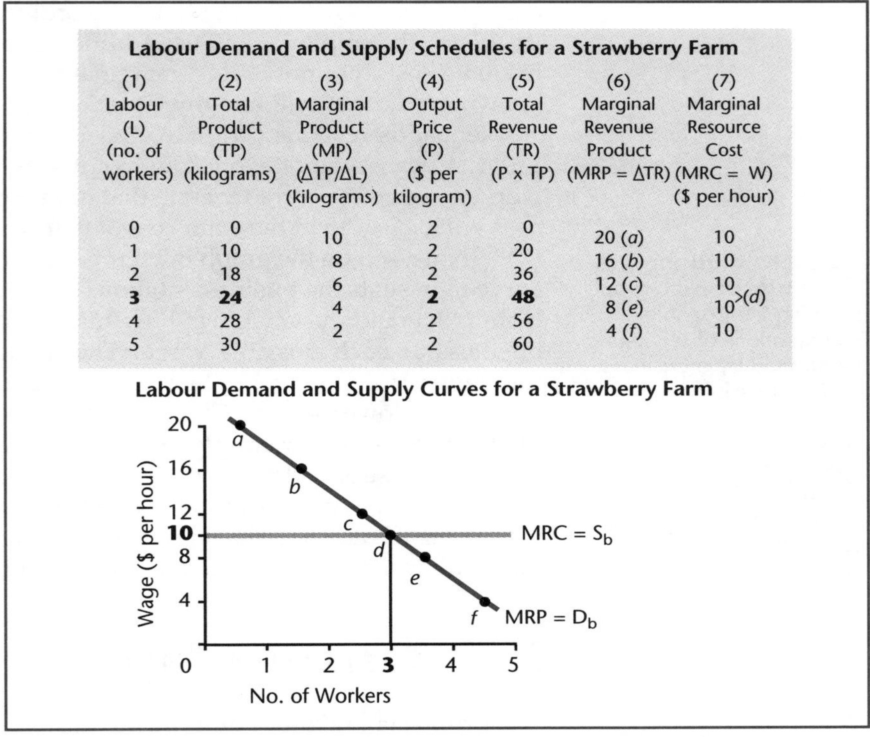

Labour Demand and Supply Schedules for a Strawberry Farm

(1) Labour (L) (no. of workers)	(2) Total Product (TP) (kilograms)	(3) Marginal Product (MP) (ΔTP/ΔL) (kilograms)	(4) Output Price (P) ($ per kilogram)	(5) Total Revenue (TR) (P x TP)	(6) Marginal Revenue Product (MRP = ΔTR)	(7) Marginal Resource Cost (MRC = W) ($ per hour)
0	0		2	0		
1	10	10	2	20	20 (*a*)	10
2	18	8	2	36	16 (*b*)	10
3	**24**	6	**2**	**48**	12 (*c*)	10
4	28	4	2	56	8 (*e*)	10 >(*d*)
5	30	2	2	60	4 (*f*)	10

Labour Demand and Supply Curves for a Strawberry Farm

The price-taking business's demand for labour, D_b, is found by calculating the marginal revenue product (MRP), or the change in the business's total revenue from hiring each new worker. The business's supply curve, S_b, is the marginal resource cost (MRC) of each new worker. Since the business can hire workers at a constant wage of $10 per hour, S_b is a horizontal line, and the business's profit-maximizing employment level of labour is 3 workers at point *d*.

table in Figure 7.1 shows total revenue in column 5 (found by multiplying each total product value by price), and the marginal revenue product (the change in total revenue) in column 6. Expressing the marginal revenue product on the graph gives us the marginal revenue product curve. So, in the strawberry farm example, total revenue is $20 (10 × $2) when employing one worker, and $36 (18 × $2) when employing two workers. Therefore, the marginal revenue product of the second worker is the difference between the two amounts, or $16 ($36 – $20), shown on the graph at point *b*.

Labour Demand and Supply

Given this information, it is a straightforward task for the strawberry farmer to find the profit-maximizing employment of labour. The extra cost of each additional unit of a resource for the business is referred to as **marginal resource cost** (MRC). In the case of the strawberry farmer who is a price-taker in the labour market, and therefore a "wage-taker," marginal resource cost is simply the prevailing wage paid to farm workers. In our

marginal resource cost: the extra cost of each additional unit of a resource

example, the wage is $10 per hour. According to the marginal productivity theory, the employer will use additional resources as long as marginal resource cost does not exceed marginal revenue product. Therefore, our strawberry farmer will hire three workers, because each of the first three workers adds revenue ($20, $16, and $12, respectively) greater than the $10 cost per worker. Beyond this point, it is not profitable to hire more workers, since the extra revenue that each worker will provide the business will be less than the extra cost of that worker.

business's labour demand curve: a graph showing the possible combinations of workers demanded by a business at each possible wage

business's labour supply curve: a graph showing the possible combinations of workers supplied to a business at each possible wage

Expressed on the graph in Figure 7.1, the marginal revenue product curve represents the **business's labour demand curve**, D_b. The business's labour demand curve shows how many workers are demanded by a business at each possible wage. The demand curve has a negative (downward) slope because businesses find it profitable to employ more workers at lower wages. The marginal resource cost curve represents the **business's labour supply curve**, or S_b. This curve shows how many workers are supplied to a business at each possible wage. Because the business is a price-taker in the resource market, this curve is horizontal. No matter what action the strawberry farmer takes, the wage is fixed at the equilibrium wage determined by the entire market.

Profit-Maximizing Employment Rule

profit-maximizing employment rule: a business should use a resource up to the point where the resource's marginal revenue product equals its marginal resource cost

The profit-maximizing point for the business occurs at the intersection of its demand and supply curves for labour, D_b and S_b. In other words, the business will hire workers up to the point where marginal revenue product and marginal resource cost are the same. This result provides a general **profit-maximizing employment rule** for resources. No matter what market a business operates in, it should use a resource up to the point where the resource's marginal revenue product equals its marginal resource cost.

Profit-maximizing employment rule:	Marginal revenue product (MRP)	=	Marginal resource cost (MRC)

Notice that the profit-maximizing employment rule parallels the profit-maximizing output rule (outlined in the previous chapter), which is used by businesses to decide levels of output. Recall that the profit-maximizing output rule states that, in order to maximize profits, a business should produce the quantity of output at which marginal revenue and marginal cost intersect, since up to this point every unit of output has a marginal revenue that exceeds its marginal cost. Similarly, a business can maximize its profits by using a resource up to the point at which marginal revenue product equals marginal resource cost. By doing so, the business employs all units that give more extra revenue than they add to the business's costs.

Thinking About Economics

Is marginal productivity theory equally applicable to economic resources other than labour?

In theory, a business should make choices about all economic resources based on each resource's marginal revenue product and marginal resource cost. In practice, however, marginal revenue product tends to be calculated for labour and for natural resources, but not for the other economic resources. This is because both labour and natural resources can be measured in standardized units—for example, an hour of a certain type of labour, or a hectare of a certain grade of land.

In contrast, it's usually harder to calculate marginal revenue product for capital goods. While it is possible to calculate the marginal revenue product of a particular material or type of machine used by a business, this cannot be done for an entire investment project—when a business contemplates building a factory, for example. One investment project differs so much from another that it is impossible to measure them in standardized units. Because they are physically indivisible, they must be counted in monetary terms—the number of dollars a business needs to undertake a certain investment project. Entrepreneurship is also difficult to measure because it is intangible. Therefore, it is not possible to calculate the marginal revenue product of a given "unit" of entrepreneurship, and its demand and supply must be treated in qualitative, not quantitative, terms.

Market Demand and Supply

labour market demand curve: a graph showing the possible combinations of workers demanded in a certain labour market at each possible wage

labour market supply curve: a graph showing the possible combinations of workers supplying their labour in a certain labour market at each possible wage

Now, if we assume that all 1000 employers of farm workers in the region have marginal revenue product curves identical to the one shown in Figure 7.1, we can derive the **labour market demand curve**, D_m. The labour market demand curve shows how many workers are demanded in a competitive labour market at each possible wage. By adding the labour demand curves of all businesses in this market, we have the labour market demand schedule and curve shown in Figure 7.2. For example, at an hourly wage of $14, each of the 1000 farmers demands two workers, which gives a total labour demand of 2000. If the wage were to drop to $10, each farmer would demand three workers, raising total labour demanded in the market to 3000.

Corresponding to this market demand for farm workers is a **labour market supply curve**, S_m, which shows the total supply of workers offering their services in a certain labour market at each wage. This curve has a positive (upward) slope because, in general, higher wages in a given market encourage more workers to offer their labour in that market. Suppose for our strawberry market that wages increase from $10 per hour to $14 per hour. Figure 7.2 shows that this wage increase would increase the quantity of farm workers supplied from 3000 to 4000. Figure 7.2 also demonstrates another feature of resource markets that is similar to that in product markets: equilibrium occurs at the intersection of the labour market supply and demand curves.

FIGURE 7.2
Demand and Supply in a Competitive Labour Market

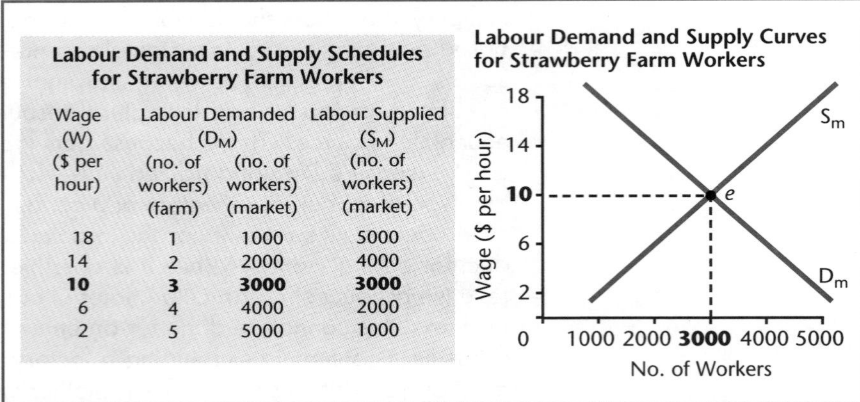

Labour Demand and Supply Schedules for Strawberry Farm Workers

Wage (W) ($ per hour)	Labour Demanded (D_M) (no. of workers) (farm)	(no. of workers) (market)	Labour Supplied (S_M) (no. of workers) (market)
18	1	1000	5000
14	2	2000	4000
10	**3**	**3000**	**3000**
6	4	4000	2000
2	5	5000	1000

The market demand curve for strawberry farm workers, D_m, is found by adding together the workers demanded by each farm at various wages. In a competitive labour market, this demand curve and the market supply curve, S_m, intersect at equilibrium point *e*, where the wage is $10 for 3000 workers employed.

BRIEF REVIEW

1. Resource markets, like product markets, are governed by the forces of demand and supply. However, the demand for resources is determined indirectly.
2. Based on marginal productivity theory, businesses decide how much of a resource to use based on the resource's marginal revenue product, or MRP (the change in total revenue associated with each new unit of resource), and marginal resource cost, or MRC (the extra cost to the business of employing each additional unit of resource).
3. The profit-maximizing employment rule states that businesses should use a resource up to the point where its marginal revenue product equals its marginal resource cost.
4. In practice, marginal productivity theory is best applied to labour and natural resources because they can be measured in standardized units.
5. In a perfectly competitive resource market, the marginal revenue product curve represents the business's resource demand curve, while the marginal resource cost curve represents the business's resource supply curve.
6. In a perfectly competitive resource market, the business is a price-taker; therefore, the business's resource supply curve is a horizontal line. In this market, the profit-maximizing employment level occurs where the business's resource demand and supply curves intersect.
7. In a perfectly competitive resource market, the market's resource demand is the sum of the individual businesses' resource demand. The market's resource supply is the sum of all the individual resource owners' resource supply. Equilibrium is the point at which the market demand and market supply curves for the resource intersect.

PRODUCT PRICE-MAKER/RESOURCE PRICE-TAKER

What happens to resource demand and supply if the business is an imperfect competitor or a monopolist in its product market? In these cases, the business has some control over the price of its product, or is a product price-maker. To see how the business's resource demand curve is determined, let's assume that the labour market is perfectly competitive, making the business a resource price-taker.

Consider the case of Nirvana Cushions, a small manufacturer that is a price-maker in the output market where it sells its product and hires unskilled workers in a competitive labour market. Nirvana Cushions decides how many workers to hire by using the concept of marginal revenue product. However, unlike a price-taker in output markets, Nirvana faces a product demand curve with a negative (downward) slope. As the business increases its output of cushions, the price it can charge for each cushion falls.

Marginal Revenue Product

As with the strawberry farmer, Nirvana Cushions must first find the total product and marginal product of each new worker. Again, we'll assume that marginal product begins to decline with the very first worker. Figure 7.3 shows the results in table columns 1 to 3. So, while the marginal product of the first worker is 4 (4 – 0), the marginal product of the second worker is 3 (7 – 4).

Next, the business must find the marginal revenue of each new worker. Because the business is a price-maker in its product market, the price is not constant at all quantities of output. So, for example, Nirvana Cushions finds that there is sufficient demand to produce four cushions per hour if they sell at a price of $8 each, but demand dictates that, if seven cushions are produced per hour, they would have to sell at a price of $6 each. The possible prices for each output level are shown in column 4 in Figure 7.3. Column 5 shows the resulting total revenues (total product multiplied by price). The change in total revenue from one production level to the next, the marginal revenue product, is shown in column 6. Expressed on a graph, the marginal revenue product figures give the marginal revenue product curve. So, the business has a total revenue of $32 (4 × $8) when employing one worker, and $42 (7 × $6) when employing two workers. The marginal revenue of the second worker, therefore, is $10 ($42 – $32), shown on the graph as point *h*.

The distinguishing feature of the marginal revenue product curve of a business that has some power to set product prices is that it is less elastic than that for a perfect competitor, which is a price-taker. At Nirvana Cushions' higher employment levels, for example, the marginal revenue product falls for two reasons. Not only does the marginal product of labour decrease, but also the price that the business can charge for its product decreases as production increases.

Labour Demand and Supply

Recall that the profit-maximizing employment rule applies to all businesses regardless of their power in the product and resource markets. This means that once Nirvana Cushions knows its marginal revenue product, it can determine its profit-maximizing employment level. According to the rule, the business should employ a resource up to the point where the marginal revenue product of the resource equals its marginal resource cost. Recall that Nirvana Cushions is assumed to be a wage-taker in a competitive labour market where individual employers have no influence. Suppose the prevailing wage for unskilled workers is \$7 per hour. Given this wage, Nirvana Cushions will hire two workers, since each provides a higher marginal revenue product than their \$7 marginal resource cost. As before, the marginal revenue product curve is the business's labour demand curve, D_b, and the horizontal marginal resource cost curve is the business's labour supply curve, S_b. The profit-maximizing employment level occurs at point *i*, where the two curves intersect in Figure 7.3.

FIGURE 7.3
Labour Demand and Supply for a Product Price-Maker/ Resource Price-Taker

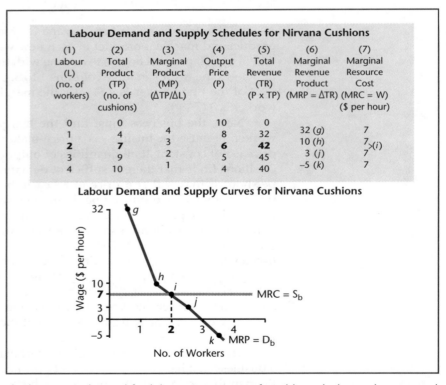

Labour Demand and Supply Schedules for Nirvana Cushions

(1) Labour (L) (no. of workers)	(2) Total Product (TP) (no. of cushions)	(3) Marginal Product (MP) (ΔTP/ΔL)	(4) Output Price (P)	(5) Total Revenue (TR) (P x TP)	(6) Marginal Revenue Product (MRP = ΔTR)	(7) Marginal Resource Cost (MRC = W) (\$ per hour)
0	0		10	0		
1	4	4	8	32	32 (*g*)	7
2	**7**	3	**6**	**42**	10 (*h*)	7 >(*i*)
3	9	2	5	45	3 (*j*)	7
4	10	1	4	40	–5 (*k*)	7

Labour Demand and Supply Curves for Nirvana Cushions

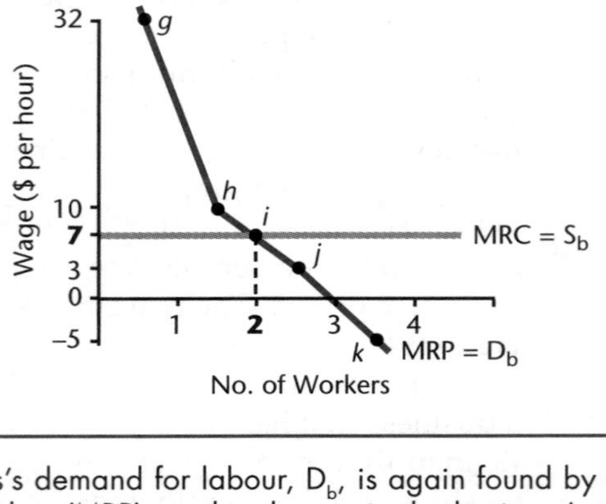

The business's demand for labour, D_b, is again found by calculating the marginal revenue product (MRP), or the change in the business's total revenue from hiring each new worker. The business's supply curve for labour, S_b, is the marginal resource cost (MRC) of new workers. Given that workers can be hired at a constant wage of \$7 per hour, S_b is a horizontal line, and the business's profit-maximizing employment level of labour is 2 workers at point *i*.

Market Demand and Supply

If the resource market is competitive, the degree of competition in the product market doesn't affect how the market demand for a resource is determined. Therefore, Nirvana Cushions' demand for unskilled workers is combined with all other businesses' demand for unskilled workers to find the market demand. As with the market for farm workers, the supply of unskilled workers will have a positive (upward) slope. Once again, the intersection of the demand curve and the supply curve gives the equilibrium point for the labour market.

CHANGES IN RESOURCE DEMAND

Resource demand can change for a variety of reasons. There are three main resource demand determinants: changes in product demand, changes in other resource prices, and technological innovation. Each demand determinant affects the business's marginal revenue product, which in turn causes a change in resource demand.

Product Demand

Recall that the demand for resources depends on the demand for the consumer products these resources help to produce. Therefore, when the demand for a certain product changes, the demand for resources used to produce the product changes in the same direction. As more people use computers in their leisure time, for example, the demand for computer programmers will increase. Meanwhile, if skiing becomes less popular as a pastime, the demand for ski-lift operators will decline.

Changes in product demand affect the demand for resources through changes in product prices. For example, if the demand for strawberries increases, their price increases, and each strawberry farm worker's marginal revenue product increases as well. Each strawberry farmer's marginal revenue product curve shifts to the right, as does the business's demand curve for labour. Therefore, the entire market demand curve for farm workers shifts to the right. In the same way, a decrease in the demand for cushions decreases the price Nirvana Cushions can charge, which, in turn, decreases each worker's marginal revenue product and reduces the business's demand for labour.

Other Resource Prices

complementary resources: resources that are used together

Resources used in a particular production process can be related in two ways. **Complementary resources** are used together, as in the case of steam shovels and steam-shovel operators. When two resources are complementary, the price for one resource and the demand for the other resource have an inverse relationship. So, for example, if steam shovels drop in price, the number of these machines will increase, and the demand for the labour of steam-shovel operators will increase as well.

substitute resources: resources that can be used in place of one another without affecting output

Substitute resources, in contrast, are resources that can be used in place of one another without affecting the business's or industry's output. The price for one resource and the demand for the substitute resource have a direct relationship. So, for example, if steam shovels drop in price, use of these machines will increase, and demand for manual labour will decrease.

Technological Innovation

A third resource demand determinant is technological innovation. Suppose a new cushion-producing machine is introduced at Nirvana Cushions. If labour and the new machinery are complementary resources, each worker's marginal product will rise and Nirvana Cushions' demand for labour will increase. In this case, there will also likely be an increase in **labour productivity**, which is the quantity of output produced per worker in a given period of time—in other words, the average product of labour. However, if Nirvana Cushions' workers and the new machinery are substitute resources, the use of this new machine will reduce the marginal product of each worker, and Nirvana's demand for labour in this industry will decrease.

labour productivity: the quantity of output produced per worker in a given period of time; the average product of labour

PRICE ELASTICITY OF RESOURCE DEMAND

Just as with demand in product markets, demand in resource markets can be elastic or inelastic. The price elasticity of resource demand indicates the responsiveness of businesses using a resource to variations in its price. In general, there are four factors that affect price elasticity of resource demand: the rate of decline in the marginal product of a resource, the price elasticity of product demand, the resource's proportion of the business's total costs, and the availability of substitute resources.

Rate of Decline in Marginal Product

The more rapid the decline in the marginal product of a resource, the steeper the business's marginal revenue product curve. Since the marginal revenue product curve equals the business's demand curve for the product, the steeper the decline in a resource's marginal product, the less elastic the resource demand becomes. For example, if introducing new robotic machinery in a car manufacturing plant causes the marginal product of auto workers to fall more rapidly than before, the marginal revenue product of auto workers becomes steeper, and the demand for auto workers becomes less elastic.

Thinking About Economics

How does the increased use of capital resources in the Canadian economy affect Canadian workers?

Recall that businesses producing a certain product can usually choose from among production processes that combine different proportions of inputs. For a given quantity of output, a labour-intensive process employs more labour and less capital resources, while a capital-intensive process employs less labour and more capital resources. The use of more capital-intensive methods of production by Canadian businesses affects parts of Canada's workforce in different ways. As a rule, highly skilled labour benefits when more capital-intensive forms of production are used. Since this labour is usually a complementary resource to new forms of machinery, the employment of more capital by Canadian businesses tends to raise the productivity as well as the demand for skilled labour, therefore boosting wages and employment for these workers.

The effects of capital-intensive production processes on semiskilled and unskilled labour are more indefinite. In the past, automated production processes in manufacturing industries often called for workers to perform simplified and highly repetitive tasks. In these cases, labour was a complementary resource to machinery: continued automation increased labour demand and raised both wages and employment levels. However, in the last few decades, new types of capital resources have increasingly been substituted for semiskilled and unskilled labour. As the use of capital resources increases, the demand for semiskilled or unskilled labour decreases, thereby decreasing the equilibrium wage and number of workers employed.

In general, the use of more capital-intensive techniques in Canadian industry has raised Canadian workers' living standards and gradually led to improved working conditions. However, because of the differential effects of automation on skilled and on semiskilled and unskilled labour, Canadian workers are being forced to become continually more skilled and productive.

Price Elasticity of Product Demand

Because the demand for resources is a derived demand, the price elasticity of a product influences the producer's decisions about the resources needed to make that product. When the demand for a product is inelastic, the company producing the product will find that at higher output levels it will charge significantly less. Therefore, the business's marginal revenue product and the associated resource demand curve will be less elastic also. So, for example, the owners of Nirvana Cushions have less elastic demand for labour than does the strawberry farmer, who faces elastic demand.

Proportion of Total Costs

When the cost of a certain resource makes up a large proportion of a business's overall costs, the demand for the resource tends to be more elastic. For example, the quantity of labour demanded by wheat farmers will not vary much when there is an adjustment in wages, since wage costs are a small percentage of total costs. In contrast, the demand for capital equipment such as combine harvesters is much more elastic because these costs represent a large percentage of wheat farmers' costs.

Substitute Resources

A resource with many substitutes has a more elastic demand curve than a resource that is indispensable to the production process. For example, the demand for labour in the auto industry tends to be more elastic than in the hotel and restaurant industry, since the opportunity to substitute capital for labour is much greater in manufacturing.

BRIEF REVIEW

1. The profit-maximizing employment rule also applies to businesses that are price-makers in their product markets. A business should use a resource up to the point where its marginal revenue product and marginal resource cost curves intersect. As long as the resource market is competitive, this point occurs where the business's resource demand and supply curves intersect.
2. The marginal revenue product is less elastic for a business that is a price-maker in its product market than for a business that is a price-taker. The decline in a resource's marginal revenue product is more rapid not only because of the diminishing marginal product but also because of price variations.
3. Resource demand can be affected by changes in product demand, changes in other resource prices, and technological innovation.
4. The price elasticity of resource demand is determined by the rate of decline in the marginal product of a resource, the price elasticity of demand for the product, the proportion of a business's total costs that the resource accounts for, and the availability of substitute resources.

KEY CONCEPTS

wage
marginal productivity theory
marginal revenue product
marginal resource cost
business's labour demand curve
business's labour supply curve
profit-maximizing employment rule
labour market demand curve
labour market supply curve
complementary resources
substitute resources
labour productivity

ANALYSIS AND APPLICATION

Production Conditions for Ham-It-Up Radios

Labour (number of workers)	Total Product (radios per week)	Marginal Product (radios per worker)	Average Product (radios per worker)
0	0		
		______	
1	120		______
		______	
2	200		______
		______	
3	270		______
		______	
4	320		______
		______	
5	340		______
		______	
6	350		______
		______	
7	340		______

1. The accompanying table gives short-run production conditions for a company that makes radios.
   a. Copy out and complete the table, and identify the ranges where marginal product is positive and where it is negative.
   b. Explain the relationships between marginal product and total product, and between marginal product and average product.
   c. On one graph, draw the total product curve. On another graph, draw the marginal product and average product curves. Why do the curves in these graphs differ from the corresponding curves portrayed in Figure 4.4 (in Chapter 4) of the text?

Labour Demand and Supply Schedules for a Salmon Fisherman

(1) Labour (no. of workers)	(2) Total Product (kilograms per hour)	(3) Marginal Product (kilograms per hour)	(4) Product Price ($ per kilogram)	(5) Total Revenue ($ per hour)	(6) Marginal Revenue Product ($ per hour)
0	0		3	____	
		____			____
1	16		3	____	
		____			____
2	28		3	____	
		____			____
3	37		3	____	
		____			____
4	44		3	____	
		____			____
5	47		3	____	

2. The accompanying table shows cost and revenue data for a salmon fisherman who sells his catch for $3 per kilogram in a perfectly competitive product market and hires boat-hands in a perfectly competitive labour market at an hourly wage of $15.
   a. Copy out and complete the table, and on a sheet of graph paper plot the fisherman's labour demand and labour supply curves.
   b. What explains the shapes of the curves you have drawn in part a.?
   c. How many full-time boat-hands will the fisherman employ? Explain using the profit-maximizing employment rule and your graph.
   d. If the wage rate rises to $24 per hour, how many full-time boat-hands will the fisherman now employ? Again, explain using the profit-maximizing employment rule and your graph.

Labour Demand and Supply Schedules for a Salmon Fisherman

(1) Labour (no. of workers)	(2) Total Product (kilograms per hour)	(3) Marginal Product (kilograms per hour)	(4) Product Price ($ per kilogram)	(5) Total Revenue ($ per hour)	(6) Marginal Revenue Product ($ per hour)
0	0		5.00	____	
		____			____
1	16		4.50	____	
		____			____
2	28		4.00	____	
		____			____
3	37		3.50	____	
		____			____
4	44		3.00	____	
		____			____
5	47		2.50	____	

3. The fisherman in the previous question begins to sell his product in an imperfectly competitive market, as shown in the accompanying table.

a. Copy out and complete the table showing the supply and demand schedule, and on a sheet of graph paper draw the fisherman's new labour demand curve.
b. Why does the curve you have drawn in part a. differ from the labour demand curve found in the previous question?
c. How many full-time boat-hands will the fisherman employ at an hourly wage of $10? at an hourly wage of $29? Explain these answers using the profit-maximizing employment rule and your graph.

4. Outline the effect of each of the following situations on the demand for labour in the production of computer chips.
   a. There is a fall in the price of silicon, which is used to make computer chips.
   b. The demand for computer chips becomes more elastic.
   c. Wages make up a smaller proportion of costs for producers of computer chips than they did previously.
   d. There is a rise in the price of machinery which can be substituted for labour in the production of computer chips.
   e. A change in production techniques means that the marginal product of labour is less affected by changes in the production of computer chips.
   f. The demand for computer chips falls.
   g. New types of automated machinery can now be substituted for labour in the production of computer chips.

5. Identify how each of the following trends will affect demand or supply in the market for unskilled labour within Canada. Also identify how the equilibrium wage and employment level for this labour will change in each case.
   a. There are a greater number of dropouts from the Canadian educational system.
   b. The equilibrium wage for unskilled labour in Mexico increases.
   c. To fund a new government pension scheme, employers must start paying a tax for each unskilled worker they employ.

6. (Advanced Question)
   In recent years, the growing use of computers has revolutionized many types of production. Give an example of capital and labour that are (a) substitute resources, and (b) complementary resources for computers, and explain the reasons for these relationships.

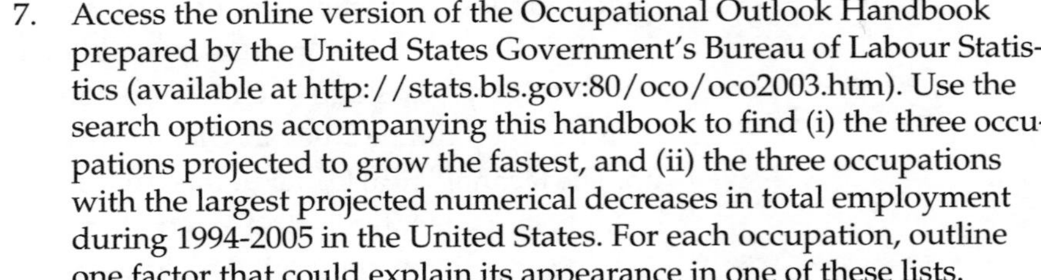

7. Access the online version of the Occupational Outlook Handbook prepared by the United States Government's Bureau of Labour Statistics (available at http://stats.bls.gov:80/oco/oco2003.htm). Use the search options accompanying this handbook to find (i) the three occupations projected to grow the fastest, and (ii) the three occupations with the largest projected numerical decreases in total employment during 1994-2005 in the United States. For each occupation, outline one factor that could explain its appearance in one of these lists.

Advancing Economic Thought

SHIFTING GEARS

Nuala Beck and the New Economy

Why are economic changes becoming more rapid? And what are the signs of this rapid change? These are the questions that Canadian economist Nuala Beck asked herself when she saw the Canadian and world economies changing in ways that didn't fit the old models and measures. In the following excerpt from her book Shifting Gears: Thriving in the New Economy, *Beck outlines how the current transformation of the Canadian economy is part of a long-term evolutionary process.*

We really only need to turn the clock back about 150 years to see how we got where we are today.

By identifying three circles, each representing an economic movement that shaped the period from 1850 to the present, I had stumbled on a key to understanding the forward movement of our economy today. I've called these models the *commodity-processing*, or C Circle; the *mass-manufacturing*, or M Circle; and the *technology*, or T Circle. Each circle contains certain key, common elements; each makes sense of vast economic changes that otherwise don't fit into a sensible pattern; each is the natural extension of the one preceding. Specific industries, even the economies of entire nations, can be defined by their place inside these circles. And once that's determined, their future—and yours—can be foretold with a remarkable degree of precision.

Nuala Beck
Source: Nuala Beck

After running my original musings through the gauntlet of hard economic analysis, it became clear that the key to each circle is a single, crucial ingredient whose abundant supply, at steadily falling prices, acts as a springboard, or catalyst, to levels of growth never before witnessed. In the commodity-processing era (the C Circle), it was cheap steel. In the succeeding mass-manufacturing era (M Circle), it was energy, specifically oil, whose discovery in vast quantities around the turn of the century fuelled the consumer-driven manufacturing boom that shifted the center of economic power to the United States from Britain.

Today, in the T (technology) Circle, the world is being driven by huge supplies of another product that was unknown outside the closely guarded doors of Texas Instruments and one or two other research laboratories thirty years ago—semiconductors, or microchips, so cheap and plentiful they can be stuck in watches to tell you when it's time to wake up. The technological leader in this circle is Japan, but America isn't nearly so far back as its internal and external critics like to think.

Besides those single, vital building blocks, each circle has other identifying traits.

- Every era has its *engines*—a handful of strategic industries that drive the entire economy and typically have risen rapidly out of humble origins. The roaring engines of the C Circle were steel, railways, textiles and coal. These were superseded in the mass-manufacturing era by autos, housing, machine tools and retailing. The T Circle, as you might guess, has been turbo-driven by computers and semiconductors, as well as telecommunications, instrumentation and the health and medical industry.
- Every era has its *virtuosos*—the innovative entrepreneurs, scientists and engineers who use existing technology merely as a stepping stone to new methods, processes and products, rather than endlessly reinventing the wheel.
- Every era can be defined by the *technology* these innovators develop. They spend their working lives looking for that better mousetrap, whether it's Henry Ford and his sturdy Model-T car or Jack Kilby and his microchips. (Ironically, Kilby, the Texas Instruments scientist who invented the first integrated circuit the size of a matchhead, never stopped using the slide rule that his pocket calculator made obsolete in 1971.) When they find it, the stage is set for the next explosive round of growth.

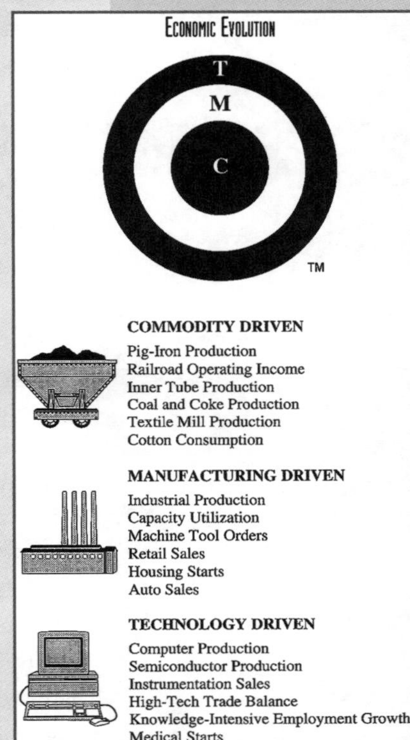

Economic Evolution
T
M
C
TM
COMMODITY DRIVEN
Pig-Iron Production
Railroad Operating Income
Inner Tube Production
Coal and Coke Production
Textile Mill Production
Cotton Consumption
MANUFACTURING DRIVEN
Industrial Production
Capacity Utilization
Machine Tool Orders
Retail Sales
Housing Starts
Auto Sales
TECHNOLOGY DRIVEN
Computer Production
Semiconductor Production
Instrumentation Sales
High-Tech Trade Balance
Knowledge-Intensive Employment Growth
Medical Starts

- Every era has its *technological pacesetters*, from Britain in the commodity-processing circle, to the United States and Germany in the manufacturing era, to Japan and the U.S. today. The key is the financial might needed to develop the better mousetraps.
- Every era has its own *management practices*. The C Circle, for example, saw the appearance of the first truly giant firms, cartels and trusts that weren't dependent on the whims of royalty or the vagaries of the trade winds. It was here that the foundation was laid for the first great industrial fortunes—a departure from the land- or merchant-based wealth of old.
- Every era has its *philosophers*, the gurus who spend most of their time formulating theories about an economy that no longer exists and may never have—except in their ideal universe.
- Every era has its *fast track*—the jobs that lead somewhere and provide the best chance of hitching dreams to reality in the workplace. In the M Circle, blue-collar workers achieved a level of prosperity beyond the wildest imaginings of previous generations. For the first time, factory laborers had the American dream within their grasp. Many acquired homes of their own, annual vacations, private transportation and other advantages that had long been the sole preserve of the rich.

Today, it's the workers in the new economy who have the best hope for a secure future. Individual computer or communication companies may come and go, but the worker with T Circle skills will still be better off than those being kicked off the assembly lines of the incredible shrinking auto industry and other outdated sectors. Seniority doesn't matter much when the company has sunk to the bottom of the lake. Everybody drowns, no matter what position they had in the boat!

- Every era has its *losers*—industries that were once a major economic force but are now more or less in permanent decline. Just ask the rail manufacturers or pig-iron producers.
- Every era has its *emerging industries*—fledgling sectors destined to carry the world into the next great period of growth, but still seeking a firm foothold. Once it was automobile manufacturing. Today, it's genetic engineering and artificial intelligence.
- Every era has its *roadblocks*, easily identifiable barriers that have to be overcome before the transition can be completed.

A natural limitation on the growth of the commodity-processing circle was the lack of standards—in everything from education and electricity to railroad tracks. In the manufacturing era, assembly-line technology overcame the severe restrictions on capacity caused by the old batch, or piecemeal, system of production, while rapid transportation removed the major roadblock to market access, and integration of design, production and marketing shunted aside idea-strangling bureaucracies. The current technology-driven circle has developed through the application of electronics and miniaturization to largely remove the limitations of existing energy and materials. Without the magic of integrated circuits, computers would be way too unwieldy and far too expensive for ordinary mortals like you and me to ever make use of them.

- Every era *organizes work* in a particular way, linked to the needs and goals of society at the time, which is why change is doubly painful. Not only does the nature of the work change, so does the social structure that underpins it. The abolition of child labor and other worker reforms in the C Circle (when some industries were known as "slaughterhouses" for the high death rate of employees, some barely out of diapers) was, in its own time, as revolutionary a move as the organization of work along assembly lines in the M Circle and the later rise of middle management and the development of a professional class.

What doesn't (and can never) work is the grafting of old approaches and structures onto the new economy. That's why companies that have failed to make the successful leap from one circle to the next seem so unbelievably incompetent. Giants like General Motors once represented all the strengths and glories of the mass-manufacturing era. Yet today they are described in unflattering terms—"bloated," "groping," "slow" and "sloppy"—prisoners caged in their own past.

The startling fact of life in Canada is that 70 percent of Canadians are already employed in the new economy, which shows just how well we have adjusted.

It pays to be a supplier of the right materials, and although many Canadians don't realize it, their country is emerging as the principal provider of many of the commodities needed by the technology-driven economy. We are so wrapped up in our wintry view of our future that we don't realize how incredibly lucky—and smart—we've been over the years. It's no secret, for example, that nickel is *the* metal of the new economy, while copper is the dark horse, and Canada happens to be one of the world's principal sources of both.

As supreme hewers of wood, miners of metals and drawers of water, Canadians have been uniquely well placed to serve both the commodity-processing centers of mother Britain and the manufacturing dynamos of the neighboring giant to the south. In return, Canada has had one of the world's fastest-growing economies for decades. The bumpy ride that we're experiencing right now is caused simply by the shifting of gears as we move from supplying the stuff to the declining old economy. For people who aren't used to driving at high speeds, that's always a challenge.

Source

Abridged from *Shifting Gears: Thriving in the New Economy* by Nuala Beck. Copyright 1992 by Nuala Beck. Published by HarperCollins Publishers Ltd., pp. 19–24, 43–44.

Photo Source: Nuala Beck is the author and Excelerate of *Shifting Gears: Thriving in the New Economy* and *Excelerate: Growing in the New Economy* and is President of Nuala Beck & Associates Inc. The New Economy is the registered trademark of Nuala Beck & Associates Inc.

1. **What are the three eras of economic development distinguished by Beck? Using the information in the article, as well as your own research, provide examples of (a) engines, (b) virtuosos, (c) characteristic technologies, (d) fast-track jobs, (e) losers, (f) emerging industries, and (g) roadblocks for each era.**
2. **Why, according to Nuala Beck, is Canada well-placed to benefit from the new economy?**

SIDELINE

POWER IN NUMBERS

The Role of Labour Unions in Canada

In this chapter, we've looked at cases in which the resource market is competitive, with many individual buyers and sellers. Because each competitive participant is small in comparison to the market, no single business has an effect on the price of a resource, and businesses are price-takers. In some resource markets, however, competition does not prevail. Most commonly this arises through the efforts of workers to use their collective power through unions and professional organizations to negotiate with employers.

The Collective Bargaining Process

The impact of Canadian labour unions is considerable. Their influence in particular labour markets extends not only to wage rates, but also to working hours, workplace standards, and employment levels. Unions represent the interests of their members primarily through collective bargaining whereby union representatives negotiate with employers over such issues as workers' wages, hours, and working conditions. As a result of collective bargaining, unions and employers make collective agreements to which both parties are bound for a set period of time. Unions also become involved in disputes over, for example, worker suspensions. Generally, unions and employers come to a settlement through face-to-face bargaining.

Mediation and Arbitration

When unions and employers cannot come to an agreement, they may seek help through a process known as mediation. An outside party known as a mediator is appointed, usually with the help of government officials. After studying the positions and proposals of union and management, the mediator makes a series of recommendations that each side is free to accept or reject.

Disputes are sometimes settled through a similar procedure called arbitration. Like a mediator, an arbitrator is an outside party, typically appointed with government help. However, the decision of an arbitrator is binding on both parties; they must accept the settlement.

Working to Rule

If no settlement is reached, a union may elect to use a tactic called working to rule, whereby union members work strictly within the bounds of their job descriptions. In a work-to-rule campaign, workers slow down normal operations, but continue to receive their pay. However, they refuse to work overtime or do anything else that is not strictly required by their jobs. A successful work-to-rule campaign pressures the employer to return to the bargaining table.

Strikes

Unions may also elect to stage a strike against the employer by effectively ceasing work. Usually, a strike forces a business to shut down, thereby pressuring management to return to the bargaining table. Unions, too, are under pressure as their members have no income except for payments from any strike funds amassed through their members' union dues, or membership payments. Sometimes unions will hold rotating strikes, with groups of workers striking for set periods of time in order to slow down work. During strikes, union members typically picket the workplace by taking strategic positions around the outside of the workplace. They may try to turn back customers, employees who are still working, and delivery people transporting goods to or from the business.

Lockouts and Replacement Workers

Employers may elect to use a lockout to speed a settlement by literally locking union employees out of the workplace and temporarily stopping work. As in the case of strikes, both sides are affected by this action: the business usually ceases operations and employees lose their incomes. In some cases, businesses that lock out employees or who have striking employees may hire replacement workers (sometimes called "scabs" by unions) to carry out the duties of permanent employees. While they can serve as powerful weapons, lockouts and replacement labour poison relations between the company and its regular employees, as well as create antagonism between the regular and the replacement workers.

Unions and the Canadian Economy

Since the 1930s, when only one out of five Canadian workers was unionized, labour unions have grown in membership. Unions now represent just under four out of ten of Canada's paid nonagricultural workers. As shown in Figure A, union membership rose substantially as a percentage of these workers during the 1940s and early 1950s. Growth fell off in the late 1950s and 1960s as most workers in easily organized manufacturing sectors were already members. Because of the growth in Canada's expanding public sector in the early 1970s, membership rose rapidly. Since the mid-1980s, relative to the total number of workers, membership has decreased slightly.

The recent stagnation in union membership results primarily from the shift of Canada's workforce from the unionized manufacturing sector to less-unionized service industries. As shown in Figure B, the role of unions in Canadian service industries varies enormously. Unions are even more prevalent in public administration, communications, and transportation than they are in manufacturing. However, there are many service industries—for example, those connected with trade and finance—in which union representation is scanty, and it is in such sectors that significant new employment has been created.

FIGURE A Union Membership in Canada

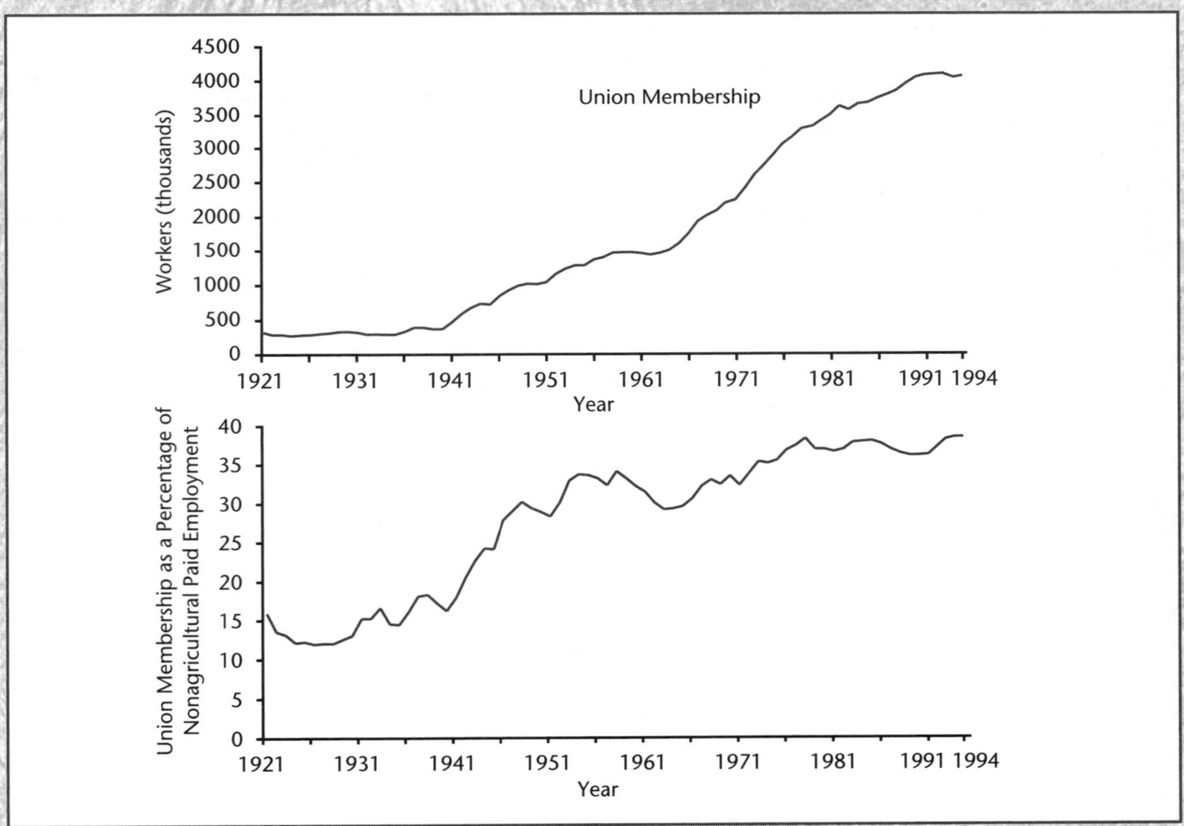

In general, the number of workers in Canada who are union members has grown steadily, as shown on the top graph. The proportion of Canadian workers — other than agricultural workers — who are union members has also risen, as shown on the bottom graph. From a low point of 12 percent in 1926, the proportion rose to its highest point of 38.8 percent in 1984.

Sources: Adapted from F.H. Leacy, ed., *Historical Statistics of Canada, 2nd ed.* (Ottawa: Statistics Canada, 1983), pp. 175–77; Labour Canada, *Directory of Labour Organizations in Canada*, 1994–95, cat. no. L2-2-1995, p. xiii. Reproduced by authority of the Minister of Industry, 1997.

There is also a notable difference in union representation based on the gender and age of workers, as illustrated in Figure B. Male workers dominate many manufacturing jobs, while women are better represented in expanding service industries. Hence, it is no surprise that the percentage of men who are union members is higher than that for women.

Studies suggest that wages in unionized occupations tend to exceed those in nonunionized occupations by about 10 to 25 percent. Unions do increase wages in unionized labour markets. However, workers who cannot find employment in unionized occupations crowd into nonunionized trades. Because the supply of labour increases in these labour markets and because workers lack the market power that unions would otherwise give them, employers are able to pay lower wages. Therefore, unions influence wages in both unionized and nonunionized occupations. Meanwhile, the extent to which union activity increases *average* wages in the entire Canadian economy is a subject of continuing controversy.

FIGURE B Union Membership by Industry and Gender (1992)

Industry	Percentage of Paid Workers Who Are Union Members
Public Administration	79.2
Communications	60.5
Metal Mines	52.0
Transportation	50.0
Manufacturing	35.2
Trade	11.9
Finance	4.7
Agriculture	1.6
Gender	
Men	38.2
Women	31.2

Union membership is most prevalent in public administration, while agriculture has the lowest percentage of union members. Males are more likely to be union members than females.

Source: Statistics Canada, *Annual Report of the Ministry of Industry, Science and Technology Under the Corporations and Labour Unions Return Act, Part 2—Labour Unions 1992* (October 1994), cat. no. 71-202, p. 38.

1. Outline the advantages and disadvantages of the following options for settling disputes. In your answer, keep in mind the interests of workers, employers, and the general public.
   a. appointment of an arbitrator, with no right to strike or work to rule for union members
   b. appointment of a mediator, with the right to strike for union members
   c. appointment of a mediator, with no right to strike, but the right to work to rule for union members

2. Which of the options in the previous question would you choose in the cases below? Explain your answer for each.
   a. a dispute involving a proposed pension scheme for retail workers
   b. a dispute involving proposed higher salaries for police

Chapter Eight

Wages, Rent, Profit, and Interest

We have only one asset, and that is people!
—Sylvia Ostry, Canadian Economist

Who gets what in an economy? In the Canadian economy, this question is decided primarily in resource markets. For most Canadians, the size of their pay cheques is the biggest determinant of income, but pay cheques vary greatly among Canadian workers. In this chapter, we'll explore the factors that affect incomes from labour. We'll also look at other resource incomes, rent and profit, and a resource-related financial income, interest.

CHAPTER FOCUS

This chapter focuses on the following:

- the factors that affect wages, including productivity, education, experience, job conditions, regional disparities, market power, and discrimination
- rent, the market for land, the equilibrium value of land rent, and changes in demand for land
- profit, and the functions it serves
- interest, how it's determined, the market for loanable funds, how the forces of demand and supply affect loanable funds, and the factors that determine the interest rate for an individual loan

WAGES AND THEIR DETERMINANTS

In the last chapter, we looked specifically at how the forces of demand and supply determine the wage in a given labour market. Recall that we're using the term "wage" generally to include salaries and other forms of payment for labour. In each labour market, the workforce constitutes a small, noncompeting group with limited opportunities to move from one labour market to another. Steelworkers, for example, can compete among themselves for many jobs in the manufacturing sector, but not likely for jobs as accountants in the financial services sector; in the same way, accountants might compete for jobs as business managers, but not for jobs as heart surgeons. Now, let's look at the big picture of many markets and of various jobs, and the factors that determine wages for Canadian workers.

Looking at the wider, national labour market highlights the tremendous differences among Canadians' incomes gained from labour. Figure 8.1 shows the distribution of earnings (defined as wages and self-employed income) in the Canadian economy. In 1995, about four out of ten Canadian earners made less than $15 000 annually. At the other end of the scale, more than one in five Canadian earners made $40 000 or more. (These figures are earnings before taxes.)

There are seven main determinants of wage levels in labour markets: labour productivity, education, experience, job conditions, regional disparities, market power, and discrimination.

FIGURE 8.1 Distribution of Earnings (1995)

Earnings	Percentage of All Earners
Under $5000	15.9
$5000–$9999	11.3
$10 000–$14 999	10.1
$15 000–$19 999	8.8
$20 000–$24 999	9.1
$25 000–$29 999	8.3
$30 000–$34 999	8.2
$35 000–$39 999	6.3
$40 000–$44 999	5.3
$45 000–$49 999	3.7
$50 000–$59 999	5.8
$60 000 and over	7.1
	100.0

Earnings of Canadians varied widely, with just under 4 out of 10 Canadian earners making less than $15 000 annually. In contrast, just over 1 in 5 Canadian earners made $40 000 or more annually.

Source: Statistics Canada, *Earnings of Men and Women*, 1995 (January 1997), cat. no. 13-217, p. 29. Reproduced by authority of the Minister of Industry, 1997.

Labour Productivity

As seen in the previous chapter, in a given job market the level of labour productivity, or the output per worker in a given time, determines the wage of that worker. Among the determinants of labour income, productivity is the most important. The output of each worker varies because of such factors as the worker's ability to do the job, the use of complementary resources, and the state of technology. With more capable workers, additional complementary resources, or a technological innovation, the marginal revenue product of each worker rises, pushing up the demand for labour as well as the prevailing wage.

Education

In general, the more education a worker needs to perform a job, the higher the pay. As Figure 8.2 shows, families headed by someone with a university degree earn about twice as much annual income as families headed by someone with only up to eight years of school. (Statistics Canada defines "family head" as the husband in families with a husband and a wife, the parent in single-parent families, or the eldest person in other families.) The most significant differences in average annual incomes are between families headed by those with eight or less years of schooling and those with some high school education ($38 569 compared to $46 627, or a 21 percent increase for the person with some high school education), and for families headed by those with postsecondary diplomas and those with university degrees ($55 973 compared to $81 756, or a 46 percent increase for the university graduate). Work that requires job-related training tends to have a higher marginal revenue product than does work that requires very little job-related training, so education is linked to labour productivity. Therefore, education has an impact on labour demand.

FIGURE 8.2 Education and Average Family Income (1995)

Education	Average Family Incomes
University degree	$81 756
Postsecondary diploma	55 973
Some postsecondary	52 268
High school graduate	52 424
Some high school	46 627
0 to 8 years of school	38 569

In general, annual family incomes rise with the educational level achieved by the family head. Average earnings for families whose heads have a university degree are double those for families whose heads have completed the eighth grade or less of schooling.

Source: Adapted from Statistics Canada, *Income Distributions by Size in Canada*, 1995 (December 1996), cat. no. 13-207, p. 79. Reproduced by authority of the Minister of Industry, 1997.

Education also has an impact on labour supply. As every student knows, education is costly and time-consuming. For example, students who undertake a full-time postsecondary program have not only out-of-pocket costs such as tuition and books, but also an important opportunity cost: the income that could have been earned by entering the workforce immediately. Of course, students who attend public postsecondary institutions do not bear the entire cost of their education (taxpayers, through government programs, pick up the remainder). Education provides benefits; acquiring skills and knowledge may itself be a reward for the work and effort involved. Just the same, a worker entering the labour force with a higher education tends to expect a return on his or her education investment.

human capital: the income-earning potential of a person's skills and knowledge

Economists view work-related education as an investment in **human capital**, which is the income-earning potential of a person's skills and knowledge. According to this perspective, an educational program is only worthwhile if the expected rise in the individual's lifetime income outweighs the sum of that education's direct and indirect costs. "Human capital" expresses the ways in which an individual's education choices correspond to businesses' investment decisions, but it is important not to let this term mask education's distinctive features. Education often has a consumption component, which is the pleasure associated with learning. This component may be especially significant in subject areas with little income-earning potential.

Thinking About Economics

Suppose three friends graduating from high school choose different career paths: the first enters the workforce directly as a clerical worker, the second enrolls in a university arts program for a major in English literature with a focus on medieval literature, and the third pursues a degree in computer science. What do these decisions suggest about the friends' economic choices?

According to the economic view of human capital, by not making a further investment in education, the first friend sacrifices possible income gains later in life for immediate earnings. In other words, receiving a dollar in purchasing power now is worth much more to this individual than receiving greater purchasing power in the future. The English major is willing to give up immediate income for future benefit, and will likely have a future income greater than the first friend's, but perhaps not as much as he would if he pursued another type of postsecondary education. From this economic viewpoint, this friend sees the knowledge he will gain from his postsecondary education primarily as a consumption item rather than as an investment in human capital. The third friend is also willing to give up immediate income for future increases in welfare. She views education as an investment in her human capital to increase future earning power and, hopefully, as a source of pleasure as well.

Experience

Experience is another determining factor of income levels. On-the-job experience increases a worker's productivity, pushing up the demand for the worker's labour and the wage rate. In many industries, workers gain certain privileges the longer they work for a single employer. Because of these **seniority rights**, older workers are often paid higher wages and can apply first for promotions and overtime work, allowing them to earn higher incomes than their younger colleagues.

seniority rights: the workplace privileges provided to workers who have the longest experience with their employer

The positive effect of workplace experience on earnings is one of the main reasons why average incomes rise with age during the first part of a person's working life. Figure 8.3 shows the relationship between age and family income for families with male heads. As the age of the head of the family rises to the 45 to 54 age range for men, average family income increases; thereafter, incomes tend to decrease as more workers retire.

FIGURE 8.3
Age and Average Family Income (1995)

Age of Family Head (years)	Average Family Income
up to 24	$33 080
25–34	52 954
35–44	62 992
45–54	70 767
55–59	66 338
60–64	51 379
65+	43 128

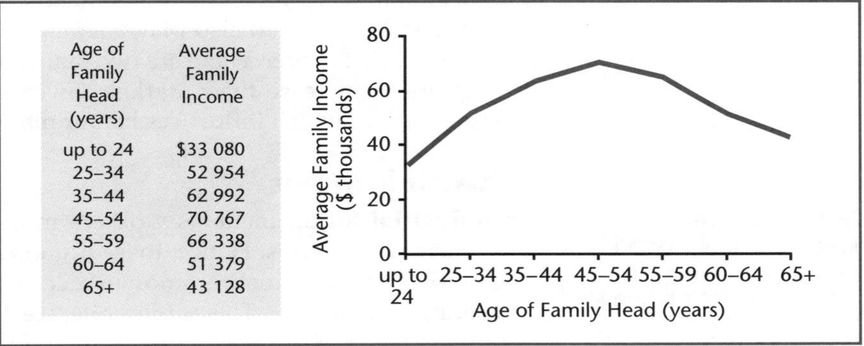

Average family incomes for families with male heads generally rise and then fall with the age of the family head, peaking at the 45 to 54 age bracket.

Source: Adapted from Statistics Canada, *Income Distributions by Size in Canada, 1995* (December 1996), cat. no. 13-207, p. 72. Reproduced by authority of the Minister of Industry, 1997.

Job Conditions

Often two occupations provide very different earnings even when productivity and education levels in each occupation are the same. One reason for this discrepancy is that working conditions in the two occupations can make one less appealing than the other. In order to attract workers to less-appealing occupations, employers must offer higher wages. For example, garbage collectors receive higher wages than most other unskilled workers, in part because of their unattractive working conditions.

Regional Disparities

Wage differences often have a geographic dimension. In Canada, workers in the same occupation often earn different incomes depending on the region they live in. For example, a fishplant worker in British Columbia may earn more than a worker doing the identical job in Newfoundland. In a perfectly functioning labour market, workers in a single occupation would move from one part of the country to another until wage disparities in this occupation were eliminated. However, labour tends to be immobile. Even when workers find moving economically feasible, they and their families may be reluctant to adjust to new jobs, schools, and surroundings. Labour immobility is especially pronounced for multiple-income families because of the added difficulty of two or more people changing jobs. Immobility is also common among older workers, who tend to be more settled in their jobs and communities.

Market Power

The market power workers have also affects their wages. As a rule, earnings in labour markets that are unionized tend to be higher than in non-unionized markets. Professional organizations for such groups as medical doctors and lawyers can also play a similar role in providing their members with market power. There are two main methods that unionized workers can use to increase their market power—industrial unions and craft unions—each of which influences labour markets in different ways.

Industrial Unions

industrial union: a labour union of workers in a certain industry, no matter what their occupations

An **industrial union** includes workers in a certain industry, no matter what their occupations. Hence, these unions are also referred to as inclusive unions, and are most common in sectors that primarily use unskilled and semiskilled labour. The automobile, steel, and forestry industries are examples. Figure 8.4 takes a look at the effect of an industrial union on the steelmaking industry. This example is based on two simplifying assumptions: all workers in the industry are assumed to perform identical tasks so that they earn the same wage, and the market for steelworkers is a competitive one. Without a union, the market for steelworkers would reach equilibrium at an hourly wage of $18, with 140 000 workers employed. By bargaining with employers, an industrial union is able to raise the wage to $22 an hour. Each member's earnings are increased, but at a cost—employment in the labour market is reduced to 120 000, creating an excess supply of 40 000 workers.

Craft Unions

craft union: a labour union of workers in a particular occupation

A **craft union** includes workers in a particular occupation. Craft unions restrict whom they allow to be members, so they are also referred to as exclusive unions. They are common in skilled trades such as printing as well as in some parts of the construction industry, such as carpentry and bricklaying. Some professional organizations, which limit numbers of newcomers in a particular occupation, can also be viewed as being similar to craft unions. In any labour market dominated by a craft union, acquiring a union card is an essential first step in being allowed to work. To become a member of such a union, a worker often must complete an apprenticeship program and write a licensing examination. While craft unions' requirements attempt to ensure craft standards, they also allow

FIGURE 8.4
The Impact of Industrial Unions

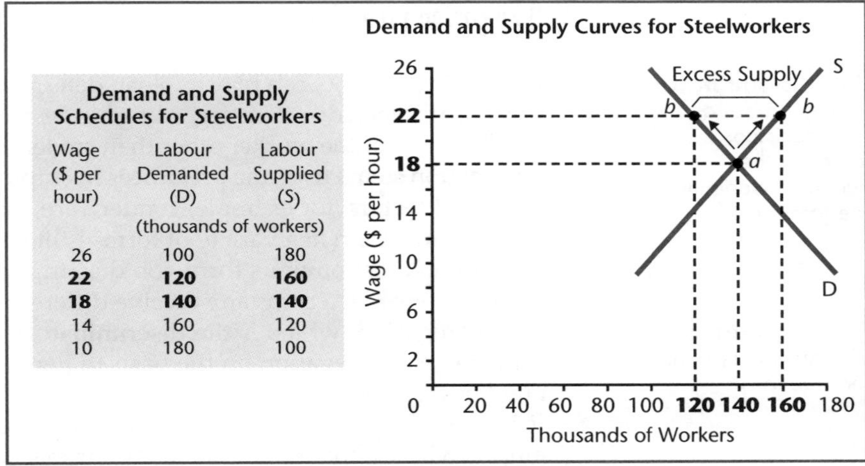

Demand and Supply Schedules for Steelworkers

Wage ($ per hour)	Labour Demanded (D)	Labour Supplied (S)
	(thousands of workers)	
26	100	180
22	**120**	**160**
18	**140**	**140**
14	160	120
10	180	100

Equilibrium in the market for steelworkers without a union would be at the intersection (point *a*) of the demand and supply curves, with a wage of $18 per hour and 140 000 workers employed. By bargaining, the industrial union raises the wage to $22 per hour, but also creates an excess supply of 40 000 steelworkers, since 160 000 are willing to work at this wage but only 120 000 jobs are available (points *b*).

unions to determine the supply of workers in the market and to negotiate higher wages for their members.

Figure 8.5 shows the results of a craft union's membership restrictions on an otherwise competitive market for bricklayers. Without a union, equilibrium in the market would occur at the intersection of D and S_0, with 18 000 bricklayers employed at an hourly wage of $20. The introduction of a craft union means the number of workers in the trade is limited to 15 000 or less. The result is a kinked supply curve, S_1, which becomes vertical at the membership limit. Market equilibrium moves to a lower employment level of 15 000 workers and a higher wage of $25 per hour.

FIGURE 8.5
The Impact of Craft Unions

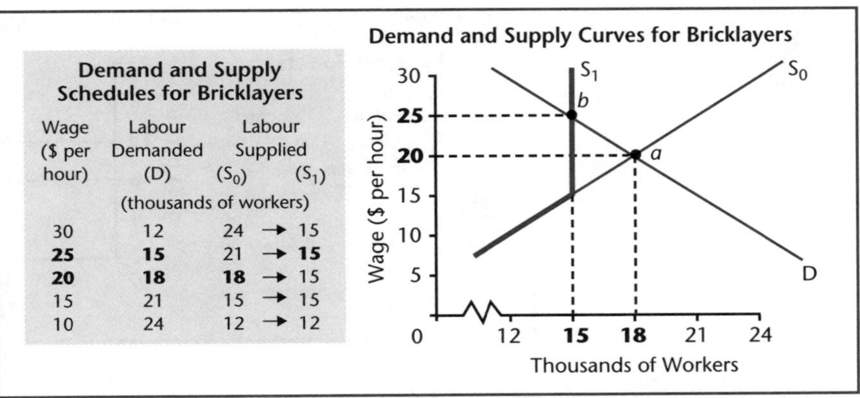

Demand and Supply Schedules for Bricklayers

Wage ($ per hour)	Labour Demanded (D)	Labour Supplied (S_0)		(S_1)
	(thousands of workers)			
30	12	24	→	15
25	**15**	21	→	**15**
20	**18**	**18**	→	15
15	21	15	→	15
10	24	12	→	12

Without a union, equilibrium in the market for bricklayers would occur at point *a*, where D and S_0 intersect, with a wage of $20 and 18 000 bricklayers employed. By restricting its membership to 15 000, the craft union imposes a new supply curve, S_1, thereby raising the wage to $25 per hour.

Discrimination

job discrimination: hiring, wage, and promotion decisions based on criteria other than a worker's credentials or performance

Discrimination, too, can play a role in determining wages. **Job discrimination** occurs when decisions regarding hiring, wages, or promotion are based on some trait of the worker other than credentials or performance. Job discrimination stems from the prejudices of employers and may be based on a variety of factors; for example, gender, race, age, or physical ability. While job discrimination in a variety of forms is illegal, it does still exist.

job segregation: the discriminatory division of occupations

In its most obvious form, job discrimination means workers doing identical work in a company receive different pay. A less obvious form is **job segregation**, which is the discriminatory division of occupations. In Canada, job segregation on the basis of gender has been widely studied, and has resulted in remedial legislation based on the notion of equal pay for work of equal value. Under such legislation, job segregation—for example, where a male-dominated labour market is paid more than a comparable female-dominated labour market—can be addressed.

Figure 8.6 shows the hypothetical example of competitive labour markets for warehouse clerks and receptionists. For convenience, we will assume that the wage rate in each occupation would be $12 per hour, at the intersection of the labour demand and labour supply curves, if the

FIGURE 8.6
The Impact of Job Segregation

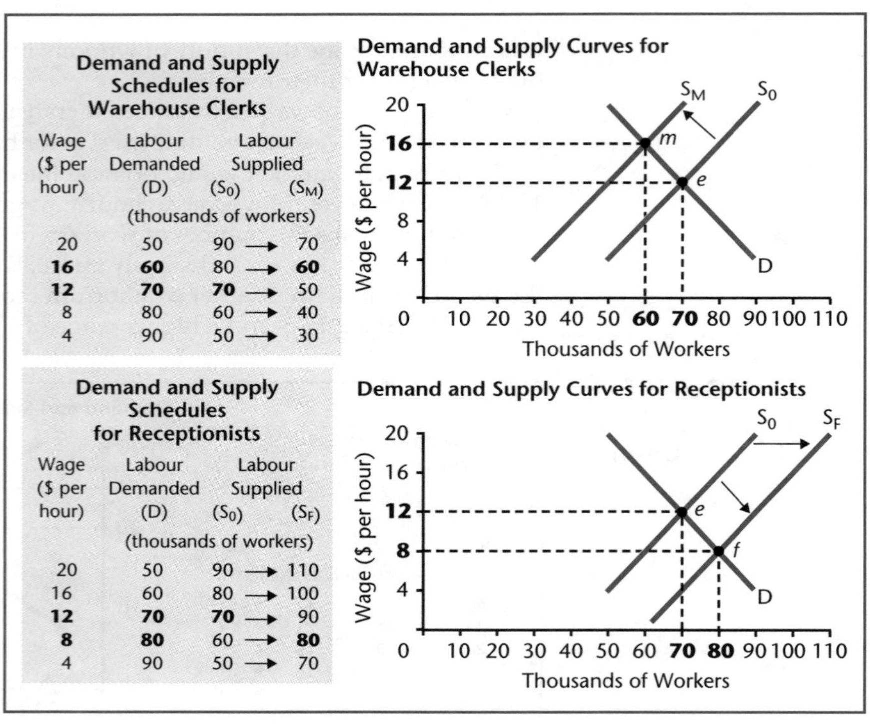

Demand and Supply Schedules for Warehouse Clerks

Wage ($ per hour)	Labour Demanded (D)	Labour Supplied (S_0)		Labour Supplied (S_M)
	(thousands of workers)			
20	50	90	→	70
16	**60**	80	→	**60**
12	**70**	**70**	→	50
8	80	60	→	40
4	90	50	→	30

Demand and Supply Schedules for Receptionists

Wage ($ per hour)	Labour Demanded (D)	Labour Supplied (S_0)		Labour Supplied (S_F)
	(thousands of workers)			
20	50	90	→	110
16	60	80	→	100
12	**70**	**70**	→	90
8	**80**	60	→	**80**
4	90	50	→	70

Without discrimination, equilibrium in the markets for warehouse clerks and receptionists would occur where D and S_0 meet at point *e*, with a wage of $12 per hour and 70 000 workers employed in each market. Job segregation shifts the supply curve for warehouse clerks to S_M and the supply curve for receptionists to S_F. Equilibrium wages increase to $16 per hour for warehouse clerks (point *m*), and decrease to $8 per hour for receptionists (point *f*).

markets weren't discriminatory. Suppose employers decide to hire men exclusively to be warehouse clerks and women exclusively to be receptionists. In the male-dominated warehouse clerk market, the supply curve shifts to the left (to S_M), thereby increasing the equilibrium wage to $16 per hour. This new supply curve reflects discrimination not only in hiring warehouse clerks, but in many other occupations as well. Because male workers face a wide range of opportunities for attractive, high-paying employment, they will only enter the market for warehouse clerks at relatively high wages. Women who would prefer to be employed in traditionally male-dominated occupations must instead apply, along with other women workers, for positions in traditionally female-dominated occupations, such as the market for receptionists. Because women are crowded into a limited range of job markets, supply curves in these markets shift to the right. Therefore, in the female-dominated receptionist market, the supply curve shifts to the right (to S_F), thereby decreasing the equilibrium wage to $8 per hour. As a result of job segregation, therefore, wages in male-dominated occupations are higher than they would otherwise be, and wages in female-dominated occupations are lower.

Job segregation is an important factor in explaining the wage gap between men and women, which in 1995 meant that women on average earned 65 percent of the average wage for men. Canadian studies suggest that, while 40 percent of this gap is related to differences in hours worked by men and women, a third is due to job segregation and another 10 percent to direct job discrimination, which involves paying men and women different amounts for substantially the same work. The remainder of the gap is explained by a variety of factors, such as differing average levels of experience, education, and unionization for men and women.

BRIEF REVIEW

1. Wages vary significantly in the Canadian labour market. Factors that determine wage levels are labour productivity, education, experience, job conditions, regional disparities, market power, and discrimination.
2. Work-related education and training can be viewed as an investment in human capital, or an individual's earning power. Ignoring the consumption aspect of knowledge, an education is worthwhile when its returns, in the form of future income gains, exceed its direct and indirect costs.
3. The positive effect of experience and seniority rights on earnings is one of the main reasons why family income tends to rise with age.
4. Industrial unions represent all workers in a certain industry, so they negotiate wages across an industry; craft unions represent workers in a particular occupation; and, they can both affect the supply of labour in the market and negotiate wages.
5. Job discrimination can be based on a variety of factors: for example, gender, race, age, or physical ability. Job segregation is one less obvious form of job discrimination.

RENT

rent: the payment for use of a productive resource that is available only in a fixed amount

So far, we have concentrated on the income from labour. Now, let's turn to a second resource income: rent. **Rent** is defined very precisely in economics as the payment for use of a productive resource that is available in only a fixed amount. Note that it is distinct from the term "rent" in more general use. For example, the total monthly payment to a landowner by a tenant often includes not only economic rent (payment for a resource in fixed supply), but also payment for utilities, maintenance, and administration, plus a normal profit for the owners. Land is the most significant resource that provides rent. With few exceptions (for example, when landfilling or drainage systems create more land), land is available in only a fixed supply. For example, Ontario has a fixed land supply of 891 190 km^2.

The Market for Land

To see how the rent for land is determined, we must make a number of assumptions. We'll assume that we can separate economic rent from payments for any buildings or improvements made on the land; we'll assume that the market for land is competitive, with many buyers and sellers; and we'll assume that each unit of land is of the same quality.

The Equilibrium Value of Rent

Figure 8.7 shows demand and supply for land in a particular region. Because there is a fixed supply of land, the supply curve is perfectly

FIGURE 8.7
Equilibrium in the Market for Land

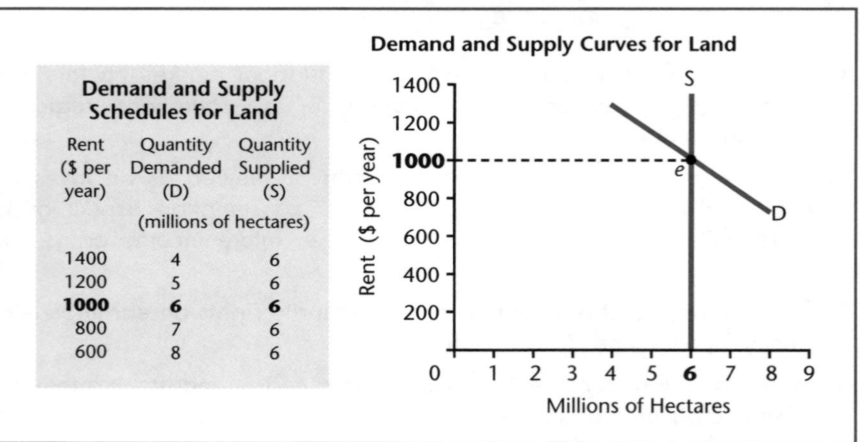

Demand and Supply Schedules for Land

Rent ($ per year)	Quantity Demanded (D)	Quantity Supplied (S)
	(millions of hectares)	
1400	4	6
1200	5	6
1000	**6**	**6**
800	7	6
600	8	6

The demand curve for land shows the total quantities of land demanded at each rent. Given that the region has a fixed supply of land (6 million hectares), the supply curve for land is a vertical line. Equilibrium occurs at point *e*, giving a rent of $1000 for each hectare of land.

inelastic, or vertical at its fixed amount. Demand, however, is variable; quantity demanded decreases at higher rents and increases at lower rents. Therefore, the demand curve for land has a negative (downward) slope. Market equilibrium occurs at a rent of \$1000, where the two curves intersect. Since we've assumed that we can separate economic rent from other payments, this \$1000 is entirely payment for the land.

Changes in Demand

Because the supply of land cannot change, only a change in demand can change the equilibrium value of rent. Recall from Chapter 7 that the demand for resources is determined indirectly, because it is derived from demand for other products. Therefore, the main factor that can change demand for land is a change in the price for the products the land is used to produce. Suppose that the land in the region we're considering is devoted entirely to cattle ranching and that all cattle ranchers are renting land from landowners. In Figure 8.8, the demand is shown as D_0 and point *a* is the equilibrium. If the price of beef rises, cattle ranchers will find they can increase their revenue for each unit of land. As a result, cattle ranchers will demand more land at every possible price, thus shifting the demand curve to the right, to D_1. The change in the demand will cause the equilibrium value of rent to rise to \$1200 (point *b*).

FIGURE 8.8
Changes in the Demand for Land

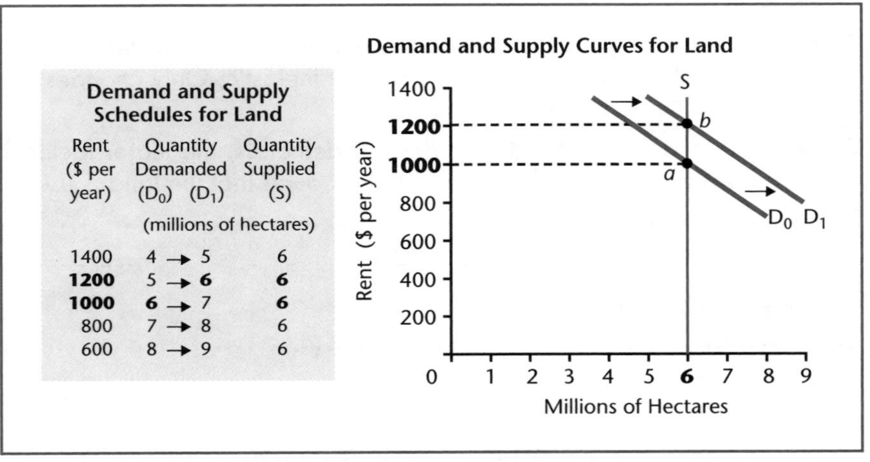

Demand and Supply Schedules for Land

Rent (\$ per year)	Quantity Demanded (D_0) → (D_1) (millions of hectares)	Quantity Supplied (S) (millions of hectares)
1400	4 → 5	6
1200	5 → **6**	**6**
1000	**6** → 7	**6**
800	7 → 8	6
600	8 → 9	6

A rise in the price of beef will increase the quantity demanded of ranch land at every possible rent, as shown by the shift from D_0 to D_1. As a result, equilibrium moves from point *a* to point *b*, and rent increases from \$1000 to \$1200 per hectare.

Thinking About Economics

Does the economic analysis for land apply to other types of productive resources?

It does only if the other resources have a fixed supply. Consider a natural resource such as minerals or water. If the known supply is limited (and therefore fixed), payments over and above the costs for extracting, processing, and distributing the resource can be called economic rents.

There is another interesting application of the economic theory of rent. A few lucky individuals, such as star athletes or entertainers, owe their success to the talents they possess. We might consider their talents as having a fixed supply. Therefore, much of the income earned by these people is really an economic rent that pays them for making their talents available in the market. Consider, for example, the hockey superstar Wayne Gretsky. We could consider a portion of his multimillion-dollar yearly salary to be a wage, but most of it is an economic rent paid by team owners who want to reap the rewards of having "The Great One" on their team.

BRIEF REVIEW

1. In economics, rent is the payment for use of a productive resource that is available in only a fixed quantity.
2. Land is an example of an economic resource that provides a rent income. Since the supply of land is fixed, the supply curve is perfectly inelastic. Only changes in the demand for land can affect the equilibrium value of its rent.
3. Because resource demands are derived demands, the major factor that can change the demand for land is a change in the price of the products that the land is used to produce.

PROFIT

Profit is another resource income. Recall that economic profit is a business's total revenue less total implicit and explicit costs. In other words, a positive economic profit is the income paid to owners of a business after all other resource payments have been made. Critics of the capitalist system attribute profit to the power of business owners rather than to their contribution to the economy. While it is true that profits can be excessive, profit can also serve some positive functions in private markets by acting as a return on risk-taking, a measure of a business's effectiveness, and a source of funds for future investment.

Return on Risk-Taking

Profit provides a return to entrepreneurs for their risk-taking. Businesses initiate change but are themselves affected by external changes. Owners attempt to predict the future—for example, consumer spending, resource costs, and the demand for their product—but their speculations are always uncertain. No one will assume such risks in a private-market economy unless they can expect at least a normal profit in return. Profit therefore provides an incentive for people to take these risks.

Measure of Effectiveness

Profits give some indication of how well a business is run, thereby giving those inside and outside the business a tool to judge the business's success. If a business makes a high economic profit while others in the same industry suffer losses or merely break even, this suggests good management of the successful business. So, profits can help investors decide what businesses to invest in. Profit levels can also indicate the health of an industry as a whole, and its future. Therefore, profits can help entrepreneurs decide whether or not to enter a particular market. If businesses in a competitive market make positive economic profits, other businesses will enter the market and try to capture some of this profit for themselves. If businesses in the market are negative, some businesses will leave over time. By performing this role, profits help ensure that an economy's scarce economic resources are allocated in a way that best serves the interests of consumers.

Source of Funds

Profits can also be used by a business to purchase assets such as buildings, plant, and equipment. Instead of borrowing money or finding new owners who are willing to invest their money, businesses can either replace or increase their assets by using past earnings. Given the return that could be made by using these funds in other ways, the business must expect sufficiently high profits to make this decision worthwhile.

INTEREST

principal: the amount of a loan, excluding interest

interest: the payment to a lender by the borrower for use of money loaned

Another form of income that contributes to the overall incomes of Canadians is interest. While related to the supply of capital resources, interest can also be viewed as a financial income. When money is lent to a consumer or business, the lender requires that not only the **principal** (the loan amount) be paid back, but also that **interest** (a payment for use of the money) be paid. Interest, in effect, is payment by the borrower to the lender for the opportunity cost of the money being used in one way over another. In other words, interest is the price of borrowing money.

interest rate: the percentage rate with which interest on loans is determined

Interest is determined as a percentage of the principal, which is known as the **interest rate**. The interest rate, or rate of return on loanable funds, is one of the key prices in the economy.

Consider the example of a travel agency, Mariposa Vacations, which decides to borrow \$2000 from a bank. The bank agrees to lend the money for a year, and sets the interest rate at 5 percent *per annum*. Interest rates are typically given as *per annum*, or per year. Therefore, at the end of the year, Mariposa Vacations will pay back the principal (\$2000), plus interest at a rate of 7 percent (0.07 × \$2000 = \$140), for a total of \$2140 (\$2000 + \$140).

The Loanable Funds Market

loanable funds: all the monies made available to lenders by borrowers

What determines the interest rate for an entire economy? According to the loanable funds theory, the interest rate is simply the price of **loanable funds**. These funds are all the monies made available by lenders to borrowers. Exchanges in the loanable funds market may take place through an intermediary or directly. In the example of Mariposa Vacations, the bank serves as the go-between in the lending process. Chartered banks, as well as other deposit-taking institutions such as trust companies and credit unions, gather funds from depositors to make loans to borrowers, charging a higher rate to borrowers than the rate they pay to depositors. Among friends and family or with a large company, lending is often done directly.

bond: a contract between a borrower and the holder of the contract that entitles the holder to interest plus repayment at the maturity date

While you and a friend might have a verbal agreement, General Motors, for example, might issue a **bond** for the amount of money it wants to borrow. Bonds are formal contracts that set out the amount borrowed, the borrower (known as the issuer), the period of time until maturity, the interest rate, and when interest is to be paid. When a bond "matures," the bond issuer pays the principal back to the bond holder. Bonds can be bought and sold among lenders.

Demand for Loanable Funds

The demand for loanable funds comes from all participants in the economy. Governments borrow so that they can finance expenditures without immediately increasing taxes. Consumers often borrow to purchase big-ticket items such as houses or cars, so that they can spread out payments over a period of time. Businesses, however, are the main borrowers in the Canadian economy.

real capital: assets such as buildings, equipment, and materials used by businesses to produce goods and services

depreciation: the decrease in value of durable real assets over time

financial capital: assets in the form of cash, bonds, and shares

Businesses borrow funds to invest in projects that they believe will make a profit. When analyzing business investment, it is important to make a distinction between a business's real and financial assets. A business's **real capital** is made up of assets such as buildings and equipment used to produce goods and services. These assets depreciate; that is, their value decreases over time, so that a business must recognize the fall in value, or **depreciation**, each year in its accounts. Investing in profit-making projects usually means adding to that store of real capital. However, to buy this real capital means using **financial capital**, or cash, bonds,

share: partial ownership of a corporation, which entitles the shareholder to dividends and, hopefully, a profit once the share is sold; also called a stock

and shares. Note that a **share** (or stock) gives partial ownership of a corporation to the shareholder, who expects to receive periodic payments in the form of dividends, and hopes to sell the share at a profit later.

Suppose that the hypothetical corporation Optimum Slide, a producer of skateboards, begins the year with real capital assets valued at $100 000. These assets depreciate 20 percent in the first year, meaning that they lose $20 000 in value. To maintain the value of its real capital, Optimum Slide must therefore spend at least $20 000 on investment projects. If the business puts $30 000 into investment projects, the year-end value of its real capital will rise to $110 000 [($100 000 – $20 000) + $30 000)]. To get the $30 000 for investment projects, the business could use past earnings, issue shares to investors, or borrow money. If Optimum Slide chooses borrowing over its other options, the company must demand $30 000 from the market for loanable funds.

In the market for loanable funds, as in all markets, those who demand funds are concerned with the price they must pay. This applies to all borrowers: businesses, governments, and consumers. As the interest rate on loans goes up, the cost of the loan (the interest payments) can exceed the loan's benefits. Therefore, the quantity of loanable funds demanded by borrowers and the interest rate are inversely related. Figure 8.9 shows the resulting demand curve with a negative (downward) slope. When, for example, the interest rate rises from 6 percent to 8 percent, the quantity of loanable funds demanded by borrowers decreases from $160 billion to $140 billion.

Supply of Loanable Funds

While businesses and governments sometimes have temporary savings, which contribute to the supply of loanable funds, the supply comes primarily from household savings. In the circular flow of markets, consumers not only purchase products and supply labour, but also save and provide funds to the loanable funds market by, for example, banking their savings. Whenever a household engages in saving, it postpones consumption and the benefits that consumption would have had. Households (as we'll call them in their role not as consumers, but as savers) provide their savings to the loanable funds market in order to make interest income.

Just as businesses may have a profit after paying all costs from their total revenues, a household may have an excess after paying all basic costs (for example, food, shelter, and clothing) from its incomes (for example, wages). The household can decide how to spend or save any excess. When deciding how much to save, the household must weigh the psychological costs of delaying consumption against the benefits of earning interest income and greater security for the future. If the interest rate rises, the income earned from each dollar of saving rises as well. Since saving provides greater benefits, it is likely that households will choose to save more, leading them to supply a greater quantity of loanable funds. Therefore, the quantity of loanable funds supplied by lenders is directly related to the interest rate, as shown in Figure 8.9. For example, a rise in the interest rate from 6 percent to 8 percent would cause the quantity of loanable funds supplied to increase from $160 to $180 billion.

FIGURE 8.9
Equilibrium in the Loanable Funds Market

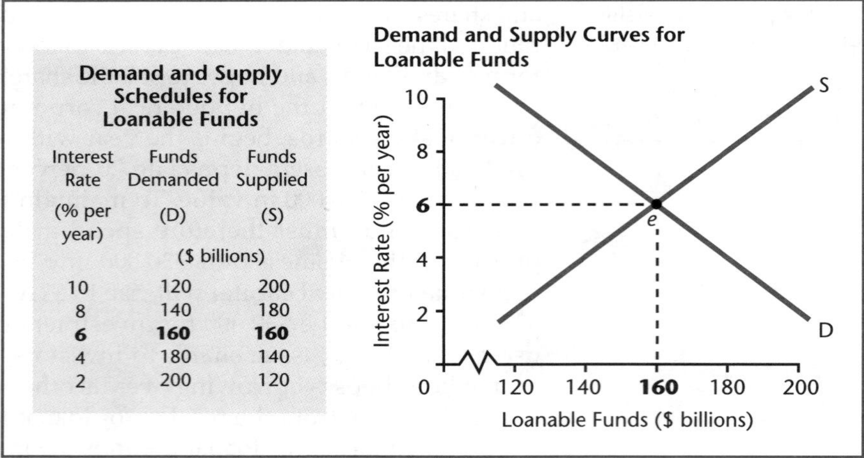

While the quantity of loanable funds demanded by borrowers is inversely related to the interest rate, the quantity of funds supplied by lenders is directly related. In this case, quantities demanded and supplied are equal at an equilibrium interest rate of 6 percent, at point *e*.

The Equilibrium Interest Rate

Equilibrium in the loanable funds market occurs at the intersection of the demand and supply curves. In Figure 8.9, equilibrium is at the interest rate of 6 percent. This equilibrium value can change depending on outside factors that affect either the demand for or supply of loanable funds.

Changes in Demand

The demand for loanable funds can change for a variety of reasons, thereby affecting equilibrium in the market. Anything that makes investment more attractive will increase the demand for loanable funds. A rise in consumer purchases of big-ticket items also raises the demand for loanable funds. Governments, too, can increase demand. In all three cases, expanding demand causes both equilibrium values for the interest rate and the quantity of loanable funds exchanged to rise, as shown in Figure 8.10.

Changes in Supply

The main factor determining the supply of loanable funds is the saving habits of households. If, for example, households decide to reduce the amount they save, they decrease the supply of loanable funds, and the interest rate rises.

Range of Interest Rates

Equilibrium in the loanable funds market does not mean that all loans have the same interest rate. At any one time, interest rates in the market will range above and below the equilibrium rate. The interest rate

FIGURE 8.10
Changes in the Demand for Loanable Funds

Demand and Supply Schedules for Loanable Funds

Interest Rate (% per year)	Funds Demanded (D_0)		Funds Demanded (D_1)	Funds Supplied (S)
	($ billions)			
10	120	→	160	200
8	140	→	**180**	**180**
6	**160**	→	200	**160**
4	180	→	220	140
2	200	→	240	120

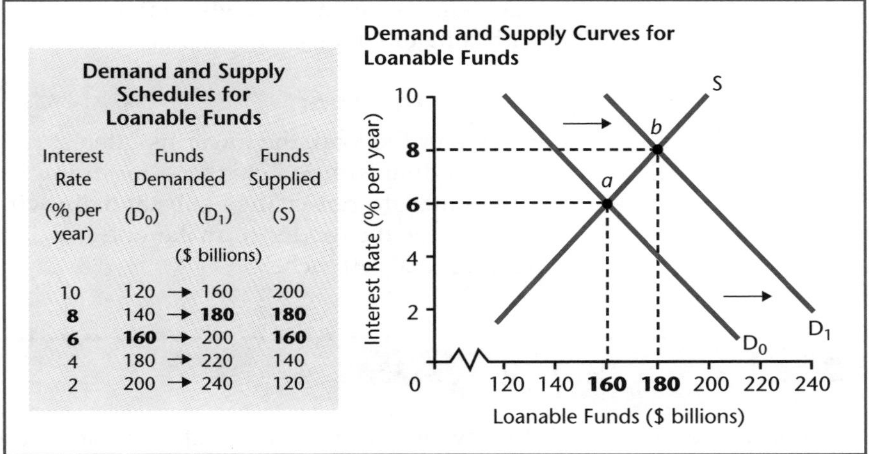

An increase in the profitability of investment projects, for example, will increase the demand for loanable funds at every possible interest rate, as shown by the shift from D_0 to D_1. As a result, the equilibrium interest rate increases from 6 percent (point *a*) to 8 percent (point *b*).

charged on a particular loan depends on four factors: the borrower's credit risk, the loan period, whether or not collateral is provided, and the size of the loan.

Credit Risk

credit risk: the assessed likelihood of a borrower not repaying a loan

When deciding whether to lend funds to a borrower, a lender tries to establish the borrower's **credit risk**, which is the assessed likelihood of the borrower not repaying the loan. In the case of a business, if the business has healthy profits, a solid history and a strong future in the industry, a small existing debt, and a record of repaying loans on time, the credit risk is low. So, for example, Bell Canada would pay a lower interest rate than would a new goldmining business with no track record.

Loan Period

In general, the shorter the time before the loan must be repaid, the lower the interest rate; the longer the time, the higher the interest rate. In effect, the borrower pays for the added time the lender won't have that money available and for the added risk of an extended loan period. For example, a lender might be willing to lend funds for a single year at an annual interest rate of 8 percent, but the same borrower would be charged an annual rate of 10 percent for a two-year period.

Collateral

collateral: assets pledged by a borrower as security against a loan; these assets can be seized by the lender if the loan is not repaid

Lenders often have the security of **collateral**, which are assets pledged by a borrower as security. If a loan is not repaid, the lender acquires these assets. Collateral can take a variety of forms. For example, a mortgage is a loan whose collateral is in the form of land and buildings. As a rule, lenders demand a higher interest rate on loans that are not secured with collateral than on those that are secured with collateral.

Size of the Loan

The larger the loan, the lower its interest rate. Because lending involves certain administration charges—for example, for paperwork and collections—that do not change substantially with the size of the loan, it is cheaper for the lender to make one loan for $1 million rather than 50 loans for $20 000 each.

BRIEF REVIEW

1. Profit is the income paid to owners of a business after all other resource payments have been made. Profit acts as a return on risk-taking, as a measure of a business's effectiveness, and as a source of investment funds.
2. Interest is the income earned on money that is lent. According to the loanable funds theory, the demand for and supply of loanable funds determines the interest rate.
3. Demand for loanable funds is determined mainly by business investment projects and by government borrowing. Supply is determined mainly by household savings.
4. The interest rate an individual borrower pays depends on the borrower's credit risk, the loan period, whether or not collateral is provided, and the size of the loan.

KEY CONCEPTS

human capital
seniority rights
industrial union
craft union
job discrimination
job segregation

rent
principal
interest
interest rate
loanable funds
bond

real capital
depreciation
financial capital
share
credit risk
collateral

ANALYSIS AND APPLICATION

1. Taking into account labour productivity, education, and job conditions, outline some of the problems that would arise if all workers in the Canadian economy received a uniform wage.

2. The hypothetical schedules in the accompanying table show the demand and supply for miners and nurses, who are assumed to be employed in perfectly competitive labour markets.

Demand and Supply Schedules for Miners			Demand and Supply Schedules for Nurses		
Wage ($ per hour)	Labour Demanded (thousands of workers)	Labour Supplied (thousands of workers)	Wage ($ per hour)	Labour Demanded (thousands of workers)	Labour Supplied (thousands of workers)
26	40	60	26	50	90
24	45	55	24	60	80
22	50	50	22	70	70
20	55	45	20	80	60
18	60	40	18	90	50

a. Using two diagrams, identify the equilibrium wage and employment level in each labour market if initially there is no job segregation in either occupation.
b. With job segregation, mining is one of a wide range of occupations that becomes male-dominated, causing supply to decrease by 20 000 workers at every possible wage rate. Nursing is one of a narrow range of occupations that becomes female-dominated, causing supply to increase by 20 000 workers at every possible wage rate. Outline the effects on equilibrium wages and employment levels in each market.
c. Gender-based job segregation benefits a large number of men as well as a few women, and it harms a large number of women as well as a few men. Explain, using miners and nurses as examples.

3. The table below shows hypothetical demand and supply schedules for stagehands in a perfectly competitive labour market before the formation of a union.

Demand and Supply Schedules for Stagehands

Wage ($ per hour)	Labour Demanded (number of workers)	Labour Supplied (number of workers)
18	2000	6000
15	3000	5000
12	4000	4000
9	5000	3000
6	6000	2000

a. Suppose stagehands form a craft union that limits membership to 3000 workers. Carefully plot a graph to show the effects on the equilibrium wage and level of employment in this labour market. Who benefits and who loses from the formation of this union?

b. Now suppose stagehands decide to form an industrial union instead. How would this union have to operate to provide its members with the same benefits gained by the craft union in part a.? Explain with the aid of your graph.
c. As a rule, which type of union has a better chance of benefiting its members? Explain using the example provided in this question.

4. Identify the direction of each of the following trends as well as the changes in demand and/or supply that cause them.
   a. An influx of immigrants causes land rents to vary in a major metropolitan area.
   b. Widespread environmental damage alters the economic rent received by owners of drinkable water.
   c. The expansion of a professional basketball league leads to an adjustment in the economic rent received by the league's star player.
   d. A major oil discovery in the Middle East influences the rent on oil-drilling properties in Alberta.

5. In 1996, chief executives of Canadian corporations received average annual earnings of over $500,000, with a third of this amount tied to the performance the companies they managed. What economic arguments can be made for and against such high average earnings for this group?

6. How will the equilibrium interest rate in the Canadian loanable funds market change as a result of the following factors? In each case, use a diagram to explain your answers.
   a. The federal government announces new tax advantages for households that save for retirement.
   b. The discovery of a safe method of generating power from nuclear fusion significantly reduces energy costs.
   c. A worldwide economic boom is expected in the near future.
   d. Prices in the Canadian economy are expected to fall.

7. (Advanced Question)
   Unions indirectly lower wages in nonunionized labour markets through a process similar to job segregation. Outline how this process can occur. In your answer, use an example of related labour markets, such as the unionized market for Canada Post employees and the nonunionized market for employees of private courier companies.

8. Access the online version *of After High School: the 1995 School Leavers Follow-up Survey* prepared by Human Resources Development Canada (available at http://www.hrdc-drhc.gc.ca). Based on this report, outline how recent changes in Canada's labour markets are affecting Canadian young people's (i) chances of employment, (ii) participation in labour markets, and (iii)education plans. (Adobe Acrobat required.)

Advancing Economic Thought

REAPING THE REWARDS

David Ricardo and the Theory of Rent

Ricardo and His Influence

In the generation after Adam Smith, several influential thinkers worked to extend his theories. Of this group, now known as the classical economists, David Ricardo (1772–1823) left the greatest mark. Unlike most who have made a study of economic questions, Ricardo had practical experience in business.

Born in Holland, Ricardo later moved to England with his parents, where he went on to amass such a great fortune on the London stock market that he retired to the country in his early forties. There, he turned his attention to the subject known as "political economy."

Like others of his time, Ricardo wanted to understand the questions of who gets what in an economy, and why. To do this, he needed a theory of rent. The issue of land rent was especially important in nineteenth-century Britain, because most farmers did not own the land they cultivated but leased it from a small group of landowners, mostly members of the aristocracy. By coincidence, in February of 1815 four British writers published pamphlets outlining theories of rent; of those theories, Ricardo's became the standard.

David Ricardo
Source: The Bettmann Archive

Ricardo's Theory of Rent

According to Ricardo's theory, the rent to a landowner for a certain piece of farmland equals the excess revenue that remains after paying all other costs, including the farmer's normal profit. Why do landowners receive all this surplus revenue? They do so because the quantity of the land is fixed. Farmers bid against one another to rent each parcel of land; this bidding process raises the rent for each parcel to its maximum possible value.

Suppose, for example, that wheat farmers lease four different grades of land. The table and graph on the next page show the output of wheat per hectare on each grade of land. While grade A land provides an annual crop of 50 kg per hectare, the other grades each produce, respectively, 40, 20, and 10 kg. For all grades of land, farmers have a cost of $100 per hectare for all other inputs. This figure includes not only explicit production costs, such as wages, but also implicit costs, such as the farmer's normal profit.

So, with the output and costs now established, we can determine rent according to Ricardo's theory. For each hectare of land, rent equals the farmer's revenue less the production costs of $100. If the price of wheat is $5, the 50 kg output from a hectare of grade A land gives the farmer a total revenue of $250 per hectare. Therefore, rent for this particular grade of land is the total revenue less the production costs, or $150 ($250 – $100). Because lower-quality land produces a lower output, and therefore lower revenue, the lower grades of land have lower rents. For example, a hectare of grade C land produces an output of 20 kg of wheat, giving the farmer a revenue of $100 (20 kg × $5 per kg); after the costs of $100 are paid from the revenue, the rent stands at zero ($100 – $100). The lowest grade of land, grade D, would not be cultivated since the production costs ($100) exceed its revenues (10 kg × $5 per kg = $50).

In Ricardo's theory, the rent of a hectare of agricultural land depends on the price of the product it produces. So, in our example, an increase in the price of wheat to $10 would increase the rents on each grade of land. For example, the rent of a hectare of grade A land would rise to $400, or the difference between the farmer's new revenue ($10 × 50 kg = $500) and the constant production costs ($100). Similarly, the rents for grades B and C land rise to $300 and $100 per hectare, respectively, and grade D land would be brought into production with a rent of zero, since its revenue now matches production costs. Grade D land therefore represents the new margin of cultivation.

Rent and Population Growth Ricardo's explanation of rent played an important part in his predictions for the future, which he outlined in

Ricardo's Theory of Rent

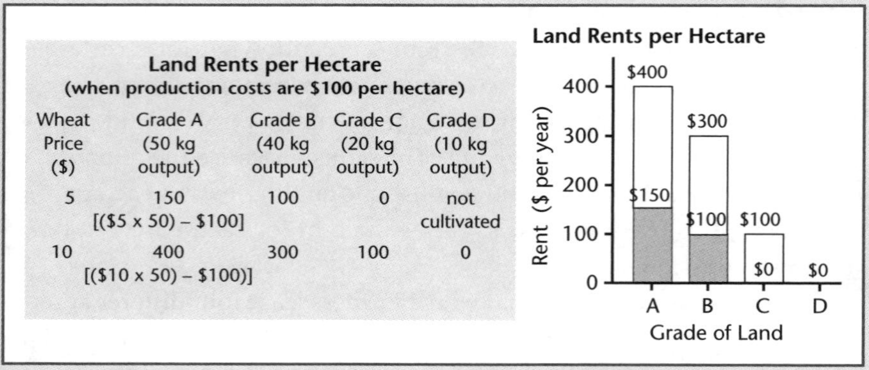

Land Rents per Hectare
(when production costs are $100 per hectare)

Wheat Price ($)	Grade A (50 kg output)	Grade B (40 kg output)	Grade C (20 kg output)	Grade D (10 kg output)
5	150 [($5 x 50) – $100]	100	0	not cultivated
10	400 [($10 x 50) – $100)]	300	100	0

The production costs are constant at $100 per hectare with different grades of land, but the output of wheat per hectare varies from 10 to 50 kg. The table and bar graph show the resulting land rents given two wheat prices: $5 and $10 per kg. If the price of wheat is $5 per kg, the rents for the three highest grades of land would be $150, $100, and $0, respectively. On the bar graph, the shaded areas indicate the rent at the $5 price. If the price of wheat increased to $10 per kg, the rents on the highest grades of land would rise and the fourth grade (D) would enter production, as indicated by the unshaded areas on the bar graph.

Source: Adapted from Stanley L. Brue, *The Evolution of Economic Thought,* 5th ed. (Fort Worth: The Dryden Press, 1994), p.116.

Principles of Political Economy and Taxation, first published in 1817. As population increased, said Ricardo, less productive land would have to be brought into production as premium-quality land became fully utilized. Wheat output per worker would therefore decline, meaning the price of wheat would gradually rise. Because bread was such an important staple in the diets of workers and their families, higher wheat prices would push up the wages that employers would have to pay. And these higher wages, said Ricardo, would lower businesses' profits.

Who would benefit from these trends? It would not be employers, whose profits would shrink, nor workers, whose higher wages would only keep up with costs. It would be well-off landowners who would reap the rewards as higher food prices forced up rents. Unlike other classes in society, said Ricardo, these landowners provided no productive service themselves, but were simply fortunate enough—probably through inheritance—to have gained ownership of an essential economic resource.

The Corn Laws Already renowned for his theories, Ricardo became famous for applying them when he served as a representative in Britain's parliament. One of the most contentious issues facing the British government in Ricardo's time was whether or not to abolish the country's Corn Laws. These laws restricted the purchase of foreign wheat (or "corn" as it was then called) through a system of tariffs, or taxes on imports. The tariffs, which were meant to aid British farmers, raised average wheat prices. Therefore, Ricardo argued, the tariffs helped no one but the wealthy landowners who benefited from increased rents. While the Corn Laws were not repealed until after Ricardo's death, his theories and political involvement were both important in the struggle against these laws.

Henry George and the Single Tax Movement

While Ricardo did not draw any radical conclusions from his theory of rent, others did. In later decades of the nineteenth century, the privileged position of landowners, both in Europe and North America, increasingly came under attack. One of the most zealous critics of landowners was the American journalist and economist Henry George (1839–1897).

Should those lucky enough to own land be able to make often lavish unearned incomes from this ownership at the expense of productive capitalist employers and workers? Like many reformers, George thought not, and in his well-known book, *Progress and Poverty* (1879), he set out his solution: all taxes should be replaced by a 100 percent tax on land rent.

According to George and his many supporters, this tax would have far-reaching benefits. Because the amount of land is fixed by nature, imposing a land rent tax would not reduce the supply of land. Moreover, the revenues from this tax would be so great that all other taxes could be repealed. Repealing all other taxes would stimulate greater production.

George's proposal was so popular that, at the end of the nineteenth century, his name was almost a household word in Britain and North America. However, no government ever adopted the single tax. Most economists criticized it, stating that such a tax would harm many poor people (for example, elderly widows) and might cause huge social upheavals as all landowners found the return on their investments completely wiped out. Critics also pointed out that much of what is classified as land rent in fact represents the landowner's payment for other items, such as interest payments and the depreciation of buildings on the land. Recent critics point to the increase in government spending, which would mean that 100 percent land rent taxes could no longer provide sufficient revenues to replace all other taxes.

1 a. According to David Ricardo's theory of rent, what would happen to the rent per hectare paid on grade A, B, C, and D land if the price of wheat increased to $30?

b. In Ricardo's theory, what causes the price of wheat to rise gradually over time?

c. According to Ricardo, which groups in society benefit, which lose, and which are relatively unaffected by the trends that accompany increasing wheat prices? Why?

2. Food prices have not continually risen as predicted by Ricardo's theory. Why not?

SIDELINE

SHAKEDOWN

The Great Wage Divide

In many industrialized countries, wage differences have been increasing since the 1970s. The following article analyses the reasons for this growing wage spread, and compares recent Canadian experience with trends in some other countries.

Tammy Davidson's mother used to earn $20 an hour at General Motors of Canada Ltd.'s van plant in Scarborough, Ontario, until she was laid off when the plant closed in 1993. Now Ms. Davidson, 25, works at one of GM's suppliers, Mackie Automotive Systems Ltd. in Oshawa, Ontario, operating a lift truck for $10.94 an hour, on which she must support three children and her unemployed husband.

The same work at GM pays more than twice as much, but she harbours no hope of getting it. "The only way to get in there is if you know people." Anyway, GM is cutting jobs, not hiring, she said. Her Grade 12 education keeps better-paying, more-demanding jobs out of reach. "I don't even know how to work a computer," she confessed, but adds, "my son does."

Mackie is one of the many companies that has thrived on the outsourcing trend. Mackie has grown by bidding for GM's traditional in-house work, such as roof liners and rear-window-shelves. But typical of the parts industry, it pays a lot less than GM.

For years, unskilled workers at GM who stapled fabric to seats worked side by side with skilled electricians repairing complete machinery for nearly the same generous wages and benefits. It was a picture repeated at many of the country's biggest employers.

For at least a decade, however, GM has been outsourcing most of its lower-value work to the parts industry, keeping a shrinking but still highly paid core work force to assemble its cars and key components.

In industries ranging from banking to lumber, employers have pushed to have wages better reflect the disparity in employees' skills.

What's Behind This?

Through most of the 20th century in the industrialized countries, household incomes rose rapidly and the gap between rich and poor narrowed. The rise of the blue-collar middle class was made possible by an ample supply of well-paying, unskilled work. That went hand in hand with the growing strength of unions, who fought to keep the salary pie as evenly shared among their members as possible.

That trend has begun unravelling. A study by McMaster University economists Peter Kuhn and Leslie Robb found that between 1977 and 1991 the richest 10 percent of men saw their real yearly income rise 2 percent while the poorest 10 percent saw it plunge 28 percent.

Professor Kuhn said a variety of factors has driven the polarization of wages, but the two most important are technological change and increased international trade and investment. New technology demands more skills and education from workers. Those with it have been rewarded, those without, penalized. Increased international trade with developing countries that have ample supplies of unskilled labour has also tended to drive down the relative demand for unskilled workers.

The automotive industry is typical of the overall trend. Between 1983 and 1995, employment in motor vehicle assembly in Canada rose by 26 percent while real wages rose 22 percent. In the parts industry, employment jumped 42 percent, but real wages were stagnant.

In the economy as a whole, and nonunionized sectors in particular, wage inequality has risen much more noticeably since the late 1970s and the working poor have seen their incomes fall the most.

Even with unionizated rates relatively stable in Canada, the breakdown of industry-wide "pattern" bargaining has allowed wage disparity to widen.

Vancouver-based MacMillan Bloedel Ltd. is trying to break the pattern in West Coast forestry collective bargaining with the eventual aim of introducing greater variance in pay.

Gary Johncox, MacMillan's vice-president of human resources, said that in Canada the wage scale is flat, running from $19 to $24 an hour, whereas in the United States, a steeper wage scale prevails, typically $12 (U.S.) to $24 an hour. He said that while the company loses competitiveness by overpaying for unskilled labour, employees also lose the incentive to improve themselves.

Another result of narrow wage differentials is higher unemployment among the unskilled, said Professor Kuhn, noting that unemployment tends to be highest in countries such as France, with more egalitarian wage structures, and lower in countries with more wage inequality, such as the United States. "You find that the increase in unemployment in Canada has been concentrated among the less-skilled workers."

Unions are fighting a rear-guard action against wage polarization. "The trade-union movement has always tried to come up with solutions that are not just what the market would say," said Sam Gindin, assistant to Canadian Auto Workers president Buzz Hargrove.

But free trade, cuts to the welfare state, deregulation and business decentralization have all tipped power in favour of companies, he said, and companies want a bigger spread in wages. "Decentralized bargaining is always about increased polarization and outsourcing is obviously part of the same thing."

Source

Adapted from "The Great Wage Divide," *The Globe and Mail*, 26 October 1996, pp. B1, B4.

1. Explain how each of the following changes can benefit employers of unskilled labour in industrialized countries:
   a. technological progress that makes production more capital-intensive
   b. expanding trade with developing countries
   c. cutbacks in government programs such as employment insurance and welfare

2. As a rule, businesses employing unionized workers try to increase the wage spread for different jobs, while industrial unions attempt to decrease this wage spread. Using evidence from the article, outline how businesses and unions try to meet these goals in today's labour markets.

Chapter Nine

The Role of Government

Government is an art, not a science, and an adventure, not a planned itinerary....

—Donald Creighton, Canadian historian

Imagine that one person enjoys all the luxuries of a consumer culture, while another can barely scrape by. Alternatively, imagine that a business's profit-making activity pollutes a resource that is shared with neighbours. What is fair? What is reasonable? What could or should be done, and how? In mixed market economies such as Canada's, governments deal not only with competition in the market, as we have seen in previous chapters, but also with the distribution of income and with spillover effects. In this chapter, we examine: the distribution of income among Canadian households; the tools the Canadian government uses to promote income equity, especially transfer payments and taxation; the extent of poverty in Canada; and spillover effects.

CHAPTER FOCUS

This chapter focuses on the following:

- the distribution of income among Canadian households, how this distribution is measured, and the factors underlying the distribution
- how government intervenes with transfer payments and taxes, and the effectiveness of this intervention
- the causes of poverty and the way poverty is measured
- the Canadian welfare society and its impact on Canadians
- spillover costs and benefits, and how the government addresses these issues

THE DISTRIBUTION OF INCOME

In the last chapter, we examined the incomes from resources, the factors that affect these incomes, and the importance of each type of income in the Canadian economy. Now we'll look at who gets what, and why.

Income Shares

To get an overview of who gets what in the economy, economists typically rank Canadian households by income and then categorize households into five groups based on their income levels. Each group therefore represents 20 percent, or one-fifth, of the total number of Canadian households. Figure 9.1 shows the pre-taxation income levels of the five groups for various years. In 1995, the fifth of Canadian households with the lowest incomes received a small proportion—a mere 4.7 percent—of all households' total pre-tax income, while the fifth of Canadian households with the highest incomes received 44.1 percent. The groups in-between the extremes received 10.2 percent, 16.4 percent, and 24.5 percent, respectively.

Looking at the figures for selected years, one can see that there has been surprisingly little change in income distribution since the 1950s. For example, in 1951 the fifth of Canadian households with the lowest incomes received 4.4 percent of all households' total pre-tax income, whereas the fifth with the highest incomes received 42.8 percent.

FIGURE 9.1 Income Distribution in Selected Years

	Percentage of Total Pre-tax Income Received by Each Fifth of Households					Average Income (1995)
	1951	1961	1971	1981	1995	
Lowest 20%	4.4	4.2	3.6	4.5	4.7	$10 760
Second 20%	11.2	11.9	10.6	10.9	10.2	23 144
Third 20%	18.3	18.3	17.6	17.6	16.4	37 192
Fourth 20%	23.3	24.5	24.9	25.2	24.5	55 563
Highest 20%	42.8	41.1	43.3	41.8	44.1	99 976
Average of total						$45 329

Selected incomes from five decades show the income distribution to Canadian households. Proportionally, the shares have not changed considerably since 1951. Consistently, the group of households with the highest income received over 40 percent of the total income, while the group of households with the lowest income received less than 5 percent.

Sources: Statistics Canada, *Incomes of Non-Farm Families and Individuals in Canada, Selected Years 1951–65* (June 1969), cat. no. 1100-506, p. 78; Statistics Canada, *Income Distributions by Size in Canada, 1983* (March 1985), cat. no. 13-207, p. 93; Statistics Canada, *Income After Tax, Distributions by Size in Canada, 1995* (May 1997), cat. no. 13-210, p. 23. Reproduced by authority of the Minister of Industry, 1997.

The Lorenz Curve

Lorenz curve: a graph showing the cumulative distribution of income among a country's households

Comparing distributions of income for different years can be a cumbersome task given the amount of information included in Figure 9.1. Therefore, economists simplify matters by summarizing the results on a graph. However, rather than simply presenting the shares of each one-fifth of households, economists present the *cumulative* distribution of income. The **Lorenz curve**, as this graph is known, conveniently summarizes how equally or unequally income is distributed.

To see how the Lorenz curve does this, take another look at the income distribution for 1995 given in Figure 9.1. Seen as separate shares of total pre-tax income, the figures—4.7 percent, 10.2 percent, 16.4 percent, 24.5 percent, and 44.1 percent—don't seem to say a lot. However, we can look at the first and second groups together; then the first, second, and third groups together; and so on. The results are shown in Figure 9.2. For example, whereas the 20 percent of Canadian households with the lowest incomes receive 4.7 percent of the total income, the 40 percent of households with the lowest incomes receive 14.9 percent, and the 60 percent of households with the lowest incomes receive 31.3 percent. Plotted on a graph—with the variables being the percentage of households and the percentage of income—these figures give the Lorenz curve. The points *a*, *b*, *c*, *d*, and *e* represent the cumulative income shares.

Interpreting the Lorenz Curve

To see what this curve tells us about the distribution of income among Canadian households, it can be compared to Lorenz curves for two hypothetical economies with income distributions at the extremes: perfectly equal, and perfectly unequal.

FIGURE 9.2 The Lorenz Curve

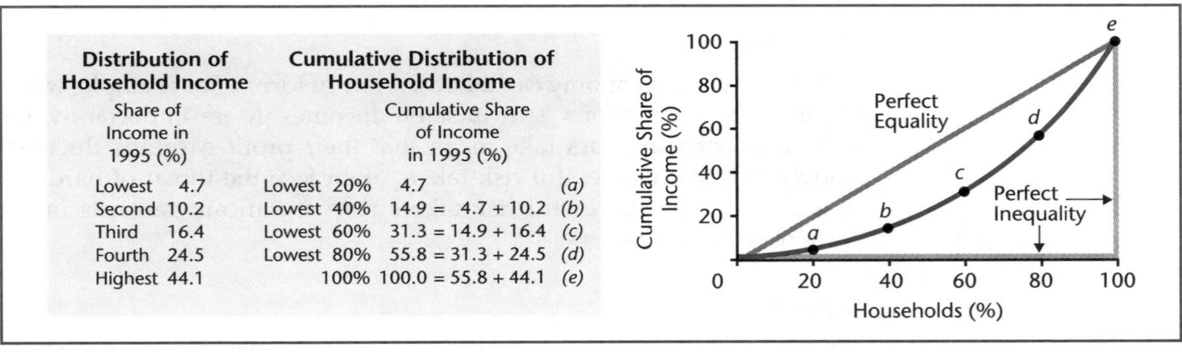

Distribution of Household Income		Cumulative Distribution of Household Income		
Share of Income in 1995 (%)			Cumulative Share of Income in 1995 (%)	
Lowest	4.7	Lowest 20%	4.7	*(a)*
Second	10.2	Lowest 40%	14.9 = 4.7 + 10.2	*(b)*
Third	16.4	Lowest 60%	31.3 = 14.9 + 16.4	*(c)*
Fourth	24.5	Lowest 80%	55.8 = 31.3 + 24.5	*(d)*
Highest	44.1	100%	100.0 = 55.8 + 44.1	*(e)*

Point *a* on the graph shows that the group with the lowest income received 4.7 percent of the total pre-tax income in 1995. Point *b* shows that the groups receiving the lowest 40 percent of pre-tax income in 1995 received 14.9 percent (4.7 + 10.2). Each subsequent point shows the cumulative income distribution; therefore point *e* shows that 100 percent of households earned 100 percent of total incomes (the numbers do not add exactly due to rounding). Connecting all the points gives the Lorenz curve. To contrast, the extremes of perfect equality and perfect inequality are shown. The closer the Lorenz curve is to the curve representing perfect equality (and the farther from the curve of perfect inequality), the more equally incomes are distributed.

Perfect Equality

The first hypothetical Lorenz curve represents the case of *perfect equality*, where each household earns an identical amount. Therefore, 20 percent of households receive 20 percent of the total income, 40 percent receive 40 percent, 60 percent receive 60 percent, and so on. The result is the 45-degree line shown in Figure 9.2 The closer the actual Lorenz curve is to this hypothetical case—in other words, the less bow-shaped it is—the more equal the distribution of incomes in the economy.

Perfect Inequality

At the other extreme of income distribution is *perfect inequality*, with only one household receiving all of the economy's income, while all other households receive nothing. The hypothetical Lorenz curve in this circumstance would follow the horizontal and vertical axes of the graph, as shown by the two thick lines in Figure 9.2 forming a right angle at the bottom right-hand corner. The closer the Lorenz curve is to this hypothetical case—meaning the more bow-shaped it is—the more unequal the distribution of income.

Reasons for Income Inequality

The differences in incomes of individual households can be attributed to a variety of causes. Wages and salaries make up over 70 percent of income earned in Canada. Hence, the factors that determine wages outlined in Chapter 8—labour productivity, education, experience, job conditions, regional disparities, market power, and discrimination—play an important role in income inequality. However, not all income inequalities are related to these factors. Profit, rent, and interest also play a part. Three main factors determine these other types of income, and can sometimes affect wages as well: risk-taking, ability, and wealth.

Risk-Taking

Risk-taking in an economy can take a variety of forms. For example, workers in some occupations earn unstable incomes. More importantly, the risks that entrepreneurs take mean that their profit earnings fluctuate widely. While unsuccessful risk-takers often face the threat of hardship and bankruptcy, successful risk-takers reap significant rewards in the form of high profits.

Ability

Because of different abilities, some individuals may pursue careers in high-paying areas while others make no earnings at all. Those individuals who find their talents in short supply—star athletes or gifted computer programmers, for instance—can sometimes earn extravagantly high incomes due to their special abilities.

Wealth

wealth: ownership of financial assets, such as stocks and bonds, or real assets, such as buildings and land

Most rent and interest incomes flow from the ownership of **wealth**. Wealth takes the form of financial assets, such as stocks and bonds, or real assets, such as buildings and land. There are two main ways to acquire wealth: through one's own saving, or by inheriting wealth from others.

Interestingly, wealth tends to be much more unequally distributed than income. Figure 9.3 shows the share of wealth held by the top 1 percent, 5 percent, and 20 percent of households in various years for four countries: Sweden, Canada, France, and the United States. In Canada, the top 1 percent owned 16.8 percent of the country's total wealth, while the top 5 percent owned 37.5 percent, and the top 20 percent owned 68.8 percent. This last figure is significantly higher than the 40.8 percent share for the top one-fifth income group after transfer payments and taxes. While less equally distributed than in Sweden, wealth in Canada is distributed more evenly among households than it is in either France or the United States.

FIGURE 9.3
Distribution of Wealth in Selected Countries

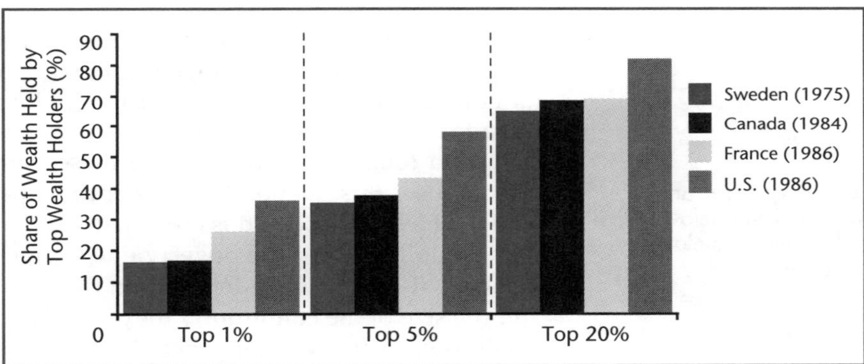

In 1984, the top 1 percent of Canadian households held 16.8 percent of Canada's wealth, the top 5 percent held 37.5 percent, and the top 20 percent held 68.8 percent. In Canada, the distribution of wealth among households is more equal than it is in France or the United States, but less so than in Sweden.

Source: Ontario Fair Tax Commission, *Wealth Tax Working Group Final Report* (Toronto, March 1993), p. A20.

Thinking About Economics

Is income inequality necessarily a bad thing?

While gross inequalities in income are undesirable, a perfect equality of incomes is not necessarily desirable because of the tradeoff between equity and efficiency. Without differences in incomes, the incentive to undertake further education, to take unpleasant jobs for greater pay, to save one's earnings, and to take risks would be severely hampered. Without some degree of income inequality, an economy's total output would be below its highest possible level. The goal of income equity is, therefore, usually interpreted as reducing, rather than eliminating, the inequalities that would exist in a pure market economy.

POVERTY

poverty: a situation in which a person's income is inadequate to provide the necessities of life

One of the main reasons behind the economic goal of income equity is the desire to minimize poverty. **Poverty** is a situation in which a person's income is inadequate to provide the necessities of life, such as food, clothing, and shelter. In practical terms, any precise definition of poverty is open to debate. All would agree that food is a necessity of life, but what sort of food should a person be able to afford? Also, should such products as TVs and radios be considered necessities in a rich industrialized country such as Canada, when they are luxuries in other countries? These are examples of questions governments must address when trying to define and minimize poverty.

The Poverty Line

poverty line: an income level below which a household is classified as poor

In Canada, poverty is defined in relation to the average Canadian income and expenditures. The average Canadian family spends 34.7 percent of its household pre-tax income on food, clothing, and shelter. Statistics Canada defines as poor any household that spends an additional 20 percent, or a total of 54.7 percent, on these items. For simplicity, Statistics Canada uses this relationship to identify a **poverty line**, or income level below which a household is classified as poor.

In dollar terms, the poverty line—which is also known as the low-income cut-off (LICO)—depends on the number of household members and the size of the community they live in, since people in rural areas or small towns can live more cheaply than those in urban centres. Figure 9.4 shows the poverty lines as determined for 1995. For example, the poverty line would be a yearly income of \$31 753 for a household of four persons living in a large city, or a yearly income of \$11 661 for an unattached individual living in a rural area.

Incidence of Poverty

How common is poverty among different groups in Canadian society? Using Statistics Canada's poverty line, an estimated 5 205 000 Canadians lived in poverty in 1995, of which 1 472 000 were children under the age of 18. As a proportion of Canada's total population, the number of poor Canadians has been falling in the last few decades. While 27.9 percent of families and 49.2 percent of unattached individuals were classified as poor in 1961, 14.2 percent of families and 39.3 percent of unattached individuals were classified as poor in 1995.

Figure 9.5 shows how the incidence of poverty among households (defined by LICO) is classified by certain characteristics: the sex of the household head, and his or her age, employment status, and education, as well as the region in which the household lives.

FIGURE 9.4 The Poverty Line for Various Households (1995)

Size of Household Unit	Urban Areas (categorized by size) ($1995)				Rural Areas
	500 000 and over	100 000 to 499 999	30 000 to 99 999	Less than 30 000	
1 person	16 874	14 473	14 372	13 373	11 661
2 persons	21 092	18 091	17 965	16 716	14 576
3 persons	26 232	22 500	22 343	20 790	18 129
4 persons	31 753	27 235	27 046	25 167	21 944
5 persons	35 494	30 445	30 233	28 132	24 530
6 persons	39 236	33 654	33 420	31 096	27 116
7 or more persons	42 978	36 864	36 607	34 061	29 702

The poverty line varies among household sizes and the households' community size. Within a given household category, a household would be considered poor if its income were below the income listed.

Source: Statistics Canada, *Income Distributions by Size in Canada, 1995* (December 1996), cat. no. 13-207, text table VIII. Reproduced by authority of the Minister of Industry, 1997.

Gender and Household Type

In general, poverty rates are considerably higher among unattached individuals of either sex than among families, with 39.3 percent of all unattached individuals being poor as opposed to 14.2 percent of all families. Unattached females are more likely to be poor than unattached males, while single-parent families tend to be poorer than two-parent families.

Age

Households headed by the youngest group (24 and under) and the oldest group (65 and over, unattached individuals) are more heavily represented among the ranks of the poor than are other households.

Employment

While poverty is more common among the unemployed, as expected, a notably high proportion of the employed are poor as well. Indeed, of families classified as poor, over half of the heads—52.8 percent in 1995—were employed for at least part of the year. This group, known as the "working poor," is often found in primary industries such as fishing, where wages are low and seasonal employment is common.

Education

Those households headed by a person with less education (no high school diploma) have the highest poverty rates. As we saw in Chapter 8, education affects wage levels. As a result, education level attained is a factor of poverty for the working poor.

Region

Poverty also varies from region to region. Historically, poor households tend to be concentrated in certain regions, particularly the Atlantic provinces and parts of Quebec. However, poverty exists throughout Canada. For example, a third of Canada's poor live in Ontario.

FIGURE 9.5 The Incidence of Poverty (1995)

	Percentage of Households Below the Poverty Line in 1995	
	Families	**Unattached Individuals**
	14.2	39.3
Gender and Household Type		
Married couples with children	7.7	
Single-parent families (female head)	45.4	
Single-parent families (male head)	22.9	
Unattached males		34.0
Unattached females		44.4
Age of Household Head		
24 and under	43.5	65.9
25-34	18.7	26.3
35-44	15.1	29.4
45-54	10.5	34.3
55-65	12.8	43.7
65 and over	7.8	45.1
Weeks Worked by Household Head in 1995		
None	27.6	58.2
1-9 weeks	52.6	88.4
10-19 weeks	34.2	75.5
20-29 weeks	26.1	49.0
30-39 weeks	18.5	43.7
40-48 weeks	12.5	34.0
49-52 weeks	6.1	15.7
Education of Household Head		
0-8 years of schooling	18.8	58.1
Some secondary education	19.2	48.9
Graduated from high school	14.4	35.2
Some postsecondary	18.2	50.3
Postsecondary certificate or diploma	11.8	29.1
University degree	7.4	23.2
Region		
Atlantic provinces	15.6	42.0
Quebec	16.7	46.8
Ontario	12.6	35.7
Prairie Provinces	14.2	36.3
British Columbia	13.0	35.9

The greatest incidence of poverty is among unattached individuals, women, single-parent families, families with a household head under 25 or over 64 in age, the unemployed, and those with minimal education. Differences in poverty rates also exist among regions.

Source: Statistics Canada, *Income Distributions by Size in Canada, 1995* (December 1996), cat. no. 13-207, pp. 180–183. Reproduced by authority of the Minister of Industry, 1997.

BRIEF REVIEW

1. The pre-tax income share of each fifth of households in Canada has not changed significantly in the last 40 years.
2. The Lorenz Curve, which expresses cumulative income distribution, demonstrates the extent to which there is perfect equality or perfect inequality in income distribution.
3. Factors that determine wages, as well as risk-taking, ability, and wealth, play a part in income inequality.
4. In Canada, poverty is defined in relation to the average Canadian income and expenditures on necessities. The poverty line, which depends on household type, is the income level below which a household is classified as poor.
5. Poverty is most prevalent among unattached individuals (especially women), single-parent families (especially those headed by women), the unemployed, and those under 25 and over 64 years old. Certain regions in Canada also have higher poverty rates.

THE CANADIAN WELFARE SOCIETY

welfare society: a society in which the government plays a major role in attempting to ensure the economic well-being of its citizens

A mixed economy such as Canada's can be described as a **welfare society**, in which the government plays a major role in attempting to ensure the well-being of its citizens. Although the welfare society has become an integral part of life in industrialized countries such as Canada, it is a relatively recent creation. Before the 1930s, Canadian government maintained the legal system, provided education up to the secondary school level, and encouraged markets to develop. Health care and universities were left largely in the hands of the private sector, and unemployment insurance was not available. In comparison to the present, a *laissez-faire* attitude characterized the relationship between government and business.

Change began with the Great Depression of the 1930s. Faced with widespread unemployment and deprivation, Canadians demanded that government attend to the economic welfare of its citizens. From the 1930s to the 1970s, the role of Canadian governments continued to expand. The question "What is fair?" has become perhaps the most important question that Canadian governments face, and their welfare programs are part of the answer. Now the welfare society in Canada includes a host of government programs: payments to adults with children, retirement funds for the elderly, insurance for unemployed workers, welfare payments for those who cannot work, subsidies for higher education, free health care, free schooling, and subsidized public housing for low-income families.

transfer payments: government payments to households or other levels of government

While all of these programs promote the general goal of ensuring Canadians' economic welfare, it is the transfer payments made to supplement incomes that most significantly address the specific goal of income equity. **Transfer payments** are government payments to either households or other levels of government. In both cases, transfer payments are not payments for goods and services, but legally granted payments. In

Canada, transfer payments are made by all three levels of government; however, the federal government takes the leading role.

Universality Versus Means Testing

universality: the principle applied to transfer payments whereby benefits are provided to all, regardless of income

means testing: a procedure whereby transfer payments vary according to a recipient's income

In the past, federal transfer payments to households were often based on the principle of **universality**. The principle of universality means that benefits apply to all individuals, no matter what their incomes. Universal programs had the advantage of treating everyone in the same way. However, universal programs also had drawbacks. Their main weakness was their expense: in order to provide substantial help to those who needed it most, a large sum of money had to be paid to *all* recipients.

In recent years, there has been a move toward **means testing**, whereby transfer payments vary according to a recipient's income. The main advantage of these programs is that benefits can be directed to those who need them most, so poor households receive the highest payments. However, governments may use means testing to limit spending by narrowing qualifications.

Federal Transfer Payments to Households

There are five main federal transfer payments to households. Old Age Security provides monthly payments to all Canadian residents 65 and over (though well-off households pay back some or all of their benefits in the form of personal income taxes). The Guaranteed Income Supplement (GIS) is a means-tested program that boosts the incomes of elderly Canadians whose only other primary source of income is Old Age Security. The Child Tax Credit provides means-tested payments to low-income parents of children under 18 years old. Employment Insurance (EI) is a federally run insurance program, funded by compulsory contributions from employees and their employers, to aid people unemployed because of job loss, temporary sickness, or the birth or adoption of a child. Finally, the Quebec and Canada Pension Plans (QPP and CPP) provide workers in Quebec and the rest of Canada with payments after retirement, financed by compulsory contributions from employees and their employers.

Starting in 2001, a single transfer payment program will begin replacing Old Age Security and the Guaranteed Income Supplement. This new Seniors Benefit will be means-tested, with low-income recipients receiving more (and high-income recipients receiving less) than the payments received under the previous two programs.

Other Transfer Payments

Provincial and territorial governments finance the costs of health care, provide subsidies for post-secondary education that translate into reduced tuition fees for students, and (with the help of municipalities)

offer welfare services to single-parent families with low incomes, individuals who are unable to find work due to disability, and families in crisis. Under the Canada Health and Social Transfer (CHST), the federal government pays for a portion of these costs by providing cash grants and personal income tax revenues to provincial and territorial governments.

Figure 9.6 shows the expenditures of three levels of government. For the federal government, the most important category of expenditure is debt charges, which are interest payments on the government's own debt, followed by transfer payments to persons. The expenditures of provincial and local governments are more heavily weighted toward purchases of goods and services, although transfers to persons are also an important component of total provincial spending.

Criticisms of the Welfare Society

While providing much-needed assistance to many households, Canada's welfare society has been the subject of widespread debate. Critics have pointed to three main problems with transfer payments to households: they discourage employment, they lead to inequities, and they are ineffective.

Disincentives to Work

According to critics, three programs in particular discourage employment: welfare, Employment Insurance, and government-run pension

FIGURE 9.6 Government Expenditures (1996–7)

Federal (1996-97) ($ billions)		Provincial (1996) ($ billions)		Local (1996) ($ billions)	
Transfers to persons		Goods and services	48.1	Goods and services	45.7
Benefits to the elderly	21.6	Transfers to		Transfers to	
Employment insurance benefits	13.1	Persons	33.9	Persons	3.0
Transfers to other levels of government	22.6	Businesses	5.1	Businesses	1.2
Subsidies and other transfers	18.3	Municipalities	28.2	Provinces	0.1
Crown corporations	4.3	Hospitals	22.1	Debt charges	4.3
Defence	9.6	Debt charges	25.2		54.3
Government operations	19.5		162.7		
Debt charges	45.5				
	154.5				

Federal government spending for the budgetary year of 1996–7 was dominated by transfer payments to persons and debt charges, which together make up almost half of federal spending. The main components of provincial spending are expenditures on goods and services, and transfers to persons, municipalities, and hospitals. Expenditures on goods and services dominate local government spending.

Sources: Department of Finance, *The Budget Plan* (February 1997), pp. 41, 43; Statistics Canada, *Canadian Economic Observer, Statistical Summary* (March 1997), cat. no. 11-010, pp. 7–8. Reproduced by authority of the Minister of Industry, 1997.

plans. Welfare plans vary across Canada, but most of them set up financial hurdles to employment, with some recipients receiving more income from welfare than they would upon initially entering the workforce.

Canada's Employment Insurance program has been criticized for worsening the very problem it is meant to counteract. By allowing repeated claims for benefits with minor penalties, the program encourages workers to stay in occupations and regions of the country in which the risk of unemployment is considerable. Moreover, the high contributions paid by employers discourage them from creating new jobs.

The QPP and CPP have been criticized largely for their funding. Both are financed on a "pay-as-you-go" basis: the benefits paid out in any given year are funded by the benefits paid in. With the aging of the "baby-boom generation" and other demographic changes, workers' and employers' payments will have to rise to 9.9 percent (or about 4.95 percent each for employers and employees) by the year 2003 to cover the costs. This projected increase, critics argue, will discourage employment and job creation and may lead to a significant scaling back of these payments—to the detriment of young people currently paying into the programs.

More generally, critics claim, Canada's welfare society indirectly discourages work by increasing taxes for individuals and businesses. With high tax rates, people have less incentive to seek employment and businesses have less incentive to hire them.

Inequities and Abuses

Some people argue against the principle of universality, which ensures that Old Age Security is paid to all households, not just those in need. The same criticism is directed at Employment Insurance; it is paid to both well-off individuals and those in need. Critics also note abuses of programs. Employment Insurance, for example, might be claimed by individuals who have little intention of acquiring a permanent job, but who may work for brief periods each year in order to claim extended benefits.

Ineffectiveness

Lastly, critics argue that Canada's transfer payment system is hampered by overlapping bureaucracies, high administrative costs, and a lack of focus. They contend that due to this lack of focus and despite the large amounts spent on maintaining Canada's welfare society, transfer payments do not sufficiently alleviate poverty. In particular, the welfare society is not well-suited to helping the large group of working poor.

BRIEF REVIEW

1. Canada's welfare society has developed since the 1930s. As well as instituting free health care, schooling, and so on, governments have established programs requiring transfer payments to households, the main purpose of which is to promote income equity.
2. In the past, transfer payments to households were often based on the principle of universality, with all Canadians receiving the same payment. Now programs are likely to be means tested; that is, benefits are determined by the recipient's income.
3. The main federal transfer payment programs to households are Old Age Security, Employment Insurance, and the Quebec and Canada Pension Plans.
4. The Federal Government shares the cost of health care, post-secondary education, and welfare service with provincial and territorial governments through the Canada Health and Social Transfer (CHST).
5. Government transfer payment programs are criticized for discouraging employment, fostering inequities and abuses, and not sufficiently alleviating poverty.

Thinking About Economics

Could Canada's current patchwork of transfer payments be replaced with a single program?

Many economists propose a *guaranteed annual income*, which could replace virtually all current transfer payments to households. Under this proposed program, Canadians would be guaranteed a certain income. Those who earn no income themselves would receive the entire amount from the government. Those who earn some private income would have their government payment decreased by a certain amount for every dollar of private income. Say, for example, the guaranteed minimum were set at $20 000 per year and the deduction for each dollar of private earnings set at 50 cents. A household with no private earnings would receive $20 000. If it started to have private earnings of $2000, its payment would be reduced by $1000 ($2000 × 0.50), for a new government payment of $19 000. Therefore, with a total income of $21 000 ($19 000 + $2000) the household would still be better off than if it did not have any private income. As private earnings rose further, the government payment would gradually drop, finally disappearing altogether.

TAXATION

tax: a payment required by government from individuals or businesses, with no direct good or service being provided in return

A **tax** is a payment required by government from individuals or businesses, with no direct good or service being provided in return. The main purpose of taxation is to finance state activity, but taxes may also be designed to promote income equity or improve outcomes in private markets. As shown in Figure 9.7, taxes by all three levels of government in Canada have increased considerably over past decades in relation to the size of the entire economy. The federal government, which plays the biggest role in operating Canada's welfare programs, takes the largest share of taxes.

Principles of Taxation

How should the burden of taxes be shared among taxpayers? Two principles can be applied in deciding whether or not the burden of a tax is distributed in a manner that is fair to all taxpayers: the principle of benefits received, and the principle of ability to pay.

Benefits Received

benefits received: the principle applied to taxation whereby taxes are geared to the benefits each taxpayer gains from government activity

The principle of **benefits received** suggests that taxes should be geared to the benefits each taxpayer gains from government activity. In this case, government services are paid for in the same ways that products are bought and sold in the private sector. The benefits-received principle is the guiding philosophy behind some taxes. The proceeds from a tax on

FIGURE 9.7
Taxes in the Canadian Economy

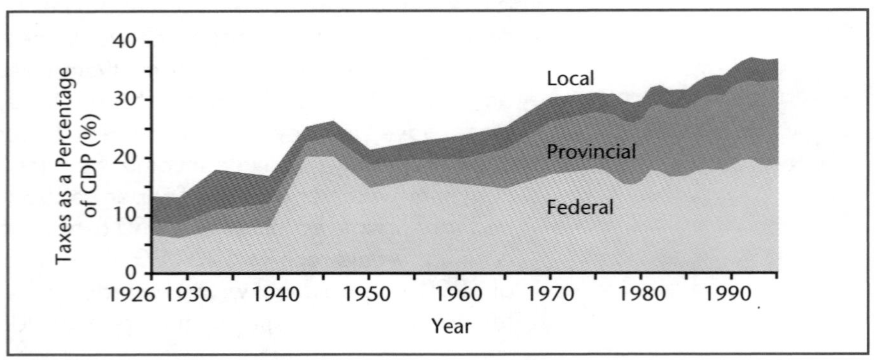

Since the 1920s, the increasing importance of the public sector in the Canadian economy has led to increased taxes (including contributions for such programs as Employment Insurance and CPP/QPP) in relation to the size of the economy. While taxes represented just over 10 percent of Gross Domestic Product (GDP) in 1926, they represented just under 40 percent by 1995.

Sources: Adapted from Statistics Canada, *National Income and Expenditure Accounts, Annual Estimates, 1926 to 1989,* cat. no. 13–511, and CANSIM matrices 2711 to 2713 and 6713 to 6714 (September 1996), reprinted in Canadian Tax Foundation, *The National Finances, 1993* (Toronto, 1993), p. 3:12 and *Finances of the Nation, 1996* (Toronto 1997), p. B:9. Reproduced by authority of the Minister of Industry, 1997.

gasoline, for example, are often earmarked for road construction and maintenance, thereby allowing governments to have drivers who use the most gasoline—and use the roads the most—pay the most for road upkeep.

Ability to Pay

ability to pay: the principle applied to taxation whereby taxes vary in proportion to a taxpayer's financial resources

A more common tax philosophy is based on the principle of **ability to pay**. According to this principle, taxes should vary in proportion to a taxpayer's financial resources—in particular, income. As sensible as the principle may be, it is difficult to measure ability to pay. For example, do all individuals earning $40 000 have the same ability to pay taxes, or does their taxpaying capacity also depend on other factors, such as the number of dependent children they support? Suppose a person's income rises by 50 percent, from $40 000 to $60 000. Should his or her tax bill also rise by 50 percent, or by some larger or smaller percentage?

Taxes and Income

Taxes are related to income in three possible ways, with a certain type of tax being either progressive, regressive, or proportional.

Progressive Taxes

progressive tax: a tax that increases as a proportion of income as income increases

A **progressive tax** is one that increases as a proportion of income as the income increases. In other words, well-off taxpayers are taxed more in both dollar terms *and* percentage terms. For example, someone making an annual income of $10 000 might pay 10 percent of total income, or $1000, for a certain tax, but a person making $20 000 a year might pay 15 percent of total income, or $3000, for that same tax.

Regressive Taxes

regressive tax: a tax that decreases as a proportion of income as income increases

In contrast, a **regressive tax** is one that decreases as a proportion of income as income increases. In other words, taxpayers with low incomes pay proportionately more of their incomes for the tax than do well-off taxpayers, even though the well-off taxpayer may pay more as a dollar amount. For example, one taxpayer making $10 000 a year might pay 8 percent in tax, or $800, while another taxpayer with an annual income of $20 000 might pay 6 percent, or $1200, for the same tax.

Proportional Taxes

proportional tax: a tax that remains constant as a proportion of income for all incomes

Finally, a **proportional tax** is one that remains constant as a proportion of income for all incomes. Therefore, while taxpayers with vastly different incomes pay proportionately the same tax, the well-off taxpayer pays a higher dollar amount. For example, with a 6 percent tax rate, one taxpayer with an annual income of $10 000 would pay $600 in tax, while another taxpayer with an annual income of $20 000 would pay $1200.

Types of Taxation

Canadian governments at the federal, provincial, and local levels use five main types of taxation to raise funds: personal income taxes, sales taxes, excise taxes, property taxes, and corporate income taxes.

Personal Income Taxes

Personal income taxes are collected by the federal government, the proceeds being shared with the provinces and territories (except in Quebec, where federal and provincial income taxes are collected separately). Households pay taxes not only on their income from supplying resources, but also on any transfer payments they receive. Households also pay income tax on **capital gains**, which are earnings from selling an asset such as a bond or a piece of land at a higher price than it was purchased for.

capital gains: earnings from selling an asset, such as land, at a higher price than it was purchased for

marginal tax rates: tax rates that are calculated as percentages of each extra dollar of taxable income

Figure 9.8 shows the federal income tax rates. Note how the tax rates go up as income increases. These rates are called **marginal tax rates**, meaning that they are calculated as percentages of each *extra* dollar of taxable income. So, for example, households in the lowest income bracket, with 1993 taxable incomes of up to $29 590, were taxed at 17 percent. Therefore, a household making the maximum would pay $5030 in taxes ($29 590 × 0.17). In contrast, a household in the next tax bracket—with taxable income between $29 591 and $59 180—would pay 17 percent on its first $29 590 of taxable income, but 26 percent on income above that amount. Thus, a household that earns the maximum for the second tax bracket, or $59 180, would pay $5030 on the first $29 590 (using the 17 percent rate), plus $7693 on the remaining $29 590 (using the 26 percent rate), for a total tax bill of $12 723. Households in the highest possible tax bracket are taxed on each new dollar of income at a marginal tax rate of 29 percent.

Households may be allowed a variety of deductions that reduce their taxable income. For example, contributions to registered retirement savings plans can reduce the dollar amount on which a household is taxed.

FIGURE 9.8 Federal Personal Income Tax Rates (1996)

Levels of Taxable Income	Marginal Tax Rate
$0 to $29 590	17%
$29 591 to $59 180	26%
$59 181 or more	29%

In 1996, households with taxable income in the first tax bracket—between $0 and $29 590—paid 17 cents on each dollar of income. Those in the second tax bracket—between $29 591 and $59 180—paid 26 cents on every dollar earned above $29 590. Those in the third income bracket paid 29 cents on every dollar earned above $59 180.

Source: Condensed from *Tax Facts and Figures 1996*, published by Coopers & Lybrand, Chartered Accountants.

In addition to these deductions, households may also claim a variety of tax credits, which directly reduce their tax bill.

Outside Quebec, provincial personal income taxes are simply a percentage of the federal tax bill added onto the taxpayer's bill. These percentages vary among the provinces and territories. Newfoundland taxes at the highest rate, with the province adding an extra 69 percent to households' tax bills in 1996. In contrast, residents of the Northwest Territories enjoy the lowest rate—45 percent in 1996.

As shown in Figure 9.9, personal income taxes made up 38.8 percent of total tax revenues for all levels of government in 1994.

FIGURE 9.9 Tax Revenues for All Levels of Government (1994)

	Percent of GDP	Percent of Total Taxes
Personal income taxes	13.9	38.8
Sales and excise taxes	5.6	15.7
Property taxes	3.8	10.6
Corporate income taxes	2.3	6.4
Miscellaneous taxes	10.2	28.5
	35.8	100.0

Personal income taxes are the most important single source of revenue for the state, followed by sales and excise taxes, property taxes, and corporate taxes.

Source: Statistics Canada, *Provincial Economic Accounts, 1961–1995*, cat. no. 13-123-XDB (May 1996), reprinted in Canadian Tax Foundation, *Finances of the Nation, 1996*. Reproduced by authority of the Minister of Industry, 1997.

Sales and Excise Taxes

sales taxes: taxes that are charged on a wide range of products, and calculated as a percentage of their prices

excise taxes: taxes that are charged on particular products, and often expressed as a dollar amount per unit of quantity

Sales and excise taxes, which made up 15.7 percent of total tax revenues in 1994, are levied by both federal and provincial governments on goods and services. **Sales taxes** are usually charged on a wide range of goods and services, and are calculated as a percentage of the prices of these products. For example, a general 7 percent sales tax means that 7 cents is paid on each $1 spent on goods and services. In contrast, **excise taxes** are charged on particular products such as gasoline, liquor, and tobacco, and are often expressed as a dollar amount per unit of quantity, rather than in terms of percentages of product price.

Property Taxes

Property taxes are charged by local governments on buildings and land. For taxation purposes, these assets are assigned a value—often not their potential price in the real estate market, but some arbitrary dollar amount set in the past. Then, each year, the local government establishes a tax rate in terms of mills (or thousands) of property value. For example, a mill rate of 80 means that property owners are charged $80 for each $1000 in property value. As shown in Figure 9.9, property taxes made up 10.6 percent of Canadian governments' total tax revenues in 1994.

Corporate Income Taxes

Corporate income taxes are paid by corporations to governments as a percentage of their annual profits. As with personal income taxes, corporations are allowed to make deductions from their total income in calculating taxable profit. The resulting dollar amount is then taxed at a constant marginal rate of 28 percent by the federal government, with most provincial governments "piggybacking" on this rate as in the case of personal income taxes. In the budget year 1994, corporate income taxes represented 6.4 percent of total tax revenues for all levels of government, as shown in Figure 9.9.

Thinking About Economics

Are Canadian taxes progressive, regressive, or proportional?

Because of the range of marginal rates for different income brackets, Canada's personal income tax system is progressive, with the rich paying a larger proportion of their incomes than do the poor. This is so despite tax shelters that the rich can use to reduce their taxable incomes. In contrast, sales and excise taxes tend to be regressive, since the poor spend a higher proportion of their incomes on consumption items than do the rich, who are more likely to save part of their incomes. Property taxes (at least those on buildings rather than those on land) are also often regressive, largely because the poor devote a higher proportion of their incomes to housing than do the rich. Corporate income taxes are more difficult to classify as either progressive or regressive. To the extent that these taxes reduce the income of shareholders—a rich group in Canadian society—they are progressive. However, corporations that have considerable market power may succeed in passing on the burden of the tax to consumers in the form of higher prices for their products. In this case, the corporate tax is regressive in a similar way to a sales tax.

BRIEF REVIEW

1. Taxes are payments required by government from individuals and businesses. Over past decades, taxation has increased as a proportion of the overall Canadian economy, with federal taxes representing the largest share.
2. Taxes may be based on the benefits received by a taxpayer from government activity, or on the taxpayer's ability to pay.
3. Taxes that are progressive increase as a proportion of income as income increases. Taxes that are regressive decrease as a proportion of income as income increases. Taxes that are proportional remain constant as a proportion of all incomes.
4. Canadian governments use five main types of taxation: personal income taxes, sales taxes, excise taxes, property taxes, and corporate income taxes.

SPILLOVER EFFECTS

spillover effects: external effects of economic activity, which have an impact on outsiders who are not producing or consuming a product

Government spending and taxation are not only geared to promoting income equity and competition. Governments also play a part in dealing with the external effects of economic activity. These spillover effects arise whenever outsiders are affected by the production or consumption of a particular product. **Spillover effects** occur in even the ideal case of a perfectly competitive market, simply because no market exists in isolation. Governments often step in to see that all costs and benefits—private and public—are accounted for. Sometimes government intervention takes the form of direct spending.

Spillover Costs and Benefits

Spillover effects may take the form of either costs or benefits.

Spillover Costs

spillover costs: negative external effects of producing or consuming a product

Spillover costs are the negative effects of producing or consuming a product that fall on outsiders, not market participants. Environmental pollution is the most common example. Recall that some resources called *free goods*, such as air, can be used free of charge. Still other resources, such as water, have prices that do not reflect the resource's value. Any damage caused to these resources through market activity creates substantial costs for society as a whole.

Producers making products that have negative external effects focus only on their private costs as they make supply decisions. Consequently, the prices for these products are insufficient to cover both private and spillover costs. Figure 9.10 illustrates spillover effects with the example of gasoline used by motor vehicles. Assuming that the market for gasoline is

FIGURE 9.10
The Impact of Spillover Costs

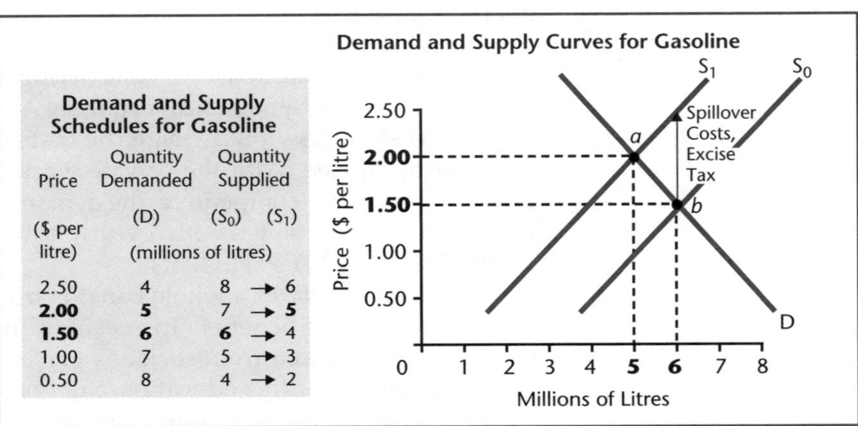

Demand and Supply Schedules for Gasoline

Price ($ per litre)	Quantity Demanded (D)	Quantity Supplied (S_0)	(S_1)
	(millions of litres)		
2.50	4	8 →	6
2.00	**5**	7 →	**5**
1.50	**6**	**6** →	4
1.00	7	5 →	3
0.50	8	4 →	2

Without government intervention, equilibrium occurs at point *b*, at a price of $1.50 per litre and a quantity of 6 million litres of gasoline. To account for spillover costs, the government may impose an excise tax of $1.00 per litre. As a result, the supply curve shifts from S_0 to S_1, moving equilibrium to point *a*, at a price of $2.00 per litre and a quantity of 5 million litres.

perfectly competitive and free of government intervention, equilibrium occurs at point *b*, the intersection of the demand and supply curves D and S_0, with a price per litre of $1.50 and a quantity of 6 million litres.

Because of the environmental damage created by both the production and the consumption of gasoline, spillover costs are associated with this product. If these spillover costs are an extra $1 for each litre of gas, a new supply curve, S_1, can be drawn that incorporates the additional cost per litre. Whereas the old supply curve, S_0, reflects the private costs of producing one more litre of gasoline, the new supply curve, S_1, reflects the *private* and *public* costs of each new litre.

Where should the market operate? Applying the rule of marginal cost pricing, price in this market should equal the height of the supply curve (which reflects marginal cost), once both private and spillover costs are accounted for. In other words, equilibrium should occur at point *a*, the intersection of D and S_1, at a price of $2 and a quantity of 5 million litres. Without government intervention, 1 million too many litres of gasoline are produced and consumed, given the environmental damage associated with both the production and consumption of gasoline. To achieve the preferred outcome, the government can impose regulations on the use of gasoline, or use its taxing powers. For example, it can levy an excise tax on gasoline equalling $1 per litre. This succeeds in shifting the supply curve from S_0 to S_1, and ensures that the oversupply of gasoline is corrected.

Spillover Benefits

spillover benefits: positive external effects of producing or consuming a product

Spillover benefits are positive external effects of producing or consuming a product. Education is an important example, since society as a whole gains from this service. From an economic perspective alone, education is considered beneficial because of the increased work and income-earning opportunities it affords each individual, and because it enriches the nation's human resources. More generally, education is seen as a social good because it helps Canadians to lead more informed, fulfilled, and productive lives.

Suppose that students are considering an education in engineering. Figure 9.11 gives a hypothetical example. As in any education and career choice, the students would weigh the costs and benefits of obtaining an engineering degree. With the private market for an engineering education being perfectly competitive, the demand and supply curves D_0 and S have equilibrium point *a*, with a yearly tuition per student of $4000 and an enrollment of 10 000 students.

Because society as a whole benefits from having trained engineers, there are spillover benefits. To see how much engineering education should be undertaken from society's perspective, we must estimate the spillover benefits of this education. Suppose the result is $2000 per student per year. As a result, a new demand curve, D_1, can be drawn that incorporates the private and public benefits.

Again applying the rule of marginal cost pricing, price in this market should equal the height of the supply curve (which reflects marginal cost), once both private and spillover benefits are accounted for. In other

FIGURE 9.11
The Impact of Spillover Benefits

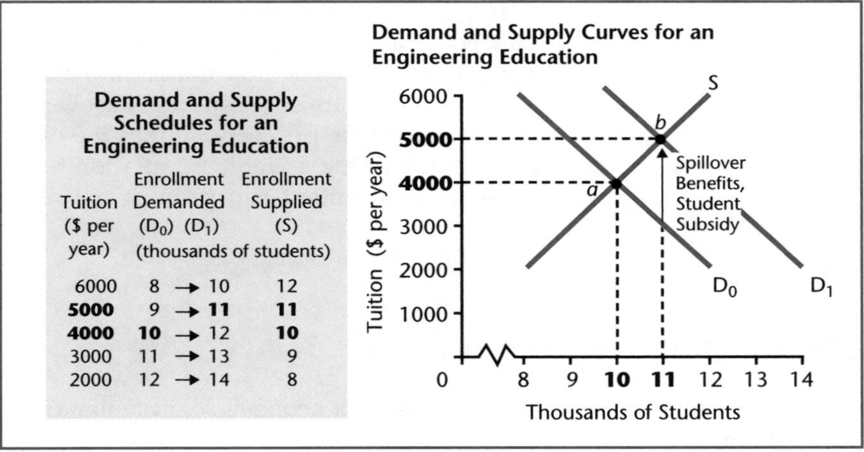

Demand and Supply Schedules for an Engineering Education

Tuition ($ per year)	Enrollment Demanded (D_0) (D_1)	Enrollment Supplied (S)
	(thousands of students)	
6000	8 → 10	12
5000	9 → **11**	**11**
4000	**10** → 12	**10**
3000	11 → 13	9
2000	12 → 14	8

Without government intervention in the market for engineering education, equilibrium occurs at point *a*, at a yearly tuition of $4000 per student and an enrollment of 10 000 students. If spillover benefits are determined to be $2000 per student, government can create a subsidy for students pursuing a career in engineering. As a result, the demand curve shifts from D_0 to D_1, and the new equilibrium is at point *b*, at a yearly tuition of $5000 per student, $2000 of which is paid by the government, and an enrollment of 11 000 students.

words, equilibrium should occur at point *b*, at the intersection of S and D_1, with an annual tuition of $5000 and an enrollment of 11 000 students. However, if private benefits alone were accounted for, only 10 000 students (point *a*) would be enrolled, thereby creating a shortfall of 1000 students. To increase enrollment to the desired level, the government could provide engineering education itself, or it could subsidize engineering education by giving prospective students vouchers to be turned in to the engineering school. The school would then turn in these vouchers to the government for $2000 per voucher. As a result, the demand curve for engineering education would shift to the right, thereby ensuring that society produces more engineers than would a fully private and competitive market.

Public Goods

public good: a product whose benefits cannot be restricted to certain individuals

At the extreme, there are some products for which private benefits and spillover benefits cannot be separated. A **public good** is a product whose benefits cannot be restricted to certain individuals. In other words, while many consumers may pay for the product, others may get a "free ride." Lighthouses are an example, since any ship making use of a lighthouse for navigation benefits whether or not the ship's owners help pay for the lighthouse's upkeep. In this situation, one option is to dispense with markets and have government provide these products. This happens in the case of national defence. Since it is impossible to restrict the benefits of this service only to those citizens who are willing to pay for it, national defence must be financed through compulsory taxation. In other cases, governments can help turn public goods into private goods. For example, increasing elephant populations in African countries can be viewed as a public good. One option is to have governments finance policing measures to stop indiscriminate hunting. Another option that has been tried with some success in several African countries is to make elephants private property, so that the owners have an economic interest in maintaining a viable population for commercial hunting. In such cases, a government can prompt the formation of workable private markets.

BRIEF REVIEW

1. Spillover effects are the external effects of economic activity that arise because no market exists in isolation.
2. Spillover effects can be negative or positive. Spillover costs, such as pollution, are the harmful effects of producing or consuming a product. Spillover benefits, such as those associated with education, are the positive effects of producing or consuming a product.
3. Governments often step in to see that public, as well as private, costs and benefits are accounted for. Governments might, for example, intervene with taxes to correct an oversupply in the case of spillover costs, or with subsidies to correct a shortfall in the case of spillover benefits.
4. Public goods are products whose benefits cannot be restricted to certain individuals. Governments often step in to provide these goods rather than leave them to private markets. Governments can also attempt to turn such goods into private goods by defining new types of property.

KEY CONCEPTS

Lorenz curve
wealth
poverty
poverty line
welfare society
transfer payments
universality
means testing
tax
benefits received
ability to pay
progressive tax
regressive tax
proportional tax
capital gains
marginal tax rates
sales taxes
excise taxes
spillover effects
spillover costs
spillover benefits
public good

ANALYSIS AND APPLICATION

Distribution of Household Income (1995)

	Income Before Transfer Payments and Taxes (1)		Pre-tax Income (2)		Income After Transfer Payments and Taxes (3)	
	Income Share	**Average Income**	**Income Share**	**Average Income**	**Income Share**	**Average Income**
Lowest 20%	0.8	1 576	4.7	10 760	5.7	10 428
Second 20%	7.5	14 681	10.2	23 144	11.5	20 883
Third 20%	16.1	31 502	16.4	37 192	17.2	31 402
Fourth 20%	26.2	51 357	24.5	55 563	24.5	44 615
Highest 20%	49.5	97 034	44.1	99 976	41.1	74 972
	100.0%	39 232	100.0%	45 329	100.0%	36 462

Source: Statistics Canada, *Income After Tax, Distributions by Size in Canada, 1995* (May 1997), cat. no. 13-210, p. 23. Reproduced by authority of the Minister of Industry, 1997.

1. The table above shows the income shares going to each one-fifth of Canadian households before government transfer payments (column 1), after the receipt of transfer payments (column 2), and after the receipt of transfer payments and the payment of personal income taxes (column 3). Using the data in this table, do the following:
   a. For each of the five income groups, calculate the changes in average income from income before transfer payments and personal income taxes, to pre-tax income, to income after transfer payments and personal income taxes.
   b. Comment on the results, noting and explaining the most significant changes.

2 a. Figure 9.2 gives the Lorenz curve based on incomes prior to taxation but after transfer payments. Using the data from the previous question, create a graph giving two Lorenz curves: one using income shares prior to transfer payments and personal income taxes, and another after both transfer payments and personal income taxes.
   b. Compare the results. Given that one of the main goals of transfer payments and personal income taxes is income equity, how effective do you think these forms of government intervention are?

Income Shares in Selected Countries

Country	Share of income received by each fifth of income earners				
	1 (lowest)	2	3	4	5 (highest)
Canada	5.7	11.8	17.7	24.6	40.2
United States	4.7	11.0	17.4	25.0	41.9
Chile	3.5	6.6	10.9	18.1	61.0
Japan	8.7	13.2	17.5	23.1	37.5

Source: *World Development Report 1996*, by the World Bank. Copyright 1996 by The International Bank for Reconstruction and Development/The World Bank. Table 5 "Distribution of Income or Consumption," pp. 196-7.

3. The table above shows the share of post-tax income received by each fifth of income earners, from lowest to highest, in selected countries for various years.
   a. Construct a table showing the cumulative distribution of income among the five groups of income earners in each country.
   b. Based on your table in part a., draw and label a Lorenz curve for each country on the same large graph. Then, rank the countries from the most equal to least equal income distribution.

4. Why is the distribution of wealth in most countries more unequal than the distribution of income?

5. Outline four common causes of poverty in Canada.

6. Some commentators suggest Canada's traditional system of transfer payments should be replaced by a guaranteed annual income (GAI) plan.
   a. To what extent could such a plan correct the problems associated with traditional transfer payments?
   b. What are some possible disadvantages of a GAI plan?
   c. Give an example of an existing transfer payment that already incorporates elements of a GAI plan. What are the similarities and differences between this transfer payment and a GAI plan?

7. Identify the following taxes as progressive, regressive, or proportional, and explain your answers.
   a. a tax on inherited wealth
   b. a 7 percent sales tax on all goods and services (with no accompanying tax credit)
   c. a personal income tax with a constant marginal tax rate (and no deductions from income)
   d. a tax on residential housing

Demand and Supply Schedules for Cigarettes

Price ($ per pack)	Quantity Demanded	Quantity Supplied	
	(millions of packs per year)		
	(D_0)	(S_0)	(S_1)
5	7	11	___
4	8	10	___
3	9	9	___
2	10	8	___
1	11	7	___

8. The table above shows hypothetical demand and supply schedules for cigarettes in the absence of government intervention.
   a. Draw a diagram showing demand (D_0), supply (S_0), and equilibrium price and quantity in the market before government intervention.
   b. Government policy-makers estimate that the spillover costs associated with cigarette smoking are an extra $2 for each pack sold. Outline the nature of these spillover costs in the case of cigarette smoking.
   c. Based on the estimate in part b., draw a new supply curve (S_1) on your graph that incorporates both private and public costs of producing and consuming cigarettes. Then, using your graph, copy out and complete the table accompanying this question. With the aid of your graph and table, identify the preferred equilibrium in this market.
   d. Outline the various ways in which government can intervene to achieve the preferred outcome in this market.

9. Identify the spillover effect in each of the following cases, and outline a government policy to deal with this effect.
   a. Impaired driving causes numerous accidents on Canadian roads.
   b. Some Canadians begin to take a new vaccine for measles.
   c. Heroin use by pregnant women is hazardous to the health of their offspring.
   d. A mosquito abatement program is established in a particular community.

10. (Advanced Question)
    An economy is made up of five individuals, whose incomes are $56 000 (person A), $50 000 (person B), $30 000 (person C), $16 000 (person D), and $8,000 (person E).
    a. Based on this data, what percentage of the economy's total before-tax income is earned by each income earner?

b. The government is considering several tax proposals to finance its expenditures on foreign-made goods and services. For each proposal below, calculate the percentage of the economy's total after-tax income received by each income earner, and identify whether the proposal is regressive, proportional or progressive.
   i. a lump-sum tax of $3200 on each income-earner
   ii. a general sales tax of 10 percent on all consumption items, assuming that each person in the economy has basic consumption needs totalling $8000 each year and then spends 75 cents of each dollar of income above $8000
   iii. a 10 percent tax on all income
   iv. a 12.5 percent tax on all taxable income, with each income-earner allowed to deduct $6400 from their income when calculating their taxable income
   v. an income tax with marginal tax rates on taxable income found in Figure 9.8, with each income earner allowed a tax credit whereby they can deduct $1000 from their tax bill

11. In 1996, the federal government instituted wide-ranging changes to unemployment insurance. Access the online version of the Guide to Employment Insurance prepared by Human Resources Development Canada (at http://www.hrdc-drhc.gc.ca/hrdc/ei/sc1236_e.html), and summarize the changes that took place to:
    a. introduce a new house-based system for calculating benefits
    b. provide extra payments for low-income families
    c. increase the clawback of benefits for high-income earners

Advancing Economic Thought

THE DOOMSDAY PROPHET

Thomas Malthus and Population Growth

Malthus and His Influence

Known as the "doomsday prophet" for his gloomy predictions of the economic and social future, Thomas Malthus (1766–1834) was an economist, as well as a clergyman. Malthus's theories and predictions sprang from an unlikely source: a reform-minded writer named William Godwin (1756–1836), who believed that future society would be transformed by science and human reason. Wars, disease, and crime would finally come to an end, Godwin thought, and the need for government would vanish. Malthus's *Essay on Population* (1798), in which he published his arguments against Godwin's vision, was destined to be one of the most influential economic works of the nineteenth century.

Malthus's basic point was that utopian visions of the future ignore the negative effects of population growth. According to Malthus, food production and population levels expand at different rates. At best, he said, food increases in what mathematicians call an algebraic progression (1, 2, 3, 4...) as more variable inputs are devoted to a certain amount of usable land. In contrast, population increases in a geometric progression (1, 2, 4, 8...), with levels doubling again and again in a set period. Malthus estimated this period to be 25 years.

Thomas Malthus

Source: By courtesy of the National Portrait Gallery

Given these assumptions, it was easy for Malthus to predict a discrepancy between food production and the needs of the population. The following time chart shows numbers taken from Malthus's *Essay*. For convenience, population and food stocks in Year 1 are set equal to 1 unit. Food production expands by 1 unit every 25 years as population doubles in the same period. After 225 years, population will have outstripped food by a factor of just over 50 (512 ÷ 10) to 1.

A Malthusian Time Chart

Year	1	25	50	75	100	125	150	175	200	225
Food	1	2	3	4	5	6	7	8	9	10
Population	1	2	4	8	16	32	64	128	256	512

If food grows by 1 unit every 25 years but population doubles over the same period, then after 225 years food production will be ten times higher but population will be 512 times higher.

Source: Henry William Spiegel, *The Growth of Economic Thought* (Durham, NC: Duke University Press, 1971), p.272.

Malthus warned of desperate circumstances if his predictions came true, and outlined how population growth could be slowed by either a decrease in the birth rate or an increase in the mortality rate. He had little faith that the number of births would decrease; however, he did feel that at some point, if birth rates did not fall, a limited food supply would bring on misery, famine, plagues, or war, thereby decreasing the population.

Implications and Influence of Malthus's Theory

Based on his assumptions, Malthus believed that aid to those in need would be self-defeating, as it would encourage larger families and therefore more population growth. In the long run, he said, this population growth would result in starvation. During the nineteenth century, Malthus's views had a powerful effect on government policies. In England, for example, aid to people who were physically able to work was restricted to those willing to give up their possessions and move into a workhouse, where prolonged labour brought them virtually no pay—only room and board.

Social reformers attacked this "Malthusian" policy, calling it misguided and cruel. The appalling conditions in English workhouses were exposed in many books and pamphlets, Charles Dickens' fictional account *Oliver Twist* being the most famous. Not surprisingly, it was because of Malthus's work that economics was dubbed "the dismal science" by its critics.

Relevance for Today

Fortunately, Malthus's dire predictions have proven to be wrong, at least in those countries with which he was directly concerned. While he later refined the logic of his arguments, their foundations were shaky. Malthus implied that the state of technology would remain fixed; however, the dramatic changes in technology since his day have increased food production in most countries. Malthus also overlooked the extent to which large families were the result of economic necessity. In his own day, high infant mortality rates and the lack of old age pensions meant that large families provided parents with security in old age. Also, during his time, child labour provided extra income to a family. Today, with social welfare programs, child labour laws, and the means to limit population growth, population growth rates in industrialized countries have been far below what Malthus imagined. Indeed, in some of these nations, the rate is close to zero.

While population growth continues to be a *global* concern (which we'll address in Chapter 18), the history of Malthus's theory has a valuable lesson: care must be taken in applying economic models to the real world and to government policy.

1 a. Briefly explain why Thomas Malthus believed the growth in living standards in countries such as Great Britain could eventually stagnate.

b. Summarize two main reasons why the pessimistic warnings of Malthus proved to be unwarranted.

2. Critics of Malthus suggested that, by assuming a set ratio between the growth rates of food and population, he was ignoring the role of food prices. Explain how this argument could be used against Malthus's theory.

SIDELINE

TAXATION BLUES

The Debate Over the Goods and Services Tax

In 1991, the federal government made a controversial change in Canada's tax system: it introduced the Goods and Services Tax (GST). Rarely has a tax been so disliked by Canadian taxpayers, so much so that many taxpayers demanded its replacement. To examine why, let's first look at why the GST was introduced.

Drawbacks of the Federal Sales Tax

Prior to the GST, the federal government had a Federal Sales Tax (FST), also known as the manufacturer's sales tax. Under the FST, a 13.5 percent tax was levied on the sales value of all Canadian manufactured goods. The tax was "hidden" to consumers in that it was built into final retail prices, rather than added on top. Therefore, most consumers were unaware of its existence.

As it stood, the FST had some major drawbacks: its narrow base, the possibility of tax avoidance, its effect on exports, and its effect on the poor.

Narrow Base Only one-third of all products bought by Canadians were taxed under the FST. Forty percent of FST revenues, for example, came from consumer spending on just five types of products: tobacco, alcohol, automobiles, auto parts, and fuels. If the government had chosen to raise the FST rate, the tax would have put an extra burden on buyers and sellers of this narrow range of products.

Tax Avoidance Businesses could avoid paying the FST because of the method used to calculate the tax, and because of an increasing number of exemptions. The FST was calculated on the basis of business costs; however, certain types of businesses had gained exemptions. So, for example, if a company created a special subsidiary to perform the marketing function for its products, this marketing subsidiary, because of exemptions, would pay no FST. In comparison, a company that had not created a subsidiary would pay more tax while producing the same product. As a result, the total dollar amount of taxation was reduced, and unfairly so. Also, by battling the federal government in court, businesses were gradually able to carve out a wider range of possible cost exemptions.

Effect on Exports The FST was applied on both products sold to Canadians and products sold in foreign markets. By raising the prices of Canadian manufactured goods in foreign markets, the tax reduced sales of Canada's exports, thereby hurting employment in the related industries.

Effect on the Poor Like all sales taxes, the FST was regressive. Because Canadians with low incomes spend a higher proportion of their incomes on consumption items, they were more affected by the FST than were Canadians with high incomes.

How the GST Operates

The GST differs from the FST in two key ways: it applies to virtually all goods and services, and it is a "value-added" tax. As a result of its broad base—which includes almost everything but food (as of 1997)—the tax rate could be kept to 7 percent. Because it is a "value-added" tax, the GST is charged on the value added by businesses to a good or service at each stage of production.

The following example illustrates how a value-added tax works. In this example, logging, paper-making, and retailing are the stages in producing and selling a pad of paper.

Transaction 1 Wood with a value of $1 is sold by the logging company to the paper-maker. Because the logging company adds the full $1 in value, the tax that is paid on this transaction is 7 cents (7 percent of $1). This tax is collected by the logging company and passed on to the federal government.

Transaction 2 The paper-maker manufactures the pad of paper, which is sold to the retailer for $4. A tax of 28 cents (7 percent of $4) is charged on this transaction. The paper-maker collects the tax, but before handing it over to the government

Calculating the GST

Transaction	Value of Sale	Tax on Sale (0.07 × value of sale)	Input Tax Credit (tax paid at previous stage)	Net Tax on Value Added (tax on sale less input tax credit)
1. Wood sold by logging company	$1.00	$0.07	—	$0.07
2. Paper sold by paper-maker	$4.00	$0.28	$0.07	$0.21
3. Paper sold to consumer	$6.00	$0.42	$0.28	$0.14
				$0.42

When the wood is sold to the paper-maker for $1, a tax of 7 cents is charged. When the paper-maker sells the resulting pad of paper to the retailer for $4, a tax of 28 cents is charged; however, the paper-maker claims a 7-cent input tax credit for tax already paid, and therefore pays a net tax of 21 cents. When the pad is finally sold to the consumer at a price of $6, the retailer collects 42 cents in tax, but claims a 28-cent input tax credit for tax already paid; therefore, the retailer pays 14 cents. The net taxes paid at each stage add up to the full 42 cents in tax paid by the consumer.

is able to claim an "input tax credit" for the 7 cents tax paid to the logging company in transaction 1. Hence, the company pays a net tax of only 21 cents (28 cents – 7 cents) to the government. This represents 7 percent of the $3 value that the paper-maker adds to production—the $4 it gains from selling the paper minus the $1 it was charged for the necessary input.

Transaction 3 When a consumer buys the pad of paper at a retail price of $6, he or she pays a tax of 42 cents (7 percent of $6). Before transferring this amount to the government, the retailer claims an input tax credit for the 28 cents in tax paid to buy the paper. Thus, the retailer's net tax is the remaining 14 cents (42 cents – 28 cents). This is 7 percent of the $2 value added by the retailer in buying the pad of paper for $4 and selling it for $6.

Impact of the GST

The response of Canadians to the GST stems from its three main attributes: multi-stage coverage, broad base, and visibility.

Multi-Stage Coverage Because the GST is levied at all stages of production, and because legal tax avoidance is not possible, the GST is more fair than the FST. The input tax credits received by businesses make it possible for the government to exempt goods and services sold outside the country, thereby keeping down the prices of exports and helping export industries. Export businesses can claim input tax credits on any taxes they pay to suppliers.

Broad Base The GST's broad base of goods and services has both positive and negative effects. On the positive side, it allows the federal government to raise more tax revenue. A portion of these revenues is channelled into a "GST credit" to taxpayers with low incomes, thereby helping to overcome the tax's regressive aspects. Another advantage of the GST's broad base—at least for government policy-makers—is that it allows for increases in the tax rate without placing an undue burden on consumers and producers of a narrow range of products.

The disadvantages of the broad base have attracted the most attention. Not only does the GST apply to more products than did the FST, it also covers many more businesses. All companies whose taxable sales exceed $30 000 have to collect the tax. For these businesses—especially the numerous small businesses in the service sector—this task adds to the cost of doing business. Many commentators suggest that the GST has led to more "under-the-table" transactions in parts of the service sector, so that unscrupulous businesses and consumers can evade the tax.

Because its broad base makes it similar to provincial sales taxes, the GST allows for the blending of sales taxes levied by the two levels of government. In 1997, this occurred in three Atlantic Provinces (Newfoundland, Nova Scotia, and New Brunswick) with the introduction of the 15 percent harmonized sales tax (HST) which reduces tax collection costs for governments and makes the payment of taxes easier for businesses in these provinces.

Visibility Ironically, one of the most contentious aspects of the GST is incidental to its operation. Unlike the FST, the GST is visible to consumers when they pay for their purchases. Supporters of this feature say that Canadians should be aware of the taxes they pay. Others point out that the tax seems more intrusive in Canadians' daily lives. Making the GST—or any replacement—more palatable to Canadian consumers seems to mean making the tax less noticeable.

Source

This material is drawn from the discussion in Evelyn Jacks' book, *Jacks on GST* (Toronto: McGraw-Hill Ryerson, 1991).

1. An artist buys $20 of materials to produce a painting that she sells to an art gallery for $140 and which is then sold to a member of the public for a price of $250.
   a. Using the table in this article as a guide, construct a table showing the net GST payment at each stage in the production of this item, given a tax rate of 7%.
   b. Using your table, calculate what percentage of the total tax payment is paid at each stage.

2. Suggest a possible way you think the GST could be amended to make this tax more palatable to Canadian taxpayers while providing the federal government with the same amount of tax revenue.

Part Three

Economic Stability

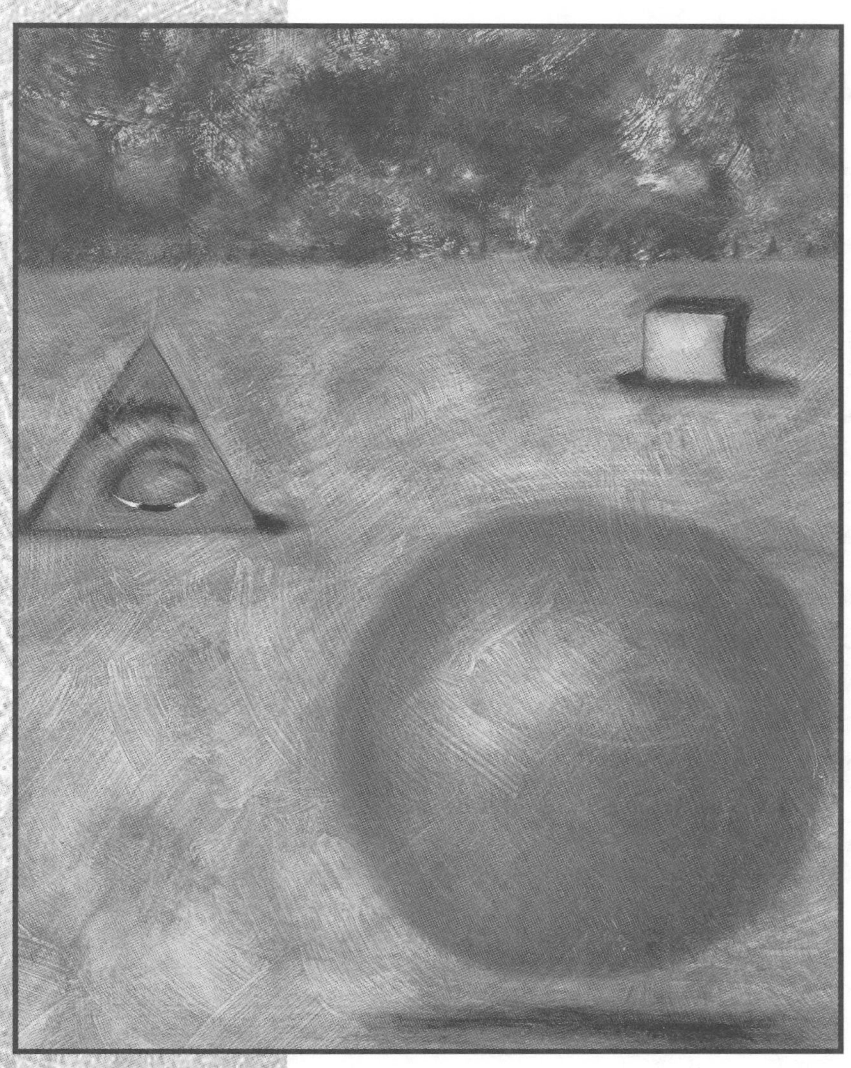

In the long run we are all dead. Economists set themselves too easy, too useless a task if in tempestuous seasons they can only tell us that when the storm is long past the ocean is flat again.

—John Maynard Keynes, English economist

Chapter Ten

Measures of Economic Activity

All progress is precarious, and the solution of one problem brings us face to face with another problem.

—Martin Luther King Jr., American civil rights and religious leader

How healthy is the Canadian economy? Are the incomes of Canadians rising or falling? How do living standards in Canada compare with those in other countries? Just as you use a thermometer to check your temperature, nations must diagnose and understand their economic health before they can respond to questions such as these ones. This chapter examines various indicators of Canadian economic health, especially the most prominent measure—Gross Domestic Product (GDP). In later chapters, we will consider GDP further and examine additional measures, what they indicate, and the economic realities of stability and instability.

CHAPTER FOCUS

This chapter focuses on the following:

- Gross Domestic Product (GDP), and the two approaches to calculating it
- the components of GDP
- real GDP and per capita GDP, and how they may be used to compare GDPs of different years or different countries
- some limitations of GDP as an economic indicator
- other economic measures developed from the national income accounts

GROSS DOMESTIC PRODUCT

National Income Accounts

national income accounts: accounts showing the levels of total income and spending in the Canadian economy

Keeping track of the Canadian economy is the task of Statistics Canada, a federal agency. This agency prepares the country's **national income accounts**, which give various measures of total income and spending in the Canadian economy. Recall that businesses track revenues and expenditures in their accounts and show any resulting profit on an income statement, thereby allowing managers and owners to pinpoint ways of improving a business's performance. National income accounts play a similar role for the economy as a whole. They allow us to evaluate the performance of the Canadian economy and to compare it with other nations' economies. National income accounts also help government policy-makers find ways to improve the economy.

Measuring Gross Domestic Product

Gross Domestic Product: the total dollar value at current prices of all final goods and services produced in Canada over a given period

A variety of measures of economic activity can be developed from the national income accounts. Of these, the most common measure in Canada is **Gross Domestic Product**, or GDP. GDP is the total dollar value of all final goods and services produced in the economy over a given period. The dollar value is calculated at current prices, and the period is typically a year. As Figure 10.1 shows, GDP uses *dollar* value because it effectively simplifies the picture; dollar value is a way to quantify and combine a wide range of goods and services.

FIGURE 10.1 Calculating Gross Domestic Product

Product	Current Price (P)	Annual Output (Q)	Total Dollar Value (P × Q)
Surgical lasers	$1000	3	$3000
Milkshakes	2	1000	2000
			GDP = $5000

It is impossible to add together the economy's annual output of surgical lasers and milkshakes without taking into account dollar values. If 3 surgical lasers and 1000 milkshakes are produced, then GDP is the sum of both outputs valued at their current prices.

Two Views of GDP

Canada's GDP is calculated using two approaches, one measuring income and the other measuring spending. Figure 10.2, which illustrates the circular flow for a simple economy where only consumer products are sold, shows both approaches. The diagram shows two economic sectors:

households and businesses. Recall that whereas the inner (clockwise) loop represents the flow of payments, the outer (counterclockwise) loop represents the flow of products and resources. The upper portion of the diagram shows the economy's resource markets, in which natural and capital resources as well as human resources (labour and entrepreneurship) are sold by households for incomes. The **income approach** to GDP involves adding together all the incomes in the economy to give GDP. The lower portion of the diagram shows the economy's product markets, in which final consumer products are sold by businesses to households. The **expenditure approach** to GDP involves adding together all consumer spending in the economy to give GDP.

income approach: a method of calculating Gross Domestic Product by adding together all incomes in the economy

expenditure approach: a method of calculating Gross Domestic Product by adding together all spending in the economy

The GDP Identity

In the simple economy shown in Figure 10.2, because all spending on final consumer products ends up as some form of household income, annual income equals annual spending. As a result, GDP found using the income approach and GDP found using the expenditure approach are the same. This relationship between the two approaches is known as the **GDP identity**:

GDP identity: Gross Domestic Product calculated as total income is identical to Gross Domestic Product calculated as total spending

GDP expressed as total income ≡ GDP expressed as total spending

The triple-lined identity sign in this formula—a stronger version of the equals sign (=)—indicates that the expressions on either side are identical.

FIGURE 10.2
Circular Flow in a Simple Economy

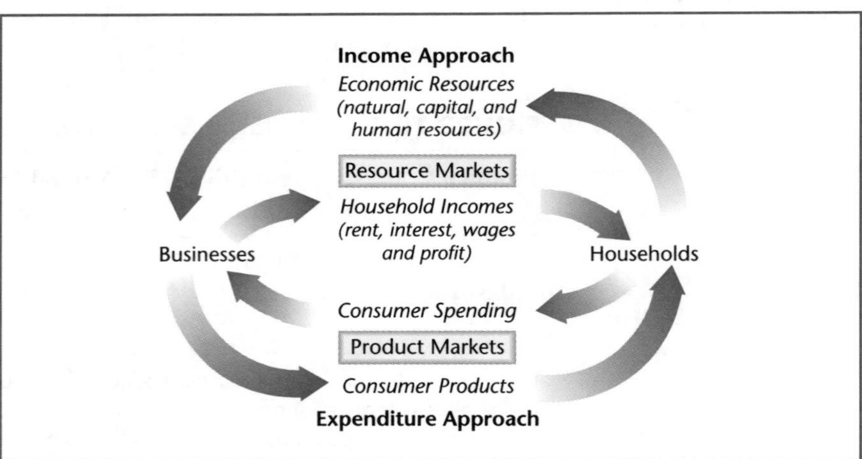

Households and businesses meet in both resource and product markets. The inner (clockwise) loop represents the flow of money. The outer (counterclockwise) loop represents the flow of products and resources. As shown in the upper portion of the diagram, in the resource markets, natural, capital, and human resources are sold by households for incomes. As shown in the lower portion of the diagram, in the product markets, final consumer products are sold by businesses to households. The income approach to GDP measures the flow of incomes in the upper portion; the expenditure approach measures the flow of spending in the lower portion.

The GDP identity applies not only to the simplified economy shown in Figure 10.2, but also to the entire Canadian economy. So, Statistics Canada uses both approaches—the income approach and the expenditure approach—to calculate GDP. As will be seen later in the chapter, the circular flows of income and spending in the Canadian economy incorporate not only the interaction of households and businesses in product and resource markets, but also flows relating to financial markets, government, and the rest of the world. This involves a wide range of goods and services. Therefore, Statistics Canada does not restrict itself to consumer products; instead, it considers incomes from and expenditures on all goods and services in Canada.

THE INCOME APPROACH

Income Components of GDP

As discussed in Chapter 8, wages, rent, profit, and interest make up Canadian incomes. These four payments form the basis of GDP calculated using the income approach. As we mentioned in Chapter 8, because of practical difficulties in distinguishing resource earnings, Statistics Canada applies its own classification system: wages and salaries, corporate profits, interest income, and proprietors' incomes (including rent).

To these four classes of income, Statistics Canada adds three other classifications: indirect taxes, depreciation, and a statistical discrepancy account. These three categories help to balance GDP that is calculated using the income approach with GDP that is calculated using the expenditure approach. Using the income approach, GDP is the sum of all seven categories.

Wages and Salaries

Wages and salaries are the largest income category, representing about 55 percent of GDP. This category includes direct payments to workers in both business and government, as well as employee benefits such as contributions to employee pension funds.

Corporate Profits

This category includes all corporate profits declared to the government, including the profits paid as corporate income tax, the profits paid out to corporate shareholders as dividends, and the profits put back into the business. The final subcategory of profits put back into the business, or **retained earnings**, represents the funds that corporations keep for new investment. Also included in the category of corporate profits are adjustments to the value of businesses' unsold products.

retained earnings: profits kept by businesses for new investment

Interest Income

Interest income includes interest paid on business loans and bonds and, to a lesser extent, income such as royalty payments. This category does not, however, include interest payments made by consumers and government, since consumer loans and government debt are viewed simply as transfers of purchasing power.

Proprietors' Incomes and Rents

Proprietors' incomes include the earnings of sole proprietorships and partnerships, including self-employed professionals and farmers. These incomes are received by owners for supplying various types of resources to their businesses. The income to landlords from renting property is also included in this category.

Indirect Taxes

Indirect taxes, such as provincial sales taxes, are charged on products rather than levied against households or businesses. Because of this, they would not be included as part of GDP using the income approach, but would be using the expenditure approach. To balance the results from the two approaches, taxes (minus any subsidies businesses receive) are added to income-based GDP.

Depreciation

Recall that durable assets—such as buildings, equipment, and tools—wear out and need to be replaced. This is considered a cost of doing business, and shows up in the expenditure approach to GDP. To balance the two approaches to calculating GDP, the income approach must also include depreciation.

Statistical Discrepancy

Because businesses' and individuals' records might be faulty or missing, GDP figures for the two approaches do differ. Therefore, the GDP figures are actually estimates, and any discrepancy between them is known as a *statistical discrepancy*. To balance the two figures, Statistics Canada divides the difference between the two approaches. As shown in Figure 10.3, the discrepancy was 0.2 billion in 1996. Half the amount (0.1 billion) is added to the lower figure, the income-based estimate of GDP, and half (0.1 billion) is deducted from the higher figure, the expenditure-based GDP estimate.

THE EXPENDITURE APPROACH

GDP found using the expenditure approach is the sum of purchases in product markets. In order to explore this in greater detail, we must first distinguish between categories of products. Later, we will examine the categories of expenditures.

Categories of Products

final products: products that will not be processed further and will not be resold

Final products are those that will not be processed further and will not be resold. How much the ultimate user pays for the product determines

FIGURE 10.3 Canada's Gross Domestic Product (1996)

Income Approach ($ billions)		Expenditure Approach ($ billion)	
Wages and salaries	434.0	Personal consumption (C)	483.0
Corporate profits	62.9	Gross investment (I)	124.4
Interest income	55.8	Government purchases (G)	165.3
Proprietors' incomes and rents	45.9	Net exports (X – M)	25.2
Indirect taxes	98.4	Statistical discrepancy	–0.1
Depreciation	100.7		
Statistical discrepancy	0.1		
Gross Domestic Product	797.8	Gross Domestic Product	797.8

With the income approach, GDP is the sum of incomes and balancing items, as shown on the left. With the expenditure approach, GDP is the sum of expenditures, as shown on the right. Both totals are reconciled with an equal amount for statistical discrepancy.

Source: Adapted from Statistics Canada, *National Income and Expenditure Accounts, Quarterly Estimates, Fourth Quarter 1996* (March 1997), cat. no. 13-001-XPB, vol. 44, no. 4, pp. 40, 41. Reproduced by authority of the Minister of Industry, 1997.

intermediate products: products that will be processed further or will be resold

the value of a final product. An example might be a pad of paper bought at the corner store. In contrast, **intermediate products** are those that will be processed further or will be resold. Advertising services bought by a soft-drink manufacturer or clothing bought by a wholesaler are examples. Something is a final product or an intermediate product based on how it is used. For example, flour that is bought by a household for home baking is a final product; however, flour that is bought by a bakery to make bread to be sold is an intermediate product.

To understand why the distinction matters, consider that some products will be sold many times in product markets—first as intermediate products, and then as final products. The products to make a pad of paper, for example, may be sold once by the logging company to the paper producer, a second time by the paper producer to the retailer, and a third time by the retailer to you. Since the cost of the wood may be $1 out of the retail price of $4, the value of the final product covers the value of the wood used to make it.

double counting: the problem of adding to GDP the same item at different stages in its production

value added: the extra worth of a product at each stage in its production; a concept used to avoid double counting in calculating GDP

If the values of all products—final and intermediate—were included in the GDP calculations, we might have the problem of **double counting**. Double counting would cause estimates of GDP to be too high and not reflect the real activity in the economy. To avoid this problem, the concept of **value added** is applied to GDP. This concept helps quantify the extra worth of the product at each stage in its production. Figure 10.4 uses the example of the pad of paper to show the results of double counting and how the concept of value added deals with it. Statistics Canada subtracts the value of all purchases of intermediate goods and services by businesses from the value for which intermediate and final products are sold.

FIGURE 10.4 Value Added in Making Paper

Production Stage	Total Value Paid/Received	Value Added	Business That Adds Value
1. Wood is cut and transported to paper mill	$1.00	$1.00	logging company
2. Paper is processed and sold to retailer	2.75	1.75 (2.75 – 1.00)	paper company
3. Paper is sold by retailer to consumer	4.00	1.25 (4.00 – 2.75)	retailer
	$7.75	$4.00	

A pad of paper is produced from wood that is (1) cut and transported, and (2) processed into paper, which is sold to a retailer. Then (3) the paper is sold by the retailer to the consumer. The value added by each business at each production stage is the value of the business's output, less its cost of intermediate products. The sum of the values added at all stages of production represents the price of the pad of paper when it is finally sold.

Categories of Purchases

Expenditure-based GDP is calculated on the basis of almost all purchases in the Canadian economy. Note, once again, that figures for GDP calculated using this approach are adjusted for any statistical discrepancy.

Excluded Purchases

Before we examine the categories of purchases included in GDP, let's examine those that are excluded because they are not related to current production. There are two types: financial exchanges and second-hand purchases.

Financial Exchanges A gift of money—between family members, for example—is not a transaction included in GDP for the simple reason that the transaction just shifts purchasing power from one party to another. Similarly, bank deposits and purchases of stocks are not included; however, payments for any financial service—bank service charges or a commission to a stockbroker—are included.

Second-Hand Purchases Purchases of second-hand, or used, goods are also excluded from GDP because these products have already been counted at their first sale to a consumer. In other words, including second-hand purchases in GDP would double count, or overestimate, the value of products sold.

Included Purchases

Purchases included in GDP calculations fall into four categories: personal consumption (C), gross investment (I), government purchases (G), and net exports (X – M). Each of these categories contributes to the circular flow of payments in the Canadian economy. The following **expenditure equation** shows that GDP is simply the sum of these four types of spending.

expenditure equation: the equation that states that GDP is the sum of personal consumption (C), gross investment (I), government purchases (G), and net exports (X – M)

$$GDP = C + I + G + (X - M)$$

Personal Consumption **Personal consumption** (C) is household spending on goods and services. These purchases make up the largest component, about 60 percent, of GDP. Of the goods and services consumed, **nondurable goods**, such as food, are consumed just once. **Durable goods**—such as automobiles—are consumed repeatedly over time.

personal consumption: household spending on goods and services

nondurable goods: goods that are consumed just once

durable goods: goods that are consumed repeatedly over time

Gross Investment The second component of expenditure in GDP is **gross investment** (I). This category includes purchases of assets that are intended to produce revenue. Gross investment varies—usually from between 15 and 25 percent of GDP—from year to year. The most important spending in this category is on equipment and machines used by businesses—for example, a carpenter's purchase of a lathe or a newspaper publisher's purchase of a printing press. Expenditures by government agencies on equipment and machines also fall into this category.

gross investment: purchases of assets that are intended to produce revenue

inventories: stocks of unsold goods and materials

Gross investment also includes changes in the dollar value of unsold goods and materials, known as **inventories**. So that businesses can meet unexpected demand for particular products without stopping production to wait for deliveries of inputs, they often keep inventories of inputs on hand. Because these inventories are income-producing assets, an increase in an economy's inventories over a given year is seen as positive investment spending. In contrast, a decrease in inventories is seen as negative investment spending.

The construction of all buildings, including houses and apartments, is considered another part of gross investment. Owner-occupied housing is added here, rather than as part of personal consumption, because owner-occupied dwellings *could* be rented out by the owner to make an income. From an economic perspective, homeowners make an investment when they purchase their properties, and then rent to themselves.

capital stock: the total value of productive assets that provide a flow of revenue

net investment: gross investment minus depreciation

Gross investment is related to the economy's **capital stock**, which is the total value of productive assets that provide a flow of revenue. Recall that capital assets, such as machinery and equipment, depreciate in value over time. Subtracting annual depreciation of an entire economy's capital assets from new gross investment gives **net investment**. Net investment therefore represents the yearly change in the economy's stock of capital.

Consider the example in Figure 10.5. An economy has $200 billion of capital stock at the beginning of a year and depreciation of $40 billion during the year. If gross investment over the same period is $100 billion, then net investment equals $60 billion ($100 billion – $40 billion). This $60 billion represents the amount by which the capital stock expands during the year. So, by year's end, the value of the economy's capital stock is $260 billion ($200 billion + $60 billion).

FIGURE 10.5
Net Investment and Capital Stock

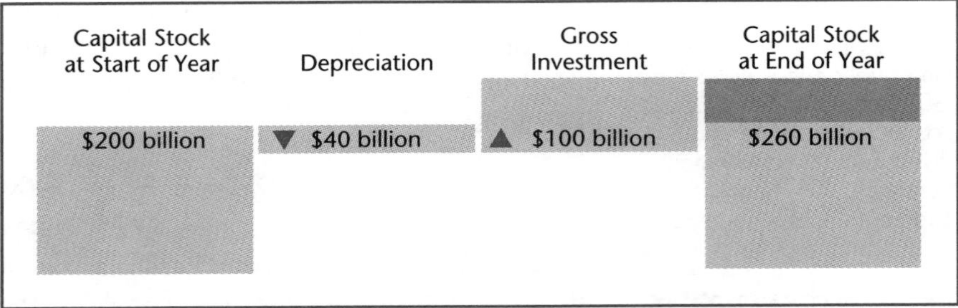

In a growing economy, the decline in the economy's capital stock during a year due to depreciation ($40 billion) is outweighed by gross investment ($100 billion) over the same period. The year-end capital stock ($260 billion) is greater than the capital stock at the start of the year ($200 billion) by the amount that gross investment exceeds depreciation ($100 billion – $40 billion). This $60 billion increase, shown by the dark rectangle, represents the economy's net investment during the year.

Thinking About Economics

Does gross investment include spending on education and training?

As discussed in Chapter 8, education can be considered an investment in human capital, with knowledge and skills representing a vital part of an economy's productive assets. Some economists argue that Statistics Canada should include at least some spending on education as part of gross investment and add human capital to its estimate of Canada's total capital stock. Statistics Canada does not do this because of the difficulty in separating out the investment component of education. Instead, education appears either as part of personal consumption or government purchases.

personal saving: funds saved by households

While they cannot be included in GDP, it is interesting to highlight the sources of funds for investment. Recall from Chapter 8 that the funds used for capital investment come not only from businesses' retained earnings but also from households' **personal saving** (S). By depositing funds in banks and by investing in stocks and bonds, households provide a flow of personal savings to businesses. Figure 10.6 shows this flow of funds for investment, as well as the flows of incomes and spending between businesses and households.

government purchases: current government spending on goods and services

Government Purchases **Government purchases** (G) include current spending by all levels of government on goods and services, and typically make up about 20 percent of GDP. The federal government buying a battleship for the armed forces and a municipality hiring a paving company to do road repairs are two examples of government spending.

Some types of government spending are not included in this category. Government transfer payments to households, such as those detailed in Chapter 9, are excluded from government purchases since they are simply a redistribution of purchasing power. For the same reason, government subsidies to businesses are also excluded. Both transfer payments and government subsidies are viewed instead as negative taxes, meaning they

FIGURE 10.6
Financial Markets and the Circular Flow

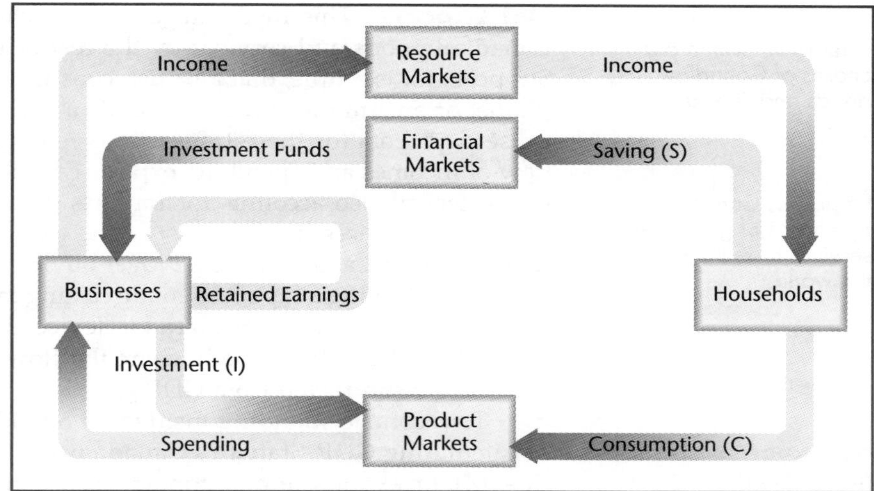

Personal saving is transformed into investment funds for businesses by financial markets. Businesses then use these funds, plus their retained earnings, to make investment. Investment and personal consumption form part of total spending.

are tax payments in reverse. Expenditures by government-owned agencies on income-producing assets—for instance, hydro-electric dams built by Ontario Hydro, or post offices built by Canada Post—are also excluded from government purchases, because these amounts are considered part of gross investment.

As outlined in Chapter 9, government spending is partly financed through taxes from both households and businesses. Governments also finance their spending through borrowing, which takes place in financial markets. Figure 10.7 shows the role of government in the economy's circular flow of incomes and spending.

FIGURE 10.7
Government and the Circular Flow

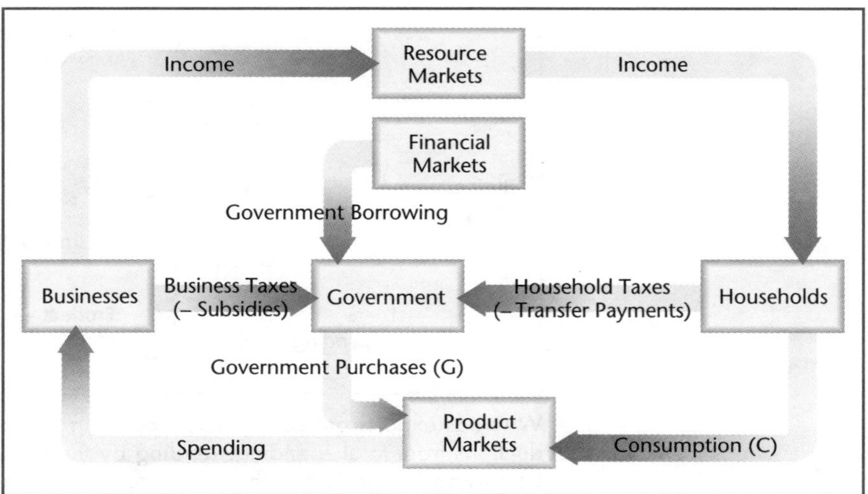

Government purchases of goods and services are part of total spending. These purchases are financed through (1) taxes on households and businesses, after deducting transfer payments and business subsidies, and (2) government borrowing in financial markets.

exports: foreign purchases of Canadian goods and services

imports: Canadian purchases of goods and services from the rest of the world

net exports: exports minus imports

Net Exports This final category of purchase includes purchases of Canadian goods and services by the rest of the world, or **exports** (X). Suppose, for example, that a British consumer buys a Canadian cellular phone, or an American tourist spends a night in a Canadian hotel. Because payments for these transactions remain in the Canadian circular flow of incomes and spending, exports contribute to GDP. This expenditure category also accounts for **imports** (M), or Canadian purchases of goods and services from the rest of the world. Such spending includes, for example, a Canadian cheese-lover buying French cheese, a Canadian steelmaker buying a Japanese-made casting machine, or a Canadian police force buying an American radar device. Because payments for these transactions leave the Canadian circular flow of incomes and spending, imports are subtracted from GDP.

To reconcile spending inside and outside the Canadian economy in calculating GDP, Statistics Canada uses the category of **net exports** (X – M), or exports minus imports. When represented as net exports, these purchases represent a small fraction of GDP; however, the values of exports and imports viewed separately each account for over 35 percent of GDP.

Figure 10.8 shows the roles of exports and imports in the circular flow of the Canadian economy. Note that the rest of the world also plays a part in the Canadian economy by lending to and borrowing from financial markets. Loans from the rest of the world to the Canadian economy are flows into the economy while Canadian loans to the rest of the world are flows out of the economy.

FIGURE 10.8
The Rest of the World and the Circular Flow

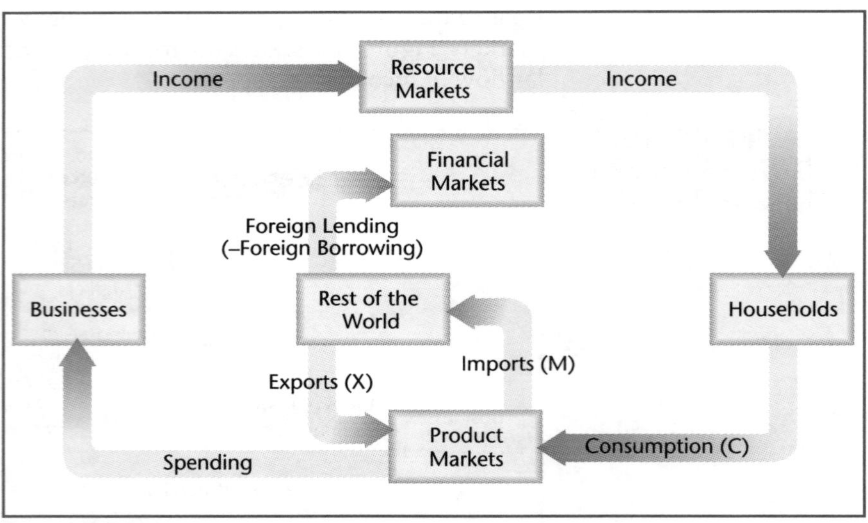

Whereas exports are part of total spending in product markets, imports are deductions from total spending. Lending by the rest of the world, after subtracting borrowing by the rest of the world, represents an inflow to Canadian financial markets.

BRIEF REVIEW

1. Statistics Canada prepares national income accounts to measure the economic health of Canada.
2. The most prominent measure of economic activity is Gross Domestic Product (GDP), which is the total dollar value of all final goods and services produced in the economy over a given period.
3. GDP can be calculated by adding all incomes in resource markets or all expenditures in product markets. After taking account of several balancing items, including a statistical discrepancy, the two approaches give the same figure.
4. Using the income approach, GDP is the sum of four main income items—wages and salaries, corporate profits, interest income, and proprietors' incomes (including rent)—plus indirect taxes and depreciation.
5. The expenditure approach depends on the concept of added value to avoid double counting of purchases.
6. Using the expenditure approach, GDP is the sum of personal consumption, gross investment, government purchases, and net exports, but neither financial exchanges nor second-hand purchases.

GDP AND LIVING STANDARDS

per capita GDP: GDP per person, calculated as GDP divided by population

What does GDP say about life in Canada? How do living standards in Canada today compare with past living standards? And how does Canadian economic performance compare with that of other countries? To answer these questions, **per capita GDP**, or GDP per person, is frequently used as a measure.

A country's GDP divided by its population is its per capita GDP. So, for example, in 1995, Canada's GDP was $776 299 million and its population was 29.615 million. Hence, per capita GDP was $26 213 per person:

$$\text{Per capita GDP} = \frac{\text{GDP}}{\text{population}}$$

$$\$26\,213 = \frac{\$776\,299\,000\,000}{29\,615\,000}$$

Adjustments to Per Capita GDP

Depending on how per capita GDP is to be used, either of two adjustments can be made to it: inflation adjustments or exchange-rate adjustments.

Inflation Adjustments

real GDP: GDP expressed in constant dollars from a given year

Because prices change over the years, per capita GDP must be adjusted when comparing economic well-being in the same country in different years. This is done by using **real GDP**, which is GDP expressed in constant dollars from a given year (currently, 1986 is the base year). When a

per capita real GDP: GDP per person, expressed in constant dollars from a given year

country's real GDP is divided by its population, the result is **per capita real GDP**, or real GDP per person. This adjustment allows comparisons to be made between per capita GDP despite changes in price. For example, Canada's 1995 real GDP, expressed in 1986 dollars, was $608 835 million. Given Canada's 1995 population of 29.615 million, per capita real GDP in 1995 was $20 558. In contrast, the per capita real GDP for 1986 was $19 297 ($505 666 million ÷ 26.2038 million).

$$\text{Per capita real GDP} = \frac{\text{real GDP}}{\text{population}}$$

$$\$20\,558 = \frac{\$608\,835\,000\,000}{29\,615\,000}$$

Exchange-Rate Adjustments

To compare various countries' per capita GDP for a given year, we must adjust for the different currencies. This is done by expressing all countries' GDPs in one currency, the standard being the American dollar. For example, per capita GDP for 1995 in the United States was $27 555 in U.S. dollars, while Canada's per capita GDP for 1995 in U.S. dollars was $19 106. When expressed in a common currency, Canada's GDP is lower than that of the United States.

Limitations of GDP

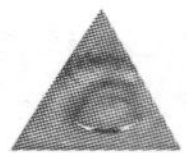

As with any economic indicator, it is important to distinguish what specifically is being *measured* by GDP and what GDP *indicates*. Recall that GDP is a *measure* of the total dollar value of all final goods and services produced in an economy over a given period. Also, GDP indicates economic activity and, to some extent, living standards. However, like all indicators, it has quantitative and qualitative limitations.

Excluded Activities

Because GDP represents the market value of goods and services produced in an economy, it does not include some types of productive activities. Excluding these activities means that GDP can understate economic activity and living standards.

nonmarket activities: productive activities that take place outside the marketplace

underground economy: all the market transactions that go unreported

Nonmarket activities—such as housework, unpaid child care, and the work of "do-it-yourselfers"—take place outside the marketplace, so they are excluded from GDP. However, these productive activities have a vital impact on the living standards of Canadians.

The **underground economy** includes all the market transactions that are unreported and, therefore, also left out of GDP. One example of a transaction in the underground economy is smuggling, which is an illegal activity. In contrast, other "under-the-table" transactions may be for legal purchases—for example, gardening services that are paid for by cash or barter so that taxes on these transactions can be avoided.

Thinking About Economics

How large is Canada's underground economy?

Estimates of the size of Canada's underground economy vary widely. Some economists have tried to measure the underground economy by studying how much cash is held by the public, since underground transactions are commonly paid for with cash to escape detection. Using this method, it has been estimated that Canada's underground economy is equal to anywhere from 10 to 25 percent of GDP, meaning that it has an annual value of $80 billion or more. Statistics Canada's own studies suggest that Canada's underground economy is much smaller—between 1 and 5 percent of GDP. Because of the difficulty in gathering data, these are only "guesstimates."

Product Quality

Today's GDP includes purchases of products not available a few decades ago—personal computers, fax machines, and VCRs, to name only a few. As well, many other products, such as cars and photocopiers, have increased substantially in quality with little or no rise in price. GDP, which can only add up selling prices, cannot fully capture these quality improvements.

Composition of Output

Another limitation related to the dollar-value basis of GDP is that it tells us nothing about what is produced and purchased. Suppose one country dedicates most of its GDP to military uses, but another country dedicates the same GDP to health care and education for its citizens. While the GDPs may be the same, the countries' living standards would differ considerably.

Income Distribution

As outlined in Chapter 9, incomes may be distributed in a range of ways, with profound effects on the living standards of individuals. GDP does not reflect how output is distributed among a country's citizens. So, for example, citizens in two countries with the same per capita GDP may have very different living standards if one country's income is equally distributed, while most of the other country's income is in the hands of a few.

Leisure

Although we might be able to work every waking hour, most of us consider leisure a requirement for a satisfactory standard of living. However, leisure is not bought and sold in the market, so it can't be accounted for by GDP. Thus, although the average Canadian work week has gradually become shorter—to almost half of what it was a century ago—GDP has no way of representing this change. Because of this, GDP understates economic well-being.

The Environment

Since GDP quantifies economic activity in terms of its dollar value, it does not adequately represent another factor: the environment. GDP does not differentiate between economic activities that are harmful to the environment and those that are not, and it may not effectively represent spillover costs and benefits. So, for example, while the clean-up following an oil spill would be added to GDP, the creation of a new nature preserve would likely not be added.

OTHER ECONOMIC MEASURES

Statistics Canada uses the national income accounts to calculate other measures, which are employed in various ways to indicate economic activity.

Gross National Product

Gross National Product: the total income acquired by Canadians both within Canada and elsewhere

Gross National Product (GNP) is the total income acquired by Canadians both within Canada and elsewhere. Note that, while GDP focuses on incomes made in *Canada*, GNP focuses on the earnings of *Canadians*.

To calculate GNP, two adjustments to GDP must be made. Income earned from Canadian financial investments by the rest of the world—interest payments on a Canadian government bond held in Japan, for example—is deducted from GDP. Although included in GDP, such earnings are not part of the earnings of Canadians. Also, income earned from financial investments by Canadians in the rest of the world—a stock dividend from an American company paid to a Canadian shareholder, for example—is added to GDP. While not included in GDP, this income is part of Canadians' earnings.

These two adjustments can be made in an investment income account. Because, traditionally, financial investment by the rest of the world in Canada has been higher than financial investment by Canadians in the rest of the world, the account gives *net* investment income to the rest of the world, and is subtracted from GDP to give GNP. As Figure 10.9 shows, Canadian GNP is less than Canadian GDP.

FIGURE 10.9 Deriving Gross National Product (1996)

	($ billions)
Gross Domestic Product (GDP)	797.8
Deduct: Net investment income to the rest of the world	(–) 26.0
Gross National Product (GNP)	771.8

GNP is less than GDP because foreign financial investments in Canada exceed Canadian financial investment in the rest of the world.

Source: Statistics Canada, *Canadian Economic Observer* (March 1997), cat. no. 11-010-XPB p. 4. Reproduced by authority of the Minister of Industry, 1997.

Net Domestic Income

net domestic income: income earned by households supplying resources in Canada

Another adjustment to GDP gives **net domestic income** (NDI), or what is earned by households supplying resources in Canada. As shown in Figure 10.10, NDI is GDP minus those amounts that are not earnings from current production—namely, indirect taxes, depreciation allowances, and the statistical discrepancy.

Personal Income

personal income: the income actually received by households

Personal income (PI) is the income actually *received* by households. To calculate it, adjustments are made to net domestic income, as shown in Figure 10.10.

Transfer Payments

One adjustment to personal income is the addition of government transfer payments to net domestic income. Even though transfer payments are unrelated to earned income, they are received by households. Thus, they are excluded from net domestic income but are part of households' personal income.

Other Payments to Persons

Other payments to persons are primarily from governments to households, the most important being interest payments paid by governments on the debt they owe. Like transfer payments, these are not part of resource earnings but are nonetheless received by households. Hence, they must be included in personal income.

Earnings Not Paid Out to Persons

Earnings not paid out to persons include taxes on corporate profits and retained earnings. These items must be subtracted from net domestic income to find personal income, since they are earned, but not received, by households.

Net Investment Income to the Rest of the World

Just as net income from Canadian financial investments going to the rest of the world must be subtracted from GDP to give GNP, this net investment income must be subtracted to give personal income. These income payments are part of both GDP and net domestic income, but are not received by Canadian households.

Disposable Income

disposable income: household income minus personal taxes and other personal transfers to government

Household income after personal taxes and other personal transfers to government have been subtracted from personal income is called **disposable income**, or DI, as shown in Figure 10.10. Households use one part of their disposable income for personal consumption and the remainder for personal saving.

Figure 10.10 Deriving Other Income Measures (1996)

		($ billions)
Gross Domestic Product (GDP)		797.8
Deduct:	Indirect taxes	(–) 98.4
	Depreciation	(–) 100.7
	Statistical discrepancy	(–) 0.1
Net Domestic Income (NDI)		598.6
Add:	Government transfer payments	113.3
	Other payments to persons	52.6
Deduct:	Earnings not paid out to persons	(–) 58.7
	Net investment income to the rest of the world	(–) 26.0
Personal Income (PI)		679.6
Deduct:	Personal taxes and other personal transfers to government	(–) 166.3
Disposable Income (DI)		513.3*

* numbers may not sum due to rounding

Net domestic income is less than GDP because some payments included in GDP do not represent resource earnings. Personal income is greater than net domestic income because amounts received by households exceed amounts earned. Finally, disposable income is less than personal income because of the effect of personal taxes.

Source: Adapted from Statistics Canada, *National Income and Expenditure Accounts, Quarterly Estimates, Fourth Quarter 1996* (March 1997), cat. no. 13-001-XPB, vol. 44, no. 4, pp. 29, 41, 49, 51, 53.

BRIEF REVIEW

1. To make comparisons among years and countries, GDP is expressed per capita, or per person. To compare GDP for different years, it is adjusted for inflation to derive real GDP, and then expressed per capita. To compare GDP among countries, a common currency must be used, usually American dollars.
2. GDP has its limitations as an indicator of living standards: it excludes nonmarket activities and the underground economy; it does not reflect changes in product quality or what specific products a country is producing; it cannot account for income distribution or leisure; and, it cannot adequately account for environmental spillover costs and benefits.
3. Other measures of economic activity and income include Gross National Product, net domestic income, personal income, disposable income, and discretionary income.

KEY CONCEPTS

national income accounts
Gross Domestic Product
income approach
expenditure approach
GDP identity
retained earnings
final products
intermediate products
double counting
value added
expenditure equation
personal consumption
nondurable goods
durable goods
gross investment
inventories
capital stock
net investment
personal saving
government purchases
exports
imports
net exports
per capita GDP
real GDP
per capita real GDP
nonmarket activities
underground economy
Gross National Product
personal income
disposable income

ANALYSIS AND APPLICATION

Metrica's National Accounts (1998)

	($ billions)
Corporate profits	55
Exports	68
Wages and salaries	546
Gross investment	157
Government purchases	184
Indirect taxes	75
Personal consumption	490
Interest income	43
Imports	27
Depreciation	79
Proprietors' incomes and rents	56
Statistical discrepancy	?

1. The data in the accompanying table apply to a hypothetical country, Metrica, during 1998.
   a. Use the data to find income-based and expenditure-based estimates of Metrica's GDP.
   b. Outline how the statistical discrepancy between the two estimates in part a. can be used to find a single GDP value.
   c. By how much is Metrica's capital stock expanding or contracting in 1998? Explain.

Cantina's National Accounts (1998)

	($ billions)
Imports	47
Government transfer payments	43
Net investment	27
Government purchases	54
Indirect taxes	37
Net investment income to the rest of the world	16
Exports	32
Personal consumption	215
Other payments to persons	21
Earnings not paid out to persons	45
Depreciation	14
Personal taxes and other personal transfers to government	61
Statistical discrepancy	0

2. The data in the accompanying table applies to a hypothetical country, Cantina, during 1998. Calculate the country's:
   a. GDP
   b. GNP
   c. NDI
   d. PI
   e. DI

3. The production of a kilogram of smoked salmon requires a fisherman to catch salmon worth $1.40, which is prepared by a food processor and sold to a retailer for $2.20, who then sells it to a consumer for $2.75. With the aid of a table similar to Figure 10.4, explain how this product appears in GDP using the concept of value added.

4. For each of following cases, give a possible example. Explain each of your answers.
   a. a product that is always a final product
   b. a product that is always an intermediate product
   c. a product that, depending on how it is used, is sometimes a final product and sometimes an intermediate product

5. For each of the following transactions, identify whether or not it would be included in GDP:
   a. an accountant receives payment for preparing a client's personal income tax return
   b. an owner of a Canada Savings Bond is paid interest on this bond
   c. a business buys a new piece of production equipment
   d. a student is paid for shovelling a neighbour's sidewalk
   e. an unemployed carpenter receives an employment insurance payment

f. a town council hires a contractor to do paving work on the town's roads
g. a newspaper publisher buys newsprint to add to its inventories of supplies
h. an electronic hobbyist sells a used computer to a friend
i. a Canadian consumer purchases a bottle of French wine
j. a fisherman receives a government subsidy to help relocate to a larger community
k. a Canadian business sells medical equipment to a Japanese hospital
l. a wealth-holder sells 1000 shares issued by a Canadian corporation
m. a cafe-owner buys a freshly baked cake to be served to her customers
n. a home-owner repairs his own leaking roof

6. Each of the following cases applies to a country whose per capita real GDP has been steadily rising at 1 percent a year. In each case, explain whether GDP overstates or understates the change in living standards.
   a. the average amount of leisure time for workers has decreased
   b. the relative importance of the nonmarket sector has risen
   c. incomes have become less equitably distributed
   d. a larger proportion of the economy's resources are devoted to recycling and the introduction of environmentally sustainable production techniques

7. (Advanced Question)
   On a single diagram, show how financial markets, government, the rest of the world can be integrated in the circular flow.

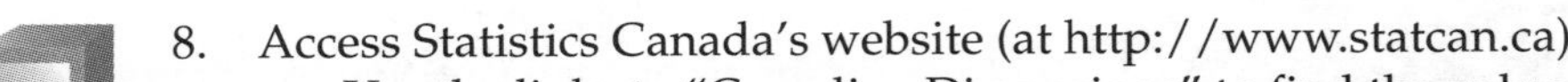

8. Access Statistics Canada's website (at http://www.statcan.ca).
   a. Use the links to "Canadian Dimensions" to find the value in the most recent year available for expenditure-based GDP at market prices.
   b. Also find the values for the most recent year available for the components of expenditure-based GDP at market prices: (i) personal consumption, (ii) gross investment, (iii) government purchases, (iv) net exports, and (v) the statistical discrepancy.

Advancing Economic Thought

THINKING GLOBALLY

Hazel Henderson and GNP

After moving to New York City with her family, Hazel Henderson saw firsthand one outcome of economic growth: pollution. Her daughter's sooty face and persistent morning cough from the pollution started Henderson's career as an environmentalist and a critic of traditional economics.

In 1964, Henderson founded one of the first grassroots environmental organizations in the U.S.—Citizens for Clean Air. Back then, pollution stood for progress. Henderson, 57, hasn't stopped fighting for a saner, greener, healthier world. She, however, treads an unbeaten path as an economic guerrilla.

The unsoapable soot on her daughter's face, she realized, stemmed from the industrial economic system—a system that has a voracious appetite for resources, then pretends it has nothing to do with environmental and health consequences.

Hazel Henderson
Source: Ian Lindsay/*The Vancouver Sun*

Economics, she realized, is politics in disguise and the environmental movement doesn't touch on the bigger problem of a bulimic economic system.

Railing at the line that she had become a "sincere lady who just doesn't understand that cleaning up the air was uneconomic," she read everything she could on economics and went into combat with condescending industrial potentates.

By 1967, the *Harvard Business Review* published her article called "Should Business Tackle Society's Problems?"

In 1978, she published *Creating Alternative Futures: The End of Economics*. In 1981, she published *The Politics of the Solar Age: Alternatives to Economics*, both as big as booster seats.

"I knew there must be something terribly wrong with economics if keeping it healthy meant people had to get sick," she said during a visit to Vancouver.

Consider this. The Exxon Valdez oil spill creates millions of dollars' worth of economic activity around the blighted Alaskan coast. Cleanup, public relations and an inquiry are *good* for the gross national product. Environmental, health, and social problems *add* to GNP rather than subtract from it.

For a real look at progress and success, the debit side has to be factored in, not ignored, she says. But the present economic system plays the denial game very well. It's a system that cannibalizes itself, a parasite that kills its host.

Henderson wants to include environmental and social costs of development in the economic accounting system. Right now, she says, the end-all, be-all, of economic success is growing GNP. It will, in the end, mean a lower standard of living and lower profit margins—but then whoever said businesses had to keep growing and growing, making bigger and bigger profits? Whoever said the privileged few have to gourmandize at the expense of the lower classes and of future generations?

Current economics rewards resource depletion rather than taxing it and values cheap land, cheap labour, low taxes and weak environmental laws, says Henderson. It rewards over-developed nations and impoverishes developing ones. It panders to greed and profits and expansion and has the pretence of science, while ignoring the simple law of thermodynamics.

Henderson says that a new economics, for example, would make the polluter, not the taxpayer, pay for pollution cleanup. Polluting products would include the cost of disposal and recycling. Prices would, in effect, reflect total costs.

"We need to encourage more green technologies and tax the hell out of waste and destruction," says Henderson.

She would redeploy and retrain workers for environmentally benign industries. She would provide guaranteed incomes for people stranded in environmental sunset industries, a cheaper alternative to corporate bailouts and continued environmental and social damage.

She would decentralize, localize and seek global cooperation in development.

"Think globally, act locally," is her favourite motto.

Henderson, a consultant to organizations in more than 30 countries, makes about 200 speeches a year to grassroots organizations, enlightened corporations, colleges, agencies, and planning groups, mostly outside the U.S. She talks to Soviet officials and meets with Chinese think-tank members regularly on how to make the shift to green technologies.

She operates on the Robin Hood principle—charge the rich and give to the poor. She fetches $3,000 for a corporate appearance but pays her own way to speak in China.

During the pit stops at home, she transports herself on an "unstealable" 20-year-old rusty five-speed Schwinn bicycle, grows flowers, writes poetry and cosies up in her 2,000-book library. Two phones and a fax machine connect her to the outside world.

She says that economics, like ecology, comes from the Greek word *oikos*, meaning house and home. It's supposed to be about providing goods and services efficiently. But it's now about artificial needs and wants, created through corporate advertising.

Henderson's metaphor for economics is a cake. The top layer is the official market economy of money transactions. But two other layers—social/familial/community activities and Mother Nature—are missing from today's "science" of looking after house and home.

"Karl Marx and Adam Smith both discount nature in exactly the same way and discount unpaid work," she says.

Economists, Henderson feels, are hired guns, like lawyers. The only difference is, economists are passed off as scientists. "An absolutely wonderful way of psyching out the ordinary citizen," she says. "Part of my message has always been: never let an economist get away with saying they are experts on efficiency. Ask 'For whom?' and 'In what time frame?' Generally you'll find it's efficiency for the client in the short term."

"Economists confuse money with real wealth and the GNP scorecard distorts the kind of debate needed about what's valuable," Henderson says. "If we paid less attention to money and more attention to real wealth—like creative people, healthy ecosystems, healthy people, education, nutrition—it will put us on track to a sustainable future," she says.

"Power flows from the economic system; power is defined by money, the control of capital, and the ability to control political processes. We allow money changers to take control in this hypnosis about money," she says. "It's a form of control that's so subtle—people are buying into disempowerment."

"The most glaring problem is, it doesn't show the poverty gap and whether it's widening or narrowing or how much energy is being used to produce a unit of GNP. We can watch money, income, GNP, and stock markets go up while everything else may be going to pot."

She wants nations to set up data banks codifying their value systems—"a cultural DNA code"—to incorporate into economics.

Solar cars, renewable energy systems, mass transit, organic agriculture, preventive health care, recyclable products, education, reforestation, information industries, desert greening, pollution control, day care, and elder care—this is the stuff of developing sustainably.

In Florida, says Henderson, conservationists offered an alternative to a coal-fired power plant meant to boost air conditioning energy. Planting shade trees would have reduced the ambient air by eight degrees Fahrenheit, just what the plant was intended to do. But the plant went ahead anyway, she says.

Despite being ignored for decades, Henderson sees the world catching up. "Mass media have discovered the environment and 20-year-old issues. For many of us in the field, things are unfolding predictably.

"Things are happening in many, many chinks and niches. Every institution is changing just a little bit and people in many institutions are rethinking and orchestrating millions of different decisions. It will eventually reach critical mass," she says. "It's time to give Karl Marx and Adam Smith a decent burial."

Source

Abridged from Mia Stainsby, "Back When Clean Air Was a Dirty Term," *The Vancouver Sun*, 3 November 1990, pp. D3, D4.

1. **List the various shortcomings that Henderson highlights in arguing that GNP (or GDP) is a deficient indicator of economic progress.**

2. **Traditional economists would oppose Henderson by suggesting that expenditures on an environmental disaster such as the Exxon Valdez should be included in GNP and GDP statistics. Summarize what you think their argument would be.**

SIDELINE

"CANADIANS LIVE BEST"

Top 10 Countries to Live in

1. Canada
2. United States
3. Japan
4. Netherlands
5. Norway
6. Finland
7. France
8. Iceland
9. Sweden
10. Spain

Source: *The Human Development Report,* published for UNDP by Oxford University Press.

Indicators of well-being are numerous. One that draws on a range of statistics is the human development index used by the United Nations. Using this index, Canada has been judged as one of the most desirable countries in which to live, as discussed in the article below.

For the fourth time this decade, Canada has been ranked as the best place in the world to live. The United Nations 1996 Human Development Index —which measures income, education and life expectancy—places Canada first among 174 countries.

We may not be the richest country in the world. The average American has an annual income $5072 higher than that of the average Canadian. We don't have the highest life expectancy. The average Japanese outlives the average Canadian by two years. And our level of adult literacy is no higher than those of 17 Western countries.

But when the three criteria are combined, Canada comes out on top with an overall score of 95.1 percent. The United States is second with 94 percent and Japan and the Netherlands are tied for third with 93.8 percent.

Despite giving Canada an excellent report card, the U.N. does point out some areas that need work:

- Canada has one of the highest youth unemployment rates in the developed world.
- We have one of the largest gaps between rich and poor among industrial nations.
- We consume more energy per person than any nation, except the United States. The average Canadian uses 1.5 times as much energy as the average Norwegian and twice as much as the average Japanese.
- We have the industrial world's third-highest rate of drug crime, behind Australia and the United States.

And we have one of the lowest proportions of scientists and researchers in our population of any industrial nation.

For most of the world, the U.N.'s annual report on the well-being of the global population is a catalogue of misery.

Eighty-nine countries are worse off economically than they were a decade ago, leading James Gustave Speth, administrator of the United Nations Development Program, to warn that polarization between the world's rich and poor is reaching alarming proportions.

"If present trends continue, economic disparities between industrial and development nations will move from inequitable to inhuman," he said.

The U.N. highlighted a second troubling development. The link between economic growth and jobs seems to have been broken. Even when a nation's output is expanding, some of its people are left struggling to survive with no work and little chance of employment.

Source

Carol Goar, "Canada Again Best Place in the World," *TheToronto Star*, 16 July 1996, pp. A1, A4.

1. The Human Development Index has three main components: per capita income, average life expectancy, and the rate of adult literacy. Outline a possible problem with each of these three statistics as a guide to living standards.

2. The United Nations calculates additional statistics to help compare living standards in various countries. Suggest a statistic you think could be used for this purpose and explain the reasoning behind your choice.

Chapter Eleven
Inflation and Unemployment

Unemployment and inflation still preoccupy and perplex economists...and everyone else.
—James Tobin, American Economist

Ask working Canadians what economic prospect concerns them the most, and the answer will likely be unemployment. Ask a pensioner the same question and, chances are, the answer will be inflation. Our anxiety over these two economic evils is not misplaced; in fact, price stability and full employment are among Canada's most important economic goals. This chapter explores the effects of a trend of rising prices, how the trend is measured, and how it often hurts most those who can afford it least. In this chapter, we'll also examine unemployment: how it is measured, its causes, and its costs, not only for individuals but for the entire economy.

CHAPTER FOCUS

This chapter focuses on the following:

- inflation, its two measures—the consumer price index and the GDP deflator—and their limitations
- nominal and real incomes, both for individuals and the entire economy
- the effects of inflation
- how the labour force and unemployment are defined
- limitations of the official unemployment rate
- frictional, structural, cyclical, and seasonal unemployment
- full employment, the reasons for recent changes in unemployment, and the costs of unemployment

INFLATION

Inflation, as introduced in Chapter 1, is a general increase in the prices of goods and services in an entire economy over time. Suppose, for example, that Canada has an annual inflation rate of 3 percent this year. Inflation does not mean that all prices are rising. Some prices are rising, others are remaining constant, while still others may be falling; however, the *overall* rise in prices is 3 percent. In exceptional cases—most notably during the 1930s—prices may remain constant, in which case the inflation rate is zero, or there may be a general decrease in prices. A general decrease in the level of prices is called **deflation**. To explain why Canadian governments stress the goal of price stability, let's first examine inflation in detail, how it is measured, and its implications for the economy.

deflation: a general decrease in the level of prices

The Consumer Price Index

consumer price index: a measure of price changes for a typical basket of consumer products

The tool most commonly used to measure overall changes in prices is the **consumer price index** (CPI). This index monitors price changes in a representative "shopping basket" of consumer products. To determine what typical Canadian households buy, Statistics Canada surveys their buying habits every few years.

A simple illustration, as given by Figure 11.1, allows us to see how the consumer price index indicates price changes. Suppose the shopping basket includes only two items—hamburgers and milkshakes. An investigator conducting a survey in 1997 finds that each month an average consumer buys 10 hamburgers at $2 each and 30 milkshakes at $1 each. In other words, the typical consumer spends $20 on hamburgers and $30 on

FIGURE 11.1 Simple Consumer Price Index

Results of 1997 Survey

	Prices	Quantity Consumed per Month	Expenditure per Month	Weights
Hamburgers	$2.00	10	$20	$20 ÷ $50 = 0.4
Milkshakes	$1.00	30	$30	$30 ÷ $50 = 0.6
			$50	

Prices in 1998

	Prices	1998 Price 1997 Quantity
Hamburgers	$2.20	$2.20 × 10 = $22.00
Milkshakes	$1.05	$1.05 × 30 = $31.50
		$53.50

In this simplified economy, 10 hamburgers and 30 milkshakes fill the monthly shopping basket of an average consumer. If the value of this basket rises from $50.00 to $53.50 during the course of a year, the annual inflation rate is 7 percent, with the consumer price index moving from 100 to 107.

milkshakes, for a total of $50 per month. Therefore, two-fifths (0.4) of the consumer's total budget is spent on hamburgers and three-fifths (0.6) on milkshakes. These fractions represent the **item weights**, or proportions of each good in the total cost of the shopping basket.

item weights: the proportions of each good in the total cost of the basket of consumer goods used to calculate CPI

base year: the survey year used as a point of comparison in subsequent years

To give a point of comparison for prices in subsequent years, the year in which the survey is conducted acts as the **base year**. The combined price of the representative products in the base year is considered the reference point, and the index in the base year is set at 100. Suppose, in our example, that the prices of hamburgers and milkshakes rise to $2.20 and $1.05 in 1998. Based on the quantities determined by the 1997 survey, the amount spent each month on hamburgers and milkshakes can be calculated. In other words, the same quantity of hamburgers at the new hamburger price (10 × $2.20) and the same quantity of milkshakes at the new milkshake price (30 × $1.05) give a total cost of $53.50 ($22.00 + $31.50). Compared with the 1997 total cost ($50.00) of the same products, prices have risen $3.50 ($53.50 – $50.00) or 7 percent from the base year [($3.50 ÷ $50.00) × 100]. Hence, the 1998 consumer price index is 107.

While it includes many more items, the actual CPI is calculated by Statistics Canada in the same way. Figure 11.2 shows the item weights for the major components of the CPI. Every month, the prices of about 600 representative products included in the CPI shopping basket are researched in a variety of Canadian communities. The index is calculated from the results. In the typical case of rising prices, the percentage increase in the consumer price index represents the inflation rate. For example, if the CPI has a value of 100 at the end of one year and a value of 110 at the end of the next year, the inflation rate over the year has been 10 percent. In other words, the change in the index (110 – 100), expressed as a percentage [(10 ÷ 100) × 100], is the inflation rate (10 percent).

FIGURE 11.2
Consumer Price Index Weights (1992)

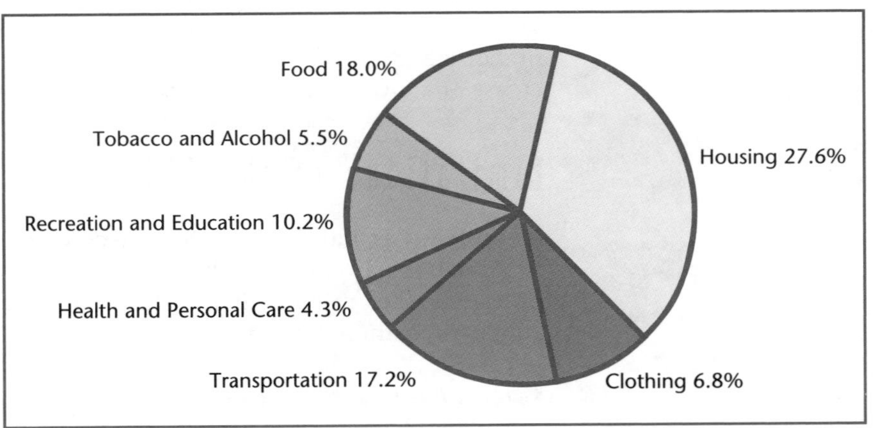

According to Statistics Canada's 1992 survey, a typical urban household's expenditures had the above weights. As shown, housing was the biggest expenditure, followed by food and transportation.

Source: Adapted from Statistics Canada, *Consumer Prices and Price Indexes* (June 1996), cat. no. 62-010-XPB, p. 114. Reproduced by authority of the Minister of Industry, 1997.

Nominal Versus Real Income

cost of living: the amount consumers must spend on the entire range of goods and services they buy

nominal income: income expressed in current dollars

real income: income expressed in constant base-year dollars

The consumer price index is useful in helping consumers determine the **cost of living**, or the amount they must spend on the entire range of goods and services they buy. In particular, the CPI allows consumers to judge how much better or worse off they are as a result of inflation. Suppose, for example, a consumer's monthly income increases from $1000 to $1050 during a year when the CPI rises from 100 to 110. If the consumer's own monthly purchases roughly correspond to those in the representative "shopping basket," he can evaluate the personal impact of inflation. To see how this consumer's purchasing power is affected by inflation, we can express his **nominal income**, or income valued in current dollars, as a **real income**, or income expressed in constant base-year dollars. To determine real income, the consumer's nominal income ($1050.00) is divided by the value of the consumer price index expressed in hundredths (1.10):

$$\text{Real income} = \frac{\text{nominal income}}{\text{CPI (in hundredths)}}$$

$$\$954.55 = \frac{\$1050.00}{1.10}$$

In other words, the consumer's monthly income of $1050.00 has a purchasing power of $954.55 when valued in constant base-year dollars. His income has not increased proportionally with the cost of living. For the consumer's purchasing power to keep up with inflation, his income would have to increase by the same percentage as the increase in prices—that is, by 10 percent, or $100 ($1000 × 0.10), to $1100 ($1000 + $100).

As our example shows, the purchasing power of a current dollar is inversely related to the consumer price index: the lower the CPI, the higher the purchasing power of nominal income; and, the higher the CPI, the lower the purchasing power of nominal income. Therefore, those whose incomes increase at a higher rate than the rise in prices have a higher standard of living. On the other hand, those whose incomes increase at a lower rate than the rise in prices are worse off than before.

Limitations of the CPI

As with any economic indicator, the consumer price index has a number of limitations. In this case, they consist of the following: consumer differences, changes in spending patterns, and product quality. In some circumstances, these limitations can severely reduce the index's usefulness.

Consumer Differences

Individual consumption patterns do not always match those of the typical urban household. Hence, the consumer price index may not apply to many consumers' individual cost of living. Consider, for example, a fashion-conscious reader. This person tends to spend a larger proportion of her budget on clothing and books than the typical consumer and, consequently, might travel less than the average consumer. For this individual consumer, the official index understates the impact of price changes in clothing and books, but overstates the impact of price changes in travel fares.

Changes in Spending Patterns

While Statistics Canada regularly surveys households to update both the contents and the item weights of the "shopping basket," changes in consumption patterns are ongoing and gradual. For example, more cellular phones and CD players were steadily purchased in the early 1990s. Also, consumers tend to buy less of items whose prices rise the most. Over time, these products have too high a weight in the CPI basket, meaning that the index overstates the rate of inflation.

Product Quality

The index cannot reflect changes in quality that are unmatched by changes in price. For example, items in the CPI shopping basket such as medicines and stereos may improve tremendously in quality, yet their prices may not increase proportionally with quality, and may even fall. So, while the standard of living may increase because of the increased quality, this will not be reflected in the CPI.

The GDP Deflator

GDP deflator: an indicator of price changes for all goods and services produced in the economy

Another indicator of price changes is the **GDP deflator**. Unlike the CPI, which focuses on a small number of consumer items, the GDP deflator measures price changes for all goods and services produced in the economy, and weights them in terms of the economy's total output. The item weights in this index are altered yearly, depending on how goods and services are represented in current GDP. While this frequent updating increases the accuracy of the GDP deflator, it means that values for this index are not as quickly available as values for the consumer price index. Because of this drawback, the GDP deflator receives less publicity than the CPI. Given the difference in the way they are calculated, the two indicators give similar but not identical estimates of inflation.

Figure 11.3 shows how the GDP deflator is calculated in a simplified economy that produces only computer microchips. In 1997, which is the base year, the GDP deflator is equal to 100. In order to calculate the value of the GDP deflator in each subsequent year, the output of each year is multiplied by the current price per microchip, divided by the same output in base-year prices and then multiplied by 100. For example, the 1998 output of microchips is 2000 and the price is 30 cents. This \$600 value of output (2000 × \$0.30) is divided by the same output in 1997 prices (2000 × \$0.20), or \$400, to give a GDP deflator of 150 [(\$600 ÷ \$400) × 100]. The result shows that the general price level has risen by one-half between 1997 and 1998. In other words, the inflation rate was 50 percent.

Nominal Versus Real GDP

Just as nominal incomes for an individual household can be adjusted to take account of price changes, so the value of the economy's entire output

FIGURE 11.3 Simple GDP Deflator

(1) Year	(2) Output of Microchips	(3) Current Price	(4) Output at Current Price (2) × (3)	(5) Output at 1997 Price (2) × $0.20	(6) GDP Deflator [(4) ÷ (5)] × 100
1997	1000	$0.20	$200	$200	100
1998	2000	0.30	600	400	150
1999	2500	0.40	1000	500	200

The GDP deflator in any year is calculated by taking the economy's annual output at current prices (column 4), dividing by this same output valued in base-year prices (column 5), and then multiplying the result by 100. While the GDP deflator has a value of 100 in 1997, which is the base year, it rises in proportion with the prices of the economy's output.

nominal GDP: Gross Domestic Product expressed in current dollars

can be adjusted for inflation. Recall that real GDP (or real output) is GDP expressed in constant dollars from a chosen base year. In contrast, **nominal GDP** (or nominal output) is GDP expressed in current dollars. Recall that real income for the individual household measures the purchasing power of that household over time. In the same way, real GDP gives an indication of the purchasing power of an entire economy. To find real GDP, economists and statisticians divide nominal GDP by the GDP deflator expressed in hundredths:

$$\text{Real GDP} = \frac{\text{nominal GDP}}{\text{GDP deflator (in hundredths)}}$$

This formula can be applied to Canada's GDP in Figure 11.4 to give GDP in constant base-year (1986) dollars. Canada's nominal GDP was $797.8 billion in 1996. This amount divided by the GDP deflator expressed in hundredths, which was 1.2914 (129.14 ÷ 100), gives a real GDP of $617.8 billion ($797.8 billion ÷ 1.2914). The same approach can be used for years prior to the base year. For example, Canada's 1968 nominal GDP was $75.4 billion. This amount divided by the GDP deflator expressed in hundredths, which is 0.3 (30.0 ÷ 100), gives a real GDP for 1968, expressed in 1986 dollars, of $251.3 billion ($75.4 billion ÷ 0.3). Notice that when the adjusting number is more than 100, as in 1996, nominal GDP is reduced or deflated to find real GDP. In the opposite case, where the index falls short of 100, as in 1968, nominal GDP is expanded or inflated when this adjustment is made.

Inflation's Effects

Figure 11.5 shows Canada's inflation record since 1926. After a period of deflation during the Great Depression of the 1930s, significant inflation occurred during and immediately after World War II. Relatively low rates of inflation during the 1950s and 1960s were then followed by gradually rising rates during the 1960s and 1970s. Since the mid-1980s, inflation rates have again gradually fallen to low levels.

FIGURE 11.4 Finding Real Gross Domestic Product

(1) Year	(2) Nominal GDP (current $ billions)	(3) GDP Deflator (1986 = 1.00)	(4) Real GDP (1986 $ billions) [(2) ÷ (3)] × 100
1968	$75.4	30.00	$251.3
1986	505.7	100.00	505.7
1996	797.8	129.14	617.8

Canada's real GDP in any year is found by dividing the economy's nominal GDP, which is expressed in current dollars, by the value of the GDP deflator. While Canada's nominal output rose from $75.4 to $797.8 billion between 1968 and 1996, the nation's real output in 1986 dollars increased by a much smaller amount, from $251.3 to $617.8 billion.

Sources: Statistics Canada, *Canadian Economic Observer, Historical Statistical Supplement, 1995/6* (July 1996), cat. no. 11-210-XPB, vol. 10, pp. 5, 7; Statistics Canada, *Canadian Economic Observer* (May 1997), cat. no. 11-010-XPB, p.4. Reproduced by authority of the Minister of Industry, 1997.

Why are high inflation rates, such as those experienced by Canadians during the 1970s and early 1980s, such a serious problem? Inflation redistributes purchasing power among different groups in ways that can be both economically harmful and unjust; in other words, purchasing power keeps pace with inflation for some individuals but not for others. To see the effects of inflation, we will look at its effects on household incomes and on borrowing and lending.

FIGURE 11.5
The Inflation Rate

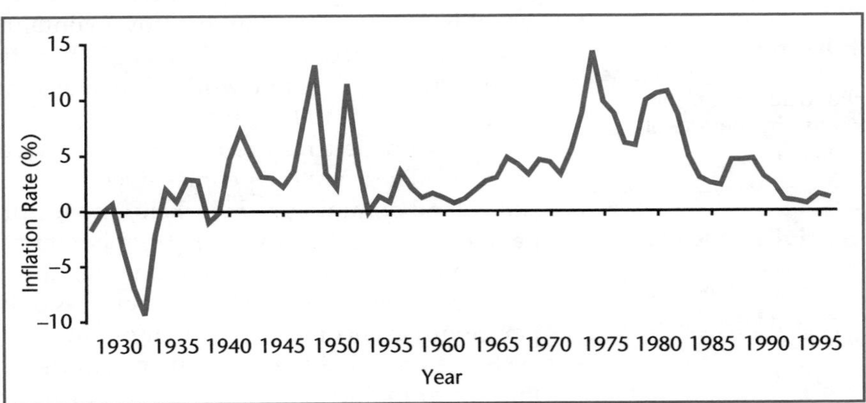

The graph shows annual inflation rates as measured by changes in the GDP price deflator. While deflation occurred during the early 1930s, inflation has been the dominant trend ever since. Inflation was most pronounced after World War II, during the 1970s, and in the early 1980s. In the late 1980s and early 1990s, the inflation rate dropped tremendously.

Sources: Adapted from Statistics Canada, *Canadian Economic Observer, Historical Statistical Supplement, 1995/6* (July 1996), cat. no. 11-210-XPB, vol. 10, p. 42; Statistics Canada, *Canadian Economic Observer, Statistical Summary* (August 1997), cat. no. 11-010-XPB, p. 4. Reproduced by authority of the Minister of Industry, 1997.

Incomes

Inflation means not only increasing prices, but expanding nominal incomes as well. The effect on households' purchasing power depends on which is greater—inflation or the increase in nominal income. If a household's nominal income increases steadily every year but inflation rises at a higher rate, the household loses purchasing power. So, for example, this year's dollars buy fewer groceries than did last year's dollars, even with the expanding nominal income. If, in contrast, the same household has a nominal income that increases at roughly the same rate as inflation, the household maintains its purchasing power. In other words, each year's dollars buy about the same amount of groceries. Therefore, whereas some households may feel the full impact of inflation on their living standards, others may have the impact cushioned by income adjustments, and there are others who may even benefit from inflation because their nominal incomes rise more quickly than inflation. One of the most costly aspects of inflation for society is that this redistribution of purchasing power occurs in an arbitrary way. The winners are often those with substantial economic resources, while the losers are commonly those least able to withstand a drop in purchasing power.

Many labour unions negotiate income adjustments for their members. As a result, workers' wages are adjusted using the consumer price index, or cost of living, as it is popularly known. In the collective agreement, provisions for these adjustments are called **cost-of-living-adjustment** (COLA) **clauses**. When workers' incomes automatically increase by the rate of inflation, they are called **fully indexed incomes**. In this case, nominal income rises at the same rate as prices, so real income stays the same. For example, if the inflation rate between 1997 and 1998 is 10 percent, a worker originally earning a monthly income of $1000 receives a new monthly income of $1100, thereby maintaining purchasing power. The worker's real income in 1997, using 1997 as the base year, is $1000 ($1000 ÷ 1.00). In 1998, the same worker's real income, expressed in 1997 dollars, is again $1000 ($1100 ÷ 1.10).

cost-of-living adjustment clauses: provisions for income adjustments to accommodate changes in price levels, which are included in wage contracts

fully indexed incomes: nominal incomes that automatically increase by the rate of inflation

Other people may receive incomes that are only partially indexed or are fixed. These are the people—including, for example, pensioners, unskilled and nonunionized workers, and recipients of government transfer payments—who lose the most from inflation. **Partially indexed incomes** rise more slowly than the inflation rate, causing real incomes to fall. Suppose, for example, that a single parent has only welfare payments of $1000 per month as income. If the inflation rate is 10 percent between 1997 and 1998, the household needs a 10 percent rise, or an extra $100, in nominal income to maintain its purchasing power. If the payments increase by only 7 percent, they rise by $70, for a total of $1070 per month. Using 1997 as the base year, the household's real income falls from $1000.00 in 1997 to $972.73 ($1070.00 ÷ 1.10) in 1998.

partially indexed incomes: nominal incomes that increase by less than the rate of inflation

In contrast to indexed and partially indexed incomes, **fixed incomes** are nominal incomes that stay at the same nominal dollar amount. In other words, these incomes do not change at all in response to inflation. Suppose, for example, that a pensioner receives a set monthly payment of $1000. Any increase in prices will cause purchasing power to decrease and, thereby, the pensioner's real income will be reduced. So, with the

fixed incomes: nominal incomes that remain fixed at some dollar amount regardless of the rate of inflation

same hypothetical 10 percent inflation rate between 1997 and 1998, the pensioner's real income, expressed in 1997 dollars, drops from $1000.00 in 1997 to $909.09 ($1000.00 ÷ 1.10) in 1998.

Borrowing and Lending

As discussed in Chapter 8, the forces of demand and supply in the loanable funds market, the duration of the loan, the loan size, the individual's credit risk, and whether collateral is provided determine the interest rate at which money is lent. Whatever interest rate is established, if the lender loans funds at an interest rate that is not adjusted for inflation, the lender may lose out.

nominal interest rate: the interest rate expressed in money terms

To illustrate, we have to distinguish between two types of interest rates. The **nominal interest rate** is the interest rate expressed in money terms. This is the interest rate stated per annum, as discussed in Chapter 8. For example, Mariposa Vacations borrows $2000 at 7 percent per annum. At the end of the year, Mariposa Vacations will pay back the principal ($2000), plus interest (0.07 × $2000 = 140), for a total of $2140 ($2000 + $140).

real interest rate: the nominal interest rate minus the rate of inflation

In contrast, the **real interest rate** is the nominal interest rate minus the rate of inflation.

$$\text{Real interest rate} = \text{nominal interest rate} - \text{inflation rate}$$

If the inflation rate is 3 percent in the year that Mariposa Vacations takes out the loan, then the loan's real interest rate is 4 percent—the 7 percent nominal interest rate minus the 3 percent rate of inflation. The real interest rate reflects the fact that, because of inflation, the funds lent (the principal) have less purchasing power at the end of the one-year term than they did at the time the loan was made. Thus, the bank lending to Mariposa Vacations receives $140 (7 percent) in nominal interest at the end of the year, but only $80 (4 percent) in real interest.

inflation premium: a percentage built into a nominal interest rate to anticipate the rate of inflation for the loan period

Once the nominal interest rate has been agreed upon, it is fixed. So, lenders try to anticipate the rate of inflation for the loan period and build it into the nominal interest rate. This rate built into the nominal interest rate is known as the **inflation premium**. Lenders, therefore, determine what real interest rate they desire and add an inflation premium to determine the nominal interest rate:

$$\text{Nominal interest rate} = \text{desired real interest rate} + \text{inflation premium}$$

For example, the manager at Mariposa Vacations' bank may have anticipated a 2 percent inflation rate and wanted a real interest rate of 5 percent. So, on the $2000 one-year loan, she expected the bank would receive real interest of $100 ($2000 × 0.05) and an inflation premium of $40 ($2000 × 0.02) to compensate for the reduced purchasing power of the original $2000 principal.

What happens if the inflation rate turns out to be higher than lenders anticipated? Suppose, in our example, the inflation rate is actually 4 percent instead of 2 percent. As a result, the bank actually receives only 3 percent real interest—that is, the 7 percent nominal rate minus the 4 percent inflation rate. This is substantially less than the 5 percent real interest rate the bank manager anticipated. Because the inflation rate is higher than anticipated, the real interest rate is lower than the desired real interest rate, and lenders are worse off.

BRIEF REVIEW

1. Inflation is a general increase in the prices of goods and services in the entire economy. A general fall in prices is known as deflation.
2. The consumer price index (CPI) is one indicator of inflation, or changes in the cost of living. The CPI measures price changes in a typical "shopping basket" of consumer products.
3. Whereas nominal income is expressed in current dollars, real income is expressed in constant base-year dollars. Real income equals nominal income divided by the current value of the CPI (expressed in hundredths).
4. The GDP deflator measures price changes for all goods and services produced in the economy, and weights them in terms of the economy's total output. Nominal GDP divided by the current value of the GDP deflator (expressed in hundredths) gives the economy's real GDP, or real output.
5. The extent to which inflation affects individuals' purchasing power varies. Those people whose incomes are fully indexed to inflation rates maintain purchasing power. However, those with partially indexed or fixed incomes lose purchasing power.
6. Lenders also lose from inflation if inflation is higher than they anticipated with the inflation premium.

UNEMPLOYMENT

Recall from Chapter 1 that another economic goal of Canada is full employment. Of all economic statistics, the unemployment rate is the one most often highlighted in the media, discussed by politicians, and noticed by Canadians. For most people, the prospect of involuntary unemployment provokes considerable anxiety. To see why, we must understand unemployment, how it is measured, and its implications for individuals and for the economy as a whole.

The Labour Force Survey

labour force population: the population, with specific exclusions, from which Statistics Canada takes a random sample for the labour force survey

labour force: all people who either have a job or are actively seeking employment

Statistics Canada keeps track of the Canadian workforce through a monthly survey of about 52 000 households. These households are a random sample of the **labour force population**, which includes all residents of Canada over 15 years of age except those living in the Northwest Territories and Yukon, on Native reserves, and in institutions (for example, jails and psychiatric hospitals), and full-time members of the armed forces. The **labour force** is made up of those people in the labour force population who either have jobs or are actively seeking employment. By its definition, the labour force leaves out such groups as pensioners who do not have jobs and are not looking for work. It also excludes those who have given up looking for a job, as well as full-time homemakers who, while they work, do not do so in the formal job market.

participation rate: the percentage of the entire labour force population that makes up the labour force

The **participation rate** is the percentage of the entire labour force population that makes up the labour force. For example, in 1996 Canada's labour force was 15.145 million and the labour force population was 23.352 million, so the participation rate was about 65 percent. In other words, of the defined labour force population, about 65 percent is participating in the labour market:

$$\text{Participation rate} = \frac{\text{labour force}}{\text{labour force population}} \times 100$$

$$64.9\% = \frac{15\,145\,000}{23\,352\,000}$$

Statistics Canada also examines the participation rates of specific groups of people. Figure 11.6 shows recent trends in labour force participation for women and men in two age groups. As shown, the participation rates for women 25 years and over have increased steadily until very recently. In contrast, the participation rates for men aged 25 years and over have decreased slightly. This decline is largely due to the growing popularity of early retirement. Overall, the participation of young people in the labour force is higher than it was in the past but it has decreased in recent years, as young people remain full-time students for longer periods to increase their chances of finding suitable jobs.

FIGURE 11.6
Participation Rates

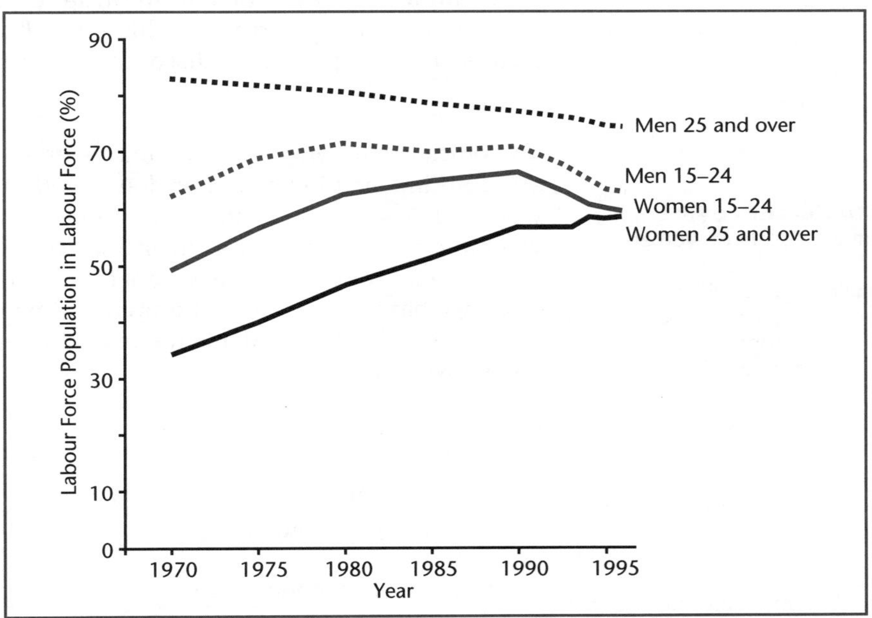

Since the 1970s, participation in the labour force by women over the age of 25 has increased substantially. In contrast, participation rates for men over the age of 25 underwent a small decrease. While participation rates for young people have fluctuated widely.

Sources: Adapted from Statistics Canada, *Canadian Economic Observer, Historical Statistical Supplement, 1992/93* (July 1993), cat. no. 11-210, vol. 7, p. 38; Statistics Canada, *Canadian Economic Observer, Statistical Summary* (February 1997), cat. no. 11-010, p. 16. Reproduced by authority of the Minister of Industry, 1997.

The Official Unemployment Rate

Once the labour force has been defined, its members can be divided into those who are employed and those who are unemployed. The official unemployment rate is the number of unemployed people in the labour force as a percentage of the entire labour force. For example, Canada's 1996 labour force of 15.145 million people was composed of 13.676 million people who were employed and 1.469 million who were not. Therefore, the unemployment rate was 9.7 percent:

$$\text{Unemployment rate} = \frac{\text{unemployment in labour force}}{\text{labour force}} \times 100$$

$$9.7\% = \frac{1\,469\,000}{15\,145\,000}$$

Figure 11.7 summarizes the relationships among Canada's population, labour force, labour force population, and unemployed labour force.

Drawbacks of the Official Unemployment Rate

Because of the way the official unemployment rate is calculated, it may either understate or overstate the true level of unemployment in the Canadian economy. Critics of this official rate point to the following factors: underemployment, discouraged workers, and dishonesty.

Underemployment

underemployment: the problem of workers being underutilized, either as part-time workers or by working at jobs not appropriate to their skills or education

The official unemployment rate makes no distinction between part-time and full-time employment, nor does it reflect the appropriateness of the work. While some part-time workers prefer part-time work, others would want full-time work if it were available. Also, in hard times, some workers may have to work at jobs that do not fully utilize their skills and education. Thus, we have the problem of **underemployment**. It is sometimes argued that the official rate understates unemployment by ignoring underemployed workers.

FIGURE 11.7 The Canadian Labour Force (1996)

$$\text{Participation rate} = \frac{\text{labour force}}{\text{labour force population}} \times 100 = \frac{15\,145\,000}{23\,352\,000} \times 100 = 64.9\%$$

$$\text{Unemployment rate (\%)} = \frac{\text{unemployed in labour force}}{\text{labour force}} \times 100 = \frac{1\,469\,000}{15\,145\,000} \times 100 = 9.7\%$$

In 1997, Canada's total population was about 30 million. Of this number, 23.352 million were considered part of the labour force population. The labour force constituted 64.9 percent of the labour force population, or 15.145 million. Of this labour force, 90.3 percent, or 13.676 million, were employed. The remaining 1.469 million in the labour force were unemployed, giving an unemployment rate of 9.7 percent.

Source: Statistics Canada, *Labour Force Annual Averages 1996* (February 1997), cat. no. 71-220, p. 8-2. Reproduced by authority of the Minister of Industry, 1997.

Discouraged Workers

discouraged workers: unemployed workers who have given up looking for work

Unemployment statistics also do not take into account people who, after searching for a job without luck, give up looking. Because they are not actively seeking employment, these **discouraged workers** are not considered part of the labour force. Again, it is sometimes argued that this causes the official rate to understate unemployment.

The number of underemployed and discouraged workers rises during an economic downturn, since job prospects—especially for full-time work—are at their bleakest. During the recession of the early 1990s, for example, estimates suggested that the numbers of underemployed and discouraged workers would have added up to 10 percent to the official unemployment rate.

Dishonesty

People responding to Statistics Canada's labour market survey may state that they are actively looking for work when, in fact, they are not. While the extent to which such dishonesty affects the unemployment rate is difficult to measure, it does make it possible for the official rate to overstate unemployment.

Types of Unemployment

When examining unemployment, we should distinguish among four types: frictional, structural, cyclical, and seasonal unemployment.

Frictional Unemployment

frictional unemployment: unemployment due to being temporarily between jobs or looking for a first job

Workers who are temporarily between jobs or have begun looking for their first jobs are experiencing **frictional unemployment**. A dental assistant who has left one job voluntarily to look for another and a recent college graduate looking for career-related work are examples. Frictional unemployment is a permanent feature of labour markets, and represents about 3 percent of the labour force at any given time.

Structural Unemployment

structural unemployment: unemployment due to a mismatch between people and jobs

Another type of unemployment arises largely from structural changes in the economy. **Structural unemployment** is due to a mismatch between people and jobs—unemployed workers cannot fill the sorts of jobs that are available. This type of unemployment occurs primarily because of gradual changes in the economy. Long-term adjustments in what items are produced (for example, the current shift from goods to services), how they are produced (largely due to technological change), and where they are produced cause such unemployment.

Because of these changes, workers lose out; they're displaced. Consider a worker who loses her job in manufacturing because of automation. She might not yet have the skills for the expanding service sector. In the same way, an unemployed fisherman living in a remote village cannot easily take advantage of employment opportunities elsewhere. Because gaining new skills, moving to obtain work elsewhere, and developing new industries in a region all take time, structural unemployment can persist for long periods.

Cyclical Unemployment

cyclical unemployment: unemployment due to the ups and downs of economies and businesses

Economies and businesses must cope with ups and downs (which we'll discuss in Chapter 12), causing unemployment to rise and fall. This type of unemployment is called **cyclical unemployment**. An auto worker, for example, may work overtime in periods of strong consumer demand for cars, but be laid off in leaner times.

Seasonal Unemployment

seasonal unemployment: unemployment due to the seasonal nature of some occupations and industries

In some Canadian industries—agriculture, construction, and tourism, for example—work is seasonal, with lower employment in the winter months. As a result, some workers experience **seasonal unemployment**. Compared with many other countries, seasonal unemployment is particularly significant in Canada, given its climate and the importance of its primary resource industries. So that month-to-month comparisons can be made without the influence of seasonal unemployment, Statistics Canada calculates seasonal changes and adjusts the official unemployment rate accordingly.

Full Employment

full employment: the highest reasonable expectation of employment for the economy as a whole

natural unemployment rate: the unemployment rate that defines full employment

Defining **full employment** is a tricky task. In effect, full employment is the highest reasonable expectation of employment for the economy as a whole, and is defined in terms of a **natural unemployment rate**. This rate includes frictional unemployment, but traditionally excludes cyclical unemployment. This rate also excludes seasonal unemployment, which is already omitted from the official unemployment rate using the seasonal adjustment.

In the 1950s and 1960s, full employment in the Canadian economy was defined by the Economic Council of Canada as a natural unemployment rate of 3 percent. In other words, full employment was 100 percent labour force employment minus 3 percent frictional unemployment. As Figure 11.8 shows, the unemployment rate, which reached almost 20 percent during the Great Depression of the 1930s, decreased considerably over the following decades. However, full employment—as it was defined—was only occasionally achieved.

Since the 1970s, the unemployment rate has been well over 3 percent. In light of recent economic trends and thinking, many economists argue that in addition to frictional unemployment—which will always exist—the definition of full employment should also accommodate at least some structural unemployment. This, they say, is because structural unemployment *can* be reduced, but only very gradually. While definitions of full employment in the 1990s vary, most include a natural unemployment rate of between 6 percent and 8 percent. Because of this, full employment does not mean what it would seem to — that everyone who wants a job has one. Indeed, a significant proportion of the labour force (6 to 8 percent) is unemployed.

FIGURE 11.8
The Unemployment Rate

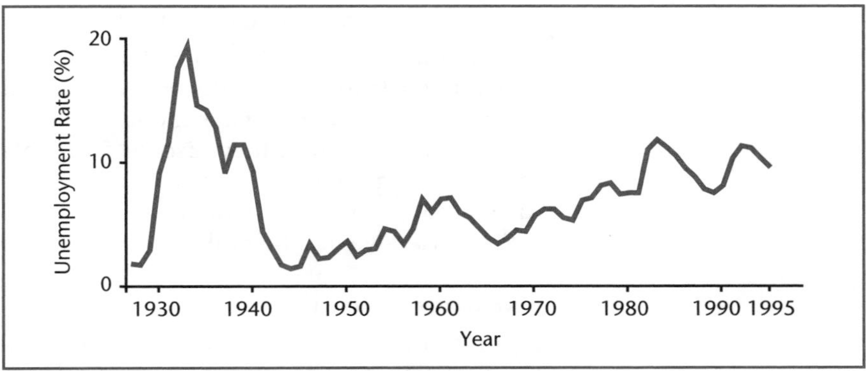

After rising significantly in the 1930s, the unemployment rate fell to 2 to 4 percent for much of the 1940s and 1950s. Since the late 1950s, the rate has gradually risen. Much of this increase can be attributed to a rise in natural unemployment.

Sources: Adapted from (for 1966–1995) Statistics Canada, *Canadian Economic Observer, Historical Statistical Supplement, 1995/96* (July 1996), cat. no. 11-210-XPB, vol. 10, p. 30; adapted from (for 1926–1965) *National Income and Expenditure Accounts, Annual Estimates 1926–1986* (June 1988), cat. no. 13-531, pp. 214–15. Reproduced by authority of the Minister of Industry, 1997.

Increases over the past few decades in both the actual and the natural unemployment rates represent worrisome trends. Several factors are often highlighted in explaining these trends.

Structural Change

Recall that structural adjustments in an economy occur whenever there are changes regarding what products are produced, as well as in how and where they are produced. Over the past few decades, the pace of structural change in the Canadian economy has accelerated. The OPEC oil crisis, the growth of the service sector and shrinking of the traditional manufacturing sector, and the removal of many international trade barriers have each led to the displacement of workers and therefore caused increases in long-term structural unemployment.

Unemployment Insurance

Most unemployed workers today have a significant advantage over those in previous generations. The financial cushion provided by unemployment insurance has allowed job seekers to devote more time and effort to searching for employment than in the past, which increases frictional unemployment. Reforms to unemployment insurance in the early 1970s also made it easier for those experiencing seasonal and structural unemployment to claim benefits. Thus, unemployment insurance can be a factor in increasing the unemployment rate. Overall, it is estimated that this factor added between 0.5 percent and 2.0 percent to the unemployment rate since the 1970s. However recent changes to the unemployment insurance system (now called Employment Insurance), which make it more difficult to claim benefit, should reduce this effect.

Changing Participation Rates

Recall from Figure 11.6 that, over the last few decades, young people have added to the labour force. Not only do they add to the supply of unskilled labour when they first enter the labour force but, as they acquire skills and work experience, they also suffer greater frictional unemployment than more experienced workers. As a result, the increased participation rates among young Canadians (which have declined somewhat in the 1990s) have swelled the ranks of the unemployed.

Minimum Wage

Minimum wage levels set by the provinces have increased a great deal in the past few decades. For young people in particular—who are more likely than others to be affected by minimum wage laws—this has meant an increase in the number of people looking for work. For example, a 1980 Canadian study suggested that a 10.0 percent increase in the minimum wage reduces employment by 1.0 percent for male teenagers and 2.7 percent for female teenagers.

Thinking About Economics

How do minimum wages cause unemployment?

A minimum wage has the same effect on the market for unskilled labour as industrial unions do in other labour markets. By creating a wage floor above equilibrium, the minimum wage creates a surplus, with a greater supply of workers than there are available jobs at that wage. In evaluating the effectiveness of minimum wages, the higher wages received by employed workers must be weighed against the unemployment caused for others.

The Costs of Unemployment

High unemployment rates hurt both individuals and the Canadian economy as a whole. As Figure 11.9 shows, the rates vary from province to province and among groups of people. To jobless workers and their families, unemployment, especially for extended periods, can create stress and discouragement, disrupt family life, lower self-esteem, and cause financial hardship. The economy as a whole loses the output the worker could have produced.

potential output: the real output, or Gross Domestic Product, associated with full employment

One way to measure the cost of unemployment for the entire economy is by calculating the extent to which **potential output**, or the real output associated with full employment, exceeds actual real output. According to Okun's Law—named after the American economist Arthur Okun—for every percentage point that the unemployment rate

FIGURE 11.9 Unemployment Rates by Province, Gender, and Age (1996)

Province		Gender and Age	
Newfoundland	19.4	Women	
Prince Edward Island	14.5	15-24	14.6
Nova Scotia	12.6	25 and over	8.4
New Brunswick	11.7		
Quebec	11.8	Men	
Ontario	9.1	15-24	17.5
Manitoba	7.5	25 and over	8.5
Saskatchewan	6.6		
Alberta	7.0		
British Columbia	8.9		

Unemployment rates vary from province to province. 1996 rates were highest among the Atlantic provinces and Quebec, and lowest in Saskatchewan. Rates for women are slightly lower than for men, and young people were more likely to be unemployed than those over the age of 25.

Source: Statistics Canada, *Canadian Economic Observer, Statistical Summary* (March 1997), cat. no. 11-010-XPB, pp. 16, 59. Reproduced by authority of the Minister of Industry, 1997.

exceeds the natural unemployment rate, the gap between potential output and actual real output is 2.5 percent.

In 1996, for example, real GDP in (constant) 1986 dollars was $617.8 billion, while the unemployment rate was 9.7 percent, or 2.2 percent above an assumed natural unemployment rate of 7.5 percent. According to Okun's Law, real output could have been 5.5 percent (2.2 × 2.5) higher if unemployment equalled the natural rate. In other words, in 1986 dollars, 1996 real GDP could have been $34.0 billion ($617.8 billion × 0.055) higher.

This method of measuring the costs of unemployment is difficult to apply both because of disagreements over the natural unemployment rate and because it can be argued that these are costs of unemployment even if actual real output equals or exceeds potential output. It gives a good indication of the substantial cost of unemployment, not just to those workers who are directly affected, but to the economy as a whole.

BRIEF REVIEW

1. The labour force population is Canada's population over age 15, with some exclusions.
2. The participation rate is the percentage of those in the labour force population who make up the labour force, which includes all those people who are employed or who are actively seeking work within the formal economy. Participation rates for women and young people have risen considerably in the last few decades.
3. The official unemployment rate is the percentage of the labour force that is unemployed.
4. The official unemployment rate, which has risen significantly in the last few decades, does not take into account underemployment, discouraged workers, or dishonest answers given in labour market surveys.
5. Unemployment can be categorized as frictional, structural, cyclical, and seasonal.
6. Full employment is the highest reasonable expectation of employment for the economy as a whole, and is defined in terms of a natural unemployment rate. Traditionally, the natural unemployment rate only accommodated frictional unemployment; now, however, many economists believe it should include at least some structural unemployment.
7. The costs of unemployment are profound and numerous for unemployed workers and their families. Unemployment costs to the economy as a whole are indicated by the extent to which potential output exceeds actual real output.

KEY CONCEPTS

deflation
consumer price index
item weights
base year
cost of living
nominal income
real income
GDP deflator
nominal GDP
cost-of-living-adjustment clauses
fully indexed incomes
partially indexed incomes
fixed incomes
nominal interest rate
real interest rate
inflation premium
labour force population
labour force
participation rate
underemployment
discouraged workers
frictional unemployment
structural unemployment
cyclical unemployment
seasonal unemployment
full employment
natural unemployment rate
potential output

ANALYSIS AND APPLICATION

1. The table below gives data on Student A's monthly purchases during 1997 and 1998.

Student A's Monthly Purchases

	Prices		Quantities Consumed per month	
	(1997)	(1998)	(1997)	(1998)
Hotdogs	$1.50	$1.60	3	2
Cans of cola	.75	.70	16	18
Chocolate bars	1.00	1.00	7	7
Magazines	3.50	4.50	3	2
Video rentals	3.00	2.75	2	3

   a. Calculate the value of Student A's 1997 shopping basket using 1997 prices. What are the item weights associated with this shopping basket?
   b. Calculate the value of Student A's 1997 shopping basket using 1998 prices. If 1997 is used as the base year, what is the 1998 value of Student A's price index? What is the 1997 value of this index? By what percentage has this index changed between 1997 and 1998?

Finding the GDP Deflator

	Output in 1998	Prices in 1998	Prices in 1997
CDs	4	$22.00	$16.00
Bags of chips	50	1.80	1.50

2. The above table shows output and prices during 1998 in an economy that produces only two goods—CDs and bags of chips.
   a. What is the total value of the economy's output in 1998 valued in 1998 prices?
   b. What is the total value of the economy's output in 1998 valued in 1997 prices?
   c. Based on your answers to parts a. and b., calculate the value of the GDP deflator in 1998 if 1997 is treated as the base year.
   d. In what ways does the calculation of the GDP deflator differ from the calculation of the consumer price index?

Finding Real Gross Domestic Product

Year	Nominal GDP (current $ billions)	GDP Deflator	Real GDP (1986 $ billions)
1978	$_____	60.000	$402.7
1982	374.4	87.887	_____
1986	505.7	_____	_____
1990	669.5	118.454	_____
1994	747.3	_____	595.0

3. a. Copy out and complete the above table.
   b. Explain why real GDP is less than nominal GDP in some years and greater than nominal GDP in other years.

4. Outline how each of the following individuals is influenced by unexpected inflation:
   a. a lawyer whose costs and revenues both rise by the inflation rate
   b. the owner of a heavily indebted restaurant
   c. a worker with a union contract that includes a COLA clause
   d. an injured worker who lives on a partially indexed transfer payment from the government

5. For each of the following years, determine the real interest rate. Find the difference between this rate and the desired real interest rate and explain how any difference affects borrowers and lenders.
   a. In year 1, the nominal interest rate is 9 percent, the inflation premium on loans is 3 percent, and actual rate of inflation is 4 percent.
   b. In year 2, the nominal interest rate is 10 percent, the inflation premium is 4 percent, and the actual rate of inflation is 2 percent.
   c. In year 3, the nominal interest rate is 8 percent, the inflation premium is 2 percent, and the actual rate of inflation is 2 percent.

Finding Participation and Unemployment Rates

Total population over 15 years of age	4.2 million
Those over 15 years of age not in the labour force population	1.4 million
Part-time workers who wish to have full-time jobs	100 000
Part-time workers who do not wish to have full-time jobs	300 000
Discouraged workers	400 000
Workers with full-time jobs	1.2 million
Unemployed members of the labour force	150 000

6. Use the hypothetical data in the table above to calculate the following variables:
   a. the labour force population
   b. the labour force

c. the participation rate
d. the unemployment rate

7. Outline how the employment conditions of the following individuals can be explained using the concepts introduced in the chapter. In each case, state whether or not the individual is included in the official unemployment rate.
   a. a laid-off typesetter who so far has had no success finding a similar job, due to the replacement of typesetters by computers
   b. a former cod fisherman who gives up looking for work and goes on welfare
   c. a farm labourer who is unemployed during the winter months
   d. a graphic artist who loses her job during an economic downturn
   e. a part-time store clerk who looks for a full-time position in the same occupation
   f. a bricklayer receiving employment insurance who works for a renovation company that operates in the underground economy
   g. a recent business school graduate who searches for her first career-related position

8. Using Okun's Law, calculate the gap between potential output and actual real output in the Canadian economy in 1992 and 1994. In your answers, assume a natural unemployment rate of 7.5 percent.
   a. In 1992, the unemployment rate was 11.3 percent and real GDP in 1986 dollars was $559.3 billion.
   b. In 1994, the unemployment rate was 10.4 percent and real GDP in 1986 dollars was $595.0 billion.

9. (Advanced Question)
   a. Using the table accompanying Question 1, calculate the value of Student A's 1998 shopping basket using 1998 prices as well as the item weights associated with this basket. What would the value of this 1998 shopping basket have been in 1997? If 1998 is used as the base year, what is the 1997 value of Student A's price index? What is the 1998 value? By what percentage has this index changed between 1997 and 1998?
   b. Why do the percentage changes in Student A's price index differ depending on which year is chosen as the base year?

10. Access Statistics Canada's website (at http://www.statcan.ca).
   a. Use the links to "Canadian Dimensions" to find the annual changes in Canada's consumer price index for the last four years for which data are available. Which component of the CPI has risen most quickly over this four-year period? Which component has fallen the most (or risen the least)?
   b. Use the links to "Canadian Dimensions" to find (i) the unemployment rate, (ii) the participation rate, and (iii) the proportion of the labour force population that is employed (known as the employment/population ratio) for Canada during the last four years for which data are available. Explain how movements in these three variables have been related over the relevant four-year period.

Advancing Economic Thought

BOOM BUST & ECHO

David K. Foot and the Economics of Age Distribution

What economic indicators can we apply to our personal lives? David K. Foot, a well-known Canadian economist and demographer, suggests that our ages can give us insights into our economic futures. In the following excerpt from his book Boom Bust & Echo *(written with Daniel Stoffman), Foot outlines some of the effects of Canada's huge "baby-boom generation" (people born from 1947 to 1966), its smaller "baby-bust generation" (people born from 1967 to 1979), and its "baby-boom echo generation" (people born from 1980 to 1995).*

Demography, the study of human populations, is the most powerful—and most underutilized—tool we have to understand the past and to foretell the future. Demographics affect every one of us as individuals, far more than most of us have ever imagined. They also play a pivotal role in the economic and social life of our country.

David Foot
Source: Footwork Consulting Inc.

What kinds of foods will people buy and what kinds of cars will they drive? Where will they choose to live? Which investments will they favour? These and many other things can be confidently predicted simply on the basis of readily available data on the age of Canadians. The two keys to these forecasts are the number of people in each age group and the probability that each person will participate in a given behaviour.

Canada's population pyramid (See Figure A) contains a massive bulge, representing the huge generation of baby-boomers born in the 20 years from 1947 to 1966. By comparison, the Depression and World War II generations that preceded the baby boom are small, as is the baby bust that followed it. But the most recently arrived group, the offspring of the boomers or the baby-boom echo, is comparatively large.

The Baby Boom (1947 to 1966)

The baby boom, both those born in Canada and those born elsewhere, totals 9.8 million people in 1996, almost 33 percent of the Canadian population.

Why did the baby boom happen? A likely explanation is that during these 20 years, Canadians knew they could afford large families. The postwar economy was robust, the future seemed full of promise, and young couples wanted to share that bright future with a big family. The second reason was the high immigration levels that prevailed during the

FIGURE A Canada's Population Pyramids, 1996

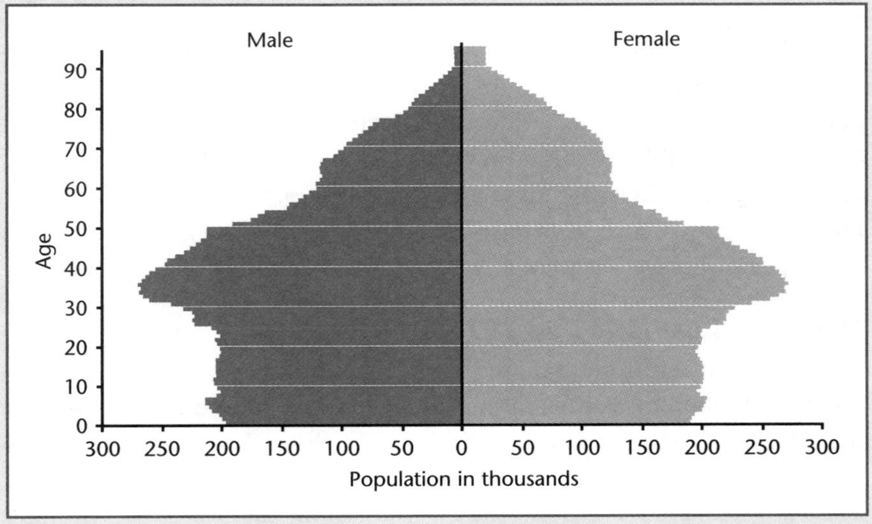

1950s; immigrants tend to be people of childbearing age, and they made an important contribution to the boom.

The front-end boomers have done pretty well for themselves. There are a lot of them, so they had to compete for jobs when they entered the workforce in the 1960s. But the entry of vast numbers of young baby-boomers into the marketplace through the 1970s and 1980s created wonderful opportunities for the front-enders already entrenched in business and government.

Those born towards the end of the 1950s also understand the baby boom but, unlike the front-enders, they are less well positioned to profit from that knowledge. Generally, most members of this boomer subgroup have just managed to get a house. But that house is in the suburbs, and during the first part of the 1990s its value crashed as the peak of the boom passed through its prime purchasing years. Most of these people are in a career, but that career seems to be going nowhere because the rungs ahead of them are clogged with older boomers who are still 15 to 20 years from retirement.

Things are tough for the late-1950s group, but not nearly as bad as they are for the back end that arrived just after them. These are the 2.6 million people born from 1960 to 1966. They are the same age as the characters in Douglas Coupland's novel *Generation X,* which gave the early-1960s group its name. Many of them are still living at home with their parents because, faced with horrendous obstacles in the labour market, they haven't been able to get their careers on track. That is why, while front-end boomers were earning 30 percent more than their fathers by age 30, back-enders were making 10 percent less than their fathers at the same age.

One of the worst things the Gen-Xers have to cope with is their parents—the Depression generation. These are the 55-to-60-year-olds sitting at the top of the corporate ladder, approaching the end of very successful careers, and unable to fathom why their 30-year-old offspring are living at home. Tension is tremendous in these families. Often the father is certain that his own success is based solely on his own merit while he sees his son's failure as a result of lack of drive and ambition.

The Baby Bust (1967 to 1979)

The commercial introduction of the birth control pill in 1961 and the rising participation of women in the labour market led to declining fertility over the 1960s. The result was a decline in births and a smaller cohort, often called the baby bust. In 1996, 5.4 million Canadians are in this cohort. The baby-busters have done pretty well so far, especially the younger ones. They had no difficulty finding part-time jobs in high school, unlike their older brothers and sisters, who had less opportunity to earn money in high school because they had so many competitors. During the 1990s, university entry standards have been falling, making it easier for busters to get into the school of their choice.

The Baby-Boom Echo (1980 to 1995)

As of 1996, there are 6.9 million members of the echo generation. What is the outlook for the echo kids? It won't be quite as smooth sailing as the baby-busters have had, but it won't be as disastrous as for Generation X either. Like the baby boom, the echo has a front end, born in the 1980s, that will have an easier ride than its back end, born in the first half of the 1990s. The latter group, Generation X-II, will experience the familiar disadvantages of arriving at the rear of a large cohort. Generation X-II will have a life experience similar to that of its parents, the first Generation X. Just as the first Gen-Xers have done, Gen X-II will have to scramble.

However, Gen X-II should be better prepared than its parents were to cope with high youth unemployment and other difficulties associated with a large cohort. That's because these kids have their Gen-X parents to teach them. By contrast, the original Generation X was the offspring of a small cohort that wasn't equipped to prepare them for the difficult world they encountered when they left home in the early 1980s.

Source

Abridged from *Boom Bust & Echo* by David K. Foot with Daniel Stoffman. Published by Macfarlane Walter & Ross, Toronto, 1996, pp. 2, 7, 9, 19 -24.

1. **Based on the demographic factors outlined in this article, predict whether (ceteris paribus) the following variables will rise or fall between 2000 and 2010. In each case, explain your answer.**
   a. **unemployment rates for youth aged 15 - 24**
   b. **interest rates**
   c. **sales of housing**
   d. **stock market prices**

2. **Access Statistics Canada's website (at http://www.statcan.ca). Then use the links to "Canadian Dimensions" to access population projections for various age groups in 2001 and 2016.**
   a. **Calculate the projected percentages of the population in the 0-24, 25-39, 40-64, and 65 + age groups, both in 2001 and 2016.**
   b. **Using the concepts introduced in Foot's article, explain the projected changes in the relative sizes of each of these age groups between 2001 and 2016.**

SIDELINE

JOBS UP BUT QUALITY DOWN

Changing conditions in Canada's labour market are creating a need for new statistics to help explain these conditions and capture current trends. A statistic recently devised by a Canadian economist is outlined in the article below.

Benny Tal, an economist with the Canadian Imperial Bank of Commerce, has come up with what he calls an employment quality index (EQI) that he has developed to capture more than just the raw growth in employment.

Mr. Tal's EQI has three components — a job's compensation, its stability, and whether or not it is a full- or part-time position. Each has its own index and the three are combined to make the full EQI.

"The economic consequences of a given rise in overall employment are not identical if a majority of the new jobs are of low quality as opposed to jobs of a higher quality," he says in his study, which the bank's economics department has published in *CIBC Observations.*

More, but less

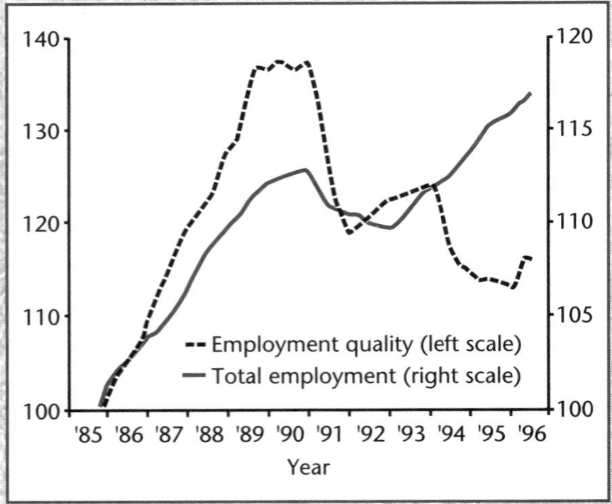

While total employment has risen in the past three years, the quality of those jobs has gone down.
Index: 3rd quarter 1985 = 100
Source: Canadian Imperial Bank of Commerce

"A full-time employee who enjoys above-average compensation and is unlikely to lose his/her job in the foreseeable future, is in a better position to maintain or improve his/her standard of living and avoid debt default (than) ... a part-time employee with lower-than-average compensation and an unstable job."

First, he looked at wage differentials among industries, which are relatively stable. Primary industries and the manufacturing sector pay good wages, so the average factory worker, for example, makes about 20 percent more than the average industrial wage. Jobs in many service industries, however, have low rates of pay, so people who work in retail and wholesale jobs make about 25 percent less than the average.

In recent years, employment in the lower-wage industries has been growing faster than employment in the higher-wage industries, so Mr. Tal's employment compensation index has fallen.

Next, he constructed an employment stability index based on an employee's likelihood of keeping a job for more than six months. Managers and professionals have the most stable jobs, and their share of total employment has been rising, so that's a plus for the index. Service-sector occupations are among the least stable jobs in the economy and their share of employment has been rising; that's a minus.

Employment stability fell during the recession (no surprise there), but it fell again in 1994 when the economy churned out some 350 000 jobs, which suggests that "many of the recently created jobs are less stable and therefore did not contribute as much to overall consumer confidence and spending as would otherwise be expected."

Finally, Mr Tal converted part-time jobs into "full-time equivalent" employment (two part-time jobs equal one full-time job). The number of full-time equivalent jobs, relative to the more familiar number for total employment, has fallen since 1989, except for a brief recovery in 1994.

When he combined these three measures into the broader EQI, Mr. Tal found that rising employment during the past two or three years was accompanied by a steady decline in the quality of those jobs.

Jobs, yes; good jobs, no. Canadians may have more jobs per se, but those jobs are lower-paying and less secure than they were even at the worst of the 1990s' recession.

Source

Abridged from Bruce Little, "The Jobs Are Up but the Quality's Down," *The Globe and Mail*, 11 November 1996, p. A6.

1. Usually total employment and the employment quality index have changed in the same direction. Why?
2. Outline the main reason why total employment and each of the three components of the employment quality index have often moved in opposite directions since 1993.

Chapter Twelve
Economic Fluctuations

It's a recession when your neighbor loses his job; it's a depression when you lose yours.

—Harry Truman, American president

For decades, real output and average living standards in Canada have gradually increased, but the economy rarely grows steadily. Sometimes, production and incomes increase sharply; at other times, they inch up or even fall. Such fluctuations occur in all free-market economies, with occasionally devastating results. During the Great Depression of the 1930s, for example, real output in Canada dropped by over 25 percent, while unemployment soared. In the late 1960s, the opposite happened: an overheated economy led to accelerating inflation, which significantly reduced some Canadians' living standards. More recently, the recession of the early 1990s led to layoffs and plant closings throughout Canada, leaving a legacy of displaced workers and lost production. This chapter analyzes the causes of these types of instability.

CHAPTER FOCUS

This chapter focuses on the following:

- aggregate demand and aggregate supply
- the effect of the general price level on total expenditures and on total output
- aggregate demand factors and aggregate supply factors
- the economy's equilibrium and how it differs from its potential
- injections to and withdrawals from the economy
- the business cycle of expansion and contraction, with its peaks and troughs

AGGREGATE DEMAND

What determines the connections among inflation, unemployment, and levels of spending and real output in the Canadian economy? As in the case of individual markets, the explanation can be given in terms of demand and supply. First, we'll look at how the concept of demand can be applied to the economy as a whole to see the relationship between the general price level and total spending in the economy, which is known as **aggregate demand** (AD).

aggregate demand: the relationship between the general price level and total spending in the economy

Recall that total spending on an economy's goods and services is the sum of four components: consumption, investment, government purchases, and net exports. The primary groups responsible for this spending are households, businesses, governments, and foreigners. Total spending in an economy, adjusted for changes in the general price level, is referred to as **real expenditures**, and is calculated using the GDP price deflator. Suppose, for example, that \$1080 billion in nominal dollars are spent in Canada in a year in which the GDP deflator has a value of 120. Therefore, real expenditures, or total output purchases, equal \$900 billion (\$1080 billion ÷ 1.2) in constant dollars.

real expenditures: total spending in an economy, adjusted for changes in the general price level

Economists attempt to identify the factors that influence real expenditures. One of the most important factors is the price level, since changes in prices cause changes in spending. In other words, not only is price level used to calculate real expenditures, it also affects real expenditures.

The Aggregate Demand Curve

aggregate demand schedule: the relationship between the general price level and total spending in the economy expressed in a table

aggregate demand curve: the relationship between the general price level and total spending in the economy expressed on a graph

Aggregate demand can be expressed in a table known as the **aggregate demand schedule**, or on a graph known as the **aggregate demand curve** (AD). Figure 12.1 shows an aggregate demand schedule and an aggregate demand curve. Just as with a demand curve for a single product, the price variable is placed on the vertical axis of the graph, and the output variable is placed on the horizontal axis.

Recall that price and quantity demanded of a single product almost always have an inverse relationship: as price rises, quantity demanded decreases, and vice versa. The same can be said for the general price level and real expenditures, although for different reasons. Whereas quantity demanded of a certain product is affected by the law of diminishing marginal utility, the amount spent in the entire economy is affected by two entirely different factors: wealth and foreign trade. Note that the response to a change in the price level is a movement along the aggregate demand curve.

Wealth

In Chapter 9, we saw that a household may have wealth in the form of financial assets, as well as real assets. The nominal values of these

FIGURE 12.1
Aggregate Demand

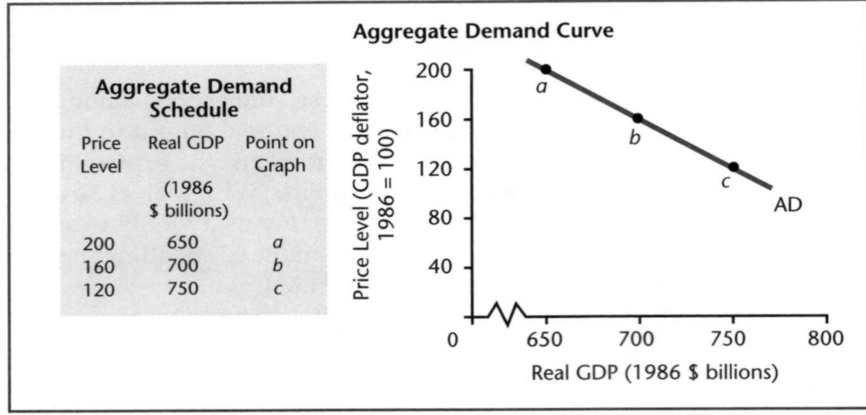

As the general level of prices increases, less real output is bought for two reasons. (1) The real value of financial assets, such as bank accounts and bonds, decreases. As a result, households feel less wealthy, so they reduce their consumption spending. (2) Net export spending is reduced as both foreigners spend less on Canadian exports and Canadian residents spend more on imports.

financial assets—such as bank accounts and retirement savings plans—stay the same no matter what the price level; however, their real values change with any rise or fall in the price level. To find the real value of financial assets, their nominal value must be divided by the price level:

$$\text{Real value of financial assets} = \frac{\text{nominal value of financial assets}}{\text{price level}}$$

When the price level rises, the real value of households' financial assets decreases. Because consumers feel they have less wealth, they spend less on consumption items. As a result of this **wealth effect**, real expenditures drop.

wealth effect: with changes in the price level, the real value of households' financial assets changes, causing households to adjust their spending

Foreign Trade

Changes in the price level also influence foreign trade. When the price level in Canada rises, Canadian exports become more expensive for foreigners. As a result, sales in foreign markets fall, causing a decrease in export expenditures. At the same time, products imported into Canada become cheaper relative to higher-priced domestic products. Therefore, import expenditures by Canadians rise. The **foreign trade effect**—as this combination of effects is known—involves a decrease in net exports (X – M), and thus a decline in real expenditures.

foreign trade effect: with changes in the price level, expenditures on imports change in the same direction, while expenditures on exports change in the opposite direction

CHANGES IN AGGREGATE DEMAND

aggregate demand factors: variables that cause changes in total expenditures at all price levels

increase in aggregate demand: an increase in total expenditures at all price levels

decrease in aggregate demand: a decrease in total expenditures at all price levels

In addition to the price level, other factors can influence total spending. However, these factors, called **aggregate demand factors**, change total spending at all price levels. In other words, they shift the aggregate demand curve. Recall that spending has four components—consumption, investment, government purchases, and net exports. When factors other than price level affect any of these components, they in turn affect total real expenditures.

Suppose, for example, that due to an increase in government purchases, the aggregate demand curve shifts to the right by $50 billion, as shown in Figure 12.2, from AD_0 to AD_1. This change is known as an **increase in aggregate demand**. Similarly, a decrease in another component of real expenditures, such as consumption spending, would cause a decrease in total expenditures. This **decrease in aggregate demand** would be represented by a shift in the aggregate demand curve to the left.

Aggregate demand factors can be categorized by the spending component they immediately affect. As we consider each in turn, we must assume that all other aggregate demand factors and the price level remain constant.

Consumption

Recall that personal consumption and saving are the two uses of disposable income. Thus consumer spending is decided when households determine how much to spend or save. Changes in disposable income, wealth, consumer expectations, and interest rates can all affect consumer spending. With any change in consumer spending, total expenditure changes also, thereby shifting the aggregate demand curve.

FIGURE 12.2
Changes in Aggregate Demand

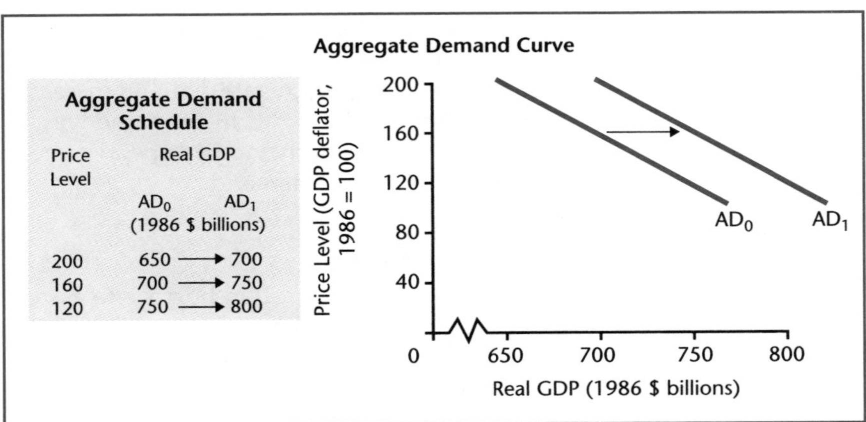

An increase in government purchases causes a $50 billion increase in real expenditures at every price level. Thus, aggregate demand increases, and the AD curve shifts to the right from AD_0 to AD_1.

Disposable Income

The most significant determinant of consumer spending is the level of disposable income (DI) in the entire economy. The economy's total disposable income may change as a result of changes in population or changes in disposable income per household. Higher income taxes, for example, decrease household disposable income. Disposable income and consumer spending have a direct relationship. So, when disposable income rises, there is a rise in consumer spending, thereby adding to total expenditures and shifting the aggregate demand curve to the right.

Wealth

In Chapter 9, we learned that wealth and income are quite different. Whereas income consists of earnings received over time, wealth is made up of financial and real assets. Real assets (such as houses and appliances) and financial assets (such as stocks and bonds) are measured at a particular point in time. We've already considered the wealth effect—the effect of the price level on the value of wealth, which then influences consumer spending. Factors other than price level can affect wealth, however, and in turn affect consumer spending. For example, if stock prices jump, households owning stocks enjoy increased wealth; as a result, these households will likely spend more of their disposable income. Aggregate demand will increase and the aggregate demand curve will shift to the right. Conversely, an increase in consumer debt means that households lose wealth. Households reduce their spending as a result, and aggregate demand decreases.

Consumer Expectations

As we saw in Chapter 2, consumer expectations influence the demand for a single product. Similarly, these expectations can affect aggregate demand by changing general consumption patterns. If consumers expect prices to rise—for example, because of a calamity such as war or a flood—they will spend more now and save less. As a result of this higher consumer spending, aggregate demand increases, and the aggregate demand curve shifts to the right. In the same way, if consumers expect their incomes to rise soon, they again spend more and save less, causing an increase in aggregate demand.

Interest Rates

Because households often borrow to purchase durable goods, such as cars and furniture, changes in real interest rates can affect their purchasing decisions. If the real interest rate falls, consumers are more likely to borrow in order to buy big-ticket items. Consumer spending rises, and the aggregate demand curve shifts to the right. Conversely, a jump in the real interest rate has the opposite effect: because consumer spending falls, aggregate demand decreases, and the aggregate demand curve shifts to the left.

Investment

The investment component of aggregate demand is limited to planned investment, which excludes unintended changes in inventories. As we saw in Chapter 8, investment represents spending on projects where earning a profit is anticipated.

real rate of return: constant-dollar extra profit provided by a project each year stated as a percentage of the project's initial cost

How does a business decide whether or not to make an investment? The business first calculates all the expected revenues and costs of the project in constant dollars. Then it calculates the project's **real rate of return**, which is the constant-dollar extra profit provided by the project each year stated as a percentage of the project's initial cost. Let's consider our example from earlier chapters, Pure 'n' Simple T-Shirts. As its owner, you are deciding whether to buy a $100 sewing machine, which is expected to last for one year. After its effects on day-to-day operating costs are taken into account, the machine is expected to add $112 in constant dollars to your business's net revenue. The extra profit gained from purchasing the machine is therefore $12 ($112 – $100). Thus, the machine's real rate of return, as a percentage of its $100 price, is 12 percent [($12 ÷ $100) × 100%].

Because most businesses borrow money to finance their investment projects, they will pursue projects for which the return on the project exceeds, or at least equals, the real interest rates they will be charged. In other words, any project is undertaken if its annual benefit is greater than or at least equal to its annual cost.

We've focused on a single business; now let's turn our attention to the entire economy. Suppose that businesses in the economy are considering four possible investment projects. Projects A, B, C, and D each have a cost of $15 billion. However, their real rates of return differ. Project A has a real rate of return of 10 percent, B a rate of 8 percent, C a rate of 6 percent, and D a rate of 4 percent. Figure 12.3 shows the projects' respective profits as rectangles. While each rectangle has the same width, representing the projects' uniform $15 billion cost, the heights differ to reflect the different rates of return.

FIGURE 12.3
Investment Demand

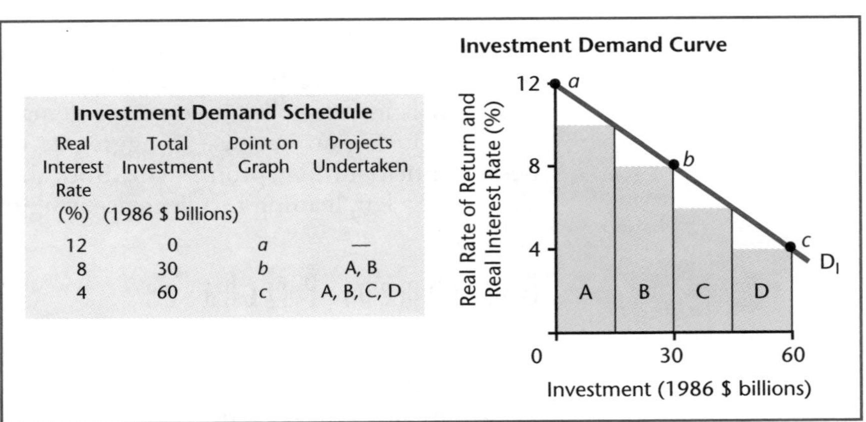

Investment Demand Schedule

Real Interest Rate (%)	Total Investment (1986 $ billions)	Point on Graph	Projects Undertaken
12	0	*a*	—
8	30	*b*	A, B
4	60	*c*	A, B, C, D

As the real interest rate decreases, more investment projects are undertaken. When the interest rate is 8 percent, only Projects A and B are carried out, since their estimated real rates of return are greater or equal. If the interest rate falls to 4 percent, Projects C and D can be pursued as well.

To see how interest rates affect investment in the economy, let's place the real interest rate on Figure 12.3, also on the vertical axis. Recall that only investment projects with a real rate of return equal to or greater than the prevailing real interest rate will be undertaken. So, if the real interest rate is 12 percent, businesses in the economy would not invest in any project since none provides a sufficient real rate of return to cover the cost of borrowing. This is shown as point *a* in Figure 12.3. If the real interest rate falls to 8 percent, businesses in the economy will invest in Projects A and B, as shown by point *b*, because their real rates of return equal or exceed the costs of borrowing. As a result, investment in the economy rises to $30 billion. Finally, if interest rates drop even further, to 4 percent, businesses in the economy will invest in Projects A, B, C, and D, as shown by point *c*, thereby increasing investment in the economy to $60 billion. This relationship between interest rates and investment is known as **investment demand**. Investment demand can be expressed in a table, called the **investment demand schedule**, or on a graph, called the **investment demand curve** (D_I).

investment demand: the relationship between interest rates and investment

investment demand schedule: the relationship between interest rates and investment expressed in a table

investment demand curve: the relationship between interest rates and investment expressed on a graph

Now that we have seen how total investment in the economy is determined, it is easier to recognize the various aggregate demand factors related to investment. A rise in investment causes an increase in aggregate demand, thereby shifting the aggregate demand curve to the right. Conversely, a fall in investment causes a decrease in aggregate demand, thereby shifting the aggregate demand curve to the left. Investment not only changes because of interest rates, as we've seen, but also because of business expectations.

Interest Rates

As shown by the investment demand curve in Figure 12.3, real interest rates and investment have an inverse relationship. Hence, a rise in real interest rates causes a decrease in aggregate demand, and a fall in real interest rates causes an increase in aggregate demand.

Business Expectations

Business expectations—whether optimistic or pessimistic—can affect the position of the investment demand curve. If businesses anticipate that profits will increase, the investment demand curve shifts to the right, thereby causing an increase in aggregate demand. Conversely, if businesses anticipate that profits will drop, the investment demand curve shifts to the left, leading to a decrease in aggregate demand.

Government Purchases

A rise in government purchases—such as highway construction, for example—causes an increase in aggregate demand, while a fall in government purchases causes a decrease in aggregate demand. Recall that this component of spending does not include government transfer payments, such as those discussed in Chapter 9; Old Age Security payments, for example, are classified as negative taxes, which flow *from* rather than *to* governments.

Net Exports

As seen earlier, net exports can vary due to changes in the price level. For example, a drop in the Canadian price level increases net exports, because Canadian exports are cheaper in the rest of the world and imports are made more expensive in Canada. As a result of this foreign trade effect, a change in the price level influences total spending in the economy, which is expressed as a movement along the aggregate demand curve.

Other factors that affect net exports—and that cause a *change* in aggregate demand—include incomes in foreign countries and foreign exchange rates. The effect of changes in these factors is represented by a shift in the aggregate demand curve.

Foreign Incomes

Suppose incomes rise in a foreign country such as France. French citizens will be able to buy more products as a result. Not only will they purchase French products, but also those of other countries. As a result, Canadian net exports to France will likely rise, thereby increasing Canada's aggregate demand. Conversely, a fall in foreign incomes will likely reduce Canadian net exports, thereby decreasing Canada's aggregate demand.

Exchange Rates

exchange rate: the value of one nation's currency in terms of another currency

An **exchange rate** is the value of one nation's currency in terms of another currency. As we will see in more detail in Chapter 16, the value of the Canadian dollar can be expressed in any other currency, but is usually compared to American dollars. So, the exchange rate can show how many American cents are needed to buy one Canadian dollar. A rise in the value of the Canadian dollar—for example, from 75 to 80 cents—means more U.S. currency is needed to purchase Canadian funds. In this example, Canada's currency becomes more expensive for Americans to purchase. At the same time, U.S. currency becomes cheaper for Canadians to purchase, since we get more of it—80 cents as opposed to 75 cents—in exchange for one Canadian dollar.

If the Canadian dollar goes up in value, exports from Canada become more expensive for Americans. So, a product priced at $1 in Canada costs not 75 cents in American funds but 80 cents. At the same time, American products imported into Canada fall in price when expressed in Canadian currency. One Canadian dollar now buys American products with a U.S. price of 80 cents, whereas before the same dollar could buy American products with a U.S. price of only 75 cents.

Because of the impact of exchange rates on prices, net exports fall when the Canadian dollar goes up in value, causing aggregate demand to decrease. A drop in the value of the Canadian dollar has the opposite effect: net exports rise, thereby increasing aggregate demand. The effects of this and other aggregate demand factors are summarized in Figure 12.4.

FIGURE 12.4 Shifts in the Aggregate Demand Curve

Aggregate demand increases and the AD curve shifts to the right, with the following:	*Aggregate demand decreases and the AD curve shifts to the left, with the following:*
(1) An increase in consumption due to (a) a rise in disposable income (b) a rise in wealth unrelated to a change in price level (c) an expected rise in prices or incomes (d) a fall in interest rates	(1) A decrease in consumption due to (a) a fall in disposable income (b) a fall in wealth unrelated to a change in the price level (c) an expected fall in prices or income (d) a rise in interest rates
(2) An increase in investment due to (a) a fall in interest rates (b) an expected rise in profits	(2) A decrease in investment due to (a) a rise in interest rates (b) an expected fall in profits
(3) An increase in government purchases	(3) A decrease in government purchases
(4) An increase in net exports due to (a) a rise in foreign income (b) a fall in value of the Canadian dollar	(4) A decrease in net exports due to (a) a fall in foreign income (b) a rise in the value of the Canadian dollar

Thinking About Economics

Which of the components of aggregate demand is most likely to vary?

While consumption, government purchases, and net exports all vary substantially, investment is the most unstable element in aggregate demand. This is because investment depends so heavily on business expectations, which can be subject to volatile swings as perceptions of the future change.

BRIEF REVIEW

1. Aggregate demand is the relationship between the price level and total spending in the economy. This relationship can be expressed in an aggregate demand schedule or on an aggregate demand curve (AD).
2. Total spending in the economy, adjusted for inflation, is known as real expenditures, and includes the spending of households, businesses, governments, and foreigners.
3. The general price level and total spending in the economy have an inverse relationship, thereby giving the aggregate demand curve a negative slope.
4. Both the wealth effect and the foreign trade effect, which arise from price level changes, cause movements *along* the aggregate demand curve.
5. In contrast, aggregate demand factors cause a change in total spending at all price levels, thereby *shifting* the aggregate demand curve. Anything other than the price level that changes consumption spending, investment, government purchases, or net exports shifts the aggregate demand curve.

AGGREGATE SUPPLY

aggregate supply: the relationship between the general price level and real output produced in the economy

aggregate supply schedule: the relationship between the general price level and real output expressed in a table

aggregate supply curve: the relationship between the general price level and real output expressed on a graph

So far in this chapter, we have focused on the role of spending in the economy. Now, let's turn our attention to the role of production. **Aggregate supply** is the relationship between the general price level and real output produced in the economy. Figure 12.5 shows aggregate supply expressed in a table, called the **aggregate supply schedule**, and on a graph, called the **aggregate supply curve** (AS).

The Aggregate Supply Curve

As Figure 12.5 shows, price level and real output are directly related, giving the aggregate supply curve a positive slope. At higher price levels in the economy, businesses are encouraged to produce more; at lower price levels, businesses may not be able to make a profit or break even in the short run, so they reduce output. Variations in an economy's output caused by changes in the price level result in movements *along* the aggregate supply curve.

Recall from Chapter 11 that unemployment reduces real output from what it could be. If full employment were achieved—in other words, if only natural unemployment occurred—the economy would reach its potential output. If, as sometimes happens, the unemployment rate temporarily falls below the natural unemployment rate, real output rises temporarily above potential output.

Let's consider the hypothetical example in Figure 12.5. Potential output—the real output associated with full employment—has a value of $725 billion. The real output level, as shown by the aggregate supply curve (AS), is much lower than its potential at point *a*, but greater than

FIGURE 12.5
Aggregate Supply

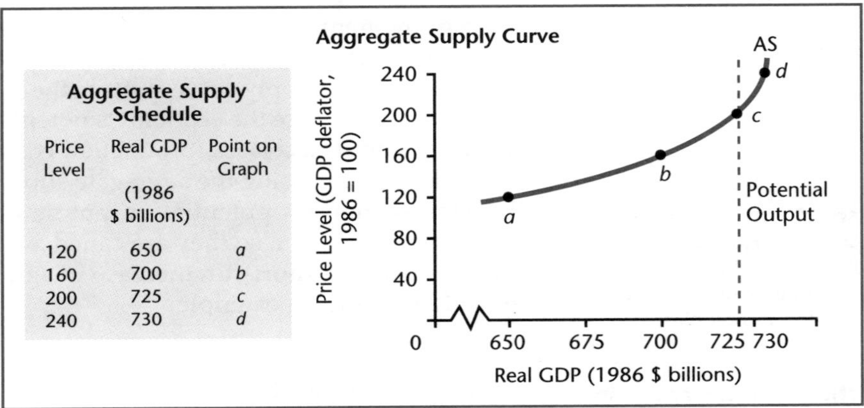

Aggregate Supply Schedule

Price Level	Real GDP (1986 $ billions)	Point on Graph
120	650	*a*
160	700	*b*
200	725	*c*
240	730	*d*

Businesses respond to increasing prices by producing more real output. At low output levels (such as point *a*), businesses produce significantly below capacity and the AS curve is relatively flat. As output increases above the potential output level of $725 billion (point *c*), businesses produce above their normal capacity and the AS curve is steep.

the potential output at point *d*. Notice that, above the potential output level, the aggregate supply curve becomes very steep. This shows that businesses are producing above their normal capacity, which is possible in the short run only if businesses employ overtime labour and temporarily rent new machinery. These temporary measures mean that any expansion in real output—for example, from $725 billion (point *c*) to $730 billion (point *d*)—requires a relatively large increase in the price level to cover businesses' additional per-unit costs. Conversely, at real output levels below the potential output, the production capacity of businesses is underutilized, with some labour and capital equipment either working part-time or sitting idle. A rise in real output, as from $650 billion (point *a*) to $700 billion (point *b*), can be made with a relatively small increase in the price level to cover additional per-unit costs.

CHANGES IN AGGREGATE SUPPLY

aggregate supply factors: variables that change total output at all price levels

Of course, other factors in addition to the price level can influence real output. However, these factors, known as **aggregate supply factors**, change real output at *all* price levels. In other words, they *shift* the aggregate supply curve. Once again, as we examine each in turn, we must assume that all other aggregate supply factors and the price level remain constant.

Input Prices

Aggregate supply assumes steady input prices for the businesses that are producing the output. Changes in input prices—an increase in wages, for example, or decreased prices for imported raw materials due to a rise in the value of the Canadian dollar—alter production costs. These changes can occur frequently over brief periods of time. When a rise in the price of an input pushes up production costs, businesses reduce their real output and the aggregate supply curve shifts to the left. Note, however, that nothing happens to change the economy's potential output. Conversely, if the price of an input decreases, production costs fall. Businesses then raise their real output, causing the aggregate supply curve to shift to the right, while the economy's potential output stays the same. These changes apply to the short run, so they are called a **short-run decrease in aggregate supply** and a **short-run increase in aggregate supply**, respectively. Figure 12.6 shows an example.

short-run increase in aggregate supply: an increase in total output at all price levels, with no change in potential output

short-run decrease in aggregate supply: a decrease in total output at all price levels, with no change in potential output

Resource Supplies

Over the long term, supplies of resources in an economy—especially human and capital resources—tend to grow. With any such increase, businesses produce more real output at every price level. In other words, more inputs over the long run increase aggregate supply, as well as the economy's potential output. Figure 12.7 shows the outcome—

FIGURE 12.6
A Short-Run Change in Aggregate Supply

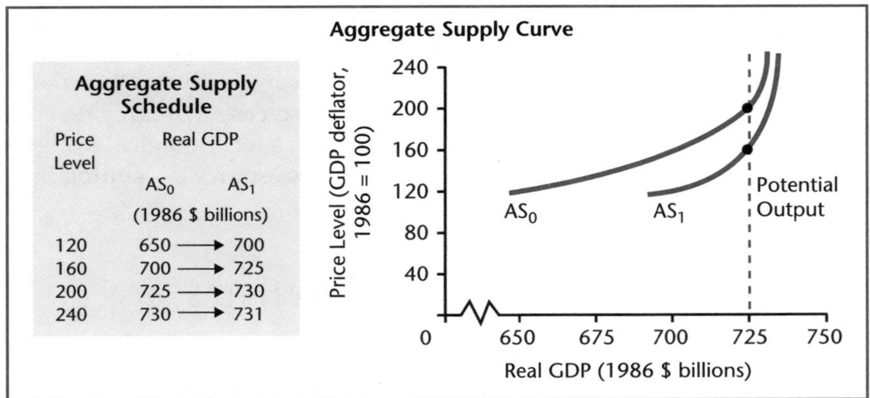
Aggregate Supply Schedule

Price Level	Real GDP AS_0 (1986 $ billions)		Real GDP AS_1 (1986 $ billions)
120	650	⟶	700
160	700	⟶	725
200	725	⟶	730
240	730	⟶	731

A drop in the wage rate results in an increase in real output at every price level, from AS_0 to AS_1. The movement is greatest at low price levels where substantial excess capacity exists. Because a decrease in wages does not affect long-run production trends, potential output stays constant at $725 billion.

long-run increase in aggregate supply: an increase in total and potential output at all price levels

long-run decrease in aggregate supply: a decrease in total and potential output at all price levels

a **long-run increase in aggregate supply**. The reverse is also possible. With a long-run reduction in the amounts of any resource, businesses will produce lower real output at all prices, thereby causing a **long-run decrease in aggregate supply**, which is accompanied by a reduction in the economy's potential output.

Productivity

Recall that productivity is the real output produced per unit of input over a given period of time. In particular, labour productivity is found by dividing a nation's real output by the total number of hours worked by its labour force:

$$\text{Labour productivity} = \frac{\text{real output}}{\text{total hours worked}}$$

FIGURE 12.7
A Long-Run Change in Aggregate Supply

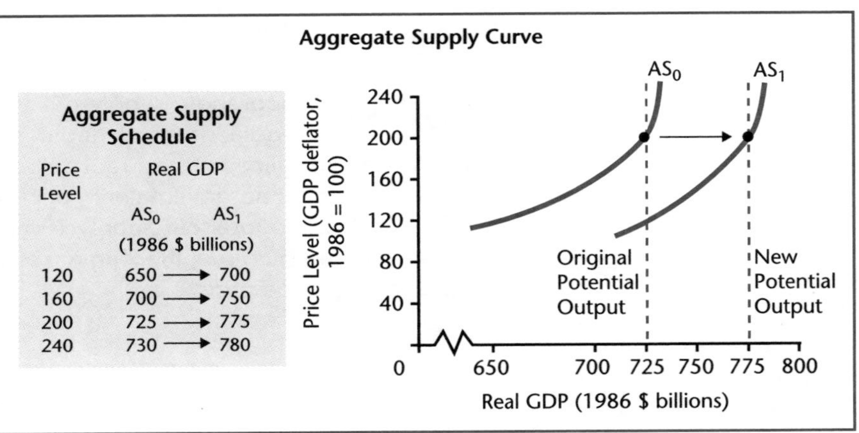
Aggregate Supply Schedule

Price Level	Real GDP AS_0 (1986 $ billions)		Real GDP AS_1 (1986 $ billions)
120	650	⟶	700
160	700	⟶	750
200	725	⟶	775
240	730	⟶	780

An increase in a country's supplies of economic resources causes both aggregate supply and potential output to increase, thereby shifting the AS curve from AS_0 to AS_1, and the potential output from $725 billion to $775 billion.

Increases in productivity are due largely to technological progress. A technological innovation raises productivity when the same amount of economic resources can produce more real output at every price level, causing a long-run increase in aggregate supply similar to that shown in Figure 12.7. Likewise, a technological decline reduces the real output produced with the same resources, resulting in a long-run decrease in aggregate supply.

Government Policies

Government policies can also influence aggregate supply through their effects on the business environment in an economy. For example, suppose that taxes rise for businesses and households. Because the after-tax returns on supplying economic resources are reduced, businesses and households may reduce the resources they supply at every price level. As a result, real output falls, causing a long-run decrease in aggregate supply. Conversely, lower taxes may encourage businesses and households to increase their supply of economic resources, leading to a rise in real output and a long-run increase in aggregate supply.

Government regulations, such as environmental and safety standards, typically raise per-unit costs for businesses. Hence, more regulation causes businesses to produce less real output at every price level, causing a long-run decrease in aggregate supply. Similarly, less regulation stimulates production, leading to a long-run increase in aggregate supply. The effects of these and other aggregate supply factors are summarized in Figure 12.8.

Thinking About Economics

How important are changes in aggregate supply in relation to changes in aggregate demand?

As a rule, production adjusts less rapidly than does spending. Therefore, changes in aggregate supply are usually slower to occur than changes in aggregate demand. Input prices, which may change quickly, often take time to affect real output. Changes in resource supplies, technology, and government policies tend to occur even more gradually. While aggregate supply is more stable than aggregate demand over the short run, the long-run effect of aggregate supply on the economy can be profound.

FIGURE 12.8 Shifts in the Aggregate Supply Curve

Aggregate supply increases, with the AS curve shifting to the right, and potential output staying the same with the following:	*Aggregate supply decreases, with the AS curve shifting to the left, and potential output staying the same with the following:*
(1) A decrease in input prices due to (a) a fall in wages (b) a fall in raw material prices	(1) An increase in input prices due to (a) a rise in wages (b) a rise in raw material prices
Aggregate supply increases, with the AS curve shifting to the right, and potential output increasing with the following	*Aggregate supply decreases, with the AS curve shifting to the left, and potential output decreasing with the following*
(2) An increase in supplies of economic resources due to (a) more labour supply (b) more capital stock (c) more land (d) more entrepreneurship	(2) A decrease in supplies of economic resources due to (a) less labour supply (b) less capital stock (c) less land (d) less entrepreneurship
(3) An increase in productivity due to technological progress	(3) A decrease in productivity due to technological decline
(4) A change in government policies: (a) lower taxes (b) less government regulation	(4) A change in government policies: (a) higher taxes (b) more government regulation

BRIEF REVIEW

1. Aggregate supply is the relationship between the price level and real output produced in the economy. This relationship can be expressed in an aggregate supply schedule or on an aggregate supply curve (AS).
2. Because higher prices encourage increased real output and vice versa, the price level and real output have a direct relationship, thereby giving the aggregate supply curve a positive slope.
3. Since real output may not reflect full use of all resources—for example, labour—an economy may not reach its potential output.
4. While changes in the price level cause movement *along* the aggregate supply curve, aggregate supply factors—changes in input prices, supplies of economic resources, productivity, and government policies—*shift* the curve and so change real output of an economy and aggregate supply.
5. Short-run changes in aggregate supply, caused by varying input prices, do not change an economy's potential output. However, long-run changes in aggregate supply do change an economy's potential output in the same direction.

EQUILIBRIUM

Aggregate Demand and Supply

So far, we've been looking at aggregate demand and aggregate supply separately. Now we'll consider them together. What happens if real output at a certain price level exceeds real expenditures? Alternatively, what happens if real output at a certain price level falls short of what participants in the economy wish to spend? Figure 12.9 presents answers to these questions. As with demand and supply in a competitive market for an individual product, the forces underlying aggregate demand and aggregate supply push the economy to an equilibrium point. An economy's equilibrium price level and real output occur at the intersection of the aggregate demand and aggregate supply curves.

Inventory Changes

Unintended changes in inventories cause price levels and real outputs to reach equilibrium. We'll look at the two possibilities: the results of an inventory increase and of an inventory decrease.

Results of an Inventory Increase

positive unplanned investment: an unintended increase in inventories; a surplus

Suppose the general price level is above the equilibrium price level, at 200 (points *a*). At this price level, real output exceeds real expenditures, meaning that more is produced than is purchased in the economy. Businesses have an unintended increase in inventories—in other words, a surplus—which represents **positive unplanned investment**. As a result of this surplus, prices of individual products decrease, pushing down the general price level.

The general decrease in prices influences both households and businesses. Because of the wealth and foreign trade effects, the response of buyers is to increase spending. So, real expenditures in our example increase toward point *b*. Meanwhile, lower prices cause businesses to decrease real output, and, since real output and unemployment are inversely related, this causes a rise in the unemployment rate. These trends continue until real output and real expenditures are equal at the equilibrium point (point *b*).

Results of an Inventory Decrease

negative unplanned investment: an unintended decrease in inventories; a shortage

Suppose, on the other hand, that the price level is below its equilibrium value, at 120 (points *c*). Expenditures exceed production, creating a shortage. This leads to an unintended decrease in inventories, known as a **negative unplanned investment**. Because particular products are in short supply, prices rise. The response of buyers is to decrease spending. Meanwhile, the higher price level causes businesses to raise real output, causing unemployment to fall. These trends continue until real output and real expenditures are equal at the equilibrium point (point *b*).

FIGURE 12.9
An Economy in Equilibrium

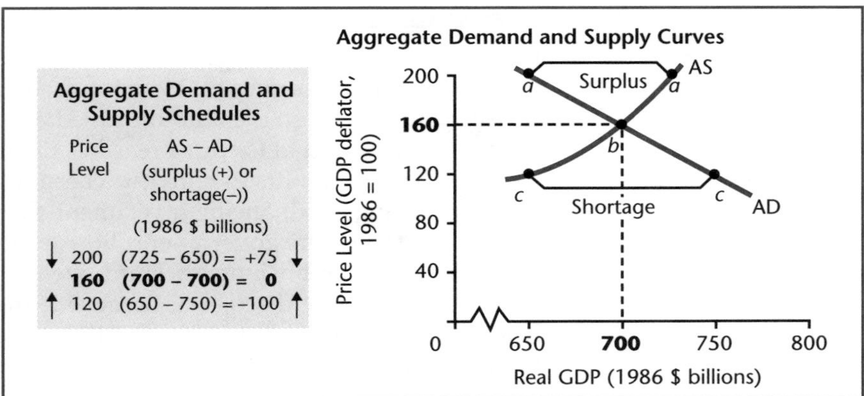

If the price level, at points *a*, is above its equilibrium level of 160, real output exceeds expenditures. An unintended rise in inventories causes businesses to lower prices until output and expenditures are the same, at $700 billion (point *b*). When the price level is below its equilibrium value (points *c*), there is an unintended fall in inventories. Businesses increase prices until equilibrium is reached (point *b*).

The Role of Unplanned Investment

Notice that, in the case of either an unintended increase or decrease in inventories, unplanned investment plays a central role in stabilizing the economy. Unplanned investment is positive when the price level is above its equilibrium value and negative when the price level is below its equilibrium value, and in each case unplanned investment is identical to the discrepancy between aggregate demand and aggregate supply.

This is illustrated by the aggregate demand and supply schedules in Figure 12.9. The $75 billion discrepancy between aggregate demand and aggregate supply at a price level of 200 means there is an unintended increase in inventories of $75 billion. Hence, there is unplanned investment of $75 billion. Likewise, the shortage of $100 billion that appears at the 120 price level translates into an unintended $100 billion drop in inventories. Unplanned investment is therefore –$100 billion.

Injections and Withdrawals

injections: additions to an economy's income-spending stream

withdrawals: deductions from an economy's income-spending stream

The tendency of an economy to move toward equilibrium can also be outlined by looking at the flows of income payments and purchases that connect resource and product markets. There are three flows, known as **injections**, that add to the main income-spending stream: investment (I), government purchases (G), and exports (X). Corresponding to these injections are three outward flows of funds, known as **withdrawals**. Withdrawals, which divert funds from the income-spending stream, are saving (S), taxes (T), and imports (M).

There is no need for these individual injections and withdrawals to be equal. Even those injections and withdrawals related to the same sector can have different values. To see why, we'll look at each related pair of injections and withdrawals in turn.

Investment and Saving

Recall that personal savings from households provide the bulk of funds in the loanable funds market. Most funds are borrowed by businesses for investment. However, the amount saved and the amount invested in an economy are not equal for three reasons. First, recall that companies keep a portion of their profits to reinvest. These retained earnings supplement personal savings in financing investment. Second, governments also borrow money. The more governments borrow, the less personal savings end up in the hands of businesses. Third, we must also consider the foreign flows we've already discussed. Because lending by the rest of the world has usually exceeded borrowing by the rest of the world, foreign funds have typically added to Canadian savings available for investment.

Government Purchases and Taxes

Recall that transfer payments and business subsidies are viewed as negative taxes. Government purchases usually exceed taxes. To make up for the discrepancy, governments borrow funds in financial markets. In the less likely case that taxes exceed government purchases, governments can use their excess revenues to pay off some of their outstanding debt.

Exports and Imports

In the past, Canada's imports of both goods *and* services have typically been greater than its exports. In other words, Canadians spent more on products from the rest of the world than they received in revenues from selling products to the rest of the world. At the same time, foreign lenders have typically provided funds to Canadian financial markets, with lending by foreigners being greater than borrowing by foreigners. So, the surplus of lending by foreigners has helped make up for the shortfall in net exports. We will explore this subject further in Chapter 16.

Total Injections and Withdrawals

While individual injections and withdrawals are not necessarily equal, there is an important connection between them that applies when an economy is at equilibrium. If the circular income-spending stream is thought of as a flow of water—a water-ride at an amusement park, for example—then it is easy to see what will happen if the amount of water flowing into this stream is more or less than the water flowing out. If inward flows exceed outward flows, the amount of water circulating in the stream must be increasing. Conversely, if inward flows are less than outward flows, the amount of water must be decreasing. Only if inward and outward flows are equal will the water-ride function well. Viewed in this way, comparing total injections and withdrawals provides a way of explaining macroeconomic equilibrium that complements the approach using aggregate demand and aggregate supply.

Total injections are the sum of investment, government purchases, and exports (I + G + X). Total withdrawals are the sum of saving, taxes, and imports (S + T + M). Just as only the planned portion of investment is included in real expenditures to find aggregate demand, only planned investment is included in total injections.

Total injections (I + G + X) and total withdrawals (S + T + M) may be equal or unequal. When total injections exceed total withdrawals, flows into the income-spending stream are greater than flows out. Hence, the income-spending stream rises and speeds up. In other words, real output and spending in the economy expand. On the other hand, if total withdrawals exceed total injections, flows into the income-spending stream are less than outflows. Hence, the income-spending stream falls and slows down. In other words, real output and spending in the economy contract. Finally, in the case of equilibrium total injections equal total withdrawals. Because inward and outward flows match, the income-spending stream circulates at a steady rate, so that real output and spending in the economy stay constant.

Equilibrium Versus Potential Output

An economy's equilibrium point can occur at its potential output, as illustrated in Figure 12.10. If so, then unemployment at equilibrium equals the natural unemployment rate.

Recessionary Gaps

While the situation shown in Figure 12.10 is possible, an economy's real output rarely equals its potential output. If equilibrium output is below its potential level, unemployment is above the natural unemployment rate. In this case, the difference between equilibrium output and potential output is known as a **recessionary gap**. Figure 12.11 shows on the left an economy with a recessionary gap of $25 billion. This is the amount by which real output would have to increase from its equilibrium value of $700 billion in order to attain its potential level of $725 billion.

recessionary gap: the amount by which equilibrium output falls short of potential output

FIGURE 12.10
An Economy at Its Potential Output

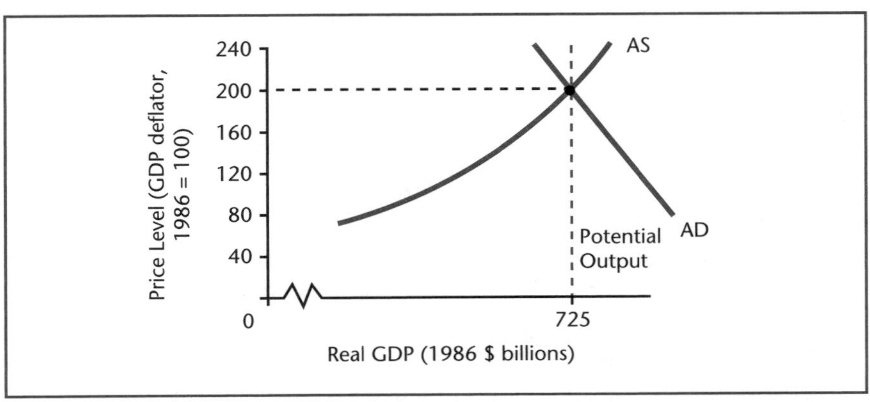

It is possible for equilibrium to occur at the economy's potential output. In this case, actual unemployment equals the natural unemployment rate.

Inflationary Gaps

inflationary gap: the amount by which equilibrium output exceeds potential output

If equilibrium output is above its potential output, unemployment is temporarily below the natural unemployment rate. Inflation will accelerate if this situation persists. When equilibrium output exceeds potential output, therefore, the discrepancy is called an **inflationary gap**. Figure 12.11 shows on the right an economy with an inflationary gap of $5 billion. In this case, the equilibrium output of $730 would have to fall by $5 billion to achieve the potential output of $725 billion.

A recession differs from the notion of a recessionary gap. During a recession, real output moves from above to below its potential level, with an inflationary gap transformed into a recessionary gap. On the other hand, a recessionary gap occurs whenever real output is below its potential level—in the latter stage of a recession as well as the first stage of an expansion or recovery.

FIGURE 12.11
Recessionary and Inflationary Gaps

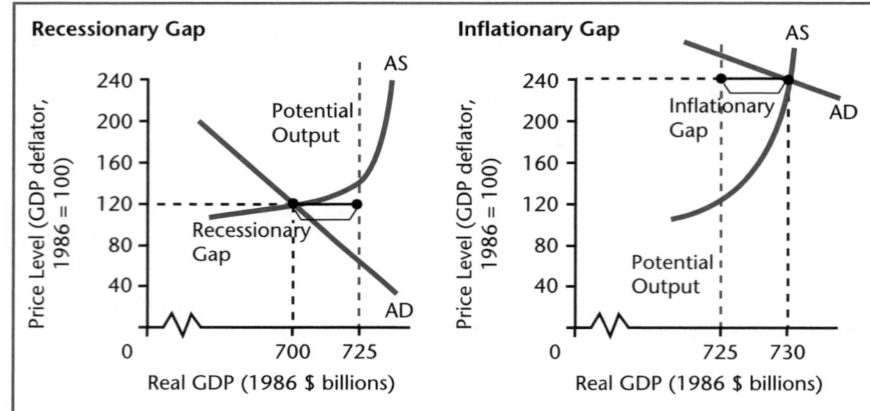

When real output falls short of potential output, the difference between the two is a recessionary gap, as shown on the left. In contrast, when real output temporarily exceeds its potential level, the difference between the two is an inflationary gap, as shown on the right.

BRIEF REVIEW

1. An economy's equilibrium price level and real output occur at the intersection of the aggregate demand and aggregate supply curves.
2. The economy moves toward equilibrium through the workings of positive and negative unplanned investment—in other words, surpluses and shortages.
3. When an economy is at equilibrium, total injections (I + G + X) equal total withdrawals (S + T + M). If total injections exceed total withdrawals, real output rises and the economy expands. If the reverse is true, real output falls and the economy contracts.
4. If equilibrium output is less than potential output, the difference between the two is a recessionary gap. When equilibrium output exceeds potential output, the discrepancy in the output levels is an inflationary gap.

BUSINESS CYCLES

expansion: a sustained rise in real output of an economy

contraction: a sustained fall in real output of an economy

business cycle: the cycle of expansions and contractions in the economy

Recessionary and inflationary gaps do not happen at random. Instead, they occur in a sequence based on fluctuations in real output and expenditures. As a rule, a sustained rise in real output, known as a period of **expansion** or recovery, is followed by an extended period of falling real output, known as a **contraction**. These rises and falls in real output constitute a pattern known as the **business cycle**.

Figure 12.12 shows the business cycle in simplified form. The long-run trend of potential output to rise is shown by a dashed line. Actual output moves toward and away from this potential output in a cycle of successive contractions and expansions.

Actual Versus Potential Output

When actual output exceeds potential output, the resulting inflationary gap is the difference between real output (point *a*) and potential output (point *b*). Real output then falls below its potential level shown by the trend line. In this case, the recessionary gap is the amount by which real output falls short of its potential—in other words, the difference between potential output (point *c*) and real output (point *d*).

Contraction

peak: the point in the business cycle at which real output is at its highest

Consider the case of an economy that has reached its **peak**. At this point (point *a*), the economy is said to be experiencing a boom, which occurs when real GDP is at its highest value in the business cycle. The inflationary gap has reached its maximum width, unemployment is at its lowest

FIGURE 12.12
The Business Cycle

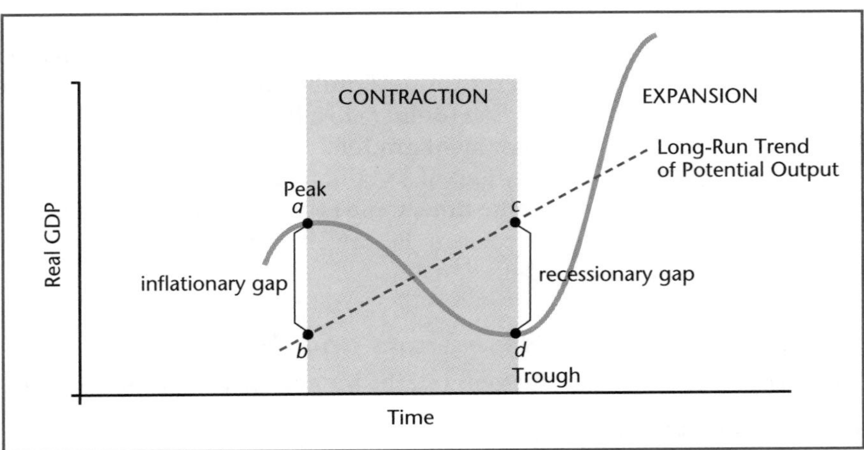

Real GDP rises and falls in a cycle of expansion and contraction. These fluctuations can be compared with a trend line that represents long-run growth potential. The distance between actual output and the trend line represents the size of either the economy's inflationary gap (as in the case of points *a* and *b*) or the economy's recessionary gap (as in the case of points *c* and *d*).

possible level, and real output can grow no larger in the short run. From this point, the economy must contract.

The Role of Expectations

Any decrease in aggregate demand can be magnified by the reactions of both households and businesses to initial reductions in spending and output. To understand how this occurs, recall that spending by both households and businesses is influenced by expectations of the future. Households vary consumption expenditures depending on their anticipation of future prices and incomes, while businesses decide how much to invest based on estimates of future profit.

Expectations of the future are often made simply by extending current trends. Sometimes this can create a self-fulfilling prophecy. That is, if the economy is experiencing reductions in real output and spending, then many households and businesses assume that income and spending will drop further. As a result, there will likely be decreases in three types of spending: consumption, investment, and exports. The prospect of lower future incomes causes households to spend less, especially on durable items. Similarly, the decline in spending that businesses expect causes a drop in real rates of return for investment projects, leading to further declines in investment. The effect on exports occurs because periods of contraction usually arrive in various countries simultaneously. Therefore, it is probable that foreign consumers and businesses are reacting in the same way as their domestic counterparts, thus reducing exports. In other words, the expectations of businesses and households create a downward spiral in which declines in real output lead to further declines in spending and in output. Enough pessimism creates the very economic conditions people fear.

Effects of a Contraction

Figure 12.13 shows the effects of a decrease in aggregate demand from AD_0 to AD_1. Equilibrium output declines from its initial value of $730 billion (point *f*) to a final value of $700 billion (point *e*). As a result, unemployment gradually rises above its natural rate, with the initial inflationary gap of $5 billion turning into a recessionary gap of $25 billion. At the same time, there is downward pressure on prices. If inflation is originally zero, as in Figure 12.13, then the price level falls from 240 to 160, causing deflation.

recession: a decline in real output that lasts for six months or more

depression: a particularly long and harsh period of reduced real output

Recessions and Depressions

In general, the longer the period of declining real output, the more serious its effects. A decline in real output that lasts for six months or more is known as a **recession**. A **depression** occurs if the reduction in real output is particularly long and harsh, as happened during the early 1930s.

FIGURE 12.13
Expansion and Contraction

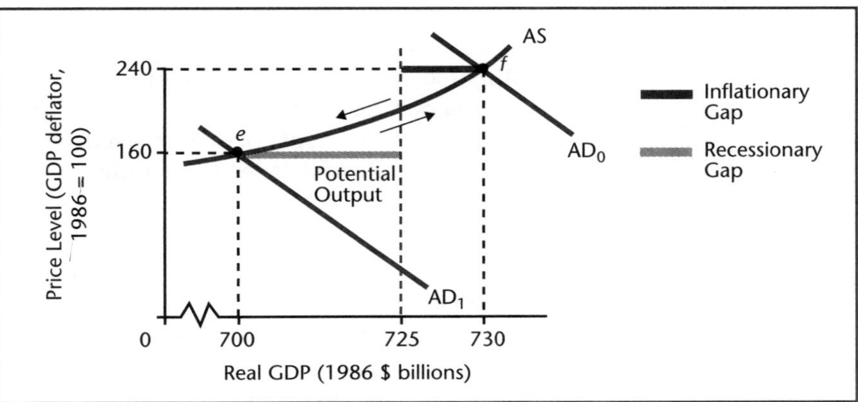

Periods of contraction lead to a decrease in aggregate demand, shifting the curve from AD_0 to AD_1. This leads to a fall in equilibrium output from $730 to $700 billion (points *f* to *e*). As a result, the initial inflationary gap of $5 billion turns into a recessionary gap of $25 billion. Periods of expansion reverse the change, causing the curve to shift from AD_1 to AD_0, and increasing equilibrium output (points *e* to *f*).

Expansion

trough: the point in the business cycle at which real output is at its lowest

The spiral of worsening expectations and declining real output does not last indefinitely. Sooner or later, the economy reaches a **trough** where real output is at its lowest possible value in the business cycle. In Figure 12.12, this occurs at point *d*. At this point, not only is the economy's recessionary gap at its widest, but unemployment is at its highest level. After this turning point, the dampening effect of expectations is counteracted by other factors, and the economy enters a phase of expansion.

Thinking About Economics

Which sectors of the economy are most affected by a downturn?

While a recession or a depression is felt in every sector, those industries that make capital goods or durable consumer goods, such as automobiles and appliances, are hardest hit. This is because purchases of these products can be postponed until after the downturn has ended. In contrast, producers of nondurable consumption items—especially necessities such as food and utilities—are less affected by the downturn. Households can reduce their spending on nondurable products, but they cannot postpone these purchases.

The Role of Expectations

As in periods of contraction, expectations play a role in maintaining a recovery. Initial increases in real output and spending lead to optimistic forecasts of continuing growth. Therefore, consumption, investment, and exports all increase. Consumers react to the prospect of higher incomes by spending more, especially on durable goods. At the same time, businesses increase their investment because optimism causes further rises in estimated real rates of return. Finally, in the case where other countries are experiencing similar trends, foreign buyers also increase their spending and buy more exports. Increased consumer spending, business investment, and exports lead to continual increases in aggregate demand, until a new peak is reached and the stage is set for another period of contraction.

Effects of an Expansion

Figure 12.13 also shows the effects of an expansion. In this case, the aggregate demand curve shifts to the right, from AD_1 to AD_0. Because of the rise in equilibrium output, the original recessionary gap is turned into an inflationary gap. Corresponding to this movement, the unemployment rate goes from above to below its natural rate, while the accompanying rise in the general price level causes inflation.

BRIEF REVIEW

1. Real output rarely equals potential output. Instead, output and expenditures generally follow a cycle of expansions and contractions, which together make up the business cycle.
2. The highest output occurs at a peak in the business cycle. From this point, the economy must contract, so aggregate demand decreases. Consumer and business expectations magnify the downward trend.
3. The lowest output occurs in a trough in a business cycle. From this point, the economy must expand, so aggregate demand increases. Again, expectations magnify the upward trend.

KEY CONCEPTS

aggregate demand
real expenditures
aggregate demand schedule
aggregate demand curve
wealth effect
foreign trade effect
aggregate demand factors
increase in aggregate demand
decrease in aggregate demand
real rate of return
investment demand
investment demand schedule
investment demand curve
exchange rate
aggregate supply
aggregate supply schedule
aggregate supply curve
aggregate supply factors
short-run increase in aggregate supply
short-run decrease in aggregate supply
long-run increase in aggregate supply
long-run decrease in aggregate supply
positive unplanned investment
negative unplanned investment
injections
withdrawals
recessionary gap
inflationary gap
expansion
contraction
business cycle
peak
recession
depression
trough

ANALYSIS AND APPLICATION

1. In a hypothetical economy, 100 investment projects worth $1 million each are undertaken when the real interest rate is 11%, and 50 more projects worth $1 million each are undertaken every time the real interest rate falls by 2%.
   a. Based on this information, construct a table showing the investment demand schedule.
   b. Draw a graph showing the investment demand curve.
   c. How much investment will be undertaken in this economy if the real interest rate is 5%? Explain.

2. Identify the impact of each of the following trends on aggregate demand. In each case, draw a graph to show the effect on the aggregate demand curve, as well as on the equilibrium price level and real output.
   a. consumers become more confident about the prospects for output growth in the Canadian economy
   b. Canadian interest rates rise
   c. political pressure causes an increase in tax rates on households earning high incomes
   d. a newly elected federal government increases its purchases of goods and services
   e. the U.S. economy experiences a boom
   f. the Canadian dollar falls in value against the U.S. dollar

3. Identify the impact of each of the following trends on aggregate supply. In each case, draw a graph to show the effect on the aggregate supply curve, as well as on the equilibrium price level and real output.
   a. Canadian workers receive higher wages
   b. a cheap new source of energy raises labour productivity in the Canadian economy
   c. the federal government reduces corporate income tax rates
   d. due to a global environmental crisis, there is a reduction in the amount of available land
   e. the price of oil decreases
   f. the Canadian dollar rises in value against the U.S. dollar

Hypothetical Aggregate Demand and Aggregate Supply Schedules

Price Level (1986=100)	Real GDP AD_0	AD_1	AS_0	AS_1
		(1986 $ billions)		
140	200	160	270	310
130	220	180	260	300
120	240	200	240	280
110	260	220	220	260
100	280	240	180	220

4. The table above shows aggregate demand and aggregate supply schedules in a hypothetical economy.
   a. Draw a graph to identify the equilibrium price level and real output in this economy, if the relevant schedules are AD_0 and AS_0.
   b. With AD_0 and AS_0 as the relevant schedules, what happens if the price level is 140? 110?
   c. Draw a new graph to show the effects on equilibrium if aggregate demand shifts from AD_0 to AD_1 while aggregate supply remains at AS_0. Describe this change in aggregate demand and outline two possible trends that could have caused the change.
   d. On the same graph you have drawn in part c., show the effects on equilibrium if aggregate supply shifts from AS_0 to AS_1 while aggregate demand remains at AD_0. Describe this change in aggregate supply and outline two possible trends that could have caused the change.

5. Outline how a fall in injections will affect the income-spending stream and equilibrium real output. Discuss how the same result can be found using aggregate demand and aggregate supply.

6. "Over time, long-run changes in aggregate supply are the key determinants of changes in real output." Evaluate this statement using evidence from the chapter.

7. Why does a $100 million decrease in aggregate demand have a greater impact on real output when the economy is below its potential output than when it is above it potential output?

Year	Annual Percentage Change in Real GDP (1986 $)
1981	3.7
1982	−3.2
1983	3.2
1984	6.3
1985	4.8
1986	3.3
1987	4.2
1988	5.0
1989	2.4
1990	−0.2
1991	−1.8
1992	0.8
1993	2.2
1994	4.1
1995	2.3
1996	1.5

Source: Statistics Canada, *Canadian Economic Observer, Statistical Summary* (May 1997), cat. no. 11-010, p. 4, *Canadian Economic Observer, Historical Statistical Supplement*, 1995/6 (July 1996), cat. no. 11-210, vol. 7, p. 7. Reproduced by authority of the Minister of Industry, 1997.

8. Study the table above. Identify the following and give support for your answer:
   - years in which the economy expanded
   - years in which the economy contracted
   - peaks
   - troughs

9. Predict how each of the following will tend to move during (i) economic expansions, and (ii) economic contractions.
   a. consumption of durable goods
   b. consumption of nondurable items
   c. planned investment
   d. exports
   e. imports
   f. wage rates
   g. unplanned investment

10. Give examples of industries that will perform well during (i) contractions, and (ii) expansions.

11. (Advanced Question)
    Discuss how changes in the following variables could affect aggregate demand in order to reduce (i) an inflationary gap, or (ii) a recessionary gap:
    a. government purchases
    b. personal and corporate tax rates
    c. interest rates
    d. the Canadian dollar's value in U.S. dollars

12. Access Statistics Canada's website (at http://www.statcan.ca/) and use the links in "Canadian Dimensions" to find the base-year values for GDP, C, I (leaving out investment in inventories), G, and (X-M) during the four most recent years available.
    a. Compute annual percentage rates of change for each of these variables.
    b. Based on your answers to a., discuss how each of the four components of aggregate demand tend to move in relation to total real expenditures.

Advancing Economic Thought

ECONOMIST EXTRAORDINAIRE

John Maynard Keynes and the Transformation of Macroeconomics

Keynes and His Influence

The best blueprint for a model economist comes from the century's most illustrious one—John Maynard Keynes (1883–1946). An Englishman, he was a well-rounded and energetic individual who wrote on mathematics, formulated economic policy as an adviser to the British government and a director of its central bank, and served as a representative at international conferences, such as the Paris Peace Conference that ended World War I. On top of all of this, Keynes found time to be a college administrator, edit a major economics journal, produce theatre, chair an insurance company, and serve as an investment trust manager, while accumulating a considerable personal fortune through his own investments.[1]

Keynes came from a privileged background—his father was an economist and his mother was a city politician. After a time at the exclusive boarding school Eton, Keynes studied mathematics at Cambridge University, where he began a lifelong association with the Bloomsbury Group, an influential circle of English writers and artists with a shared taste for the unconventional and a reputation for snobbery.

John Maynard Keynes
Source: The Bettmann Archive

In response to the Great Depression plaguing North America and Europe, Keynes published his book *The General Theory of Employment, Interest, and Money*. By 1936, when the book was published, millions of jobless people had given up hope of finding work, and capitalism seemed to many to be on the verge of self-destruction, just as Karl Marx had predicted decades earlier. There was a widespread call for government intervention to combat the Depression. Keynes, however, went one step further: he supported the call for government intervention with a coherent theory, which stressed the role played by aggregate demand in determining output in the macroeconomy.

Keynes and his followers were able to convince most politicians and economists that action was needed. The government programs they advocated were later viewed as crucial in hastening the end of the Depression. Keynesian ideas dominated macroeconomics from after World War II to the 1970s, when events brought about a new period of questioning and debate.

Neoclassical Theory

Prior to Keynes' influence, most economists held the opinion that economic slowdowns—even those as severe as the Great Depression—are self-correcting. This view of the economy, referred to as neoclassical theory, is based on two major assumptions: flexible labour markets and Say's Law.

Flexible Labour Markets According to neoclassical economists, both the demand and supply of labour depend on the real wage rate, or wages expressed in constant base-year dollars, rather than the nominal wage rate, which is valued in current dollars. Neither workers nor employers are fooled by price changes; therefore, they adjust their behaviour only when the purchasing power of wages changes. Employers demand less labour at higher real wage rates, while workers choose to supply more. As Figure A illustrates, the labour market can be shown using the demand and supply curves D_L and S_L.

Neoclassical economists distinguished between two types of unemployment: voluntary and involuntary. Voluntary unemployment exists whenever workers decide that real wages are not high enough to make work worthwhile. In contrast, involuntary unemployment—when someone wants to work at the current real wage rate but cannot find a job—is of much greater concern to policy-makers. According to neoclassical economics, involuntary unemployment occurs when market demand and supply create a surplus—for example, at a $6 real wage rate, as shown in Figure A. As long as labour markets are flexible, the market forces of demand and supply eradicate the surplus—for example, when market forces push wages toward an equilibrium point of $5. Because markets are flexible, involuntary unemployment is no more than a short-run problem.

FIGURE A A Flexible Labour Market

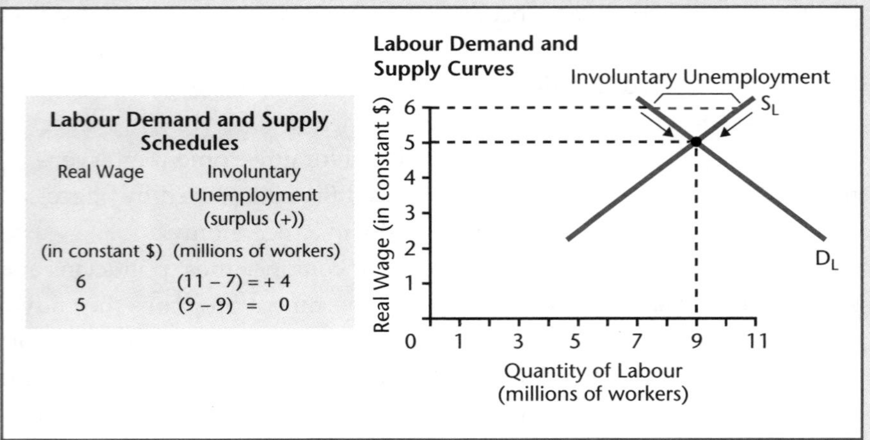

Labour Demand and Supply Schedules

Real Wage (in constant $)	Involuntary Unemployment (surplus (+)) (millions of workers)
6	(11 – 7) = + 4
5	(9 – 9) = 0

If the real wage is $6 per hour, the quantity supplied of labour exceeds the quantity demanded, resulting in 4 million workers involuntarily unemployed. According to neoclassical economics, the forces of demand and supply push the wage to the equilibrium level of $5 per hour, eliminating the surplus.

Say's Law Neoclassical economists also assumed that periods of underspending in the economy are short-lived. Their view was based on a principle known as Say's Law, first outlined by the French economist Jean-Baptiste Say. Using the circular flow of money in the economy, Say argued that supply automatically creates its own demand. That is, we produce goods and services in order to purchase others. A tailor makes clothes, for example, in order to have funds to buy other products.

Even if some of these funds are withdrawn from the circular flow, the production of goods and services generates enough funds to purchase them, as long as total withdrawals and total injections are equal. Neoclassical economists believed that this occurs since total withdrawals and injections can be equal *at any output*. According to their view, interest rates charged in financial markets will vary until withdrawals leaving the circular flow are matched by injections. Therefore, reduced spending is only temporary; total expenditures and production soon balance each other out.

Keynesian Theory

Keynes challenged both of the assumptions of neoclassical economics. Having done so, he provided a theory that explained how involuntary unemployment and underspending had become chronic problems during the Depression.

Challenge to Flexible Labour Markets Keynes believed, unlike the neoclassical economists, that workers were influenced by *money illusion*. By this, he meant that workers would respond to changes in nominal wages, rather than real wages and purchasing power.

Consider a case in which prices fall, as they did during the Great Depression. If the price level drops by 10 percent, workers should not mind if their nominal wages are cut by 10 percent as well, because real wages and purchasing power are not affected. However workers *do* mind, according to Keynes. Workers see a decrease in nominal income as a drop in living standards, and trade unions tend to reject nominal wage cuts. Therefore, the nominal wage rate does not move despite downward pressure.

Figure B illustrates Keynes' view of labour markets. The quantity demanded and supplied of labour both vary with the nominal wage rate. Because the nominal wage will not decrease despite market pressure, the involuntary unemployment caused by a nominal wage such as $8 can last indefinitely. Only if there is an increase in spending, shifting demand to the right, will this unemployment be reduced.

Challenge to Say's Law Keynes proved that, despite its superficial appeal, Say's Law is not always valid. Output levels—not interest

FIGURE B An Inflexible Labour Market

Labour Demand and Supply Schedules

Nominal Wage (in current $)	Involuntary Unemployment (surplus(+)) (millions of workers)
8	(12 – 8) = +4
7	(10 – 10) = 0

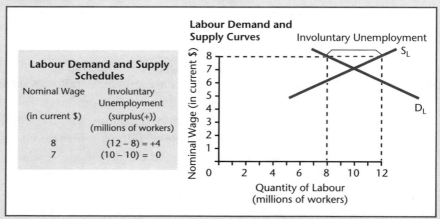

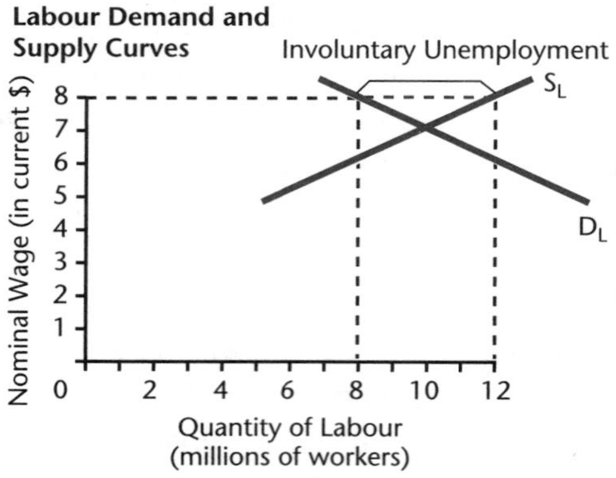

Labour Demand and Supply Curves

Involuntary Unemployment

S_L

D_L

Nominal Wage (in current $)

0 2 4 6 8 10 12

Quantity of Labour (millions of workers)

At a nominal wage of $8 per hour, 4 million workers are involuntarily unemployed. According to Keynesian economics, because these nominal wages will not respond to downward pressure, the market does not move toward the equilibrium wage of $7 per hour. Instead, involuntary unemployment persists.

rates—adjust to bring about a balance between total injections and withdrawals. When injections are less than withdrawals, output falls until a new equilibrium level is reached. It is only *at this equilibrium output* that Say's Law is true, with injections and withdrawals the same. Also, this output is quite possibly associated with high unemployment. Hence, Keynes concluded that underspending is not necessarily self-correcting. So governments must step in to create the needed jobs.

Note

[1]D.E. Moggridge, *Keynes* (London: Macmillan, 1976), p. 12.

1. Outline how the neoclassical economists and Keynes would differ in their interpretation of the following trends:
   a. a fall in wages (measured in both real and nominal terms)
   b. an increase in injections

2 **a. Why did neoclassical economists believe government intervention to be unnecessary during periods of low output and high unemployment?**
   b. Why did Keynes disagree with neoclassical economists on this issue?

CRYSTAL BALL ECONOMICS

Forecasting the Future

Attempting to predict the future is a popular, though often futile, pastime. Accurate forecasts of economic conditions benefit households, businesses, and governments. A home-buyer who can correctly predict changes in interest rates, for example, can decide on the best time to take out a mortgage. Similarly, if business managers can successfully predict the future spending on the items their companies sell, they are able to make more cost-effective decisions. Finally, government officials can use predictions of the business cycle to plan economic policy.

Statistical Models

One way to predict economic conditions is with statistical models. These models are composed of equations that summarize macroeconomic behaviour in numerical terms. For example, one equation is an estimate of aggregate demand. The slope and position of the aggregate demand curve are approximations based on past economic behaviour. Possible values of the variables in the equation can then be "plugged in" to forecast movements of the curve.

There are several well-known models of the Canadian economy, including one formulated by the Bank of Canada known as RDX2. These models require large amounts of data and use sophisticated statistical techniques. However, the models are not always reliable indicators of the future. The complexity of an economy can only be approximated by a model, especially when the model is based on past economic relationships.

For example, a study of leading Canadian forecasters found that, for six out of ten important indicators, the range of predictions provided by the forecasters turned out to be incorrect more than half the time.[1] Figure A shows the discrepancies found in the forecasters' annual predictions of economic growth between 1981 and 1993.

Composite Index One forecasting tool that is used to predict turning points in the business cycle is the Statistics Canada composite index. This index is calculated monthly, and is a weighted average of 10 *leading indicators* which show movement that precedes changes in GDP. The stock market is one example of a leading indicator,

FIGURE A How the experts forecast the GDP

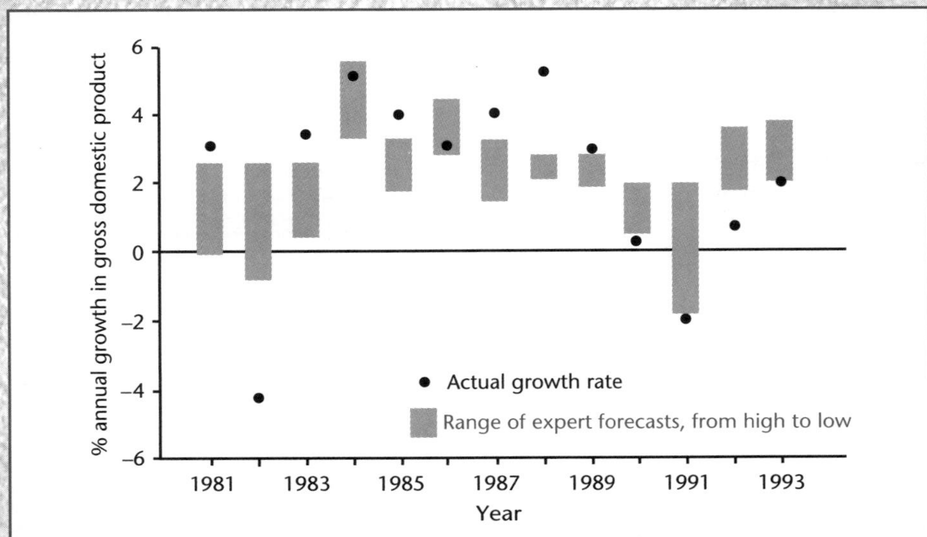

Source: *The Globe and Mail*, 31 July 1996, pp. B1, 9; adapted from *Canada Business Economics*, Spring 1996.

SIDELINE

since share prices reflect expectations of the future.

Five indicators that are included in the composite index—furniture and appliance sales, retail sales of other durable goods (such as automobiles), new orders for durable goods, a shipment-to-inventory ratio of finished goods, and a house-spending index—highlight consumer demand for durable goods as well as factors that affect investment. Changes in any of these indicators point to corresponding future changes in GDP.

Future GDP movements are also directly related to current employment trends. This link is captured by two other indicators that are part of the composite index: employment in business and personal services, and the average work week in the manufacturing sector.

Because Canadian exports form part of GDP and are dependent on the health of foreign economies, one key foreign economy is reflected in the composite index. The most recent value of the American composite index is included in the Canadian composite index.

The final ingredients of the composite index, which represent financial and money markets, are the Toronto Stock Exchange 300 share price index (known as the TSE 300, which includes the 300 most influential firms trading on the Exchange) and a measure of money supply called M1. While movements in share prices reflect expected changes in corporate profits, alterations in the money supply are directly tied to future spending plans. Changes in either measure point to similar future changes in GDP.

Generally, the composite index must move in the same direction for three consecutive months before it is said to forecast changes in GDP. In the past, the composite index has often successfully

FIGURE B Forecasting with the Composite Index

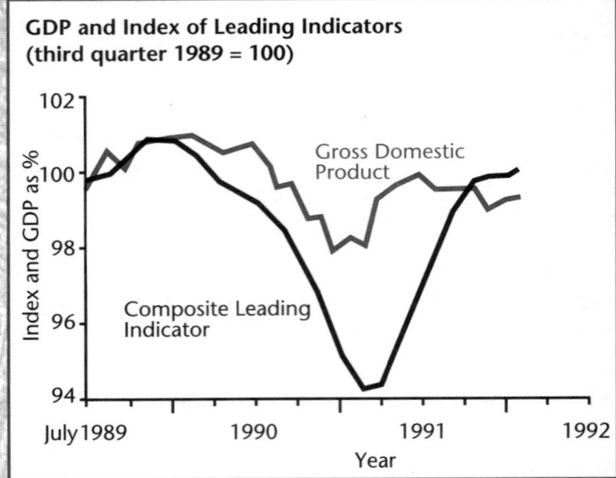

Source: *The Globe and Mail,* 9 May 1992, p. 821; adapted from Statistics Canada.

forecast turning points in the business cycle. However, use of the index is complicated by the length of time it takes to collect values for all of its 10 components. Also, the index can give false predictions. The following example from the late 1980s and early 1990s illustrates both successes and failures.[2] As shown in Figure B, the index successfully predicted the start of the recession of the early 1990s, since it began falling four months before the sustained drop in GDP in 1990. However, the index failed to give adequate warning of the rise and fall that occurred in 1991.

Notes

[1] Bruce Little, "To Err Is Forecaster's Forte," *The Globe and Mail,* 31 July 1996, pp. B1, 9.

[2] Bruce Little, "Leading Indicators Lag Sometimes," *The Globe and Mail,* 9 May 1992, p. B21.

1. Give an illustration of how an economic model based on past relationships can produce an incorrect prediction of the future.

2. Unlike leading indicators, lagging indicators show movements that follow changes in GDP. Identify two lagging indicators.

Chapter Thirteen
Fiscal Policy

Democracy will defeat the economist at every turn at its own game.

—Harold Innis, Canadian economist and historian

Should governments sit idly through the upheavals caused by the business cycle? Certainly not, according to John Maynard Keynes, the founder of modern macroeconomics. Governments can do plenty to stabilize the economy—not only during downturns when unemployment is high, but also during inflationary upswings. Governments can use certain policies to achieve economic stability; for example, they can spend more money or reduce taxes to cause changes in total spending and aggregate demand. This chapter examines the theory behind such policies and their outcomes.

CHAPTER FOCUS

This chapter focuses on the following:

- expansionary and contractionary fiscal policies, which are used by governments seeking economic stability
- the effects of automatic stabilizers
- the multiplier effect of fiscal policy, as determined by the marginal propensities to consume and withdraw
- the benefits and drawbacks of fiscal policy, and principles that may guide such policy
- budget surpluses and deficits, and their impact on public debt and public debt charges

FISCAL POLICY

The Goal of Stabilization

stabilization policy: government policy designed to lessen the effects of the business cycle

expansionary policies: government policies designed to reduce unemployment and stimulate output

contractionary policies: government policies designed to stabilize prices and reduce output

To lessen the effects of downs and ups in the business cycle—particularly unemployment and inflation—governments use stabilization policies. A **stabilization policy** attempts to influence the amounts spent and produced in an economy. The goal of such a policy is to keep the economy as close as possible to its potential output. At this point, only natural unemployment exists and inflation is restrained.

Stabililization policies fall into two categories, depending on the state of the economy and the effect on the economy the policy is meant to have. When total output is below its potential, policy-makers want to eliminate the recessionary gap—in other words, reduce unemployment and stimulate total output. Policies with these goals are called **expansionary policies**.

In contrast, if the economy is booming, policy-makers want to cut the inflationary gap—in other words, stabilize prices and bring the economy back down to its potential output. Policies with these goals are called **contractionary policies**.

Stabilizing the Business Cycle

Assuming that it can be applied quickly and effectively, stabilization policy may be used to smooth out the business cycle. Figure 13.1 shows how stabilization policy can reduce the severity of economic troughs and peaks, and the recessionary and inflationary gaps associated with them. The closer the economy stays to the long-run trend of potential output, the lower will be the social costs of unemployment and inflation to the country's citizens.

In general, governments can affect spending and output levels in an economy through two sets of instruments. First, recall that governments

FIGURE 13.1 Stabilization Policy and the Business Cycle

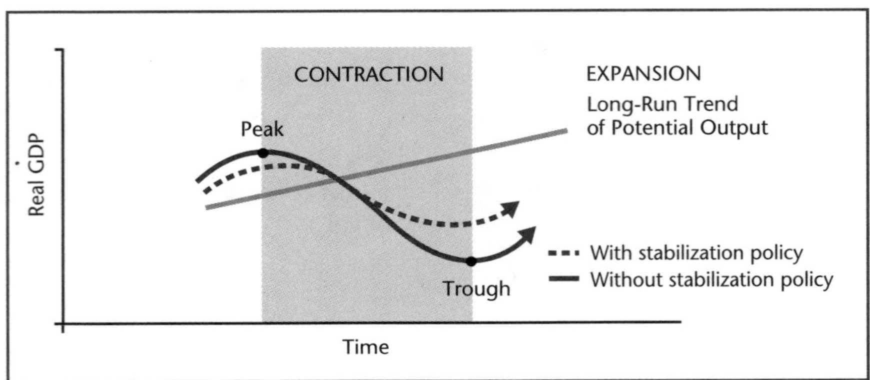

Effective stabilization policy minimizes the severity of the peaks and troughs in the business cycle. Differences between actual output and the long-run trend of potential output are therefore smaller, thus reducing recessionary and inflationary gaps.

have an extensive impact on the economy through taxation and government purchases. Because a government's annual budget sets out what the government will tax and spend, the budget becomes an instrument of stabilization policy. Such a policy is called **fiscal policy**, "fiscal" meaning "budgetary." The twelve-month period to which the budget applies is called the **fiscal year**. Governments can also exert their influence on interest rates and the economy's money supply. A policy that uses these tools is called monetary policy. We'll focus on fiscal policy in this chapter, and turn our attention to **monetary policy** in the next chapter.

fiscal policy: government stabilization policy that uses taxes and government purchases as its tools; budgetary policy

fiscal year: the twelve-month period to which a budget applies

monetary policy: government stabilization policy that uses interest rates and the money supply as its tools

Use of Fiscal Policy

Governments apply fiscal policy during any part of the business cycle. So, during a recession or depression, government action is geared toward increasing spending and output in the economy. Such **expansionary fiscal policy** involves increasing government purchases, decreasing taxes, or both. In contrast, during an inflationary boom, government policy-makers concentrate on restraining output and spending. Such **contractionary fiscal policy** involves decreasing government spending, increasing taxes, or both.

expansionary fiscal policy: government policy that involves increasing government purchases, decreasing taxes, or both to stimulate spending and output

contractionary fiscal policy: government policy that involves decreasing government purchases, increasing taxes, or both to restrain spending and output

Injections and Withdrawals

One way to see how fiscal policy works is to look at injections and withdrawals. Recall from Chapter 12 that investment, government purchases, and exports make up injections to the income-spending stream; saving, taxes, and imports are withdrawals from the stream.

With expansionary fiscal policy, governments increase their purchases and so raise injections to the circular flow. As a result, injections rise relative to withdrawals, and the total flow increases. Reducing taxes has the same effect. By withdrawing less from the income-spending stream, withdrawals decrease relative to injections, and the total flow increases. As the total flow rises, equilibrium output is pushed up.

Contractionary fiscal policies have the opposite effect. Governments that reduce their purchases reduce injections to the circular flow. As a result, injections fall relative to withdrawals, and the total flow decreases. Raising taxes has the same effect; withdrawals rise relative to injections, and the total flow decreases. As the total flow falls, equilibrium output is pushed down.

Aggregate Demand

Another way to look at fiscal policy is through its effects on aggregate demand and aggregate supply. To increase aggregate demand so that the economy expands to its potential, policy-makers raise government purchases, cut taxes, or both. Increasing government spending has an immediate effect on aggregate demand since government purchases are a component of real expenditures. As Figure 13.2 demonstrates, the equilibrium price level and output are pushed up as a result.

FIGURE 13.2
Expansionary Fiscal Policy

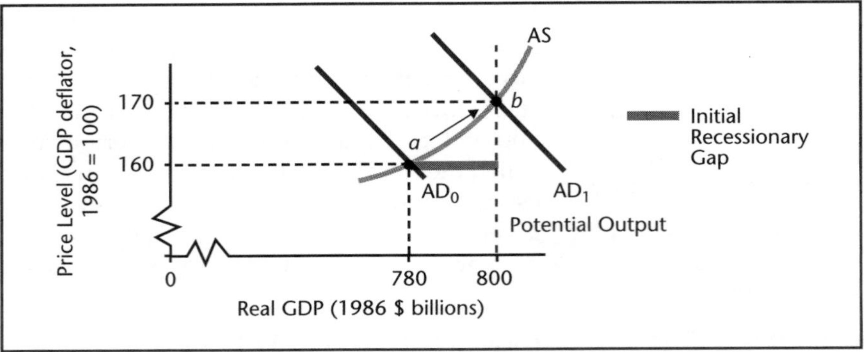

A rise in government purchases or a cut in taxes increase aggregate demand, shifting the aggregate demand curve from AD_0 to AD_1. This causes a rise in the equilibrium price level and output (from point *a* to point *b*). Output rises from $780 billion to the potential level of $800 billion. As a result, the economy's $20 billion recessionary gap is eliminated.

The effect of tax cuts is less immediate, because there is no guarantee that households and businesses will alter spending in response to a tax change. Cutting taxes enables households and businesses to spend more, so both consumption and investment should increase, thereby shifting the aggregate demand curve to the right. Again, Figure 13.2 illustrates the results.

If a government has a contractionary fiscal policy—in other words, if it wants to decrease aggregate demand so that the economy contracts to its potential—policy-makers will reduce government purchases, raise taxes, or both. As with expansionary fiscal policy, the effect of decreasing government purchases is immediate, while the effect of increasing taxes is less so. Figure 13.3 illustrates both cases. A fall in government purchases reduces aggregate demand, thereby shifting the aggregate demand curve to the left. Higher taxes reduce households' disposable income and businesses' profits. Consumption and investment both decline,

FIGURE 13.3
Contractionary Fiscal Policy

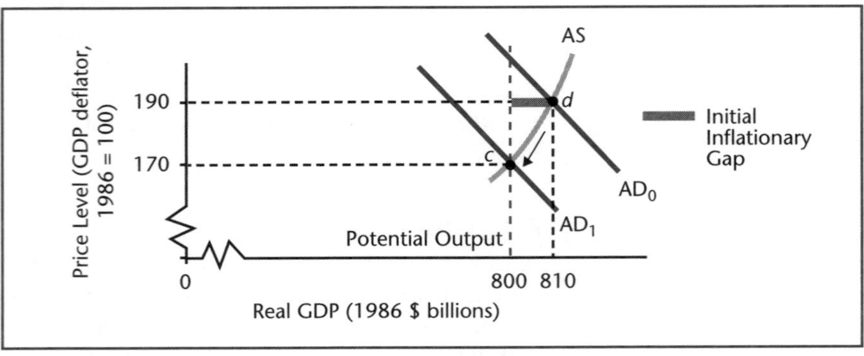

A fall in government purchases or a rise in taxes decrease aggregate demand, shifting the aggregate demand curve to the left from AD_0 to AD_1. This causes a fall in the equilibrium price level and output from point *d* to point *c*. Output falls from $810 billion to the potential level of $800 billion. As a result, the economy's $10 billion inflationary gap is eliminated.

thereby reducing aggregate demand and shifting the aggregate demand curve to the left.

Automatic Stabilizers

discretionary policy: intentional government intervention in the economy, such as budgeted changes in spending or taxation

automatic stabilizers: built-in measures, such as taxation and transfer payment programs, that lessen the effects of the business cycle

net tax revenues: taxes collected, minus transfers and subsidies

As we've seen, fiscal policy involves adjusting government purchases or taxes. These actions are intentional; laws must be passed and budgets brought down. Because it is up to a government's discretion to take these actions, fiscal policy is known as **discretionary policy**. In contrast, some stabilizing forces are automatic—that is, they do not involve the direct involvement of government decision-makers.

Recall from Chapter 9 the taxation and transfer payment programs such as progressive income taxes, Employment Insurance, and welfare payments. These established programs act as **automatic stabilizers** in the business cycle. In a period of contraction, **net tax revenues** (taxes minus transfers and subsidies) decrease; during a period of expansion, net tax revenues increase. As a result, spending and aggregate demand are stimulated in a downturn and suppressed in an upswing, thereby helping to smooth out the business cycle.

To see how automatic stabilizers work, let's first consider an economy that is contracting. Because household incomes and business profits fall, the taxes that a government can collect from households and businesses also fall. As jobs are lost and businesses suffer, government transfer payments and subsidies are increased. Both trends cause a decline in net tax revenues. Because incomes are bolstered by one program and taxes are reduced by the other, spending increases over what it would have been, helping to push the economy toward its potential output.

When the economy expands, the opposite happens. Personal incomes and business profits increase. As a result, governments collect more in taxes. Because the nation is more prosperous and employment is high, transfer payments and subsidies are reduced. Both trends cause a rise in net tax revenues. Because taxes have risen, spending and aggregate demand decrease, helping to push the economy back down to its potential output.

Thinking About Economics

How significant are automatic stabilizers in the Canadian economy?

As discussed in Chapter 9, the expanding role of Canadian governments since World War II has led to a substantial increase in rates of taxation as well as rising expenditures on transfer payments. Higher tax rates and more generous transfer payments have both served as important automatic stabilizers in the Canadian economy during recent decades—a point that is stressed by economists who support greater government involvement in the economy.

BRIEF REVIEW

1. Governments use stabilization policies to minimize ups and downs in the business cycle. Such policies are categorized as expansionary or contractionary policies depending on the state of the economy and the effect of the policy on the economy.
2. Fiscal policy affects spending and output through taxes and government purchases. Monetary policy affects spending and output through interest rates and the economy's money supply.
3. Expansionary fiscal policy involves increasing government purchases, decreasing taxes, or both. Such a policy increases aggregate demand and pushes up the equilibrium price level and output.
4. Contractionary fiscal policy involves decreasing government purchases, increasing taxes, or both. Such a policy decreases aggregate demand and pushes down the equilibrium price level and output.
5. In contrast to discretionary policies, automatic stabilizers are built-in factors that affect aggregate demand and minimize the impact of inflationary and recessionary gaps.

THE SPENDING MULTIPLIER

Government decision-makers must have some way of estimating, in terms of dollar values, the impact that their policies will have on the economy. In general, a certain dollar change in government purchases or taxation does not cause the same dollar change in total real output. Like a pebble dropped in a pond causes ripples, fiscal policy has a multiplier effect.

The Multiplier Effect

multiplier effect: the magnified impact of a spending change on aggregate demand

The **multiplier effect** is the magnified impact of any spending change on aggregate demand. It assumes that the price level stays constant. So, the multiplier effect is the change in spending at one price level, multiplied by a certain value to give the resulting change in aggregate demand.

Let's consider an example. Suppose the government institutes an expansionary fiscal policy. As part of this policy the government pays Spender A, a trade consultant, $1000 for her services. The economy's output rises by $1000, and the consultant's revenues rise by $1000. (We'll assume for this example that the consultant incurs only negligible costs.) This consultant spends half of the amount she earns on a Canadian product and uses the rest for saving, imports, and taxes. In other words, she pays $500 to the supplier of a Canadian product, Spender B, thereby increasing Spender B's income (assuming that B also has negligible costs). The economy's total output has been expanded again by $500, with the remaining $500 withdrawn from the income-spending stream by Spender A in the form of saving, imports, and taxes. Spender B, with his $500 in new income, spends $250 on Canadian products and uses the other $250 on saving, imports, and taxes. His $250 purchase also has an impact on the Canadian economy and provides income to someone else. And on it goes. Any given purchase made by the government has an initial effect, a secondary effect, and so on.

As the example illustrates, the inclination to spend and the inclination to save or otherwise withdraw funds from the economy both determine the multiplier effect. These factors are summarized by the concepts of marginal propensity to consume and marginal propensity to withdraw.

Marginal Propensity to Consume

marginal propensity to consume: the effect on domestic consumption of a change in income

Marginal propensity to consume (MPC) is the effect on domestic consumption of a change in income, and applies to individual households and the economy as a whole. In effect, MPC answers the question: "If income increases this amount, how much extra will be spent on domestic goods and services?" MPC is defined as the change in consumption on domestic products as a proportion of the change in income.

$$\text{MPC} = \frac{\text{change in consumption on domestic items}}{\text{change in income}}$$

Marginal Propensity to Withdraw

marginal propensity to withdraw: the effect on withdrawals—saving, imports, and taxes—of a change in income

As the earlier example illustrated, not all income is spent, and what is may not be spent on domestic products. As a result, some income does not reappear in the circular flow. Recall from Chapter 12 that there are three types of withdrawals: saving, taxes, and imports. Part of income is saved, part is paid out in taxes, and part is used to buy imports. The **marginal propensity to withdraw** (MPW) is the effect on withdrawals of a change in income. It is defined as the change in total withdrawals as a proportion of the change in income.

$$\text{MPW} = \frac{\text{change in total withdrawals}}{\text{change in income}}$$

Let's consider the concepts of MPC and MPW together. Suppose a person's income rises by \$1000. Of that, the consumer spends \$300 on domestic products but saves the rest. In this case, the marginal propensity to consume is 0.3 (\$300 ÷ \$1000), while the marginal propensity to withdraw is 0.7 (\$700 ÷ \$1000). Note the relationship between the values of the marginal propensities to consume and withdraw: their sum equals 1.0. This is always the case because income is either spent on domestic consumption or withdrawn from the circular flow as saving, imports, or taxes.

$$1.0 = \text{MPC} + \text{MPW}$$
$$1.0 = 0.3 + 0.7$$

To see in detail how the multiplier effect works, let's consider our example of the trade consultant again. The marginal propensities to consume and withdraw in each round, or stage, of spending help to determine the multiplier effect. Figure 13.4 illustrates the example.

First Round

Recall that the government pays Spender A, the trade consultant, $1000. Not only does her income rise, but the economy's output also rises by $1000. The effect is illustrated on the left in Figure 13.4.

Second Round

Spender A starts the second round of spending by using the extra $1000 in income. Because her marginal propensity to consume is 0.5 ($500 ÷ $1000) and her marginal propensity to withdraw is also 0.5 ($500 ÷ $1000), she puts an extra $500 into the circular flow, but withdraws $500 in the form of saving, imports, and taxes. As a result, the economy's real output undergoes a further rise of $500.

Third Round

Recall that Spender B spends $250 of his $500 in income on domestic products, and an equal amount on saving, imports, and taxes. Therefore, Spender B's marginal propensity to consume is 0.5 ($250 ÷ $500), and his marginal propensity to withdraw is also 0.5 ($250 ÷ $500). Figure 13.4 shows that he adds another $250 to the economy's real output.

Later Spending Rounds

The same process of spending providing income, which is then spent domestically or withdrawn, repeats, with expenditures and withdrawals getting smaller in each round. For example, if the spender in the fourth

FIGURE 13.4
The Effect of a Rise in Government Purchases

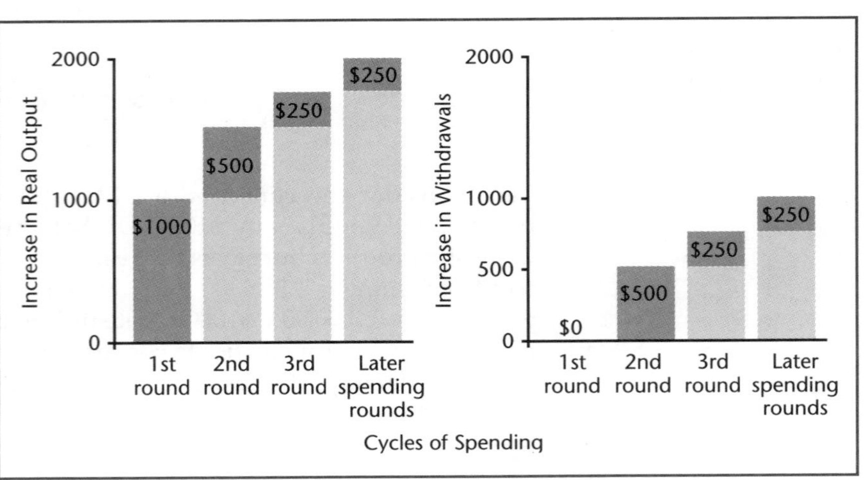

On the left, a $1000 rise in government purchases gradually pushes up real output by $2000, with each round of spending adding successively smaller amounts (as indicated by the darker rectangles). On the right, each successive round of spending involves greater amounts of withdrawals, until new withdrawals equal the initial rise in spending.

round also has a marginal propensity to consume of 0.5, another \$125 (\$250 × 0.5) will be added to the economy's real output. This process finally ends when real output has risen by a total of \$2000.

Injections and Withdrawals

To see why total output grows by \$2000, let's turn our attention to the withdrawals that have occurred with each spending round, shown on the right in Figure 13.4. Notice that with each subsequent round of spending, there are new withdrawals. Eventually, total withdrawals equal \$1000. This result can be interpreted in terms of injections and withdrawals, or leakages.

Before the expansionary fiscal policy, the economy was in equilibrium, with injections and withdrawals equal. As a result of the government's discretionary policy—that is, its \$1000 planned increase in government purchases—total injections exceed total withdrawals, causing output to rise. In each round of spending, withdrawals increase. This expansion continues until withdrawals equal the initial discretionary injection. At this point, injections and withdrawals are both \$1000 higher than they were before government purchases were increased.

The Spending Multiplier

spending multiplier: the value by which an initial spending change is multiplied to give the total change in real output

Now that we've seen the multiplier effect in action, we'll give it a numerical value. The **spending multiplier** is the value by which the initial spending change is multiplied to give the total change in output—in other words, the shift in the aggregate demand curve.

$$\begin{matrix}\text{Total change in output} \\ \text{(shift in AD curve)}\end{matrix} = \begin{matrix}\text{initial change} \\ \text{in spending}\end{matrix} \times \begin{matrix}\text{spending} \\ \text{multiplier}\end{matrix}$$

In our example, because initial spending rose by \$1000 and total output increased by \$2000, the spending multiplier equals 2. This figure can be found by rearranging the above equation to isolate the multiplier:

$$\text{Spending multiplier} = \frac{\text{total change in output (shift in AD curve)}}{\text{initial change in spending}}$$

$$2 = \frac{\$2000}{\$1000}$$

If total output increased instead by \$3000 as a result of a \$1000 rise in government purchases, then the multiplier would be 3 (\$3000 ÷ \$1000).

To see what determines the value of the spending multiplier, recall that the economy's total output expands until new withdrawals equal the initial government purchase—the new injection. In our original example, the marginal propensity to withdraw was 0.5, meaning that 50 cents were withdrawn for every \$1 of new output in the economy. Output therefore had to expand by \$2000 to create the needed \$1000 in new withdrawals, giving a spending multiplier of 2. If the marginal propensity to withdraw had been 0.33, then 33 cents would have been withdrawn for each dollar of new output. Hence, output would have had to increase by $3000 to create $1000 in extra withdrawals, giving a spending multiplier equal to 3.

These examples point to the inverse relationship between the marginal propensity to withdraw and the spending multiplier. If MPW is 0.5, the multiplier equals 2. If MPW is 0.33, the multiplier is 3. Therefore, the spending multiplier is the reciprocal of the marginal propensity to withdraw.

$$\text{Spending multiplier} = \frac{1}{\text{MPW}}$$

$$2 = \frac{1}{0.5}$$

Effect of a Tax Cut

The multiplier effect can be applied to the other stimulus that governments use: tax cuts. Recall that tax cuts can also be applied to expand the economy. Lower taxes leave households and businesses with more funds to spend and invest. In this case, the initial spending stimulus of the tax cut is multiplied by the spending multiplier, or the reciprocal of MPW. The result is an increase in total output, shown as a shift in the aggregate demand curve.

In contrast to government purchases, a tax adjustment has a smaller initial effect on spending. Recall our example of a $1000 government purchase from Spender A. Spender A's initial transaction with the government was added directly to real output before taking into account further rounds of spending. If a reduction in taxes increases Spender A's disposable income by $1000, however, some of this amount would be withdrawn from the circular flow before its first effect on real output. Only that amount used to buy domestic products represents the initial spending increase. For example, if the marginal propensity to consume is 0.5, then the initial change in spending on domestic items is $500 ($1000 × 0.5). This $500 spending increase is then multiplied by the spending multiplier, or 2 (1.0 ÷ 0.5). As a result, the aggregate demand increases by $1000 ($500 × 2), which is less than the $2000 increase caused by an initial $1000 government purchase.

Relevance of the Spending Multiplier

Recall that throughout our discussion of the multiplier effect, we've assumed that the price level is constant. However, what happens to the spending multiplier if price levels vary?

As shown in Figure 13.5, fiscal policy affects the price level as well as output. Recall from Chapter 12, that the slope of the aggregate supply curve is steep as it reaches or surpasses the potential output level. So, as shown in Figure 13.5, when the aggregate demand curve shifts to the right from AD_0 to AD_1, it moves to a steep portion of the aggregate supply curve. In this case, the change in the equilibrium point, from point *a* to point *c*, means that while both price levels and output rise, the price level rises proportionally more than does output. So, in general, when the economy is close to its potential level, the increase in aggregate demand translates into higher price levels more than into expanded production. In other words, with the stated goal being a stable economy and expanded output, expansionary fiscal policy is less effective the closer the economy is to its potential. Similar reasoning applies to contractionary fiscal policy. When the economy is above its potential, a decrease in aggregate demand means that both price level and total output fall. However, price level falls proportionally more than total output does.

In summary, because of possible changes in the price level, the multiplier effect is less definite than the use of a simple formula would indicate. However, the multiplier calculation is nonetheless useful in indicating the *maximum* change in equilibrium output following a certain fiscal policy.

FIGURE 13.5
The Multiplier Effect and Price Changes

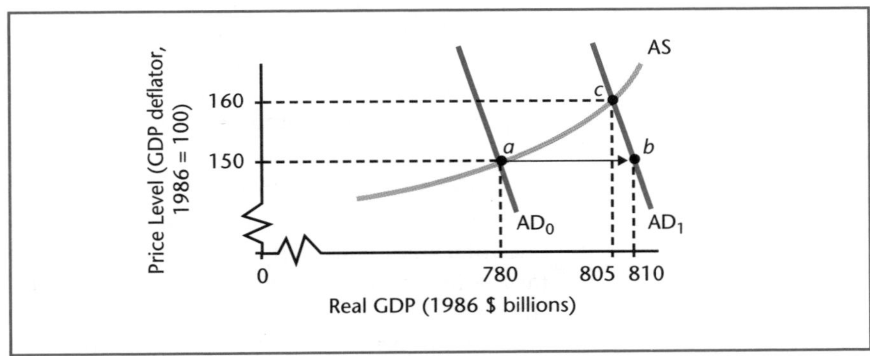

If spending affected output alone, with a spending multiplier of 1.5, a $20 billion rise in government purchases would push the output from $780 billion (point *a*) to $810 billion (point *b*). However, since price level is also affected, the shift from AD_0 to AD_1 causes equilibrium to move to point *c*, with an output of $805 billion and a price level of 160. Because of the slope of the AS curve, the closer an economy is to its potential, the greater impact a change in aggregate demand will have on the price level instead of output.

Thinking About Economics

How large is the spending multiplier in the Canadian economy?

Several estimates of the Canadian spending multiplier have been made. The average value is about 1.5. If this figure is correct, then, as Figure 13.5 illustrates, a $20 billion jump in government purchases shifts the aggregate demand curve to the right by $30 billion. However, given the positive slope of the aggregate supply curve, this change means a rise in the price level as well as in total output. In this case, output would rise by $25 billion.

Benefits of Fiscal Policy

Fiscal policy has two benefits as a stabilization tool: its regional focus, and the direct impact it has on spending.

Regional Focus

Parts of Canada may be more affected than others by the business cycle. Fortunately, discretionary fiscal policy can focus on particular regions. For example, during a recession, new government purchases or programs to reduce the amount of tax paid can be targeted to regions where unemployment rates are highest. In a boom, spending cuts and tax hikes can be concentrated on the regions where inflation is at its worst. Similarly, automatic stabilizers have the greatest effect in regions that need them the most. During recessions, net tax revenues drop most in regions hardest hit by unemployment and falling output. For example, the greatest rise in Employment Insurance payments is in areas with the highest growth in unemployment. During booms, the largest increase in net tax revenues occurs in regions where the economy is most overheated. For example, revenues from personal income tax expand most quickly in areas where employment and incomes are most buoyant.

Impact on Spending

As indicated by the previous discussion of the multiplier effect, the influence of a stabilization policy is tied to its initial effect on spending. Monetary policy influences spending through a fairly elaborate chain of events. In contrast, fiscal policy has a more straightforward impact—at least when altering government purchases. The first spending adjustment is then assured, since the government itself initiates the change.

Drawbacks of Fiscal Policy

Offsetting the benefits of fiscal policy are three main drawbacks: policy delays, the political visibility of this policy, and its effects on public debt.

Delays

While automatic stabilizers work promptly to stabilize the economy, discretionary measures are sometimes delayed. Three time lags can slow down fiscal policy-makers: the recognition lag, the decision lag, and the impact lag.

recognition lag: the amount of time it takes policy-makers to realize that a policy is needed

The **recognition lag** is the amount of time it takes policy-makers to realize that a policy is needed. Suppose that economic growth suddenly slows. A few months may pass before statistical evidence of this becomes available. It may then take several more months for policy-makers to decide whether this represents a minor fluctuation or the start of a recession.

decision lag: the amount of time needed to formulate and implement an appropriate policy

The **decision lag** is the period that passes while an appropriate response is formulated and implemented. Suppose policy-makers have decided that, indeed, the economy is entering a recession. They must then decide what to do about it. Should they increase government purchases, reduce taxes, or use some combination of the two measures? Once they've decided, the policy must be passed into law and included in a budget.

impact lag: the amount of time between a policy's implementation and its having an effect on the economy

Finally, once the policy is implemented, there is an **impact lag**—the time that elapses between implementing the policy and its having an effect on the economy. In the case of government spending to combat a recession, for example, the many rounds of spending must take place before the full multiplier effect is felt in the economy.

As a result of these time lags, a year or more may pass between the cause and the effect of a fiscal policy. Meanwhile, the economy may already have moved to a completely different point in the business cycle. In the extreme case, the use of fiscal policy may worsen the business cycle by stimulating output during upswings and suppressing it during downturns.

Political Visibility

Discretionary fiscal policy is a highly visible element of government activity. Not surprisingly, therefore, it is often affected by political as well as economic considerations. Voters are likely to respond more favourably to increases in government purchases and cuts in taxes than they are to spending decreases and tax hikes, regardless of the appropriateness of these policies for the economy. As a result, political parties understandably favour expansionary fiscal policy, especially when an election is coming up.

Public Debt

public debt: the total amount owed by the federal government as a result of its past borrowing

While there remains a political bias toward expansionary policy, the federal government has used stimulative measures more sparingly in recent recessions. This reluctance to increase government purchases or decrease taxes is related to Canada's **public debt**, which is the total amount owed by the federal government as a result of its past borrowing. This differs from total government debt, which includes the debts of individual provinces and territories—and sometimes local governments and hospitals as well. Given the growth in provincial debt during the 1990s, this distinction can be important. Public debt, which is owed by Canadian taxpayers to owners of Canadian government bonds, totalled $593.3 billion at the end of 1996.

public debt charges: the amounts paid out each year by the federal government to cover the interest charges on its public debt

The federal government spends large sums related to its debt. **Public debt charges** are the amounts paid out each year by the federal government to cover the interest charges on its public debt. Just as payments of interest on a bank loan do not reduce the principal of the loan, public debt charges do not reduce the overall size of the public debt.

In 1996–97, for example, the federal government's public debt charges were $45.5 billion. This figure represented an average interest rate of about 8 percent [($45.5 billion ÷ $593.3 billion) × 100%] that the federal government paid to the bondholders who owned its $593.3 billion debt.

Public debt grew rapidly in recent decades, so that now public debt charges are by far the largest single expenditure made by the federal government. In 1996–97, for example, a third of every federal tax dollar went to pay interest on Canada's public debt. Because the government has not yet been able to significantly reduce the public debt, when an individual bondholder cashes in a Canadian government bond the government replaces the funds by selling more bonds. Recently, worries over this trend have constrained the use of expansionary fiscal policy. As a result, such a policy—which has the potential to increase Canada's public debt further—has been used less.

BRIEF REVIEW

1. The multiplier effect—the magnified impact of fiscal policy on aggregate demand—is determined by the marginal propensity to consume and the marginal propensity to withdraw.
2. Assuming a constant price level, the spending multiplier is the value by which an initial spending change is multiplied to give the total change in real output.
3. Because a new injection brings about new withdrawals that equal the initial injection, the spending multiplier is the reciprocal of the marginal propensity to withdraw.
4. In the case of a tax cut, the initial spending adjustment is less than the change in taxes because a portion of the tax cut represents withdrawals from the circular flow of spending and income.
5. While fiscal policy can target certain regions and have a direct impact on spending, it also suffers from delays, problems associated with political visibility, and its impact on public debt.

IMPACT OF FISCAL POLICY

Budget Surpluses and Deficits

Government expenditures and revenues are affected both by discretionary fiscal policy and by the workings of automatic stabilizers. In the unlikely case where a government's expenditures and revenues are equal, the government is running a **balanced budget**.

balanced budget: the situation where a government's expenditures and revenues are equal

In general, government expenditures and revenues are not equal. When a government's revenues exceed its expenditures, there is a **budget surplus**. For example, in 1969–70 the federal government's total expenditures were $14.2 billion and its total revenues were $14.4 billion. Therefore, the budget surplus was $0.2 billion.

budget surplus: the situation where a government's revenues exceed its expenditures

$$\text{Budget surplus} = \text{government revenues} - \text{government expenditures}$$

$$\$0.2 \text{ billion} = \$14.4 \text{ billion} - \$14.2 \text{ billion}$$

In contrast, when a government's expenditures exceed its revenues, there is a **budget deficit**. For example, in 1996–97 the federal government's total expenditures were $154.5 billion and its total revenues were $135.5 billion. Therefore, the budget deficit was $19.0 billion:

budget deficit: the situation where a government's expenditures exceed its revenues

Budget deficit = government expenditures – government revenues

$19.0 billion = $154.5 billion – $135.5 billion

The size of a government's surplus or deficit in relation to the economy's overall GDP gives an indication of what type of discretionary fiscal policy is in operation, as well as the built-in effects of automatic stabilizers.

A government's deficit should not be confused with its debt. A budget deficit occurs when a government's expenditures exceed its revenue during a given period. The government's debt, on the other hand, represents the sum of all its past budget deficits – minus any budget surpluses.

Surpluses

In some unusual cases, budget surpluses are related to discretionary fiscal policy. For example, a government might decide to suppress the inflationary effects of an economic boom by cutting defence spending and raising income taxes. However, it is more likely that budget surpluses are the result of built-in factors. During a boom, for example, rising tax revenues that outweigh transfer payments can sometimes cause provincial budgets to show a surplus.

Deficits

Budget deficits sometimes indicate active expansionary policies that increase government expenditures or reduce revenues. During an economic downturn, for example, the federal government may increase its spending on roads and bridges, or it may institute a temporary sales-tax cut to stimulate household spending. Budget deficits more often come about as a result of automatic stabilizers. For instance, fewer jobs and less spending during a recession lead to rising Employment Insurance benefits and sagging income tax revenues. Both of these trends push the federal budget into a deficit position.

Impact on Public Debt

Because federal surpluses and deficits have not balanced each other over the long run, they have had a tremendous impact on the size of Canada's public debt. When the federal government has a budget deficit, which is most common, the public debt increases by the same amount. For example, Canada's public debt at the start of the 1996-97 fiscal year was $574.3 billion. Because the federal government ran a budget deficit of $19.0 billion in 1996–97, its public debt at the start of the 1997–98 fiscal year increased to $593.3 billion ($574.3 billion + $19.0 billion). In the rare case of a federal budget surplus, the public debt can be reduced by the same amount. For example, when the federal government ran a $0.2 billion budget surplus in 1969–70, its public debt was reduced from $18.7 billion at the beginning of the fiscal year to $18.5 billion (18.7 billion – $0.2 billion) at the beginning of the next fiscal year.

Fiscal Policy Guidelines

There are three principles that guide government fiscal policy: annually balanced budgets, cyclically balanced budgets, and functional finance.

Annually Balanced Budgets

annually balanced budget: the principle that government revenues and expenditures should balance each year

Those who criticize government intervention in the economy tend not to support fiscal policy. In general, these critics suggest that any fiscal policy that is used must be guided by the principle of an **annually balanced budget**. In other words, revenues and expenditures should balance every year. So, for example, new spending programs must be matched with higher taxes. In essence, by advocating an annually balanced budget, these critics dismiss active fiscal policy as an option.

Opponents of this principle suggest that it is based on faulty reasoning. While an annually balanced budget might make sense for a particular household, it is not necessarily appropriate for society as a whole. After all, the business cycle does not span one year, but many. During an economic contraction, for example, tax revenues decrease. To balance the budget, a government would have to reduce government purchases, thereby worsening the slump in spending. This problem occurred during the early years of the Great Depression in Canada.

Cyclically Balanced Budgets

cyclically balanced budget: the principle that government revenues and expenditures should balance over the course of one business cycle

A less stringent principle—and one that has more supporters—is that of a **cyclically balanced budget**. In other words, government revenues and expenditures need not be balanced every year, but they should balance over one business cycle. The deficits from periods of contraction should roughly equal the surpluses from periods of expansion.

Functional Finance

functional finance: the principle that government budgets should be geared to the yearly needs of the economy

The principle of **functional finance** stems from the view that policy-makers should concern themselves primarily with correcting fluctuations caused by the business cycle. Rather than trying to balance budgets either annually or over the business cycle, governments should base a year's fiscal policy on the needs of the economy.

In practice, the choice of fiscal policy guidelines depends on the government's belief in fiscal policy as an effective tool for stabilizing the economy. The defenders of functional finance are those who see fiscal policy as a powerful stabilization tool, while economists who back a cyclically or annually balanced budget tend to be less convinced of fiscal policy's effectiveness.

Recent Fiscal Policy

The predominant view of fiscal policy in Canada has undergone a profound change since the mid-1980s. Similar changes have taken place in other industrialized nations. In the 1970s and early 1980s, functional finance was the guiding principle behind fiscal policy in Canada and many other countries. Since then, there have been attempts to move toward cyclically balanced budgets.

In Canada, this change in view relates primarily to increased budget deficits and their impact on the economy as a whole. Figure 13.6 shows the federal budget deficits and the combined deficits of provincial and territorial governments as proportions of Canada's nominal GDP for the years 1981–82 to 1996–97. For example, in relation to Canada's 1996 nominal GDP of $797.8 billion, the federal government's $19.0 billion budget deficit in 1996–97 was 2.4 percent [($19.0 billion ÷ $797.8 billion) × 100%]. Similarly, provincial and territorial governments, when viewed as a single unit, had a combined budget deficit in 1996–97 of $9.0 billion, which as a share of nominal GDP was 1.1 percent [($9.0 billion ÷ $797.8 billion) × 100%]. Because this period spans two recessions and two periods of expansion, it illustrates the changing view of fiscal policy.

Total government deficits were highest during the periods corresponding to the recessions of the early 1980s and early 1990s. However, there were significant differences in fiscal policy. During and just after the slump of the early 1980s, the overall budget deficits of Canadian governments were about 10 percent of Canada's nominal GDP. The budget deficits of the lower levels of government, which were relatively small, came about largely because of automatic stabilizers as tax revenues fell with slumping output and incomes. The large federal deficits were due not only to automatic stabilizers, but also to the use of discretionary expansionary policy by government policy-makers. In particular, the federal government increased purchases of goods and services to counteract the effects of sagging output and incomes.

Following the recession of the early 1980s, the Canadian economy experienced a prolonged period of economic growth, with first a recovery and then a boom occurring in the later years of the decade. By 1988, when the unemployment rate was under 8 percent, the Canadian economy was at or above its potential output. Despite these boom conditions, budgets did not show an overall surplus. In fact, the combined deficits of federal, provincial, and territorial governments were still about 5 percent of nominal GDP in 1988 and 1989.

During and just after the downturn of the early 1990s, the combined deficits of the lower levels of government were much more significant in comparison to the size of the federal deficit. As a result, the overall budget deficits of all levels of government were again nearly 10 percent of Canada's nominal GDP. However, these deficits were less a result of discretionary policy than of automatic stabilizers. This difference resulted from worry over the increased public debt and reduced confidence in the effectiveness of discretionary fiscal policies to counteract a recession. As the economy expanded in the mid-1990s, the impact of automatic stabilizers, falling interest rates, and deficit-cutting by all levels of government led to a reduction of the overall budget deficits of Canadian governments to 3.5 percent of nominal GDP by 1996-97.

FIGURE 13.6 Budget Deficits Relative to GDP

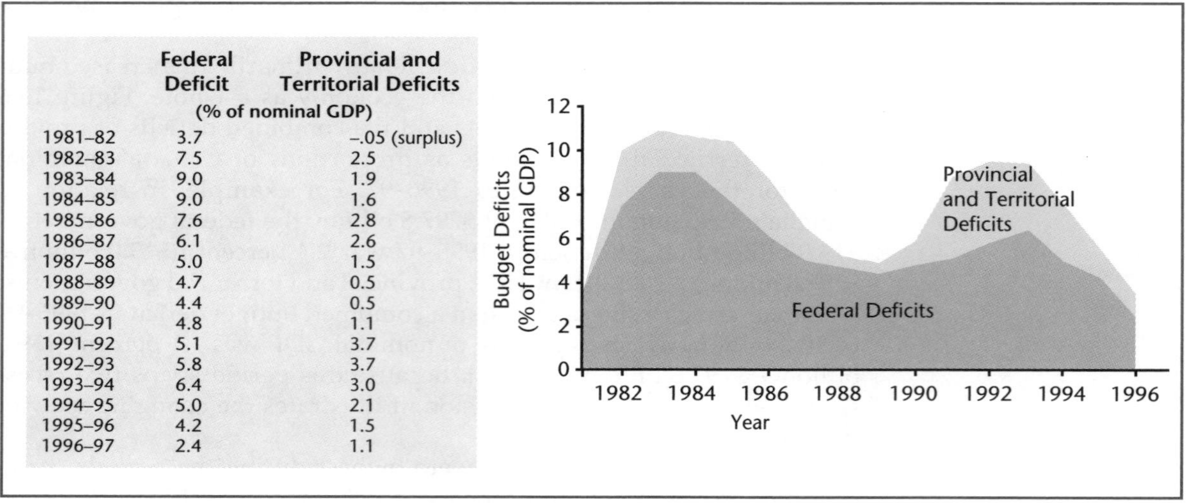

	Federal Deficit	Provincial and Territorial Deficits
	(% of nominal GDP)	
1981–82	3.7	–.05 (surplus)
1982–83	7.5	2.5
1983–84	9.0	1.9
1984–85	9.0	1.6
1985–86	7.6	2.8
1986–87	6.1	2.6
1987–88	5.0	1.5
1988–89	4.7	0.5
1989–90	4.4	0.5
1990–91	4.8	1.1
1991–92	5.1	3.7
1992–93	5.8	3.7
1993–94	6.4	3.0
1994–95	5.0	2.1
1995–96	4.2	1.5
1996–97	2.4	1.1

Federal budget deficits (darker area) and the combined budget deficits for provincial and territorial governments (lighter and darker areas) are shown as percentages of Canada's nominal GDP. Recessions in the early 1980s and early 1990s each caused an increase in budget deficits. While the increase in the early 1980s was mainly due to the federal government, the increase in the early 1990s was split between the federal and the lower levels of government.

Source: Statistics Canada, *Public Sector Finance* (March 1996), cat. no. 68-212-XPB, p. 5; Department of Finance, *The Budget Plan* (February 1997), p. 6; Department of Finance, *Provincial Fiscal Monitor* (February 1997), p. 2. Reproduced by authority of the Minister of Industry, 1997.

Thinking About Economics

Why are budget deficits so common for Canadian governments through all phases of the business cycle?

Many observers believe that between the early 1980s and mid-1990s Canada entered a harmful deficit–debt spiral. Past dependence on federal budget deficits expanded Canada's public debt, which in turn raised annual interest payments on the public debt. The same trend was also noticeable for provincial governments. Greater debt charges for all levels of government increased their spending, which in turn raised deficits even more. Without the deficit-cutting measures pursued by all levels of government in the mid-1990s, this trend could have led to even higher government deficits and debt levels in the future.

BRIEF REVIEW

1. When government expenditures equal revenues, the budget is balanced. Budget surpluses—when revenues exceed expenditures—rarely occur. Most frequently, expenditures exceed revenues, resulting in a budget deficit.

2. Repeated budget deficits—in periods of both expansion and contraction—caused Canada's public debt to balloon.

3. Fiscal policy may be based on three possible guidelines: annually balanced budgets, cyclically balanced budgets, or functional finance. At the federal level, functional finance has been the guiding principle in Canada since the 1970s, although cyclically balanced budgets are increasingly favoured.

KEY CONCEPTS

stabilization policy
expansionary policies
contractionary policies
fiscal policy
fiscal year
monetary policy
expansionary fiscal policy
contractionary fiscal policy
discretionary policy
automatic stabilizers
net tax revenues
multiplier effect
marginal propensity to consume
marginal propensity to withdraw
spending multiplier
recognition lag
decision lag
impact lag
public debt
public debt charges
balanced budget
budget surplus
budget deficits
annually balanced budget
cyclically balanced budget
functional finance

ANALYSIS AND APPLICATION

1. In each of the following cases, state whether the economy faces a recessionary or inflationary gap, outline possible fiscal policies, and explain how each of these policies affect aggregate demand:
   a. the unemployment rate is 7 percent and inflation is rising
   b. real output is falling and unemployment is 9.5 percent
   c. the unemployment rate is 7.5 percent and prices are stable

2. In each of the following cases, calculate the values of MPC, MPW, and the spending multiplier:
   a. a $1 million increase in income leads to a $350 000 rise in consumption on domestic items
   b. a $4 million decrease in income results in a $1 million drop in consumption on domestic items
   c. a $5 million decrease in income causes a $3 million drop in withdrawals

3. "The more regressive Canada's tax system, the less effective automatic stabilizers become." Discuss.

4. Assume that Canadian governments tax away 40 cents of each dollar of new income, that 30 percent of the remaining 60 cents of disposable income is spent on imports, and that 5 percent of disposable income is saved.
   a. What is the value of the marginal propensity to withdraw?
   b. How much of each new dollar of income is spent on domestic consumption items?
   c. What is the value of the Canadian spending multiplier?

5. Draw charts similar to those in Figure 13.4 to show the changes in real output and withdrawals that occur in the first three spending rounds when there is a $810 increase in government purchases in an economy with an MPC of 0.33.

6. For each of the following cases, calculate the spending multiplier and find the direction and size of the shift in the AD curve:
   a. government purchases increase by $2 billion in an economy with an MPW of 0.65
   b. government purchases decrease by $5 billion in an economy with an MPC of 0.45
   c. a tax rise causes an initial $3 billion decrease in spending on domestic items in an economy with an MPW of 0.7
   d. a $4 billion tax cut causes an initial $1.5 billion increase in spending on domestic items

7. A decrease in government purchases of $8 billion leads to an initial $4.4 billion decrease in withdrawals.
   a. Find the values of MPW, MPC and the spending multiplier in this economy.
   b. State the direction and size of the shift in the AD curve.
   c. Draw a graph showing the policy's possible effects, given an initial equilibrium price level and real output of 130 and $650 billion.

8. Explain the effects of a rise in personal and corporate tax rates on (a) the equilibrium real output and price level, (b) the spending multiplier, (c) the effectiveness of automatic stabilizers in smoothing out the business cycle.

9. Provincial governments sometimes pursue discretionary fiscal policies. How does the spending multiplier for this type of policy within a provincial economy differ from the corresponding multiplier for federal fiscal policy within the entire Canadian economy? Explain.

10. With the aid of aggregate demand/aggregate supply graphs, outline how the principle of an annually balanced budget can increase the severity of recessionary and inflationary gaps through the business cycle.

11. Explain how a series of federal budget surpluses can lead to a spiral of larger surpluses and rapidly decreasing public debt.

12. (Advanced Question)
Using two aggregate demand/aggregate supply graphs, show why the estimate of potential output is so crucial in determining the size of an economy's recessionary and inflationary gaps.

13. Access the Department of Finance s website (at http://www.fin.gc.ca/), and use the links provided to find the most recent budget documents for the federal government.
    a. Explain how the annual federal deficit or surplus is related to changes forecast in net public debt in the current fiscal year.
    b. Is net public debt expected to rise or fall relative to GDP in the current year? Explain.

Advancing Economic Thought

CAUSES OF HIGH UNEMPLOYMENT

Paul Krugman and Rising Natural Unemployment Rates

Though in the short run governments are concerned with stabilizing the economy at its potential output, in the long run they can focus instead on raising potential output by reducing the economy's natural unemployment rate. Noted American economist Paul Krugman, who is a professor at the Massachussetts Institute of Technology, has put forward important theoretical insights on a range of contemporary economic topics. In the following article, he evaluates why the natural unemployment rate in many countries, including Canada, has risen over the past few decades. He also offers tentative solutions to reverse this trend.

The starting point for most analytical discussion of unemployment trends is the hypothesis that at any given time a national economy is characterized by a "natural rate" of unemployment. Expansion of aggregate may push unemployment below this rate, but only at the cost of higher and accelerating inflation.

It follows from this hypothesis that changes in unemployment must be separated into two components: "cyclical" fluctuations around the natural rate, which can be attributed to changes in aggregate demand, and "structural" movements in the natural rate itself, which can result from changes in labour market institutions, demographic shifts and so on. What policies one advocates to reverse a rise in unemployment depends crucially on whether the rise is cyclical or structural.

For the U.S., at least, the natural rate hypothesis has a very solid basis in experience. Inflation consistently accelerates when the unemployment rate is low, and decelerates when that rate is high. Admittedly, a simply relationship like this can be contructed only for the U.S. among advanced countries. The reason is that the U.S. is unique in having no visible long-term trend in its unemployment rate, suggesting that the natural rate has been more or less constant. For other industrial countries it is necessary to attempt to estimate shifts in the natural rate.

The unemployment rates consistent with stable inflation have unambiguously risen, in Canada and especially in Europe. Inflation in the European Community was stable in the early 1960s, despite an average unemployment rate of little more than 2 percent; it was rising in the late 1980s, in spite of an average unemployment rate of more than 8 percent, suggesting that the natural rate of unemployment has risen by at least six percentage points.

Why Has The Natural Rate Risen?

A wide variety of explanations have been offered for the apparent rise in the natural rate of unemployment. I will offer just one explanation, in two parts. The first part is that persistent high unemployment can be explained by the disincentive effects of welfare state policies. The second part is that market forces pushing toward greater inequality have worsened the unemployment consequences of the welfare state.

The Welfare State and Unemployment

By just about any measure, the U.S. taxes less and provides less support to the unemployed than do European nations. The U.S. has also, of course, been able to avoid the upward trend in unemployment that has afflicted Europe. It is only natural to suspect that the two facts are related: that the generosity of Europe's welfare states is in some sense responsible for the rise in their unemployment rates.

How might a welfare state create unemployment? Taxes and regulations may raise the costs to firms of offering jobs, and thus reduce the wages they are willing to pay. And benefits such as unemployment insurance may reduce the incentive for workers to accept jobs, and thus raise the wages they demand.

This scenario implies that, across countries, there should be a positive relationship between unemployment and both the level of benefits to the unemployed and the tax wedge. It also implies that within countries unemployment should be higher among low-productivity workers. Both propositions have some empirical support.

But this is a story about the level of the unemployment rate, rather than its trend. It does not explain why unemployment rates in Europe should have risen so much, since European welfare states were already notably generous in the low-employment era of the early 1970s. Most analysts have therefore looked for the explanation of the upward trend not in changed policies but in a changed environment. In particular, it has become increasingly common to argue that the upward trend in unemployment is the result of market forces that "want" to produce greater inequality of earnings. The collision between these market forces and the attempts of the welfare state to limit inequality then lead to higher unemployment.

Inequality and Unemployment If the wages that the market is willing to pay workers of low productivity fall relative to the level of unemployment benefits, more workers will find that, at available pay rates, it is not worth working. In a strong welfare state the increase in underlying pressures toward inequality may not be clearly visible in the actual distribution of earned wages, since those workers whose relative wages would have fallen the most are instead priced out of the labour market. In a weak welfare state, the market push toward greater inequality will simply result in greater inequality.

These observations suggest two points. First, if a tendency toward greater inequality is an important cause of rising unemployment, we might expect to see less of that trend in countries with niggardly welfare states. Second, in those countries where there is no upward trend in unemployment, we should expect to see a marked rise in wage inequality. The dramatic increase in wage inequality in the U.S. has led many observers to conclude that growing U.S. inequality and growing European unemployment are different sides of the same coin.

The Market Forces Behind Greater Inequality

The evidence clearly rejects the view that growing competition from the Third World has been the source either of growing inequality in the U.S. or of rising unemployment in Europe.

Although the relative wages of skilled workers have risen, most sectors have increased the ratio of highly skilled to less-skilled workers in their labour force; this immediately indicates a change in production that raises the marginal product of the skilled relative to the unskilled. And virtually all of the rise in the relative demand for skilled workers seems to have been a result of this change in demand. The growth of earnings inequality in the U.S.—and quite possibly therefore much of the rise in structural unemployment in Europe—would thus seem to have been the result of technological changes that just happen to work against unskilled workers.

This answer may, however, seem unsatisfying. It is far from clear just what technological changes have devalued unskilled work. It is hard to believe that the dramatic progress in information and communications technology over the past two decades have not somehow played a central role. The supporting evidence is mixed, however, and the actual linkages are not at all well understood—a point that is important to remember when we turn to policy.

What Can Be Done?

If the European unemployment problem and the U.S. inequality problem are, indeed, two sides of the same coin, there are a limited number of sensible strategies available.

Human Capital The most optimistic viewpoint on the inequality/unemployment problem is that investment in human capital—both in basic education and in retraining for older workers—can reverse the tendency toward greater inequality.

Is it realistic to expect government education and training programs to make a large enough impact on the wage distribution to have any noticeable effect? It is unclear how much of the spread in the earnings distribution is actually tied to formal eduaction. Second, improvements in basic education will, by definition, take a very long time to be reflected in the actual labour market. As a result, human capital optimists tend to stress retraining, which might have a more immediate payoff; but there is little evidence suggesting that retraining schemes are actually particularly effective in raising worker productivity. Above all, it is hard to see any evidence in the data that good education and retraining are rewarded with good labour market performance.

Pruning the Welfare State Theory, experience, and evidence all suggest that unemployment can be cut by reducing both the generosity and duration of benefits to the unemployed, thereby increasing the desperation with which the unemployed must search for jobs. The experience of the U.K., which has lowered its social safety net part way from European towards U.S. levels, suggest that the U.K.'s natural rate has in fact declined both absolutely and relative to those of its European neighbours.

There is a cost to this approach, and the tradeoff is not very pleasant. When the welfare state is scaled back, the lowest-income members of society are in fact hurt. The new jobs created are, predictably, low-wage. And those who are still unemployed after the reduction in benefits are especially hard hit.

Subsidizing Employment Until recently, smaller European countries, and especially Sweden, seemed to escape both Eurosclerosis and the American affliction of growing inequality. The key element was an "active manpower policy," in which the government was prepared to make large outlays in an effort to keep unemployment low. Unemployed workers were sent to expensive retraining programs; employers were offered substantial subsidies for hiring the long-term unemployed; and the government itself acted as an employer of last resort. Unfortunately, this record of success ended in the 1990s. The Swedish unemployment rate, less than 2 percent in 1990, has nearly quadrupled, and many Swedes attributed the country's slide in economic rankings to the long-term effects of its social policies.

As a matter of economic principle, subsidized employment for those who would otherwise be unemployed should be a way to cut through the otherwise agonizing tradeoff between mass unemployment and mass poverty. As a practical matter of political economy, is it possible to carry out such a policy in a way that targets the groups that really need it, and thus avoids a runaway growth of expenditure? Five years ago, one might have said yes, and pointed to the Swedish example; at this point, the apparent unravelling of that model makes it difficult to argue for implementation of Swedish-style labour market policies.

Conclusion

Unfortunately, it is hard to offer any comforting predictions. The unemployment problem of the advanced nations has no painless solutions, and we should not expect effective action to solve the problem until or unless it becomes a true crisis.

Source

"The Causes of High Unemployment," *Policy Options*, July-August 1996, pp. 20-24.

1. **Estimates in the mid-1990s suggest that the average natural unemployment rate in European countries is close to 10 percent, while it is 6 percent (or lower) in the United States. According to Krugman, what accounts for this difference?**

2. **Explain how rising income inequality in the United States and high unemployment in European countries may be connected.**

MOUNTAIN OR MIRAGE

The Debate Over Public Debt

At first sight, the figures are astounding. From 1982, when public debt was under $5000 per Canadian, the federal government's debt rose by 1996 to about $20 000 per capita. And supplementing this 1996 figure is another amount over $6000 that each Canadian owes because of the debts of provincial and territorial governments—making a total of over $26 000 a head.

Has public debt skyrocketed out of control, are the potential costs of this debt exaggerated by those who want less government involvement in the economy, or does the truth lie somewhere in-between? Because the costs are great whatever the truth—huge debt at one extreme, potentially reduced government programs at the other—this is a question not only for economists and policy-makers, but also for the public as a whole. Let's take a look at opposite perceptions.

Debt Problems Are Overemphasized

People who believe that the negative aspects of public debt have been exaggerated give four main arguments: public debt can increase current output, most of this debt is owed to ourselves, we should take into account the assets created by this debt, and as a percentage of GDP the debt is still lower than it has sometimes been in the past.

Benefits of Public Debt As discussed in Chapter 12, the amount by which real output falls short of its potential level represents the permanent loss of output due to high unemployment. To the extent that expansionary fiscal policy minimizes this gap, it provides a significant benefit—both by supplementing the economy's output and by reducing the human costs of unemployment. According to this argument, any disadvantages caused by the increases in federal debt are minor in comparison to its positive contribution to economic growth.

Debt to Ourselves The federal government issues bonds to deal with the debt. However, most bonds—about three-quarters of the total value—are actually a liability Canada owes to Canadian bondholders. Supporters of fiscal policy stress this number's significance. They argue that, when interest is paid on Canadian-owned public debt, funds are simply taken from one group of Canadians in the form of taxes or new borrowing and given to another group of Canadians. In other words, the total "economic pie" doesn't get bigger or smaller—just the sizes of the slices.

Assets Versus Liabilities When debt is used to create productive assets, it can be defended in the same way as the debt acquired by businesses for investment purposes. While Canadian government investment in capital goods—at least as defined in the national accounts—has fallen in recent decades as a percentage of GDP, supporters of fiscal policy suggest that the problem lies in the definitions. They believe that we should define productive assets more widely to include the country's human resources, whose worth is promoted through such expenditures as education. Unfortunately, it is difficult to put a value on a country's stock of productive assets when they are broadly defined in this way.

Comparisons With the Past Because of substantial inflation and economic growth over the years, debt trends expressed in current-year dollars are inadequate. A much better indication of the economy's ability to bear public debt is to express the debt as a percentage of nominal GDP, as shown in the figure below. For example, the $593.3 billion public debt at the end of the 1996–97 year equalled 74 percent of the 1996 nominal GDP of $797.8 billion [($593.3 ÷ $797.8) × 100%]. In contrast, the federal government's debt charges of $45.5 billion equalled 5.7 percent [$45.5 ÷ $797.8) × 100%]. It is interesting to note that, when measured in this way (column 3), public debt has sometimes been at higher levels than in the mid-1990s. For example, Canada's public debt in 1936–37, while only $3.1 billion in nominal dollars, was 67 percent of that year's GDP. By 1946–47, after federal borrowing to help finance Canada's involvement in World War II, public debt was over 100 percent of that year's GDP—a figure much higher than the 1996–97 level of 74 percent.

Public Debt Is a Major Problem

People who are concerned about present levels of public debt concentrate on a different set of

SIDELINE

Public Debt and GDP (billions of current dollars)

(1) Year	(2) Public Debt (billions of current-year $)	(3) Public Debt (% of nominal GDP)	(4) Public Debt Charges (% of nominal GDP)
1926-27	2.3	46	2.5
1936-37	3.1	67	3.0
1946-47	12.7	107	3.9
1956-57	11.4	35	1.5
1966-67	17.2	27	1.8
1976-77	39.9	20	2.4
1986-87	271.7	54	5.3
1996-97	593.3	74	5.7

As a percentage of nominal GDP, public debt rose between the 1920s and 1940s, and then fell until the 1970s. However, high interest rates during the 1980s and the first part of the 1990s meant that, as a percentage of nominal GDP, public debt charges were higher than ever before.

Source: Department of Finance, *Quarterly Economic Review: Special Report* (March 1992), pp. 33-34, and *The Budget Plan* (February 1997), p. 6. Reproduced by authority of the Minister of Industry, 1997.

arguments: the growth of public debt charges in relation to the size of the economy, the recent significance of provincial and territorial government debt, the apparent limits to future tax increases, and the potential future burdens that government debt may place on Canadians.

Public Debt Charges Although public debt as a proportion of GDP is lower today than during some other periods in Canada's history, public debt charges—or the annual interest payments on this debt—rose substantially until recent years. As shown in column 4 of the figure, public debt charges as a percentage of GDP were much higher in the 1980s and 1990s than in any previous decade since the 1920s, with public debt charges reaching almost 6 percent of nominal GDP in the mid-1990s. This trend was due to high real interest rates during the 1980s and the first part of the 1990s. A subsequent drop in real interest rates in the 1990s has eased the problem, but public debt charges remain high when compared to the past.

Provincial and Territorial Debt The comparison of public debt and nominal GDP shown in the figure underestimates the overall expansion of debt for all levels of government in Canada. In former decades, the debts of provincial and territorial governments in Canada tended to be relatively minor. At the end of the 1981–82 fiscal year, for example, the combined net debts of provincial and territorial governments represented only 4 percent of Canada's GDP. By the end of the 1996–97 fiscal year, however, this combined debt stood at $203 billion, or 25 percent of the country's GDP. Adding this debt to the federal debt means that the total debt of all levels of government had reached over 100 percent of GDP.

Tax Limits When total government debt charges rise, Canadian governments can keep their budget deficits in check either by increasing taxes or by reducing other expenditures, known as program spending. In the past, tax increases have commonly been used as a way of limiting budget deficits. However, in recent years, Canadians have grown more reluctant to shoulder further tax burdens, making it unlikely that tax rates can rise much beyond present levels. As a result, governments have been forced to engage in unpopular cuts in program spending.

Potential Future Burdens Many economists argue that public debt imposes future burdens on the entire Canadian economy. According to the *crowding out effect,* higher levels of government borrowing raise demand in the market for loanable funds, which we considered in Chapter 8. This leads to an increase in interest rates, causing businesses to reduce their investment spending. The result is a lower future stock of real capital in the economy and hence a lower rate of economic growth.

Another potential burden of public debt is the portion owed to foreigners. While just over one-quarter of Canada's combined federal and provincial/territorial debt is now foreign-held, this proportion has risen considerably in recent decades. Unlike the case of domestically held debt, interest payments on this debt represent a transfer of purchasing power from Canadians to foreigners. The higher the proportion of public debt owed to foreigners, therefore, the greater this transfer will be in the future.

1. During a certain fiscal year, the interest rate is 6 percent, federal spending (excluding public debt charges) is $180 billion, and federal tax revenues are $200 billion.
   a. What is the federal government s budget deficit if public debt at the start of the year is $500 billion? $600 billion? What conclusions can you draw concerning the relationship between budget deficits and the size of the public debt?
   b. How would your answers in part a. differ if the average interest rate on the public debt were 5 percent instead of 6 percent? What conclusions can you draw concerning the relationship between budget deficits and interest rates?
2. "A reduction in public debt should cause an increase in investment." Evaluate this statement using arguments provided in the article.

Chapter Fourteen
Money

The two greatest inventions of the human mind are writing and money—the common language of intelligence and the common language of self-interest.

—Honoré-Gabriel Mirabeau, French statesman and orator

Money talks, and, depending on who is listening, it can say a variety of things. Money's allure is undeniable. However, it is neither static nor easy to define; it has taken many forms and continues to evolve today. This chapter highlights three main issues: the functions money performs in modern economies, the connection between money and interest rates, and how banks help create money.

CHAPTER FOCUS

This chapter focuses on the following:

- the functions of money, its components, and the various definitions of money
- the Canadian financial system, types of deposits, cash reserves, and reserve ratios
- the demand for and supply of money, and equilibrium in the money market
- how money is created, and the money multiplier

MONEY AND ITS USES

The Functions of Money

Money serves three separate functions in any economy. It provides a means of exchange, a store of purchasing power, and a measure of value.

Means of Exchange

The most important function of money is that it acts as a means of payment whenever items are bought and sold. Without money, market participants must trade one product for another product, a transaction known as **barter**.

barter: a system of trading one product for another

coincidence of wants: the situation where someone purchasing an item finds a seller who wants what the purchaser is offering in return

Barter is an unwieldy method of exchanging products. Someone purchasing an item must find a seller who wants what the purchaser is offering in return. In other words, there must be a **coincidence of wants** between both parties. For example, a barber who wants to buy a clock must find a clockmaker who wants a haircut. Because a coincidence of wants is usually difficult to achieve, trade is discouraged, so most people living in a barter system produce many items for themselves.

Money overcomes these problems. The barber can deal with any clockmaker and pay in money, which the clockmaker can then use to purchase a wide range of items.

The benefits of money as a means of exchange are far-reaching. People can minimize the time they spend finding others with whom they can buy and sell. They can also focus their productive activity by devoting themselves to economic pursuits in which they are most adept. The barber can stick to cutting hair and the clockmaker to making clocks. Specialization promotes the division of labour and allows an economy to achieve higher levels of output. Therefore, the use of money not only facilitates transactions of goods and services—it also raises living standards.

Store of Purchasing Power

Money's second function is providing a safe and accessible store of wealth. Money is an attractive store of purchasing power during the period between the time it is earned and the time it is spent.

liquidity: the ease with which an asset can be converted into a means of payment

There are both benefits and drawbacks associated with holding wealth as money. Money's major advantage is its **liquidity**, or the ease with which it can be turned into a means of payment. Assets are most liquid when they can be quickly turned into money with little loss in value. All financial assets are liquid to some degree, but none as much as money, which is perfectly liquid by its very nature.

Recall, however, that for any economic choice there is an opportunity cost. In this case, the cost of holding wealth in the form of money is the income sacrificed by not holding it in some other form. For example, someone who holds wealth by stashing a thousand-dollar bill in a cookie jar is sacrificing the income the wealth could earn if it were converted into a stock or bond. As a result, people hold wealth as money when the benefits of liquidity outweigh the income that could be earned by holding it in another form.

Measure of Value

unit of account: a pricing standard that allows all products to be valued consistently

Money also provides buyers and sellers with a **unit of account**, or pricing standard. The unit of account allows all products to be valued consistently against a common measure—in other words, it provides a point of comparison between, for example, apples and oranges. So, if apples cost $2 per kilogram and oranges cost $4 per kilogram, it is easy to see that oranges cost twice as much as apples. Recall from Chapter 10 that the unit of account does the same on a grander scale; expressing Gross Domestic Product (GDP) as a dollar value simplifies the picture by allowing a wide range of products to be quantified and combined.

In contrast, a barter economy requires many measures of value. The question, "How much does this cost?" would bring the inevitable reply, "It depends on what you've got." A clock, for example, might be exchanged for 100 apples, 50 oranges, 20 loaves of bread, 2 haircuts, or some number of any other product a market participant is offering. As well as creating a confusion of prices, a barter economy is difficult to measure.

The Canadian Financial System

deposit-takers: institutions or businesses that accept funds provided by savers and lend these funds to borrowers

Now that we've defined the functions money serves, we will consider the system in which it operates as well as the supply of money. The supply of money is closely associated with institutions known as **deposit-takers**, which accept funds provided by savers and lend these funds to borrowers. For the deposit-taker, the deposits it accepts and owes back to savers are its liabilities; the funds it lends to borrowers, and which borrowers owe the deposit-taker, are its assets. These institutions make a profit by paying lower interest rates on deposits than they charge on loans.

cash reserves: funds kept on hand by deposit-takers to meet the needs of depositors withdrawing funds

Not all funds flowing into the institution flow out. Deposit-takers also keep on hand some amount, known as **cash reserves**, so that depositors can withdraw funds when they request them. Because deposit-takers make little or no income from cash reserves, they hold only the minimum of their assets in this form.

Deposit-takers fall into two categories: chartered banks and near banks.

Chartered Banks

chartered banks: deposit-takers allowed by federal charter to offer a wide range of financial services

Chartered banks form the backbone of Canada's financial system. Unlike other deposit-takers, these institutions are allowed, through a charter they receive from the federal government, to sell a wide range of financial services.

While there are over 50 chartered banks in Canada, 6 big banks dominate the sector—the Royal Bank of Canada, the Canadian Imperial Bank of Commerce, the Bank of Montreal, the Bank of Nova Scotia, the Toronto-Dominion Bank, and the National Bank. Each of these banks has many branches, following what is known as a branch banking system.

Together, the "big six" control about 90 percent of Canada's chartered bank deposits and assets. Most of the remaining chartered banks are relatively small foreign-owned banks. Apart from American and Mexican banks, which are exempt because of recent trade agreements, these banks are limited by law to 12 percent of Canadian chartered bank assets.

The Canadian chartered banking system is therefore an oligopoly. While the reduced competition may lead to some market inefficiencies, it also enhances the financial soundness of the Canadian system. By comparison, in the United States there are well over 10 000 commercial banks. About a third of them operate under federal law and are known as national banks. The others, called state banks, are controlled by state governments. Many of these state banks are relatively small and have few branches. While competition is enhanced by the number of players, the modest size of each bank can increase the chance of financial difficulties.

Near Banks

near banks: deposit-takers that are not chartered and have more specialized services; mainly trust companies, mortgage loan companies, and credit unions

In contrast to chartered banks, **near banks** are not chartered and have more specialized services. The most important are trust companies, mortgage loan companies, and credit unions.

Trust companies administer various types of accounts, including estates and trust funds. They also compete with chartered banks by taking deposits and granting loans, mainly to households.

As their name suggests, mortgage loan companies specialize in granting mortgages, and raise some of their funds through deposit-taking. Recall from Chapter 8 that a mortgage is a loan whose collateral is in the form of land and buildings.

Credit unions (called *caisses populaires* in Quebec, where they are particularly prevalent) are nonprofit institutions that take deposits and grant loans to their members.

FIGURE 14.1 Chartered Banks and Near Banks in Canada

(total assets, $ billions, 31 October 1996)

Chartered Banks		**Near Banks**	
Royal Bank	$ 218.0	Trust and mortgage loan companies	$ 72.1
CIBC	199.0	Credit unions and caisses populaires	103.9
Montreal	169.8	Total	$176.0
Scotiabank	157.3		
Toronto-Dominion	125.7		
National	53.1		
Others	90.8		
Total	$1013.7		

The "big six" chartered banks dominate the financial services market. These banks hold about 90 percent of all chartered bank assets, and their combined assets are more than five times that of near banks.

Sources: Bank of Canada, *Bank of Canada Review* (Spring 1997), Tables D1–D2; Canadian Bankers Association, *Domestic Banks' Financial Results* 1995/96 (Dec. 1996), p. 1.

Other Financial Institutions

In addition to deposit-takers—especially chartered banks—there are other types of financial institutions: insurance companies and investment dealers. Insurance companies offer insurance policies to their clients and use the funds to buy various types of income-producing financial assets. Investment dealers buy and sell financial securities such as stocks and bonds for their customers.

The Financial System

Traditionally, chartered banks, trust companies, insurance companies, and investment dealers formed the four pillars of the financial system. Each group had its specialized functions. Now, however, regulations governing financial institutions in Canada and in other countries have been loosened. Financial deregulation, as it is called, has allowed each institution to perform a wider range of functions.

For example, chartered banks are taking on some of the functions of other financial institutions. "Financial supermarkets" have sprung up to give a complete range of financial services under one corporate roof. While deregulation has promoted competition and efficiency, some critics fear it will lead to several giant companies controlling most of the Canadian financial system.

The Supply of Money

The supply of money is made up of currency and some deposits.

Currency

currency: paper money and coins

Currency includes paper notes, such as twenty-dollar bills, issued by Canada's central bank, the Bank of Canada. It also includes coinage produced by the Royal Mint.

Deposits

Recall that deposits are given to deposit-takers and lent out to borrowers, who pay interest. In this way, chartered banks and near banks make their profits. Deposits can be classified according to the conditions of their use. In general, the access the depositor has to his or her funds determines the interest rates paid on deposits. The longer a deposit-taker can make use of the funds, and the fewer the services the deposit-taker provides, the higher the interest rate.

demand deposits: accounts of funds to which depositors have immediate access

Demand Deposits In some cases, depositors can demand immediate access to their money. Such deposits are called **demand deposits**, and take the form of current and personal chequing accounts. Depositors can withdraw money directly from the bank or can write cheques, which are a convenient way for depositors to authorize banks to pay a certain sum to a named person or institution. In return for easy access to their deposits and because processing cheques is a relatively expensive operation, depositors receive a lower interest rate, or no interest, on their money.

notice deposits: accounts of funds for which deposit-takers may require notice before withdrawals can be made

Notice Deposits Deposit-takers can require notice before depositors withdraw funds in certain cases. **Notice deposits**, as these are called, pay substantial rates of interest but limit or exclude cheque-writing. Traditionally, both chartered banks and near banks accept notice deposits.

term deposits: accounts of funds to which depositors have no access for a fixed period of time

Term Deposits When depositors guarantee that they will not withdraw their funds for a fixed period of time, deposit-takers can pay a higher interest rate. **Term deposits**, as these are called, are traditionally accepted by chartered banks and near banks. Term deposits made by households are called personal term deposits, and those made by businesses are known as nonpersonal term deposits.

Foreign Currency Deposits

foreign currency deposits: accounts of funds held by Canadian residents that are valued in foreign currency

Some deposits provided by chartered banks in Canada are valued in terms of a foreign currency—usually the U.S. dollar. These **foreign currency deposits**, which are held by Canadian residents, are treated as a separate class of deposit.

Money Defined

What *is* money? The definitions range from the very narrow to the broad. In the following sections and in Figure 14.2, we'll examine the four most common definitions used by economists and government decision-makers: M1, M2, M3, and M2+.

M1

M1: the narrowest definition of money, consisting of currency outside chartered banks and publicly held demand deposits at chartered banks

The narrowest definition of money is **M1**. Its two components—publicly held currency and publicly held demand deposits at chartered banks—are the two most intensively used forms of money. Note that only currency circulating outside chartered banks is part of M1; cash reserves held by chartered banks are not included. Also note that only demand deposits held by the public at chartered banks are included; government-owned deposits are left out. Because of their importance, currency outside chartered banks and demand deposits appear in all other money definitions also.

M2

M2: a broader definition of money, consisting of M1 plus notice deposits, and personal term deposits at chartered banks

M2 is a broader definition of money that includes not only currency outside chartered banks and demand deposits at chartered banks (M1), but also funds from notice deposits and personal term deposits at chartered banks. While currency and demand deposits are perfectly liquid, notice deposits and personal term deposits are often converted into another form before being used as a means of payment.

M3

M3: the definition of money consisting of M2 plus nonpersonal term deposits and foreign currency deposits at chartered banks

An even broader definition of the money supply is **M3**. M3 includes the components of M2 (currency outside chartered banks, plus demand deposits, notice deposits, and personal term deposits at chartered banks), as well as nonpersonal term deposits and foreign currency deposits at chartered banks. These additional types of deposits are relatively liquid, although less so than those included in M2.

M2+

M2+: the definition of money consisting of M2 plus corresponding deposits at near banks and some other liquids assets

With the growing similarity between chartered banks and near banks in the Canadian financial system, economists have been paying more attention to a fourth definition of the money supply. **M2+** includes currency outside chartered banks, plus demand deposits, notice deposits, and personal term deposits at both chartered banks and near banks. Some similar assets issued by other financial institutions are also included. It does not, however, include any nonpersonal term deposits or foreign currency deposits.

near money: all deposits not included in M1, plus some other highly liquid assets

Note how the definitions build on one another, all including the most narrow definition, M1. In contrast to M1, other definitions of money include what is sometimes called **near money**. Near money includes all deposits at chartered banks except publicly held demand deposits (which are included in M1), all deposits at near banks, and some other highly liquid assets such as Canada Savings Bonds. While relatively easily converted to a means of payment, near money is less frequently used than money as defined by M1.

Choosing a Definition

Since currency and demand deposits are used solely as means of payment, they seem to fit best the definition of money. Therefore, many economists view M1 as the most accurate measure of the money supply.

FIGURE 14.2
The Canadian Money Supply

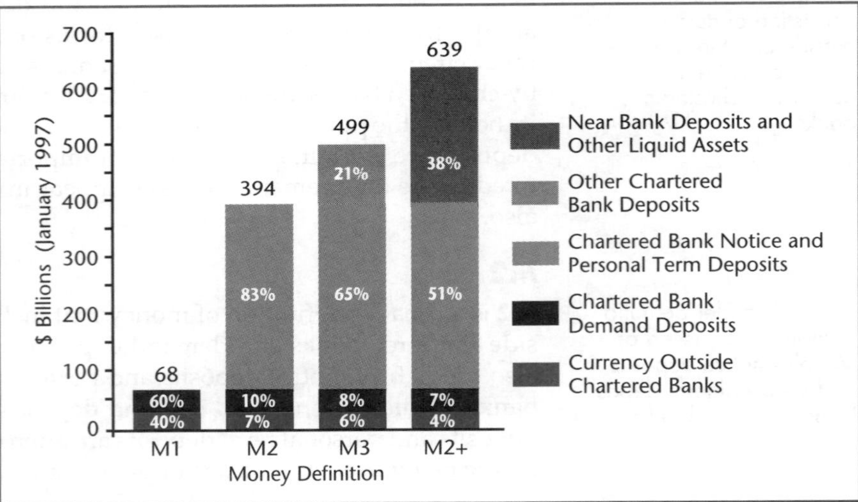

Currency and demand deposits make up approximately equal shares of M1 while M2 is dominated by notice and personal term deposits. These deposits also dominate M3. M2+ is by far the broadest of the four money definitions, with deposits made in near banks (as well as other liquid assets) rivalling in size similar deposits made in chartered banks.

Source: Bank of Canada, *Bank of Canada Review* (Spring 1997), Table E1.

Others believe that M1 is too narrow; these economists prefer broader definitions—especially M2 and M2+. They point to recent innovations in payment methods that have made the accounts included in M2 and M2+ more liquid.

The Role of Credit Cards

credit card: a means of payment that provides instantly borrowed funds

One of the main causes of the increasing liquidity of M2 and M2+ is the ability many consumers now have to pay with "plastic." A **credit card** provides its holder with the opportunity to buy goods and services with instantly borrowed funds. When a credit card is used for a purchase, the lending institution makes a loan or "credit" to the user equal to the amount of the sale. This loan lasts as long as it takes the credit card user to pay off the monthly bill.

Contrary to popular perception, credit cards are not money. They are simply an easy way for buyers to borrow funds for short periods. However, credit cards do have an indirect effect on the money supply by altering the way depositors use their deposit accounts.

Well-timed purchases made with credit cards do not have to be settled for over a month. So, for example, a person making a $50 purchase with a credit card is essentially taking out a short-term loan for the same amount. As long as this loan is paid back promptly, the purchaser is charged no interest. If credit card balances are not cleared monthly, however, the interest rate charged is higher than on most other consumer loans.

About half of all credit card users pay off their outstanding balances each month. Rather than paying currency for purchases throughout a month, card users can keep their funds in their deposit accounts until credit card payments are due. Because they can maintain their deposit accounts longer, they can accumulate more interest. If card users pay off their balance monthly (and so incur no interest charges), they can profit by using credit cards effectively. This trend to use deposit accounts in combination with credit cards has led some economists to suggest that M2 and M2+ are increasingly accurate measures of the money supply.

The Introduction of Debit Cards

debit card: a means of payment that instantaneously transfers funds from buyer to seller

Some buyers now use a new way of paying with plastic. A **debit card** allows a payment to be made through an instantaneous transfer of funds. While similar in appearance to credit cards, debit cards represent a different type of transaction, because the buyer's account is instantly reduced or "debited" by the amount of the purchase.

Debit cards are part of a widespread financial revolution that also includes the use of automated teller machines. This revolution is based on the ability of computers to move information electronically. For example, a supermarket customer might settle her $30 grocery bill with a debit card. With the use of a cash register linked electronically to financial institutions, the amount of $30 is automatically moved from her account to the supermarket's account.

Unlike credit cards, which are issued only to people who have an acceptable credit history, debit cards can be employed by virtually any depositor. They can be of particular benefit to people who are tempted to overuse the instant spending power provided by credit cards. There are costs associated with debit cards, however. In the short term, the retail sector must pay for a sophisticated computer system. In some cases, this is leading to higher prices for the consumer. However, in the long term, there will be a downward pressure on prices as business costs associated with handling cash are reduced.

Thinking About Economics

Will cash eventually disappear?

Because everyone with a deposit account can use a debit card, it's possible that paper currency may be phased out. A cashless society would bring with it some significant benefits. Conceivably, consumers would face lower prices as the costs associated with handling cash fall, while the problems of theft would be reduced. Also, since records would exist for all transactions, it would be easier for governments to collect taxes and stamp out illegal activities.

However, a cashless society has potential drawbacks. Critics point out that governments may intervene unduly, that computer records of citizens' transactions and activities would mean a loss of privacy, and that the expense and complexities of cashless business would shut down some businesses and deter others from starting. And, of course, those involved in the underground economy, which depends on cash, would not welcome its demise.

BRIEF REVIEW

1. Money serves as a means of exchange, a store of purchasing power, and a measure of value. In contrast, barter is a cumbersome system of exchange.
2. Canada's financial system includes chartered banks, near banks, insurance companies, and investment dealers. Increasing deregulation is changing the functions of financial institutions.
3. Deposit-takers accept deposits and grant loans. Deposits vary according to their conditions.
4. Money may be defined narrowly as currency outside chartered banks and demand deposits at chartered banks (M1), or it may be defined more broadly to include less liquid assets sometimes known as near money.
5. Credit and debit cards are not directly part of the money supply, but are gradually changing the use of money.

THE MONEY MARKET

The Demand for Money

Recall that money functions as a means of exchange, a store of purchasing power, and a measure of value. In the economy as a whole, money is demanded for reasons related to the first two functions.

Transactions Demand

If there is a rise in an economy's real output or price level, the total value of transactions expands. This increases the demand for money. Conversely, a fall in real output or the price level decreases the total value of transactions and the demand for money. In other words, changes in the total value of transactions affect the **transactions demand** for money, which is connected to money's use as a means of exchange.

transactions demand: the demand for money that is related to its use as a means of exchange

Asset Demand

asset demand: the demand for money that is related to its use as a store of purchasing power

In contrast, the **asset demand** for money is associated with money's function as a store of purchasing power. As discussed earlier, the main cost of holding money is the added income that could have been earned by converting it into a higher-paying asset such as a bond.

Recall that bonds are formal contracts that set out the amount borrowed, by whom, for what period of time, and at what interest rate. Most bonds can be bought and sold among lenders on the open market. When bonds "mature," or reach the end of their term, the bond issuer pays the principal to the bondholder.

On the bond market, prices for bonds are inversely related to the prevailing interest rate. To see why, suppose you purchased a $1000 bond with an interest rate originally specified as 6 percent per annum. In other words, you expect an annual interest payment of $60 until the bond matures, at which time you, or whoever else holds the bond, will be repaid the $1000 principal. Two years later, you want to sell the bond, but the prevailing interest rate is 12 percent. In other words, newly issued $1000 bonds are promising annual interest payments of $120, while the bond you own promises only a $60 annual interest payment. Because its annual payment is half that of new bonds, your bond will fall in price to about $500, or half of the value of a newly issued $1000 bond. Similarly, if the interest rate declines from its initial value of 6 percent to 3 percent, the price of your bond will double from its original value of $1000 to about $2000, since it provides twice the annual interest payment ($60) than the payment found on a newly issued $1000 bond ($30).

Bonds are the most popular way for governments and large businesses to raise funds. They are also attractive assets. Because they can be easily bought and sold before their term has ended, they offer liquidity as well as relatively high rates of return in exchange for the risk associated with changes in bond prices. For individuals who hold wealth, therefore, bonds offer the likeliest alternative to holding money—depending on how individuals view the tradeoff between bonds' higher rates of return and higher risk.

For these reasons, the asset demand for money is inversely related to the nominal interest rate on bonds. When this interest rate increases, the prices of bonds fall. Lower bond prices cause some individuals to convert their money into bonds, reducing the asset demand for money. Similarly, a reduction in the nominal interest rate means that the prices of bonds rise. Higher-priced bonds become a less attractive option for wealthholders, causing more of them to hold money rather than bonds, thus pushing up the asset demand for money.

money demand: the amounts of money demanded at all possible interest rates

money demand schedule: money demand expressed in a table

money demand curve: money demand expressed in a graph

Money demand is the amounts of money demanded, unadjusted for inflation, at all possible interest rates. Money demand expressed in a table gives the **money demand schedule**; expressed in a graph, it gives the **money demand curve**, D_m. As Figure 14.3 shows, the money demand curve has a negative slope. This slope is determined by the asset demand for money, which is inversely related to interest rates. As we have just seen, a rise in the nominal interest rate on bonds reduces the asset demand for money, while a fall in the nominal interest rate increases the asset demand. Therefore, a change in the asset demand causes a change in the quantity of money demanded, or a movement along the money demand curve.

In contrast, a change in transactions demand changes the amounts demanded at all interest rates—that is, it causes a shift in the money demand curve. An increase in either real output or the price level raises the transactions demand for money at every possible interest rate. Hence, the money demand curve shifts to the right, from D_{m0} to D_{m1}, as shown in Figure 14.3. Conversely, a decrease in either real output or the price level shifts the money demand curve to the left.

FIGURE 14.3 The Demand for Money

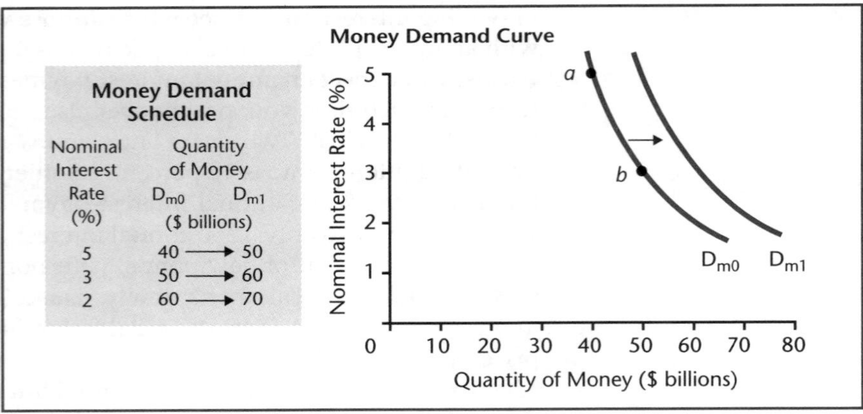

Money Demand Schedule

Nominal Interest Rate (%)	Quantity of Money ($ billions) D_{m0}	→ D_{m1}
5	40	50
3	50	60
2	60	70

Because a greater quantity of money is demanded at lower nominal interest rates, the money demand curve has a negative slope. A change in the interest rate causes a change in the asset demand for money, which is shown as a movement along the money demand curve. For example, a rise in the interest rate from 3 to 5 percent causes a decrease in the quantity of money demanded (from point *b* to point *a*). An increase in real output or the price level causes money demand to increase at all interest rates, as shown by the shift from D_{m0} to D_{m1}.

The Supply of Money

money supply: a set amount of money in the economy, as determined by government decision-makers

money supply schedule: money supply expressed in a table

money supply curve: money supply expressed in a graph

While money demanded is inversely related to interest rates, the **money supply** is a set amount (unadjusted for inflation) determined by government decision-makers. As Figure 14.4 shows, money supply can be expressed in a table, giving the **money supply schedule**, or in a graph, giving the **money supply curve**, S_m. No matter what the nominal interest rate, the amount of money supplied is a constant value, as depicted by the vertical supply curve, S_{m0}. Only when government decision-makers decide to change the money supply does the supply curve shift. Therefore, the supply curve shifts to the right, from S_{m0} to S_{m1}, only when the government increases the money supply. Likewise, the money supply curve shifts to the left only when the government decreases the money supply.

FIGURE 14.4
The Supply of Money

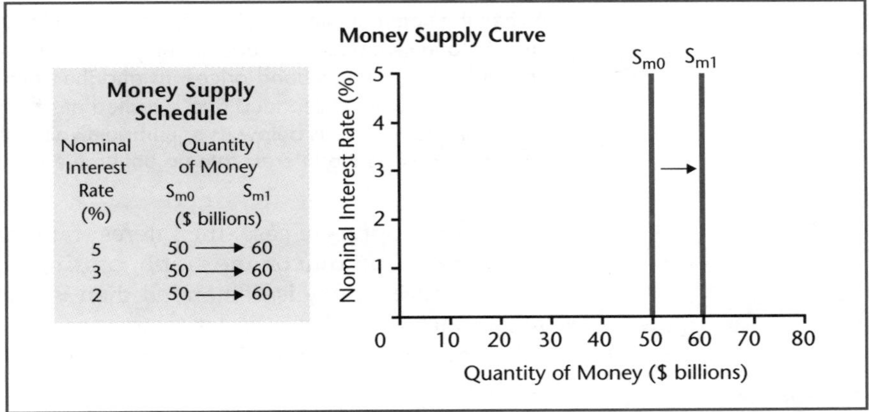

Money Supply Schedule

Nominal Interest Rate (%)	Quantity of Money ($ billions) S_{m0}		S_{m1}
5	50	⟶	60
3	50	⟶	60
2	50	⟶	60

Because government policy-makers determine the supply of money at any given time, the money supply curve is a vertical line at that amount. Any change in the money supply results in a shift of the vertical line, as shown, for example, by the shift from S_{m0} to S_{m1}.

Equilibrium in the Money Market

The demand and supply of money interact in the money market to bring about a state of equilibrium. As shown in Figure 14.5, the equilibrium level of the nominal interest rate is found at the intersection of the money demand and money supply curves. As usual, surpluses and shortages help bring about equilibrium in the market.

When the interest rate is above its equilibrium level—for example, at 5 percent as opposed to 3 percent in Figure 14.5—there is a surplus of money. In other words, more money is supplied than is demanded. As people try to rid themselves of money and buy assets that will provide high earnings, the demand for these assets rises, pushing up their price and causing the nominal interest rate to fall. This trend of falling interest rates continues until the discrepancy between the demand and supply of money is eliminated.

FIGURE 14.5
Equilibrium in the Money Market

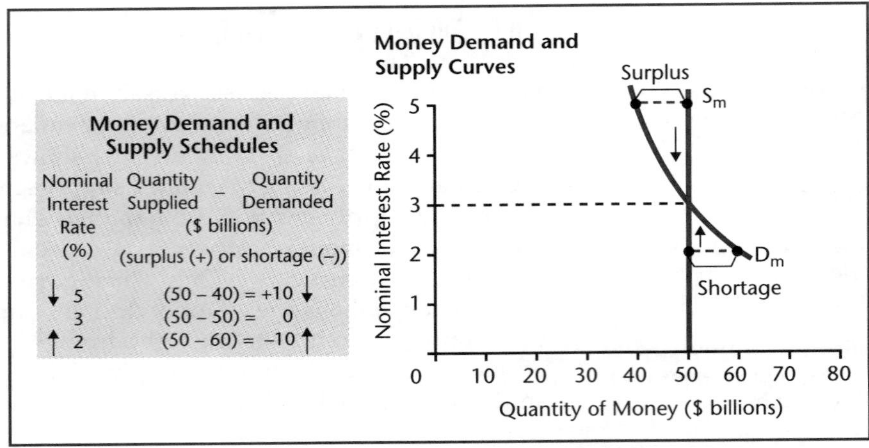

When the nominal interest rate exceeds its equilibrium value of 3 percent, the quantity of money supplied exceeds quantity demanded. This surplus leads to more buying of bonds, forcing bond prices up and the nominal interest rate down until the quantity of money demanded and supplied are the same at $50 billion. When the nominal interest rate is below its equilibrium value, the opposite occurs. A shortage of money pushes the interest rate up until the equilibrium point is reached.

In the opposite case, the interest rate falls short of the equilibrium value, as at 2 percent on the graph, causing a shortage of money. In other words, more money is demanded than is supplied. As people try to sell assets such as bonds in order to acquire money, the price of these assets falls, causing the nominal interest rate to rise until the equilibrium point is attained.

BRIEF REVIEW

1. Demand for money is of two types, each of which is related to a function of money. Transactions demand relates to the function of money as a means of exchange; asset demand relates to the function of money as a store of purchasing power.
2. Money demand is the amounts of money demanded at all possible interest rates, which can be expressed in a table or a graph. The money demand curve has a negative slope because of the inverse relationship of money demanded to interest rates.
3. Money supply is a set amount that is determined by government decision-makers. As a result, the money supply curve is a vertical line at this set amount.
4. The economy's equilibrium interest rate and money supply occur at the intersection of the money demand and money supply curves.

MONEY CREATION

When setting the money supply, government policy-makers must take into account the actions of deposit-takers. This is because a substantial portion of money in the economy is held in the form of deposits.

Recall that deposit-takers receive deposits from savers and lend to borrowers, while keeping some cash reserves on hand for withdrawals by depositors. By charging higher interest rates to borrowers than they pay to depositors, deposit-takers make profits. In a sense, through this process of receiving deposits and lending funds, chartered banks and near banks create deposit money. This is not by some trick of magic, but by the roles played by cash reserves and the profit motive.

Desired Reserves

desired reserves: minimum cash reserves that deposit-takers hold to satisfy anticipated withdrawal demands

Until 1994, chartered banks were legally required to hold certain levels of cash reserves, more than near banks were required to hold. Since then, both chartered banks and near banks have kept only **desired reserves**, which are the minimum amounts of cash necessary to satisfy anticipated withdrawal demands.

The Reserve Ratio

reserve ratio: desired reserves expressed as a percentage of deposits or as a decimal

In general, the more money a deposit-taker holds in deposits, the greater the withdrawals it can expect. Therefore, the best way to deal with anticipated withdrawals is for the deposit-taker to hold a certain portion of deposits in the form of cash reserves. This portion, which can be expressed as a percentage or in decimal terms, is the **reserve ratio**. Suppose, for example, that a bank has a reserve ratio of 0.10. If the bank has deposits of $100 million, then it will hold 10 percent of this dollar value as desired reserves ($100 million × 0.10):

$$\text{Reserve ratio} = \frac{\text{desired reserves}}{\text{deposits}}$$

$$0.10 = \frac{\$10 \text{ million}}{\$100 \text{ million}}$$

Different types of deposits have different reserve ratios. For example, demand deposits require a higher reserve ratio than do other types of deposits. However, to examine the process of money creation, we'll simplify matters by assuming a uniform reserve ratio.

Excess Reserves

excess reserves: cash reserves that are in excess of desired reserves

At times, deposit-takers find that their cash reserves exceed desired levels, or they have **excess reserves**. For example, a chartered bank with deposits of $100 million and desired reserves of $10 million may find itself holding $14 million in actual cash reserves:

Excess reserves = cash reserves – desired reserves
$4 million = $14 million – $10 million

Because idle cash reserves earn no profit, deposit-takers will try to transform any excess reserves into income-producing assets as quickly as possible. They therefore lend out the full amount of excess reserves. In our example, the bank will lend out the $4 million excess to borrowers.

The Money Creation Process

To see how lending out excess reserves "creates" money, let's consider an example. For the time being, we will make two key assumptions. First, the public holds money in the form of deposits and uses only cheques for transactions. Second, all deposits are made to one sort of deposit-taker, which we'll simply call banks, and all deposits are of one type, which allows cheques to be written against them. We'll also assume the banks' reserve ratio for their deposits to be 0.10, or 10 percent.

First Transaction

At the outset, Cabot Bank has cash reserves equal to desired reserves. However, Saver A receives $1000 in currency and immediately deposits it in Cabot Bank. As shown in Figure 14.6, Cabot Bank has a new cash asset as well as a new deposit liability to Saver A, each equalling $1000. So far, there has been no change in the amount of money in the economy, only in who holds it. Because the $1000 in currency is transformed into $1000 held in a deposit, no money is added to the money supply. (Recall that the $1000 in currency sitting in the vault of Cabot Bank is not considered part of the money supply.)

FIGURE 14.6 Opening a Deposit

Cabot Bank			
Assets		**Liabilities**	
Cash Reserves	*+$1000*	Saver A's Deposit	*+$1000*

Saver A deposits $1000 at Cabot Bank. As a result, Cabot Bank has new cash assets and deposit liabilities of $1000.

Second Transaction

Because of Saver A's deposit, Cabot Bank's total deposits increase by $1000. At the same time, the actual cash reserves increase by $1000 as well. However, with a reserve ratio of 0.10, Cabot Bank really only wants to keep $100 of the newly deposited $1000 on hand as desired reserves ($1000 × 0.10). As a result of this new deposit, Cabot Bank has excess reserves of $900 ($1000 – $100).

The bank responds by lending $900 to Borrower X. As Figure 14.7 demonstrates, the new loan increases Cabot Bank's deposit liabilities by

$900. In other words, by lending out its excess reserves, Cabot Bank creates $900 in new money.

FIGURE 14.7 Granting a Loan

Cabot Bank

Assets		**Liabilities**	
Cash Reserves	$1000	Saver A's Deposit	$1000
Loan to Borrower X	*+$900*	Borrowers X's Deposit	*+$900*

Cabot Bank lends out its $900 in excess reserves to Borrower X, creating new loan assets and deposit liabilities of $900. Since Borrower X's new deposit is money, the money supply has risen by $900.

Third Transaction

Now that he has the money, Borrower X uses his $900 loan to purchase goods or services. Figure 14.8 shows the resulting changes in both Cabot Bank's cash assets and the new deposit to Borrower X—they are both reduced by $900.

FIGURE 14.8 Withdrawing a Deposit

Cabot Bank

Assets		**Liabilities**	
Cash Reserves	$100 ($1000 – *$900)*	Saver A's Deposit	$1000
Loan to Borrower X	$900	Borrower X's Deposit	$0 ($900 – *$900)*

When Borrower X withdraws the $900 from his deposit, Cabot Bank's cash assets and deposit liabilities each fall by $900.

Fourth Transaction

So, does reducing Cabot Bank's deposits mean the newly created money suddenly disappears? It doesn't if we take into account Borrower X's $900 purchase. Suppose Borrower X bought something for $900 from Saver B. Saver B, in turn, deposits the $900 from the sale in her account at Fraser Bank. As a result, Fraser Bank's cash assets and deposit liabilities increase by $900, as shown in Figure 14.9. This means that the $900 deposit originally created by Cabot Bank has simply moved to Fraser Bank. As a result of this transaction, there is no change in the money supply.

FIGURE 14.9 Accepting Deposit Funds

Fraser Bank

Assets		**Liabilities**	
Cash Reserves	*+$900*	Saver B's Deposit	*+$900*

Saver B deposits the $900 from Borrower X's purchase in her account at Fraser Bank. The bank's cash assets and deposit liabilities both rise by $900.

Fifth Transaction

Now, let's consider Fraser Bank. Because Saver B's deposit to Fraser Bank increases the total deposits of the bank, desired reserves should increase by $90 ($900 × 0.10). Once again, however, the deposit of $900 also increases the cash reserves, thereby giving excess reserves of $810 ($900 – $90).

Because the excess reserves can be put to use to earn profits, Fraser Bank lends the $810 to Borrower Y. As a result, Fraser Bank's loan assets and deposit liabilities have jumped by $810, as shown in Figure 14.10. Because of this rise in deposits, more new money has been created, so the money supply has been boosted by another $810.

FIGURE 14.10 Granting a Loan

Fraser Bank			
Assets		**Liabilities**	
Cash Reserves	+$900	Saver B's Deposit	+$900
Loan to Borrower Y	*+$810*	Borrower Y's Deposit	*+$810*

Fraser Bank lends out its $810 in excess reserves to Borrower Y. This creates added loan assets and deposit liabilities of $810. Since Borrower Y's new deposit is money, the money supply increases by $810.

The Money Multiplier

The possible transactions are endless. However, we can see the process of money creation in the few transactions outlined. Recall that the quantity of money increased once, when Cabot Bank lent out its $900 in excess reserves to Borrower X, and again, when Fraser Bank lent out its excess reserves of $810 to Borrower Y. In other words, the money supply increases $1710 in these few transactions. Money will continue to be created as long as banks find they have excess cash reserves to lend out.

Notice how the process of money creation is similar to the process of the spending multiplier, as outlined in Chapter 13. In this money creation process, an initial change in money has a magnified effect on the money supply. The **money multiplier** is the value by which the initial change is multiplied to give the maximum total change in money supply. Suppose, for example, that the initial change in excess reserves is $900 and the final change in the money supply is $4500; the money multiplier therefore has a value of 5:

money multiplier: the value by which the amount of excess reserves is multiplied to give the maximum total change in money supply

$$\text{Change in money supply} = \text{change in excess reserves} \times \text{money multiplier}$$

$$\$4500 = \$900 \times 5$$

The Multiplier Formula

The value of the money multiplier is determined in the same way as the size of the spending multiplier. Recall that the spending multiplier is the reciprocal of the marginal propensity to withdraw (MPW), which indicates how much is taken out of the income-spending stream with each spending cycle.

In the case of the money creation process, deposit-takers hold back a certain portion of the funds in each lending cycle. As we've seen, this portion is determined by the reserve ratio. So, in money creation, the multiplier is the reciprocal of the reserve ratio. In our example, with banks reserving 10 percent (or 0.10) of deposits, the money multiplier is 10 (1.00 ÷ 0.10). In other words, the initial change in excess reserves ($900) eventually causes an increase in the money supply of $9000:

$$\text{Money multiplier} = \frac{1}{\text{reserve ratio}}$$

$$10 = \frac{1}{0.10}$$

$$\text{Change in money supply} = \text{change in excess reserves} \times \text{money multiplier}$$

$$\$9000 = \$900 \times 10$$

Adjustments to the Money Multiplier

In order to see how money is created, we temporarily assumed that all money is in the form of deposits, and all deposits are made to one sort of deposit-taker offering only a single type of deposit. However, these assumptions don't hold true in reality. Let's consider the implications in turn.

Publicly Held Currency

The public, of course, does use currency, and currency is a part of all definitions of money. So, rather than all money going to deposit-takers, who then keep some as reserves and lend the rest, some money does circulate and is unaffected by the money multiplier. Thus, in our example, the money supply would not increase by $9000 but by a lesser amount.

Differences in Deposits

As we've noted, there is a wide range of deposit types, and not all types are represented in the narrowest definition of money, M1. Therefore, as deposit money expands in the succession of transactions, not all of it will be reflected as an increase in money supply defined as M1. So, the money supply in our example would increase by an amount less than $9000.

Thinking About Economics

How relevant is the money multiplier in the Canadian monetary system?

The money multiplier represents the maximum possible effect of money creation. Returning to our example, the money multiplier formula allows us to specify the maximum amount ($9000) by which the quantity of money rises as a result of the infusion of $900 in new excess cash reserves into the economy. Because of the various factors that influence this increase, the exact size of the money multiplier can vary significantly.

BRIEF REVIEW

1. Deposit-takers reserve a certain percentage of deposits to satisfy withdrawal requests from depositors. This percentage is known as the reserve ratio, and the resulting dollar amount equals the desired reserves.
2. Cash reserves in excess of desired reserves are lent out to borrowers in order to create profit.
3. In the same way that spending is magnified, lending excess reserves magnifies deposits.
4. The money multiplier is the reciprocal of the reserve ratio and the maximum value by which an initial change in excess reserves changes the money supply.

KEY CONCEPTS

barter
coincidence of wants
liquidity
unit of account
deposit-takers
cash reserves
chartered banks
near banks
currency
demand deposits
notice deposits
term deposits
foreign currency deposits
M1
M2
M3
M2+
near money
credit card
debit card
transactions demand
asset demand
money demand
money demand schedule
money demand curve
money supply
money supply schedule
money supply curve
desired reserves
reserve ratio
excess reserves
money multiplier

ANALYSIS AND APPLICATION

1. Identify which of the three functions of money is most relevant in the following situations:
   a. a consumer compares prices on various brands of clothing
   b. a restaurant-owner writes a cheque to pay for food purchases
   c. a wealth-holder temporarily keeps part of her financial assets in a chartered bank deposit
   d. a borrower deposits currency in his chartered bank to pay off a loan

Total value of corporate shares	\$500 billion
Currency outside chartered banks	\$28 billion
Notice and personal term deposits at chartered banks	\$288 billion
Publicly held demand deposits at chartered banks	\$31 billion
Federal government bonds	\$623 billion
Notice and personal term deposits at near banks	\$235 billion
Other liquid assets included in M2+	\$18 billion
Nonpersonal term and foreign-currency deposits at chartered banks	\$254 billion

2. Use the hypothetical data provided in the table above to calculate (a) M1, (b) M2, (c) M3 and (d) M2+.

Money Demand and Supply Schedules

Nominal Interest Rate (%)	Money Demanded (D_m) ($ billions)	Money Supplied (S_m)
5.0	90	130
4.0	110	130
3.0	130	130
2.0	150	130
1.0	170	130

3. a. Use the schedules in the above table to draw a graph showing the money demand and money supply curves. Identify the equilibrium point.
   b. What happens in this market if the prevailing interest rate is initially 5 percent? 1 percent?
   c. With the aid of your graph, outline the effects of a \$20 billion decrease in the money supply.
   d. In which direction will the equilibrium interest rate move if real output in the economy increases? if the price level decreases? Why?

4. A bond is initially worth $10 000 and provides an interest rate of 4 percent.
   a. Explain how this bond's price changes if the prevailing interest rate falls to 2 percent.
   b. What happens to the bond's price if the prevailing interest rate rises to 6 percent?

5. Hudson Bank has a reserve ratio of 5 percent and $10 million issued in deposits.
   a. If the Bank's actual reserves are $600 000 then what are its excess reserves?
   b. By how much can this Bank increase the money supply?

6. Champlain Bank has a reserve ratio of 4 percent, $5 million issued in deposits, and $200 000 in actual reserves. What is the effect on the Bank's excess reserves if $15 000 in currency is deposited in the Bank?

7. A wealth-holder withdraws $200 from her bank and stashes this currency in a cookie jar. Assume that other economic participants hold their money in one type of deposit in a financial system with a single type of deposit-taker with a reserve ratio of 5 percent.
   a. Outline the first two transactions that occur as a result of this withdrawal.
   b. What is the final change in the money supply? Explain.

8. (Advanced Question)
   a. How can the value of deposit-takers' assets be negatively affected during economic downturns?
   b. How might the reactions of depositors intensify the problems outlined in part a.?
   c. Suggest some ways these financial risks faced by deposit-takers can be minimized either by government policy-makers or by deposit-takers themselves.

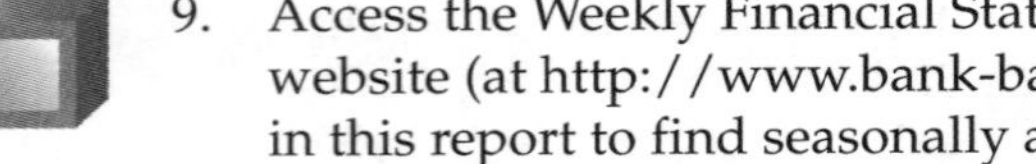

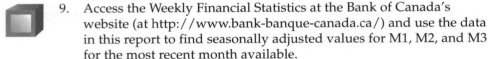

9. Access the Weekly Financial Statistics at the Bank of Canada's website (at http://www.bank-banque-canada.ca/) and use the data in this report to find seasonally adjusted values for M1, M2, and M3 for the most recent month available.

Advancing Economic Thought

LENDER WITH A MISSION

Muhammad Yunus and Micro-Lending

Lending policies tend to follow a "top-down" approach: they are set by managers of banks and near banks, who determine which individual players in the economy—businesses and households—are elegible to receive loans. In some cases, another stage is added. As we will see in Part 4, the World Bank (known officially as the International Bank for Reconstruction and Development) has traditionally lent funds to nonindustrialized nations for large projects such as hydro-electric dams. However, this is not the only approach that can be taken. By asking the questions, "What function does money have for the most needy, how is it lent, and to whom?" Muhammad Yunus, a Bangladeshi economist, offers a grass-roots alternative.

Yunus is the founder of Grameen Bank, a Bangladeshi credit organisation that has pioneered lending to the rural poor—and in the process stood normal banking conventions on their head.

The customers of Grameen (whose name means rural in Bengali) are almost exclusively those who have no collateral to offer against their loans. Yet defaults are so low its repayment rates would be the envy of most mainstream lenders. "Compared to Grameen Bank," says Yunus, "other banks look like charity outfits for the rich."

Muhammad Yunus
Source: Far Eastern Economic Review

Two other things are immediately striking about Grameen. First, the vast majority of its customers are women—a fact not unconnected with the low number of defaults—and, second, its vision extends beyond mere finance. Grameen is perhaps the only bank in the world that encourages birth control, sanitation, and a clean environment as part of its lending policy.

As a pioneer in the growing field of "micro-lending," Grameen has shown that the rural poor—even in a country virtually synonymous with deprivation—can make productive use of credit. To many, this approach is a more effective antidote to poverty than traditional giveaways.

The bank's success since it was set up in 1983 has spawned Grameen-type institutions in 30 countries. A group of U.S. politicians recently urged President Bill Clinton to make micro-enterprise development efforts, modelled specifically on Grameen, the "hallmark" of his foreign-aid programme. Yunus already has the admiration of Clinton, who once met Yunus in Washington and deems him worthy of a Nobel prize. "He made enterprise work. He promoted discipline, not dependence," Clinton says.

That, in a nutshell, was the idea. It began 17 years ago, when Yunus, an economics professor at Chittagong University, found himself frustrated at the irrelevance of textbook development theory to the poverty all around him. What bedevilled even the diligent poor around Chittagong, he could see, was the absence of cheap credit. Aside from loan sharks, they could turn to commercial banks, but they demanded collateral.

How, then, to direct credit to those who most need it: the assetless poor? Yunus' answer was to channel loans through wealthier intermediaries like himself. While shunning the peasant farmer and the bamboo-stool maker, the banks happily lend to the more affluent. In turn, Yunus reasoned, these borrowers could lend to the poor, in effect assuming risk that banks would not.

The risk, it turned out, was minimal. Experimenting initially on his own, Yunus acted as guarantor for loans to impoverished village-dwellers, who responded with a surprisingly high repayment rate. Encouraged, but eventually tired of running to the banks, Yunus decided to start his own. The government initially owned 60% of Grameen and the borrowers the rest. Today, its 1.4 million borrowers, each with a mandatory share (Taka 100, or US$2.50 each), own 88%.

Grameen's average loan size is US$75, its maximum except for housing loans. It charges simple interest at a rate of 20% a year, compared with compound interest of 13–16% at Bangladesh's commercial banks. Principal is repaid first, so that a borrower of Taka 2,500 would typically repay Taka 50 a week over 50 weeks. Interest, calculated weekly on the diminishing principal, is repaid only after the principal is paid off, making for an effective interest rate of 10–12%, Grameen sources say.

Home loans are repayable over 10 years at the same weekly rates. The maximum home loan is Taka 12,000, which will build a tin-roofed house.

Borrowers are formed into groups of five—the basic unit—and are indoctrinated in Grameen social values, known as the "sixteen decisions." Borrowers vow to observe the bank's four basic principles: discipline, unity, courage, and hard work "in all walks of life." They also pledge to "keep our families small," shun child marriage and the "curse" of wedding dowries, "build and use pit-latrines," and "plant as many seedlings as possible during the plantation seasons."

Grameen is effective partly because it is self-policing. Rather than bank officials, it is the assetless themselves, meeting weekly, who approve the loans. Group members are residents of the same village, perhaps next-door neighbours. It is this familiarity that provides transparency, guaranteeing that the recipients are truly those who need it most. A bank official attends the meeting, but group members decide who receives a loan, and they assume responsibility for ensuring its repayment.

A typical case: Sahera Khatun, 25, with a six-month-old baby, receives a loan through Grameen Gazipur-Sripur branch, about 95 kilometres north of Dhaka. She receives only Taka 2,375 of the Taka 2,500 approved. Taka 125 is deducted as a 5% contribution to her group fund, and a further Taka 1 per week to her own emergency savings fund. The loan is repaid over a year.

Shaheen Ara Begum became manager of Gazipur-Sripur branch in 1990, since when its lending has increased manyfold. The branch currently has about 1,900 members and has disbursed about Taka 16.6 million (about Taka 5.6 million is outstanding). By year's end, Shaheen expects membership of the branch to reach about 2,100.

A stroll through the village is instructive. Amid an otherwise depressing landscape there stand out some obvious improvements, brought about since the Grameen branch was established in December 1988. Houses are small but immaculate; families, too, are small and the children relatively healthy; and confident-looking women are busy at work in various cottage industries.

Grameen Bank's default rate is about 2%, astonishingly low compared with what Bangladesh's commercial banks suffer: about 70% for agricultural loans and 90% for industrial loans.

The difference, Yunus says, lies in the psychology of the borrowers. The rich can evade the consequences of non-payment; the poor cannot. They value access to credit so highly, and dislike the loan sharks so much, that they are only too grateful for a once-in-a-lifetime opportunity to improve themselves. And, by design, 92% of Grameen's borrowers nationwide are women. The bank targets them because it considers them more reliable than men. Children order their priorities, making them less likely to squander funds, and more likely to use them for household or capital improvements. "If being poor is tough, being a poor woman is toughest," says Yunus.

Today, Grameen has more than 1,000 branches conducting operations in about half of Bangladesh's 68,000 villages. It also runs about 18,000 feeder schools preparing children for government primary schools. It disburses about Taka 750 million in loans each month and has paid-up capital of Taka 120 million.

Grameen posted modest profits until government-mandated pay rises for the bank's staff forced losses of Taka 8.3 million in 1991 and 10 million in 1992. It may break even in 1993.

To be sure, the Grameen approach has its detractors. Some say micro-lending takes place on too small a scale to promote economic growth, and does little to teach skills. For the poor in Bangladesh, however, Grameen is delivering in a way that other banks are not.

Grameen, meanwhile, has become the model for micro-lending programmes in countries as diverse as Kenya, Ethiopia, and Sri Lanka. Its experience is not unique. In the Philippines, for example, Tagay sa

Pagunlad (Bridge to Progress) has provided credit to the poor since 1982, learning in the process that they can make money go a long way, "precisely because they have so little of it," in the words of director Benjamin Montemayor.

Elsewhere, Malaysia's Projek Ikhtiar, uses the Grameen approach too, and has also shown that small loans at affordable terms can greatly reduce extreme rural poverty.

Back in Bangladesh, Yunus wants to put more emphasis on Grameen's housing projects, which have won praise abroad. The bank has helped build more than 153,000 low-cost, tin-roofed houses with built-in latrines, each costing about US$300. Demand for 10-year loans to pay for them is rising fast.

Yunus is also working on a Grameen health project, planning up to four health centres on an experimental basis, each costing Taka 200,000 annually. He plans to charge Taka 5 a week for each Grameen member, whose family would receive free treatment. Non-members would pay more. Yunus believes the programme could eventually become self-financing. The centres could also become crucial to family planning, helping the government toward its goal of zero population growth.

Source

Abridged from S. Kamaluddin, "Lender With a Mission," in *Far Eastern Economic Review*, 18 March 1993, pp. 38, 40.

1. a. Outline four reasons why such a low proportion of Grameen Bank's borrowers default on their loans.

b. Would a conventional chartered bank have similar success in lending to Grameen Bank's borrowers? Why or why not?

2. Could Grameen Bank's innovative mix of small-scale lending and support for business development be applicable to the Canadian economy? If so, how?

AS GOOD AS GOLD

The Evolution of Money

In early societies, a wide assortment of items—for example, cloth, seashells, and cattle—served as money. The following article outlines how money has evolved since then.

Coinage

About seven thousand years ago, precious metals such as silver and gold began to be used as money. Because of their high intrinsic value and durability, they gradually became the dominant type of money in many parts of the world.

The first coins were invented during the 7th century BCE in the ancient kingdom of Lydia (in what is now Turkey). Early coins differed from previous types of metal money in that they bore stamps or symbols indicating the weight and purity of the metal from which they were made.

Early coins were supposed to be full-bodied, so that their face value matched their worth as pieces of metal. However, because users tended to accept coins at face value, cheaters could make a profit by employing practices known as clipping and hollowing. Clipping was conducted by shaving metal from the edges of a coin, while hollowing involved trimming a coin's two faces. Slivers of metal collected in this way could be sold to make new coins. Governments sometimes made matters worse. Political rulers sometimes engaged in a practice known as debasement, reducing the value of metal in the coins they issued. Until this dishonest behaviour became common knowledge, their coinage was accepted at face value. For a while, rulers were therefore able to buy products worth more than the metal used to make their coins.

Because many coins were worth less than their face value, people tended to hoard full-bodied coins, while passing on other coins to buy goods and services. This behaviour is described by one of the earliest laws in economics. Gresham's Law is named after its originator— Sir Thomas Gresham, England's Chancellor of the Exchequer during the reign of Queen Elizabeth I. According to Gresham's Law, "cheap money" always replaces "dear money" in circulation because full-bodied money is saved.

Paper Money

The next development of money involved the use of paper. Unlike previous types of commodity money, paper money has no intrinsic value and is more convenient and cheaper to produce than coins. Paper money first appeared during the 7th century CE in China, and in succeeding centuries its use spread to other parts of Asia. In the 13th century, for example, the Italian traveller Marco Polo recorded with wonderment the use of paper currency in the empire of the Mongol ruler Kublai Khan. In medieval Europe, the introduction of paper money was closely tied to the development of banking. Over time, the paper receipts issued by banks began to circulate as a means of payment. Depositers found it convenient to settle transactions by exchanging banks' receipts rather than withdrawing and redepositing coins. These receipts—which were endorsed by each holder as they passed from hand to hand—were an early form of the bank cheque.

By the 17th century, the certificates of deposit issued by banks were generally accepted as money— first in England and the Netherlands, and then in other parts of Europe. Bank deposits still make up the bulk of the money supply in most nations, including Canada.

Like bank deposit money, government-issued paper currency dates back to the 17th century. An early use of paper currency occurred in Canada during the colonial period. Starting in 1685, a shortage of coins forced colonial administrators in New France (now Quebec) to issue card money. Playing cards endorsed by colonial officials were assigned different denominations and then used in the colony as a means of exchange.

For a time, this card money was a success, and its use spread to some of the English colonies in North America. But the system finally broke down when colonial officials issued too many cards in order to pay for government purchases. This caused a cycle of inflation. As playing card money became less valuable, the prices of products in terms of this money increased.

The temptation for governments to distribute too much currency led to the adoption by many countries of a gold standard. Under this system, which prevailed in Europe and North America during the 19th and early 20th centuries, a unit of paper currency could be exchanged for a coin containing a given amount of gold. For example, the Canadian dollar could be converted into 23.22 grains of gold. This option ensured there were constraints on the amount of paper currency that could be issued.

While minimizing the risk of inflation, the gold standard did not allow governments to vary the money supply as a tool of stabilization policy. During the Great Depression, when stimulating economic activity was a prime concern, the gold standard was allowed to lapse in Canada as well as most other countries. Since then, Canadian paper currency has not been convertible into any other form, but possesses a set value by law. The same applies to Canada's coins, whose face value does not depend on their metallic worth.

1. "Any commodity can act as money as long as all participants in an economy agree to use it." Discuss.
2. Explain the advantages and disadvantages of the following types of money: a. coinage b. bank deposits c. paper currency.

Chapter Fifteen
Monetary Policy

There were warnings of apprehension from economists. There always are; apprehension is their business.

—Stephen Leacock, Canadian writer and economist

According to an old joke, ask two economists the same question and you'll get three answers. Economists—like any social scientists—do disagree and, very often, their disagreements revolve around stabilization policy—especially monetary policy. In this chapter, we explore the workings of monetary policy and then study some of the issues that are key to the use of both fiscal and monetary policies.

CHAPTER FOCUS

This chapter focuses on the following:

- the Bank of Canada, its functions, and the tools it uses to conduct monetary policy
- demand-pull inflation, and the tradeoffs between inflation and unemployment as expressed by the Phillips curve
- cost-push inflation and stagflation
- wage and price controls, and wage and price guidelines

THE BANK OF CANADA

The moving force behind Canada's monetary policy is the Bank of Canada, which since 1935 has served as Canada's central bank. A wholly government-owned institution, the "Bank" as it is known has been given a mandate to perform four basic functions relating to money and the financial system: managing the money supply, acting as "the bankers' bank," acting as the federal government's fiscal agent, and ensuring the stable operation of financial markets.

Managing the Money Supply

The most important role of the Bank of Canada is to conduct monetary policy by controlling the amount of money circulating in the economy. Not only does it issue paper currency, but more importantly it affects the activities of chartered banks and near banks so that it can vary the supply of money and interest rates. In managing the money supply, the Bank is concerned with three goals: minimizing inflation in order to preserve the purchasing power of the dollar; maintaining real output as close as possible to its potential level, and regulating the external value of the Canadian dollar on foreign exchange markets.

Acting as the Bankers' Bank

The Bank of Canada holds the deposits of financial institutions that are members of the Canadian Payments Association (CPA). The association includes the chartered banks and some near banks—in particular, the larger trust companies and representatives of credit unions and *caisses populaires*.

The Canadian Payments Association acts as a clearing house for cheques of both chartered banks and near banks. Suppose, for example, that Depositor A has a chequing account with Tecumseh Trust. He writes a $50 cheque to Depositor B, who deposits this cheque in her account at Elgin Bank, increasing her deposit balance by $50. Elgin Bank delivers the cheque to Tecumseh Trust, and receives $50 in return. This payment between the two banks is actually made by using the accounts kept by both institutions (or larger banks acting as their representatives) at the Bank of Canada. The $50 is transferred from Tecumseh Trust's account to Elgin Bank's account at the Bank of Canada. To complete the entire exchange, Tecumseh then cancels the cheque it has received and reduces Depositor A's deposit account by $50. Each day, every cheque transaction like this is added up, and the accounts of CPA members are all "cleared" at once. This procedure vastly simplifies the transactions that are made necessary by the use of cheques among various deposit-takers.

The accounts of CPA members at the Bank of Canada, which are part of their cash reserves, are kept so that funds are available to meet the daily clearing of payments. When a CPA member finds its account is too low, it can borrow from the Bank of Canada. The Bank provides an overnight loan, or an "advance" as it is usually known, by depositing the required funds in the CPA member's account. The interest rate charged on these advances is called the **bank rate**. Because the bank rate is higher than interest rates on other overnight loans, CPA members try to minimize their advances from the Bank of Canada. Nonetheless, they are a necessary backup to guarantee that CPA members always have sufficient funds in their accounts at the Bank of Canada.

bank rate: the interest rate CPA members are charged on advances from the Bank of Canada

Acting as the Federal Government's Fiscal Agent

In Chapter 13, we discussed the fiscal, or budgetary, policy that Canadian governments institute in order to level out the business cycle. In order to conduct the business of spending, taxing, and so on, the federal government needs a bank to manage its transactions and financial assets. In its role as the government's fiscal agent, the Bank of Canada engages in three main tasks: the Bank holds some of the government's bank deposits and decides where the other deposits should be held, it acts as the government's banker by clearing federal government cheques, and it handles the financing of the federal government's debt by issuing bonds. Government bonds fall into various categories, the most notable being Canada Savings Bonds and treasury bills.

Canada Savings Bonds are popular with household savers. These bonds differ from others in that they are not bought and sold after they have first been issued. Instead, holders of Canada Savings Bonds who want their funds back before the bonds have matured must "cash in" the bonds with the Bank of Canada at a set price. Since savers know exactly how much they will receive for the bond during its entire term, this feature of Canada Savings Bonds increases their attractiveness. Recall that ordinary bonds, in contrast, fluctuate in price before their maturity date depending on the value of interest rates in the economy. Hence, they are somewhat riskier than Canada Savings Bonds.

Canada Savings Bonds: federal government bonds that have a set value throughout their term

Treasury bills are an important type of short-term federal government bond. They have terms of three months to a year, and are usually issued in large denominations. Unlike other government bonds, treasury bills provide no interest payments. Rather, they are sold at a marked down price. For example, a one-year treasury bill worth $100 000 might be bought—usually by banks and other financial institutions—for $95 000. Once the treasury bill matures, the holder receives the face value of $100 000, thereby earning an income of $5000 ($100 000 – $95 000). Viewed in another way, the $5000 earned at maturity can be seen as interest on the original purchase price, or as a nominal rate of interest of 5.3 percent [($5000 ÷ $95 000) × 100%]. The price for federal treasury bills is decided at an auction conducted each Tuesday by the Bank of Canada.

treasury bills: short-term federal government bonds that provide no interest, but are sold at a discount

Thinking About Economics

How is the auction of treasury bills conducted?

The main buyers in the treasury bill market are the chartered banks, the large near banks, and investment dealers. The Bank of Canada also buys treasury bills to become part of its bond holdings. Buyers provide written bids, which outline the price they are willing to pay and the number of bills they want. As in any auction, the bills go to the highest bidders; those who bid highest have their orders filled first. The average price per week is therefore determined by the supply of bills and the expectations of buyers.

Ensuring the Stability of Financial Markets

In tandem with other agencies, the Bank of Canada supervises the operation of financial markets to ensure their stability. The Bank has a particular responsibility in overseeing the activity of chartered banks. By doing so, it helps protect the safety of depositors' funds and the soundness of the financial system.

MONETARY POLICY

Recall that monetary policy involves the Bank of Canada changing interest rates, altering the money supply, or both, in order to stabilize the economy. Our analysis of money and deposit-takers allows us to examine the way in which monetary policy is conducted.

Expansionary Monetary Policy

expansionary monetary policy: a policy of increasing the money supply and reducing interest rates to stimulate the economy

When real output falls short of its potential level, a recessionary gap is created. To stimulate output and increase employment, the Bank of Canada can use **expansionary monetary policy**. Such action is referred to informally as an "easy money policy."

The Bank of Canada applies an easy money policy by expanding the money supply. As shown on the left in Figure 15.1, increasing the money supply shifts the money supply curve, S_m, to the right, causing a drop in the equilibrium interest rate.

To see how this lower interest rate affects aggregate demand, remember that a fall in interest rates makes borrowing funds cheaper. With a decline in the nominal interest rate, the real rate of interest falls as well. Businesses respond by increasing their investment spending, and households purchase more durable goods, raising consumption. Both adjustments spur an initial increase in spending that is then magnified by the same successive cycles of new spending as seen in the case of an expansionary fiscal policy, as discussed in Chapter 13.

FIGURE 15.1
An Expansionary Monetary Policy

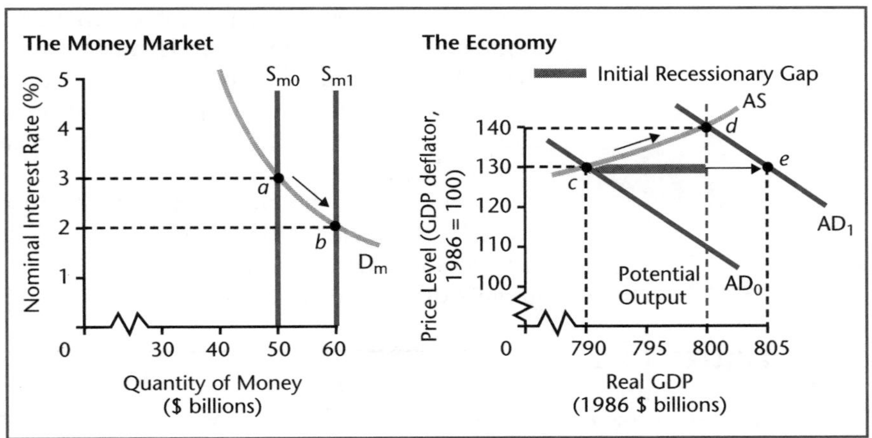

When the economy is in a recession, the Bank of Canada can increase the supply of money, shown by the shift from S_{m0} to S_{m1} on the left, thereby pushing down the interest rate from 3 percent to 2 percent (point *a* to point *b*). Because of the initial spending increase and the spending multiplier, the result in the economy as a whole is an increase in aggregate demand, as shown on the right as the $15 billion shift from AD_0 to AD_1. Output does not rise by $15 billion (from point *c* to point *e*); rather, the price level and output both rise to give a new equilibrium at point *d*, with output at the potential level of $800 billion and the recessionary gap eliminated.

The effect is the same as when government purchases increase. The change in aggregate demand, or total spending, is found by calculating the product of the spending multiplier and the initial spending change. Suppose, for example, that the initial increase in investment and consumption totalled $9 billion and the value of the economy's spending multiplier is 1.67. The total change in aggregate demand is then $15 billion:

$$\text{Total change in output (shift in AD curve)} = \text{initial change in spending} \times \text{spending multiplier}$$

$$\$15 \text{ billion} = \$9 \text{ billion} \times 1.67$$

As shown on the right in Figure 15.1, the $15 billion shift in the aggregate demand curve causes equilibrium output to rise by a smaller amount—$10 billion—because of the accompanying price level rise.

Contractionary Monetary Policy

contractionary monetary policy: a policy of decreasing the money supply and increasing interest rates to dampen the economy

Conversely, during an economic boom, the Bank of Canada can inhibit spending and inflation with a **contractionary monetary policy**. Such action, also known as a "tight money policy," decreases the money supply. The result, as shown on the left in Figure 15.2, is that the money supply curve, S_m, shifts to the left, driving up the equilibrium interest rate.

The higher nominal interest rate results in a higher real interest rate as well. This discourages investment spending by businesses as well as consumption spending on durable items by households, so it influences aggregate demand. Both trends cause an initial reduction of spending that is then magnified by the spending multiplier. Suppose, for example, that investment and consumption spending decline initially by $9 billion, and the spending multiplier is 1.67. As a result, the total decrease in aggregate demand is $15 billion.

Once again, the change in output causes a lesser change in actual spending because of the change in price level at the same time. In this case, as shown on the right in Figure 15.2, the $15 billion decrease in aggregate demand causes a $5 billion decrease in equilibrium output.

FIGURE 15.2
A Contractionary Monetary Policy

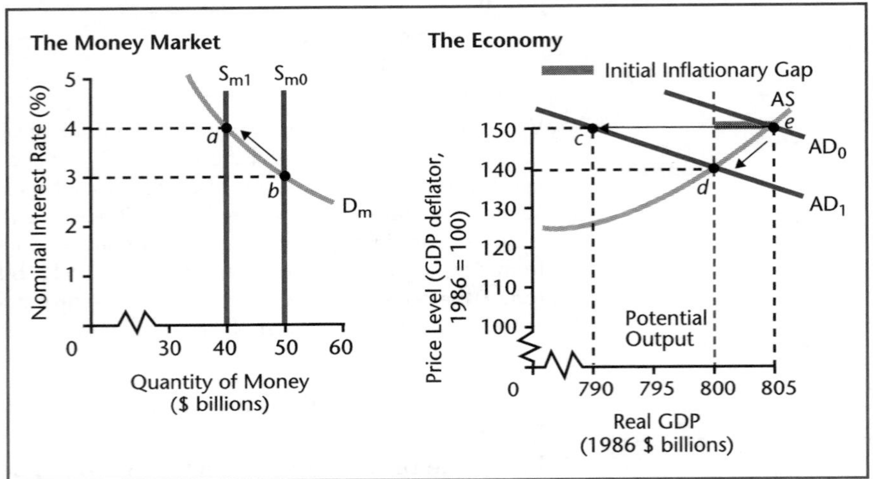

During an economic boom, the Bank of Canada can decrease the supply of money, shown by the shift from S_{m0} to S_{m1} on the left, thereby pushing up the interest rate from 3 percent to 4 percent (point *b* to point *a*). Because of the initial spending decrease and the spending multiplier, the result in the economy as a whole is a decrease in aggregate demand, as shown on the right as the $15 billion shift from AD_0 to AD_1. Output does not fall by $15 billion (from point *e* to point *c*); rather, the price level and output both fall to give a new equilibrium at point *d*, with output at the potential level of $800 billion and the inflationary gap eliminated.

BRIEF REVIEW

1. Canada's central bank—the Bank of Canada—manages the money supply, serves as a bank for chartered banks and some near banks, acts as the federal government's fiscal agent, and helps to ensure the stability of financial markets.
2. An expansionary monetary policy raises real output toward its potential level by increasing the money supply and decreasing interest rates. The resulting increase in investment and consumption are magnified by the spending multiplier to give an even greater increase in aggregate demand.
3. A contractionary monetary policy reduces real output toward its potential level by decreasing the money supply and increasing interest rates. The resulting decrease in investment and consumption are magnified by the spending multiplier to give an even greater decrease in aggregate demand.

TOOLS OF MONETARY POLICY

The Bank of Canada has three different tools it can use to conduct monetary policy: open market operations, government deposits, and (as a signal of its intentions) the bank rate.

Open Market Operations

Recall that the Bank of Canada sells and buys back federal government bonds. Its role in the bond market is a major tool with which the Bank of Canada conducts monetary policy. Through selling and buying back federal and other bonds, the Bank of Canada can use deposit-takers' cash reserves as a lever to influence both the money supply and interest rates. Because these transactions take place in the open bond market, they are called **open market operations**.

open market operations: the buying and selling of bonds by the Bank of Canada

Bond Sales

Consider the sale by the Bank of Canada of a $1000 bond to Bondholder A. When the sale takes place, Bondholder A pays for the bond with a cheque written against his deposit account at Cartier Bank. The Bank of Canada sends the cheque to Cartier Bank, which then cancels the cheque and reduces Bondholder A's account by $1000. Most importantly, Cartier Bank pays the Bank of Canada for the cheque by having $1000 taken out of its Bank of Canada account, as shown in Figure 15.3.

FIGURE 15.3 A Bond Sale

Bank of Canada

Assets		Liabilities	
Bonds	–$1000	Cartier Bank's Deposit	–$1000

Cartier Bank

Assets		Liabilities	
Reserves at Bank of Canada	–$1000	Bondholder A's Deposit	–$1000

When the Bank of Canada sells a bond to Bondholder A, its bond assets fall, as do its deposit liabilities to Cartier Bank. Meanwhile, Cartier Bank's cash assets at the Bank of Canada decrease, as do its deposit liabilities to Bondholder A. The drop in Bondholder A's deposit immediately reduces the money supply by $1000. With a reserve ratio of 10 percent, Cartier Bank's excess reserves fall by $900 and the money multiplier has a value of 10. Because reductions to deposits are magnified, the money supply drops by as much as an extra $9000 (the $900 decrease in excess reserves multiplied by the money multiplier).

The money supply immediately falls by $1000 due to the loss of the deposit previously held by Bondholder A. Assuming that the reserve ratio is 0.10, Cartier Bank's excess reserves are cut by $900, causing a multiple reduction of the money supply. Cartier Bank has less money available to lend. With a reserve ratio of 0.10 and a maximum money multiplier of 10, the further decline in the supply of money could be as much as $9000 ($900 × 10).

Therefore, the sale of bonds reduces the cash reserves of deposit-takers, which, in turn, cuts back on lending, and finally decreases the supply of money. By selling bonds, the Bank of Canada engages in contractionary monetary policy.

Bond Purchases

Now, consider the implications of the Bank of Canada buying back bonds from members of the public in the open market. Suppose the Bank of Canada buys back a $1000 bond from Bondholder B. Bondholder B receives a cheque from the Bank of Canada, which she deposits in her account at Cartier Bank. On acquiring the cheque, Cartier Bank delivers it to the Bank of Canada, and receives in return a $1000 addition to its Bank of Canada deposit.

As Figure 15.4 shows, both the money supply and Cartier Bank's cash reserves increase by $1000 due to the new deposit held by Bondholder B. However, the bank, with a reserve ratio of 0.10, need only hold back $100. Therefore, the bank has excess reserves of $900 ($1000 – $100). Cartier Bank will lend this money, which in turn will increase the money supply in a series of transactions similar to those outlined earlier in this chapter. Assuming a uniform reserve ratio of 0.10, we can see that the money multiplier (10, or the reciprocal of 0.10), creates a further increase in the money supply of up to $9000 ($900 × 10).

Therefore, buying back bonds allows the Bank of Canada to practise expansionary monetary policy. Cash reserves increase, resulting in increased lending, which causes the money supply to expand.

FIGURE 15.4 A Bond Purchase

Bank of Canada

Assets		Liabilities	
Bonds	+$1000	Cartier Bank's Deposit	+$1000

Cartier Bank

Assets		Liabilities	
Reserves at Bank of Canada	+$1000	Bondholder B's Deposit	+$1000

If the Bank of Canada purchases a bond from Bondholder B, its bond assets rise, as do its deposit liabilities to Cartier Bank. From Cartier Bank's perspective, its cash assets at the Bank of Canada increase, as do its deposit liabilities to Bondholder B. The new deposit from Bondholder B immediately adds $1000 to the money supply. With a reserve ratio of 0.10, Cartier Bank's excess reserves increase by $900, while the money multiplier has a value of 10. Because deposits expand, the money supply increases by as much as an extra $9000 (the $900 increase in excess reserves multiplied by the money multiplier).

Government Deposits

Recall that the Bank of Canada acts as the federal government's banker. However, the federal government's deposits are held in both the Bank of Canada and in CPA members. This gives the Bank an important tool of monetary policy, by moving some deposits from the Bank of Canada to CPA members, or vice versa.

Suppose, for example, that the Bank of Canada moves a $1000 government deposit to Cartier Bank. As shown in Figure 15.5, Cartier Bank receives payment by having $1000 added to its account at the Bank of Canada. As a result, Cartier Bank's reserves increase by $1000. While the new government deposit is not held by the public, and so is not included in the definition of money, it does affect Cartier Bank's dealings. If Cartier Bank has a reserve ratio of 0.10, then only $100 of the $1000 new deposit need be kept as cash reserves; the remaining $900 can be lent out. Given the money multiplier of 10 (the reciprocal of 0.10), these excess reserves may be magnified to increase the money supply by a maximum of $9000 ($900 × 10).

FIGURE 15.5 Movements of Government Deposits

Bank of Canada

Assets		Liabilities	
		Government Deposits	–$1000
		Cartier Bank's Deposit	+$1000

Cartier Bank

Assets		Liabilities	
Reserves at Bank of Canada	+$1000	Government Deposit	+$1000

When the Bank of Canada moves a federal government deposit from itself to Cartier Bank, Cartier Bank's deposits increase. Cartier Bank's cash assets at the Bank of Canada rise, as do its deposit liabilities to the government. Meanwhile, the Bank of Canada's deposit liabilities to the federal government fall, while the Bank of Canada's deposit liabilities to Cartier Bank rise. With a reserve ratio of 10 percent, excess reserves increase by $900 and the money multiplier has a value of 10. Because of the movement of government deposits, the money supply can increase by as much as $9000.

Therefore, by moving federal government deposits from the Bank of Canada to CPA members, the Bank of Canada conducts expansionary monetary policy. Conversely, by moving deposits from CPA members back to the Bank of Canada by calling in deposits, the Bank of Canada conducts contractionary monetary policy.

The Bank Rate

Recall that the bank rate is the interest rate paid by members of the Canadian Payments Association when they receive Bank of Canada advances. Because this rate acts as a signal of Bank of Canada intentions, it plays an important role in monetary policy.

overnight rate: the interest rate on overnight loans between chartered banks and other financial institutions

The bank rate is tied to the **overnight rate**, which is the interest rate on overnight loans between chartered banks and other financial institutions. At any given time, the Bank makes sure the overnight rate stays within a publicized target range of 50 basis points (a basis point is one-hundredth of a percentage point). The Bank keeps the overnight rate within the desired range by using its two main monetary policy tools. When the Bank buys bonds on the open market or moves government deposits out into the banking system, the accounts of CPA members at the Bank increase in value, which reduces the need for overnight borrowing and pushes down the overnight rate. On the other hand, when the Bank engages in an open-market sale of bonds or switches government deposits back from the banking system, the accounts of CPA members at the Bank are reduced, raising the need for overnight borrowing as well as the overnight rate.

Since 1996, the bank rate has been set at the ceiling of the 50-basis-point target range for the overnight rate. Whenever the Bank changes this target range, the bank rate is adjusted automatically, which signifies where monetary policy is heading in the near future.

prime rate: the lowest possible interest rate charged by deposit-takers on loans to their best corporate customers

If the change in the bank rate is substantial, deposit-takers may decide to alter their own interest rates in the same direction. In particular, they adjust their **prime rate**, which is the lowest possible rate charged by deposit-takers on loans to their best corporate customers. When the prime rate varies, so do all other rates for depositors and borrowers.

Benefits of Monetary Policy

Monetary policy has two main benefits: its separation from politics, and the speed with which it can be applied. These benefits have made monetary policy the most important stabilization tool in recent years.

Separation From Day-to-Day Politics

Unlike fiscal policy, which is usually a well-publicized element of the political process, monetary policy is detached from immediate political influence. While the Bank of Canada is under the control of Parliament, as represented by the Prime Minister and cabinet, in practice the Bank of Canada is controlled by appointed officials—the most important being its governor, who serves a seven-year term—and its operations are veiled from public view. Thus, monetary policy tends to be focused on economic rather than political goals.

Speed

Recall that fiscal policy suffers from recognition, decision, and impact lags. While recognizing a problem can also cause a delay in monetary policy and the impact of any policy may also be delayed (by anywhere between 12 and 18 months), decisions regarding monetary policy can be made speedily.

Drawbacks of Monetary Policy

Monetary policy does have two major drawbacks: its relative weakness as an expansionary tool, and its broad impact.

Weakness as an Expansionary Tool

The Bank of Canada is quite capable of restraining an overheated economy during a boom period. By squeezing deposit-takers' excess reserves through open market sales of bonds and shifts of government deposits to the Bank of Canada, it can be assured that the money supply will fall, pushing up interest rates and reducing spending and output.

However, matters are not necessarily so straightforward during a severe recession or depression. While the Bank can increase deposit-takers' cash reserves through open market purchases of bonds and shifts of government deposits to CPA members, there is no guarantee that this will translate into more bank loans and an expansion of the money supply. If deposit-takers hold on to their extra cash reserves, the desired increase in the money supply will not occur, which can make the use of expansionary monetary policy seem like"pushing a string."

Broad Impact

Unlike fiscal policy, which can be focused on particular regions, monetary policy affects every region of the country uniformly. When the Bank of Canada raises interest rates during a boom, for example, the impact is felt not only in those parts of the economy with overheated economies, but also in areas that have been relatively unaffected by the upswing. As a result, regions already enduring high rates of unemployment experience even more.

BRIEF REVIEW

1. One major way the Bank of Canada pursues monetary policy is through open market operations. Buying bonds from the public is an expansionary policy that increases chartered bank reserves, leading to a magnified increase in the money supply. In contrast, selling bonds reduces the money supply.
2. By moving government deposits from its own holdings to CPA members, the Bank of Canada increases CPA members' excess reserves, which increases the money supply and thus expands the economy. In contrast, the Bank of Canada can reverse the process to conduct contractionary policy.
3. The Bank of Canada signals its intentions by setting the bank rate, which in turn influences the prime rate. A rise in the bank rate signals contractionary policy. A fall in the bank rate signals expansionary policy.
4. While monetary policy has the benefits of its isolation from politics and the speed with which decisions can be made, it is less effective for expansion than for contraction, and it cannot be focused on particular regions as can fiscal policy.

INFLATION AND UNEMPLOYMENT

Stabilization policies—both fiscal and monetary—are usually applied to affect inflation and unemployment. The task of policy-makers is complicated by the fact that the relationship between inflation and unemployment is usually an inverse one. So, for example, an increase in aggregate demand during an economic expansion means that equilibrium between aggregate demand and aggregate supply is found at a higher price level and higher output, as shown in Figure 15.6. The increase in price level translates into inflation, and the increase in output translates into lower unemployment. In other words, there is a tradeoff—higher prices for more jobs. Because increased demand pulls up prices, economic expansion that causes inflation is known as **demand-pull inflation**.

demand-pull inflation: inflation that occurs as increased aggregate demand pulls up prices

The Phillips Curve

Recall from Chapter 12 that Keynesian economics stresses the inverse relationship between inflation and unemployment as found in demand-pull inflation. Based on the assumption that there is a fixed and predictable inverse relationship between unemployment and inflation, one Keynesian economist—A.W.H. Phillips—created a curve that expresses this relationship. This **Phillips curve** is shown in Figure 15.7.

Phillips curve: a curve expressing the assumed fixed and predictable inverse relationship between unemployment and inflation

According to the Keynesian perspective, if an economy with an inflation rate of 2 percent and an unemployment rate of 8 percent (point *b* in Figure 15.7) experiences demand-pull inflation, the inflation rate will rise at the same time that unemployment decreases to, for example, point *a*. Increased aggregate demand creates shortages in labour markets, which put upward pressure on wages, thereby boosting inflation. In the same way, decreased aggregate demand increases unemployment, which puts downward pressure on wages, thereby reducing the rate of inflation. We see this in the shift from point *b* to point *c*.

FIGURE 15.6
Demand-Pull Inflation

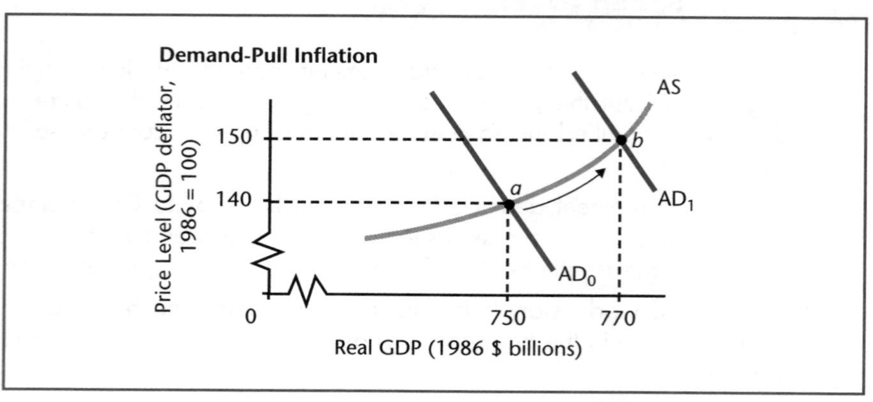

During expansionary times, aggregate demand increases, shifting the aggregate demand curve from AD_0 to AD_1. The result is that the price level rises from point *a* to point *b*. In other words, increased demand *pulls* up prices.

FIGURE 15.7
The Phillips Curve

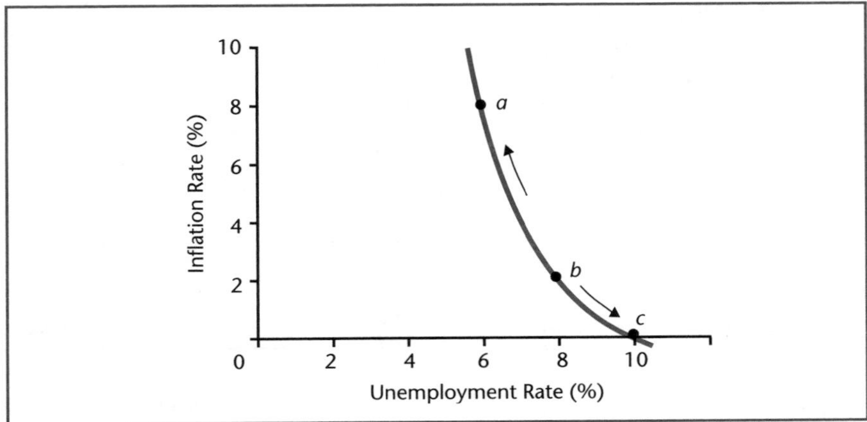

The Phillips curve expresses the Keynesian belief in the fixed and predictable inverse relationship between unemployment and inflation that occurs with demand-pull inflation. When the economy moves from point *b* to point *a*—which may happen as a result of expansionary stabilization policies—inflation increases and unemployment decreases. In contrast, contractionary policies cause the economy to move from point *b* to point *c*.

In the past, the Phillips curve was often treated by governments as a "policy menu." Governments using expansionary fiscal or monetary policies would anticipate a move up the curve, for example from point *b* to point *a*; governments using contractionary fiscal or monetary policies would expect a move down the curve, for example from point *b* to point *c*.

The extent to which Phillips curves are applicable can be seen using historical data for Canada. Figure 15.8 plots annual unemployment and inflation rates for 1960 to 1996. Let's consider the relevance of the Phillips curve to three periods.

From 1960 to 1972

For the years 1960 to 1972, in general, higher inflation accompanied lower unemployment, and vice versa. In other words, inflation during this period was of the demand-pull variety. Therefore, the points indicating inflation and unemployment rates fall in a broad band from which we can draw a Phillips curve, shown in Figure 15.8 with a solid line. Because inflation and unemployment had a predictable inverse relationship, Canadian federal governments were able to use the curve when trying to predict how their stabilization policies would affect the economy.

From 1973 to 1982

In the years between 1973 and 1982, the previously predictable relationship between inflation and unemployment in Canada broke down. Most notably, inflation rose from 1973 to 1974 while unemployment remained about the same. This trend was repeated in the years 1979 to 1981. The Phillips curve for the Canadian economy during this period, shown as a dashed line in Figure 15.8, demonstrates that inflation and unemployment overall were greater in this period than in the last.

FIGURE 15.8
Shifts in the Phillips Curve

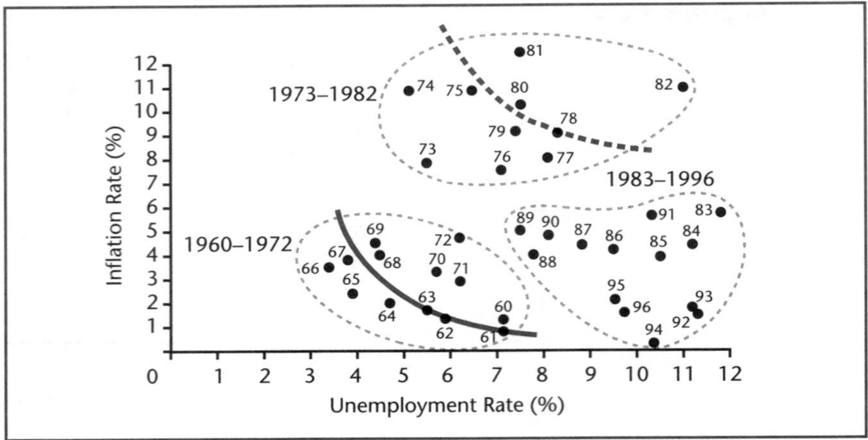

During the years 1960 to 1972, inflation and unemployment rates fell in a broad band, from which a Phillips curve can be drawn (shown as a solid line). In the period from 1973 to 1982, the predictable relationship broke down. However, it seems that the Phillips curve moved to the right (shown as a dashed line) as both inflation rates and unemployment rates were above those in the previous period. In the period from 1983 to 1996, the trend was to lower inflation, but unemployment rates remained high. As a result, the new position of the Phillips curve was not clear for this period.

Sources: Adapted from Statistics Canada, *National Income and Expenditure Accounts, Annual Estimates 1926–1986* (June 1988), cat. no. 13-531, p. 214–15; *Canadian Economic Observer, Historical Statistical Supplement, 1995/96* (July 1996), cat. no. 11-210-XPB, vol. 10, pp. 30, 43; *Canadian Economic Observer, Statistical Summary* (March 1997), cat. no. 11-010-XPB, pp. 16, 23. Reproduced by authority of the Minister of Industry, 1997.

As this period illustrates, sometimes unemployment and inflation have a direct relationship rather than an inverse relationship. A rising rate of inflation associated with constant or expanding unemployment—that is, consistently low output—is known as **stagflation**. This name refers to the combination of *stag*nation and in*flation*.

stagflation: a combination of consistently low output (and so constant or expanding unemployment) and rising inflation

Stagflation can be caused by a decrease in aggregate supply. During the period from 1973 to 1982, for example, businesses faced rising prices for inputs, largely due to rising oil prices. Oil prices were ten times higher in 1981 than they were at the start of 1973 because of the cartel behaviour of OPEC—the Organization of Petroleum Exporting Countries. In response to increases in input prices, businesses decrease their output, thus reducing aggregate supply. The result, shown in Figure 15.9, is a fall in equilibrium output and a rise in the price level. Because the increased costs push price levels up, this situation is known as **cost-push inflation**. During the 1970s, demands for increased wages further decreased aggregate supply and worsened cost-push inflation.

cost-push inflation: inflation that occurs as increased production costs decrease aggregate supply, which then pushes up prices

From 1983 to 1996

From 1983 to 1996, the stagflation of the previous period was partly reversed. While unemployment rates remained stubbornly high in Canada through most of the 1980s and 1990s, by the mid-1990s inflation had fallen

FIGURE 15.9
Cost-Push Inflation

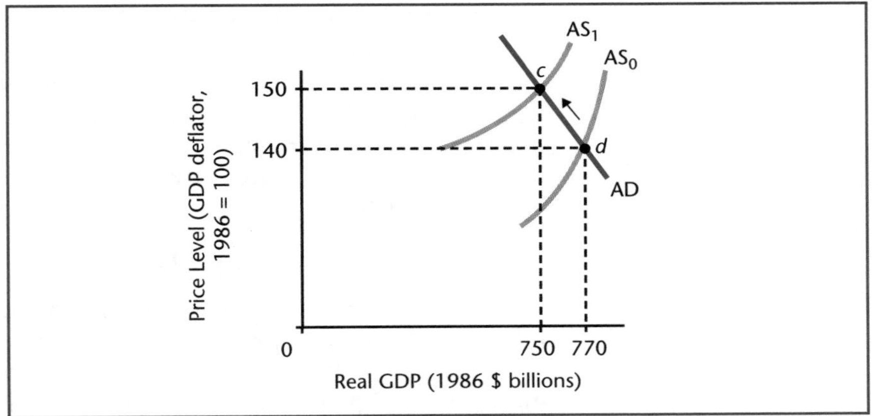

Increased input prices cause businesses to decrease output. The resulting decrease in aggregate supply shifts the supply curve from AS_0 to AS_1. The result is that the price level is pushed up from point *d* to point *c*. In other words, increased costs *push* up prices.

to levels not seen since the early 1970s. Note, however, that there was no consistent relationship between inflation and unemployment during this period. While the new Phillips curve was presumably below the Phillips curve for the previous period, its position was not apparent from the behaviour of the economy between 1983 and 1996, as illustrated in Figure 15.8.

Two main factors account for Canada's lower inflation since 1983. Oil prices fell dramatically in the mid-1980s, increasing aggregate supply and restraining increases in the price level. In addition, the recessions of 1981–82 and 1990–91 had a major impact on reducing inflation rates by decreasing aggregate demand. This impact was especially strong given the contractionary monetary policies conducted by the Bank of Canada during both recessions.

Wage and Price Policies

In the 1970s and early 1980s, macroeconomic policy-makers faced both increased inflation and rising unemployment. Because fiscal and monetary policies can reduce *either* inflation or unemployment but not both at the same time, policy-makers had to find new solutions to stagflation.

By the late 1960s, there was widespread concern that wage demands by trade unions had become unreasonable and that large businesses were increasing prices unjustifiably, thus fuelling inflation. As a result, governments in Canada and various other countries tried to intervene in the form of **wage and price controls** and **wage and price guidelines**. Wage and price *controls* involve governments passing laws that impose maximum allowable increases in wages and prices. Wage and price *guidelines* involve governments encouraging voluntary caps on wages and prices. Canadian governments tried both policies.

wage and price controls: government-imposed restrictions on wage and price increases

wage and price guidelines: voluntary restrictions on wage and price increases

Wage and Price Guidelines

In 1969, a federal Prices and Incomes Commission was formed. Its mandate, from 1969 to 1975, was to co-operate with businesses and private-sector labour unions to limit wage and price increases. However, because of a lack of support from businesses and labour unions, the Commission had little success. Inflation, which had been 5 percent in 1969, rose to 10 percent by 1975.

Wage and Price Controls

In late 1975, the federal government introduced another, harsher policy. It legislated wage and price controls and created the Anti-Inflation Board to enforce them. By law, wages and salaries were allowed to increase by a maximum of 8 percent in 1976, 6 percent in 1977, and 4 percent in 1978. Workers in industries where productivity was rising rapidly or where previous wage increases had been lower than average were allowed an extra 2 percent. Also by law, businesses were allowed to increase prices only to cover increased costs, and restrictions were placed on profits. To save on the administrative costs of the program, small businesses—including those in farming and fishing—were exempt from the controls.

Inflation did subside in the years 1976 to 1978, during the time the controls were in place. While the inflation rate in 1975 had been over 10 percent, in the next three years it varied between 7.5 percent and 9 percent. However, this fall in the inflation rate was largely the result of changes in food prices, which were not included in the control program. By 1980, two years after the controls were lifted, inflation was again above 10 percent.

"Six and Five" Guidelines

In 1982, the federal government applied wage and price restrictions again. This time, however, the government attempted to limit wages and prices it controlled *directly* while making the restrictions voluntary for the rest of the economy. Six percent was the limit in the 1982–83 fiscal year, and 5 percent in the 1983–84 fiscal year. Provincial governments and the private sector were encouraged to follow the federal lead. While inflation fell dramatically between 1982 and 1984, the consensus among economists is that this was due to the dampening effect of the 1981–82 recession as well as the contractionary monetary policies of the Bank of Canada, rather than the "six and five" guidelines.

The Debate Over Wage and Price Policies

Many economists oppose policies restricting wage and price levels on the basis of their effectiveness, fairness, and efficiency.

Effectiveness

Voluntary guidelines have shown little success in decreasing inflation in the private sector, because businesses and unions are reluctant to follow them. Also, although legislated wage and price controls may reduce inflation in the short run, Canadian experience shows that inflation rises again after the controls have been removed.

Fairness

Because some sectors are easier to regulate than others, wage and price restrictions are unfairly applied. For example, workers in the public sector and in large regulated businesses bear the brunt of government restrictions, while workers in less easily regulated sectors enjoy higher wage increases. Price restrictions, and the shortages they bring, can also lead to inequities, with output in some markets being distributed in unfair and arbitrary ways. For example, product shortages tempt some buyers to offer "under-the-table" incentives in addition to the product's legal price to assure that purchases are made.

Efficiency

Wage and price restrictions disrupt the functioning of free markets. Since the direct link between labour productivity and income is broken with wage restrictions, workers have less incentive to maximize the amount of real output they produce. Because restricted prices cannot operate as signals of changes in demand and supply, resources may be inefficiently distributed among different sectors. Hence, the long-term growth of the economy may be harmed.

BRIEF REVIEW

1. Inflation and unemployment have often had an inverse relationship. In periods of expansion, the result is demand-pull inflation.
2. The Phillips curve represents the Keynesian assumption of an inverse and predictable relationship between inflation and unemployment. While the Phillips curve applied to Canada in the period from 1960 to 1972, it has been less relevant since.
3. Since the 1970s, inflation and unemployment in Canada have frequently had a direct relationship. Stagflation has been caused largely by decreases in aggregate supply due to price increases of inputs. The result is cost-push inflation.
4. Overall inflation and unemployment rates in Canada increased in the period from 1973 to 1982, shifting the Phillips curve to the right. From 1983 to 1996, unemployment continued to be high but inflation declined.
5. Various types of wage and price restrictions have been applied in Canada since 1969. Critics suggest that these programs show little success, while fostering inequities and inefficiency.

KEY CONCEPTS

bank rate
Canada Savings Bonds
treasury bills
expansionary monetary policy
contractionary monetary policy
open market operations
overnight rate
prime rate
demand-pull inflation
Phillips curve
stagflation
cost-push inflation
wage and price controls
wage and price guidelines

ANALYSIS AND APPLICATION

1. Changes in real output caused by monetary policy have their own effect on interest rates.
   a. Using graphs like those shown in Figure 15-1, explain whether this effect intensifies or partly counteracts the initial impact of an expansionary monetary policy on the equilibrium interest rate.
   b. What does your analysis in part a. suggest about the effectiveness of monetary policy?

2. Using T-accounts like those in Figure 15-5, show how a move of $1 million in government deposits from Frontenac Bank to the Bank of Canada will affect Frontenac Bank's excess reserves given a reserve ratio of 5 percent. What is the maximum final effect on the money supply? Explain.

3 a. What is the nominal rate of interest on a one-year $1 million treasury bill if its purchase price is $975 000? if its purchase price is $960 000?
   b. Given your answers to part a., how can the Bank of Canada adjust supply in the auction of treasury bills to increase the nominal rate of interest on treasury bills?
   c. How can the Bank of Canada adjust its own purchases in the auction of treasury bills to decrease the nominal rate of interest on treasury bills?

4. When would it be more advantageous to hold Canada Savings Bonds than to hold regular bonds? When nominal interest rates are rising or falling? Explain.

5. Calculate the maximum amount by which the following policies will change the money supply:
   a. $100 million of bonds are bought by the Bank of Canada when the reserve ratio is 5 percent
   b. $10 million of government deposits are moved from CPA members to the Bank of Canada when the reserve ratio is 6 percent
   c. $50 million of bonds are sold by the Bank of Canada when the reserve ratio is 7.5 percent

d. $20 million of government deposits are moved from the Bank of Canada to CPA members when the reserve ratio is 8 percent

6. "Changes in the bank rate can only affect the money supply if backed up by the use of open market operations and/or the switching of government deposits." Discuss, using either expansionary or contractionary monetary policy as an example.

Inflation and Unemployment in Macronia

Year	Inflation Rate	Unemployment Rate
1998	4	5
1999	2	8
2000	3	6

7. a. Draw a Phillips curve based on the hypothetical information in the above table.
   b. What types of stabilization policies could have caused the change that takes place between 1998 and 1999? between 1999 and 2000?
   c. What are the benefits and costs of the changes that take place between 1998 and 1999?
   d. What are the benefits and costs of the changes that take place between 1999 and 2000?
   e. Suppose that in 2001 the inflation rate is 5 percent and the unemployment rate is 10 percent. What has happened to the Phillips curve? What could explain this change?

8. (Advanced Question)
American economist Alan Blinder has popularized what he calls Murphy's Law of Economic Policy: "Economists have the least influence where they know the most and are most agreed; they have the most influence on policy where they know the least and disagree most vehemently." Using evidence from this chapter, state whether you agree or disagree with Blinder's statement.

9. Access the summary of the most recent Monetary Policy Report at the Bank of Canada's website (at http://www.bank-banque-canada.ca/).
   a. Based on this summary, state whether monetary policy during the relevant time period covered by the report has been expansionary or contractionary.
   b. Summarize the reasons why the Bank believes such a policy was needed.

Advancing Economic Thought

MONEY MATTERS

Milton Friedman and Monetarism

Friedman and His Influence

The leading supporter of monetarism has been the American economist, Milton Friedman (born in 1912). He was both a student and a long-time professor at the University of Chicago, an institution where the ideas of the neoclassical economists lived on despite the Keynesian revolution of the 1930s and 1940s.

Friedman is perhaps most famous as a promoter of *laissez-faire* capitalism in the tradition of Adam Smith. He has popularized his views in his books *Capitalism and Freedom* (1962) and *Free to Choose* (1980) as well as in numerous magazine articles and TV appearances. Friedman's pro-market outlook stems from his belief that wages and prices in private markets are fairly close to their most efficient perfectly competitive values, while externalities such as pollution can best be dealt with through private lobbying and negotiation, rather than through government intervention. Since governments are inefficient by their very nature, says Friedman, and because they hinder individual freedom, their intervention in private markets should be minimized.

Milton Friedman
Source: The Bettmann Archive

Friedman would replace income-support programs such as welfare and unemployment insurance with a single guaranteed annual income system (as outlined in Chapter 9). He also argues that many functions currently performed by governments could be performed more efficiently by the private sector, if businesses are chosen to fulfil each specified task at the lowest possible cost.

The Role of Money Friedman has contributed to various aspects of macroeconomics, but his most wide-ranging work is associated with the economic perspective known as monetarism, which emphasizes the influence of money on the economy.

Monetarism is a recent extension of the theories that dominated macroeconomics before John Maynard Keynes. Like the neoclassical economists, such as William Stanley Jevons and Alfred Marshall, monetarists believe that the economy is able to adjust to shocks *without* government intervention. While admitting that the economy can be temporarily set off course, monetarists argue that, usually, misguided government intervention just makes economic fluctuations worse. Because they stress the importance of money, monetarists blame unwise use of monetary policies in particular.

The experience in Canada and other countries during the 1970s and 1980s has not provided convincing evidence for the overriding importance of money in influencing the economy. As a result, most economists do not support monetarist theory.

The Self-Stabilizing Economy

However, an important element of Friedman's argument has made its way into mainstream economic theory. This is his description of the economy's capacity to stabilize itself in the long run. According to Friedman, forces push the economy toward its potential output, where unemployment is at its natural level. While the economy may rarely reach this long-run equilibrium, economic fluctuations can be fully understood only if this self-stabilizing tendency is taken into account.[1]

The figure below illustrates a simplified version of Friedman's argument for a hypothetical economy. The short-run tradeoff between output and the price level is shown by the aggregate supply curve. But only at point *b*, which is associated with the economy's potential output, is the economy stationary in the long run. At any other point on the curve, the economy will sooner or later display its built-in tendency to stabilize.

During an economic boom, the economy's equilibrium may be at a point such as *c*, where output is above its potential level. Because unemployment is below its natural rate, tight labour markets allow workers to bargain for higher nominal wages. These wage hikes raise business costs, leading to a decrease in aggregate supply. Equilibrium therefore moves back toward the economy's potential output, and unemployment rises toward its natural rate.

According to Friedman, the opposite occurs when an economy's equilibrium is below its potential output, as at point *a* on the graph, with

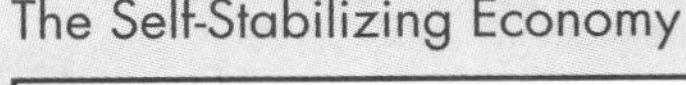
The Self-Stabilizing Economy

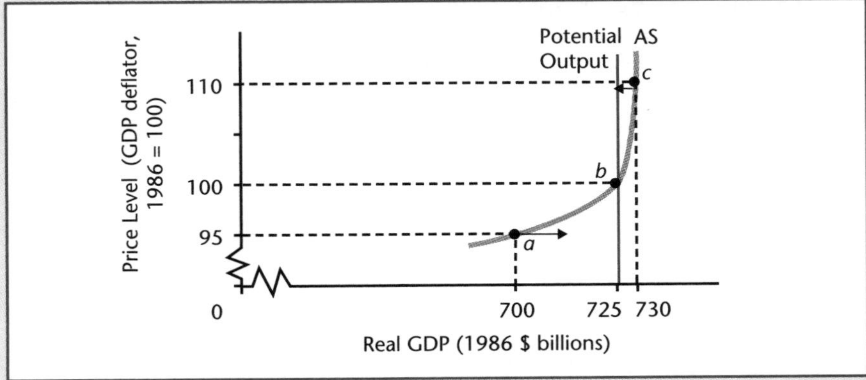

At point *b*, the economy could remain indefinitely at its potential output. However, when equilibrium is at point *c* in a boom, the economy's self-stabilizing tendency will push the aggregate supply curve to the left, so that the potential output can be resumed. The same is true if the economy's equilibrium is at point *a* in a recession. The self-stabilizing tendency will push the aggregate supply curve to the right.

a high unemployment rate. Workers initially resist any attempts to reduce their nominal wages, as was pointed out originally by Keynes. However, over time, unemployment puts downward pressure on nominal wages. This causes an increase in aggregate supply, boosting output back toward its potential level and lowering unemployment toward its natural rate.

The Long-Run Supply Curve In either case, the vertical line shown on the graph at the potential output level can be interpreted as this hypothetical economy's long-run aggregate supply curve, since it shows all those points consistent with stable equilibrium in the long run. The presence of this curve, and the self-stabilizing process that underlies it, are now accepted by most economists, although its importance is disputed. Those such as monetarists who see little need for government stabilization policy believe the economy adjusts quickly by itself toward its potential output level. In contrast, Keynesian economists see the self-adjusting process as a slow one, which means government stabilization policy can still play an important role in reducing the severity of ups and downs in the business cycle.

Note

[1] Milton Friedman, "The Role of Monetary Policy," *The American Economic Review*, March 1968, pp. 1–17. The modern theory of the self-stabilizing economy also owes its roots to Edmund S. Phelps, "Phillips Curves, Expectations of Inflation and Optimal Unemployment Over Time," *Economica*, August 1967, pp. 254–81.

1. **Do the shifts in the AS curve that occur when an economy is pushed towards its potential output represent short-run or long-run changes in aggregate supply? Explain with the aid of a graph.**

2. **If Friedman's description of the self-stabilizing economy is correct, then what shape does the Phillips curve have in the long run? Explain.**

ZEROING IN

Canadian Monetary Policy

Milton Friedman's view of the self-stabilizing process at work in the macroeconomy has had an important impact on Bank of Canada policy-makers, who believe their major task is minimizing inflation. In the words of Bank governor Gordon Thiessen:

> There is no question that monetary policy has a short-term influence on demand, production, and employment, but surely the notion of a long-run inverse trade-off between inflation and unemployment has been widely discredited. In the long run the impact of monetary policy is on inflation, and the central bank must set its objective in terms of the variable it can expect to influence.[1]

Long-Term Interest Rates

The Bank's emphasis on reducing inflation is strengthened by its view (not shared by all economists) that long-term interest rates are increasingly determined by global forces.[2] Important factors include the global demand and supply of loanable funds, which set a global equilibrium interest rate, and Canada's risk premium, which is the extra interest rate demanded by lenders to make up for the uncertainty associated with Canadian economic prospects.

Canada's risk premium is based partly on fiscal policy and partly on political conditions. For example, a rise in Canada's government debt or heightened uncertainty over Canada's political future lead international lenders to demand a higher return on Canadian-dollar bonds to make up for the added risk of future repayment difficulties and volatile financial markets. Inflation may also affect Canada's risk premium. If lenders expect Canada's inflation to stay low, they accept not only a smaller inflation premium on *nominal* interest rates, but also lower *real* interest rates as well, since low inflation enhances stability in financial markets. If this analysis is valid, then the main way the Bank can reduce long-term real interest rates (since fiscal policy and political conditions are out of their hands) is by reducing inflation.

Zero-Inflation Policy

Given this view of contemporary monetary policy, Mr. Theissen's predecessor, John Crow, adopted what he called a zero-inflation policy, though a better term might be a "low inflation" policy. In 1991, specific targets for inflation (based on rises in the CPI) were introduced—3 percent by the end of 1992, 2.5 percent by the middle of 1994, and a range between 1 to 3 percent by 1995. In 1993, the 1 to 3 percent range was extended to 1998, and it is likely to be continued for the forseeable future.

While the Bank has met its inflation targets, opinions differ on the wisdom of this policy. Some economists oppose what they see as the Bank's single-minded obsession with reducing inflation. For these economists, the Bank does have a role to play in reducing unemployment, especially during economic contractions. They also criticize the Bank's timing in its pursuit of low inflation, arguing that unemployment was pushed up just when the economy was least able to withstand it—during a recession and the fragile recovery that followed.

Supporters of the Bank's strategy contend that low inflation could not have been reached without a short-term rise in unemployment, and they credit the Bank with having promoted the future stability and competitiveness of the Canadian economy. In the long run, say these economists, lower interest rates will cause employment and real output in Canada to be higher than otherwise because of the Bank's inflation medicine.

Another issue has also entered this debate—the effects of the Bank's zero-inflation policy on government debt. By pushing down output and employment, say the critics of the policy, the Bank caused tax revenues to decline for all levels of government. A vicious cycle was created in the early 1990s, with the sagging tax intake for Canadian governments leading to ever higher budget deficits, debts, and debt charges. Supporters of the Bank admit that the short-term effect of the zero-inflation policy was to increase government deficits and debts, but they contend

SIDELINE

that lower real interest rates resulting in the long run from the Bank's policy will have a dampening effect on government deficits and debts.

Notes

[1] Gordon Thiessen, "Uncertainty and the Transmission of Monetary Policy," the HERMES-Glendon Lecture reprinted in *Bank of Canada Review*, Summer 1995, p. 51.

[2] Ibid., pp. 45-46.

1. Explain how each of the following events would affect the risk premium on long-term Canadian-dollar bonds:
   a. Canada's federal government introduces a large tax cut
   b. a constitutional accord in Canada improves the prospects for national unity
   c. Canada's inflation rate rises against its American counterpart
2. Using the concepts outlined in "Money Matters," explain the statement by Gordon Theissen quoted in this article.

Part Four

Canada in the Global Economy

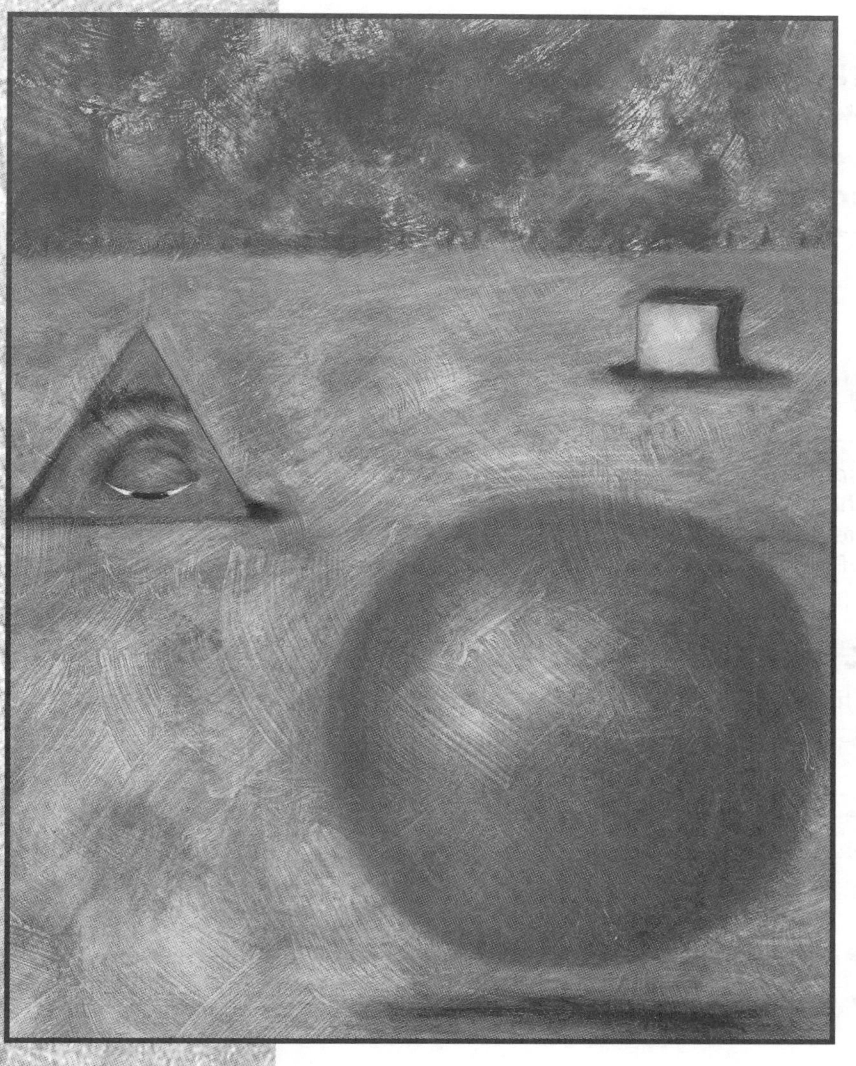

Like other animals, we find and pick up what we can use, and appropriate territories. But unlike the other animals, we also trade and produce for trade.

—Jane Jacobs, American urban affairs expert and author

Chapter Sixteen
The Foreign Sector

That knowledge has become the key resource means that there is a world economy, and that the world economy, rather than the national economy, is in control.

—Peter F. Drucker, American social philosopher

For all nations, including Canada, the move toward a global economy is bringing about changes in living standards, employment patterns, and prospects for growth. In this chapter, we examine how foreign transactions are summarized in the balance-of-payments accounts, and we study the influence of currency exchange rates. We will also see how international financial investment has affected Canada's external debt and levels of foreign ownership in the Canadian economy.

CHAPTER FOCUS

This chapter focuses on the following:

- the balance-of-payments accounts, which include the current account and the capital account
- exchange rates and how they're determined
- demand and supply for Canadian dollars, how equilibrium is reached in foreign exchange markets, and the factors that change demand and supply for currencies
- trends in balance-of-payment accounts and exchange rate systems
- the variety of exchange rate systems and policies

THE BALANCE OF PAYMENTS

As seen in earlier chapters, the rest of the world is linked with the Canadian economy through trade. Foreigners enter Canadian product markets by buying Canadian exports. In turn, Canadians buy foreign imports. Foreign spending on Canadian exports represents a monetary inflow for Canada's product markets, while Canadian spending on imports represents a monetary outflow from the Canadian economy.

Recall also that the same principles apply to trading financial assets, such as stocks and bonds. Foreigners enter Canadian financial markets by buying Canadian stocks and bonds, therefore creating an inflow of funds to Canadian financial markets. Of course, foreigners also sell foreign stocks and bonds to Canadians, thereby creating an outflow of funds from Canadian financial markets.

The Balance-of-Payments Accounts

The connections between the Canadian economy and the rest of the world are shown in detail using Canada's balance-of-payments accounts. Recall from Chapter 1 that these accounts provide a summary of all transactions between residents of Canada and those of foreign countries that involve exchanging Canadian dollars for some other international currency. At any given time, a statement of the accounts will show how the inflows and outflows "balance."

Receipts and Payments

Transactions in the accounts are divided into receipts and payments. The receipts represent monetary inflows to the Canadian economy, including both foreign purchases of Canadian exports and inflows from foreigners when they buy Canadian financial assets. Receipts are considered positive, so they are given a plus sign (+) in the accounts.

Payments, on the other hand, represent monetary outflows from the Canadian economy. They include outlays by Canadians for foreign imports and foreign financial assets. Payments are considered negative, so they are given a minus sign (–) in the accounts.

The Current Account

current account: the summary of all foreign transactions associated with current economic activity in Canada and involving Canadian dollars

Figure 16.1 shows the portion of the balance-of-payments statement that is called the **current account**. This account summarizes all foreign transactions associated with current economic activity in Canada and involving Canadian dollars. The current account includes four types of transactions: trade in merchandise (in other words, tangible goods) as well as in three "invisible" items—trade in services, flows of investment income, and transfers.

FIGURE 16.1 Canada's Current Account (1996)

	(Canadian $ billions)				
	Receipts (+) (Canadian $ inflows)		Payments (–) (Canadian $ outflows)		Balance (net) (Canadian $ inflows – outflows)
Merchandise trade	267.6	–	233.0	=	+34.5
Trade in services	39.0	–	48.3	=	–9.3
Balance of trade (net exports)				=	+25.2
Investment income	17.8	–	45.8	=	–28.0
Transfers	5.3	–	4.1	=	+1.1
Current account surplus (+) or deficit (–)					–1.7

The current account details receipts (Canadian dollar inflows) and payments (Canadian dollar outflows) for merchandise trade and nonmerchandise transactions (trade in services, investment income, and transfers). In contrast to the +$34.5 billion 1996 merchandise balance of trade, Canada had a +$25.2 billion 1996 balance of trade (net exports). Overall, for 1996, the difference between total receipts and total payments gave a current account deficit of $1.7 billion.

Source: Adapted from Statistics Canada, *Canada's Balance of International Payments, Fourth Quarter 1996* (March 1997), cat. no. 67-001-XPB, vol. 44, no. 3, pp. 28-29. Reproduced by authority of the Minister of Industry, 1997.

Trade in Merchandise

merchandise balance of trade: merchandise export receipts minus merchandise import payments

The most significant and obvious components of the current account are Canadian exports and imports of goods, or "visibles" as they are known. Canadians sell a broad range of merchandise exports and buy an equally broad range of merchandise imports. In years when the dollar value of Canadian exports of visibles outweighs that of Canadian imports of visibles, the current account shows a positive **merchandise balance of trade**. For example, in 1996, payments for Canadian exports of merchandise were $267.6 billion and payments for Canadian imports of merchandise were $233.0 billion, giving a positive merchandise balance of trade of $34.5 billion. In contrast, in years when imports of goods outweigh exports, the current account shows a negative merchandise balance of trade.

$$\text{Merchandise balance of trade} = \text{merchandise export receipts} - \text{merchandise import payments}$$

$$+\$34.5 \text{ billion} = +\$267.6 \text{ billion} - \$233.0 \text{ billion}$$

Nonmerchandise Transactions

The three remaining "invisible" components of the current account—trade in services, investment income, and transfers—are known collectively as nonmerchandise transactions.

Services Not only do Canadians import and export goods, but they also exchange services with foreigners. One important type of traded service is tourism. Spending by foreign tourists travelling in Canada represents a service export that creates an inflow of funds from foreign countries. Conversely, when Canadians travel outside Canada, their spending in foreign countries is considered a service import that causes an outflow of Canadian funds to foreign hands.

Canadians also import services when they pay foreigners to provide freight and shipping for goods. Likewise, Canadians export services when they transport goods on behalf of foreigners. In addition, a host of other invisible service items, such as insurance and telecommunications, are traded between Canadians and other countries. In 1996, the service account had a net balance of –$9.3 billion, showing that more services were imported by Canadians than were exported.

Investment Income Dividends to owners of company stocks appear as investment income in the current account, as do interest payments to owners of bonds. An American company's dividends received by a Canadian stockholder, for example, are treated as a receipt in the current account, or a positive figure. In contrast, payments to a German owner of a Canadian government bond are shown as a payment in the accounts, or a negative figure.

Because of extensive foreign ownership of Canadian stocks and bonds, payments of investment income usually overwhelm receipts, giving Canada a large negative balance on its investment income account. This is illustrated by the 1996 balance of –$28.0 billion.

Transfers Funds entering and leaving Canada as gifts and inheritances, as well as government foreign aid to low-income countries, are considered to be transfers. When new immigrants to Canada bring funds with them, these funds are considered an inflow to the Canadian economy. In contrast, federal government spending on foreign aid is considered an outflow. In 1996, transfers showed a net balance of +$1.1 billion.

current account deficit: a negative net balance in the current account resulting from lower receipts than payments for merchandise and nonmerchandise transactions

Current Account Balance

When the receipts represented in Canada's current account are lower than the payments, this results in a negative net balance, which is known as a **current account deficit**. In 1996, this shortfall totalled –$1.7 billion. On the other hand, when receipts on the current account outweigh payments, Canada has a **current account surplus**.

current account surplus: a positive net balance in the current account resulting from higher receipts than payments for merchandise and nonmerchandise transactions

The Balance of Trade

balance of trade: for both goods and services, receipts (inflows of Canadian dollars) less payments (outflows of Canadian dollars)

Two of the four components of the current accounts can be viewed in another way. Canada's **balance of trade** represents both goods *and* services, so it is identical to net exports (X – M), which was discussed in previous chapters. In recent years, Canada's surplus in merchandise trade has been greater than the deficit in trade in services, giving a surplus in the balance of trade of all products. Note that the two terms, "balance of trade" and "merchandise balance of trade" are quite different; despite this, the terms are frequently and inaccurately interchanged by the media, leading to some confusion.

The Capital Account

capital account: the summary of all international transactions of financial assets involving Canadian dollars

Figure 16.2 shows another portion of the balance-of-payments statement called the **capital account**. This account summarizes the international transactions of financial assets involving Canadian dollars. Suppose a foreigner buys a Canadian government bond and holds bank deposits valued in Canadian dollars. This ownership of financial assets is being *exported* from Canada, so an inflow of receipts is shown on the capital account. Note, however, that the interest paid on bonds or deposits appears as an outflow on the current account.

Suppose also that a Canadian purchases stock in a foreign company. In this case, the Canadian's ownership is seen as an import of ownership, so the transaction is considered to be an outflow from the capital account. Once again, note that any payment on the financial asset—in this case, a dividend—would appear as an inflow on the current account.

FIGURE 16.2 Canada's Capital Account (1996)

	(Canadian $ billions)				
	Receipts (+) (Canadian $ inflows)		Payments (–) (Canadian $ outflows)		Balance (net) (Canadian $ inflows – outflows)
Portfolio investment	26.2	–	18.4	=	+7.8
Direct investment	9.1	–	10.3	=	–1.2
Other capital flows	10.4	–	15.4	=	–5.0
Capital account surplus (+) or deficit (–) (excl. official reserves)					+1.6

The capital account details receipts and payments for financial investment (portfolio and direct investment) and other capital flows. In 1996, there was a large positive balance for each portfolio investment, which more than offset negative balances in the other categories, giving a capital account surplus of +$1.6 billion.

Source: Adapted from Statistics Canada, *Canada's Balance of International Payments, Fourth Quarter 1996* (March 1997), cat. no. 67-001, vol. 44, no. 3, pp. 28-29. Reproduced by authority of the Minister of Industry, 1997.

Portfolio and Direct Investment

The most significant transactions on the capital account are associated with the buying and selling of stocks and bonds. These capital flows are often referred to as financial investment, and can be divided into portfolio

investment and direct investment. Note that financial investment differs from investment, as defined by economists. While investment refers to businesses' purchases of real assets, financial investment refers to the buying of stocks and bonds.

portfolio investment: financial investment (purchases of stocks and bonds) that does not give the buyer a controlling interest in the institution issuing the assets

When the financial investment does not give the buyer a controlling interest in the institution issuing the assets, it is called **portfolio investment**. Suppose, for example, a Japanese resident buys a Canadian federal government bond. This would be shown as a receipt, or positive entry, on the capital account. Conversely, if a Canadian purchases a few hundred shares in a large American corporation that trades on the New York Stock Exchange, the transaction would be shown as a payment, or negative entry, on the capital account. Portfolio investment in and out of Canada usually produces a positive balance. This is primarily because of the substantial receipts that arise from foreign purchases of Canadian bonds. In 1996, for example, there was a net balance of +$7.8 billion.

direct investment: financial investment (purchases of stocks) that gives the buyer of the financial assets a controlling interest in the institution issuing the assets

In contrast to portfolio investment, **direct investment** is financial investment that gives the buyer of the financial assets a controlling interest in a company. In the case of a corporation, this may be 50 percent of the company's voting shares, or even less if ownership of the other shares is widely scattered. For example, an inflow of direct investment would occur if an Australian financier gained control of a Canadian goldmining company. An outflow would arise if a Canadian retailer acquired majority ownership of a British competitor.

Canada's net balance of direct investment varies widely from year to year. If Canada is viewed as an attractive place in which to do business, heavy inflows of direct investment lead to an overall positive balance. If other countries seem more appealing to foreign and Canadian investors, there can be an overall negative balance, as was the case in 1996 when direct investment totalled –$1.2 billion.

Other Capital Flows

Most of the remaining transactions on the capital account are connected with day-to-day fluctuations in bank deposits. If, for example, a foreigner puts funds into a Canadian-dollar bank account, a positive receipt is created in Canada's capital account. Likewise, a negative payment on the account can be caused by a Canadian adding more to a U.S.-dollar bank account.

capital account surplus: a positive net balance in the capital account, demonstrating lower investments by Canadians in foreign markets than by foreigners in the Canadian economy

capital account deficit: a negative net balance in the capital account, demonstrating higher investments by Canadians in foreign markets than by foreigners in the Canadian economy

Capital Account Balance

When receipts on Canada's capital account exceed payments, this results in a positive net balance known as a **capital account surplus**. In 1996, for example, this balance was +$1.6 billion. Such a surplus means that there are lower investments by Canadians in foreign markets than by foreigners in the Canadian market. It is also possible to show a **capital account deficit**, with a negative net balance and capital outflows exceeding inflows. Such a deficit means that there are higher investments by Canadians in foreign markets than by foreigners in the Canadian market.

Thinking About Economics

In the past, Canada has habitually run current account deficits and capital account surpluses. Why?

The frequency of deficits in Canada's current account is closely tied to the high degree of foreign ownership in the Canadian economy. To compensate for this outflow of interest and dividend payments, there has to be a sizable inflow of investment funds from foreigners on the capital account, which means more foreign ownership of Canadian financial assets and higher investment outflows in the future. Capital account inflows are achieved by making Canadian bonds especially attractive to foreign buyers. Traditionally, this has been accomplished through higher real interest rates than in other countries—particularly the United States.

Balance-of-Payments Surpluses and Deficits

balance-of-payments surplus: a positive net balance on the balance-of-payments statement, demonstrating greater receipts than payments for the current and capital accounts combined; balanced with changes in official reserves

balance-of-payments deficit: a negative net balance on the balance-of-payments statement, demonstrating lower receipts than payments for the current and capital accounts combined; balanced with changes in official reserves

Adding Canada's current and capital account balances (as well as a statistical discrepancy, which accounts for hidden transactions that are impossible to measure) gives a relatively small figure known as a **balance-of-payments surplus** if it is positive and a **balance-of-payments deficit** if it is negative. This surplus or deficit shows whether or not inflows are higher than outflows on all foreign transactions involving trade and financial assets. In 1996, for example, Canada had a balance-of-payments surplus of $7.3 billion, as shown by the positive balance in Figure 16.3. In other words, for that year, inflows exceeded outflows on the combined current and capital accounts.

FIGURE 16.3 Canada's Balance of Payments (1993)

(Canadian $ billions)	Balance (net)
1. Current account	–1.7
2. Capital account	+1.6
3. Statistical discrepancy	+7.4
Balance of payments surplus (+) or deficit (–)	+7.3
4. Changes in official reserves	–7.3

The sum of the current and capital accounts, adjusted for the statistical discrepancy, gives Canada's balance of payments. In 1996, the result was a balance of payments surplus of $7.3 billion. Because there must be change in the official reserves of foreign currency to balance any deficit or surplus, the 1996 balance of payments shows a –$7.3 billion change to the reserves.

Source: Statistics Canada, *Canada's Balance of International Payments, Fourth Quarter 1996* (March 1997), cat. no. 67-001, vol. 44, no. 3, pp. 28-29. Reproduced by authority of the Minister of Industry, 1997.

Changes in Official Reserves

change in official reserves: use of the government's reserves of foreign currency to influence the international value of the Canadian dollar, as shown on the balance-of-payments statement

To influence the international value of the Canadian dollar (as we'll discuss later), the Bank of Canada sometimes buys and sells foreign currencies, using the government's reserves of foreign currency. The effect of these operations on the flow of Canadian dollars is known as the **change in official reserves**. As shown in Figure 16.3, the change in official reserves is equal in value (and opposite in sign) to the surplus or deficit noted in the balance of payments. In 1996, for example, the –$7.3 billion change in reserves matches the +$7.3 billion balance-of-payments surplus. This negative change in official reserves indicates that the Bank of Canada *sold* Canadian dollars (creating an outflow) by buying foreign currency for the government's official reserves. In the same way, if there were a balance-of-payments deficit, there would be a positive change in official reserves equal to that amount. This positive change in official reserves would indicate that the Bank of Canada *bought* Canadian dollars (causing an inflow) and sold foreign currency.

Once the change in official reserves is added to the balance-of-payments surplus or deficit, the balance-of-payments accounts sum to zero. In other words, the inflow of funds from foreigners matches the outflow of funds from Canadians, ensuring that the accounts balance. This balance occurs because holders of Canadian dollars who buy foreign currency must engage in transactions of equal value with holders of foreign currency buying Canadian dollars. For example, $1 in Canadian currency can be sold for Japanese yen only if someone is willing to purchase this Canadian dollar in return for yen.

BRIEF REVIEW

1. Because products and financial assets are exchanged between Canadians and foreigners, foreigners participate in the Canadian economy.
2. The current account summarizes all receipts and payments from international trade in merchandise, trade in services, flows of investment income, and transfers of funds. The current account has typically shown payments exceeding receipts, giving a current account deficit.
3. Because Canada's balance of trade is the exports of goods and services less imports of goods and services, it is the same as net exports (X – M).
4. The capital account summarizes all international transactions related to the buying and selling of financial assets. Large inflows of funds from foreigners buying Canadian bonds mean that Canada typically has a capital account surplus.
5. The current account (which has usually shown a deficit) and the capital account (which has usually shown a surplus) are adjusted for statistical discrepancy, but balanced by changes in the official reserves. The Bank of Canada either sells or buys Canadian dollars to adjust the monetary flows.

EXCHANGE RATES

Any transaction that appears in the balance-of-payments accounts involves trading Canadian dollars for another currency. Transactions that are classified as receipts involve foreign currency being sold to buy Canadian dollars. For example, a company that purchases Canadian paper sold in France trades French francs for Canadian dollars to pay the Canadian paper company. In contrast, transactions that are classified as payments involve Canadian dollars being sold to buy foreign currency. A Canadian buying the services of a German architect, for example, exchanges Canadian dollars for German marks to pay the architect.

foreign exchange market: the global market in which national currencies are traded

Currencies are traded in the global **foreign exchange market**. In the Canadian sector of this market, which is run by the chartered banks, Canadian dollars are exchanged for U.S. dollars, Japanese yen, French francs, and other international currencies. The recent revolution in communications technology has made the foreign exchange market a truly global one, with currency prices internationally consistent and immediately available. For example, if the Canadian dollar is trading at a price of 80 cents in Toronto, then the same price applies in London and Tokyo.

Recall from Chapter 12 that the exchange rate is the value of one nation's currency in terms of another currency, and it becomes the price at any location where the two currencies are being exchanged. There are many exchange rates for a certain currency. For example, at any given moment one Canadian dollar may trade for 80 U.S. cents, 130 Japanese yen, or 1200 Italian lire. Because most of Canada's trade is with the United States, the price of the Canadian dollar is commonly related to U.S. dollars. We'll be using the example of Canadian and U.S. dollars in the rest of the chapter, although the same principles apply to all currencies.

Two exchange rates can be used to compare any two currencies—for example, a Canadian dollar with its U.S. counterpart. The first tells us how many U.S. dollars it takes to buy one Canadian dollar—for example, one Canadian dollar may cost 80 U.S. cents. The other way to express the exchange rate is to ask how many Canadian dollars are needed to purchase one U.S. dollar. This amount can be calculated from the first exchange rate using the following formula:

$$\text{Canadian dollars to buy US\$1} = \frac{1}{\text{U.S. dollars to buy CDN\$1}}$$

$$\text{CDN\$1.25} = \frac{1}{\text{US\$0.80}}$$

In other words, the second exchange rate—CDN$1.25 buys US$1—is the reciprocal of the first exchange rate.

Exchange Rates and Prices

One important application of exchange rates is to determine prices of products in terms of a foreign currency—either the U.S. dollar price of a

Canadian product, for example, or the Canadian dollar price of an American item.

Foreign prices of Canadian products are calculated by applying the exchange rate to the goods' Canadian dollar prices. For example, when a Canadian export with a Canadian price of $20.00 is sold in the United States, its U.S. dollar price is found by multiplying its Canadian price by the exchange rate expressed as the number of U.S. dollars it takes to buy one Canadian dollar. When the exchange rate has a value of US$0.80 for each Canadian dollar, the American price of this product is therefore US$16.00:

$$\text{U.S. dollar price} = \text{Canadian dollar price} \times \text{U.S. dollars to buy CDN\$1.00}$$
$$\text{US\$16.00} = \text{CDN\$20.00} \times \$0.80$$

Canadian prices of foreign goods are calculated in reverse. As an example, an American product imported to Canada has a U.S. price of $40.00. The import's Canadian dollar price is found by multiplying the American price by the exchange rate expressed as the number of Canadian dollars it takes to buy one U.S. dollar. When the exchange rate has a value of CDN$1.25 for each U.S. dollar, the item's Canadian price is CDN$50.00:

$$\text{Canadian dollar price} = \text{U.S. dollar price} \times \text{Canadian dollars to buy US\$1.00}$$
$$\text{CDN\$50.00} = \text{US\$40.00} \times \$1.25$$

Foreign Exchange Markets

To see how exchange rates are set, we must look at the demand for and supply of Canadian currency in foreign exchange markets. In doing so, we concentrate on the number of U.S. dollars needed to purchase a Canadian dollar.

Demand for Canadian Dollars

demand for Canadian dollars: the relationship between the price of a Canadian dollar and the quantity demanded in exchange for another currency

The **demand for Canadian dollars** is the relationship between the price of a Canadian dollar and the quantity of Canadian dollars demanded in exchange for another currency. The relationship can be expressed in a schedule and a curve. As Figure 16.4 shows, this relationship is inverse, so the curve has a negative slope. For example, a jump in the price of the Canadian dollar in terms of the U.S. dollar reduces the quantity of Canadian dollars demanded.

Canadian dollars are demanded on foreign exchange markets to finance foreign purchases of either Canadian exports or Canadian financial assets. Foreigners buying Canadian exports of goods and services exchange their own currencies for Canadian dollars in order to pay Canadian producers. Likewise, foreigners acquiring Canadian financial assets buy Canadian dollars to settle their purchases.

The negative slope of the demand curve is determined by the first of these two groups—foreign export buyers. A higher Canadian dollar means that Canadian goods and services have higher American prices.

FIGURE 16.4
A Foreign Exchange Market

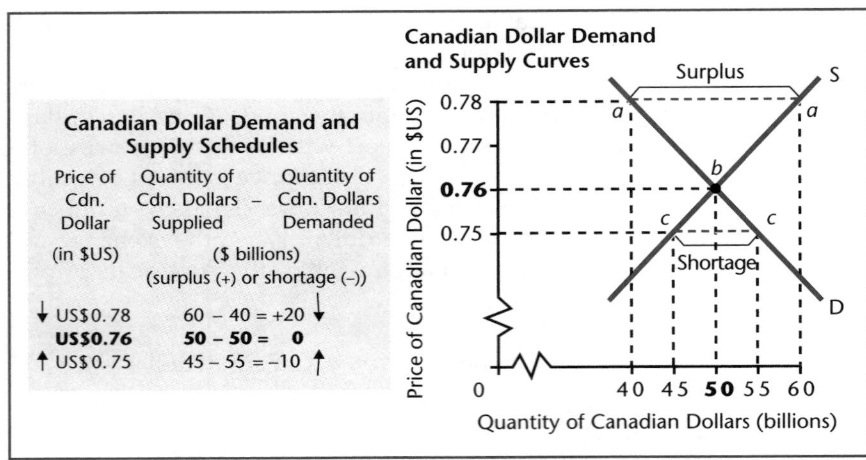

Canadian Dollar Demand and Supply Schedules

Price of Cdn. Dollar (in $US)	Quantity of Cdn. Dollars Supplied – Quantity of Cdn. Dollars Demanded ($ billions) (surplus (+) or shortage (–))
↓ US$0.78	60 – 40 = +20 ↓
US$0.76	**50 – 50 = 0**
↑ US$0.75	45 – 55 = –10 ↑

The demand and supply curves for the Canadian dollar determine its equilibrium value, which equals its exchange rate. If the price falls (to points *c*) below the equilibrium value (point *b*), a shortage of Canadian dollars results. Without government intervention, the forces of demand and supply push the price up to equilibrium (point *b*), causing the Canadian dollar to appreciate. A price above the equilibrium value (at points *a*) causes a surplus of Canadian dollars. Without government intervention, the Canadian dollar would depreciate, returning to its equilibrium value.

Suppose, for example, the exchange rate for Canadian dollars is US$0.75. As a result, a Canadian export with a price of CDN$2.00 originally has an American price of US$1.50 ($2.00 × $0.75). If the value of the Canadian dollar increases from US$0.75 to US$0.80, the American price of this export rises to US$1.60 ($2.00 × $0.80). Because American buyers find Canadian exports more expensive, they purchase fewer of them, decreasing both Canadian export receipts and the quantity of Canadian dollars demanded in exchange for U.S. dollars.

Supply of Canadian Dollars

supply of Canadian dollars: the relationship between the price of a Canadian dollar and the quantity supplied in exchange for another currency

In contrast, the **supply of Canadian dollars** is the relationship between the price of the Canadian dollar and the quantity of Canadian dollars supplied in exchange for another currency. Once again, the relationship can be expressed in a schedule or a curve. As Figure 16.4 shows, the relationship is direct, as is typical in supply relationships. A rise in the price of the Canadian dollar causes an increase in the quantity supplied of Canadian dollars.

Canadian dollars are supplied in foreign exchange markets for Canadian purchases of foreign products and financial assets. Canadians buying imported products or foreign financial assets sell Canadian dollars for another currency to complete their transactions.

The positive slope of the supply curve is determined by the first of these two groups—Canadian import buyers. For example, a higher Canadian dollar lowers domestic prices of imported goods and services from the United States. If the Canadian dollar rises from US$0.75 to US$0.80, the U.S. dollar falls in terms of the Canadian dollar from

CDN$1.33 ($1.00 ÷ $0.75) to CDN$1.25 ($1.00 ÷ $0.80). An American import that costs $3.00 in the United States therefore drops from CDN$4.00 ($3.00 × $1.33) to CDN$3.75 ($3.00 × $1.25). Canadians respond to these lower prices by purchasing more imports, increasing both Canadian import payments and the quantity of Canadian dollars supplied in exchange for U.S. dollars.

Market Equilibrium

Recall that, in competitive markets, the forces of demand and supply bring the market to an equilibrium point, where demand and supply intersect. The same is true of foreign exchange markets. So, when a government allows the value of its currency to vary, foreign exchange markets will move toward an equilibrium point where any discrepancy between amounts demanded and supplied is eliminated. Figure 16.4 provides a hypothetical example.

If (at points *c*) the Canadian dollar exchange rate is below its equilibrium price of US$0.76 (point *b*), the quantity demanded of Canadian dollars on this foreign exchange market is greater than the quantity supplied of Canadian dollars. This causes a $10 billion shortage of Canadian currency, as shown at the exchange rate of US$0.75 ($55 billion – $45 billion). When exchange rates are allowed to vary, the price of the Canadian dollar is forced up to its equilibrium value. In this case, when one currency's price increases against another, the increased currency is said to **appreciate**. The movement to equilibrium is very rapid because foreign exchange markets are highly competitive and involve large numbers of price-conscious buyers and sellers.

appreciate: to increase, as when a currency's price rises in comparison to the price of another currency

In contrast, if (at points *a*) the Canadian dollar is above its equilibrium price, the quantity supplied of Canadian dollars exceeds the quantity demanded on this foreign exchange market. The result is a $20 billion surplus of Canadian currency as shown at the exchange rate of US$0.78 ($60 billion – $40 billion). When exchange rates are allowed to vary, this excess soon pushes down the price of the Canadian dollar until it reaches its equilibrium value. In this case, the Canadian dollar is said to **depreciate** when compared to the U.S. dollar. Again, the movement toward equilibrium happens very quickly.

depreciate: to decrease, as when a currency's price falls in comparison to the price of another currency

Note that both preceding examples involve the variations in exchange rates that bring about changes in quantities demanded or supplied. In other words, the examples demonstrate movements *along* the Canadian dollar demand and supply curves.

Changes in Demand and Supply

Of course, other factors can cause the Canadian dollar demand and supply curves to *shift*. Demand and supply shifts in foreign exchange markets are related either to trade or to financial conditions. As a result of shifts in the curves, the equilibrium exchange rate changes. Four main factors affect the equilibrium value of the exchange rate: price differences, product demand, interest rates, and speculation.

Price Differences

A country's price level may rise more rapidly than price levels in other countries, so that its own products become more expensive than foreign products. The left graph in Figure 16.5 illustrates a hypothetical example of what happens when Canada's rate of inflation outpaces inflation in the United States.

At any given exchange rate between the two currencies, increases in the prices of Canadian products mean that Americans will purchase fewer Canadian exports, reducing the amount of Canadian currency demanded on this foreign exchange market. This reduces the demand for Canadian dollars, shown as a shift in the demand curve for Canadian dollars from D_0 to D_1. A lower U.S. inflation rate also means that American products become cheaper relative to Canadian products. As a result, Canadian buyers purchase more American imports at any given exchange rate. This increases the supply of Canadian dollars, thereby shifting the supply curve from S_0 to S_1. As a result of these demand and supply changes, the Canadian dollar depreciates, or falls in value, from point *a* to point *b*.

Product Demand

The appeal of a country's products to prospective buyers can also affect exchange rates. Suppose, for example, the quality of Canadian products improves. As a result, the demand for Canadian products in both foreign and domestic markets increases. The result is illustrated on the right graph in Figure 16.5.

In this case, Americans increase their purchases of Canadian products, thereby shifting the demand curve for Canadian dollars from D_2 to

FIGURE 16.5
Exchange Rate Changes

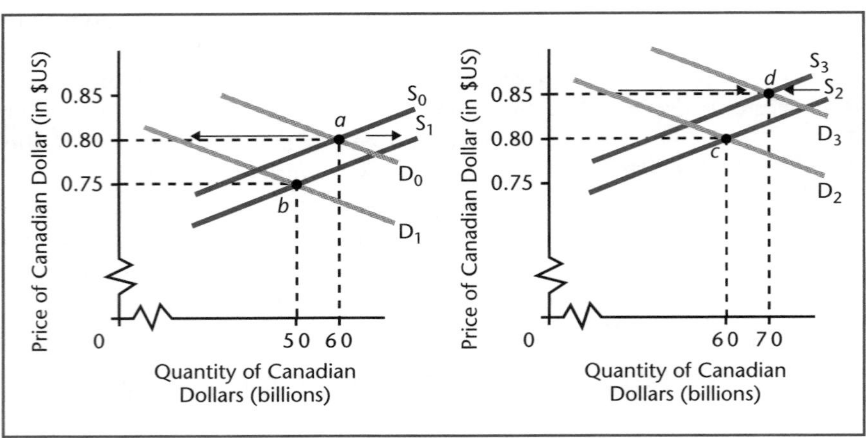

On the left graph, a decrease in demand, shown as the shift from D_0 to D_1, and an increase in supply, shown as the shift from S_0 to S_1, cause the Canadian dollar to depreciate from point *a* to point *b*. Conversely, as shown on the right graph, an increase in demand (from D_2 to D_3) and a decrease in supply (from S_2 to S_3), cause the Canadian dollar to appreciate from point *c* to point *d*.

D_3 in this foreign exchange market. Also, Canadians buy more domestic products and fewer American imports. This reduces the sale of Canadian dollars on this foreign exchange market and so shifts the supply curve to the left, from S_2 to S_3. Both trends cause the Canadian dollar to appreciate, or rise in value, from point *c* to point *d*.

Interest Rates

Suppose that the Bank of Canada implements an expansionary monetary policy, causing Canadian interest rates to fall in comparison to corresponding American rates. As shown in Figure 16.5, on the left, this has implications for the Canadian dollar.

With the drop in the Canadian interest rate, Canadian bonds become less appealing to financial investors in both Canada and the United States. Fewer American purchases of Canadian bonds mean that the demand for Canadian dollars decreases, thereby shifting the demand curve from D_0 to D_1. Meanwhile, Canadians also reduce their purchases of domestic bonds *and* are more likely to buy foreign financial assets. In order to buy the foreign financial assets, Canadians must sell additional Canadian dollars on foreign exchange markets. The result is an increase in the supply of Canadian dollars, shown as a shift to the right of the supply curve from S_0 to S_1. The movements in demand and supply both cause the Canadian dollar to depreciate.

Speculation

Some individuals, but more often financial institutions, buy and sell on foreign exchange markets simply in order to profit from short-run changes in currency values. The activities of these profit-seekers, known as **speculators**, affect the demand and supply of particular currencies, and so lead to changes in exchange rates.

speculators: individuals or organizations that buy and sell currencies for profit

For example, if there are signs that the Canadian dollar will soon rise in value against the U.S. dollar, speculators enter the market in such a way as to make this expectation a reality. Figure 16.5, on the right, shows the effects. Lured by potential profits, American speculators demand the currency that is expected to rise in value, so they purchase Canadian dollars by selling their holdings of U.S. dollars. As a result, the demand curve for Canadian dollars shifts from D_2 to D_3. At the same time, Canadian speculators hold onto, and perhaps buy more, Canadian dollars rather than buying U.S. dollars. As a result, the supply curve for Canadian dollars shifts from S_2 to S_3. As a result of both trends, the Canadian dollar appreciates and speculators make a tidy profit.

Thinking About Economics

What factors prompt speculators to enter foreign exchange markets?

Speculators respond to three factors: interest rates, inflation rates, and the political climate. Because of the influence of interest rates on exchange rates, speculators pay particular attention to monetary policy. Any indication that the Bank of Canada is following a contractionary policy, for example, leads speculators to forecast a rise in Canadian interest rates and a resulting increase in the value of the Canadian dollar. Speculation therefore hastens the Canadian dollar's appreciation in the foreign currency market. Speculators also act on the basis of expectations about inflation. For example, they may expect that the Canadian inflation rate will fall compared to inflation rates in other countries. As a result, speculators expect a future rise in the Canadian dollar's value. This prediction again causes intervention in the foreign exchange market that immediately raises the value of the Canadian dollar. Finally, speculators pay attention to political factors—especially their possible impact on foreign-held debt. Suppose, for example, there is a risk that Canada will become politically unstable. Speculators will expect that instability to make Canadian bonds less attractive to foreign investors, thereby reducing the demand for Canadian dollars on the foreign exchange market. In anticipation of the possible fall in the Canadian dollar's value, speculators will sell Canadian dollars immediately, thus hastening the change they predict.

BRIEF REVIEW

1. Exchange rates are prices of currencies in terms of other currencies. They are determined in global foreign exchange markets.
2. The demand for Canadian dollars is the relationship between the price of a Canadian dollar and the quantity of Canadian dollars demanded in exchange for another currency. The relationship is inverse, so, for example, an increase in price causes a decrease in quantity demanded. This is shown as a movement along the demand curve. Demand for Canadian dollars in foreign exchange markets is created by foreigners' purchases of Canadian exports and financial assets.
3. The supply of Canadian dollars is the relationship between the price of the Canadian dollar and the quantity of Canadian dollars supplied in exchange for another currency. The relationship is direct; so, for example, an increase in price causes an increase in quantity supplied. This is shown as a movement along the supply curve. Canadian dollars are supplied in foreign exchange markets for Canadian purchases of foreign products and financial assets.
4. When currency values are allowed to vary, a currency's exchange rate will move toward its equilibrium value, the point of intersection of the demand and supply curves for the currency.
5. Factors that shift the demand and supply curves for a particular currency, and so the equilibrium point as well, are price differences, product demand, interest rates, and speculation.

EXCHANGE RATE SYSTEMS

Flexible Exchange Rates

flexible exchange rates: currency exchange rates that are allowed to move freely to their equilibrium levels; also called floating rates

Governments that allow the exchange rate of their currency to vary freely, as assumed in Figures 16.4 and 16.5, are following a system of **flexible exchange rates**, or floating rates as they are sometimes known.

Flexible exchange rates offer one main advantage: market forces quickly eliminate shortages or surpluses so that inflows and outflows soon match each other. However, flexible rates also have an important disadvantage. Dramatic changes in exchange rates mean considerable risks for businesses involved in importing or exporting.

Consider, for example, a Canadian importer of American-made products. If the Canadian dollar depreciates suddenly, the price of the products is pushed up to the point that the products become too expensive for Canadian consumers and quantity demanded decreases. Canadian exporters and their suppliers face similar uncertainty. Suppose, for example, the Canadian dollar jumps in value in comparison to the American dollar. The exporter who exports Canadian products to the U.S. market finds that they become too expensive for the American market and quantity demanded decreases. Because of these fluctuations, incomes and employment in the import and export industries are harmed.

Fixed Exchange Rates

fixed exchange rates: currency exchange rates set or "pegged" to a certain value by each country's government

To avoid the uncertainty caused by flexible exchange rates, governments often intervene directly in foreign exchange markets. **Fixed exchange rates** offer the most striking alternative to floating rates. When a government establishes a fixed exchange rate, it sets or "pegs" the value of the country's currency at a certain price in terms of another currency.

Impact of Market Intervention

The effects of fixed exchange rates on a foreign exchange market are illustrated by the hypothetical example in Figure 16.6. This shows that whenever the government's target rate differs from the equilibrium level, either a balance-of-payments surplus or deficit is created.

Suppose the federal government sets a target exchange rate of 82 cents in U.S. currency (at points *c*). Because this rate is below its equilibrium level of 84 cents (point *b*), it creates excess demand for Canadian dollars, with more sought than are available on the market. This means that the inflows represented on the current and capital accounts, which are associated with buying Canadian dollars, exceed the outflows represented on these accounts, which are tied to sales of Canadian dollars. This shortage leads to a balance-of-payments surplus of CDN$20 billion.

FIGURE 16.6
Fixed Exchange Rates

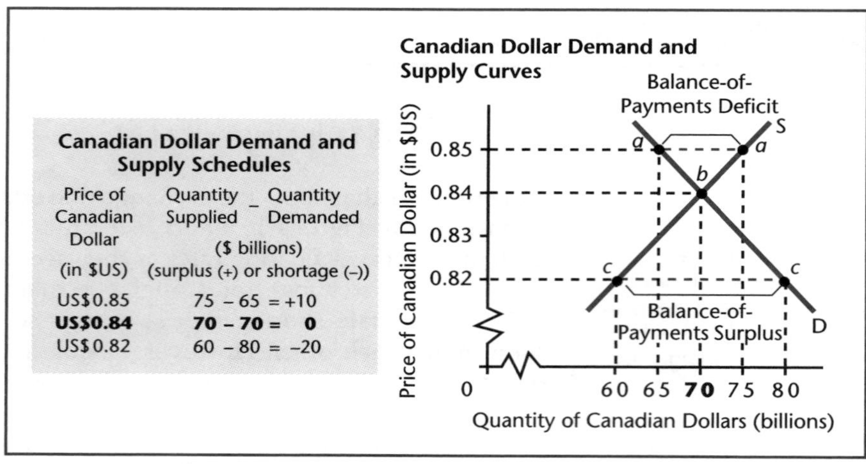

Canadian Dollar Demand and Supply Schedules

Price of Canadian Dollar (in $US)	Quantity Supplied − Quantity Demanded ($ billions) (surplus (+) or shortage (–))
US$0.85	75 – 65 = +10
US$0.84	**70 – 70 = 0**
US$0.82	60 – 80 = –20

With fixed rates, the target value of the Canadian dollar can differ from the equilibrium determined by the market demand and supply curves. A target level above (at points *a*) the equilibrium value (point *b*) produces a balance of payments deficit. A target level below (at points *c*) the equilibrium value (point *b*) results in a balance of payments surplus.

To make up for the excess demand of Canadian currency in the foreign exchange market, the Bank of Canada intervenes by selling CDN$20 billion and purchasing U.S. currency in return. In doing so, the Bank is able to curb any rise in the value of the Canadian dollar above the desired level of US$0.82.

Suppose, instead, the federal government set the target level of the Canadian dollar at 85 cents in U.S. currency (points *a*), above the market equilibrium price (point *b*). As a result, a $10 billion surplus of Canadian dollars translates into a $10 billion balance-of-payments deficit. To prop up the Canadian dollar at this preferred rate of US$0.85, the Bank of Canada intervenes by buying CDN$10 billion and selling American currency in return. In this way, it eliminates the excess supply of Canadian dollars.

Exchange Rate Policy

Sometimes governments use fixed exchange rates to affect domestic output and prices. To see how policy-makers can use exchange rate policy to different ends, let's consider the impact of low exchange rates, high exchange rates, and monetary policy.

Low Exchange Rates

A low target rate for the Canadian dollar, such as US$0.82 in Figure 16.6, makes Canadian exports cheap and imports of American products expensive. This policy stimulates export revenues and inhibits import spending, thereby increasing net exports. Recall from the discussion of aggregate demand and supply in Chapter 12 that a rise in net exports increases aggregate demand. Hence, lowering the exchange rate serves as an expansionary policy. Both real output and employment are boosted, and any recessionary gap that exists is reduced.

However, there are several problems in setting a low exchange rate. First, there is the danger of inflation. This hazard is especially acute if the economy is near its potential output, when shifts in the aggregate demand curve primarily affect prices. Second, there is a chance that a country's trading partners may respond by reducing *their* exchange rates to maintain their own export markets. When this happens, currencies return to their original relative values, and the original policy achieves nothing.

Despite these risks, a policy of low exchange rates has sometimes been pursued with success. For example, Pacific Rim countries such as Taiwan and South Korea have depressed the values of their currencies as a way of encouraging export-driven growth. Evidence of this strategy is found in their large holdings of foreign currency, which have resulted from the balance-of-payments surpluses associated with a low exchange rate policy.

High Exchange Rates

Setting a high target for the Canadian dollar, such as US$0.85 in Figure 16.6, has the opposite effect: high exchange rates make imports cheaper and boost the prices of Canadian exports. Therefore, raising the exchange rate serves as a contractionary policy by reducing net exports and decreasing aggregate demand. This puts downward pressure on inflation as well as on real output and employment.

Using a high exchange rate as an anti-inflationary tool has its problems, however. Not only is there a reduction in output and employment—especially in exporting industries—but also a reduction in the government's foreign currency holdings. Sooner or later, through continual balance-of-payments deficits, the holdings are depleted. In this situation, countries sometimes attempt to bolster their currency reserves by such measures as forcing citizens to sell their foreign currency to the government rather than allowing them to trade it privately. These laws produce underground foreign exchange markets, with prices set at equilibrium levels determined by demand and supply.

Monetary Policy and Exchange Rates

The Bank of Canada can use monetary policy to back its intervention in the foreign exchange market. Recall that interest rates and the price of the Canadian dollar move in the same direction. If the Bank wishes to raise the exchange rate without incurring a balance-of-payments deficit, it can force up interest rates using contractionary monetary policy. Conversely, an easy money policy of low interest rates can be applied to depreciate the exchange rate. In either case, the Bank of Canada influences the Canadian dollar by adjusting its equilibrium value.

Unfortunately, applying monetary policy in this way can complicate stabilization policy. If the Bank of Canada focuses its monetary policy excessively on maintaining a certain target exchange rate, it may end up worsening the business cycle. Therefore, the Bank must make sure its target value for the Canadian dollar allows the economy to move toward its potential output.

Evolution of Exchange Rate Systems

During the past century, there have been three major exchange rate systems used by industrialized countries: a fixed gold standard, a structure of adjustable fixed rates, and the widespread use of the managed float, which offers a middle ground between the extremes of fully flexible and fixed exchange rates.

The Gold Standard (1879–1934)

Except for a brief time connected with the financial turmoil caused by World War I, the international gold standard was in place for over five decades. With this system, each country set the value of its currency in terms of an amount of gold. (For example, the Canadian dollar traded for 23.22 grains of gold.) Because these standards were not adjustable, maintaining a constant exchange rate took precedence over stabilization policy. The gold standard finally broke down under the strains of the Great Depression of the 1930s as governments unsuccessfully attempted to stimulate their exports and domestic employment levels by depreciating their currencies.

The Bretton Woods System (1945–1971)

The disarray caused by exchange rate movements in the latter half of the 1930s led to the creation of the Bretton Woods system after World War II. (Bretton Woods is the name of the place in the United States where the conference to establish an international monetary system was held.) This system was based on adjustable fixed exchange rates. Governments set an official exchange rate for their currency until persistent surpluses or shortages in the foreign exchange market forced an adjustment. The currency then underwent a **devaluation** (reduction in value) when there were surpluses, or a **revaluation** (an increase in value) when there were shortages.

devaluation: a reduction in the value of a currency by the government that sets the exchange rate

revaluation: an increase in the value of a currency by the government that sets the exchange rate

The organization known as the International Monetary Fund (IMF) was also established at this time. Among other tasks, it promotes the stability of exchange rates through loans to countries that are running out of foreign currency reserves in order to stabilize their currencies.

From 1950 to 1962, the Canadian government chose to diverge from the international Bretton Woods system and adopted floating rates instead. Substantial inflows of foreign financial investment kept the value of the Canadian dollar high during these years. During most of this period, the Canadian dollar traded above the price of US$1.

Canada returned to a fixed exchange rate system from 1962 to 1970, pegging its dollar at a relatively low value of US$0.925. This action was prompted by speculators who were driving down the Canadian dollar's value. The Canadian experience in the 1960s points out an interesting problem with fixed exchange rates. With such a system, it is difficult for a country to shield itself from foreign inflation. In Canada's case, rising inflation experienced by the United States during this period was automatically "imported" to Canada as prices for American items sold in Canada increased.

Managed Float (1971–1997)

The stability provided by the Bretton Woods system helped promote the high growth rates experienced by most countries in the postwar period. However, the system fell apart in 1971 when the United States—whose dollar had come to serve as an "international currency"—was forced to adopt a **managed float**. Under this system, the foreign value of a currency is allowed to vary over time, but the effects of short-run demand and supply movements in the foreign exchange market are sometimes lessened through government intervention. The move to a partially floating exchange rate provided the American government with the leeway needed to deal with imbalances in the foreign exchange market. By 1974, most other major economies had also switched away from fixed exchange rates.

managed float: a flexible exchange rate system that sometimes involves short-term government intervention

Canada preceded most other countries in adopting a managed float in 1970. During the early 1970s, high prices for many of Canada's resource exports boosted the demand for Canadian currency. As a result, the Canadian dollar traded above US$1.00. Relatively rapid inflation in Canada during the late 1970s and early 1980s, however, caused the Canadian dollar to decline to an all-time annual low of US$0.72 by 1986. In the late 1980s and the first half of the 1990s, the dollar rose and then fell in response to interest rate adjustments by the Bank of Canada. The behaviour of the U.S. price of the Canadian dollar in the last few decades is indicated in Figure 16.7.

FIGURE 16.7
Canadian Exchange Rates

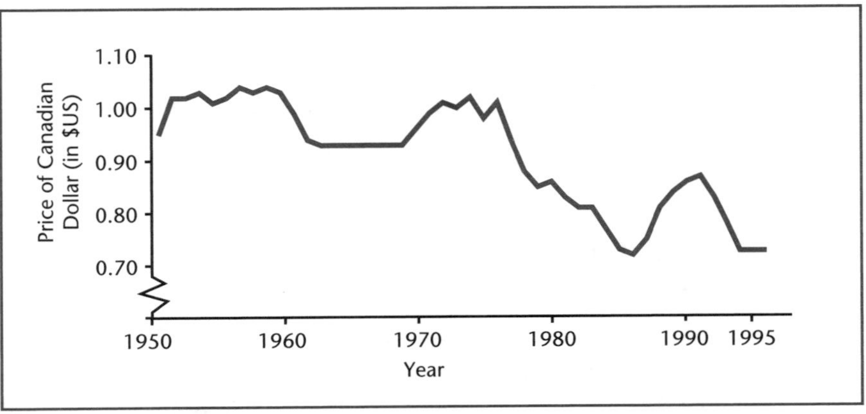

With floating rates, the Canadian dollar rose above US$1.00 in the 1950s. Between 1962 and 1970, it remained close to its fixed value of US$0.925. With a managed float in place since 1970, the Canadian dollar has fluctuated widely.

Sources: Adapted from Statistics Canada, *Canadian Economic Observer, Historical Statistical Supplement, 1995/96* (July 1996), cat. no. 11-210-XPB, vol. 10, p. 89; *Canadian Economic Observer, Statistical Summary* (March 1997), cat. no. 11-010-XPB, p. 52. Reproduced by authority of the Minister of Industry, 1997.

Thinking About Economics

What are the trends in exchange rate systems?

Because of two factors—the uncertainty of fluctuating currency prices and multinational trade arrangements—some countries started moving back to pegged exchange rates in the 1990s. For example, various member nations of the European Union (EU), including Germany and France, synchronized their currencies through a system of adjustable fixed exchange rates. With the growing integration of national economies, these types of regional exchange rate arrangements will probably become more common. Many economists have predicted that the integration of national economies will bring about a single international currency. While it would simplify the financing of international trade and investment, critics point out that individual countries would lose the ability to conduct their own monetary policies.

BRIEF REVIEW

1. While flexible exchange rates allow the foreign exchange market to correct imbalances automatically, this system can create instability in the domestic economy, especially for businesses involved in importing or exporting.
2. By fixing, or pegging, an exchange rate, a government can create balance-of-payments surpluses and deficits.
3. Governments can use exchange rate policy as a means of influencing output and price levels. A lower exchange rate fosters more domestic output and employment, while a higher exchange rate reduces inflation. Governments can also use monetary policy to influence exchange rates by adjusting interest rates.
4. Three main exchange rate systems have prevailed worldwide over the past century: the fixed gold standard, the Bretton Woods system of adjustable fixed rates, and the recent preference for the managed float.

KEY CONCEPTS

current account
merchandise balance of trade
current account deficit
current account surplus
balance of trade
capital account
portfolio investment
direct investment
capital account surplus
capital account deficit
balance-of-payments surplus
balance-of-payments deficit
change in official reserves
foreign exchange market
demand for Canadian dollars
supply of Canadian dollars
appreciate
depreciate
speculators
flexible exchange rates
fixed exchange rates
devaluation
revaluation
managed float

ANALYSIS AND APPLICATION

1. Outline the effects of the following situations on Canada's balance of trade:
   a. a boom in the American economy
   b. a rise in the value of the Canadian dollar in terms of U.S. dollars
   c. an expansion of transnational corporations' production facilities in Canada
   d. a "made-in-Canada" recession

2. Despite the large negative balance on Canada's investment income account, it is possible for Canada's current account to show a surplus and the capital account to show a deficit. Give one possible reason to explain this situation.

3. For each transaction below, identify where it appears on Canada's current account and whether it is classified as a receipt or payment:
   a. a Canadian furniture dealer buys an antique clock in France
   b. a German bondholder is paid interest by the Canadian government
   c. an Italian immigrant to Canada transfers funds to his Canadian bank account
   d. a Canadian shareholder receives dividends from a Mexican company
   e. a Canadian spends her holidays in Switzerland
   f. an Australian television network buys a weekly series from a Canadian program producer
   g. a Canadian sends funds to relatives living in Somalia
   h. an Israeli consumer buys paper stationery produced in Canada

4. For each transaction below, identify where it appears in Canada's capital account and whether it is classified as a receipt or payment.
   a. a British retailer opens a chain of stores in Canada
   b. a Canadian buys 1000 IBM shares on the New York Stock Exchange
   c. a Japanese investment company adds funds to its Canadian bank account
   d. an American purchases a bond issued by a Canadian provincial government
   e. a Canadian media company takes over a British newspaper
   f. a Canadian mining firm opens a bank account in Chile

Delphi's Balance-of-Payments Accounts (Delphi $ millions)

	Receipts	Payments	Balance
Current Account			
Merchandise trade	183.4	323.6	_____
Trade in services	187.9	_____	+90.5
Investment income	192.3	157.9	_____
Transfers	_____	24.5	+32.3
Capital Account			
Portfolio investment	65.9	_____	–20.2
Direct investment	32.7	45.8	_____
Other capital flows	_____	15.2	+22.9

5. a. What is Delphi's balance of merchandise trade? balance of trade?
   b. Calculate the surplus or deficit on Delphi's current account and the surplus or deficit on its capital account.
   c. If the statistical discrepancy in Delphi's balance of payments accounts is $24.5 million, is Delphi running a balance of payments surplus or deficit? Explain.
   d. Calculate the "changes in official reserves" that appears in Delphi's balance of payments accounts. Is this figure positive or negative? Why?

6. Calculate the following:
   a. the U.S. dollar price of an item priced at $520 in Canadian currency when the exchange rate is CDN$1.00 = US$0.81
   b. the Canadian dollar price of an item priced at $24 000 in U.S. currency if the exchange rate is US$1.00 = CDN$1.22
   c. the U.S. dollar price of an item priced at $3.00 in Canadian currency when the exchange rate is US$1.00 = CDN$1.25
   d. the Canadian dollar price of an item priced at $82 in U.S. currency when the exchange rate is CDN $1.00 = US$0.80

Canadian Dollar Demand and Supply Schedules

Price of Cdn. Dollar (in $US)	Quantity of Cdn. Dollars Supplied ($ billions)	Quantity of Cdn. Dollars Demanded ($ billions)
.81	75	35
.80	65	45
.79	55	55
.78	45	65
.77	35	75

7. a. Use the hypothetical data in the table above to draw demand and supply curves for the Canadian dollar in exchange for U.S. dollars.
   b. With a flexible exchange rate, what will the value of the Canadian dollar be?
   c. If the Canadian government sets a target exchange rate of US$0.81, will a balance of payments surplus or deficit result? Calculate the "changes in official reserves" that would appear in Canada's balance of payments accounts, presuming that the U.S. dollar is the only foreign currency traded with the Canadian dollar.
   d. If instead the Canadian government sets a target exchange rate of US$0.78, will a balance of payments surplus or deficit result? Again calculate the "changes in official reserves" that would appear in Canada's balance of payments accounts, again presuming that the U.S. dollar is the only foreign currency traded with the Canadian dollar.

8. For each of the following trends, draw a demand and supply graph to show the effect on the price of the Canadian dollar in terms of U.S. dollars:
   a. a contractionary monetary policy initiated by the Bank of Canada raises Canadian interest rates
   b. Canada's real output rises at a time when real output in the United States is falling
   c. a new Canadian constitutional accord reduces the threat of Quebec separation
   d. Given Canada's aging population, more Canadian "snowbirds" travel to the U.S. each winter

9. (Advanced Question)
   Given the close links between the Canadian and U.S. economies, some commentators suggest that the Canadian dollar should be fixed against the U.S. dollar. What would be the main advantages and disadvantages of this arrangement to Canadians?

10. Access the Penn World Tables (at http://cansim.epas.utoronto.ca:5680/pwt/pwt.html).
    a. Use the tables to retrieve data on Canada's exchange rate for the last five years for which data are available.
    b. Identify any trends shown by the data you have retrieved and discuss which Canadian groups are hurt and which are helped by the trends you have identified.

Advancing Economic Thought

GLOBAL WARNINGS

Homer-Dixon and the Environment

In recent decades, the goal of environmental sustainability has received increasing attention in economics and other social disciplines. Many global problems are now directly related to the environment. The article below offers some fresh insights into the connections between international economic and environmental trends, as outlined in the work of an influential Canadian thinker, Thomas Homer-Dixon.

It was a standard news story out of Washington: a group of senior officials had been briefed on global security and America's ever-dominant role therein. The adviser was a Canadian, a 40-year-old assistant political science professor at the University of Toronto, one Thomas (Tad) Homer-Dixon. He may not be a household name yet, but his analyses of the environmental causes of violent conflict have become much sought after in the White House, not to mention the CIA.

Thomas Homer-Dixon
Source: *Thomas Homer-Dixon*

But still, this crowd listening to an assistant professor? And a Canadian? Since when?

Since the old solutions ran out of gas. Since the start of an understanding that the problems of the developing world are so complex and horrific that conventional interventions do not and will not work.

He may be an assistant poli-sci prof in the lecture rooms of University College but down in the basement, in a bunker of utilitarian offices, the lanky 40-year-old reigns as the director of U of T's peace and conflict studies program, 60 cream-of-the-crop graduate students under his command.

It's from there, over the last five years, that he's fanned out into the Third World to do on-the-ground research in countries that are at risk of civil breakdown—with all that entails for the rest of the planet.

What Homer-Dixon told U.S. officials, put simply, is this: from here on in, the causes of conflict in the world are going to be environmental in the broadest sense. Growing scarcities of water, forests for fuel, cropland for food, and soil itself—linked with unchecked population growth—are going to result in violent breakdown in the Third World, produce a chaotic unravelling that will, one way or another, spill over into the rest of the planet.

And it will happen, he says, with a speed and scale unprecedented in history. "My work is a red light flashing, 'Pay attention, people. If we don't do something now when we still have the opportunity, we're going to be faced with a lot more Haitis down the road.' We are already living cheek-by-jowl on this planet and we're not going to escape the problems that arise. It's as simple as that."

Unless, that is, policymakers intervene to address the underlying causes of scarce resources. What Homer-Dixon does believe is that a big part of the solution in the developing world is markets. Not in the ideological sense that free enterprise will fix all problems, that once government is out of the way, economic growth will happen. But markets with prices that reflect the scarcity of a resource, that result in conservation and people substituting relatively abundant resources for the scarce one.

"Scarce resources in a country with a weak government give incentives to elites to speculate on them," he says. "They have a profit incentive to prevent the institutional reform that would deal with the underlying scarcity." In Haiti, for example, forest now covers only 2 percent of the island and is disappearing at a rate of 4 to 5 percent a year. Fuel wood is therefore scarce and valuable. The military has established a monopoly over it and when reforestation projects are undertaken by the government, the military often moves in and rips out the seedlings. "It's exactly that kind of reinforcing loop of behaviour that undermines the political will of the state to deal with the scarcity, and it's exactly what we want to avoid."

Getting markets to work right in the Third World requires strong, competent, and ingenious governments, just as it requires them in the West, he says. For example, China is already in a dangerous behaviour loop. Every metre of cropland is being used to feed the ever-growing population—even a low 1.1 percent birth rate adds 14 million annually—but thousands of acres are lost to erosion and urban expansion every year. "In a sense, China has sold its soul to economic growth," he says. "It's in a race between economic growth that maintains state legitimacy and stability and growth that provides opportunity to deal with the problems that it simultaneously creates. Growth undermines the environment."

China and other countries now attempting economic transformation, and hurtling toward mammoth pollution and environmental disintegration may say, "'You had yours, now we want ours.' After feasting at the table who are we to say they can't?" Homer-Dixon says. "But what we might reasonably say is, 'You're not advised to do it in the same way we did. You can use the technology and knowledge we've gained in the last decade and become industrialized and wealthy in a different way than we did.' It is in their interest as well as ours."

It staggers many in the West that birth rates continue unabated in states where people are plagued by recurrent famine, drought, and unimaginable psychological stress. Even a 3 percent growth rate, common in Third World countries, means six and seven children per family, a doubling of the population every 20 years.

There is no single, magic-bullet solution—not poverty alleviation, not democracy, not family planning. Multiple interventions or combinations of them are needed, and they needn't be expensive.

"You don't have to build a huge dam or install a big electrification program," he says. "Set up enterprises like the banks in Bangladesh that provide small amounts of capital to women's co-ops. Or family-planning programs where people drive in and talk to individual women. In this kind of micro-level work you get a tremendous return for every dollar invested."

The premium must be on prevention of scarcity, not after-the-fact adaptation to it: "The optimism of those who have great faith in the potential of human ingenuity when spurred by necessity is, I believe, imprudent, a huge gamble."

Source

Abridged from Lynda Hurst, "The Global Guru," *The Toronto Star*, 20 July 1996, pp. C1, C5.

1. **According to Homer-Dixon, governments can help make markets work more effectively. Taking the case of Haiti, where the military controls the essential resource of fuel wood:**
    a. **Explain how the government could help encourage markets to help overcome this predicament.**
    b. **Outline some potential problems with the government actions you suggested in part a.**

2. **In what ways is Homer-Dixon's outlook on contemporary trends similar to Malthus's perspective on trends in his day? How do the perspectives of Homer-Dixon and Malthus differ?**

GOING GLOBAL

International Finance in Canada

Foreign Liabilities

The capital account surplus and current account deficit that were once typical on Canada's balance-of-payments accounts demonstrate a key characteristic of the Canadian economy: foreigners own more financial assets in Canada than Canadians own in foreign markets. For the Canadian economy as a whole, the financial assets that Canadians hold in other nations, such as stocks and bonds, are considered "foreign assets," while those that foreigners hold in Canada are considered "foreign liabilities."

As Figure A shows, foreign assets equalled \$485 billion in contrast to foreign liabilities of \$818 billion in 1996. Of financial assets that Canadians held in other countries, the majority (51.3 percent) were stocks held in foreign corporations. In contrast, the largest percentage of financial assets that foreigners held in Canada (43.5 percent) were various types of bonds. Another 27.1 percent of foreign liabilities took the form of corporate stocks.

Note that the two concepts—foreign assets and foreign liabilities—can be consolidated. "Net foreign assets" are foreign liabilities subtracted from foreign assets to give a positive or negative figure. If foreign assets outweigh foreign liabilities, the number is positive; if the reverse is true, the number is negative. So, for Canada in 1996, net foreign assets were –\$333 billion (\$485 billion – \$818billion):

Net foreign assets = foreign assets – foreign liabilities
–\$333 billion = \$485 billion – \$818 billion

Foreign Ownership

How does Canada compare with other countries? To answer this, we have to consider foreign ownership—summarized by net foreign assets—in the context of each country's economy. To do this, we use GDP. As Figure B shows, net foreign assets, expressed as a proportion of the country's GDP, range for seven countries from Germany's *positive* net foreign assets equalling just over 20 percent of its GDP to Canada's *negative* net foreign assets equalling 40 percent. The United Kingdom, Japan, and Germany all have positive net foreign assets— in other words, residents of these countries own more assets internationally than

FIGURE A Canada's Foreign Assets and Liabilities (1996)

Foreign Assets	$ Billions	% Foreign Assets	Foreign Liabilities	$ Billions	% Foreign Liabilities
Stocks	249	51.3	Stocks	222	27.1
Bonds	21	4.3	Corporate bonds	87	10.6
Government reserves and loans	66	13.6	Federal bonds	95	11.6
Other	149	30.7	Provincial bonds	120	14.7
			Municipal and government enterprise bonds	54	6.6
			Other	240	29.3
Total foreign assets	485	100.0	Total foreign liabilities	818	100.0

Of the foreign assets owned by Canadians—split among stocks, bonds, government reserves and loans, and other short-term assets such as bank accounts—stocks in corporations make up the majority (51.3 percent). In contrast, of the liabilities that Canadians owe to foreigners—in other words, the financial assets in Canada owned by foreigners—43.5 percent are bonds of various types.

Source: Adapted from Statistics Canada, *Canada's International Investment Position, 1926-1996* (May 1997), cat. no. 67-202-XPB, pp. 35, 36, 55. Reproduced by authority of the Minister of Industry, 1997.

SIDELINE

FIGURE B Net Foreign Assets as a Percentage of GDP (1992)

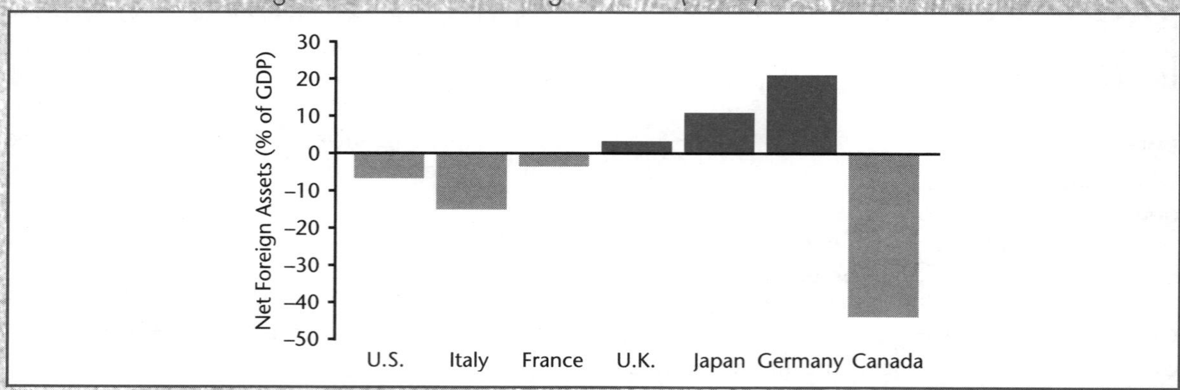

Comparing net foreign assets (foreign assets – foreign liabilities) as a percentage of a country's GDP demonstrates the degree to which foreign ownership in Canada exceeds that in many other nations. For example, while Canada's foreign assets are negative and account for over 40 percent of Canada's GDP, Germany's net foreign assets are positive and account for 20 percent of Germany's GDP.

Source: Department of Finance, Canada, *The Budget 1993* (April 26, 1993), p. 26.

they owe to foreigners. As a result, these three countries are net foreign lenders.

Many economists see Canada's foreign liabilities as a source of concern. The result of Canada's negative net foreign assets is twofold. While great amounts of foreign investment are made in the Canadian economy income from this investment leaves Canada.

This large outflow of investment income from Canada each year means that funds that could have stayed in the country to produce and buy domestic products or that could have left the country to purchase foreign goods and services are instead being used to make payments to foreigners. Since this outflow is a loss of Canadian purchasing power, it represents a drain on the Canadian economy. This is especially true for the foreign debts of Canadian government, since annual outflows of interest payments on these debts are not tied to profitable capital assets, as with most corporate liabilities.

Foreign Control of the Canadian Economy

Much of the controversy surrounding Canada's foreign liabilities has focused on foreign direct investment, which involves controlling interests in Canadian companies. Because of past high rates of foreign direct investment in Canada, a relatively high percentage of the country's economy is controlled by outsiders. As depicted in Figure C, the percentage of nonfinancial industries dominated by foreigners rose during the 1950s and 1960s, reaching a high of 37 percent in the early 1970s. After falling to 23 percent by 1986, the figure increased gradually, reaching 28 percent by 1991. Preliminary evidence suggests that it has remained relatively constant since then.

Direct investment by foreigners has been particularly significant in some sectors of the Canadian economy. Figure D shows that foreign control is most prevalent in such industries as chemicals, chemical products, and textiles (65.6 percent) and machinery and equipment (41.1 percent). In contrast, foreign control is relatively insignificant in such areas as construction and real estate (11.3 percent), and communications (8.7 percent).

The debate over foreign direct investment in the Canadian economy is closely tied to the role of so-called *transnational corporations*, such as General Motors and IBM, which have operations in many countries.

Benefits and Drawbacks

Supporters of foreign ownership point to two potential benefits: overall benefits to the Canadian economy, and efficiency.

FIGURE C Share of Foreign Control of Capital Employed in Nonfinancial Industries in Canada

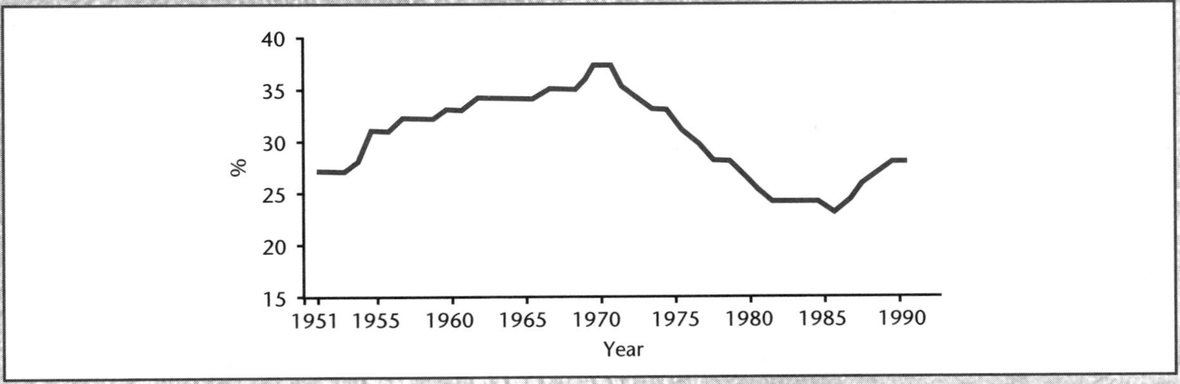

Sources: Statistics Canada, *Canadian Economic Observer* (April 1993), cat. no. 11-010, pp. 3-7.Statistics Canada. Reproduced by authority of the Minister of Industry, 1997.

FIGURE D Foreign Control in Nonfinancial Industries (1995)

	Industry Assets that Are Foreign-Controlled (%)
Chemicals, chemical products, and textiles	65.6
Machinery and equipment	41.1
Wood and paper	35.4
Metallic minerals and metal products	21.8
Energy	17.4
Services	13.8
Construction and real estate	11.3
Communications	8.7
Nonfinancial industries as a whole	24.3

Overall, 24.3 percent of the assets of nonfinancial industries in Canada are foreign-controlled. Of these industries, chemicals, chemical products, and textiles have the highest proportions of foreign control, while construction, real estate, and communications have the lowest.

Source: Adapted from Statistics Canada, *Report of the Minister of Industry, Science and Technology under the Corporations and Labour Unions Return Act, Part 1—Corporations 1995* (February1997), cat. no. 61-220-XPB, pp. 56-60, 63, 65-6, 71. Reproduced by authority of the Minister of Industry, 1997.

Overall Benefits to the Canadian Economy Supporters argue that direct investment by foreign companies in Canada benefits the Canadian economy by increasing the stock of capital assets, thereby raising the productivity and living standards of Canadian workers.

Efficiency To the extent that transnational corporations concentrate particular types of production in countries where they can be carried out most efficiently, these businesses also help to cut production costs and prices not just for Canadians but for consumers in all countries.

However, critics of direct foreign investment point to the drawbacks of increased foreign liabilities of the Canadian economy, loss of Canadian economic sovereignty, and low levels of research and development expenditures in Canada.

Increased Foreign Liabilities The first criticism is quite obvious: a high level of any foreign investment increases Canada's debt to foreigners.

Canadian Economic Sovereignty Canadian governments lose some of their power to govern when foreign-controlled companies are forced to comply with foreign legislation. The most publicized cases have involved U.S. laws that forbid American-owned companies—no matter where they operate—from trading with communist countries such as Cuba.

FIGURE E Largest Foreign-Owned Companies in Canada, 1996

Company	Revenue ($ millions)	% Foreign-Owned	Parent
General Motors of Canada	28 079	100	General Motors (U.S.)
Ford Motor Co. of Canada	25 537	100	Ford Motor (U.S.)
Chrysler Canada	17 060	100	Chrysler (U.S.)
IBM Canada	9 500	100	IBM (U.S.)
Imperial Oil	9 240	82	Exxon (U.S.)
Amoco Canada Petroleum	6 270	100	Amoco (U.S.)
Shell Canada Ltd	5 140	80	Shell (Netherlands)
Canada Safeway	4 795	100	Safeway (U.S.)
Sears Canada	3 956	55	Sears Roebuck (U.S.)
Total Petroleum (N.A.)	3 565	55	Total (France)

Source: *The Financial Post 500 Magazine,* 1997, p. 150.

Decreased Research and Development Expenditures on research and development by Canadian business tend to be lower than in most other countries. Critics of foreign ownership claim that this is so because foreign-owned business conduct such activities at their international head offices rather than in Canada. The result is fewer jobs for Canadian scientists and technicians as well as a lower rate of technological progress in the Canadian economy.

Whatever the benefits and drawbacks of foreign investment, most countries are facing higher levels of foreign investment than ever before. Given Canada's history of high foreign ownership and the related policies that go with it, Canada's experience will provide lessons for the many countries that are "going global."

1. How will Canada's net foreign assets be affected by the following trends? In each case, explain your answer:
   a. the decreasing attractiveness of Canada as a location for direct investment
   b. a drop in borrowing by Canadian governments
   c. a fall in Canadian interest rates relative to those in other countries
2. "The benefits of foreign direct investment in Canada outweigh the costs." Discuss, using the concepts outlined in this article.

Chapter Seventeen
Foreign Trade

It is very odd that, enjoying one of the highest living standards in the world, Canadians in all walks of life should nevertheless believe that their economy is a frail, hothouse creation.
—John H. Dales, Canadian economic historian

Foreign trade is an everyday part of our lives. Consider, for example, what you are wearing or what you ate today. It's likely that many of these products come from outside Canada's borders. The role of exports in our lives is less obvious, but still significant, through the effect that export industries have on Canada's economic activity and employment. In this chapter, we will see why nations exchange goods and services and how governments influence foreign trade. We will also study how the trend toward freer trade is affecting Canada's economy and the well-being of individual Canadians.

CHAPTER FOCUS

This chapter focuses on the following:

- globalization and its effects on trade
- Canada's foreign trade, trade relationships, and trading patterns
- the factors that determine what is traded among countries
- the gains from trade, including product variety, competition, and specialization
- absolute and comparative advantage, and the terms of trade
- forms of trade protection and the arguments for and against it
- Canada's trade policies from its beginnings as a country
- recent international trade arrangements, including the Auto Pact, the European Union, GATT, the WTO, the FTA, and NAFTA

CANADA'S FOREIGN TRADE

The Importance of Trade

globalization: the trend of growing foreign trade and investment and the spread of international businesses and markets

The rapid growth of foreign trade and investment flows and the resulting spread of international businesses and markets are all part of a trend known as **globalization**. In recent decades, reductions in transportation costs have helped increase the worldwide importance of foreign trade. Between 1950 and 1995, for example, world trade grew almost three times as fast as world GDP. The revolution in communications technology has caused an even more rapid increase in foreign investment flows. For example, global foreign direct investment has tripled from 1986 to 1995. Transactions in foreign exchange markets have soared, and now total over US$1 trillion a day.

Because of these changes, markets are no longer contained within national boundaries and businesses are more likely to buy resources and sell products internationally. For example, a business with its headquarters in Canada may choose to borrow from Japanese savers, purchase German-made machinery, employ Mexican workers, and sell the bulk of its output in the United States. In both its resource markets and product markets, this Canadian company probably competes with businesses from all over the world.

Within this international trend, Canada has shown a heavy reliance on trade. Figure 17.1 compares the value of exports of various countries as a percentage of their GDP. Canada's exports have a value equal to 37

FIGURE 17.1 The Importance of Trade

(exports as a percentage of GDP, 1995)

	Percent
Belgium	74
Canada	37
Switzerland	36
United Kingdom	28
Germany	23
France	23
China	21
United States	11
Japan	9
World average	22

The exports of a small country such as Belgium are high in comparison to its level of GDP. In contrast, the exports of large countries such as China and the United States are lower as a proportion of overall economic activity. When compared to the world average of 22 percent, Canada's exports account for a fairly high proportion of its GDP.

Source: From *World Development Report 1997*, by the World Bank. Copyright © 1997 by The International Bank for Reconstruction and Development/The World Bank. Table 13, "Structure of Demand," pp. 238–39.

percent of its GDP, above the world average of 22 percent and considerably higher than the United States' 11 percent and Japan's 9 percent, whose large and diversified economies allow them to be less dependent on exports and imports. However, Canada's reliance on foreign trade is not so great as that of some small industrialized countries, such as Belgium (74 percent).

Canada's Trading Partners

With whom is Canada trading? As Figure 17.2 demonstrates, the United States is Canada's principle trading partner. In 1996, 81 percent of Canada's merchandise exports went to the United States and 76 percent of its merchandise imports came from the United States. The remaining merchandise trade was shared among nations that are part of the European Union (a group of European nations we'll discuss later in the chapter), Japan, other countries in the Organization for Economic Co-operation and Development (which we'll discuss in the next chapter), and all other nations.

Canada's Trade Patterns

Canada's merchandise trade is made up of exports and imports of both natural resources and manufactured products. As Figure 17.3 shows, Canada's 1996 merchandise exports included almost equal portions of raw or processed natural resources (agricultural and fish products, energy products, forest products, and industrial goods such as minerals and metals) and manufactured products (machines and equipment, automobile products, consumer goods, and other). In contrast, merchandise imports of manufactured goods are more than double that of natural resources. In

FIGURE 17.2 Canada's Merchandise Trade by Region (1996)

	Merchandise Exports ($ millions)		Merchandise Imports ($ millions)	
United States	217 029	(81%)	176 369	(76%)
European Union (EU)	15 276	(6%)	20 271	(9%)
Japan	10 478	(4%)	7 178	(3%)
Other OECD countries	4 818	(2%)	8 812	(4%)
All others	19 549	(7%)	20 397	(8%)
Total	267 151	(100%)	233 026	(100%)

The bulk of Canada's merchandise trade is with the United States. The remaining merchandise trade is shared among the member countries of the European Union, Japan, other countries in the Organization for Economic Co-operation and Development, and all other nations.

Source: Adapted from Statistics Canada, *Canadian Economic Observer, Statistical Summary* (March 1997), cat. no. 11-010-XPB, pp. 31–32. Reproduced by authority of the Minister of Industry, 1997.

FIGURE 17.3
Canada's Merchandise Trade by Type of Product (1996)

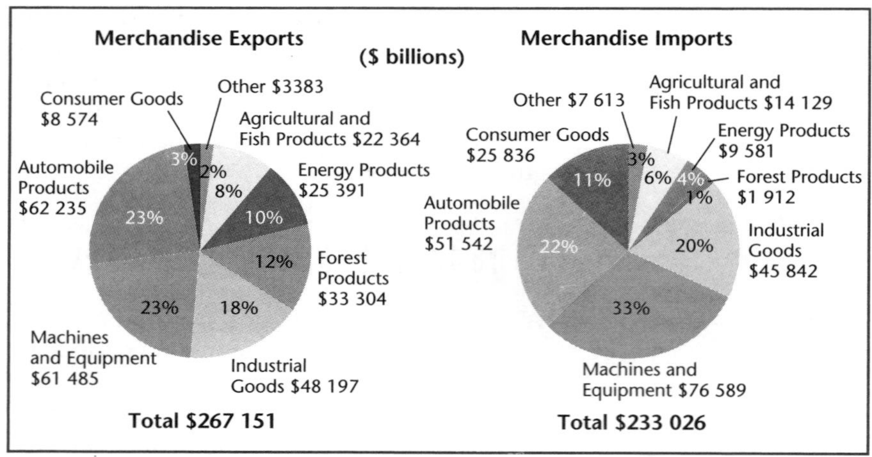

Agricultural and fish products, energy products, forest products, and industrial goods such as minerals and metals together accounted for about half of Canada's 1996 merchandise exports. Machines and equipment, automobile products, consumer goods, and other products made up the rest. In terms of merchandise imports, natural resources formed a third of the total, whereas manufactured goods formed about two-thirds.

Source: Adapted from Statistics Canada, *Canadian Economic Observer, Statistical Summary* (March 1997), cat. no. 11-010-XPB, pp. 31–32. Reproduced by authority of the Minister of Industry, 1997.

total, Canada had merchandise exports of about $267 151 billion and merchandise imports of $233 026 billion.

However, this isn't the whole picture. Recall from Chapter 16 that Canada trades not only merchandise but also services. Of these—involving travel, transportation, and commercial and government services—Canada exported $38.9 billion but imported $48.8 billion in 1996.

Historically, Canada has been considered a significant exporter of natural resources. Recently, though, the proportion of natural resources in Canada's merchandise exports has decreased while the proportion of manufactured goods has increased. For example, in comparison to the roughly equal proportions of manufactured and natural resource exports in 1996, just over a third of Canada's merchandise exports were manufactured goods in 1971. In the same period, the ratio of natural resources to manufactured goods in Canada's imports has varied only slightly, with manufactured goods expanding.

Within Canada's service trade, business services such as insurance, management services, and research and development have increased most quickly as a proportion of both imports and exports. Overall, Canada's trade in services has not grown as quickly as its merchandise trade. Between 1971 and 1996, service exports as a percentage of total exports fell from 15 to 13 percent, while service imports fell from 21 to 17 percent of total imports. These figures are surprising given the recent growth in Canada's service sector. Between 1967 and 1989, for example, Canada's service sector grew from 55 to 64 percent of Canada's real GDP while the goods sector fell from 45 to 36 percent. Employment growth in the service sector has been even more rapid. Service sector employment now represents over 70 percent of all jobs in the Canadian economy.

Thinking About Economics

Why hasn't the rise of a service-based economy been reflected in Canada's international trade?

One reason is that services are usually bought and sold within national borders. For example, in 1989 less than 10 percent of services produced in Canada were exported. In comparison, almost a third of all Canadian-made goods were destined for foreign markets. Another reason for the apparent slow growth in service trade relates to measurement problems. Because services are intangible, foreign trade in these products often escapes detection, especially in the common case where services are traded within a single company. Furthermore, goods and services are often sold in "bundles," and it is the merchandise part of the bundle that is counted. For example, new computer software is usually exchanged in physical form, and is therefore counted as a good rather than as a service. These problems make it difficult to collect trade statistics that adequately reflect the importance of services.

What Is Traded

In general, countries export the commodities they produce most efficiently and import those they would produce least efficiently. Whether or not a country can produce a particular product efficiently is determined by the country's resources, market size, and climate.

Resources

A country's pool of resources is the main factor affecting what it exports and imports. For example, Canada has been endowed with plentiful and rich natural resources that have allowed it to be a major exporter of such products as paper, wheat, and natural gas. As well, Canada has developed its human resources and capital resources in such a way that it can export capital-intensive goods. In contrast, countries with less abundant natural resources, such as Belgium, tend to be major importers of unprocessed products, and countries with a huge pool of labour and relatively few capital resources, such as Bangladesh, tend to be major exporters of labour-intensive goods. For example, almost two-thirds of Bangladesh's exports consist of textiles and clothing, whose production tends to be labour-intensive.

Market Size

Recall that some products exhibit economies of scale—that is, the cost of inputs per unit of output decreases as production increases. As a result, these products tend to be produced in markets where businesses can take advantage of economies of scale. So, for example, cars tend to be produced in countries with large markets of car buyers rather than in small countries or those where few people own cars.

Climate

Climate plays a key role in determining where some goods are produced, especially agricultural products. While tropical fruit could be grown in Canada—in climate-controlled greenhouses, for example—it makes little sense to do so, since tropical fruit can be imported cheaply from countries that are internationally competitive in producing them.

THE CASE FOR TRADE

Gains From Trade

Having determined what Canada trades and with whom, the question of "Why trade?" still remains. International trade brings significant economic gains: it increases product variety for consumers, promotes competition in each country's markets, and adds to output by allowing countries to specialize in commodities in which they are internationally competitive.

Product Variety

When countries trade, the number of products available to consumers expands. Consider one category of products you purchase regularly—for example, clothing, CDs, or magazines. You will probably notice that many of your purchases were produced in other countries. Adding imports to domestic products gives you greater choice.

Competition

International trade increases the number of businesses selling in a country's product markets. Added competition encourages all businesses to produce goods as efficiently as possible. This results in lower prices for consumers.

Specialization

The most important gain from trade comes from specialization. Without international trade, a country would have to produce everything its citizens need. With international trade, however, a country can use its resources to specialize in the products it makes most efficiently, allowing it to compete in the expanded market. The income from exporting the products that the country has made so efficiently can then pay for imported products that would be more expensive to make domestically. By increasing the output gained from various countries' resources, specialization raises world living standards. In the next sections, we will see how these gains from specialization can be quantified using two related economic concepts: absolute advantage and comparative advantage.

Absolute Advantage

Specialization is easiest to see in the case of two trading partners, each of whom is better than the other at one activity. Suppose a lawyer wants custom-made wooden furniture. At the same time a carpenter wants to prepare a will. As shown in Figure 17.4, the lawyer could build the furniture herself in 20 hours or she could hire the carpenter to do the job in 5 hours. Similarly, the carpenter could prepare the will for himself in 10 hours or hire the lawyer to do it for him in 2 hours. If the two were to trade their products, each product would be produced in the most efficient way possible.

absolute advantage: the benefit enjoyed by a producer who can supply a certain quantity of an item more efficiently than can other producers

In the example, the lawyer and the carpenter each have an **absolute advantage**. That is, each trading partner is able to produce one product using fewer resources than would other producers. The resources—in this case, time—saved by trading partners specializing in what they each do most efficiently is summarized in the third column of Figure 17.4.

The same principle applies to countries that engage in trade. For example, Canada may be more efficient than Japan in producing wheat, while Japan is more efficient than Canada in producing stereos. Canadians should therefore specialize in wheat production, leaving the Japanese to concentrate on stereo production. Through trade, both Canada and Japan can use their economic resources to produce the greatest possible output of each commodity. As a result, living standards in both countries increase.

FIGURE 17.4 Gains From Trade Based on Absolute Advantage

	Time Spent Building Furniture	Time Spent Preparing a Will	Time Saved Through Specialization
Lawyer	20 hours	2 hours	20 – 2 = 18 hours
Carpenter	5 hours	10 hours	10 – 5 = 5 hours

A carpenter can build furniture in less time than it would take a lawyer, while the lawyer can draw up a will in less time than it would take the carpenter. Each has an absolute advantage in one task. To use the resources most efficiently, the carpenter should specialize in building the furniture, while the lawyer should specialize in preparing the will. The carpenter works for 5 hours rather than 10 hours, saving 5 hours. Meanwhile, the lawyer works for 2 hours instead of 20 hours, saving 18 hours.

Comparative Advantage

Because of the varying strengths of countries, trade advantages are sometimes not so clear-cut as in the case of absolute advantage. Let's consider a hypothetical case. Both Canada and Mexico can produce paper and computers, but Canada has an absolute advantage over Mexico in both products. As shown in Figure 17.5, using equal resources, Canada can produce 12 t of paper compared with Mexico's 3 t or 12 computers to Mexico's 9.

FIGURE 17.5 Gains From Trade Based on Comparative Advantage

	Hypothetical Output per worker		Opportunity Cost	
	Paper	Computers	of 1t of paper	of 1 computer
Canada	12 t	12 computers	1 computer	1.0 t paper
Mexico	3 t	9 computers	3 computers	0.33 t paper

Although a Canadian worker can produce more paper than a Mexican worker (12 versus 3 t) or can make more computers than a Mexican worker (12 versus 9 computers), paper has a lower opportunity cost in Canada (1 computer versus Mexico's 3 computers). Thus, Canadians have a comparative advantage in producing paper while Mexicans have a comparative advantage in making computers. In other words, each has the lower opportunity cost of producing one product.

For the sake of efficiency, it would seem that both paper products and computers should be produced in Canada. However, trade is a two-way street. So, each of the two trading partners must produce and trade a product. To determine what each trading partner should produce, they must determine the opportunity cost of each product, and then produce the product for which they have the lowest opportunity cost. The trading partner with the lowest opportunity cost for a given product has the **comparative advantage**. This name reflects the fact that this benefit can be determined only after comparing opportunity costs in both countries.

comparative advantage: the benefit enjoyed by a producer who can supply a certain item with a lower opportunity cost than can other producers

In our example, the opportunity cost of producing 12 t of paper in Canada is 12 computers, and the opportunity cost of 12 computers is 12 t of paper. This gives a cost ratio of one to one between paper and computers, so that the opportunity cost of 1 t of paper is 1 computer. In Mexico, the cost of producing 3 t of paper is 9 computers, and the opportunity cost of producing 9 computers is 3 t of paper. This gives a cost ratio of one to three between paper and computers in Mexico, so that the opportunity cost of 1 t of paper is 3 computers and the opportunity cost of 1 computer is only 0.33 t of paper. Because paper has a lower opportunity cost in Canada than in Mexico, Canada has a comparative advantage in paper production. Conversely, since each computer has a lower opportunity cost in Mexico than in Canada, Mexico has a comparative advantage in computer production.

Given the comparative advantages in our hypothetical example, the opportunity costs would be lowest if Canada produced paper and Mexico produced computers. This conclusion follows the **law of comparative advantage**, which states that output is maximized when producers specialize in what they can make at a lower opportunity cost than can other producers.

law of comparative advantage: states that maximum output is achieved when producers specialize in what they can make at a lower opportun-ity cost than can other producers

Let's assume that there are twice as many workers in Mexico as in Canada. The gains from each country fully specializing in the product in which it has a comparative advantage are shown in Figure 17.6. If there is a total of 10 workers in Canada and 20 workers in Mexico, then before trade each country may devote half of its labour force to each product.

FIGURE 17.6 Total Gains From Specialization

	Before Trade		After Trade	
	Paper	**Computers**	**Paper**	**Computers**
Canada	60 t	60 computers	120 t	0 computers
Mexico	30 t	90 computers	0 t	180 computers
	90 t	150 computers	120 t	180 computers

Supposing that there are 20 workers in Mexico and 10 in Canada, and supposing that production in both Mexico and Canada were equally split between paper and computers before they began to trade, the combined countries would produce 90 t of paper and 150 computers. By specializing through trade, combined production would rise to 120 t of paper and 180 computers.

The combined paper output of both countries is therefore 90 t—60 t from Canada (5 workers × 12 t per worker) and 30 t from Mexico (10 workers × 3 t per worker). At the same time, the combined computer production of both countries is 150 computers, with 60 from Canada (5 workers × 12 computers per worker) and 90 from Mexico (10 workers × 9 computers per worker).

When both countries specialize completely in the product in which they have a comparative advantage, Canada produces 120 t of paper (10 workers × 12 t per worker) and Mexico makes 180 computers (20 workers × 9 computers per worker). World paper production has therefore risen by 30 t and world computer production by 30 computers. By specializing on the basis of comparative advantage, the two countries are therefore able to raise their total output of both items, with this added production being shared through trade.

Terms of Trade

terms of trade: the international price of one product in terms of another

The benefits of specialization are distributed between trading partners on the basis of the **terms of trade**, or the international price of one product in terms of another product. This price depends partly on the opportunity costs of the products in each country, since producers must get at least the opportunity cost that applies in domestic transactions if they are to engage in foreign trade.

Returning to our hypothetical example, recall that in Canada tonnes of paper and units of computers have a cost ratio of one to one. In order to make trading with Mexico worthwhile, Canadian paper producers demand one or more computers for each unit of paper they sell to Mexico. At the same time, in Mexico the cost ratio of tonnes of paper and units of computers is one to three. To make trading with Canada worthwhile, Mexican computer producers demand 1 t of paper for every 3 or fewer computers they sell to Canada. As a result, the international price of one product in terms of the other must fall somewhere between these limits in order for the two countries to trade:

Limits to terms of trade	1 t of paper : 1 computer
	1 t of paper : 3 computers

The actual terms of trade are then set by the international demand for each product. So, for example, when the demand for paper is high in both countries, the international price of paper in terms of computers will be close to the limit of 3 computers for 1 t of paper. If instead the demand for computers is high in both countries, the international price of computers will be pushed towards the limit of 1 computer for 1 t of paper.

Since Canadians export paper to purchase Mexican computers, they will be best off when paper has the highest possible international price in terms of computers—in other words, when 1 t of paper has its maximum value of 3 computers. In contrast, Mexicans are best off when the terms of trade have reached their lowest limit. In this case, each 1 t of paper imported by Mexicans has an international price of 1 computer, which is the minimum possible value for paper in terms of computers.

BRIEF REVIEW

1. With the recent trend toward globalization, there has been substantial growth in foreign trade and investment and international businesses and markets.
2. In comparison with other countries, Canada depends extensively on international trade. Its most significant trading partner is the United States.
3. Canada's merchandise exports include almost equal portions of natural resources and manufactured products. In contrast, its merchandise imports of manufactured products are double that of natural resources. In addition to merchandise, Canada also has significant trade in services.
4. Canada's exports of natural resources are becoming less significant than they used to be. Since the early 1970s, manufactured goods have grown considerably as a proportion of merchandise exports and slightly as a proportion of merchandise imports. While the service sector has been growing in Canada, international trade in services has not grown as much as international trade in merchandise. This is because services tend to be bought and sold within national economies and because of problems in measuring service trade.
5. What specific products a country produces for trade depends on what it produces most efficiently. Three factors affect efficiency: resources, market size, and climate.
6. Trade among nations brings significant gains: product variety, increased competition, and specialization.
7. The gains of specialization can best be seen in the cases of absolute advantage and comparative advantage. The law of comparative advantage states that output is maximized when producers specialize in what they can make at a lower opportunity cost than can other producers.
8. The terms of trade are the international price of a product in terms of another product. The terms of trade are determined by both the opportunity costs of the products for the trading partners and the international demand for the products.

THE IMPACT OF TRADE PROTECTION

Despite the benefits of international trade, countries often try to block imports or subsidize domestic industries. First we'll examine how governments intervene in international trade. Later, we'll consider the arguments against trade that motivate such intervention.

Tariffs

To see the role that foreign trade plays in markets for a specific product, let's consider a hypothetical competitive market for bicycles in Canada. The left graph in Figure 17.7 shows the demand (D) and domestic supply curves (S_{d0}) for bicycles in the unlikely case where there is no foreign trade. Market equilibrium would occur at a price of $150 and a quantity of 90 000 (point *c*).

FIGURE 17.7
The Impact of Import Barriers

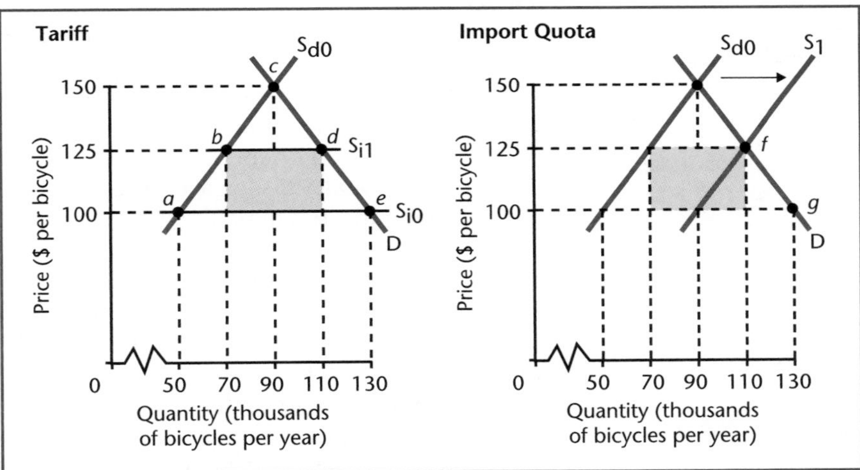

The graph on the left illustrates a domestic bicycle market without international trade, with unrestricted trade, and with tariffs. Without trade, equilibrium price in the market for bicycles is at $150 (point *c*), the intersection of the domestic demand curve (D) and the domestic supply curve (S_{d0}). With unrestricted imports of bicycles priced at $100, as shown by the import supply curve (S_{i0}), consumers demand 130 000 bicycles (point *e*), but domestic producers will supply only 50 000 bicycles (point *a*). Imports make up the 80 000 difference. With a $25 tariff, the price rises to $125 (shown by S_{i1}) at which consumers demand 110 000 bicycles (point *d*), but domestic producers will supply only 70 000 bicycles at this price (point *b*). Imports make up the 40 000 difference and the government gains extra revenue shown by the shaded rectangle.

The graph on the right illustrates the same market with an import quota. With an import quota of 40 000 bicycles, supply shifts from S_{d0} to S_1. Compared with the case of unrestricted trade, the change in price and the quantity of imports (from point *g* to point *f*) is identical to those resulting from tariffs, but now the shaded rectangle indicates extra revenue to foreign producers. This extra revenue from a higher price at least partially offsets the loss that is due to fewer sales.

If international trade in bicycles existed and this trade were unrestricted, then Canadian consumers would have the opportunity to buy either domestic or imported bicycles. Assuming for our example that the cost of transporting the product is zero, Canadians would be able to purchase foreign-made bicycles for $100, which is the prevailing world price. Since Canadian consumers make up a small proportion of the world bicycle market, their purchases do not affect equilibrium in this market. Hence, an unlimited quantity supplied is available from foreign bicycle producers at $100, as shown by the horizontal line (S_{i0}) at this price.

As shown on the left in Figure 17.7, at a price of $100 Canadian consumers would demand 130 000 bicycles (point *e*). However, Canadian suppliers are only willing to supply 50 000 bicycles at this price (point *a*). The 80 000 difference between domestic supply (S_{d0}) and domestic demand (D) represents the quantity foreign producers could sell in this market. As a result of the international trade, the price has fallen and a significant number of consumers are buying foreign-produced bicycles.

tariff: an excise tax on imported goods

Governments may respond to such a situation by imposing a **tariff**, which is an excise tax on imported goods. Until recent years, tariffs were a major tool of trade protection in Canada as well as in many other countries, especially against foreign manufactured goods. In our example, if a $25 tariff is applied on foreign-made bicycles, Canadian consumers must pay an additional $25—or a total price of $125. The result of this price increase is again shown on the left in Figure 17.7. The supply of imported bicycles is now depicted by a horizontal line (S_{i1}) at a price of $125. At this price, Canadian consumers demand 110 000 bicycles (point *d*). Since Canadian suppliers are willing to supply 70 000 bicycles at this price (point *b*), the difference between domestic demand and domestic supply at this price is 40 000, which foreign producers supply.

When compared to the case of unrestricted trade, tariffs affect consumers and the government in opposite ways. Consumers pay a higher price ($125 instead of $100) and buy fewer bicycles (110 000 instead of 130 000) than they did before the tariff was introduced. However, the government benefits from the tariff through the additional tax revenue it is able to raise. With a $25 tariff per bicycle and 40 000 bicycles imported, the government's extra revenue is $1 million ($25 × 40 000). This is shown on the left graph by the area of the shaded rectangle, whose height represents the tariff per bicycle and whose width indicates the quantity of imports once the tariff is in place.

Domestic and foreign producers are also affected in opposite ways by the tariff. Canadian bicycle producers and their resource suppliers benefit because of the extra earnings tied to the increase in price from $100 to $125 and the rise in domestic production from 50 000 to 70 000 bicycles. Foreign bicycle producers, however, are harmed by the tariff. They face an unchanged after-tax price for each bicycle they sell ($100) while accepting a reduction in imports—from 80 000 to 40 000 bicycles.

Import Quotas

non-tariff barriers (NTBs): trade barriers other than tariffs that are used to restrict imports; include import quotas, voluntary export restraints, and domestic regulations

import quota: a set limit on the quantity of a good that can be imported in a given year

voluntary export restraints (VERs): import quotas that are voluntarily put in place by the exporting country

If tariffs are not an option, a government may use other trade restrictions, known as **non-tariff barriers (NTBs)**, to limit imports. Recently, these barriers have become more popular since governments find it harder to levy tariffs because of international trade agreements.

The most common non-tariff barrier is an **import quota**, which is a set limit on the quantity of a good that can be imported in a certain year. Import quotas can work in two ways. A government can impose an import quota itself, or it can use the threat of trade restrictions to force foreign producers to set their own "voluntary" quotas, which are known as **voluntary export restraints (VERs)**. One well-known illustration of a voluntary export restraint involves Canada's imports of Japanese cars. In 1981, an agreement limiting annual Japanese exports of automobiles to Canada was worked out between the two countries. In 1986, when the agreement expired, Japanese automakers continued to limit their exports to Canada voluntarily to stop the Canadian government from taking other types of trade action.

Generally, foreign producers find import quotas preferable to tariffs. To see why, we return to our hypothetical example of the bicycle market in Figure 17.7. The impact of an import quota on this market is portrayed on the right graph, in which the domestic demand and supply curves, D and S_{d0}, as well as the prevailing world price, are identical to those on the left graph. As before, a situation of unrestricted trade (point *g*) leads to an original $100 price, with consumption exceeding domestic production by 80 000, which represents the initial amount of bicycles imported.

By imposing a maximum level of imports of 40 000, this number of bicycles is added to the domestic supply (S_{d0}) at every price, thereby giving the combined domestic and foreign supply curve S_1. Domestic demand (D) and the new supply (S_1) intersect at the new equilibrium price of $125 and quantity of 110 000 (point *f*). Again, production is split between domestic and foreign producers. Canadian businesses produce 70 000 bicycles, leaving 40 000 for foreign businesses, shown as the shaded area.

The policy's effect on consumers and domestic producers is the same as with a tariff. The results for the government and foreign producers are different, however. With an import quota, the government no longer receives tax revenue. Instead, the extra revenue indicated by the shaded rectangle on the graph on the right flows to foreign producers in the form of higher prices on the bicycles they still sell in Canada. This extra revenue partly counteracts the loss that foreign producers bear because of the lower quantity they supply in the Canadian market.

Domestic Regulations

Regulations in particular markets can make trade within them expensive for foreign producers, therefore acting as obstacles to trade. For example, Canada has certain licensing procedures, and imposes relatively high safety and environmental standards. Also, rules controlling government purchases—known as government procurement policies—may require that, whenever possible, domestic rather than foreign items should be bought by governments. If imports are successfully restricted through these practices, the results are the same as in the case of an import quota.

Export Subsidies

export subsidies: payments by a government to domestic exporters so that these exporters can reduce the prices they charge in foreign markets

Export subsidies are payments by a government to domestic exporters so that they can reduce the prices they charge in foreign markets. These programs are intended to raise the amount of exports, thus increasing output and employment in the domestic economy. Besides helping domestic exporters and foreign consumers, an export subsidy imposes a cost on foreign producers, who lose sales to the new low-priced competition, and on the exporting country's own taxpayers, who must foot the bill for the program. Such subsidies have been used by many countries, including Canada, and have been especially common in agricultural markets. Indeed, these programs were a major reason for low prices in global agricultural markets during the 1980s.

THE CASE FOR TRADE PROTECTION

The gains in economic welfare associated with specialization and the law of comparative advantage are generally large enough to make a compelling case for free trade. Consequently, it is common for economists to oppose government policies that protect trade. Nonetheless, particular cases of trade protection can be defended with either economic or noneconomic arguments. We will look at each of these arguments in turn.

Economic Arguments

Six economic arguments can be applied to support various types of trade protection. According to these arguments, trade barriers help to stimulate domestic employment, diversify export-dominated economies, foster infant industries, improve a country's terms of trade, protect a country's environmental and safety standards, and shield domestic workers from imports produced with cheap foreign labour.

Domestic Employment

Because imports are a withdrawal from an economy's circular flow, they have a dampening effect on total spending and output. Thus, a reduction in the level of imports through trade barriers can potentially increase the level of economic activity in the country and provide more jobs for domestic workers.

This argument is legitimate only in certain circumstances, however. Because a strategy of import reduction causes foreign countries' exports to diminish, output and employment levels in these foreign nations will fall. Hence, the new domestic employment in the country imposing trade barriers comes at the expense of jobs elsewhere. The threat of foreign retaliation means that this policy can easily backfire—other nations may try to recapture some of their lost exports and jobs by imposing new trade barriers of their own. Such behaviour makes everyone worse off by limiting the opportunities for each country to specialize based on comparative advantage.

Diversification

Trade barriers can help diversify the economy of a country whose prosperity is closely tied to just a few export products. Examples include Saudi Arabia, which depends on oil, and Barbados, which relies on revenues from tourism. In each case, changes in the international demand for these main exports can lead to wide fluctuations in the economy's total output.

Trade barriers allow for the development of new industries in which the country does not possess a comparative advantage. Traditionally, this reasoning has been used to foster a domestic manufacturing sector. The result, according to supporters of this policy, is an economy that is better able to withstand fluctuations in export markets. Critics point out that the industries created in this fashion represent an inefficient employment of the economy's resources. In the absence of international competition in protected markets, domestic consumers pay high prices for what may be substandard goods.

Infant Industries

infant industry: a domestic industry that is young in comparison to its foreign competitors

Closely related to the argument for diversification is the view that trade barriers should be used to shield infant industries. An **infant industry** is made up of domestic producers that are young in comparison to competitors in foreign countries. Because of their recent origin and small size, domestic producers are not able to take full advantage of economies of scale. Until they are able to, according to supporters, lower-priced foreign imports must be blocked. Such reasoning is valid only if other countries do not retaliate with their own trade barriers. Even if retaliation does not occur, the argument is open to abuse. Once imposed, trade barriers in a given industry are difficult to eliminate. Industry groups—representing both business and labour—tend to fight any reduction in barriers, even once their industry has fully matured.

strategic trade policy: the use of programs such as export subsidies to help domestic producers enter potentially lucrative markets

In recent years, the argument relating to infant industries has gained new importance in high-technology markets, such as the jet aircraft industry, where a few large businesses are able to take advantage of economies of scale. **Strategic trade policy** is the use of programs such as export subsidies to help domestic producers gain a foothold in these industries so they can reap high economic profits in the future. Supporters of this policy suggest that such long-term profits aid the entire country. Also, support of high-technology industries can help prepare the country for structural changes in the global economy. Lastly, the businesses involved can provide spillover benefits to the economy because of their contribution to product development in other industries. As with traditional trade incentives for infant industries, strategic trade policy works only if foreign governments choose not to retaliate with similar policies of their own.

Terms of Trade

If a country's volume of trade is large enough to affect prices in a world product market, then it can use trade barriers to improve its terms of trade. For example, the United States could impose a tariff on its imports of Canadian lumber. This would decrease the global demand for lumber, pushing down lumber's international price. As a result, Americans would be able to acquire the same amount of Canadian lumber with a smaller quantity of American products. As long as Canada does not retaliate with its own trade barriers, the terms of trade move in the United States' favour.

Environmental and Safety Standards

In order to address spillover costs, in particular those related to the environment and safety, many governments impose standards that can be quite costly to certain businesses. However, standards vary. While some countries may regulate industry either to reduce or to compensate for spillover costs, other countries—especially those with low per capita GDP—may have very lax environmental and safety regulations to allow exporters there to reduce their expenses and product prices.

Critics of lax environmental standards suggest that, without trade protection, increased globalization will be accompanied by an increase in environmental damage. Similarly, critics of lax safety standards believe that without trade protection, workers in all countries are hurt. Those in countries with low safety standards face increased risks of injury on the job, while those in countries with strict standards face a reduction in the demand for labour and therefore fewer available jobs.

According to critics of low environmental and safety standards, countries should maintain high standards and set up trade barriers against exports from countries with lower standards. They argue that, without these two measures, businesses operating in countries with lax standards will continue to profit, other businesses will move their operations to such countries in order to gain a competitive edge, and spillover costs will increase internationally.

Cheap Foreign Labour

A related argument suggests that imports produced by cheap foreign labour need to be blocked from entering an industrialized country in order to protect the jobs of domestic workers. In its basic form, this argument is flawed because it ignores the key reason for the differences among wage rates in various countries. Workers in countries with a higher per capita GDP tend to earn more than workers elsewhere because of their higher productivity, as defined in Chapter 8. Workers in industrialized countries tend to be highly skilled and are employed along with larger amounts of capital per worker. Once average wages in various countries are compared to these different productivity levels, workers in industrialized nations still possess a comparative advantage over low-wage foreign labour in many types of production. Nonetheless, it is likely that certain groups of workers in industrialized countries—especially those in low-productivity sectors—will be hurt by increased trade with less-developed countries.

Noneconomic Arguments

The two remaining arguments in favour of trade barriers are based on noneconomic factors: national security and cultural sovereignty.

National Security

The oldest argument for trade barriers relates to national security. A country's citizens may wish to be self-sufficient in producing certain strategic commodities such as basic food items and military equipment. If a war breaks out, supplies of these commodities will then be guaranteed. The way to ensure that domestic industries can develop in these sectors is to insulate them from foreign competition. This argument has been applied in countries such as Israel, where military threats to national security have been a major concern, but its relevance to Canada seems limited.

Cultural Sovereignty

Another noneconomic argument for certain types of trade protection relates to culture. Some countries, including Canada, have felt the need to protect and nurture their own cultural industries by, for example, restricting the imported content of radio and TV programming, limiting broadcast licences, subsidizing "home-grown" authors and visual artists, or purchasing only domestically produced textbooks. In one recent incident, in order to help the French movie industry withstand foreign competition—especially from Hollywood—France blocked American attempts to liberalize international trade in movies. However, critics suggest that, in an age of satellite communications, trade barriers relating to many cultural industries can no longer be enforced.

BRIEF REVIEW

1. Governments may intervene in international markets through a variety of means, including tariffs, non-tariff barriers (import quotas, voluntary export restraints, and domestic regulations), and export subsidies.
2. Tariffs are excise taxes on imported goods. In contrast, import quotas and voluntary export restraints are limits on the quantity of a product that can be imported in a certain year. These barriers result in higher prices, lower consumption, fewer imports, and more domestic production of the item affected. With a tariff, governments gain extra tax revenue; with an import quota or voluntary export restraint, revenues from the resulting higher prices flow to the foreign producers, partly offsetting the effect of the decrease in sales.
3. Domestic regulations can present obstacles to trade. When successful, the results parallel the effects of an import quota.
4. Export subsidies are another form of trade intervention. In this case, governments make payments to domestic exporters so that exporters can lower the prices they charge in foreign markets. The results are lower sales of foreign products and higher domestic taxes.
5. The economic arguments in favour of trade barriers relate to domestic employment, diversification, infant industries, the terms of trade, environmental and safety standards, and cheap foreign labour.
6. The noneconomic arguments in favour of trade barriers relate to maintaining national security and cultural sovereignty.

TRADE POLICIES

Recall that Canada's most significant trading partner now and throughout much of its history is the United States. As a result, trade between the two countries has played an important role in determining Canadian trade policy.

Early Canadian Trade Policy

In 1854 British and American diplomats signed the Reciprocity Treaty, establishing favourable trade relationships between British North America and the United States. So, for the duration of this treaty, tariff rates were relatively low between the United States and what is now Canada.

This reciprocal trade relationship broke down in 1866 due to a number of political and economic factors. Thereafter, trade between Canada and the United States became increasingly restrictive. As portrayed in Figure 17.8, the average Canadian tariff rate as a percentage of total merchandise imports rose in the years after Confederation.

The National Policy

National Policy: a Canadian policy initiated in 1879 that included high Canadian tariffs on manufactured imports in order to stimulate a domestic manufacturing sector

In 1879, Canada's first prime minister, Sir John A. Macdonald, instituted a wide-ranging tariff policy based on the infant-industry argument for trade protection. The **National Policy** led to high tariffs on manufactured imports to stimulate the development of a domestic manufacturing sector. Without this policy, supporters argued, Canadian manufacturers would be swamped by low-priced American competition produced with the benefits of economies of scale. Due to the National Policy, Canada's average tariff rate in succeeding decades stayed above 15 percent. As a result, many American manufacturers chose to "jump the tariff wall" by setting up branch plants in Canada to allow them to continue selling in Canadian markets.

The Great Depression

While Canada's tariffs gradually fell after World War I, the Great Depression sparked a new round of protectionism. Such a trend is common during economic downturns. With falling output and employment, domestic producers see trade barriers as a way of maintaining their sales despite shrinking markets. In the early 1930s, governments in most industrialized countries raised tariffs—partly for domestic reasons, and partly to retaliate against foreign trade barriers placed on their own exports. Not surprisingly, all countries were made worse off by this move because of the resulting decline in world trade.

Once the damaging effects of this protectionism became evident, Canada and the United States signed two trade-liberalizing agreements in the 1930s, reducing Canada's average tariff rate to below its pre-Depression level.

FIGURE 17.8
Average Tariff Rates in Canada

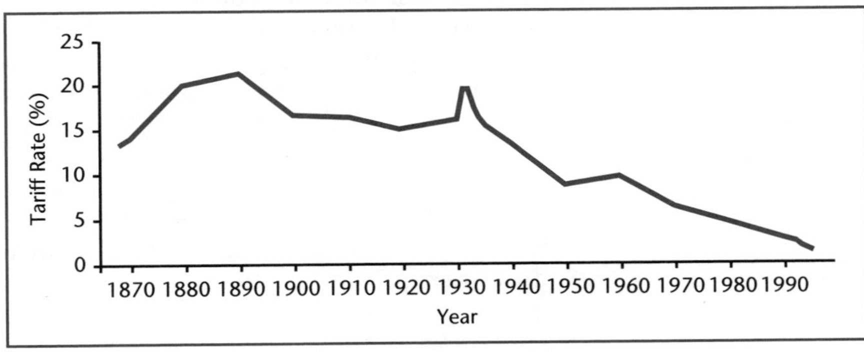

Since 1868, tariffs as a percentage of total merchandise imports have varied from above 20 percent to below 5 percent. The National Policy, which began in 1879, pushed up the average tariff rate. While the rate gradually fell from the early 1890s, it rose again during the Great Depression. Since the early 1930s, the rate has declined considerably due to the effects of various GATT agreements as well as regional agreements that Canada has entered.

Sources: F.H. Leacy (ed.), *Historical Statistics of Canada*, 2nd ed. (Statistics Canada, 1983), cat. no. CS11-516E, Series G473–487; adapted from Statistics Canada, *Canadian Economic Observer, Historical Statistical Supplement, 1995/96* (July 1996), cat. no. 11-210, vol. 8, p. 56; Statistics Canada, *Public Finance Historical Data 1965/66–1991/92* (March 1992), cat. no. 68-512, pp. 2–3; Statistics Canada, *Public Sector Finance, 1995-1996*, cat. no. 68-212-XPB, p. 113. Reproduced by authority of the Minister of Industry, 1997.

General Agreement on Tariffs and Trade

General Agreement on Tariffs and Trade (GATT): a multilateral trade agreement that lessened the degree of trade protection among member countries, including Canada

World Trade Organization (WTO): a multilateral trade organization that has replaced GATT

The liberalizing trend in global trade continued after World War II ended. Canada joined in this movement, partly because many of its manufacturing industries had matured sufficiently to be able to compete against imports without tariffs. In 1947, Canada was one of 22 nations that signed the **General Agreement on Tariffs and Trade (GATT)**, which until recently was the most important example of a "multilateral" trade agreement involving many countries. In 1995, GATT was replaced by the **World Trade Organization (WTO)**. This organization, with over 120 members, continues GATT's task of lessening trade protection among member countries, including Canada.

The WTO is based on the principle that trade policies of member countries should treat all other members equally. Complaints by one country against the trade policies of another are subject to formal rules and judged by impartial panels. If a settlement cannot be reached through compromise, then the complainant country has recourse to limited forms of trade retaliation. In the past GATT was the most important cause of liberalized global trade.

Through rounds of negotiation among GATT members, both tariff and non-tariff barriers were gradually reduced. The most important of these negotiations was the Kennedy Round, completed in 1967, which cut average tariffs by about a third, and the Tokyo Round, completed in 1979, which cut tariffs by another third. The result has been a marked reduction of tariffs—especially on manufactured products. Average tariffs for these products in industrialized countries, which were above 50 percent in the 1930s, have since fallen to below 5 percent.

The last GATT negotiations, which produced an agreement in 1993, caused GATT's replacement with the WTO. In addition, remaining tariffs on some manufactured products, such as prescription drugs and medical equipment, are being reduced, while trade in services such as computer software is being liberalized.

Previously protected agricultural products are also affected. Export subsidies to farmers are being cut, while import quotas on agricultural products are being gradually phased out. The agreement will have mixed effects on Canadian farmers. Because other countries must reduce their subsidies on grain exports, Canada's farmers will benefit from higher world prices for grain. At the same time, some Canadian farmers will be hurt. In the past, Canadian prices for eggs, poultry, and dairy products have been maintained above world levels through import quotas on these products. Because such quotas are now disallowed, the Canadian government has replaced them with tariffs—some at levels close to 300 percent given the large difference between Canadian and world prices. Over time, the Canadian government is being forced to reduce these tariffs. The result is increased foreign imports.

Recent Trading Blocs

trading bloc: a relatively small number of countries involved in a trade agreement

A wish to pursue closer economic ties has led some groups of countries to liberalize trade among themselves. A **trading bloc** is a relatively small group of countries involved in a trade agreement. There are three types: free trade area, customs union, and common market. Each type involves increased integration of trade policies.

Free Trade Area

free trade area: an area in which trade is tariff-free, although member countries are able to impose separate trade barriers on outside countries

Trade within a **free trade area** is tariff-free, although member countries are able to impose separate trade barriers on outside countries. A contemporary example of a free trade area is the North American Free Trade Agreement among Canada, the United States, and Mexico.

Thinking About Economics

How could Canada's trade be further liberalized in the future?

Canada signed bilateral trade agreements with Chile and Israel (both in 1996) and is participating in WTO negotiations on agricultural trade (beginning in 1999) and services (beginning in 2000). It is also a member of the Asia-Pacific Economic Cooperation forum (APEC), whose goal is to liberalize trade with Asian countries, and it is involved in Pan-American talks whose aim is to form a Free Trade Agreement of the Americas (FTAA) by 2005.

Customs Union

customs union: a group of countries with common trade barriers with outside countries as well as a free trade area

A **customs union** is a stronger form of regional integration that includes not only free trade among member countries, but also common trade barriers with the rest of the world. An example of an emerging customs union is Mercosur, which has six member countries, including Brazil and Argentina.

Common Market

common market: a group of countries with not only a free trade area and common trade barriers with outside countries, but also free movement of labour and capital

European Union (EU): an expanding common market of European countries first formed in 1956, formerly known as the European Economic Community (EEC)

A **common market** is a customs union that allows for the free movement of labour and capital among member nations. The best-known example of an emerging common market is the previously mentioned **European Union (EU)**, formerly known as the European Community (EC), which was first formed in 1956 by six countries—Germany, France, Italy, the Netherlands, Belgium, and Luxembourg. Since then, the European Union has expanded to include a majority of countries in Europe. In 1992, a treaty was signed among member countries that sets them on a path to even closer economic and political integration. Once this process is completed, there will be freer movement of economic resources, standardized economic regulations, and probably a common currency throughout the EU.

Supporters of the EU suggest that the gains from past trade liberalization among members have helped boost recent living standards in West European countries. For example, a study on the effects of the EU's single market suggested that in its first six years it should reduce prices in member countries by 6 percent, increase real output by 4.5 percent, and create 2 million new jobs. Critics point out the loss of national sovereignty that has accompanied the EU's evolution, and argue that European living standards would have risen with or without freer trade.

The Auto Pact

Auto Pact: the 1965 agreement establishing free trade in autos and auto parts between Canada and the United States; formerly known as the Canada–U.S. Automotive Products Agreement

The Canada–U.S. Automotive Products Agreement, or **Auto Pact**, of 1965 is an example of a free trade area in one class of products—autos and auto parts. Until 1965, high tariffs meant that Canada had an inefficient branch-plant auto industry with high prices for Canadian consumers. The pact eliminated tariffs on both sides of the border for the "Big Three" auto companies as long as their sales in North America had at least 50 percent North American content and their Canadian sales had 60 or more percent of their value added in Canada. The pact was beneficial for the companies involved, allowing them to increase their efficiency. As costs and prices for Canadian-made autos fell, output and employment rose, aiding Canadian workers and the Canadian economy as a whole.

The Free Trade Agreement

Free Trade Agreement (FTA): the 1988 pact between Canada and the United States to form a free trade area

Like the Auto Pact, the Canada–U.S. **Free Trade Agreement (FTA)** is an example of a "bilateral" free trade agreement, which involves two partners. Unlike the Auto Pact, the FTA includes trade in virtually all products between the two countries. It was signed by Canada and the United States in 1988 and came into effect in 1989. Under the terms of the agreement, all remaining tariffs on trade between the two countries have been phased out by 1998, and non-tariff barriers have been reduced. Services are also included, with a national treatment principle being adopted so that service industries in either country can compete in both national markets. Licensing procedures in the two countries are being standardized to help ease this liberalization of services. Canada's ability to screen foreign direct investment has been reduced, while non-North American car companies can trade autos and auto parts freely across the Canada–U.S. border if they meet a revised 50 percent North American manufacturing content rule. There is also greater access for U.S. wine and liquor producers—and, more gradually, for American brewers—in the Canadian market. A continental market for energy has been created. While Canada may still limit its energy exports to the United States during a period of global shortages, Canadians will have to limit their own energy consumption by the same proportion. Of particular note, Canadian cultural policies are largely exempted from the agreement, allowing Canada to impose policies that affect the trade and ownership of its cultural industries. Finally, a dispute settlement procedure is in place so that when either country retaliates against the other's trade policies, the dispute is judged by an impartial panel using the trade legislation of the retaliating country.

As usual, supporters of free trade point out the potential economic benefits from increased specialization and trade between the two countries. Canadian advocates of the agreement also suggest that it reduces the risk of American protectionist measures directed against Canadian exports. Critics of the deal focus on the possible loss of political sovereignty for Canada, especially because of the restrictions placed on government attempts to screen foreign investment and restrict energy exports. While either country can end the agreement with six months' warning, the gradual strengthening of trade ties between the two countries will make it difficult for any Canadian government to do so. Critics also stress that Canadian jobs have been lost in previously protected manufacturing industries as foreign companies closed their remaining branch plants so they could centralize their production and take advantage of economies of scale. In the important auto industry, the phasing out of tariffs means that there are no longer penalties for companies that do not meet the Auto Pact guidelines, which critics say could work to the disadvantage of Canadian producers.

Effects of the Free Trade Agreement

As expected, in the early years of the Free Trade Agreement Canada and the United States had greater trade flows. From 1989 to 1992, for example, Canadian merchandise exports in sectors liberalized by the agreement increased by 33 percent, while Canadian merchandise imports in the same sectors rose by 28 percent. The increase in Canada's exports was most pronounced in manufacturing industries such as office and telecommunications equipment, as well as in resource-based industries such as chemical products and paper. Meanwhile, Canada's merchandise imports grew most in industries such as processed food, clothing, and furniture. So far, the impartial dispute settlement procedure has often worked in Canada's favour, although the American government has shown a tendency to reintroduce trade complaints if a panel decision goes against its perceived interests.

There also have been costs associated with the agreement, which it is hoped are only the short-term costs of adjustment. The bulk of these costs have fallen on workers who lost their jobs in formerly protected industries. It is important to remember that other factors were also causing unemployment to rise during the years immediately after the FTA took effect. The first was the continuing shift of Canadian jobs away from manufacturing and toward the service sector. Second, the agreement came into effect just before the start of a significant global recession. In the long run, trade theory suggests, jobs lost in declining industries hurt by free trade should be replaced by employment in expanding export industries.

The North American Free Trade Agreement

North American Free Trade Agreement (NAFTA): the 1993 pact among Canada, the United States, and Mexico to form a free trade area

The **North American Free Trade Agreement (NAFTA)**, which was settled in 1993 and came into effect in 1994, is an illustration of a "trilateral" trade accord, which is among three countries. It extends most of the provisions of the Free Trade Agreement to include Mexico. If we consider only trade with this new partner, it seems that NAFTA will not have a significant impact on either Canada or Mexico because their trade relationship has never been significant. For example, in 1996 trade with Mexico made up only 0.5 percent of Canada's exports and 3 percent of its imports, and much of this trade was virtually tariff-free even before NAFTA.

However, critics of NAFTA suggest possible problems of including a country with a lower GDP per capita in the same free trade area as wealthier, more industrialized countries. They point to the loss of Canadian jobs that occur when businesses move to Mexico to take advantage of low-wage labour. Concern has also been expressed over Mexico's lax enforcement of labour and environmental standards. This last concern prompted the addition of two side-agreements to NAFTA. Under the side-agreements, two NAFTA members can set penalties on the third member if that country is not enforcing its labour and environmental laws. So far, these provisions have not been invoked, and it is difficult to judge the relevance of the criticisms made against NAFTA.

BRIEF REVIEW

1. Up until the 1860s, Canada had a favourable trade agreement with the United States with low tariff rates.
2. Canada became increasingly restrictive after 1866, particularly with the adoption of the National Policy in 1879. The National Policy raised tariffs to stimulate Canada's own manufacturing sector.
3. High tariff rates continued to the Great Depression, at which point this approach to trade was reassessed.
4. The General Agreement on Tariffs and Trade (GATT) was a multilateral trade agreement created in 1947 and based on the principle that member countries should treat all other members equally. Until its replacement in 1995 by the World Trade Organization (WTO), GATT was a major force in liberalizing international trade.
5. Trading blocs, which are trade agreements among a small number of countries, take a variety of forms: free trade areas, customs unions, and common markets.
6. Trade within a free trade area is tariff-free, although member countries can impose separate trade barriers on outside countries. The Free Trade Agreement (FTA) and its extension, the North American Free Trade Agreement (NAFTA), are examples of free trade areas. Another example of such an area is the Auto Pact between Canada and the United States, which deals only with automobile products.
7. A customs union is an even stronger form of regional integration. Not only is the free trade area tariff-free, but members have common trade barriers with the rest of the world. An example is Mercosur.
8. A common market is a customs union that allows for the free movement of labour and capital. The European Union (EU) is an example of a common market. The EU is moving toward even closer economic and political integration.

KEY CONCEPTS

globalization
absolute advantage
comparative advantage
law of comparative advantage
terms of trade
tariff
non-tariff barriers
import quota
voluntary export restraints
export subsidies
infant industry
strategic trade policy
National Policy
General Agreement on Tariffs and Trade
World Trade Organization
trading bloc
free trade area
customs union
common market
European Union
Auto Pact
Free Trade Agreement
North American Free Trade Agreement

ANALYSIS AND APPLICATION

1. Ada can prepare a tax return in 4 hours and paint a kitchen in 10 hours, while it takes Paulo 12 hours to prepare a tax return and 20 hours to paint a kitchen.
   a. Who is more efficient at preparing a tax return? at painting a kitchen?
   b. What are the opportunity costs for the two activities for Ada? for Paulo?
   c. Who should specialize in each activity? Why?

2. The table below shows how many computer games or radios can be produced daily by one worker in Country C and Country D.

	Daily Output per Worker	
	Computer Games	**Radios**
Country C	8	4
Country D	10	2

   a. Which country is more efficient at producing computer games? radios?
   b. On the basis of absolute advantage, which country should specialize in the production of each good? Explain.
   c. Identify the limits of the terms of trade for these two goods.
   d. Suppose there are 3 million workers in Country C and 4 million workers in Country D. Before trade, half of each country's labour force makes each good. Outline how specialization and trade lead to a gain in the two countries' total output of both goods.

3. The table below shows how many T-shirts or jeans can be made daily by one worker in Country E and Country F.

	Daily Output per Worker	
	T-Shirts	**Jeans**
Country E	40	4
Country F	30	2

   a. Which country is more efficient at producing T-shirts? jeans?
   b. What the opportunity costs for each good in Country E? Country F?
   c. On the basis of comparative advantage, which country should specialize in the production of each good? Explain.
   d. Identify the limits of the terms of trade for these two goods.
   e. Suppose there are 200 000 workers in Country E and 300 000 workers in Country F, and before trade half of each country's labour force makes each good. Outline how specialization and trade lead to a gain in the total output of both goods.

4. Suppose that 1 telephone has an opportunity cost of 5 tonnes of wheat in Canada and an opportunity cost of 10 tonnes of wheat in France.
   a. Identify the terms of trade for these two goods and the factors that determine the exact international price of one good in terms of another.
   b. What international price would be preferred by Canadians? by the French? Explain each of your answers.

5. The table below shows hypothetical data for the Canadian market for watches, presuming this market is perfectly competitive.

Domestic Demand and Supply Schedules for Watches

Price ($)	**Quantity Demanded (D_d) (millions)**	**Quantity Supplied (S_d) (millions)**
80	1.4	1.8
70	1.6	1.6
60	1.8	1.4
50	2.0	1.2
40	2.2	1.0

   a. Draw a graph showing the domestic demand and supply curves for watches. Identify the equilibrium point in the absence of foreign imports.

b. On your graph, show the effects of allowing unrestricted foreign imports of watches at a constant world price of $50.
c. Use your graph to explain how a $10 tariff on imported watches affects consumers, domestic producers, foreign producers, and the Canadian government.
d. On a separate graph, show how an import quota of 400 000 watches a year affects consumers, domestic producers, and foreign producers.

6. Explain how the requirement by the Canadian government that there be English and French labelling of products sometimes operates as an "invisible" non-tariff barrier, and give a possible example.

7. Participants in so-called infant industries are like Peter Pan — they do not want their industry to be seen as "grown up." Why?

8. "Incorporating more countries within NAFTA is in Canada's best long-term interests." Discuss.

9. What are the special advantages and disadvantages of trade agreements between countries with significantly different levels of per capita GDP?

10. (Advanced Question)
In many cases, countries import and export the same products. For example, automobiles and auto parts are traded both ways across the Canada-U.S. border. Why?

11. Access the website of the World Trade Organization (at http://www.wto.org/). Use information at this site to explain the following principles of the WTO's multilateral trading system:
a. most favoured nation (MFN) status
b. national treatment
c. dumping
d. plurilateral agreements

Advancing Economic Thought

WE ARE WHAT WE MAKE

The Theories of Harold Innis

There are few things rarer than an original thinker. The Canadian economist Harold Innis (1894-1952) was one. Raised in rural Ontario, he planned to become a lawyer, but his legal studies were waylaid by his growing interest in economics, which he studied at the University of Chicago — a well-known centre of economic research. He then taught for many years at the University of Toronto, while his writings exerted a growing influence not only on the study of Canadian economic history but also other related areas.

Staples Thesis

Innis's researches took him far beyond the usual domain of economics. His first aim was to explain the guiding forces of Canada's economic history. Why has development been concentrated in certain regions and during particular eras?

Harold Innis
Source: Public Archives Canada

His answer was an intriguing one. Innis focused on what he called staple products—natural resources that could be exploited by Canadians, and sold in foreign markets for export revenues. According to Innis's staples thesis, several natural resources have played crucial roles in the evolution of the Canadian economy. In each case, development has been shaped by where and how the resource has been extracted and used. Innis's emphasis on staple products led him to highlight geographical aspects of development, as well as the linkages between staple industries and other parts of the economy.

Innis's own work concentrated on the role of fish and furs in encouraging European settlement in Canada. Cod fish provided the first impetus to this settlement, and fishing continued to serve as the primary staple industry on much of Canada's east cost until recent times. In central Canada, development centred on the lucrative fur industry, where high European prices allowed for a high markup and generous export revenues.

Furs remained central Canada's dominant staple item until early in the 19th century, when the growing demands of ship-building and construction industries in both the U.S. and Europe meant that forestry took over as Canada's major staple industry. After the 1860s, however, lumber exports declined, and there was no staple item to take its place. Not surprisingly, this was a time of economic stagnation in Canada. Then, in the two decades leading up to World War I, wheat prices rose, encouraging the large-scale agriculture expansion that accompanied the settlement of the Prairie provinces.

After World War I, new natural resources—minerals, oil and gas and hydroelectric power—have served as staple goods, but none with the same dominance as in previous eras. The Canadian economy's current shift from manufacturing to services is difficult to interpret using Innis's theory. Nonetheless, the staples thesis offers insights into Canada's economic history, and is still applicable in some regions of the country.

Communications Theory

In his later years, Innis turned to a more basic and wide-ranging question. What is the central factor determining the type of society we live in? Nothing less than the way we communicate. This was later popularized by the famous Canadian thinker Marshall McLuhan—who was heavily influenced by Innis's ideas—as "the medium is the message."

Some types of communication exhibit a space bias, meaning they are well suited for conveying messages across geographical distances. An example is a lightweight paper letter. Other ways of communicating show a time bias, working best when communication spans time, as with a message carved on a stone monument.

Innis divided history into periods based on the dominant medium of communication. Time-biased communication in a society leads to an emphasis on tradition and religious belief. A space-biased medium causes an interest in short-lived worldly matters, and aids in the formation of geographical empires.

For example, Innis believed that early pre-literate cultures exhibited a vitality that matched their dominant form of communication. Speech is more effective in passing on information from one generation to another than it is in bridging space. Cultures depending on the spoken word were therefore time-biased, with custom playing an important role.

In about 3000 BCE, writing was invented in ancient Mesopotamia (present-day Iraq). Early writing was preserved in clay and stone. These materials are durable but cumbersome to transport. Hence the societies that used them were time-biased, stressing the supernatural and tradition. As Innis pointed out, both the yearly calendar and the pseudo-science of astrology were developed in these early time-centred cultures.

Papyrus is a portable but fragile plant material. It was first used for writing in Egypt, and became popular throughout the Mediterranean. A space-biased means of communication, it made possible the expansion of the Roman Empire and the flowering of secular culture.

Parchment, also known as vellum, is made from animal skins. From about the 8th century CE, it became the dominant writing medium in Europe. Durable but difficult to move, it represented a return to time-biased means of communication. Using Innis's theory, this accounts for the renewed emphasis on tradition and religious faith during the Middle Ages.

Paper—light, portable and space-biased—was invented in China during the 2nd century CE, and by the 12th century CE it had arrived in Europe. Its use made feasible the development of printing and, according to Innis, encouraged an interest in commerce and worldly culture that, at about 1500 CE, ushered in the modern era in Europe. Paper-based communication also facilitated the empire-building of countries such as Spain and Portugal, and later France and Britain.

What of today's communications revolution that has accompanied the introduction of TV, radio, telephones, and computers? If anything, our culture's bias towards space has been intensified. While political empires have gone out of fashion, the entire world is fast becoming one vast "information empire" in which geographical distance has lost its significance. And how is this new global order held together? Not by sea-power or trade routes, but by optical-fibre cables, radio waves, and satellites. If anything, the continuing development of instantaneous forms of communication make the space-biased aspects of our culture ever more powerful.

1. **Using one of the staple resources from Canada's past as an example, explain some possible ways that the extraction or use of this resource affected the development of Canada and its economy.**

2. **How would Innis explain the fact that contemporary societies are so consumed by passing fads and the present moment?**

NO CHILD'S PLAY

Global Trade and Labour Standards

Globalization has unpleasant aspects. Most disturbing is the way it sustains—and even encourages—the exploitation of low-wage labour. The article below discusses some of the abuses related to global sourcing and outlines the complex issues surrounding this problem.

It's a perfect Kodak moment. On Christmas morning under the tree, Amanda is thrilled with her trendy new pair of Guess jeans and her Songbird Barbie doll. Joey thinks his new Nike cross-trainers are way cool, and he's in love with his Disney 101 Dalmatians jogging gear.

But if the kids knew how some of these gifts were made, it might cast a decided pall on their holiday cheer. Former workers and union organizers allege that some Guess clothing is made by suppliers who use underpaid Latino immigrants in Los Angeles, sometimes in their own homes. Mattel makes tens of millions of Barbies a year in China, where young female Chinese workers, who have migrated thousands of miles from home, are alleged to earn less than the minimum wage of $1.99 a day. Nike is criticized for manufacturing many of its shoes in tough labour conditions in Indonesia, and some of Disney's hottest seasonal products are being made by suppliers in Sri Lanka and Haiti—countries with unsavoury reputations for labour and human rights.

In an era when the economy is necessarily a global one, it is impossible for consumers to avoid products made under less than ideal labour conditions. Moreover, what may appear to be horrific working environments are not just acceptable but actually attractive to others who live overseas.

Still, a growing number of manufacturers and retailers are coming under fire for how the goods they make and sell are produced. Labour, civic, religious, investor, and consumer groups are pushing to improve the conditions of workers at the lowest end of a global supply chain. Some of these groups are advancing their own self-interests, to be sure—including labour unions that for decades have seized on arguments to oppose imports. But the cumulative effect of their campaigns is growing. Aided by Internet connections, for example, student groups are joining in, publishing lists of companies that allegedly make or sell goods produced in abysmal working conditions.

What makes the issue so staggeringly complex is that the current system of global sourcing isn't all bad. The search for inexpensive labour benefits U.S. consumers, who enjoy far lower prices than their European and Japanese counterparts. Apparel prices have actually declined in real terms in recent years, thanks in large part to global sourcing. That eases inflationary pressures for the whole economy. In many cases, global procurement networks provide badly needed income, and often the only chance of work at all, for workers overseas.

Moreover, today's Third World nations can be tomorrow's developmental success story. Take South Korea. A decade or so ago, Nike had most of its sneakers manufactured there: now, South Korea has evolved into an industrial powerhouse with a higher living standard, and Nike makes most of its shoes in Indonesia and China.

Even the most zealous advocacy groups urge major U.S. manufacturers abroad not to shut down their factories, just to improve them. Some manufacturers and retailers are already responding. A four-year-old San Francisco-based group, Business for Social Responsibility, is teaching 800 member companies how to better manage their international purchasing. Concerns have even given birth to a new industry. There are now businesses, such as California Safety Compliance, that charge companies for monitoring work conditions in their plants around the world.

One icon of American culture whose manufacturing practices seem out of sync with its brand name is Disney. Disney maintains almost 4,000 contracts with other companies that assume the right to manufacture Disney paraphernalia, some of which are then sold in Disney stores. These licensees go to some of the world's lowest-cost-labour countries, including Sri Lanka and Indonesia, to produce stuffed animals and clothes. Disney itself rarely takes a direct hand in manufacturing.

SIDELINE

Disney's main nemesis is Charles Kernaghan, executive director of the National Labor Committee. In his office, Kernaghan points to a pile of clothes. Most of it is children's wear made in Haiti, all prominently displaying the latest Disney themes. He picks up one item — a handsome child-size sweatshirt and sweat pants outfit manufactured at a factory in Port-au-Prince. According to Kernaghan, workers in Haiti receive 6 cents for producing this item, which retails for $19.99 in the United States. The wages are attractive in a country with overwhelming unemployment but would surprise many American purchasers of the goods.

Kernaghan acknowledges that conditions have improved—workers are now being paid at least the minimum wage of 32 cents an hour, or about $2.50 a day, and factories have been cleaned up somewhat. But, he says, much more needs to be done.

Unfortunately, it's not so simple. "If the Haitian government were to raise the minimum wage much higher, then they would have to wonder what that would do to the companies that are operating there," says Cynthia Knobel, a spokesperson for VF Corp., parent of H. H. Cutler, one of the two key contractors for Disney in Haiti. "The margin we make on those products is so slim, I'm not sure we could afford to continue to manufacture there."

Does a global economy mean consumers face no choice but to buy products made under conditions Americans don't want to think about? A number of U.S. companies say that intense global competition is no excuse for keeping working standards at the lowest possible level. Levi Strauss, for example, imposes its own "terms of engagement" on manufacturers who make its jeans products in 50 countries. The company's employees were the driving force in launching a major shake-up of Levi's sourcing standards starting in 1991. Aside from introducing guidelines and actively monitoring how they are observed, the company narrowed down the number of countries where it would operate so that it could better understand local conditions. It shut down three factories in Burma and decided against operating in Haiti or El Salvador because of concerns over labour standards. It also decided to conduct only minimal business in China through a Hong Kong affiliate. Levi's reputation as a socially conscious firm has received a boost, and Levi's executives say the company s sales have been enhanced as a result of its efforts.

At the end of the day, it s not likely that sweeping solutions will emerge, because the industry is so huge and fractured. But what does seem possible are small steps and innovations, over a period of time, that will add up to an improvement of global sourcing standards.

Source

Abridged from "Santa's Sweatshop," *U.S. News and World Report*, 16 December 1996, pp. 50-60.

1. Suggest several ways that citizens in rich countries can help overcome the workplace abuses outlined in the article.

2. Access the website of the Council on Economic Priorities (at http://www.accesspt.com/cep). Based on the information provided at this site, identify at least two projects geared to eradicating child labour. Outline some of the problems hindering the success of these projects.

Chapter Eighteen

Economic Growth

If we do not build economic growth that helps sustain communities, cultures and families, the results will be harsh.

—Anita Roddick, English entrepreneur

The distinguishing feature of life in present-day Canada, compared with many other parts of the world, is the prosperity that most Canadians enjoy. Economic growth has transformed Canadian living standards in just a few generations, with real GDP per Canadian about five times higher in the 1990s than it was in the 1920s. Can this trend continue? Why are there such vast differences between rich countries such as Canada and poor countries? How can these differences be addressed? What are the implications of growth and development? These questions are explored in this final chapter.

CHAPTER FOCUS

This chapter focuses on the following:

- economic growth, as indicated by both national output and national output per capita
- a country's production choices and the implications for growth
- economic growth in Canada
- sources of economic growth and the debate over growth
- high-, middle-, and low-income countries and the economic circumstances that characterize each category
- the gap between rich and poor countries
- economic development, its dynamics, the vicious circle of poverty, and the strategies used to break the circle

ECONOMIC GROWTH

Recall from Chapter 1 that economic growth is an increase in the total output of goods and services. The term can refer to the percentage increase in an economy's total output, usually measured by real GDP, or it can refer to a percentage increase in the per capita real GDP. For example, Canada's real GDP, valued in 1986 dollars, was $608.835 billion in 1995 and $617.795 billion in 1996, while the country's population expanded from 29.615 to 29.964 million during the same period. Using the first definition, Canada's annual rate of economic growth was 1.5 percent [($617.8 billion − $608.8 billion) ÷ $608.8 billion). Since per capita real GDP rose from $20 558 ($608.835 billion ÷ 29.615 million) to $20 618 ($617.795 billion ÷ 29.964 million), economic growth using the second definition was 0.3 percent. Use of each definition depends on the context. The first definition of economic growth is most appropriate when measuring an economy's overall productive capacity, while the second definition better indicates long-term changes in living standards, since more output per capita means an average individual is better off than before.

Economic Growth and Its Impact

In terms of the aggregate demand–aggregate supply model outlined in Chapter 12, economic growth can be caused by a long-run increase in aggregate supply (which is accompanied by a rise in an economy's potential output), or by short-run changes in aggregate demand or aggregate supply.

Economic growth can also be portrayed using the production possibilities curve. In Chapter 1, we saw that this curve demonstrates the combination of outputs that an economy *can* produce, assuming constant economic resources and technology. Economic growth occurs either when there is an outward shift in the production possibilities curve (due to technological change or an increase in economic resources), or when there is movement towards the curve (in the case where the economy is inside the curve because all resources are not employed or used to their full capacity).

Consider the hypothetical economy illustrated in Figure 18.1. This economy produces consumer goods (hamburgers) and capital goods (lasers). Initially, its production is limited to the combinations of consumer goods and capital goods demonstrated by the curve PPC_0. The economy chooses to produce 40 hamburgers and 2 lasers (point *a*).

Because the curve represents all production combinations that are attainable, this hypothetical economy is producing the most it can, given its preferences for hamburgers and lasers. Only by increasing economic resources and/or improving the state of technology to use the resources more efficiently can production possibilities be increased. In Figure 18.1, the shift from PPC_0 to PPC_1 demonstrates an increase in production possibilities. Now, the economy is able to produce more of either good and economic growth can take place.

FIGURE 18.1
The Process of Economic Growth

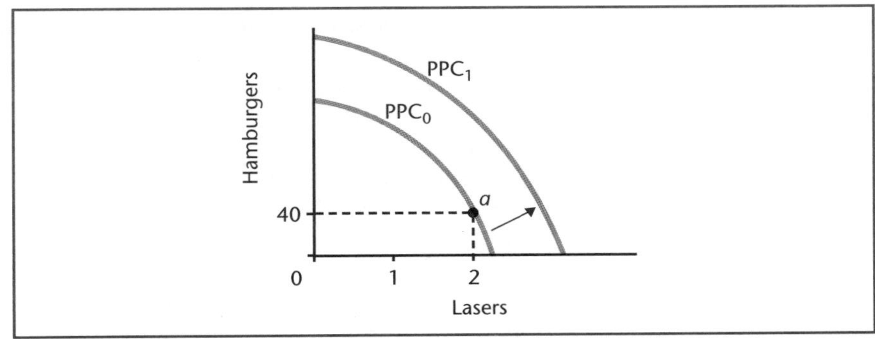

Initially the economy has production possibilities as shown by the curve PPC_0 and chooses to produce 40 hamburgers and 2 lasers (point *a*). Only by increasing economic resources and/or improving the productivity of these resources can the economy grow. By doing so, the economy can expand the production possibilities from PPC_0 to PPC_1.

Note that the production possibilities model highlights not only the limits of any economy but also the tradeoffs between various goods. Expanding our example in Figure 18.2, a country can choose to produce 40 hamburgers and 2 lasers (point *a*) on the left graph. Alternatively, it can choose to produce 100 hamburgers and 1 laser (point *c*) on the right graph.

Although a simplification, the two options demonstrate that economies can focus their resources on the production of consumer goods (hamburgers) or the production of capital goods (lasers). In contrast to

FIGURE 18.2
Production Options and Their Implications

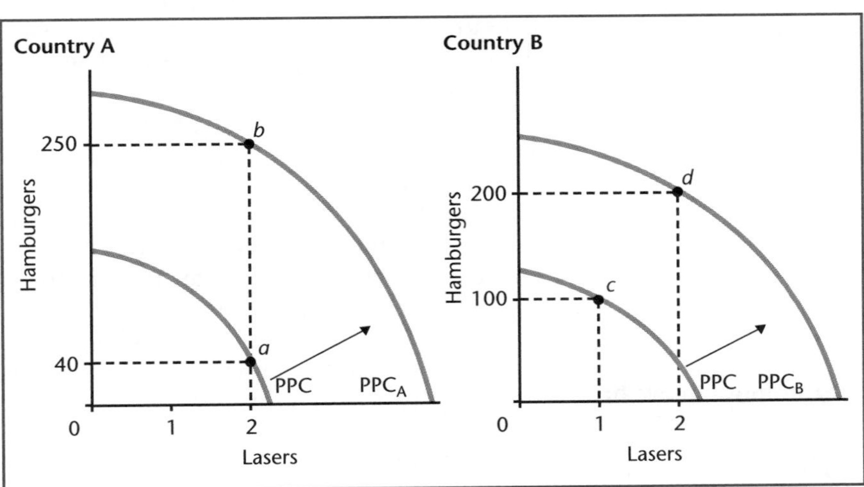

Suppose Countries A and B have the same initial production possibilities (PPC). However, Country A chooses to produce 40 hamburgers and 2 lasers (point *a* on the left) and Country B chooses to produce 100 hamburgers and 1 laser (point *c* on the right). Because Country A focuses more of its resources on producing a capital good (lasers) than does Country B, which focuses on a consumer good (hamburgers), Country A encourages greater growth. Within the same time period, Country A's production possibilities expand to PPCA, so that it may choose to produce 250 hamburgers and 2 lasers (point *b*). Country B's production possibilities expand less so, to PPC_B, so that it may produce 200 hamburgers and 2 lasers (point *d*).

consumer goods, which are simply consumed, capital goods can be used to produce more products. As such, capital goods are an investment in further production. Because of this, the choices that an economy makes between the production possibilities affect its future growth.

To demonstrate this, let's consider the hypothetical Countries A and B in Figure 18.2, which initially have identical production possibilities curves. By producing 40 hamburgers and 2 lasers (point *a* on the left graph), Country A adds to its economic resources, which in turn fuels economic growth and can mean that more of both consumer and capital goods will be produced in the future. As shown on the left, the production possibilities curve shifts from PPC to PPC_A. While the opportunity cost of focusing on capital goods is fewer consumer goods, production of both consumer and capital goods is enhanced in a year. So, for example, Country A can have an output of 250 hamburgers and 2 lasers (point *b*).

In contrast, Country B produces 100 hamburgers and 1 laser (point *c* on the right graph). Because of this choice the country has more consumer goods for its citizens immediately. However, the opportunity cost of more consumer goods is fewer capital goods, which means that the economy grows considerably less than Country A's. As shown on the right, the production possibilities curve shifts—from PPC to PPC_B—but less so than Country A's curve. So, for example, Country B can have an output of 200 hamburgers and 2 lasers (point *d*).

By consuming fewer hamburgers in the first year, Country A's citizens have gained an advantage in the second year. If they wish, they can now consume more hamburgers and match the production of lasers in Country B. Moreover, Country A now starts from a position of even greater production possibilities as it seeks further economic growth in future years.

The benefits of a high-growth strategy multiply over time. To see why, imagine what happens if, instead of choosing point *b*, the citizens of Country A continue their emphasis on capital goods by again choosing a point on PPC_A with fewer hamburgers and more lasers produced. The longer they follow this policy, the more their production possibilities curve expands and the greater their future potential consumption compared to consumption in Country B. With the passage of time, Country A reaps increasing benefits from high-growth strategy, while Country B's policy of favouring current over future consumption has an increasing opportunity cost in terms of sacrificed economic growth.

exponential growth: growth that is based on a percentage change and that builds on itself

Rule of 72: states that the number of years it takes a variable to double can be estimated by dividing 72 by the variable's annual percentage growth rate

Even small differences in growth rates can have a major long-run effect on a country's prosperity and living standards. This is because economic growth, like population growth, builds on itself, thereby showing a pattern of **exponential growth**. To see the effects, we can use a handy mathematical rule, the **Rule of 72**, which states that the number of years it takes a variable to double can be estimated by dividing 72 by the variable's annual percentage growth rate. A variable that grows exponentially at 4 percent a year therefore doubles its value in 18 years:

$$\text{Rule of 72:}\quad \text{Number of years for variable to double} = \frac{72}{\text{annual percentage growth rate}}$$

$$18 \text{ years} = \frac{72}{4\%}$$

Because of their long-term impact, small discrepancies in growth rates are treated seriously by economists and government policy-makers. Consider the hypothetical example in Figure 18.3. Two countries both have a 1998 output of $100 billion, but different growth rates (2 and 4 percent). After only 10 years, the difference between Country X's and Country Y's output is $26.12 billion.

FIGURE 18.3 GDP and Growth Rates

	Real GDP in Country X (2% annual growth in real GDP)	**Real GDP in Country Y (4% annual growth in real GDP)**
1998	$100.00 billion	$100.00 billion
1999	102.00 billion	104.00 billion
2000	104.04 billion	108.16 billion
2001	106.12 billion	112.49 billion
2002	108.24 billion	116.99 billion
2003	110.41 billion	121.67 billion
2004	112.62 billion	126.53 billion
2005	114.87 billion	131.59 billion
2006	117.17 billion	136.86 billion
2007	119.51 billion	142.33 billion
2008	121.90 billion	148.02 billion

Two countries, X and Y, have the same initial GDP in 1998, but different growth rates. Because growth is exponential, Country X's GDP falls behind Country Y's by an increasing margin. For example, while Country X's GDP rises from $100.00 billion to $102.00 billion [($100.00 billion × 0.02) + $100.00 billion] to $104.04 billion [($102.00 billion × 0.02) + $102.00 billion], Country Y's rises from $100.00 billion to $104.00 billion [($100.00 billion × 0.04) + $100.00 billion] to 108.16 billion [($104.00 billion × 0.04) + $104.00 billion].

Economic Growth in Canada

Historically, Canada has had high rates of economic growth. As a result, Canada had the fifteenth-highest per capita output of any country in the world in 1995. However, while Canada's long-term growth has been impressive, Figure 18.4 shows that increases in per capita real output have varied widely since Confederation.

Before World War I (1870–1914)

In the 44 years from just after Confederation to World War I, Canada's per capita output, measured in 1986 dollars, rose from $1713 to $3917. The

FIGURE 18.4
Canada's Economic Growth

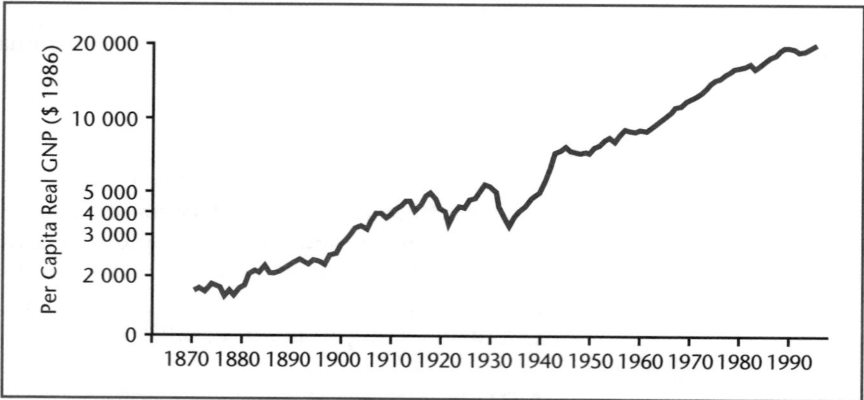

In terms of real output per capita, Canada's growth was gradual between 1870 and 1914. There were steep upswings in both the 1920s and early 1940s, but an abrupt decline in the early 1930s. Until 1973, there was steady growth in per capita income, averaging about 2 percent per year. Since then, the average rate of growth has been less. Note that the scale on the vertical axis is *logarithmic* to highlight change.

Sources: Adapted from A.G. Green and M.C. Urquhart, "New Estimates of Output Growth in Canada: Measurement and Interpretation," in Douglas McCalla and Michael Huberman (eds.), *Perspectives on Canadian Economic History* (Toronto: Copp Clark Longman, 1994), pp. 160–61; adapted from Statistics Canada, *Canadian Economic Observer, Historical Statistical Supplement, 1995/96* (July 1996), cat. no. 11-210, vol. 8, pp. 8, 25, 42. Reproduced by authority of the Minister of Industry, 1997.

economy's lacklustre growth record in the 1870s was followed by a more rapid rise in per capita real output in the 1880s and 1890s—sometimes attributed to Prime Minister John A. Macdonald's National Policy, which stimulated Canadian manufacturing through high tariffs on imports. The gradual increase in growth rates during these decades was also a part of the worldwide trend toward greater prosperity, as well as a rapid expansion of staple exports, such as wheat, that accompanied the settlement of the Canadian West.

The Interwar Period (1914–1945)

World War I ushered in a period of more unstable growth, with a lower long-term growth trend than in the previous period. After a period of negative growth just after World War I, Canada's per capita real output rose and then fell sharply during the 1920s and early 1930s, before increasing rapidly during the latter part of the 1930s and World War II. Overall, between 1914 and 1945, per capita real output almost doubled from $3917 to $7291.

The Postwar Period (1945–)

Between 1945 and 1973, Canada shared in the worldwide rise in prosperity, achieving a fairly steady growth in living standards of about 2 percent annually. Since the OPEC-spurred oil crisis of 1973, however, there has been a worrisome decrease in the rate of Canadian growth, except between 1983 and 1989, when growth in per capita real output again exceeded 2 percent. Overall, since 1945, per capita real output in Canada has increased over two and a half times to $19 865 by 1995.

Sources of Economic Growth

The production possibilities model shows that the main causes of growth in an economy's total real output are the stock of economic resources and how productively these resources are used. One of the most important causes of growth in Canada's total output—accounting for an estimated 35 percent of the growth in Canada's real GDP between 1961 and 1989—has been the increase in the quantity of labour. Some of this increase is due to higher participation rates for women in the labour force. However, most of it arises from population growth, which now runs at just over 1 percent annually.

The long-term growth in Canada's living standards, as measured by per capita real output, is determined by the other main source of growth, labour productivity. Recall from Chapter 7 that labour productivity is the quantity of output produced per worker in a certain period of time. Labour productivity can be applied not only to businesses and industries but also to countries' economies. Consider, for example, a hypothetical economy with a labour force of 5 workers who are employed for 2000 hours annually. In other words, the economy uses 10 000 hours of labour per year (5 × 2000). If real GDP in the economy is $200 000, labour productivity is $20 ($200 000 ÷ 10 000):

$$\text{Labour productivity} = \frac{\text{real output}}{\text{total hours worked}}$$

$$\$20 = \frac{\$200\ 000}{10\ 000}$$

If real GDP in this economy rises to $202 000 in the following year and the number of labour hours remains constant, then the new level of labour productivity is $20.20 ($202 000 ÷ 10 000 hours), representing an increase of 1 percent [($20.20 – $20.00) ÷ 20.00) × 100%].

Given the close association between changes in labour productivity and per capita real output, increases in Canadian labour productivity closely follow Canada's record of economic growth. There has been a significant slowdown in Canadian productivity growth over recent decades. As shown in Figure 18.5, Canada's annual rate of productivity growth in the overall business sector between 1979 and 1994 has surpassed only that of the U.S. among the big seven industrial economies. Growth in labour productivity is dependent on the quantity of capital, technological progress, the quality of labour, efficiency in production, the quantity of natural resources, and social and political factors.

FIGURE 18.5 Labour Productivity Growth in Selected Countries (1979-1994)

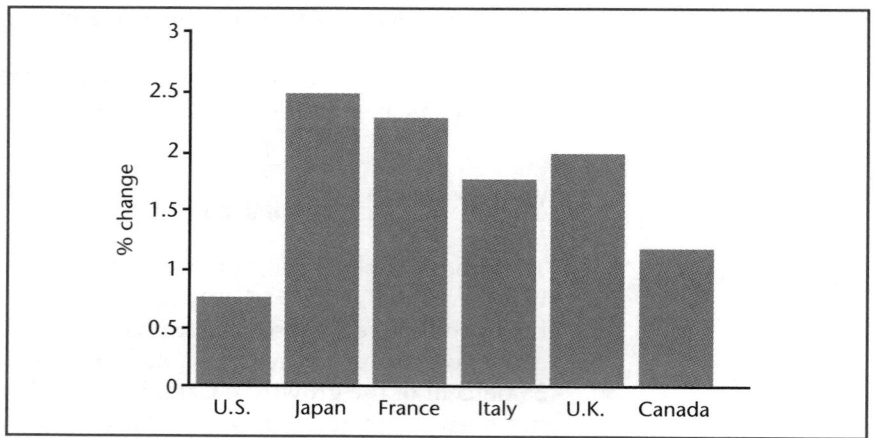

Source: Industry Canada, *Monthly Economic Indicators,* March 20, 1996, p.6. Reproduced by authority of the Minister of Industry, 1997.

Quantity of Capital

As indicated by the production possibilities model, an economy's supply of capital resources plays a central role in enhancing economic growth. By saving a higher proportion of their disposable incomes, Canadians can increase investment and accelerate the accumulation of capital resources, which, in turn, fuel economic growth. On average, the rates of Canadian saving and investment as a proportion of GDP have been higher than in the United States, but lower than in high-growth countries such as Japan and Germany.

Nonetheless, increases in the quantity of capital goods in Canada were high enough to account for an estimated 40 percent of total growth in its real GDP between 1961 and 1989. Because capital inputs have risen more quickly than labour inputs in the Canadian economy, each Canadian worker is employed with a gradually increasing amount of capital. Since 1961, for example, it is estimated that the ratio of capital to labour in Canada has risen by over 80 percent.

Technological Progress

technological progress: consists of scientific discoveries and their application, advances in production methods, and the development of new types of products

research and development expenditures (R&D): spending that is meant to accelerate the pace of technological progress

Technological progress is a broader term than the technological innovation discussed in Chapter 7 and encompasses scientific discoveries and their application, advances in production methods, and the development of new types of products. Technological progress—in all its forms—can cause economic growth. Over the long term it plays an important role in increasing labour productivity, often by raising the quality of capital resources with which labour is employed.

Some technological advances occur because of the ingenuity of individuals. Nonetheless, most technological progress is closely tied to **research and development expenditures (R&D)**, or spending whose purpose is to accelerate the pace of technological progress. Canadians have been relatively successful in taking advantage of international technological progress, but R&D expenditures by Canadian businesses have historically been relatively low compared to those of other countries. For example, R&D expenditures in 1995 represented 2.0 percent of GDP in Japan and 1.9 percent in the United States, but only 1.0 percent in Canada. It has been argued that, because of a small national market, the potential benefits of R&D expenditures are lower in Canada than in other countries. To the extent that freer trade is creating larger product markets for Canadian businesses, however, this argument is no longer relevant. Predictably, Canadian R&D expenditures have shown an upward trend in recent years.

Quality of Labour

The productivity of labour is tied not only to investment in capital goods but also to investment in human capital through education and training. Since the 1950s a growing proportion of young people have been completing high school and then pursuing postsecondary education. While 67 percent of those 15 years and older had finished high school in 1995, just over 20 percent of the comparable age group had done so in 1960. During the same period, the percentage of those between the ages of 18 and 24 enrolled full-time in universities and community colleges increased from 10 to 34 percent. To the extent that these trends augment the quality of Canada's labour force, they are raising its productivity as well as the economy's rate of growth.

Efficiency in Production

Economic growth is also influenced by changes in the efficiency of production through economies of scale and the reallocation of resources among different sectors. Canadian businesses—especially those in manufacturing—have traditionally been unable to take full advantage of economies of scale due to the small size of the Canadian market. Recent moves to freer trade are gradually removing this disadvantage, stimulating both labour productivity and the rate of economic growth—especially since the recession of the early 1990s. However, the shift of Canadian workers from the higher-productivity manufacturing sector to the lower-productivity service sector has, at least in the short run, dampened the rate of economic growth.

Quantity of Natural Resources

Canada's rich supplies of natural resources have doubtless contributed to its past economic growth, as during the boom period of rapidly expanding Western settlement between 1896 and 1914. During most periods, however, the stock of exploitable natural resources in a country remains constant, so that their impact on economic growth is minimal—especially in the modern Canadian economy, which is no longer dominated by primary sectors.

Social and Political Factors

There are a variety of social and political factors that can affect economic growth. Growth will be enhanced in a society that promotes competition, innovation, and entrepreneurship, and by social institutions geared toward enterprise and profit-making. In the political sphere, government regulations and taxes sometimes inhibit economic growth, especially through their impact on levels of saving and investment in the economy.

Thinking About Economics

What factors have led to low average growth rates in per capita real income since the mid-1970s?

The lacklustre growth performance of the Canadian economy since the mid-1970s stems from low increases in labour productivity. The exact cause of this lagging productivity growth has not been determined, but it is probably related to relatively low rates of investment and technological progress (due to the reluctance of many Canadian companies to adopt advanced technologies and contractionary government policies to combat inflation during much of this period) and also to shifts of workers from the manufacturing to the service sector. Whatever its exact causes, this productivity slowdown has had important long-term consequences for the prosperity of Canadians.

The Debate Over Growth

Is economic growth necessarily desirable? There are arguments both for and against the emphasis placed on economic growth.

Arguments for Economic Growth

Supporters of economic growth point to three main advantages: its effect on living standards, the opportunities it provides for social improvements, and its psychological benefits.

Living Standards The main benefit of economic growth is its positive effect on living standards. With rising incomes and output, more wants can be satisfied, both for individuals and for society as a whole. Indeed, the main reason life for most Canadians today is more pleasant than for Canadians of three generations ago is due to the tremendous material benefits that economic growth has provided.

Social Improvements Economic growth can be channelled not only into more consumption and investment by private households and businesses, but also into higher government spending, allowing for greater expenditures in such areas as health, education, and the promotion of income equity. Such programs are easier to implement when they can be funded from the proceeds of growth rather than through reductions in existing incomes.

Supporters of growth point out that the supposed tradeoff between income equity and economic growth has often been broken in recent decades. In the period between 1965 and 1989, countries with high growth rates tended to have a *more* equal distribution of income than countries with low growth rates. For example, the ratio of income shares of the richest and poorest 20 percent of the population was just under 10 to 1 in Singapore, while the average annual growth rate in the country's per capita real GDP was 7 percent. In contrast, Brazil's ratio of richest to poorest income shares was almost 35 to 1, while its comparable growth rate was a much lower 4 percent.

Psychological Benefits Some people suggest that there are intangible psychological benefits of economic growth as well. A growing economy helps create a mood of optimism and a sense of expanding opportunities.

Arguments Against Economic Growth

Critics of the emphasis on economic growth point to its direct opportunity cost, and to its indirect environmental and social costs.

Opportunity Cost of Growth Economic growth has a direct opportunity cost, as indicated by the production possibilities model. To promote growth, a country must devote more of its scarce resources to investment in capital goods rather than to current consumption. While this cost is not an overwhelming one for a rich country such as Canada, it is far more significant for citizens of poor countries as they choose an appropriate growth strategy.

Environmental Costs One of the main indirect costs of economic growth is damage to the environment. Higher levels of economic activity lead to greater exploitation of the world's limited supply of natural resources, as well as causing higher levels of pollution and waste. Supporters of growth suggest that environmental damage is the result of flaws in private markets rather than of economic growth itself. Proper government programs, they contend, can create the conditions for sustainable growth in the future. Critics argue that the dynamics of growth tend to swamp the impact of government regulations and controls. Environmental damage cannot be corrected through tinkering with the market system, they say, but only by a shift in values to end the quest for never-ending increases in living standards.

Social Costs The social costs of growth are related to the insecurity and risks that come with technological progress. While the general quality of life may be enhanced by technological advances, some resource suppliers will be hurt, and these individuals are often the members of society who are least able to adapt easily to change. At the same time, the pursuit of economic growth may not allow for traditional methods and lifestyles to be maintained. For some, the losses far outweigh any economic benefits.

BRIEF REVIEW

1. Economic growth refers to either increases in an economy's real output or increases in its real output per capita.
2. Economic growth expands production possibilities, so this growth can be expressed as a shift to the right of the production possibilities curve. Such growth is caused by an increase in economic resources or by technological progress, which increases the efficiency of production.
3. An economy might choose to focus on producing consumer or capital goods. A high-growth strategy involves focusing production on capital goods at the expense of consumer goods in the short run.
4. Because economic growth is exponential growth, the Rule of 72 applies. Even small differences in percentage rates of growth make a significant difference over time.
5. Overall, Canada's rates of economic growth have been high, giving Canada the fifteenth-highest per capita GDP worldwide in 1995.
6. Population growth and labour productivity have been the sources of Canada's economic growth. In turn, labour productivity is determined by the quantity and quality of capital, technological progress, efficiency, and social and political factors.
7. Arguments for growth concern living standards, social improvements, and psychological benefits. Arguments against growth concern its direct opportunity cost, and the indirect environmental and social costs.

ECONOMIC DEVELOPMENT

The World's Rich and Poor

Most Canadians live in relative comfort. In contrast, one-fifth of the world's population—about 1 billion people who live mainly in Southeast Asia and sub-Saharan Africa (meaning African countries south of the Sahara desert)—must live on US$370 or less each year.

To consider the disparities between rich and poor countries, the **World Bank** (a key international lending institution whose official title is the International Bank for Reconstruction and Development) classifies nations into three groups based on their annual per capita GNP: high-income, middle-income, and low-income countries.

World Bank: an international lending institution known officially as the International Bank for Reconstruction and Development

High-Income Countries

High-income countries are nations with per capita incomes substantial enough to provide their citizens with widespread prosperity. In 1995, the World Bank classified as high-income countries those with a per capita GNP of US$9386 or more. All of these nations have modern mixed economies based on capital-intensive production and the use of skilled labour. In 1995, there were 26 countries in this "rich club" of nations.

high-income countries: countries with per capita incomes substantial enough to provide their citizens with widespread prosperity

Middle-Income Countries

middle-income countries: countries in which a sizable minority of the population no longer lives in acute poverty

Middle-income countries are those in which a sizable minority of the population no longer lives in acute poverty. In 1995, this category was composed of nations with per capita GNP between US$766 and US$9385. Included are the former members of the Soviet Bloc—those countries in Eastern Europe and the former Soviet Union that until recently were command economies—as well as other countries primarily in Latin America, the Middle East, and the extreme northern and southern parts of Africa.

Low-Income Countries

low-income countries: the poorest countries in the world, as defined by per capita incomes

Finally, the **low-income countries** include the 50 poorest countries of the world. In 1995, this group included all nations with per capita GNP of US$765 or less. Along with China and India—the two most populous countries in the world—this category includes countries in sub-Saharan Africa and some nations in Latin America and Southeast Asia. These countries tend to have low levels of capital resources and use labour-intensive processes. Their economies tend to emphasize agriculture and other primary resource industries. Many of these countries share a history as colonies. In some cases, the national boundaries devised and the economies developed under colonialism have made the development of modern national economies difficult and often strife-ridden.

In addition to high-, middle-, and low-income countries, other terms are used to identify categories of countries with similar economies. For example, countries in Western Europe and North America (with the exception of Mexico), plus Japan, Australia, and New Zealand, are considered **industrially advanced countries (IACs)** because of their degree of industrialization. Hong Kong, Singapore, Thailand, Indonesia, South Korea, Malaysia, and Taiwan are sometimes called **newly industrializing countries (NICs)**—or, more colourfully, the "little dragons"—because of their recent strong economic growth and rapid industrialization. Another term, **less-developed countries (LDC)**, is sometimes used to describe countries with traditional mixed economies and low per capita incomes.

industrially advanced countries (IACs): countries that have a high degree of industrialization

newly industrializing countries (NICs): countries that recently have exhibited strong economic growth and rapid industrialization

less-developed countries (LDCs): countries with traditional mixed economies and low per capita incomes

Points of Comparison

Figure 18.7 presents some points of comparison that together indicate the living standards in selected countries that are high-, middle-, and low-income.

Per Capita Income

The average per capita GNP for high-income countries is over US$25 000. In contrast, the corresponding figure for low-income countries is US$430, or just over $1 a day.

FIGURE 18.6
Countries Classified by Per Capita Income

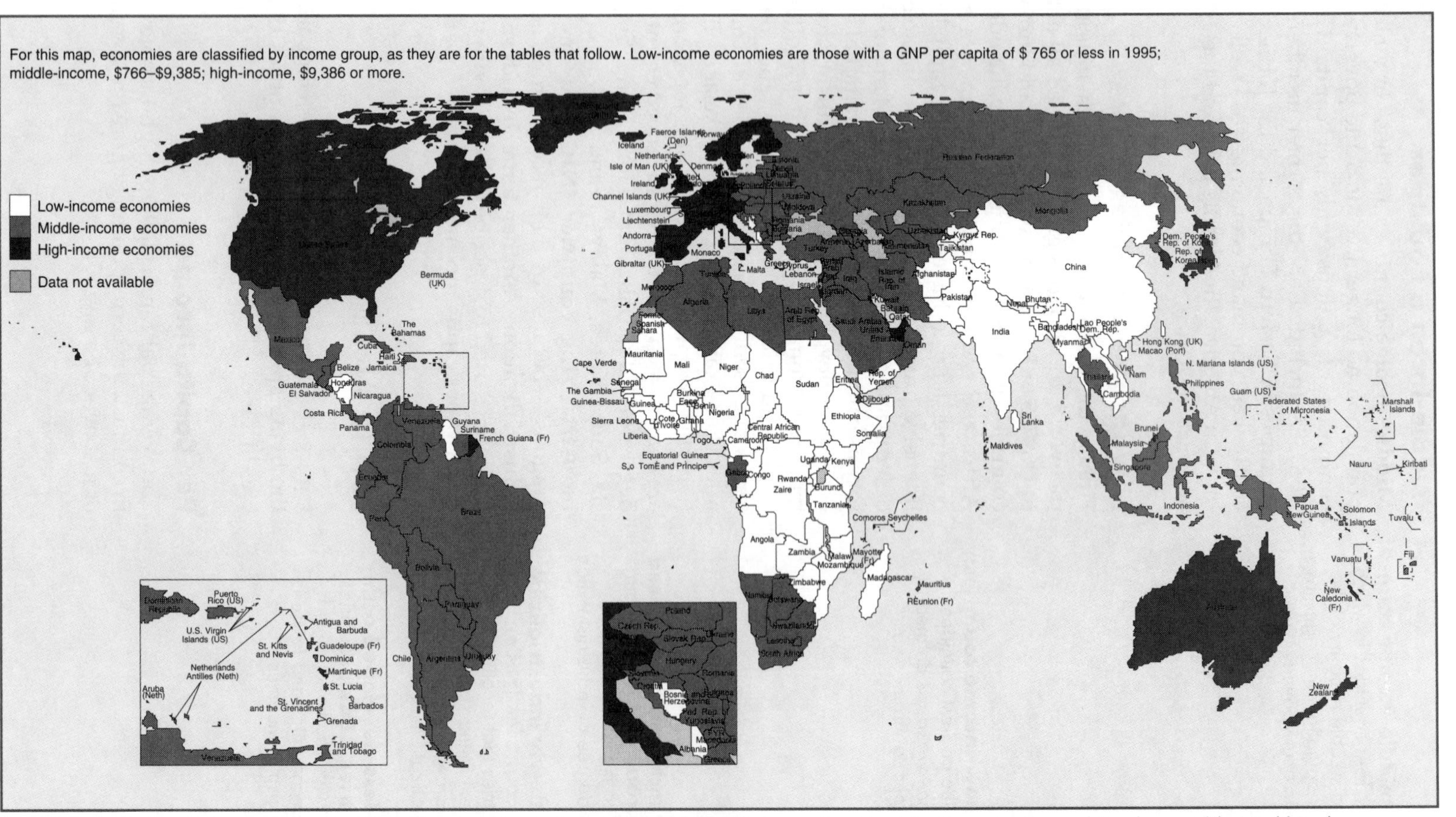

Source: From *World Development Report 1997*, by The World Bank. Copyright © 1997 by The International Bank for Reconstruction and Development/The World Bank. "Groups of Economies," pp. 209.

Health and Social Indicators

Not surprisingly, there are wide disparities in health and social indicators, such as life expectancy and infant mortality. While average life expectancy in high-income countries is 77 years, it is 63 years in low-income countries and under 50 years in the poorest countries, such as Ethiopia. Similarly, less than 5 percent of adults in high-income countries are illiterate, compared to an average 34 percent in low-income countries.

Energy Consumption

The world's poor use less energy. Average per capita consumption in high-income countries is about 14 times that in low-income countries, with Canadians (who are among the highest per capita energy users in the world) each consuming more than 21 times what citizens of low-income countries consume.

FIGURE 18.7 Indicators of Living Standards for Selected Countries (1995)

	Per Capita GNP (1995 $ US)	Average Annual Growth Rate (%) (1985-1995)	Population (millions) (1995)	Average Annual Growth Rate of Population (%) (1990-1995)	Life Expectancy at Birth (years)	Infant Mortality (per 1000 live births, 1995)	Adult Illiteracy (%) (1995)	Per Capita Energy Consumption (kg of oil equivalent) (1994)
High-Income Countries								
1. Japan	39 640	2.9	125	0.3	80	4	<5	3 856
2. U.S.	26 980	1.3	263	1.0	77	8	<5	7 819
3. Sweden	23 750	–0.1	9	0.6	79	4	<5	5 723
4. Canada	19 380	0.4	30	1.3	78	6	<5	7 854
All high-income countries	24 930	1.9		0.7	77	7	<5	5 066
Middle-Income Countries								
5. Saudi Arabia	7 040	–1.9	19	3.7	70	21	37	4 566
6. Hungary	4 120	–1.0	10	–0.1	70	11	n.a.	2 383
7. Mexico	3 320	0.1	92	1.9	72	33	10	1 561
8. Indonesia	980	6.0	193	1.6	64	51	16	366
All middle-income countries	2 390	–0.7		1.4	68	39	18	1 475
Low-Income Countries								
9. China	620	8.3	1 200	1.1	69	34	19	664
10. Honduras	600	0.1	6	3.0	67	45	27	204
11. India	340	3.2	929	1.8	62	68	48	248
12. Ethiopia	100	–0.3	56	1.9	49	112	65	22
All low-income countries	430	3.8		1.7	63	69	34	369
World	4 880	0.8		1.5	67	55		1 433

While the average per capita real GDP of high-income countries is about 60 times that for low-income countries, the average growth rates per capita are greater in low-income countries than for high- and middle-income countries. Whereas overall low-income countries have population growth rates higher than the world average, middle- and high-income countries have lower population growth rates. Overall, life expectancy and energy consumption rise with per capita income, while infant mortality and adult illiteracy fall with per capita income.

Source: From *World Development Report 1997*, by The World Bank. Copyright © 1997 by The International Bank for Reconstruction and Development/The World Bank.
Table 1, "Basic Indicators," pp. 214–15; Table 4, "Population and Labor Force," pp. 220–21; Table 6, "Health," pp. 224–25; Table 8, "Commercial Energy Use," pp. 228–29.

The Gap Between Rich and Poor

When measured by increases in per capita income, recent average rates of economic growth in poorer countries have exceeded those in rich countries. Between 1950 and 1989, for example, the average annual growth rate of per capita GDP for all low-income and middle-income countries was 2.7 percent, compared with the 2.3 percent average for high-income countries.

However, there was a tremendous range of growth rates. Asian nations not included in the high-income category achieved an average growth rate of 3.6 percent in their per capita GDP between 1950 and 1989, largely due to the performance of Asia's "little dragons" and, more recently, China. In contrast, per capita incomes grew by only 1.2 percent on average in Latin American countries and by only 0.8 percent in sub-Saharan African countries. In fact, some incomes in Latin America and sub-Saharan countries fell during the 1980s—a period often called the "lost decade" for the poor.

Despite higher average growth rates in poor countries since 1950, per capita incomes in most of these countries have risen less quickly in dollar terms than in industrially advanced countries. This apparent paradox stems from the relative size of per capita incomes in each group of countries and the fact that growth is exponential. So, for example, a hypothetical country with a per capita income of $1000 growing at 6 percent annually adds $60 to this figure in one year. In contrast, a rich country like Canada with a $20 000 per capita income can add a much higher amount of $200 simply by growing at 1 percent a year.

Thinking About Economics

Is expressing a country's per capita GDP or GNP in American dollars enough to indicate the average income of the country's citizens?

Not necessarily, for two reasons. Recall from Chapter 10 that these statistics have limitations—both quantitative and qualitative—when used as indicators of living standards. For example, neither GDP nor GNP reflect certain nonmarket activities, the quality of products, the distribution of income, and the various environmental consequences of growth. While expressing various countries' incomes in U.S. dollars allows us to compare their value on international markets, this does not tell us what an income will buy within the domestic economy. As any traveller knows, the equivalent in local currency to US$1 can buy significantly different products in one country than in another; for example, the United States and India. So that incomes can be compared more effectively, economists have developed the concept of purchasing-power parity (PPP), which is a method of adjusting for these differences in domestic prices. As a result, the incomes of most low-income countries are adjusted upward. Using this method, it has been estimated that the industrially advanced countries, with 15 percent of the world's population, account for just over 55 percent of world GDP, while countries of the former Soviet Bloc account for 11 percent, and other countries make up the remaining 33 percent.

The Dynamics of Development

economic development: an increase in a country's per capita income that is accompanied by a general rise in living standards

Economic development is an increase in a country's per capita income that is accompanied by a rise in living standards for the bulk of its population. In other words, it requires both economic growth and a widespread improvement in living standards. For most economists and planners, economic development is desirable and is associated with a structural change from a traditional mixed economy to a modern mixed economy. However, not everyone embraces economic development or the modernization that accompanies it—especially those people who wish to maintain tradition and who oppose the upheaval caused by social and economic change. People who are concerned about the environmental effects of rapid industrialization may also oppose certain aspects of economic development.

vicious circle of poverty: a cycle whereby low standards of living result in slow growth, thus keeping standards of living low in the future

Low-income countries face a daunting task in attempting to foster economic development. Many of these countries find themselves trapped in a **vicious circle of poverty**—a cycle whereby low standards of living lead to slow growth, thus keeping standards of living low in the future. As Figure 18.8 illustrates, low per capita incomes tend to cause both low investment and rapid population growth. These, in turn, perpetuate the focus on labour-intensive production, which restrains productivity, which dampens economic growth and keeps incomes low.

Low Investment

Low incomes mean that households must use most of their earnings for consumption. Thus only a minor proportion of income is saved in most low-income countries, which makes the financing of investment projects difficult. Widespread poverty also means that product markets in most low-income countries are relatively small, reducing the opportunities for business to engage in profitable investment.

FIGURE 18.8
The Vicious Circle of Poverty

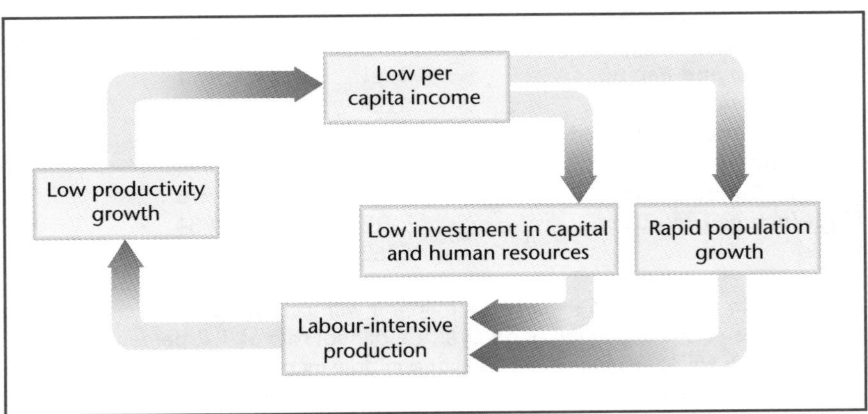

Low per capita income leads to rapid population growth and low investment, which in turn perpetuates the focus on labour-intensive production. This focus restrains productivity growth, which keeps incomes low.

Economic and social conditions in most low-income countries constrain investment in other, more subtle ways as well. Traditions that do not encourage competition or profit-making, for example, can inhibit entrepreneurship.

Rapid Population Growth

Not only are population levels in most low-income countries high relative to supplies of capital and natural resources, but current rates of population growth are increasing this discrepancy. Figure 18.9 outlines population levels in various parts of the world, along with estimates of how these levels will change in coming decades. Among the poorer countries, those in Africa and the Middle East have the highest estimated growth rates between 1990 and 2000, while those in Europe and Central Asia have the lowest. With only one exception, these rates are higher than the expected average growth rates in high-income countries.

As these data suggest, low incomes and rapid population growth tend to go together. They are linked for a number of reasons. To some extent, large families are seen as an economic necessity in low-income countries: given that poor families in these countries tend to have no income security nor pension, more children can provide more labour now to help the family and later to give the parents some security in old age. At the same time, high infant mortality encourages greater birth rates. These factors, combined with little birth control (due to economic and social factors), result in rapid population growth.

FIGURE 18.9 Global Population Trends

	Population (millions)			Estimated Annual; Growth Rate (%)	
	1990	2000 (estimated)	2030 (estimated)	1990-2000	2000-2030
Low- and Middle-Income Countries	4445	5294	7736	1.8	1.3
Sub-Saharan Africa	474	635	1313	3.0	2.4
East Asia and Pacific	1641	1891	2442	1.4	0.9
South Asia	1128	1368	2004	1.9	1.3
Europe and Central Asia	489	517	566	0.6	0.5
Middle East and Northern Africa	236	315	600	2.9	2.2
Latin America and the Caribbean	438	516	721	1.7	1.1
High-Income Countries	817	864	920	0.6	0.2
World	5262	6157	8664	1.6	1.2

According to estimates, the world's population will increase at an average annual rate of 1.6 percent to 6.157 billion in the year 2000, then at an average annual rate of 1.2 percent to 8.664 billion in the year 2030. Most of this growth will take place in the low- and middle-income countries, with estimated average annual growth rates of 1.8 percent (years 1990 to 2000) and 1.3 percent (years 2000 to 2030) and the highest rates in Africa and the Middle East.

Source: From *World Development Report 1993*, by The World Bank. Copyright © 1993 by The International Bank for Reconstruction and Development/The World Bank.
Table A.1, "Population (midyear) and average annual growth," p. 199.

The combination of higher incomes and government-sponsored birth control programs is gradually reducing population growth in many low-income countries, and this trend should continue, as shown in Figure 18.9. However, the projected increases in world population levels over the next few decades are still staggeringly high. The global population is expected to grow from 5.2 billion in 1990 to 8.7 billion by 2030, of which 7.7 billion will live in poorer countries.

Labour-Intensive Production

Low investment means that capital accumulates slowly, while rapid population growth leads to large increases in the supply of labour. Both factors are jointly responsible for creating large supplies of labour in relation to capital resources, thereby causing production in most low-income countries to be labour-intensive.

Low Productivity Growth

Because of labour-intensive production, it is difficult for producers to make use of technological innovations or to achieve the high levels of capital often needed to take advantage of economies of scale. Production remains less efficient, constraining growth in productivity. Without productivity growth, higher per capita incomes are impossible.

Strategies for Development

While difficult, it is possible to break the vicious circle of poverty, as the recent success of the "little dragons" shows. Breaking the cycle involves three domestic strategies: ensuring a stable political and economic system, investing in resources, and controlling population growth. At the same time that low-income countries are using such domestic strategies, other, higher-income countries can assist with two international strategies: trade liberalization and foreign aid.

Political and Economic Stability

A stable political system and economy are preconditions for development, since political turmoil and wide swings in output and prices both inhibit saving and investment. One of the most important development tasks of governments in low-income countries therefore is to ensure a stable political system and a smoothly running economy. Frequent changes in the country's laws discourage business activity, as do "quick-fix" schemes by governments that involve public spending financed through persistent budget deficits or inflationary monetary policy. In some countries, such as China, economic development has been associated with political repression. However, some recent studies suggest that, in general, economic development is enhanced if it is accompanied by political freedom and democracy. This is because a democratic political system tends to contribute to long-run political and economic stability.

Investing in Resources

For all low-income countries, government investment in human capital through education, health, and social programs is an important component of development. For example, greater education increases the supply of trained labour, which leads to long-term improvements in productivity. As a start, ensuring basic literacy through universal primary education enhances the opportunities for citizens to improve their own living standards.

Many governments in low-income countries also employ programs to stimulate investment in capital goods by trying to encourage the saving that is needed to finance this investment. In market economies, public policy-makers can impose taxes that promote private saving and discourage consumption. These savings can then be made available through financial markets to domestic businesses for investment. However, there is no guarantee that private saving will flow to domestic businesses. All too frequently, these savings leave the country. This problem, known as capital flight, is most acute in countries where internal conditions hinder the potential for profitable investment. While this problem has diminished in the 1990s, the estimated flight of private savings from poorer countries in the 1980s sometimes exceeded $100 billion annually.

In command economies, the investment process is carried out by public authorities themselves, who channel government revenues to public enterprises for investment. Again, these programs have possible drawbacks, since public investment projects can be chosen for political reasons rather than for their potential economic benefits.

Population Control

Governments in low-income countries can use several approaches to limit population growth. One way is to introduce voluntary birth control programs, which operate by providing incentives for those who participate. Such programs have been used in many low-income countries with varying degrees of success. In India, for example, where such programs have been common for several decades, the annual rate of population growth between 1990 and 1995 remained at a relatively high 1.8 percent. A more stringent approach is illustrated by China's "one-child" policy, which imposes financial penalties on parents who have more than one child. This program has successfully reduced the country's annual rate of population growth between 1990 and 1995 to 1.1 percent. However, the success of this type of compulsory approach must be weighed against the loss of freedom for citizens to make their own decisions regarding family size.

Additional policies and programs can indirectly affect population growth. For example, governments can provide basic social services to the poor involving health care, nutrition, and primary education, as well as family planning. These—alongside other policies and programs that develop new markets, enhance employment opportunities, stimulate investment, generate higher incomes, and improve income distribution—tend to encourage smaller families. Although powerful, such policies and programs can be difficult to implement when they clash with traditions.

Trade Liberalization

The export-driven growth of the "little dragons" shows that self-sustaining development in most low-income countries depends on making efficient use of their own resources, especially labour, to gain the benefits that flow from international trade. Therefore, one of the most important forms of assistance that industrially advanced countries can provide is to make their own markets more open to the exports of low-income countries—especially manufactured goods, which are often subject to trade barriers. This causes short-run adjustment costs for higher-income countries, but economists generally believe that the long-term benefits to low-income countries of such freer trade—as well as to the higher-income countries themselves—far outweigh the costs.

Foreign Aid

While liberalized trade has important long-term implications for international development, direct aid from higher-income countries is essential to breaking the vicious circle of poverty, especially for the poorest of the low-income countries. Most high-income countries run aid programs through their own national agencies; in Canada, government aid is administered by the Canadian International Development Agency (CIDA). A co-ordinated program of development assistance is also provided by two important international lending institutions: the International Monetary Fund (IMF) and the World Bank. While the IMF concentrates on short-term loans to governments, the World Bank uses its financial support from high-income countries to make loans to low-income countries for long-term investment projects that would otherwise not be funded. In particular, it focuses on basic health and education programs as well as on projects that provide utilities such as electrical power and running water. Nongovernmental organizations (NGOs) in high-income countries also provide aid. Recently, governments have begun to fund the work of several NGOs.

Despite the benefits that foreign aid programs can bring, certain programs have been criticized for being misdirected and badly implemented. Another criticism is that the aid is sometimes biased toward particular political aims or development paths, given for the political or commercial ends of the donor country, or designed to favour future markets. For example, in the past, donors tended to favour industry over agriculture, and showed a bias toward large-scale projects rather than more basic, but essential, assistance to small-scale producers.

The IMF and the World Bank have been criticized for such large-scale bias. Also, both commonly require recipient countries to cut back on government spending, reduce their trade barriers, and promote competition within their domestic product markets before they can receive further loans. These organizations believe that these types of constraints are necessary to ensure that aid is effectively used. However, critics argue that these requirements often hurt the poorest groups within the low-income countries and represent interference in the internal affairs of independent nations.

BRIEF REVIEW

1. Countries may be classified as high-income, middle-income, and low-income. At one extreme, high-income countries have modern mixed market economies based on capital-intensive production and the use of skilled labour. At the other extreme, low-income countries tend to have traditional mixed economies, use labour-intensive processes, and may have a history of colonialism.
2. Other classifications used are industrially advanced countries, newly industrializing countries, and less-developed countries.
3. While, on average, the economic growth rates of middle- and low-income countries are high, the gap between rich and poor countries continues to widen in dollar terms.
4. Economic development occurs when there is a rise in a country's per capita income accompanied by a general improvement in living standards. It is associated with a structural change from a traditional mixed to a modern mixed economy.
5. In the vicious circle of poverty, low incomes, low investment, and rapid population growth tend to perpetuate labour-intensive processes, which restrains productivity and economic growth and keeps incomes low.
6. Strategies for breaking the circle of poverty include domestic strategies (ensuring political and economic stability, investing in resources, and controlling population) and international strategies (liberalizing trade and foreign aid).

KEY CONCEPTS

exponential growth
Rule of 72
technological progress
research and development expenditures
World Bank
high-income countries
middle-income countries
low-income countries
industrially advanced countries
newly industrializing countries
less-developed countries
economic development
vicious circle of poverty

ANALYSIS AND APPLICATION

1. Binomia produces only milkshakes (a consumer good) and shovels (a capital good). With the aid of a graph, show the effects of each of the following trends on Binomia's production possibilities — both in the present and in the future:
   a. Binomians decide to produce more shovels and fewer milkshakes
   b. more economic resources become available in the Binomian economy
   c. a technological innovation occurs in the production of shovels

2. Calculate the following values with the aid of the Rule of 72:
   a. the number of years it will take a country's real GDP to double if the annual growth rate of real GDP is 1.5 percent
   b. the average annual rate of inflation if the general price level doubles each 27 years
   c. the approximate number of times a country's population will double in a 100 years if the annual growth rate is 3 percent.

3. In Ergonia, 8 million workers produce a real output of $500 billion in 1998 and the same number of workers produce $540 billion in 1999.
   a. Calculate Ergonia's labour productivity in each year.
   b. What is Ergonia's rate of productivity growth between 1998 and 1999?

4. From 1945 to 1973, the growth in Canada's per capita real GDP was relatively high. What were some of the reasons for this impressive performance?

5. Summarize the main advantages of stable democratic government in fostering economic development. Are there any disadvantages associated with this form of government? Explain.

6. Outline the steps whereby a government investment strategy or program of population control can break the vicious circle of poverty in a low-income country.

7. "The greatest contribution industrially advanced countries can make to economic development in low-income countries is through trade liberalization rather than through foreign aid." Discuss.

8. (Advanced Question)
   a. Outline what you consider to be the three most likely sources of economic growth (defined in terms of real GDP) in the Canadian economy over the next decade.
   b. For each source of economic growth you have identified, give an example of a government policy that can promote its performance.

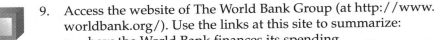

9. Access the website of The World Bank Group (at http://www.worldbank.org/). Use the links at this site to summarize:
   a. how the World Bank finances its spending
   b. the interest rate and average maturity period of World Bank loans
   c. the "graduation process" that determines which countries are eligible for loans

Advancing Economic Thought

MAKING AN ECONOMY GROW

Paul Romer and New Growth Theory

Foreign trade has many spinoffs, one of the most important being the spread of knowledge. Recently, the role of knowledge has been highlighted in economics. Part of this new emphasis is due to the contemporary American economist Paul Romer, whose theory of economy growth is discussed in the following article.

The knowledge economy. Knowledge workers. Knowledge-based industries. Ideas-driven growth. The words trip off the tongue with ease, not just in academic circles but in the mainstream population as well.

These new economic buzzwords reflect the fact that knowledge and ideas have become the vital engines of economic growth. The boom in such fields as computer software, telecommunications, pharmaceuticals, and biotechnology clearly shows that the jobs of the future, and Canada's overall prosperity, depend on wise investments in the new knowledge-based economy.

Paul Romer
Source: Courtesy of Gillian Cosgrove

The brain behind the buzzwords is Paul Romer, an intense, 40-year-old economist who has had a revolutionary impact on economic thinking and, in the process, upset the apple cart of traditional economic theories of growth.

Romer is a professor of economics at the University of California at Berkeley, a visiting fellow at the Hoover Institution, and the Royal Bank Fellow at the Canadian Institute for Advanced Research (CIAR). The praise for Romer's work is lavish and, for him, slightly embarrassing. *The Economist* has said historians will date the revival of growth theory in economics to Romer. The effect of his work has been likened to the intellectual upheavals caused by Adam Smith and John Maynard Keynes.

Romer's New Growth Theory is now widely accepted, but back in 1979, when he was a 25-year-old graduate student at Queen's University in Kingston, Ontario, it was tantamount to claiming the emperor had no clothes. Romer was at Queen's because his wife, Virginia Langmuir of Toronto, was returning to complete her residency as a physician there.

Left alone, with little academic supervision, Romer began to ponder the question that has intrigued economists for decades: what are the causes of long-term growth?

> "One of the features of that year at Queen's was that there was no one to tell me that this is how you have to think about growth," Romer recalls. "So I started, in a sense, from a clean piece of paper

> and said: 'Gee! How should I try to go about understanding this really interesting phenomenon?'
>
> "Economists had built up a relatively sophisticated and productive way of thinking about growth, but we weren't learning much more from that framework. So as much by trial and error as by chance, I started out on a new path."

Traditional economic theory held that growth was the result of two factors of production: labour and capital. But there was a nagging problem with this so-called neoclassical theory: it couldn't explain why Third World countries, given liberal amounts of labour and capital, failed to grow as fast as the industrialized nations.

Romer had the answer: knowledge. He made it the third—and most important—factor of production. By knowledge, he meant new and better ways of doing things, as well as ideas, innovation, invention, and discovery. Knowledge entails taking objects that are relatively worthless and rearranging them in new combinations to create value. For example, the sand on a beach has little value, but turn it into a silicon chip and it becomes immensely valuable.

Another compelling example is Bill Gates. He can walk through a customs barrier anywhere in the world and swear he has nothing to declare when, in fact, his brain carries the multi-billion-dollar secrets of Microsoft, which have made him the wealthiest man on earth.

> "The key issue is to understand knowledge or ideas as economic goods." Romer explains. "Ideas are very different from things. When you're dealing with things, the best institutions to use are prices, free markets and strong property rights."

But you can't just transfer these same governing principles to the market-place of ideas, he says. Objects tend to have relatively fixed costs per unit, while ideas have high upfront costs but low reproduction costs. Developing an idea—say a new piece of software—might take $100 million, while producing a copy of it on a floppy disk can cost less than 50 cents.

This raises the question of how to set the right price for the discovery of an idea. Romer cites the example of polymerase chain reaction (PCR)—a way of getting tiny amounts of DNA to multiply—which won the Nobel Prize in chemistry for Kary Mullis in 1993.

> "At the start, we put a very high price on PCR because it's extremely valuable," Romer says. "But after the idea has been produced, the most efficient thing for society as a whole is to let that idea be freely used by other scientists and researchers in the hope that it will lead to the discovery of more new ideas."

Romer's New Growth Theory seems to have struck a chord with academia and the general public alike, because it carries with it the message of optimism. Traditional economic theory held that since the way of doing things was relatively constant, no matter the capital and labour expended, over time society would get smaller and smaller returns. This was known as the law of diminishing returns. New Growth Theory, by contrast, embraces a law of increasing returns.

To illustrate the mind-boggling opportunities that ideas can generate, Romer uses the example of a manufacturing process in which 20 different parts must be attached to a frame. You could attach them in a given order: part one first, part two second, part three third, etc. Or you may attach them in another order: part one first, then part 20, then part seven, and so on. If you calculate all the possible sequences for attaching those parts, you get 10 to the 18th power, a number that's larger than the total number of seconds that have elapsed since the Big Bang created the universe. So the possibilities out there are virtually limitless.

What lies ahead for Paul Romer? Plenty of different things. At the CIAR, he's descending from the ivory tower and examining practical policy questions about restructuring financial incentives for universities so graduates can find better niches in the knowledge economy.

But this influential economist is, at heart, a loner: "People like me don't work very well in structured environments. A colleague of mine says that trying to work with us (economists) is like trying to herd cats."

Asked about leisure time, he replies with a laugh, "What's that?" And the future? "Oh, more of the same," Romer says. "I'll continue to be an intellectual bomb-thrower."

Indeed.

Source: Gillian Cosgrove, "Knowing about Growing," *Canadian Banker*, (May/June, 1996), pp. 20-22.

1 a. Give an example of a Canadian company that has experienced the increasing returns associated with knowledge.

b. Summarize how the company can benefit from these increasing returns.

2. Does Romer's theory provide an argument for or against free trade? Explain.

LESS INTO MORE

Canada's Productivity Challenge

How can Canadian businesses and governments help overcome the slow growth in labour productivity over the past few decades? The article below highlights the importance of this issue and gives some tentative answers.

Something disturbing is happening in our economy, and, unless we deal with it, we can expect little improvement in our standard of living. This is the continuing weakness in our productivity performance—our slowness to adjust to global economic changes and to become more innovative.

Productivity is the main source of rising living standards, but Canada has stagnated for the past 15 years. The pursuit of strong productivity growth does not have strong public appeal. Many people see productivity improvements as a threat to their jobs although highly productive and innovative companies are more likely to add jobs than to shed them.

Moreover, productivity is often misunderstood. It does not mean forcing workers to work at ever-increasing speed. It is all about innovation—adopting new technologies and putting these new technologies at the disposal of workers, investing in research and development, creating (as Wal-Mart did) new ways of providing services, removing regulatory barriers to competition (as happened in long-distance telephone service), retraining workers, and coming up with new methods of work organization.

At Industry Canada, policy analysts working with Andrei Sulzenko, the assistant deputy minister for industry and science policy, have highlighted our weak productivity performance, the weakest among the G-7 nations, as a critical challenge facing the country.

It's true Canadian companies have been investing more in new technology. The problem is that their competitors in the United States and elsewhere have been investing even more. On average, the executives who run Canadian companies are not as innovative as their U.S. and other foreign competitors.

As a result, productivity in U.S. manufacturing in 1995 was on average 48 percent higher than Canadian manufacturing, the largest gap since 1965, according to Industry Canada. Canada also lost "substantial ground" to other G-7 countries in this period.

Over the past 30 years, according to one analytical paper prepared within Industry Canada, growth in real or inflation-adjusted per capita incomes has been due mainly to three key factors:

- Improvements in productivity, which accounted for about 60 percent of real per capita Gross Domestic Product growth since 1961.
- Rising labour force participation, mainly of women.
- The growth in the labour force as a percentage of the Canadian population, as baby boomers finished school and entered the work force.

Since 1973, productivity growth has slowed significantly. At the same time, the days of rising labour force participation are largely over, while demographic change means there will be fewer new workers each year in the future.

So, as the Industry Canada experts point out, Canada faces a future of little growth in per capita incomes unless we can raise our productivity performance.

In effect, constant innovation has to become a way of life if Canadians want a better life. Conversely, failure to be more innovative will lead to a further decline in Canada, compared to other G-7 countries.

Likewise, poor productivity means governments have less money to spend on health, education, social programs, early childhood development, culture, the environment, and other areas affecting our quality of life.

Industry Canada estimates that if productivity growth had averaged 2 percent a year since 1974, the federal budget would have been in surplus since 1988 and the federal debt would be about 9 percent lower, and this could have been achieved without having to cut public spending.

In other words, the Industry Canada paper says, "the effects of productivity slowdown are

SIDELINE

highly significant," and "continuation of the weak productivity record of the recent past would further aggravate the serious economic and social problems in Canada today."

That's why boosting productivity has to become the front and centre goal of economic policy in Canada.

Source: Abridged from David Crane, "Lack of Innovation Plagues Economy," in *The Toronto Star*, 19 January 1997, p. F2.

1. a. Identify three possible problems that can explain Canada's lacklustre record of productivity growth since 1973.
   b. For each of the problems cited above, outline a government policy that could counteract its effects.
2. What arguments can be made against the policies that are suggested in the article to improve Canada's productivity performance?

GLOSSARY

ability to pay: the principle applied to taxation whereby taxes vary in proportion to a taxpayer's financial resources

absolute advantage: the benefit enjoyed by a producer who can supply a certain quantity of an item more efficiently than can other producers

accounting-profit rate: a measure of a business's profitability, calculated as its accounting profit divided by owner's equity

aggregate demand: the relationship between the general price level and total spending in the economy

aggregate demand curve: the relationship between the general price level and total spending in the economy expressed on a graph

aggregate demand factors: variables that cause changes in total expenditures at all price levels

aggregate demand schedule: the relationship between the general price level and total spending in the economy expressed in a table

aggregate supply: the relationship between the general price level and real output produced in the economy

aggregate supply curve: the relationship between the general price level and real output expressed on a graph

aggregate supply factors: variables that change total output at all price levels

aggregate supply schedule: the relationship between the general price level and real output expressed in a table

annually balanced budget: the principle that government revenues and expenditures should balance each year

appreciate: to increase, as when a currency's price rises in comparison to the price of another currency

arbitration: the process of having an outside party determine and dictate a settlement to employers and unions

asset demand: the demand for money that is related to its use as a store of purchasing power

Auto Pact: the 1965 agreement establishing free trade in autos and auto parts between Canada and the United States; formerly known as the Canada–U.S. Automotive Products Agreement

automatic stabilizers: built-in measures, such as taxation and transfer payment programs, that lessen the effects of the business cycle

average cost: the sum of average fixed cost and average variable cost at each quantity of output

average-cost pricing: the practice of setting price where it equals average cost

average fixed cost: the fixed cost per unit of output

average product: the quantity of output produced per worker

average revenue: a business's total revenue per unit of output

average variable cost: the variable cost per unit of output

balance-of-payments accounts: a summary of all transactions between Canadians and foreigners that involve exchanging Canadian dollars for other currencies

balance-of-payments deficit: a negative net balance on the balance-of-payments statement, demonstrating lower receipts than payments for the current and capital accounts combined; balanced with changes in official reserves

balance-of-payments surplus: a positive net balance on the balance-of-payments statement, demonstrating greater receipts than payments for the current and capital accounts combined; balanced with changes in official reserves

balance of trade: for both goods and services, receipts (inflows of Canadian dollars) less payments (outflows of Canadian dollars)

balanced budget: the situation where a government's expenditures and revenues are equal

bank rate: the interest rate CPA members are charged on advances from the Bank of Canada

barter: a system of trading one product for another

base year: the survey year used as a point of comparison in subsequent years

benefits received: the principle applied to taxation whereby taxes are geared to the benefits each taxpayer gains from government activity

bond: a contract between a borrower and the holder of the contract that entitles the holder to interest plus repayment at the maturity date

breakeven point: the profit-maximizing output where price (or average revenue) equals average cost

budget deficit: the situation where a government's expenditures exceed its revenues

budget surplus: the situation where a government's revenues exceed its expenditures

business: an enterprise that brings individuals, financial resources, and economic resources together to produce a good or service for economic gain

business cycle: the cycle of expansions and contractions in the economy

business's demand curve: the demand curve faced by an individual business, as opposed to an entire market

business's labour demand curve: a graph showing the possible combinations of workers demanded by a business at each possible wage

business's labour supply curve: a graph showing the possible combinations of workers supplied to a business at each possible wage

business's supply curve: a curve that shows the quantity of output supplied by a business at every possible price

Canada Savings Bonds: federal government bonds that have a set value throughout their term

capital account: the summary of all international transactions of financial assets involving Canadian dollars

capital account deficit: a negative net balance in the capital account, demonstrating higher investments by Canadians in foreign markets than by foreigners in the Canadian economy

capital account surplus: a positive net balance in the capital account, demonstrating lower investments by Canadians in foreign markets than by foreigners in the Canadian economy

capital gains: earnings from selling an asset, such as land, at a higher price than it was purchased for

capital-intensive process: a production process that employs more capital and less labour

capital resources: the processed materials, equipment, and buildings used in production; also known as capital

capital stock: the total value of productive assets that provide a flow of revenue

cartel: a union of oligopolists who have a formal market-sharing agreement

cash reserves: funds kept on hand by deposit-takers to meet the needs of depositors withdrawing funds

ceteris paribus: the assumption that all other things remain the same

change in official reserves: use of the government's reserves of foreign currency to influence the international value of the Canadian dollar, as shown on the balance-of-payments statement

change in quantity demanded: the effect of a price change on quantity demanded

change in quantity supplied: the effect of a price change on quantity supplied

chartered banks: deposit-takers allowed by federal charter to offer a wide range of financial services

closed shop: a specific labour market in which all workers covered by a collective agreement must be union members

coincidence of wants: the situation where someone purchasing an item finds a seller who wants what the purchaser is offering in return

collateral: assets pledged by a borrower as security against a loan; these assets can be seized by the lender if the loan is not repaid

collective bargaining: the process of union representatives negotiating with employers over workers' wages, hours, and working conditions

collusion: oligopolists acting together as if they are a monopoly

command economy: an economic system based on public ownership and central planning

common market: a group of countries with not only a free trade area and common trade barriers with outside countries, but also free movement of labour and capital

comparative advantage: the benefit enjoyed by a producer who can supply a certain item with a lower opportunity cost than can other producers

complementary goods: products that are consumed together

complementary resources: resources that are used together

concentration ratio: the percentage of total sales revenue earned by the largest businesses in a market

constant-cost industry: an industry that is not a major user of any single resource

constant returns to scale: a situation in which a percentage increase in all inputs results in an equal percentage increase in output

consumer price index: a measure of price changes for a typical basket of consumer products

consumer sovereignty: the effect of consumer needs and wants on production decisions

contraction: a sustained fall in real output of an economy

contractionary fiscal policy: government policy that involves decreasing government purchases, increasing taxes, or both to restrain spending and output

contractionary monetary policy: a policy of decreasing the money supply and increasing interest rates to dampen the economy

contractionary policies: government policies designed to stabilize prices and reduce output

corporation: a company that has a legal status independent of its owners

cost of living: the amount consumers must spend on the entire range of goods and services they buy

cost-of-living adjustment clauses: provisions for income adjustments to accommodate changes in price levels, which are included in wage contracts

cost-push inflation: inflation that occurs as increased production costs decrease aggregate supply, which then pushes up prices

craft union: a labour union of workers in a particular occupation

credit card: a means of payment that provides instantly borrowed funds

credit risk: the assessed likelihood of a borrower not repaying a loan

crowding-out effect: the effect of more government borrowing raising interest rates, which reduces or "crowds out" private investment spending

currency: paper money and coins

current account: the summary of all foreign transactions associated with current economic activity in Canada and involving Canadian dollars

current account deficit: a negative net balance in the current account resulting from lower receipts than payments for merchandise and nonmerchandise transactions

current account surplus: a positive net balance in the current account resulting from higher receipts than payments for merchandise and nonmerchandise transactions

customs union: a group of countries with common trade barriers with outside countries as well as a free trade area

cyclical unemployment: unemployment due to the ups and downs of economies and businesses

cyclically balanced budget: the principle that government revenues and expenditures should balance over the course of one business cycle

debit card: a means of payment that instantaneously transfers funds from buyer to seller

decision lag: the amount of time needed to formulate and implement an appropriate policy

decrease in aggregate demand: a decrease in total expenditures at all price levels

decrease in demand: a decrease in the quantity demanded of a product at all prices

decrease in supply: a decrease in the quantity supplied of a product at all prices

decreasing returns to scale: a situation in which a percentage increase in all inputs causes a smaller percentage increase in output

deflation: a general decrease in the level of prices

demand: the relationship between the various possible prices of a product and the quantities of that product consumers are willing to purchase

demand curve: a graph that expresses possible combinations of prices and quantities demanded of a product

demand deposits: accounts of funds to which depositors have immediate access

demand determinants: factors that can cause an increase or a decrease in a product's demand

demand for Canadian dollars: the relationship between the price of a Canadian dollar and the quantity demanded in exchange for another currency

demand-pull inflation: inflation that occurs as increased aggregate demand pulls up prices

demand schedule: a table that shows possible combinations of prices and quantities demanded of a product

dependent variable: the variable in a causal relationship that is affected by another variable

deposit-takers: institutions or businesses that accept funds provided by savers and lend these funds to borrowers

depreciate: to decrease, as when a currency's price falls in comparison to the price of another currency

depreciation: the decrease in value of durable real assets over time

depression: a particularly long and harsh period of reduced real output

desired reserves: minimum cash reserves that deposit-takers hold to satisfy anticipated withdrawal demands

devaluation: a reduction in the value of a currency by the government that sets the exchange rate

direct investment: financial investment (purchases of stocks) that gives the buyer of the financial assets a controlling interest in the institution issuing the assets

direct relationship: a relationship in which a change in the independent variable causes a change in the same direction of the dependent variable

discouraged workers: unemployed workers who have given up looking for work

discretionary policy: intentional government intervention in the economy, such as budgeted changes in spending or taxation

disposable income: household income minus personal taxes and other personal transfers to government

double counting: the problem of adding to GDP the same item at different stages in its production

durable goods: goods that are consumed repeatedly over time

economic costs: a business's total explicit and implicit costs

economic development: an increase in a country's per capita income that is accompanied by a general rise in living standards

economic efficiency: employing scarce resources in such a way as to derive the highest benefit

economic growth: an increase in an economy's total output of goods and services

economic models: generalizations about or simplifications of economic reality; also known as laws, principles, or theories

economic problem: the problem of having unlimited wants, but limited resources with which to satisfy them

economic profit: the excess of a business's total revenue over its economic costs

economic resources: basic items that are used in all types of production, including natural, capital, and human resources

economic system: the organization of an economy, which represents a country's distinct set of social customs, political institutions, and economic practices

economics: the study of how to distribute scarce resources among alternative ends

elastic demand: demand for which a percentage change in a product's price causes a larger percentage change in quantity demanded

elastic supply: supply for which a percentage change in a product's price causes a larger percentage change in quantity supplied

entrepreneurship: initiative, risk-taking, and innovation necessary for production

entry barriers: economic or institutional obstacles to businesses entering an industry

equation of exchange: the money supply multiplied by the velocity of money equals the price level multiplied by real output

European Union (EU): an expanding common market of European countries first formed in 1956, formerly known as the European Economic Community (EEC)

excess reserves: cash reserves that are in excess of desired reserves

exchange rate: the value of one nation's currency in terms of another currency

excise taxes: taxes that are charged on particular products, and often expressed as a dollar amount per unit of quantity

expansion: a sustained rise in real output of an economy

expansionary fiscal policy: government policy that involves increasing government purchases, decreasing taxes, or both to stimulate spending and output

expansionary monetary policy: a policy of increasing the money supply and reducing interest rates to stimulate the economy

expansionary policies: government policies designed to reduce unemployment and stimulate output

expenditure approach: a method of calculating Gross Domestic Product by adding together all spending in the economy

expenditure equation: the equation that states that GDP is the sum of personal consumption (C), gross investment (I), government purchases (G), and net exports (X – M)

explicit costs: payments made by a business to businesses or people outside of it

exponential growth: growth that is based on a percentage change and that builds on itself

export subsidies: payments by a government to domestic exporters so that these exporters can reduce the prices they charge in foreign markets

exports: foreign purchases of Canadian goods and services

fair rate of return: the maximum accounting-profit rate allowed for a regulated monopoly

final products: products that will not be processed further and will not be resold

financial capital: assets in the form of cash, bonds, and shares

fiscal policy: government stabilization policy that uses taxes and government purchases as its tools; budgetary policy

fiscal year: the twelve-month period to which a budget applies

fixed costs: economic costs for inputs that remain fixed at all quantities of output

fixed exchange rates: currency exchange rates set or

"pegged" to a certain value by each country's government

fixed incomes: nominal incomes that remain fixed at some dollar amount regardless of the rate of inflation

fixed inputs: inputs whose quantities cannot be adjusted in the short run

flexible exchange rates: currency exchange rates that are allowed to move freely to their equilibrium levels; also called floating rates

foreign currency deposits: accounts of funds held by Canadian residents that are valued in foreign currency

foreign exchange market: the global market in which national currencies are traded

foreign trade effect: with changes in the price level, expenditures on imports change in the same direction, while expenditures on exports change in the opposite direction

Free Trade Agreement (FTA): the 1988 pact between Canada and the United States to form a free trade area

free trade area: an area in which trade is tariff-free, although member countries are able to impose separate trade barriers on outside countries

frictional unemployment: unemployment due to being temporarily between jobs or looking for a first job

full employment: the highest reasonable expectation of employment for the economy as a whole

fully indexed incomes: nominal incomes that automatically increase by the rate of inflation

functional finance: the principle that government budgets should be geared to the yearly needs of the economy

GDP deflator: an indicator of price changes for all goods and services produced in the economy

GDP identity: Gross Domestic Product calculated as total income is identical to Gross Domestic Product calculated as total spending

General Agreement on Tariffs and Trade (GATT): a multilateral trade agreement that lessened the degree of trade protection among member countries, including Canada

globalization: the trend of growing foreign trade and investment and the spread of international businesses and markets

government purchases: current government spending on goods and services

Gross Domestic Product: the total dollar value at current prices of all final goods and services produced in Canada over a given period

gross investment: purchases of assets that are intended to produce revenue

Gross National Product: the total income acquired by Canadians both within Canada and elsewhere

high-income countries: countries with per capita incomes substantial enough to provide their citizens with widespread prosperity

human capital: the income-earning potential of a person's skills and knowledge

immediate run: the production period during which none of the resources required to make a product can be varied

impact lag: the amount of time between a policy's implementation and its having an effect on the economy

implicit costs: the owner's opportunity costs of being involved with a business

import quota: a set limit on the quantity of a good that can be imported in a given year

imports: Canadian purchases of goods and services from the rest of the world

income approach: a method of calculating Gross Domestic Product by adding together all incomes in the economy

increase in aggregate demand: an increase in total expenditures at all price levels

increase in demand: an increase in the quantity demanded of a product at all prices

increase in supply: an increase in the quantity supplied of a product at all prices

increasing-cost industry: an industry that is a major user of at least one resource

increasing returns to scale: a situation in which a percentage increase in all inputs causes a larger percentage increase in output

independent variable: the variable in a causal relationship that causes change in another variable

industrial concentration: market domination by one or a few large businesses

industrial union: a labour union of workers in a certain industry, no matter what their occupations

industrially advanced countries (IACs): countries that have a high degree of industrialization

inelastic demand: demand for which a percentage change in a product's price causes a smaller percentage change in quantity demanded

inelastic supply: supply for which the percentage change in a product's price causes a smaller percentage change in quantity supplied

infant industry: a domestic industry that is young in comparison to its foreign competitors

inferior goods: products whose demand changes inversely with income

inflation: a rise in the general level of prices

inflation premium: a percentage built into a nominal interest rate to anticipate the rate of inflation for the loan period

inflationary gap: the amount by which equilibrium output exceeds potential output

injections: additions to an economy's income-spending stream

inputs: the resources used in production

interest: the payment to a lender by the borrower for use of money loaned

interest rate: the percentage rate with which interest on loans is determined

intermediate products: products that will be processed further or will be resold

inventories: stocks of unsold goods and materials

inverse relationship: a relationship in which a change in the independent variable causes a change in the opposite direction of the dependent variable

investment demand: the relationship between interest rates and investment

investment demand curve: the relationship between interest rates and investment expressed on a graph

investment demand schedule: the relationship between interest rates and investment expressed in a table

item weights: the proportions of each good in the total cost of the basket of consumer goods used to calculate CPI

job discrimination: hiring, wage, and promotion decisions based on criteria other than a worker's credentials or performance

job segregation: the discriminatory division of occupations

kinked demand curve: a demand curve with two segments, one fairly flat and one steep, that is typical of rival oligopolists

labour: human effort employed directly in production

labour force: all people who either have a job or are actively seeking employment

labour force population: the population, with specific exclusions, from which Statistics Canada takes a random sample for the labour force survey

labour-intensive process: a production process that employs more labour and less capital

labour market demand curve: a graph showing the possible combinations of workers demanded in a certain labour market at each possible wage

labour market supply curve: a graph showing the possible combinations of workers supplying their labour in a certain labour market at each possible wage

Laffer curve: a curve that expresses the assumed relationship between tax rates and tax revenues

laissez faire: the principle that governments benefit society the most by not interfering in economic activity

law of comparative advantage: states that maximum output is achieved when producers specialize in what they can make at a lower opportunity cost than can other producers

law of demand: states that there is an inverse relationship between a product's quantity demanded and its price

law of diminishing marginal returns: at some point, as more units of a variable input are added to a fixed input, the marginal product will start to decrease

law of increasing opportunity costs: the concept that as more of one item is produced by an economy, the opportunity cost of additional units of that product rises

law of supply: states that there is a direct relationship between a product's quantity supplied and its price

less-developed countries (LDCs): countries with traditional mixed economies and low per capita incomes

liquidity: the ease with which an asset can be converted into a means of payment

loanable funds: all the monies made available to lenders by borrowers

lockout: the employer tactic of barring workers from the workplace

long run: the production period during which all resources required to make a product can be varied, and businesses may either enter or leave the industry

long-run average cost: the minimum short-run average cost at each possible level of output

long-run decrease in aggregate supply: a decrease in total and potential output at all price levels

long-run increase in aggregate supply: an increase in total and potential output at all price levels

Lorenz curve: a graph showing the cumulative distribution of income among a country's households

low-income countries: the poorest countries in the world, as defined by per capita incomes

M1: the narrowest definition of money, consisting of currency outside chartered banks and publicly held demand deposits at chartered banks

M2: a broader definition of money, consisting of M1 plus notice deposits, and personal term deposits at chartered banks

M2+: the definition of money consisting of M2 plus corresponding deposits at near banks and some other liquid assets

M3: the definition of money consisting of M2 plus nonpersonal term deposits and foreign currency deposits at chartered banks

macroeconomics: the branch of economics that takes a wide-ranging view of the economy, studying the behaviour of economic sectors

managed float: a flexible exchange rate system that sometimes involves short-term government intervention

marginal cost: the extra cost of producing an additional unit of output

marginal-cost pricing: the practice of setting price where it equals marginal cost

marginal product: the extra output produced by an additional worker

marginal productivity theory: the theory that businesses use resources based on how much extra profit these resources provide

marginal propensity to consume: the effect on domestic consumption of a change in income

marginal propensity to withdraw: the effect on withdrawals—saving, imports, and taxes—of a change in income

marginal resource cost: the extra cost of each additional unit of a resource

marginal revenue: the extra total revenue earned from an additional unit of output

marginal revenue product: the change in total revenue associated with employing each new unit of a resource

marginal tax rates: tax rates that are calculated as percentages of each extra dollar of taxable income

market: a set of arrangements between buyers and sellers of a certain item

market demand: the sum of all consumers' quantity demanded for a product at each price

market economy: an economic system based on private ownership and the use of markets in economic decision-making

market equilibrium: the stable point at which demand and supply curves intersect

market power: a business's ability to affect the price of the product it sells

market share: a business's proportion of total market sales

market supply: the sum of all producers' quantity supplied at each price

means testing: a procedure whereby transfer payments vary according to a recipient's income

mediation: the process of having an outside party determine and propose a settlement to employers and unions

merchandise balance of trade: merchandise export receipts minus merchandise import payments

microeconomics: the branch of economics that focuses on the behaviour of individual participants in various markets

middle-income countries: countries in which a sizable minority of the population no longer lives in acute poverty

minimum-cost pricing: the practice of setting price where it equals minimum average cost

modern mixed economy: an economic system that combines aspects of a market economy and a command economy; production decisions are made both in private markets and by government

monetarism: an economic perspective that emphasizes the influence of money on the economy and the ability of private markets to accommodate change

monetary policy: government stabilization policy that uses interest rates and the money supply as its tools

monetary rule: a law that forces the central bank to increase the money supply by a constant rate each year

money demand: the amounts of money demanded at all possible interest rates

money demand curve: money demand expressed in a graph

money demand schedule: money demand expressed in a table

money multiplier: the value by which the amount of excess reserves is multiplied to give the maximum total change in money supply

money supply: a set amount of money in the economy, as determined by government decision-makers

money supply curve: money supply expressed in a graph

money supply schedule: money supply expressed in a table

monopolistic competition: a market structure characterized by many buyers and sellers of slightly different products and easy entry to, and exit from, the industry

monopoly: a market structure characterized by only one business supplying a product with no close substitutes and restricted entry to the industry

multiplier effect: the magnified impact of a spending change on aggregate demand

mutual interdependence: the relationship between oligopolists, in which the actions of each business affect the other businesses

national income accounts: accounts showing the levels of total income and spending in the Canadian economy

National Policy: a Canadian policy initiated in 1879 that included high Canadian tariffs on manufactured imports in order to stimulate a domestic manufacturing sector

natural monopoly: a market in which only one business is economically viable because of economies of scale

natural resources: the resources from nature that are used in production, including land, raw materials, and natural processes

natural unemployment rate: the unemployment rate that defines full employment

near banks: deposit-takers that are not chartered and have more specialized services; mainly trust companies, mortgage loan companies, and credit unions

near money: all deposits not included in M1, plus some other highly liquid assets

negative unplanned investment: an unintended decrease in inventories; a shortage

net domestic income: the total income earned by Canada's households

net exports: exports minus imports

net investment: gross investment minus depreciation

net tax revenues: taxes collected, minus transfers and subsidies

newly industrializing countries (NICs): countries that recently have exhibited strong economic growth and rapid industrialization

nominal GDP: Gross Domestic Product expressed in current dollars

nominal income: income expressed in current dollars

nominal interest rate: the interest rate expressed in money terms

nondurable goods: goods that are consumed just once

nonmarket activities: productive activities that take place outside the marketplace

nonprice competition: efforts to increase demand through product differentiation, advertising, or both

non-tariff barriers (NTBs): trade barriers other than tariffs that are used to restrict imports; include import quotas, voluntary export restraints, and domestic regulations

normal goods: products whose demand changes directly with income

normal profit: the minimum return necessary for owners to keep funds and their entrepreneurial skills in their business

normative economics: the study of how the economy ought to operate

North American Free Trade Agreement (NAFTA): the 1993 pact among Canada, the United States, and Mexico to form a free trade area

notice deposits: accounts of funds for which deposit-takers may require notice before withdrawals can be made

oligopoly: a market structure characterized by only a few businesses offering standard or similar products and restricted entry to the industry

open market operations: the buying and selling of bonds by the Bank of Canada

open shop: a specific labour market in which union membership is not compulsory

opportunity cost: the utility that could have been gained by choosing an action's best alternative

output: the quantity of a good or service that results from production

overnight rate: the interest rate on overnight loans between chartered banks and other financial institutions

partially indexed incomes: nominal incomes that increase by less than the rate of inflation

participation rate: the percentage of the entire labour force population that makes up the labour force

partnership: an unincorporated business that is owned by two or more people

peak: the point in the business cycle at which real output is at its highest

per capita GDP: GDP per person, calculated as GDP divided by population

per capita real GDP: GDP per person, expressed in constant dollars from a given year

perfect competition: a market structure characterized by many buyers and sellers of a standard product and easy entry to and exit from the industry

perfectly elastic demand: demand for which a product's

price remains constant regardless of quantity demanded

perfectly elastic supply: supply for which a product's price remains constant regardless of quantity supplied

perfectly inelastic demand: demand for which a product's quantity demanded remains constant regardless of price

perfectly inelastic supply: supply for which a product's quantity supplied remains constant regardless of price

personal consumption: household spending on goods and services

personal income: the income actually received by households

personal saving: funds saved by households

Phillips curve: a curve expressing the assumed fixed and predictable inverse relationship between unemployment and inflation

picketing: the practice of striking workers taking positions around the outside of the workplace, usually with signs, to publicize their cause to others

portfolio investment: financial investment (purchases of stocks and bonds) that does not give the buyer a controlling interest in the institution issuing the assets

positive economics: the study of economic facts and how the economy operates as it does

positive unplanned investment: an unintended increase in inventories; a surplus

potential output: the real output, or Gross Domestic Product, associated with full employment

poverty: a situation in which a person's income is inadequate to provide the necessities of life

poverty line: an income level below which a household is classified as poor

predatory pricing: an unfair business practice of temporarily lowering prices to drive out competitors in an industry

price ceiling: a maximum price set below equilibrium

price elasticity of demand: the responsiveness of a product's quantity demanded to a change in its price

price elasticity of supply: the responsiveness of a product's quantity supplied to a change in price

price floor: a minimum price set above equilibrium

price leadership: an understanding among oligopolists that one business will initiate all price changes in the market and the others will follow by adjusting their prices and output accordingly

prime rate: the lowest possible interest rate charged by deposit-takers on loans to their best corporate customers

principal: the amount of a loan, excluding interest

product differentiation: efforts to make a product distinct from that of competitors

product markets: markets in which consumer, or final, products are traded

production: the process of transforming a set of resources into a good or service that has economic value

production possibilities curve: a graph that illustrates the possible output combinations for an economy

production possibilities schedule: a table that shows the possible output combinations for an economy

productive efficiency: making a given quantity of output at the lowest cost

profit-maximizing employment rule: a business should use a resource up to the point where the resource's marginal revenue product equals its marginal resource cost

profit-maximizing output rule: produce at the level of output where marginal revenue and marginal cost intersect

progressive tax: a tax that increases as a proportion of income as income increases

proportional tax: a tax that remains constant as a proportion of income for all incomes

public debt: the total amount owed by the federal government as a result of its past borrowing

public debt charges: the amounts paid out each year by the federal government to cover the interest charges on its public debt

public good: a product whose benefits cannot be restricted to certain individuals

quantity demanded: the amount of a product consumers are willing to purchase at each price

quantity supplied: the amount of a product businesses are willing to supply at each price

quantity theory of money: a theory stating that the velocity of money and real output are relatively stable over short periods

real capital: assets such as buildings, equipment, and materials used by businesses to produce goods and services

real expenditures: total spending in an economy, adjusted for changes in the general price level

real GDP: GDP expressed in constant dollars from a given year

real income: income expressed in constant base-year dollars

real interest rate: the nominal interest rate minus the rate of inflation

real rate of return: constant-dollar extra profit provided by a project each year stated as a percentage of the project's initial cost

recession: a decline in real output that lasts for six months or more

recessionary gap: the amount by which equilibrium output falls short of potential output

recognition lag: the amount of time it takes policy-makers to realize that a policy is needed

regressive tax: a tax that decreases as a proportion of income as income increases

rent: the payment for use of a productive resource that is available only in a fixed amount

research and development expenditures (R&D): spending that is meant to accelerate the pace of technological progress

reserve ratio: desired reserves expressed as a percentage of deposits or as a decimal

resource markets: markets in which economic resources are traded

retained earnings: profits kept by businesses for new investment

revaluation: an increase in the value of a currency by the government that sets the exchange rate

Rule of 72: states that the number of years it takes a variable to double can be estimated by dividing 72 by the variable's annual percentage growth rate

sales taxes: taxes that are charged on a wide range of products, and calculated as a percentage of their prices

seasonal unemployment: unemployment due to the seasonal nature of some occupations and industries

self-interest motive: the assumption that people act to maximize their own welfare

seniority rights: the workplace privileges provided to workers who have the longest experience with their employer

share: partial ownership of a corporation, which entitles the shareholder to dividends and, hopefully, a profit once the share is sold; also called a stock

short run: the production period during which at least one of the resources required to make a product cannot be varied

short-run decrease in aggregate supply: a decrease in total output at all price levels, with no change in potential output

short-run increase in aggregate supply: an increase in total output at all price levels, with no change in potential output

shortage: an excess of quantity demanded over quantity supplied

shutdown point: the level of output where price (or average revenue) equals minimum average variable cost

sole proprietorship: an unincorporated business that is owned by a single person

speculators: individuals or organizations that buy and sell currencies for profit

spending multiplier: the value by which an initial spending change is multiplied to give the total change in real output

spillover benefits: positive external effects of producing or consuming a product

spillover costs: negative external effects of producing or consuming a product

spillover effects: external effects of economic activity, which have an impact on outsiders who are not producing or consuming a product

stabilization policy: government policy designed to lessen the effects of the business cycle

stagflation: a combination of consistently low output (and so constant or expanding unemployment) and rising inflation

strategic trade policy: the use of programs such as export subsidies to help domestic producers enter potentially lucrative markets

strike: the union tactic of members ceasing to work

structural unemployment: unemployment due to a mismatch between people and jobs

substitute goods: products that can be consumed in place of one another

substitute resources: resources that can be used in place of one another without affecting output

supply: the relationship between the various possible prices of a product and the quantities of the product that businesses are willing to supply

supply curve: a graph that expresses possible combinations of prices and quantities supplied of a product

supply determinants: factors that can cause an increase or a decrease in a product's supply

supply of Canadian dollars: the relationship between the price of a Canadian dollar and the quantity supplied in exchange for another currency

supply schedule: a table that shows possible combinations of prices and quantities supplied of a product

supply-side economics: the view that adjustments in aggregate supply are the most critical element of government activity

surplus: an excess of quantity supplied over quantity demanded

tariff: an excise tax on imported goods

tax: a payment required by government from individuals or businesses, with no direct good or service being provided in return

technological progress: consists of scientific discoveries and their application, advances in production methods, and the development of new types of products

term deposits: accounts of funds to which depositors have no access for a fixed period of time

terms of trade: the international price of one product in terms of another

total cost: the sum of all fixed and variable costs at each quantity of output

total product: the overall quantity of output produced with a given workforce

total revenue: the total income earned from a product, calculated by multiplying the product's price by its quantity demanded

trading bloc: a relatively small number of countries involved in a trade agreement

traditional economy: an economic system in which economic decisions are made on the basis of custom

traditional mixed economies: economic systems in which a traditional sector co-exists with modern sectors

transactions demand: the demand for money that is related to its use as a means of exchange

transfer payments: government payments to households or other levels of government

treasury bills: short-term federal government bonds that provide no interest, but are sold at a discount

trough: the point in the business cycle at which real output is at its lowest

underemployment: the problem of workers being underutilized, either as part-time workers or by working at jobs not appropriate to their skills or education

underground economy: all the market transactions that go unreported

unemployment rate: the percentage of a labour force that is involuntarily unemployed

union shop: a specific labour market in which all workers covered by a collective agreement must become union members after a certain period of employment

unit-elastic demand: demand for which a percentage change in price causes an equal change in quantity demanded

unit of account: a pricing standard that allows all products to be valued consistently

universality: the principle applied to transfer payments whereby benefits are provided to all, regardless of income

utility: the satisfaction gained from any action

value added: the extra worth of a product at each stage in its production; a concept used to avoid double counting in calculating GDP

variable costs: economic costs for inputs that vary at each quantity of output

variable inputs: inputs whose quantities can be adjusted in the short run

variables: factors that have measurable values

velocity of money: the number of times, on average, that money is spent on final goods and services during a given year (a concept that is central to monetarism)

vicious circle of poverty: a cycle whereby low standards of living result in slow growth, thus keeping standards of living low in the future

voluntary export restraints (VERs): import quotas that are voluntarily put in place by the exporting country

wage: the amount earned by a worker for providing labour for a certain period of time

controls: government-imposed restrictions on wage and price increases

wage and price guidelines: voluntary restrictions on wage and price increases

wealth: ownership of financial assets, such as stocks and bonds, or real assets, such as buildings and land

wealth effect: with changes in the price level, the real value of households' financial assets changes, causing households to adjust their spending

welfare society: a society in which the government plays a major role in attempting to ensure the economic well-being of its citizens

withdrawals: deductions from an economy's income-spending stream

working to rule: the union tactic of members slowing down work by adhering strictly to their job descriptions

World Bank: an international lending institution known officially as the International Bank for Reconstruction and Development

World Trade Organization (WTO): a multilateral trade organization that has replaced GATT

INDEX

Absolute advantage, 449
Accounting-profit rate, 152
Advertising, 112–13, 119
  as entry barrier, 112–13
  in nonprice competition, 119
  top ten advertisers, 120
Aggregate demand, 33–36, 299–300
  changes in, 33–36, 301–306
  and consumption, 301–302
  decrease in, 301
  definition of, 299
  and disposable income, 302
  and equilibrium, 312
  factors, 301
  and fiscal policy, 333–35
  and foreign trade effect, 300
  and government spending, 304
  increase in, 301
  and interest rates, 302, 304
  and investment, 303–304
  and net exports, 305–306
  shifts in, 306
  and wealth, 299–300
Aggregate demand curve, 299–300
Aggregate demand schedule, 299
Aggregate supply, 37–40, 307–308
  changes in, 37–40, 308–309
  definition of, 307
  and equilibrium, 312
  factors, 308
  and government policy, 310
  and input prices, 308
  long-run decrease in, 309
  long-run increase in, 309
  and productivity, 309–10
  and resources, 308
  short-run decrease in, 308
  short-run increase in, 308
Aggregate supply curve, 307–308
Aggregate supply schedule, 307
Agriculture:
  price supports in, 63–66
    effects of, 65
Annually balanced budget, 346
Anti-combines legislation in Canada, 131–32
Appreciate, 423
Arbitration, of labour disputes, 184
Assumptions, 6
  ceteris paribus, 6
  role of, 28
Auto Pact, 464
Automatic stabilizers, 335
Average cost, 90–98
  definition of, 93
  fixed, 92–93
  long-run, 96–97, 98
  short-run, 90–94
  variable, 92–93
Average-cost pricing, 152
Average product, 86, 88–89

B

Balance of payments, 413–19
  Canada, 418
  capital account, 416–17
  capital account balance, 417
  capital account deficit, 417
  capital account surplus, 417
  current account, 413–15
  current account balance, 415
  current account deficit, 415
  current account surplus, 415
  nonmerchandise transactions, 414
Balance-of-payment accounts, 18, 413
  definition of, 18
Balance-of-payments deficit, 418–19
Balance-of-payments surplus, 418–19
Balance of trade, 415–16
Balance sheet, 106
Balanced budget, 344
  annually, 346
  cyclically, 346
Bank of Canada, 388–90, 393–95, 419
  and the bank rate, 389, 396
  change in official reserves, 419
  and federal government deposits, 395
  functions of, 388–90
    bankers' bank, 388
    ensuring stability of financial markets, 390
    federal government's fiscal agent, 389
    managing money supply, 388
  and open market operations, 393–94
Bank rate, 389, 396
Banks, 362–64. *See also* Bank of Canada; Money
  chartered banks, 362–63
  near banks, 363
Barter, 361
Beck, Nuala, 180–83
Bonds, 200, 389, 393, 394
Breakeven point, 138
Bretton Woods system, 430–31
Budget deficit, 344–45, 348
  in Canada, 345
  and fiscal policy, 344–46
  and public debt, 345
Budget surplus, 344–45
  and fiscal policy, 344–46
  and public debt, 345
Business:
  expectations, 304
  performance, 106–108
  and nonprice competition, 119–20
Business closure, 138–39
Business cycle, 317–20
  contraction of, 317–19
  depression, 318
  expansion of, 317, 319–20
  recession, 318
  stabilizing, 332–33
  troughs, 319

Business organizations, 81–82
corporations, 81, 82
definition of, 81
expectations, 304
partnerships, 81, 82
sole proprietorships, 81, 82

C

Canada Pension Plan, 222
Canada Savings Bonds, 389
Canada-U.S. Free Trade Agreement, 464–65
Canadian banking system, 362–63, 373–78, 388–90
and Bank of Canada, 388–90
chartered banks, 362–63
and money creation, 373–78
near banks, 363
Capital account, 416–17
Capital account balance, 417
Capital account deficit, 417
Capital account surplus, 417
Canadian financial system, 362–64
Capital, financial, 200
Capital gains, 228
Capital, real, 200
Capital stock, 253, 254
Cartel, 130–31. *See also* Organization of Petroleum Exporting Countries (OPEC)
Ceteris paribus, 6
Chartered banks, 362–63
Child Tax Credit payment, 222
Circular flow, 13, 255–56
in financial markets, 255
and foreign markets, 256
and government spending, 255
and measuring GDP, 256
with product markets, 13,
with resource markets, 13
Coincidence of wants, 361
Collateral, 203–204
Collective bargaining, 184
Collusion, 118
Common market, 463–64
Communications theory, 471–72
Comparative advantage, law of, 450
Competition, 119–20, 131–32
and market economy, 13
nonprice, 119–20
and business, 119–20
and the consumer, 120
Composite Index of Leading Indicators (Statistics Canada), 329–30
Complementary resources, 173–74
Concentration ratio, 121–22
Constant-cost industry, 62
Constant returns to scale, 95
Consumer expectations, 35, 302
Consumer preferences, 35
Consumer Price Index (CPI), 272–74
base year, 273
definition of, 272
item weights, 273
limitations of, 274–75
Consumer sovereignty, 13
Consumption, 253
Controls, price, 63–67
Controls, rent, 66–67
Corn Laws, 209
Corporations, 81–82
Cost of living, 274
Cost of living adjustment (COLA) clauses, 278
Costs of the business, 82–84, 85–89, 90–98
average, 93
average fixed, 92–93
average variable, 92–93
fixed, 90
in the long run, 96–97, 98
marginal, 91–92
per-unit, 92–94
in the short run, 90–94
total, 90
variable, 90
Craft union, 192–93
Credit risk, 203
Critical thinking, xi–xiv
Cultural sovereignty, 459
Currency, 364
Current account, 413–15
Current account balance, 415
Current account deficit, 415
Current account surplus, 415
Customs union, 463
Cyclical unemployment, 284
Cyclically balanced budget, 346

D

Debit cards, 367–68
Decision lag, 342
Decreasing returns to scale, 95–96
Deflation, 272
Demand. *See* Aggregate demand; Demand curve
changes (shifts) in, 34–36, 42–43
decrease in, 34
definition of, 31
determinants, 34
elasticity of, 54–59
increase in, 34
law of, 31–32
market, 33, 169–70
for products, 173, 175
for resources, 165, 173–74
Demand curve, 31, 32–35, 54–59, 115, 168
of business, 115
of business's labour, 168
kinked, 118
Demand for Canadian dollars, in foreign trade, 421, 422
Demand for labour, 172
market demand for labour, 169–70
Demand for money, 369–70
asset demand, 369–70
and money market, 371–72
transactions demand, 369
Deposits, 364–65
demand deposits, 364
foreign currency deposits, 365
notice deposits, 365
term deposits, 365
Deposit-takers, 362
Depreciate, 423
Depreciation, 106–107, 200, 250
and GDP, 250
Devaluation, 430
Diminishing marginal returns, law of, 87

Diminishing marginal utility, law of, 48–49
Direct investment, 417
Discouraged workers, 283
Discrimination, 194–95
Diseconomies of scale, 95–96
Disposable income, 261–62, 302
Distribution of income. *See* Income distribution
Double counting, and GDP, 251

E

Early Canadian trade policy, 460–61
Economic costs, 83–84
  explicit, 83
  implicit, 84
Economic development, 486–95
  definition of, 491
  dynamics of, 491–93
  energy consumption, 489
  foreign aid, 495
  health and social indicators, 489
  high-income countries, 486
  indicators of living standards for selected countries, 489
  industrially advanced countries, 487
  investing in resources, 494
  labour-intensive production, 493
  less-developed countries (LDCs), 487
  low-income countries, 487
  low investment, 491–92
  low productivity growth, 493
  middle-income countries, 487
  newly industrialized countries, 487
  per capital income, 487–88
  political and economic stability, 493
  population control, 494
  rapid population growth, 492–93
  strategies for, 493–95
  trade liberalization, 495
  vicious circle of poverty, 491
  World Bank, 486
Economic efficiency, 17
Economic goals, 17–19
  complementary, 19
  and conflicts, 19
  economic growth, 19
  environmental sustainability, 19
  full employment, 18
  income equality, 18
  price stability, 18
  viable balance of payments, 18
Economic growth, 18, 19, 476–85
  arguments against, 485
  arguments for, 484–85
  benefits of, 484–85
  in Canada, 479–81
    before World War I, 479–80
    interwar period, 480
    postwar period, 480–81
  and command economy, 15
  costs of, 485
  definition of, 19
  impact of, 476–79
  sources of, 481–84
Economic models, 5–6
Economic problem, 3–4
Economic profit, 84
  calculation of, 84
  definition of, 84
  normal, 84
Economic reasoning, 6, 28
Economic systems, 11–19
  definition of, 12
  and the three basic economic questions, 11–12
  range of, 16
  types of,
    command, 14–15
    market, 12–14
    mixed, 16–17
    modern mixed, 16
    traditional, 12
    traditional mixed, 17
Economics, 3–7, 28–29
  as an art, 28–29
  and critical thinking, xi–xiv
  definition of, 4
  normative, 6
  positive, 6
  and scientific method, xii, 5–6
  as a second language, xiv
Economies of scale, 94–95, 111–12, 123
  constant, 95
  decreasing, 95–96
  definition of, 94
  division of labour, 95
  increasing, 94–95
  limited natural resources, 96
  long-run costs, 96
  management difficulties, 96
  specialized capital, 95
  specialized management, 95
Elasticity of demand, 54–59
  calculation of, 54
  definition of, 54
  factors affecting, 58–59
Elasticity of supply, 60–62
  calculation of, 75
  definition of, 60
  factors affecting, 61–62
    immediate run, 61
    long run, 62
    short run, 61–62
Employment, 284–86
  full-time, 284–86
  participation rate, 281, 286
Employment Insurance, 222, 285
Employment Quality Index (EQI), 296
Entrepreneurship, 4
Entry barriers, 453, 455
Equilibrium, 312–16
  and aggregate demand and supply curves, 312
  changes in demand, 42–43
  changes in supply, 43–44
  and injections and withdrawals, 313–15
  and inventory changes, 312–13
  of market, 41–42
  of money market, 371–72
  value of rent, 196–97
  versus potential output, 315–16
European Union (EU), 463–64

Exchange rate, 305, 420–25, 429–30
  calculating, 420–21
  Canadian, 421
  policy, 428–30
  and prices, 420–21
Exchange rate systems, 427–31
  Bretton Woods system, 430–31
  evolution of, 430–32
  fixed, 427–28
  flexible (or floating), 427
  gold standard, 430
  managed float, 431
  trends in, 432
Excise taxes, 229
Expenditure approach to measuring GDP, 248, 250–56
Explicit costs, 83
Exponential growth, 478
Export subsidies, 456
Exports, 256, 445–57
  as a component of GDP, 256
  merchandise, 414

F

Fair rate of return, 152
Federal Sales Tax, 242–44
Final product, and GDP, 250
Financial capital, 200
Fiscal Policy, 332–35, 346–48
  and aggregate demand, 333–35
  benefits of, 342
  and the budget, 344–46
  contractionary, 332
  definition of, 333
  discretionary, 335
  drawbacks of, 342–44
  expansionary, 332
  guidelines, 346
  impact of, 344–48
  monetary, 333
  and multiplier effect, 336–37
  stabilization, 332–35
Fiscal year, 333
Fixed exchange rates, 427–28
Flexible (or floating) exchange rates, 427
Foot, David, 292–95
Foreign aid, 495
Foreign exchange market, 420, 421–23
  changes in demand and supply, 423–25
  demand for Canadian dollars, 421, 422
  and market equilibrium, 423
  supply of Canadian dollars, 422–23
Foreign investment and control, in Canada, 439–42
  benefits of, 440–41
  and Canadian economic sovereignty, 441
Foreign trade. *See* International trade
Free Trade Agreement (FTA), 464–65
  effects of, 465
Free trade area, 463
Frictional unemployment, 283
Friedman, Milton, 406–408
Full employment, 284–86
Functional finance, 346

G

Galbraith, John Kenneth, 104–105
GDP deflator, 275–76
GDP identity, 248–49
General Agreement on Tariffs and Trade (GATT), 462
George, Henry, 209–10
Global population trends, 492
Globalization, 444, 473
Gold standard, 430
Goods and Services Tax (GST), 242–44
  calculation of, 243
  debate over, 242–244
Goods, 35, 253
  complementary, 35
  durable, 253
  inferior, 35
  nondurable, 253
  normal, 35
  substitute, 35
Government, 63–67, 131–32, 152–53, 272–80, 332–35, 413–19, 427–31, 460–66. *See also* Bank of Canada; Fiscal policy; International trade; Monetary policy; Unemployment
  expenditures of, 222–24, 250–56, 304
  public debt, 343, 357–59
  revenues of, 226–30, 335, 249–50, 305
Government purchases, 254–55, 304, 314
Government spending, 222–24, 250–56, 304
  and circular flow, 255
  transfer payments and, 221–23, 261
Great Depression, 461
Gross Domestic Product (GDP), 247–50, 257–60
  definition of, 247
  and distribution of income, 259
  and the environment, 260
  and exchange-rate adjustments, 258
  expenditure equation, 253
  and inflation adjustments, 257–58
  and leisure, 259
  limitations of, as measure of economic well-being, 258–60
  measurement of, 247–49
  measurement of, expenditure approach, 248, 250–56
  measurement of, income approach, 248, 249–50
  and nonmarket activities, 258
  and standard of living, 257–60
  statistical discrepancy and, 250
  and underground economy, 258
Gross National Product (GNP), 260–62
  calculation of, 260
  definition of, 260
Guaranteed annual income, 225
Guaranteed Income Supplement payment, 222

H

Henderson, Hazel, and GNP, 266–69
High-income countries, 487
Human capital, 190

I

Impact log, 343
Import quotas, 455
Imports, 256, 445–57
  as a component of GDP, 256
  merchandise, 414
Income, 35, 278–79
  of average family and education, 189
  fixed, 278
  fully indexed, 278
  partially indexed, 278
  real, 274
Income approach to measuring GDP, 248, 249–50
Income distribution, 214–17 *See also* Lorenz curve
  and command economy, 15
  and GDP, 259
  and market economy, 14
Income inequality, reasons for, 216–17. *See also* Lorenz curve
Income statement, 106, 107
Increasing-cost industry, 62
Increasing opportunity costs, law of, 9–10
Increasing returns to scale, 94–95
Indirect taxes, in GDP, 250
Industrial concentration, 121–23
  debate over, 122–23
  definition of, 122
Industrial Revolution, 24
Industrial union, 192
Industrially advanced countries, 487
Industries, 97–98
  craft, 97–98
  manufacturing, 97
  primary, 98
Inelastic demand, 54, 56–57
  definition of, 54
Inelastic supply, 60
Inflation, 272–80, 398–403
  definition of, 18
  and incomes, 278–79
  and interest rates, 279–80
  measurements of,
    Consumer Price Index, 272–74
    GDP deflator, 275–76
    GDP deflator, in Canada, 276
  and Phillips curve, 398–401
  types of,
    cost-push, 400, 401
    demand-pull, 398
  and unemployment, 398–403
  and wage and price policies, 401–403
Inflation premium, 316
Inflationary gaps, 316
Injections, 313–15, 339
  definition of, 313
  exports, 314
  government expenditures, 313–14
  investment, 314–15
Innis, Harold, 470–72
Innovation, and market economy, 14
Instability, and market economy, 14
Interest, 199–204
  determination of, 200
  income and GDP, 249–50
  loanable funds, 202–204
  and principal, 199
Interest rate, 200, 302, 304
Intermediate product, and GDP, 249–50
International trade, 412–32, 443–66
  absolute advantage of, 449
  balance of payments, 413–19
  Canada, 444–48
  capital account, 417
  comparative advantages of, 449–52
  current account, 413–15
  gains from, 448
  importance of Canada, 444–45
  and labour standards, 473–74
  merchandise traded, Canada, 414, 445–47
  services traded, Canada, 414, 415
  terms of trade, 451–52
  trading partners, Canada, 445
  trading patterns, Canada, 445–47
Internet, xx
Inventories, 253
Investment, 303–304
  and business expectations, 304
  as a component of GDP, 253
  and interest rates, 304
Investment demand, 304
Investment demand curve, 303, 304
Investment demand schedule, 304
"Invisible hand," 25–26, 37

J

Jevons, William Stanley, 48–51
Job discrimination, 194
Job segregation, 194

K

Keynes, John Maynard, 325–28
  on flexible labour markets, 326
  on Say's law, 327
Krugman, Paul, 352–56

L

Labour, 4, 157–68, 172
  demand and supply, 167–68, 172
Labour force, 280–81
  definition of, 280
  participation rate in, 281
  population, 280
Labour productivity, 174
Labour unions, 184–86, 192–93
  arbitration, 184
  and collective bargaining, 184
  craft, 192–93
  impact of, on wages, 192–93
  industrial, 192

lockouts, 184
and McDonald's, 162–63
mediation, 184
membership in Canada, 185
strikes, 184
and wages, 211-12
working to rule, 184
Laissez faire, 26
Law of comparative advantage, 450
Law of diminishing marginal returns, 87
Law of diminishing marginal utility, 48–49
Law of increasing opportunity costs, 9–10
Less-developed countries (LDCs), 487
Liquidity, 361
Living standards for selected countries, 489
Loan period, 203
Loan, size of, 204
Loanable funds, 200
demand for, 200–201
supply of, 201–202
Lockouts, 184
Lorenz curve, 215–16
Low-income countries, 487

M

Macroeconomics, definition of, 4
Malthus, Thomas, 239–41
Marginal costs, 91–92
Marginal product, 86, 88–89, 166–67, 174
Marginal productivity theory, 165
Marginal propensity to consume, 337, 339–41
calculation of, 337
and the multiplier, 339–41
Marginal propensity to withdraw, 337–41
calculation of, 337
and the multiplier, 337–41
Marginal resource cost, 167
Marginal revenue, 166–67
Marginal revenue product, 166, 171
Marginal revenue product curve, 167
Marginal tax rates, 228
Marginal utility, 48–51
Marginal-cost pricing, 143
Market, 13, 31, 33, 41–42, 169–70, 173
and circular flows, 255–56
competitive, 41–42
demand and, 33, 169–70, 173
demand and supply, 169–70, 173
equilibrium, 41–42
product, 13
resource, 13, 165
supply and, 169–70, 173
Market demand, 33
Market power, 113–14, 123, 192–93
Market share, 116
Market structures, 110–14
monopolistic competition, 110–11
monopoly, 111
oligopoly, 111
perfect competition, 110
Market supply, 37
Marshall, Alfred, 71–74
on benefit, 71, 72
on consumer expenditure, 72
on consumer surplus, 71, 72
Marx, Karl, 126–28
on Communist Revolution, 128
labour theory of value, 126–27
theory of capitalism, 126–267
theory of exploitation, 127
McDonald's, 162–63
Means testing, 222
Mediation, of labour disputes, 184
Merchandise balance of trade, 414
Microeconomics, definition of, 4
Middle-income countries, 487
Minimum wage, 286
Minimum-cost pricing, 142
Monetarism, 406–408
Keynesian view of, 406–408
monetarists' view of, 406–408
Monetary policy, 390–92, 393–97, 409–10
benefits of, 396–97
contractionary (tight), 391–92
drawbacks of, 397
and exchange rates, 429–30
expansionary (easy), 390–91
Keynesian view of, 406–408
monetarists' view of, 406–08
Money, 360–78
creation of, 373–78
definition of, 364, 365–66
demand for, 369–70
and equilibrium, 371–72
evolution of, 385–86
and the financial system, 364
functions of, 361–62
M1, 365, 366
M2, 365, 366
M2+, 366
M3, 365–66
market for, 369–72
multiplier, 376–78
near, 366
supply of, 364–65, 371
Money demand curve, 370
Money demand schedule, 370
Money supply curve, 371
Money supply schedule, 371
Monopolistic competition, 110–11, 115–16, 144–46
demand curve of businesses under, 115–16
long-run profit maximization for, 146
revenue conditions of, 144–45
short-run profit maximization for, 145–46
Monopoly, 111, 118, 149–53
characteristics of, 111
definition of, 111
demand curve of, 118
entry barriers, 111–13
natural, 111
regulations of, 152–53
profit maximization for, 149–50
revenue conditions of, 149
versus perfect competition, 151–52

Multiplier effect, 336–337, 339–41

N

National income accounts, 247
National Policy, 461
National security (trade protection), 459
Near banks, 363
Near money, 366
Net domestic income, 261
Net exports, 305–306
  and foreign incomes, 305
Net tax revenues, 335
Newly industrializing countries, 487
Nominal GDP, 275–76
  definition of, 276
Nominal income, 274
Nonmarket activities, 258
Nonprice competition, 119–20
  and business, 119–20
  and the consumer, 120
North American Free Trade Agreement (NAFTA), 466

O

Old Age Security payment, 222
Oligopoly, 116–18, 146–48
  cartel, 118
  collusion in, 118
  co-operation in, 118
  definition of, 111
  entry barriers, 111–13
  kinked demand curve of, 118
  mutual interdependence, 116
  price leadership, 118
  profit maximization for, 147–48
  revenue conditions in, 147
Open market operations, 393–94
Opportunity cost, 7
Organization of Petroleum Exporting Countries (OPEC), 130–31
Overnight rate, 396

P

Partnerships, 81, 82
Per capita GDP, 257
Per capita real GDP, 258
Perfect competition, 115, 134–43
  benefits of, 142–43
  definition of, 110
  demand curve of business under, 135–36
  long-run profit maximization for, 140–42
  revenue conditions in, 134–35
  short-run profit maximization for, 136–40
  supply curve of business under, 139–40, 141
  versus monopoly, 151–52
Perfectly elastic demand, 55
Perfectly elastic supply, 62
Perfectly inelastic demand, 55
Perfectly inelastic supply, 61
Personal income, 261
Personal income tax, 228–29
Phillips curve, 398–401
Poverty, 218–20
  definition of, 218
  incidence of, in Canada, 218–20
Poverty line, 218, 219
Predatory pricing, 112
Presentations, xx–xxi
Price, 14, 58–59, 60, 75, 76, 174–76
  definition of, 60
  and elasticity of demand, 54–59, 75, 174–76
  and elasticity of supply, 76
  factors affecting, 58–59
  in a market system, 14
Price ceiling, 63
Price controls, 63–67
Price floor, 63
Price level, 299–300, 301–306, 401–403, 420
  and aggregate demand and supply, 299–300
  and exchange rates, 420
  and shifts in aggregate demand, 301–306
  and wage and price policies, 401–403
Price and wage policies, 401–403
  effectiveness of, 402–403
  efficiency, 403
  fairness of, 403
  "six and five" guidelines, 402
Prime rate, 396
Principal, 199
Product demand, 173
Product differentiation, 119
Production, 82–89, 94–98
  average product, 86–89
  capital-intensive, 82
  definition of, 82
  inputs, 82
    fixed, 85
    variable, 85
  labour-intensive, 82
  in the long run, 94–98
  marginal product, 86–89
  outputs, 82
  in the short run, 85–89
  total product, 85–89
Production costs. *See* Costs of the business
Production possibilities curve, 8
Production possibilities model, 8–10
Production possibilities schedule, 8
Productive efficiency, 82–83
  capital-intensive process, 82
  definition of, 83
  labour-intensive process, 82
Productivity challenge, 501–502
Profit, 198–204, 249
  corporate and GDP, 249
  as a measure, 199
  for risk-taking, 199
Profit maximization, 136–38, 145, 149–50
  in monopolistic competition, 145
  in monopoly, 149–50
  in oligopoly, 147–48
  output rule, 136
  in perfect competition, 136–38
Profit-maximizing employment rule, 168
Property taxes, 229
Proprietor's incomes and rent, and GDP, 250
Public debt, 343, 345, 357–59

Public debt charges, 343, 358
Public good, 233–34

Q

Quantity demanded, 31
 change in, 32
Quantity supplied, 37
 change in, 37–38
Quebec Pension Plan, 222

R

Real capital, 200
Real GDP, 257–58
Real expenditures, 299
Real income, 274
Real rate of return, 303
Recessionary gaps, 315
Recognition lag, 342
Relationships:
 direct, 5
 inverse, 5
Rent, 196–98
 controls, 66-67
  effects of, 66
 David Ricardo's views on, 207–208
 Henry George's view on, 209–10
 and population growth, 208–209
Research, xviii–xix
Research and development expenditures, 482–83
Reserve ratio, 373
Reserves, 373–74
 desired reserves, 373
 excess reserves, 373–74
Resource income, 4
Resource markets, 164–76
 operation of, 165
Resource prices, 38–39
Resources, 3, 165, 173, 174, 176
 capital, 3
 complementary, 173
 demand for, 165, 173–74
 economic, 3
 natural, 3
 substitute, 174, 176
Revenue, 55, 134–36, 144–45, 147, 149, 226–30
 average, 134
 of federal government, 226–30
 marginal, 134
 in monopolistic competition, 144–45
 in monopoly, 149
 in oligopoly, 147
 in perfect competition, 134–36
 total, 55
Ricardo, David, 207–10
Romer, Paul, 498–500
Rule of 72, 478

S

Sales taxes, 229
Saving, and GDP, 254
Say's law, 327
Scarcity, 9
Schumpeter, Joseph, 159–61
Seasonal unemployment, 284
Self-interest motive, 7
Seniority rights, 191
Shares, 201
Shortage, in competitive markets, 42
Shutdown point, 139
Skills resource, xi–xxi
Smith, Adam, 24–27
 on division of labour, 24–25
 and the Industrial Revolution, 24
 and the "invisible hand," 25–26
 and *laissez faire*, 26
Software, 52
Sole proprietorships, 81, 82
Specialization, 448, 451
Speculators, 425
Spending multiplier, 339–41
Spillovers, 231–34
 benefits, 232–33
 costs, 231–32
 demand and supply curves, 231
 effects, 231–34
Stabilization policy, 332–33. *See also* Fiscal policy; Monetary policy; Wage and price policies
Staples thesis, 470–71
Statistical models, 329
Strikes, 184
Structural unemployment, 283
Supply, 37–44, 60–62, 167–72. *See also* Aggregate supply
 changes (shifts) in, 37–40, 43–44
 decrease in, 38
 definition of, 37
 determinants, 37
 elasticity of, 60–62
 increase in, 38
 of labour, 167–68, 172
 law of, 37
Supply of Canadian dollars, in foreign trade, 422-23
Supply curve, 37, 38
 of business, 115
 of business's labour, 168
Supply schedule, 27
Surplus, in competitive markets, 41–42

T

Tariffs, 453–54
 and Auto Pact, 464
 definition of, 454
 and early Canadian trade policy, 460–61
 and FTA, 464–65
 and GATT, 462
 during the Great Depression, 461
 and the National Policy, 461
 and NAFTA, 466
 and WTO, 462
Tax, 226–30, 242–44. *See also* Tariffs
 corporate income, 230
 definition of, 226
 Federal Sales, 242–44
 Goods and Services (GST), 242–44
 personal income, 228–29
 progressive, 227
 property, 229
 proportional, 227
 regressive, 227
 sales and excise, 229
Taxation, 226–30

principles of, 226–27
types of, 228–30
Technological innovation, 123, 174
Technological progress, 482–83
Total product, 85–89
Total revenue, 55
Trade policies, 460–66
Auto Pact, 464
early Canadian trade policy, 460–61
Free Trade Agreement (FTA), 464–65
General Agreement on Tariffs and Trade (GATT), 462
Great Depression, 461
National Policy, 461
North American Free Trade Agreement (NAFTA), 466
World Trade Organization (WTO), 462
Trade protection, 453–59
barriers, impact of, 453
domestic regulations, 455–56
economic arguments for, 456–59
diversification, 457
domestic employment, 456
environmental and safety standards, 458
infant industries, 457–58
job protection, 458–59
terms of trade, 458
export subsidies, 456
import quotas, 455
noneconomic arguments for, 459
cultural sovereignty, 459
national security, 459
non-tariff barriers, 455
voluntary export restraints, 455
Trading blocs, 463–64
common market, 463–64
customs union, 463
definition of, 463
European Union (EU), 463–64
free trade area, 463
Transfer payments, 221–23, 261
means testing, 222
universality, 222
Treasury bills, 389
Troughs, 319

U

Underemployment, 282
Underground economy, 258
Unemployment, 280–87, 352–56, 398–403
Unemployment insurance benefit, 285
Unemployment rate, 282–87, 352–56
definition of, 18
natural, 284, 353
official, 282–83
drawbacks, 282–83
by province, 1996, 287
types of, 283–84
cyclical, 284
frictional, 283
seasonal, 284
structural, 283
and welfare state, 353
Unions. *See* Labour unions
Unit of account, 362
United States, 464–66
and Auto Pact, 464
and free trade with Canada, 464–65
and NAFTA, 466
Universality, 222
Utility, 7
diminishing marginal utility, 48–51
maximization of, 7, 50

V

Value added, and GDP, 251, 252
Variables:
dependent, 5
independent, 5
Veblen, Thorstein, 32
Vicious circle of poverty, 491
Visual materials,
graphs, xviii
tables, xv

W

Wage and price controls, 401, 402
Wage and price guidelines, 401, 402
Wage and price policies, 401–403
effectiveness of, 402–403
efficiency, 403
fairness of, 403
"six and five" guidelines, 402
Wages, 165, 188–95, 211–12
definition of, 165
determinants of, 188–95
discrimination, 194–95
education, 189–90
experience, 191
job conditions, 191
labour productivity, 189
market power, 192–93
regional disparities, 191–92
distribution of, 188
and GDP, 249
Wealth, 217, 302
distribution of, 217
Welfare society, 221–24
criticisms of, 223–24
definition of, 221
Withdrawals, 313–15, 337–39
definition of, 313
imports, 314
saving, 313–15
taxes, 314
Working to rule, 184
World bank, 486
World Trade Organization (WTO), 462

Y

Yunus, Muhammad, 381–84